Modern Chinese New Poetry and Classical Poetry Traditions

Li Yi

Modern Chinese New Poetry and Classical Poetry Traditions

Translated by Wang Sue

New York · Berlin · Bruxelles · Chennai · Lausanne · Oxford

Library of Congress Cataloging-in-Publication Data

Names: Li, Yi, author.
Title: Modern Chinese new poetry and classical poetry traditions / Li Yi.
Other titles: Zhongguo xian dai xin shi yu gu dian shi ge chuan tong. English
Description: New York : Peter Lang, 2024. | Includes bibliographical references and index.
Identifiers: LCCN 2023056030 (print) | LCCN 2023056031 (ebook) | ISBN 9781433198953 (hardback) | ISBN 9781433198960 (ebook) | ISBN 9781433198977 (epub)
Subjects: LCSH: Chinese poetry—20th century—History and criticism. | Chinese poetry—History and criticism. | LCGFT: Literary criticism.
Classification: LCC PL2332 .L46813 2024 (print) | LCC PL2332 (ebook) | DDC 895.11/509—dc23/eng/20240126
LC record available at https://lccn.loc.gov/2023056030
LC ebook record available at https://lccn.loc.gov/2023056031
DOI 10.3726/b20061

Bibliographic information published by the Deutsche Nationalbibliothek.
The German National Library lists this publication in the German
National Bibliography; detailed bibliographic data is available
on the Internet at http://dnb.d-nb.de.

Cover design by Peter Lang Group AG

ISBN 9781433198953 (hardback)
ISBN 9781433198960 (ebook)
ISBN 9781433198977 (epub)
DOI 10.3726/b20061

This edition is an authorized translation from the third revised edition of the book originally published in Chinese

Published by arrangement with Foreign Language Teaching and Research Publishing Co., Ltd.
All rights reserved.

© 2024 Peter Lang Group AG, Lausanne
Published by Peter Lang Publishing Inc., New York, USA
info@peterlang.com - www.peterlang.com

All rights reserved.
All parts of this publication are protected by copyright.
Any utilization outside the strict limits of the copyright law, without the permission of the publisher, is forbidden and liable to prosecution.
This applies in particular to reproductions, translations, microfilming, and storage and processing in electronic retrieval systems.

This publication has been peer reviewed.

Whirling and twisting, this mark
Branded all over him with a bruise,
Free flying wings, the nurture of the sunshine
His pursuit
Thwarted with the fall into darkness,
Surrounded by the walls of tradition, and the powerful
Daylight buttresses all its victorious convention.

—*Crevice*, Mu Dan

CONTENTS

Foreword by Wang Furen — xiii

Introduction: Modern Chinese New Poetry and Classical Poetry Traditions — 1
    I. Modern Chinese New Poetry: Challenges in Writing and Interpretation — 1
    II. Focusing on the Noumenon of Chinese New Poetry — 6
    III. Tradition: A Key Word in the Chinese New Poetry Development in the Past Century — 7
    IV. Modern Chinese New Poetry and Classical Poetry Traditions — 12
    V. Old Traditions and New Traditions — 17

Chapter 1 Objectification and the Cultural Characteristics of Modern Chinese New Poetry — 23
    I. *Xing* and Modern Chinese New Poetry Generating — 23
    Two Cultural Origins of Modern Chinese New Poetry Generating — 24

		Patterns of Poetry Expressions: Evoking Emotions with Objects and Emotions Flowing with the Changing Objects	29
		The Creative Subjectivity Mechanism of Modern Poets	31
		Xing and the Symbol Technique	34
	II.	Bi and Rhetoric Devices of Modern Chinese New Poetry	36
		Distant Metaphor and Near Metaphor	36
		Two Features of Near Metaphor	39
		Variations of Tradition	43
	III.	The Tradition of Bi-Xing and Objectification of Modern Chinese New Poetry	47
		Objectification Analysis	47
		Objectification of Modern Chinese New Poetry	52
	IV.	The Rival Growth of Subjectivity and Objectification	56
		Subjectivity Analysis	56
		Subjectivity Trend of Modern Chinese New Poetry	58
		Rival Growth of Subjectivity and Objectification	61
Chapter 2		Historical Forms of Modern Chinese New Poetry	67
	I.	Qu Sao and Free Forms of Modern Chinese New Poetry	68
		"A refuge to outlive the longest night"	68
		Free Qu Sao Style in Modern Chinese New Poetry	70
		Freedom Comparison in Chinese and Western Contexts	75
	II.	Poetry of the Wei, Jin, and Tang Dynasties, Ci of the Song Dynasty, and Conscious Forms of Modern Chinese New Poetry	79
		Towards Pure Poetry	80
		Life and Art	83
		Challenges	90
	III.	Poetry of the Song Dynasty and the Anti-traditional Tendency of Modern Chinese New Poetry	92
		Poetry of the Song Dynasty: A Cultural Prototype of Anti-traditional Poetry	93
		Anti-traditional Chinese New Poetry	97
		Limitations, Transformation, and Transcendence	101

	IV. *Airs of the States, Yuefu,* and Ballad Tendency of Modern Chinese New Poetry	107
	Ballad Tendency of Modern Chinese New Poetry	108
	Historical Foundation of Ballad Tendency of Chinese New Poetry	111
	Features of Ballad Tendency of Chinese New Poetry	118
	Freedom, Consciousness, Anti-tradition, and Ballad Tendency	123
Chapter 3	Traditional Culture and Text Structures of Modern Chinese New Poetry	133
	I. "Discernment" and "Forgetting": The Literary Pursuit of Modern Chinese New Poetry	133
	"Discernment" and "Forgetting" Cycling	134
	Two Modes of Thinking under Two Kinds of Poem Rules	140
	Between "Discernment" and "Forgetting"	144
	II. Harmony and Dissonance: Metrical Features of Modern Chinese New Poetry	150
	Harmony and Dissonance	150
	Harmony Pursuit of Modern Chinese New Poetry	156
	Dissonance Features of Modern Chinese New Poetry	169
Chapter 4	Individual Poets in Chinese Cultural Traditions	177
	I. Hu Shih: Slow Flow of Two Poetry Cultures	178
	Between Contingency and Clear Direction	179
	Two Poetry Cultures: The Living and the Dead	181
	From Dead Poetry to Living Poetry	186
	II. Guo Moruo: Free and Conscious Forms of Chinese Poetry Culture	192
	Free and Conscious Styles of Poetry	193
	Cycling of Free and Conscious Forms: Guo Moruo's Poetry	195
	Rival Growth of Free and Conscious Forms: A Glimpse of Guo Moruo's Spiritual Structures	200
	III. Wen Yiduo: Self-deconstruction of the Traditional, Psychological Structure	205
	"A Simple Chinese"	205

	Coexistence of Two Kinds of Poetic Ideas	209
	Conflicts: From Emotions to Art	213
IV.	Xu Zhimo: Modern Reconstruction of Classical Ideals	218
	A Son of Nature	219
	A Soul of Nature	220
	Natural Ideal	224
V.	Li Jinfa: Communication and Non-communication	229
	Symbolism: Baudelaire and Mallarmé?	230
	Tradition as a Personality Temperament	234
	Obscurity and Non-communication	237
VI.	Dai Wangshu: *The Century of Sickness* of a Chinese Soul	240
	Love and Privacy: A Sample Analysis	240
	A Sentimental and Worried Tone	244
	Pure Poetry or Prose Poetry	248
VII.	He Qifang: "*Jiaren Fangcao*" in the Western Storm	251
	Self-satisfaction, Self-respect, and "*Jiaren Fangcao*"	251
	Chinese and Western Cultures, and the Modern Choice	254
	Characteristics of He Qifang	256
VIII.	Bian Zhilin: The Sight Downstairs	260
	A "Cold-Blooded Animal" Label	261
	A Cold, Detached Tone	264
	Cultural Characteristics of Bian's Poetry	269
IX.	Liang Zongdai: Glory of Subjectivity and Enchantment of Objectification	274
	Starting from "Subjectivity"	274
	Misreading of "Objectification"	278
	Interaction and Intertwining of Chinese and Western Poetics	282
X.	Ai Qing: "An Abandoned Child" and Rebel of Chinese Tradition	285
	Ai Qing, "An Abandoned Child"	286
	Anti-tradition of the Avant-garde Art	288
	Ai Qing's "Reed Flute"	290
	Maturity during the War of Resistance against Japanese Aggression	292

XI.	Feng Zhi: Distant Metaphor and "The Most Outstanding Lyric Poet"	293
	Beyond Emotional Sensations	294
	Distant Metaphor and Organization of Ideas	297
	Cycling of the Subjectivity Process	299
XII.	Mu Dan: Anti-tradition and New Traditions of Chinese New Poetry	301
	Obscurity and Modern Poetics	303
	Vernacular, Spoken, and Prose Poetry	308
	Traditions: Past, Present, and Future	314
XIII.	Yuan Kejia: Modernization in Chinese Context	317
	Modernization of Chinese New Poetry	317
	Modernization Is Not Westernization	320
	Democratic Poetry and People's Poetry	324
	Dramatization and Experience	326
XIV.	Ren Hongyuan: Choice of a Contemporary Academic Poet	331
	A Chinese Academic Poet	332
	Ren Hongyuan as an Academic Poet	335
	"Double Transcendence"	339
	Of Life and Culture	344
XV.	Lu Xun: "Cheering for New Poetry" against Tradition	347
	Rationality and Dialogue	348
	Divergence from Early Vernacular New Poetry	351
	Lu Xun's New Poetry Criticism: An Evaluation	354
	A Critique of History and a Reflection of Reality	358

Appendix: Modern Characteristics of Chinese Modern Poetics	377
Postscripts for the Previous Chinese Editions	393
Index	397

FOREWORD BY WANG FUREN

When I was directed to the field of modern literary studies, I had passed the stage of loving poem reading and writing. Rough life has blunted my keen senses toward poetry. Therefore, I cannot say I read extensively in the field of modern poetry research. Yet, to my knowledge, Li Yi's book *Modern Chinese New Poetry and Classical Poetry Traditions* is an excellent piece of modern poetics. I read the manuscripts he sent me all at once, although I have already delayed the publication of this book. Each chapter made me feel amazed and I enjoyed the pleasure of fresh ideas. It is no exaggeration to say his book is full of inspiring sparkles throughout. This is much beyond my expectations.

Poetry appreciation requires poetry critics to be as sensitive and imaginative as poets, easily to be touched by specific objects. This is a challenge in poetry studies. But, such poetry critics are often described as somewhat narrow-minded or stubborn, which, of course, is a perception from some of our slower readers. If we do not feel what they feel or cannot imagine what they imagine, it is hard for us to understand they could talk much about a single image or word of a very short poem. It is like the amplification of a tiny thing as the whole big world. However, at the same time, poetry critics are responsible for helping readers understand the meanings and ideas of poems because poetics is always for those who do not understand poetry so well. If the poetry critics themselves are super emotional in every detail, sad at the sight of the moon, tearful at the sight of the flowers, and showing all kinds of human feelings associated with any plain verses, readers may not be able to follow their thoughts. In such a case, it would be reasonable if they feel the poetics is too narrow and too romantic. Poetics, as a theory, should have a theoretical depth, a bird-view position, and an overarching framework that accommodates subcategories of different varieties. In my opinion, such a framework for the study of Chinese new poetry has been absent. When studying Guo Moruo, Guo Moruo's standards would be applied. When studying Feng Zhi, Feng Zhi's standards would be applied. Consequently, such research became fragmentary and disorderly. It either probed into just one poet ignoring all others, or praised all poets along the way; thus, losing the value of research. The greatest contribution of Li Yi's book to the study of Chinese new poetry is to establish a powerful framework of modern poetics. It might not be the only reasonable framework; yet, it is a frame with its own logic. This framework is not imposed arbitrarily on its targets but reflects the features of Chinese new poetry development. One such remarkable feature is the comprehensive integration of three different forces: (1) the Chinese classical poetry tradition, (2) the Western poetry tradition, and (3) the individual pursuit of modern poets. When Li Yi analyzed Chinese new poetry from this framework, his research gained a grand view and no longer made people feel trivial. However, this macroscopic tolerance did not make Li Yi lose his keen sense of poetry but rather made him feel more nuanced and specific about modern poetry. I believe everyone who reads the complete book without any bias will feel the same.

No poets' writing can be separated from their traditions, but in our previous understanding, traditions seem to be confined to the traditions of Chinese classical poetry. Traditions are the integrated foundation on which poets rely their writing. Both ancient Chinese poetry and Western poetry are the poetic traditions on which modern Chinese poets set off, yet they play different roles in different historical periods. Poets have different perspectives on them. When new poetry emerged, poets saw an opportunity to develop Chinese new poetry with the traditions of Western poetry. Therefore, they advocated learning from Western poetry by introducing works and theories of Western poets. They also attempted to apply experience and theories of Western poetry to their poetry writing. However, when they did, they could not eliminate the traditions of classical Chinese poetry. Furthermore, they could not escape the restraints of traditional thoughts and the Chinese language.

On the other hand, when Western traditions were introduced to Chinese poetry, variations occurred and different characteristics formed. While it became a trend to draw from Western poetry, poets still believed they could not discard the traditions of classical Chinese poetry. Thus, the achievements of classical Chinese poetry continued to work in new poetry development. At such times, poets would turn to classical Chinese poetry and transform Chinese new poetry with theories of Chinese classical poetry. However, at the same time, authors of Chinese new poetry were already influenced by Western poetry. They were bound and did not want to leave these influences. Not only would it be impossible for the cultural traditions to be fully copied in modern times without changes, but also the Chinese foundation of classical poetry was fundamentally different from the modern vernacular language. Some aesthetic features of classical poetry have been irretrievably lost with the changes in classical Chinese metrical poetry. In my opinion, these two traditions are lit like traffic lights in the minds of modern poets. When one is lit, the other is dark, and vice versa. These two traditions take turns playing their roles, leading to the continuous evolution and development of Chinese new poetry. However, in this switch between light and dark, different corresponding points of Eastern and Western poetry are also formed. Lighting does not mean lighting the entire tradition, and darkening does not mean the whole traditional darkening. When the Western romantic poetry tradition and the works of foreign poets, such as Walt Whitman, William Wordsworth, and Rabindranath Tagore lit up for Guo Moruo, the ancient Chinese poetry tradition dimmed as a whole; but the classical poetry tradition of Qu Yuan, Tao Yuanming, Li Bai, and Wang Wei became more prominent against the background of the overall darkening. This constitutes the corresponding points of the East-West poetry tradition. Guo Moruo's poetry vacillated between these two corresponding points, sometimes closer to the Western poetry tradition and sometimes closer to the Chinese classical poetry tradition. The choice of these corresponding points changed with the poet's personality and the different situations of the Chinese and foreign poetry development at that time. In my opinion, Li Yi's work is extremely meticulous in describing the development context of modern Chinese new poetry—often missing and neglected. Many talented discussions are based on the process of describing the context. His theories about poets are quite solid, which is directly related to his strong aesthetic experience of poetry. However, if the specific poets' writings had not been analyzed in such a development context, I am afraid it would be impossible to achieve the current success.

Chinese new poetry is built on two poetic traditions of East and West, but it is the spiritual development of modern Chinese poets that ultimately plays the key role. Poetry is the purest language art. We say it is purest, not because of the opinion of some poetry critics who claim poets are completely ideal or poets can completely separate themselves from social life, politics, and material life. This is only an illusion of some poets and poet-critics. It is a kind of escape where they cannot face reality and the distress of life. Poetry is pure because it should or should try its best to eliminate the intermediate links, except language, and directly present the poets' spiritual feelings. Novels, dramas, and essays must resort to the strength of non-language factors, such as plots and characters more or less, while poetry is a purer art of language transmitting the spiritual feelings in tense relationships between language implications and expansion in forms. It is precisely because of this poetry feature that the poet's spirit plays a more direct, important role. Compared with novelists, essayists, and dramatists, the poet's spirit is purer and more explicit, although his language might be hazier, his feelings about the world, mankind, and various specific things in the surrounding world are more unobstructed in poems. Otherwise, he would not be able to write great poems. Novelists, dramatists, and essayists can speak in other people's languages and bury themselves in other people's words, but a poet can only speak for himself in his language. Nothing can shelter his inner feelings except his language. It is in such a sense that Li Yi has emphatically revealed the inextricable aesthetic connection between modern Chinese poetry and traditional Chinese poetry. After reading his book, you will definitely agree with his argument that modern Chinese poetry is closer to traditional Chinese poetry than Western poetry, although it is closer to Western poetry superficially and completely different from classical Chinese metrical poetry.

Many believe intuition is not restricted by social culture and it is the same among all human beings without any essential differences. It is probably based on such an understanding that literary theorists, such as Liang Shiqiu, established their theories of human nature, and connected Eastern and Western cultures with Eastern and Western literature based on the human nature theory. It is believed a unified standard has been found to evaluate Eastern and Western literature and culture. The more intuitive one feels, the more it reflects the great differences between different cultures—even between different individuals. Accumulated through long-term aesthetic experiences, intuition is the presentation of cultural concepts under a completely natural situation, while rationality can help us understand the intuitive and direct experiences of other people and other cultures. There is no need to understand or think about one's intuition and directness. It is presented in a flash and realized in a flash. Intuition is integral and does not need reorganization. The overall characteristics of an object can be felt at a glance. In the thousands of years of independent development of Eastern and Western cultures, feelings have been fostered in different ways, due to their different understanding of the world and human beings. These feelings not only reside in people's hearts but also are shown in their respective languages.

In the West, the transcendental God created the world and it, therefore, embodies the creation will and spirit of the transcendental God. However, this kind of spirit and the will to create is not directly manifested. They are contained in the material shell of entities in the world. The material shell does not have its spiritual characteristics, it imprisons a kind of transcendental spirit in its material shell, covering its mystical spirit with the material shell. In this way, everything in the world has two levels of significance at the same time—material and spiritual. The material shell is human, secular, and utilitarian, and has real value in the present world, but it is not a spiritual value. Spiritual value is transcendental, non-human, and non-utilitarian. It has the spiritual significance of unrealistic and non-utilitarian meaning. Material and spiritual aspects coexist in the same object, but they are not unified, and they have different connotations. The external material shell is only relative and the spiritual value is absolute. However, this absoluteness and eternity could only be reflected in a relative form. Only God, a non-human creator from the other world, presents absoluteness in absolute terms. It cannot be perceived by our intuition because it does not have a relative form. It only exists in our spiritual feelings. Intuition and direct observation can only perceive the material form with relativity, and only the inner spirit can perceive the absolute inner spirit. Man, as a kind of creation of God, also has the spiritual quality of God, but the will of God to create is not directly displayed, but confined to the limited, vulgar, human body. All desires, wisdom, and moral concepts of human beings are secular characteristics of human beings. They are different from God's will to create and imprison the transcendental spirit. One cannot grasp one's inner spirit only from one's understanding of his reason. One can only approach it through one's spiritual feelings. Man is never pure but born sinned. Man's spirit is always confined to the limited form of his own physical and material desires. To find one's inner spirit, one must transcend one's physical existence and one can only find one's existence in one's spirit.

There is no completely transcendental spirit concept in Chinese culture. We do not think everything in the world has another spiritual entity that does not belong to material with material characteristics. The world in front of us is unified, and the material and spirit are not separated. The spirit is the material spirit and the material is the material that embodies the specific spirit. When you affirm its material, you also affirm its spirit. If you affirm its spirit, it means you affirm its material. Beauty is beautiful, and ugliness is ugly. When we say the peony is beautiful, its substance and spirit are both beautiful. It does not have any rough physical shell that imprisons and restricts beauty itself, so the peony flower in our intuition is beauty itself. The crow is ugly. Its ugliness is not only material but also spiritual. It does not have any locked-up beauty. People feel its ugliness intuitively. The same is true of people. Westerners do not think people in this world will be perfect from the binary material and spirit concepts, while Chinese culture tells us people can become saints in the present world. One does not become a saint because he is not working hard enough, or because he does not strictly discipline himself. So, if one shows anything that is not true, good, and beautiful, it is his fault. He should be ashamed of himself.

The differences in cultural concepts between China and other countries are also epitomized by their languages. With the Western cultural concept, no language concept is absolutely true, good, and beautiful, nor is it absolutely false, evil, and ugly. Besides material, secular, vulgar, real, and formal characteristics, they also have spiritual, transcendental, and non-human characteristics. In the Chinese language, even polysemy is on the same level. There is no difference between the outside and the inside. We find its essence through unified phenomena. All these make the aesthetic characteristics of Chinese traditional poetry and Western poetry fundamentally different, as shown in the basic concepts of poets and poems. In China, poetry is a language form to express emotions and poets are people who master the language form of poetry. You cannot express your love for the motherland through poetry if you cannot write poetry, while I can if I could write poetry, though we both love our country. In the West, it is different. The poet is different from ordinary people and has a different ability because he can feel his inner spirit through the material shell of the world. For a long period, poetry was regarded as the voice of God and was created by the poet with the inspiration of God. Poetry was not only beyond ordinary people but also beyond the poet. It was only in a flash that God (or absolute spirit) showed himself through the spirit of the poet. Therefore, poetry is the poet's spiritual pursuit and the sublimation of spirit, rather than the realistic display of the poet's thoughts and emotions. Poetry is not ordinary because poetry is the spiritual pursuit of mankind. Poets are not mediocre because poets are people who continuously transcend themselves and reality, and enter another perfect spiritual world. Of course, they enter this world in different ways. However, in China, poetry is the expression of the poet's realistic thoughts and feelings. Poetry completely represents the poet's moralities and personality. He is not a guessing man of the world, but a describer of the world. He is not an explorer in the spiritual field, but a cultured person who reaches a certain spiritual height. In my opinion, if we understand Li Yi's comparison of the aesthetic characteristics of Chinese and Western poetry in terms of the fundamentally different characteristics of Eastern and Western cultures, we find they are quite profound and accurate. To save space, I will not quote his specific discussions of the different aesthetic characteristics of Chinese and Western poetry.

If I have to find fault with this book and single out some minor issues that any academic book would inevitably have, I think the author could be more specific in his analysis of the different aesthetic characteristics of classical metrical poems and modern vernacular poems, which is inadequate compared to his summary and analysis of the different characteristics of Chinese and Western poetry. The reason I raised this point is only by elaborating on this aspect fully can readers realize that not only is it impossible for modern Chinese poets to leave their own culture behind and completely adopt the Western culture, it is no longer possible for them to go out of modern times and completely go back to ancient times. For a culture as well as poetry writing, while complete Westernization is impossible, complete tradition restoration is also an illusion. Being pushed into modern China, we can only be modern Chinese. The differences between us can only be some possible differences in modern China. Foreign and traditional elements are only our cultural references, not the essentials of our choices. Wen Yiduo's proposition of new metrical poems does not mean writing poems for the ancients, nor are Feng Zhi's sonnets written on behalf of foreigners. They are attempts to write modern poems for the modern Chinese people.

Wang Furen
Beijing Normal University
April 10, 1994

INTRODUCTION: MODERN CHINESE NEW POETRY AND CLASSICAL POETRY TRADITIONS

Modern Chinese New Poetry: Challenges in Writing and Interpretation

Even today in the new century, probably no one can deny the trailblazing contributions of modern Chinese poetry to modern Chinese literature as a whole. No one can ignore the courage, agility, and enthusiasm shown constantly by modern Chinese poets in responding to various trends of world literature during the 20th century. Among varied evaluations, it is universally acknowledged that modern Chinese poets explored poetic ideas and artistic techniques extensively. Their diligent footprints can be found in every corner of modern art—from ideas to art forms, from self-expression to popularization, from the West to the East, from prose to pure poetry, and from romanticism and modernism to realism.

In the meantime, modern Chinese new poetry embarked on a bumpy road from the day it was born. All diligence seemed insufficient to enable it to be proud in the global poetry community. Besides, it apparently could not compete with the classical Chinese poetry it was trying to surpass. Continuous criticism runs through the history of Chinese modern poetry, constantly revealing the difficulties in new poetry writing. Hu Shih, a Chinese philosopher and writer, said of his contemporary early vernacular poets in 1919, "Most of the 'new poets' I know carried with them traces of Chinese traditional poems, ci and qu,[1] except the Zhou brothers from Kuaiji."[2] As a response to his comments, some Chinese poets, such as Mu Mutian and Wang Duqing, fought back in 1926: "The Chinese are writing poems badly now .... ." "I think Hu Shih is the biggest sinner in the new poetry movement in China." "The Chinese people, like those in social work recently, are unwilling to take things seriously or to tackle the most challenging. Therefore, the poems they produced are neither fish nor fowl in terms of techniques."[3] In 1931, when editing the *Crescent Moon School Poetry Anthology*, Chen Mengjia reviewed the achievements of the new poetry in the past ten years: "China's new poetry is more like a volcano that has been silent since ancient times. Now, the flames of the sand and sulfur mixture suddenly burst forth. Yet, its pure brilliance could not last in spite of its brightness."[4] Left-wing Chinese poets of the Chinese Poetry Association also lamented: "The Chinese poetry community remains silent. Some are pushing for Westernization, while others are immersed in such sentimental trivial as wind, flowers, and snow."[5] In the mid-1930s, when talking about the evolution of new poetry in the prior ten years, Sun Zuoyun, a historian and folklore studies scholar, argued, "If you put it sharply, there is still no new poems written in this decade that we would remember forever."[6] Shortly thereafter, Lu Xun (literary name of Zhou Shuren, commonly considered the greatest Chinese writer in 20th-century Chinese literature), put forward a harsher argument when meeting with the American reporter, Edgar Snow. Lu Xun believed even the works of some of the best modern poets "could not be highly acclaimed, but just innovative experiments." "So far, modern Chinese poetry has not been successful."[7] Likewise, Li Guangtian, an essayist and poet, commented on poetry in the 1940s: "When talking about the development of literature and art since the May Fourth Movement in 1919, most people agree modern Chinese new poetry achieved the least among all literature genres."[8] In the mid-1990s, the famous "Review at the End of the Century" by Zheng Min (a Nine Leaves poet) triggered extensive debates. Zheng Min's questioning of modern Chinese new poetry was only an extension of Mu Mutian and Wang Duqing's evaluations during their time.[9]

It is indeed a fact that the performance of new poetry often arouses more doubts among various genres of modern Chinese literature. For many, Chinese modern novels and prose, such as *Call to Arms*, *Wandering*, and *Wild Grass* by Lu Xun, have probably proven their unique values, while *Thunderstorm* and *The Wilderness* by Cao Yu show the vitality of modern drama. These works established their respective modern forms different from Chinese classical literature and started dialogues from the periphery with the center of world cultures. In contrast, the achievements of Chinese new poetry seem more ambiguous. Some people's love for new poetry is found side by side with others' cacophonous disapproval, from the early days of its founding to the maturity period during the 1930s or 1940s. Regardless of the kind of schools chosen as the benchmark, new poetry has been continuously criticized, which seems to indicate modern Chinese new poetry has not fully secured a basic readership. Compared with previous explorations and passions, we can truly feel the difficulties that modern Chinese poetry development is confronted with.

The difficulties in artistic development can also be manifest in the challenges of artistic interpretation. There is a great difference between the interpretation of an artistic form stabilized in value and the interpretation of an artistic form not yet stabilized in value. The stabilized artistic form has self-sufficiency and integrity. It fully absorbs historical and realistic cultural information, and properly melds and combines the information. When the interpreter approaches the stable, artistic form with the information of history and reality, the fusion of vision between the interpreter and the interpreted can be achieved. It seems the elucidation is just about right without much hindrance. Meanwhile, the interpreter's self-realization is also achieved. The interpretation of other genres of modern Chinese literature (such as modern novels) should be somewhat convenient, which does not mean these artistic forms are simple and transparent. Rather, it means as stable artistic forms to be interpreted, they are relatively mature—convenient for the superposition of the subjects and objects. Also, literary critics can stick to their strengths. Facing these rich objects, the interpreters seem to have gained some sense of freedom. In contrast, modern Chinese new poetry, an artistic form still struggling to find its way forward, is not yet stable. In other words, it is full of uncertainty in our public artistic value standard. Bewildered interpreters must pay attention to this and that, and, therefore, approach the interpretation with difficulty. During such times, their rich experiences and feelings of reality cannot be released and projected freely, and the disengagement between the subjects and objects may occur more frequently, which either distorts the interpretation or wrongs the interpreters.

Looking back at the interpretation history of modern Chinese new poetry, we can see this tension. For example, a series of interpretations of new poetry by Chinese left-wing poets in the 1930s, such as Pu Feng, led to a certain way of thinking. Along this track of thinking, most of the poems during the early 1920s were deeply influenced by bourgeois ideas. For example, *The Goddesses* by Guo Moruo was described as "truly reflecting the rapid development of China's rising capitalism." Xu Zhimo's works were accused of being jammed with feudal aristocracy and bourgeois clichés divorced from reality. It was claimed that only with the emergence of proletarian literature in the late 1920s and the foundation of the Chinese Poetry Association during the 1930s could Chinese new poetry embark on "a brand-new road of new realism" (socialist realism).[10] The proletarian consciousness developed in conflict with feudal aristocratic, bourgeois consciousness, which seemed to indicate a promising future for Chinese new poetry. Despite this way of thinking, one may ask, are the poets' writings of the Chinese Poetry Association represented by Pu Feng, as well as the poems about the Chinese People's War of Resistance against Japanese Aggression in the 1940s, in line with the realistic principle of objectivity and detachment? Are not these vivid emotional factors also among the characteristics of romanticism? If we say new realism has both realistic and emotional elements, then this means we must redefine realism. Besides, the Chinese poetry community was very complicated in the 1930s and 1940s. The realism of the Chinese Poetry Association was different from the realism of the July Poetry School. When these were placed under the same label, it would not make the targets of interpretation clearer, nor the process of interpretation easier, but plunged us into new confusion.[11]

Let me provide another example. A claim of poetry history emerged through the analyses of Shen Congwen, Liang Shiqiu, Yu Guanying, and other scholars during the 1920s and 1930s, which still has extensive influence even today. According to this claim, a general trend of Chinese new poetry, from the initial period to its relative maturity, is a decrease in traditional poetry elements and an increase in modern elements. Or, as argued, "Foreign literature influenced Chinese new poetry unconsciously" in its initial period while "the basic principles of new poetry are explicitly pursued from foreign literature"[12] during its maturity period. This opinion resulted from the observations and analyses of modern Chinese new poetry against the context of Chinese literature's efforts of connecting with the world. Chinese literature is true, in general, moving from a closed feudal corner to an open modern world during the 20th century, where modern Chinese new poetry is a participant. However, literature always has unexpected developments. When we set aside all external, and historical concepts and carefully examine the course of Chinese new poetry, it is not difficult to see with the increasing influence of foreign literature in the modern Chinese new poetry evolution, the influence of classical poetry also increased from the initial period to its maturity period. For example, in the relatively pure artistic explorations of the Crescent Moon School, the Symbolist School, and the Modernist School, Chinese traditional literary influence may be more notable in comparison with foreign influence. As Shi Ling (a writer) commented, the Crescent Moon School "established an indispensable bridge between the traditional and the new poetry."[13] Bian Zhilin, a Modernist poet, further concluded, "After the vernacular new poetry gained a solid foothold, it has deliberately connected the long-term traditions of China's poetry to take advantage of the artistic heritage handed down over the ages and through continuous genre changes."[14] Consequently, we would once again encounter difficulties in interpretation, if we only examine the issue from the perspective of globalization of Chinese literature.

Besides various difficulties with the interpretation of poetry's history, we are also faced with a series of basic problems in new poetry criticism. For example, both pure poetry tendency and prose poetry tendency are important phenomena in the development of Chinese new poetry. What exactly is pure poetry then? Is pure poetry pursued by modern Chinese new poetry similar to the pure poetry of French symbolism? Are the pure poems advocated by Mu Mutian, Liang Zongdai, and Li Jianwu consistent? What is the relationship between the proposition of pure poetry and its practice?[15] Similarly, how does the prose poetry of Hu Shih's "prose as poetry" connect with Ai Qing's prose beauty? Judging from the development of Chinese new poetry, is it pure poetry that points to poetry noumenon? Should prose poems written by some poets (e.g., Ai Qing and Mu Dan) be excluded from poetry? Even modern Chinese poets failed to reach a consensus on these important poetic concepts, not to mention interpreters. In addition to this, imported concepts often produce unpredictable variations. Interpreters must adjust frequently to address multifarious poetic phenomena. Therefore, some basic concepts inherent to Western poetry development may not be applicable in the Chinese literary context.

All this seems to herald our interpretation to be challenging. We not only have to eliminate the cultural traces of Other in Chinese modern poetry concepts but also to identify a myriad of ambiguities brought about by various misunderstandings and distorted readings by Chinese poets themselves. In this sense, I think the solution to the challenges of interpretation is this:

Focus on the noumenon of new poetry!

Focusing on the Noumenon of Chinese New Poetry

"Focusing on the ... noumenon" and "returning to the ... self" were important calls in modern Chinese literature studies during the 1980s. Two meanings were implied: (1) to eliminate all kinds of rigid dogmas imposed on literature by the long-term left trend of thoughts, such as excessive emphasis on class struggle theory, and (2) to restore the true face of literature as an individual activity. What I mean by "focusing on the noumenon" and "returning to the ... self" is in line with these implied meanings; but, at the same time, also goes further. In my opinion, how to restore the true face of literature as an individual activity and how to focus on the so-called noumenon of literature are only relatively abstract ideals. Ultimately, the existence of any historical form does not have a pure, objective original state nor a pure, objective internal noumenon. The so-called "focus" and "return" are only interpretations close to the fact when they are not subject to other non-literary pressures. There could be more than one interpretation of "noumenon" and "itself." Different interpretations can be found from different angles of observation. Thus, "the noumenon" or "itself" will have different sides. In a sense, the fluid, dynamic features of Chinese new poetry could pit our one-sided observation into a difficult situation. The best strategy should be the integration of multiple perspectives. A focus on and returning to the noumenon of new poetry means recovering the inherent three-dimensional characteristics of new poetry from the value standards of various cultures. We should focus on the stylistic features of poetry and explore the historical existence of poetry, mainly with the linguistic and cultural codes of the new poetry (instead of starting with external social and cultural concepts). This is not to deny external social and cultural concepts. Rather, all external social and cultural concepts are meaningful and worthy of exploration only after they have been accepted, melted, and re-compiled by poetry which has specific artistic forms. In such a process, the linguistic and cultural codes of Chinese new poetry would emerge as we define them.

For instance, the concept of realism is frequently mentioned when we critique Chinese new poetry. For the time being, we will not become involved in the debate on whether there is realism in poetry. From the perspective of the "ideal type" of realism advocated by the Chinese left-wing revolutionary poets, it is different from the realism of Western poetry. In Western poetry history, the influence of realism mainly lies in some kind of restraint and suppression of personal emotions. An objective narrative tone is often employed to view the world of life in a detached manner. For example, the Parnassian School in France and the Victorian poets in England would reject the ideal precisely because of this realism. We also consider some early *Baihua* ("plain speech," vernacular) poems realistic, but it is obvious the early vernacular poets in China never had the intentional detachment of Western poets. They did not regard detachment and objectivity as a personal attitude toward life. What does this mean? In my opinion, this shows that Chinese new poetry has its specific language codes. Foreign concepts are often very different from the Chinese code of language, where concepts have been compiled and adjusted. Should we study modern Chinese new poetry from several external concepts or from the codes of Chinese new poetry itself? The answer is self-evident.

We must change our approach. Focusing on the noumenon of new poetry is not only an approach change but also an opening of a broad research area. Many topics are waiting for exploration and discussion:

> New poetry generating in the history of Chinese poetry.
> Internal motivations for the development of new poetry.
> Divergence and convergence of new poetry.
> Connotations of new poetry.
> Relationship between the poetic pursuit of new poetry and artistic creation.
> Awareness of new poetry forms
> …
> The list continues. I attempted to itemize part of it, a very small part.
> This book is just the beginning.

In my opinion, there is a key issue that needs to be addressed before we focus on the noumenon. That is, in the course of Chinese poetry development during the 20th century, what is the significance of Chinese poetry traditions?—Not those requirements by history and politics, but the changes Chinese poetry traditions have undergone. This is our simplest assumption about focusing on the noumenon of new poetry.

Tradition: A Key Word in the Chinese New Poetry Development in the Past Century

What we need to tackle first is the relationship between Chinese new poetry and tradition when we start to examine the noumenon of Chinese new poetry. The fact that Chinese new poetry entangled with classical traditions in the course of its birth and development has triggered heated exchanges for almost a century. As we all know, diverse flags of anti-tradition are often found in the development of Chinese new poetry. The contention among schools of Chinese new poetry repeatedly centered on the "Western or traditional" modes. However, on the other hand, the discussion of the tradition of Chinese new poetry has given rise to many different interpretations today.

First, anti-tradition is regarded as the banner of Chinese new poetry development. Here, tradition naturally means conservatism, backwardness, and stagnation, which need to be condemned and removed during development.

Second, tradition is regarded as the object of our imagination and appeal. Because anti-tradition does not guarantee the smooth development of Chinese new poetry, many difficulties and problems encountered during the process are always analyzed by those in connection with tradition. Alienation from tradition perplexes us, causing us to get lost. When faced with some setbacks in poetry development, we start pondering: Is this reality the revenge of tradition? Is it the bitter fruit of our rejection of tradition?

In this way, tradition is constantly mentioned, with which we have both hopes and disappointments. However, various discussions about tradition do not seem to have brought about a logical solution to the numerous problems of Chinese new poetry. In the mid-1990s, when Zheng Min put forward the "Review at the End of the Century" in China, her questions and analysis set us back more than 70 years:

> Hu Shih, a top scholar educated in China and the West, abandoned his homeland's thousands of years of cultural heritage like dirt. Such a distorted mentality is worth pondering.[16]

As mentioned earlier, nearly 70 years ago, Mu Mutian, who advocated "ethnic style" for Chinese new poetry, made a similar famous accusation: "I think Hu Shih is the biggest sinner in the new poetry movement in China."[17] Here, problems in the development of Chinese new poetry were attributed to the abandonment of classical traditions. Such assertion was found not only at the end of the 20th century but also at the beginning of the 20th century. Hu Shih was not the only target of criticism. For example, Wen Yiduo, a famous poet, and scholar, also criticized Guo Moruo who wrote *The Goddesses*:

> The modern spirit, that is Western culture, unfortunately, runs counter to our country's culture. Therefore, one cannot have much sympathy and understanding for the latter if one is obsessed with the former. In this way, the author of *The Goddesses* is not someone who could be able to understand our Chinese culture and show deep sympathy for it.[18]

It is not the criticism itself, but the popularity of such thinking that reveals a sobering fact. That is, most of the century's criticism does not seem to have alerted our modern poets. Many modern new poems still forge their path, drifting away from the so-called tradition with miscellaneous issues and criticism. The traditions that have been constantly called upon fail to play a role in setting things correctly.

It must be pointed out that the keyword, tradition, which repeatedly appears in the critical discourse of Chinese new poetry, is rather ambiguous. It has been used in multiple meanings. However, due to the differences in the value positions approved by critics, many topics triggered by the abstract tradition could not reach a common understanding, nor could the issues be enriched or deepened through discussions for more than half a century.

If analyzed carefully, the so-called tradition repeatedly discussed today can be summarized into two aspects: One is the traditions formed by Chinese classical poetry as the precondition for the existence of Chinese new poetry. The second is the new "traditions" formed during the development of Chinese new poetry. Tradition in these two senses is related to our understanding of the core of Chinese new poetry and affects our evaluation of its future development.

The traditions of Chinese classical poetry, which correspond to the formation of Chinese new poetry, are foundational. The relationship between Chinese new poetry and the traditions of Chinese classical poetry has been understood in completely different ways at various times, which directly affects the positioning of tradition.

One basic judgment scholars have held for a long time is tradition means conservative and anti-tradition Chinese new poetry implies the most positive progress. Now, this reasoning is questionable. But after the 1990s with the continuous debate, new problems have arisen. Is tradition equal to opposing Western cultural hegemony? Is anti-tradition of Chinese new poetry equal to silence in its submission to Western cultural hegemony?

When we interpret the May Fourth New Literature Movement, which includes vernacular new poetry as a component, into the confrontational context of new/old, progressive/conservative, and revolutionary/feudal dualities, we naturally highlight the anti-traditional elements therein. In the past, we admired these anti-traditional images greatly and even believed Hu Shih's reform was insufficient compared with Chen Duxiu's more radical revolution. Hu Shih's foot-unbinding poems were too conservative in comparison with Guo Moruo's radical breakthrough, which truly started a new poetic style. However, by the 1990s, these same anti-traditional images had encountered unprecedented doubts. The thinking modes of the May Fourth writers were relegated to the absurd logic of either/or. Their choice to rebel against the classical traditions and imitate Western poetry was even condemned as submission to Western cultural hegemony and considered the root cause of all defects in Chinese new poetry.

To tackle this issue of tradition, it is best to return to history and let the historical facts of Chinese new poetry speak for themselves. If we interpret modern Chinese poetry without any prior prejudice, we can easily find its strong connections with Chinese classical poetry, which has been established in all aspects, from feelings and tastes to language forms. Even in the antitraditional Chinese new poetry, the indirect influence of the Song Dynasty poetry, which represents an anti-traditional model of Chinese classical poetry can be found, though we lack more systematic and convincing proof for this issue.

Indeed, the new traditions of Chinese new poetry and our long-standing traditions of classical poetry are two interrelated components. These two are almost parallel:

1. The classical poetry traditions experienced variations and transformations on the modern journey of Chinese poetry.
2. Foreign poetic concepts and modern living conditions have a variety of influences on the modern orientation of Chinese new poetry. At the same time, they are also restricted, eroded, and selected by the Chinese classical poetry traditions.

The first component is an interpretation of traditional culture, known as archetypal criticism in the West. However, within Western culture, archetypes are usually associated with myths. Their collective unconsciousness is the memory of the birth, adventure, suffering, and resurrection of gods. Literature is the repeated narrations of this ancient, often renewed, mythological pattern. However, in China, the highly mature Confucian culture has long removed many of our memories of the gods in primitive times. Therefore, our so-called archetype is mainly a typical social and cultural mentality passed from generation to generation. As far as poetry is concerned, this refers to the aesthetic ideal and artistic pursuits established by Chinese classical poetry during its development and maturity. After the pinnacle and decline of the Tang and Song dynasties, the aesthetic ideal and artistic pursuits seemed to become the most unattainable peaks. They secure a place in people's hearts and affect new creative activities in different ways. The establishment of modern Chinese new poetry is closely associated with the input of Western poetry. However,

> One culture and its aesthetic horizon do not easily disappear merely because of the adoption of alien models. Very often, the poets may accept alien forms, attitudes, and thoughts only on the surface, whereas subconsciously the traditional aesthetic sense may continue to affect and condition the selection and operation of the alien models.[19]

The second component seems to have always been the topic of our discussions when in reality this is not the case. When Liang Shiqiu claimed "new poetry is foreign poetry written in Chinese,"[20] he regarded Chinese new poetry as a simple response to Western poetry. This simplistic point of view limits the interpretations of Chinese new poetry. Our elaboration of Western influence should be based on the prerequisite that Chinese poetry would always be considered a part of Chinese culture. The influence of Western poetry on modern Chinese poetry is the dialogue between these two cultures. It should be noted that in this process, we are more concerned about the concepts of Western poetry culture accepted by the Chinese poetry culture in the dialogue.

Since acceptance takes place in dialogue, I think it is necessary to determine the connotation of Chinese poetry culture first. What position and role did it play in the history of modern poetry? Only by carefully reviewing our cultural system can we find the basis for the dialogue between Chinese and foreign poetry cultures in modern China. This allows us to truly explain where the external influence took place and where the influence was rejected. This means exploring the relationships between Chinese classical poetry and modern Chinese new poetry from the perspective of interpretation of traditional culture is the first step in our work. With this unfolding, we would have a new, in-depth elucidation of the historical characteristics of modern Chinese new poetry.

A thorough, detailed answer to the question of Chinese new poetry can help us effectively reveal the challenges of some skeptics of the modernization of new poetry and the challenges of those who question the legitimacy of the vernacular new poetry. This will help us further investigate the profound roots of Chinese modern poetry and pinpoint the possible problems in these roots more objectively.

Modern Chinese New Poetry and Classical Poetry Traditions

Among all literary genres, poetry has the deepest, most resilient relationship with the traditional culture of its nation. From the perspective of aesthetic ideals, poetry is different from narratives in literature, such as novels or dramas. Poetry abandons the imitation and reconstruction of realistic pictures and reveals people's deepest life experiences and aesthetic ideals directly. While the realistic movement could drive narratives in literature to a quick transition to reflect a new historical era, poetry cannot betray the most stable side of people's hearts. At such times, poetry would be stranded, which makes people see the unconscious collective mentality of the nation. According to Thomas Stearns Eliot:

> ... poetry has primarily to do with the expression of feeling and emotion; and that feeling and emotion are particular, whereas thought is general. It is easier to think in a foreign language than it is to feel in it. Therefore no art is more stubbornly national than poetry.[21]

From the linguistic perspective, each kind of poetry has the tendency of solidification in the literati extraction and the tendency of variability in social activities. Relatively speaking, narrative literary language—convenient to track real social activities—may be more popular, more direct, and more prone to change with time, while the language of poetry is closer to the prototype of traditional culture after repeated deliberation and polishing due to its solidification.

If we argue the traces of national culture can only be recognized by careful identification in the spiral development of self-denial in Western poetry, Chinese poetry is different. Classical ideals established throughout the long history of China are often repeatedly and openly praised by modern Chinese people. Furthermore, it is the wish of the multitude to restore the poetry prosperity of the Tang Dynasty. In China, the prototype of the national poetry culture does not exist in secret nor just in dreams. On the contrary, it seems to have infiltrated from unconsciousness to consciousness. Recalling, calling for, and deliberating with the ideals of classical poetry are components of Chinese people's practical needs. It is their conscious pursuits to maintain and identify with the modes of classical poetry. Yu Pingbo (a vernacular poem pioneer) said, "We may be dissatisfied with traditional Chinese poetry in many aspects, but we are always amazed by its artistic ingenuity."[22] Ye Gongchao (also known as George Kung-chao Yeh, a diplomat, and scholar) represents the experiences of some poets, "... the diction and rhythm of the classical poems are so refined and skilled that you could not help envying them if you read them very often. It is only a natural result to imitate."[23] Zhou Zuoren (Chinese essayist, critic, and literary scholar, the younger brother of the renowned writer Zhou Shuren) also commented:

> I am not a disciple of traditionalism, but I agree the power of tradition cannot be despised. There is quite some negativity in traditional thoughts, which we should naturally try our best to remove. Yet, there are equally, if not more, parts of tradition that transcend good and evil, and cannot be ruled out. For example, there are various rhetorical techniques created by Chinese characters. We cannot remove them when we use Chinese characters to write.[24]

All these scholars vividly reveal the mental state of modern Chinese people. This mentality exists not only among poets but also among ordinary readers, with writers and readers jointly expecting the realization of the ideal of Chinese classical poetry. Writers' expectations determine the potential trend of poetry writing, while readers' expectations encourage and consolidate this trend.

On the whole, the relationship between modern Chinese new poetry and classical poetry is sometimes hidden, sometimes explicit, sometimes conscious, and sometimes unconscious. It may be directly inherited from history at some moments, and in others, it is the indirect match of reality and practice.

The early vernacular new poetry represented by Hu Shih inherited the tradition of "prose as poetry" of the Song Dynasty. According to Hu Shih, "Most poets today write in styles similar to those in the Poetry Movement of the Song Dynasty."[25] He "argued the trends in the history of Chinese poetry from Tang to Song dynasties as nothing mysterious, but only closer to the vernacular."[26] However, how did the Chinese traditional pattern of "prose as poetry" integrate with the strong impact of Western poetry rushing in during this period? The vernacular poets had not thought about this issue carefully in the early days. What we see in *A Book of Experiments* by Hu Shih are the juxtaposition of Eastern and Western poetry ideals. Similar situations can also be found in Guo Moruo's *The Goddesses*. Guo Moruo highly praised the dynamic cultural spirits of the Pre-Qin (221–207 BC) period and showed his passion for the *Qu Sao* style originated from Qu Yuan (340–278 BC), the founder of romanticism of Chinese literature. However, he also appreciated the simple, elegant style of Tao Yuanming (365–427) and the free, natural spirit of Wang Wei (701–761). Poets, such as Walt Whitman, George Gordon Byron, Percy Bysshe Shelley, and Johann Wolfgang von Goethe, were also among his favorites.[27] As a result, these complicated poetic ideals of ancient and modern China, and foreign countries intermingled in his works. The more conscious absorption from tradition began with the short poems by Bing Xin, Zong Baihua, and other writers. In June 1923, Wen Yiduo made the famous proposition of "local colors," advocating a child of Chinese and Western arts marriage,[28] which means maintaining the ethnic features of Chinese new poetry. This nationalization proposition of introducing Western poetry to highlight local colors was fully practiced in the poetry writing of the Crescent Moon School. From the Crescent Moon School and the Symbolist School to the Modernist School, modern Chinese new poetry reproduced well the various rhymes and styles of classical poetry ideals (poetry of the Tang Dynasty and *ci* of the Song Dynasty) in its heyday. At the same time, modern Chinese new poetry readjusted the functions of modern Western poetry for its better use. This fundamentally changed the mixed situation of multiple cultures in poetry during the May Fourth period and accomplished a return to classical poetry through integration. However, this attempt was doubted and criticized by other poets during the 1930s and 1940s. The left-wing revolutionary poets attacked this return with the proposal of poetry popularization, accusing this return of aristocratic narrowness. The Nine Leaves poets (such as Xin Di, Chen Jingrong, Tang Qi, and Mu Dan) also criticized the romantic sentimentality prevailing among poets and advocated the modernization of new poetry. These critics seemed to set themselves apart from poems of the Tang and Song dynasties. However, when folk songs and ballads were collected on a large scale to maintain the Chinese style and Chinese elements by the left-wing Chinese Poetry Association and the poets in the liberated areas in the 1940s, it reminds us of the collection of ballad tunes, such as *Airs of the States* and *Yuefu* in ancient China. When the Nine Leaves poets expressed their emotions and feelings in narrative and argumentative verses, it also reminds us of the Song Dynasty poetry. Indeed, the poetry of the Chinese Poetry Association, the poetry of the liberated areas, and the poetry of the Nine Leaves have indirect or hidden relationships with classical poetry when compared with the Crescent Moon School, the Symbolist School, and the Modernist School. It is a kind of long-distance communication and correspondence through writing practice, especially so for the relationship between the Nine Leaves works and the Song Dynasty poetry.

Through the above brief review of the influence of classical traditions on new poetry history, we can summarize several features of the revival of classical poetry prototypes in modern times:

1. The influence of classical poetry was realized by specific schools and poets. Variety and individuality are outstanding features of modern schools and their poets. The poets in each school (or those outside) have different understandings and feelings about tradition. Therefore, Chinese classical poetry as a whole can't have a comprehensive influence on modern Chinese new poetry. We see modern new poetry often shows only a component of the connotation of the classical poetry ideal, with different schools and poets only remembering some part of the classical poetry ideal. This is its "incomplete feature."
2. The revival of the prototype does not mean simple restoration or replication of traditional ways. It often appears along with the development of the trend of the times and is linked to some characteristics of the times. With the development of the times, some repressed parts of the classical traditions may be strengthened and become especially prominent, such as the *Qu Sao* style, poetry of the Song Dynasty, and the ballad tendency of poetry. Indeed, these classical poetry forms are not as dazzling and refined as the poetry of the Tang Dynasty nor the *ci* of the Song Dynasty, nor are they the best representatives of Chinese classical poetry aesthetics. However, it is precisely because of the atypical features they could be restored and carried forward in the new poetry movement against the decadent tradition. Also, the anti-traditional new poetry seems to have gained some support from tradition. This is exactly what some Chinese poets are requesting. This is its "feature of the times."
3. Modern Chinese poets face the ebb and flow of poetry in the entire world, not just a distant traditional culture. They should not only satisfy the unconscious expectations of poetic beauty but also meet the various challenges of the 20th century. As a result, when the influence of classical poetry is expressed in various forms in twists and turns, it is likely to undergo various transformations and reorganization at the same time. Sometimes, the connection between ancient and modern times is quite hidden and indirect. It showed the influence of other poetic factors. For instance, the influence of Western 20th-century poetics can be detected clearly amid the connections between Nine Leaves poems and the poetry of the Song Dynasty. We cannot assert

how much the achievement of the Nine Leaves poets can be credited to the poetry of the Song Dynasty. We can only argue the works by the Nine Leaves poets had a distant resonance with the poetry of the Song Dynasty. This is the "transformed feature."

4. In connection with the previous two points, the embrace of Chinese classical traditions by modern Chinese new poetry may occur along with its adoption of Western poetry. We have noticed Western poetry is often considered the modern proof of classical aesthetics. For example, the Crescent Moon School, the Symbolist School, and the Modernist School were delighted with the Eastern elements of some Western poetry in the 19th and 20th centuries. Thus, they took the integration of the East and the West as a transition, rightfully drawing nourishment from the classical poetry traditions of China. In other words, we can say in the view of some poets, the Chinese classical poetry traditions provide the foundation for the integration of Western poetry by its modern Chinese counterpart. This is the feature of "Chinese and Western integration."

In brief, the main features of modern Chinese new poetry influenced by classical poetry traditions include incompleteness, features of the times, transformation, and the Chinese and Western integration. These are the main ways in which classical poetry traditions continue to act on modern new poetry. In the elaboration of each chapter of this book, we can see such influences throughout.

That being said, what is the significance of these classical poetry traditions that influence the development and perfection of modern Chinese new poetry? The significance is multi-faceted.

The most obvious is the Chinese poets' conscious inheritance of the classical poetry ideal that promoted the maturity of Chinese new poetry and won it a wide readership. When vernacular poetry came into existence, the voice of opposition rose. As Yu Pingbo noted, "Since the birth of new poetry, people who expressed doubts outnumbered those who expressed sympathy, based on my observations as well as those of my friends."[29] This fully demonstrates the Chinese readers' unfamiliarity and resistance to this new art, according to their own aesthetic needs. Thus, when did Chinese readers begin to recognize and accept new poetry? Some argued it started with Xu Zhimo.[30] As we know, the active inheritance of modern Chinese new poetry to the classical traditions began with the Crescent Moon School represented by Xu Zhimo. Undoubtedly, Chinese readers believed Xu's poems are more approachable because of their conscious inheritance of classical poetic beauty. We mentioned earlier that expectations from writers and readers are the main motives for the revival of the Chinese poetic beauty prototype. These can also be expressed since only new poetry meets the expectations in some way can it win its readers, because only in the readers can the artwork finally become complete.

There is also the issue of the extent of adaptation to these expectations. When Chinese modern poets blindly follow the expectations of the beauty of such poems, they are likely to slip into a state of self-restraint in the process of tracking the classical appeal. We noticed Xu Zhimo, Shao Xunmei, and other Crescent Moon School poets once wrote indiscreet romantic poems, just as the romantic gifted scholars in ancient China would doodle a few palace poems. In the late stage of their writing careers, Modernist poets also fell into a state where their literary thoughts desiccated, their poems turned rigid, and they faced premature career aging.[31] This could be the negative impact of traditional poetry. The influence of classical poetry would be more positive if modern Chinese poets regarded the beauty of classical poetry as only a potential, a poetic potential that does not possess modern characteristics, and consciously makes transformative use of it with the development of modern culture. If the cultural factors of traditional poetry can exist on a deeper level and provide more new cultural thoughts, then let unfamiliarity and familiarity coexist. In this regard, the Nine Leaves poets of the 1940s may have set a good example. Still, looking at the history of modern Chinese new poetry, I think I should point out that the negative influence of classical poetry seems more problematic, which might be responsible for the challenges in the writing and interpretation of modern Chinese new poetry.

Old Traditions and New Traditions

Finally, another point I would like to put forward is that the search for traditional and modern connections should not appear as a defense of false accusations, nor should we fall into the simplistic duality thinking of yes/no. Furthermore, we should not forget, even unconsciously, to continue to study the many noumenon issues in the development of Chinese new poetry. We do not need to prove the legitimacy of Chinese new poetry through the traditions of classical poetry, nor can we falsify it by the loss of these traditions. So is our relationship with the artistic experience of Western poetry. The legitimacy of Chinese new poetry can only be articulated by its artistic practice.

Just as Mr. Wang Furen (a scholar and professor at Beijing Normal University) pointed out:

> Unlike a pile of coal transported by conveyor belts, culture has changed after being processed through the minds of Chinese intellectuals in the past and present. They are not assemblers either, who only assemble different parts of Chinese culture and Western culture into a new type of machine with all the predetermined parts. Human beings are creative. Every culture is a product of human creation. The nature and function of Chinese modern and contemporary cultures cannot be determined only by their sources. Therefore, it is impossible to conduct effective research, while assuming the binary opposition between China's inherent cultural traditions and Western culture.[32]

This tells us the historical significance of tradition in poetry is not necessarily as confrontational as we understand it. Rather, it is just one of the elements of poetry. At some tense moments in history, we may be able to see the anxiety toward tradition. However, a retrospect at the long history of Chinese poetry will show us that tradition is only a kind of gentle existence as an element of personal choices in the genre. This is quite prominent in poetry's history in the Taiwan region. From the 1950s to the 1970s, there was large-scale Westernization versus tradition debates by poets in Taiwan. However, both sides have developed and adjusted their standing since then. Traditional-style poems by Yu Guangzhong have developed, while Westernized poems by Luo Fu have evolved as well. At the turn of the century, poets in Taiwan seem quite mature—at least they no longer needed to develop themselves along the debates over tradition.

Since tradition is only an element of poetry writing resources, it is not a scale of value today for us to establish the legitimacy of poetry. When we argue that Chinese new poetry does not depart from the traditions of Chinese classical poetry, the purpose is to illustrate the fact that Chinese new poetry has never surrendered to the hegemony of Western culture rather than prove the eternal charm of Chinese classical poetry models. Chinese new poetry is still the expression of Chinese poets' life perceptions in their own living space. In such a shared living space, some similarities between traditional and modern Chinese poetry are the natural products of shared life and spiritual experiences. Chinese poets speak in their own space and express what they should do in their world. They do not merge into the West nor do they write the Chinese versions of Western poetry just because of their communications with the Western world. Even poets like Mu Dan undeniably elucidate China's life experiences, which is a significant fact in spite of his rational expressions of his rejection of Chinese traditions and the similarities we have found between his poetry and Western poetry. If we accept this fact without prejudice, we can find the anti-traditional Mu Dan still bears the marks of tradition. For example, connections are found between his "Eight Poems" and Du Fu's "Autumn Meditations" as discussed by Professor Wang Yi of modern literature at Huazhong University of Science and Technology.

However, there is another aspect to this issue. That is, the independent value of modern Chinese new poetry lies precisely in its ability to break through powerful traditions and set its new artistic forms. It is in this sense that we say it is futile to provide one-way proof of the influences of classical poetry traditions on new poetry; this is because fundamentally, the value of Chinese new poetry does not depend on these classical factors. It can only rely on itself and its unprecedented artistic creativity. Or in other words, what matters is not whether Chinese new poetry has inherited the traditions of Chinese classical poetry, but whether it can open up new traditions in its unprecedented creative activities.

When we evaluate Chinese new poetry as a whole, the entirety of Chinese poetry history is taken into consideration. In such a context, we must admit that Chinese new poetry has formed a series of features different from classical Chinese poetry.

First, the freedom and independence of the creative subjects are pursued. In the foreword of the first issue of *New Youth*, which published the largest number of early vernacular poems, it was noted the human rights theory is among the first characteristics of modern civilization. The different meanings of subjects have been presented from Hu Shih's "The Raven" and "You Must Not Forget" to Guo Moruo's "Tiangou" (the Heavenly Dog), from the early proletarian poems to Hu Feng and his July School. What is especially noteworthy is the emphasis on self by these poets has radically different meanings from the emphasis on self-cultivation by Chinese classical poets.

Second, a series of poetry texts showing the poets' subjectivity is created. That is, Chinese poetry has begun to depart from the traditional modes of expressing emotions through visible objects and scenes and to take a more abstract subjectivity as its ideas of expression. Compared with "poetry should have its distinctive subject and artistic taste" (Yan Yu, *Canglang Shihua*) in traditional Chinese poetics, this is a striking breakthrough. Under such modes of writing, the poets' charms could be presented, and they could use subjectivity to experiment with and mold objective images. Furthermore, the poets' illusive expressions of the object images could also be presented.

Third, a variety of free forms are created. Diversified poetic styles have been widely employed, such as the introduction of Western sonnets, stair poems, the exploration and application of folk songs, prose poems, and drama poems. Although achievements vary, these attempts are undoubtedly extremely valuable. In this regard, Guo Moruo made some thought-provoking comments:

> Quite a few people think new poetry has not established a form, which showed its failure, but I cannot agree with this. I would argue it is like a paradox—it is a great achievement of new poetry that it does not establish just one form ... Not instituting forms is a new type of poetry.[33]

Undoubtedly, for Guo Moruo, a pioneer of new poetry, the fluid and dynamic Chinese new poetry has assumed an unprecedented free posture, which provides modern poets with more room to maneuver. Isn't this a precious tradition? Compared with classical Chinese poetry which has faded, the traditions of modern Chinese new poetry are more fluid and, therefore, more growth-oriented. With its constant flowing and growth, Chinese new poetry has indeed shown its differences from the historical forms as a whole, regardless of how many problems and defects it might still have. As Li Jianwu, a writer and critic, pointed out:

> During the nearly twenty years of the new literature movement, poetry writing experienced hard times when compared with prose. Even now, the forms and ideas of new poetry are still challenging for many active and established poets ... However, a fact is poems are more difficult to compose even there are many get engaged in such activities. The experiments by these early modern poem writers showed the disorientation and uncertainty of trailblazers. Yet, the absence of a definite path means a world with all possibilities. This is incredible and spectacular. It is usually thought that the achievements of poetry in the new literature movement are not as outstanding as that of prose. Yet, judging from the term "modern," I am afraid prose is lagging far behind.[34]

The traditions of Chinese new poetry are still providing momentum for Chinese new poetry development today. At the same time, they also require our better understanding.

Notes

1 *Ci* (lyrics) and *qu* (melody) are Chinese traditional poetic forms.
2 Hu Shih, "On New Poetry," in *Collection of Theory Development, China's New Literature Series* (Liangyou Books Company, 1935), 300.

3   Mu Mutian, "On Poetry—A Letter to Moruo"; Wang Duqing, "On Poetry Again—to Mutian and Boqi," *Creation Monthly* 1, no. 1 (Mar. 1926).
4   Chen Mengjia, "Preface to *Selected Poems of the Crescent Moon School*," in *Selected Poems of the Crescent Moon School* (Xinyue Bookstore, 1931).
5   The First Issue of *New Poetry Journal* (Feb. 1933), cited from Chen Shouli, *Digest of Chinese Modern Literature History* (Beijing Publishing House, 1985), 406.
6   Sun Zuoyun, "On Modernist Poetry," *Tsinghua Weekly* 43, no. 1 (May 1935).
7   "Lu Xun and Snow's Talk Transcript," *Historical Materials of New Literature*, no. 3 (1987).
8   Li Guangtian: "On the Ideas and Forms of New Poetry," in *Art of Poetry* (Kaiming Bookstore, 1943).
9   Zheng Min, "Review at the End of the Century: The Changes of Chinese Language and the Writings of Chinese New Poetry," *Literary Review*, no. 3 (1993).
10 See Pu Feng, "A Bird's-eye View of Chinese Poetry from the May Fourth Movement to the Present," *Poetry Quarterly* 1, no. 1–2 (Dec. 1934–Mar. 1935).
11 Many years ago, some poets noted there was no "realism" in poetry when faced with such difficulties in interpretation, but it did not attract sufficient attention of the academic community. See Lan Dizhi's "On Realism in Poetry," *Guizhou Social Sciences*, no. 2 (1987).
12 Liang Shiqiu, "The Style of New Poetry and Others," *Shi Kan* (*Poetry Journal*), no. 1 (Jan. 1931).
13 Shi Ling, "The Crescent Moon School Poetry," *Literature* 8, no. 1 (Jan. 1937).
14 Bian Zhilin, "Preface to *Dai Wangshu's Poetry Anthology*," in *People and Poetry: Retrospect and Prospect* (Joint Publishing Company, 1984), 64.
15 In recent years, some people have begun to study this in depth. For example, Wu Xiaodong's "From Prose Tendency to Pure Poetry," published in *Series of Modern Chinese Literature Studies*, no. 3 (1993).
16 Zheng Min, "Review at the End of the Century: The Changes of Chinese Language and the Writings of Chinese New Poetry," *Literary Review*, no. 3 (1993).
17 Mu Mutian, "On Poetry—A Letter to Moruo," *Creation Monthly* 1, no. 1 (Mar. 1926).
18 Wen Yiduo, "Local Colors of *The Goddesses*," *Creation Weekly*, no. 5 (June 1923).
19 Wai-lim Yip, "The Use of Models in East West Comparative Literature," in *Diffusion of Distances: Dialogues between Chinese and Western Poetics* (University of California Press, 1993), 27.
20 Liang Shiqiu, "The Style of New Poetry and Others," *Shi Kan* (*Poetry Journal*), no. 1 (Jan. 1931).
21 Thomas Stearns Eliot, "The Social Function of Poetry," in *On Poetry and Poets* (Farrar, Straus and Giroux, 2009), 8.
22 Yu Pingbo, "Psychological Views on New Poetry," *New Trend* 3, no. 1 (Oct. 1919).
23 Ye Gongchao, "On New Poetry," *Literary Journal* 1, no. 1 (May 1937).
24 Zhou Zuoren, "Preface to *Yangbian Ji* (*Spurring Collection*)," *Yu Si*, no. 82 (June 1926).
25 See *Hu Shih's Anthology* (2) (Taipei Far East Book Company, 1975), 214.
26 Hu Shih, "Forced Rebellion," in *Collection of Theory Development, China's New Literature Series*, 8.
27 See Guo Moruo, "Past and the Present, Paintings Scripts," in *Moruo's Collected Works*, vol. 12 (People's Publishing House, 1959).

28 Wen Yiduo, "Local Colors of *The Goddesses*," *Creation Weekly*, no. 5 (June 1923).
29 Yu Pingbo, "Psychological Views on New Poetry," *New Trend* 3, no. 1 (Oct. 1919).
30 See Bian Zhilin, "Preface to *Anthology of Xu Zhimo's Poems*," in *People and Poetry: Retrospect and Prospect* (Joint Publishing Company, 1984), 34.
31 Ke Ke, "Essays on New Poetry," *New Poetry* 2, no. 3 and no. 4 (1937).
32 Wang Furen, "Questions on a Research Mode," *Journal of Foshan University*, no. 1 (1996).
33 Guo Moruo, "Exploring the New Poetry Path," see *Guo Moruo on Writing* (Heilongjiang People's Publishing House, 1982), 58.
34 Li Jianwu, "*Yumu Collection*: Bian Zhilin's Works," in *Li Jianwu's Literary Criticism Essays* (Zhuhai Publishing House, 1998), 104, 107.

· 1 ·
OBJECTIFICATION AND THE CULTURAL CHARACTERISTICS OF MODERN CHINESE NEW POETRY

What is objectification? What are the national cultural characteristics of modern Chinese poetry in the world poetry history of the 20th century? These need some discussion. Let us return to modern Chinese new poetry and examine it from several aspects.

First, we will discuss the origin and growth of Chinese new poetry, and see how it is generated and what inspirations Chinese new poetry could provide us during its maturity period.

Xing and Modern Chinese New Poetry Generating

> Since ancient times, no poet could write without *Xing*.
> *Xing* would be employed if one was inspired by the sight of something.
> —Ge Lifang of the Song Dynasty, *Yunyu Yangqiu* (*Poetics of Ge Lifang*)

The so-called generating has two meanings: one is the origin of the new literary style and the second is the production of new literary works. Origin refers to a new style of modern Chinese poetry. Production refers to specific new poetry works. For both, the generation of new poetry reflects significant national characteristics.

Two Cultural Origins of Modern Chinese New Poetry Generating

The exploration of modern Chinese poetry origin did not begin today. Guo Moruo first proposed in his *On Poetry* in 1921, "People who study poetry should not study it from the perspective of Chinese textual research but from psychological, anthropological, or archaeological perspectives. Only by focusing on its historical origin could it become a scientific study."[1] Scholars, such as Yu Pingbo, Kang Baiqing, and Zhou Zuoren in the 1920s, and Liang Shiqiu, Chen Mengjia, and Zhu Ziqing, etc. in the 1930s also embarked on the studies of the origin of Chinese new poetry. However, until today, we almost invariably believe the Chinese new poetry movement originated from the West. This is most typically represented by Liang Shiqiu's comments in 1931, "I always think the influence of foreign literature is the main cause of the new literary movement. The new poetry is foreign poems written in Chinese."[2] Regardless of the true motives of this Babbittist, this assertion is unquestionable and should be the basis for our new interpretation.

However, with full respect to this assertion, I would like to propose another perspective: Can foreign inspiration replace the generation of the Chinese new poetry self? The generation of a new life always uses inherent elements of life. External energy is important, but external influence must also mobilize the intrinsic life system to make a difference.

An important fact in the history of modern Chinese poetry is those who translated and introduced Western poetry in the early days of the May Fourth Movement in 1919 were later criticized to varying degrees. For example, Wen Yiduo thought that Guo Moruo's *The Goddesses* lost "local colors." Mu Mutian even attacked Hu Shih as the "biggest sinner" of the Chinese new poetry movement. From its birth to its maturity, the external influence of new poetry faded or was suppressed, rather than becoming stronger and deeper, as shown in some of the Western-style early vernacular poetry. For example, Hu Shih's translation of the poem *May Wind* by S. Teasdale signified the beginning of Chinese new poetry.

我说"我把心收起,
像人家把门关了,
叫'爱情'生生的饿死,
也许不再和我为难了。"

但是屋顶上吹来,
一阵阵五月的湿风,

更有那街心琴调，
一阵阵的吹到房中。

一屋里都是太阳光，
这时候"爱情"有点醉了，
他说，"我是关不住的，
我要把你的心打碎了！"
(The Chinese version by Hu Shih)

I SAID, "I have shut my heart
As one shuts an open door,
That Love may starve therein
And trouble me no more."

But over the roofs there came
The wet new wind of May,
And a tune blew up from the curb
Where the street-pianos play.

My room was white with the sun
And Love cried out in me,
"I am strong, I will break your heart
Unless you set me free."
(The original version)

This poem is about a "battle" between "I" and "love." Its most striking feature is the abstract concept love is regarded as the subject of expression. Although the original work by S. Teasdale could not represent the best of modern Western poetry, it is obvious the deep concern about rationality and abstract concepts has always been the focus of Western poetry. When examining new Chinese poetry during the mature period, few works make such abstract expressions of love. The popular Chinese new poetry theme on love often has specific characters, tangible backgrounds, and vivid plots (or close-up shots), such as "I Came to the Yangtze River to Buy a Bouquet of Lotus Seeds" by Xu Zhimo:

> I came to the Yangtze River to buy lotus seeds.
> I peeled the lotus seed dressing by hand,
> River seagulls flying in front of me,
> I was choking with sad tears,
> I was thinking about you, I was thinking about you, ah Dear Little Long!

Besides love poetry, the new poetry of the mature period tends to focus on feelings and emotions, and too much rationality would be considered a serious taboo. It is particularly noteworthy that since the mid-1920s, the poetic views of Chinese poets and poetry theorists have demonstrated distinctive national characteristics. Many ideals of Chinese classical poetics, such as spirit, verve, artistic conception, etc. became the goals poets consciously pursued once again. Bian Zhilin, a poet, said, "After the vernacular new poetry gained a solid foothold, it deliberately got connected with our long-cherished tradition of poetry. It took advantage of the artistic heritage passed down through the long-term and long-lasting changes." "The tendency to absorb from Western poetry was transferred to the focus on the inheritance of Chinese traditional poetry."³

We could argue that Chinese new poetry did not become mature completely in the direction of Western poetics. Chinese new poetry achieved its maturity through its turn in the poetic pursuit. Without the return of the national cultural spirit, there is no such maturity in Chinese new poetry. Thus, in terms of history development as a whole, we think the generation of Chinese new poetry has a certain dual nature or at least two different cultural foundations.

From the perspective of Chinese classical poetics, a source of this generating is *Xing*, a heritage of the Chinese classical poetry culture. "*Xing* means beginning or evoking" (Liu Xie, *Wenxin Diaolong, The Literary Mind and the Carving of Dragons*). "*Xing* means to mention something else before the elicitation of the real intention" (Zhu Xi, *Poetry Collection*). Chinese classical poetry writing tends to focus on specific objects with specific emotions and feelings. The unfounded reasoning as well as abstract descriptions, in particular, would be considered taboo. Jiao Ran, a poet-monk in Tang Dynasty, said in his *Poetry Styles*:

> The similarities between images make *Bi* possible, and the similarities between meanings make *Xing* possible. The meaning is what lies behind the images. Anything that has a name, including birds, fish, flowers, trees, people, and objects could be compared with those that share similar characteristics, which became the sources of *Bi* and *Xing*." In the history of classical poetry, "with *Xing*, the poetry art officially embarked on the path of objectification of the subject emotions, and gradually reached the perfect position of the subjective and objective unity of scenes, objects, and thoughts, ultimately fulfilled special requirements for poetry.⁴

An Experimental Collection by Hu Shih is a simple, straightforward narrative. *The Goddesses* by Guo Moruo are direct expressions of emotions and feelings. Early Chinese new poetry was unaware of the necessity of turning emotions into images, that is, using objects to express feelings. By consciously digging into the consistency between subjects and objects, and through the search for "the meaning of the images," the art of Xing where "the words refer to this while the meaning refers to that" (Luo Dajing, 1196—? 1252, a writer of the Southern Song Dynasty) gradually showed its value during the reflection period of the May Fourth Poetry Movement. Eventually, the Movement formed the second generation of artistic resources in the history of Chinese new poetry. The regeneration of new poetry reserved previous foreign inspirations, but was very consciously reluctant to stop at this. The Movement strived to find nutrients from the Chinese poetry tradition and explore the poetic value of Xing. Therefore, on the whole, the second generation, which originally contained previous inspirations, consciously reversed some of the pursuits of its predecessors.

This kind of backlash can first be found in the series of practices by Crescent Moon School poets. Shi Ling said the merits of the Crescent Moon School "established an indispensable bridge between classical poetry and new poetry."[5] The Crescent Moon School poetry is an important representative of the regeneration of Chinese new poetry.

If we compare poems by the Crescent Moon School poetry with poems during the May Fourth era (1915–1927), we can see the inspirational significance of Xing in the following three aspects.

First, the representation of abstract ideas is greatly reduced. In the vernacular new poems in the early days of the May Fourth Movement, abstract ideas once attracted the interest of many poets. The following are some examples of this trend: "the bitterness, joy, beauty, and ugliness" by Lin Sun ("Bitterness-Joy-Beauty-Ugliness"), Kang Baiqing's "the river of love" ("Add No More!"), Huang Zhongsu's "mind" ("Questioning the Heart"), Lu Xun's "cultural conflict" ("Their Garden"), Hu Shih's "active thinking" ("One Thought"), Liu Bannong's "soul" ("Soul"), Liu Dabai's "elimination" ("Here Comes Elimination"), Guo Moruo's "expression of Nirvana, the Eastern concept of life" ("Phoenix Nirvana"). Similarly, a large number of translated poems that were popular at the time also focused on abstract concepts. However, starting with Crescent Poetry, such tendencies were significantly suppressed. Take the common theme of love as an example. In the May Fourth new poems, the abstract expression of "starving love" is quite representative. Xu Zhimo's masterpieces included "Happy Snowflakes," "Laments," and "Coincidence" as a member of the Crescent Moon School, although he also wrote, "This is a Timid World."

Second, purely scenery description and realistic poetry could hardly be found. In the first collection of modern poems in modern literature history,

Selected Vernacular Poems, the poems are classified according to scenery writing, realism, and writing of emotions and thoughts, which are sufficient to see the trend of objective reality pursuit at the time. Yu Guanying once divided the new poems into two periods with *Poetry* (*Shi Juan*, a journal) as the dividing line:

> It was most obvious the number of philosophical poems was reduced, compared to those written during the previous period. There were very few scenery poems. The evidence for this tendency can be found everywhere. For example, if we browse through the first, second, and third issues of *Poetry Periodical* (*Shi Kan*), no scenery poems could be found among almost 90 poems. They are all lyric poems.[6]

Third, purely imaginative objects also decreased. In the May Fourth vernacular new poems, purely imaginative images were in harmony with purely realistic scenery descriptions, such as Lu Xun's "Peach Blossom," Guang Fo's "Shadow of Heart," Chen Jianlei's "Tree and Stone," etc., not to mention many of the poems in Guo Moruo's *The Goddesses*. The purely imaginative images fully demonstrate the poets' creativity and manipulative power in the objective world. Except for a few works, the Crescent poems are mainly based on the images in their "native" state. This native state also contains certain emotions. Different from realistic descriptions, the emotions naturally blended with the nature of the images, rather than the mandatory mixture and juxtaposition of the poems. Crescent poets, such as Xu Zhimo and Wen Yiduo, emphasized the importance of imagination, but their so-called imagination diverted from that of Western poetics. The search for harmony, unity, and self-emotional restraint is the key to their poetic spirit, or the so-called "meaning of the poem should be felt as natural as the natural growth of leaves on the trunk."[7]

The series of changes reflected in the second generation of Chinese new poetry could be understood like this. Abandoning abstract ideas is obstructing the path of poetry to a purely inner world. By directing the vision of poetry to the objective world, while avoiding a single view and realism, it is possible to retain the position of a subjective mind in the objective world. Finally, when the objective world is presented in our peaceful state of mind and the poets no longer need to destroy its original image with the power of personal imagination, but pursue the harmony between things, a new, charming poetic world was born. In such circumstances, poetry covers both images and meanings or the meaning behind the images. This is what the ancients called "writing because of the stimulation of objects, and writing because of similarities between the objects and ideas" (Mei Yaochen, *Wanling Ji: Works of Mei Yaochen*).

When modern Chinese new poetry was generated for the second time under the inspiration of *Xing* and approached maturity, modern Chinese poetry theory also made a timely elaboration and summary, thus delineating and popularizing the meaning of this generation. In 1926, Zhou Zuoren explicitly raised the issue of *Xing* in the preface to Liu Bannong's *Yangbian Ji* and linked it to another foreign art symbol popular at that time. Thus, he accomplished a timely exchange between different cultures. Zhou Zuoren was very aware of such an occurrence at the time. He envisioned "if new poetry should go this way," "real Chinese new poetry can be produced."[8]

History later confirmed the prediction of Zhou Zuoren. From the Crescent Moon School to the Symbolist School to the Modernist School in the 1930s, artistic thinking of harmony between humans and the world has become the basic feature of the new poetry writing. *Xing* completed the most far-reaching regeneration in the history of Chinese new poetry.

Patterns of Poetry Expressions: Evoking Emotions with Objects and Emotions Flowing with the Changing Objects

On a macro level, *Xing* guided the poets' pursuits of "the meaning of the images"; thus, opening up a brand new era in the history of modern Chinese poetry. In terms of specific artistic techniques, the expression pattern represented by *Xing*, which arouses emotions with images and follows with images has also won people's hearts and become one of the basic features of modern Chinese new poetry writing.

"*Xing* is the technique of speaking something else before the elicitation of one's real intentions" (Zhu Xi). "Speaking of something else before expressing one's feelings" was once the earliest, most common initiating model of Chinese classical poetry. In modern Chinese poetry, this model still received extensive attention and application. For example, when Xu Zhimo hand-peeled lotus seeds, the sight of river gulls reminded him of his love ("I Came to the Yangtze River to Buy a Bouquet of Lotus Seeds"). His thoughts went flying because of the tranquility of the courtyard, and the bright moon in the sky ("In the Mountains"). Wen Yiduo associated chrysanthemums in a bottle with the "superb" and "free elegance" of the distant motherland and the Eastern civilization ("A Gathering of Chrysanthemums"). Lin Huiyin submitted herself to an infinite sadness because of the music heard late at night ("Music in the Late Night"). Fang Weide triggered a storm in his own heart in the storm of nature ("Storm"). Li Jinfa, caught in a drizzle, thought of his hometown ("Rain"). Feng Naichao wrote, "Looking at the dying candlelight /Reminded me of the faded joy in the past" ("Dying Candlelight"). After seeing some children throwing stones, Bian Zhilin realized the fact life had been "thrown into the world" ("Throwing"). Dai Wangshu had an autumn dream when he saw the fallen leaves and a shepherdess ("Autumn's Dream"). With the "breath of the sea," came the "homesickness of the wanderer" ("The Wanderer"). He Qifang sighed over his loneliness at the sight of the dampness of the rainy gloomy days ("A Rainy Day"). Further, we find some traces of this kind of lyric model in the May Fourth vernacular new poems (that is, before the second generation of Chinese new poetry), such as Hu Shih's "April 25 Night" and Luo Jialun's "See Off Chu Seng (Xu Deyan) to France at the Qianmen Gate" and so on. It can be seen that *Xing* has a wide influence as an artistic expression model.

In correspondence with the objective form of modern Chinese poetry in separate paragraphs, the model of "speaking of something else before expressing one's feelings" also made some new adjustments. There might be more than one elicitation and the emotions caused by it are no longer consistent from the beginning to the end. In a poem, other images rich in ideas can be found frequently, generating rising and falling poetic feelings. For example, in Xu Zhimo's "Farewell to Cambridge," the golden willow trees of the riverside elicited the reverie of the hometown fellows; the green weeds on the soft mud brought out soft feelings; the deep whirl under the shade evoked past dreams. In "Reflections," Li Jinfa was reminded of the wretched passing of life at the sight of falling leaves and reflected on the necessity of immediate pleasure when he heard drunk songs under the moon. Feng Zhi reflected on the trapping of human beings after the observation of the vast, deep oceans. He was reminded of the transiency of life by the breeze on his hair ("Seaside"). If the one-time "speaking of other things before expressing one's feelings" can be called "evoking emotions with objects," then this multiple uses of "evoking emotions with objects + speaking of other things before expressing one's feelings" should be called "the flow of the emotions with the changing objects."

"Evoking emotions with objects" is a simple mode of *Xing* initiating, while "the flow of the emotions with objects" is more complicated and mature. At this time, the images of *Xing* not only would evoke emotions, but also naturally go with the flow of poetry and become an organic part of poetry. "The flow of the emotions with objects" is not only a product of the new style of modern poetry but also coincides with the development clues of the Chinese classical poetry model. The mechanical rhythmic beginning is turned to changing metaphors in the poetry and harmony of humans and the objective world, with complete natural integration of scenes and emotions.

In Chinese classical poetry, the objects used to elicit emotions are integrated with the emotions delivered, suggesting the flow of emotions in the visual representation of objects, which is the real high-level mode. We could also regard it as a more advanced, more ideal flow of emotions with objects. In the modern poetry of Lin Huiyin during the 1920s, He Qifang, and Dai Wangshu during the 1930s, it is difficult to find one or more such elicitations. They have become part of the emotional delivery, an advanced form of emotional flow through objects. For example, in "Joy" by He Qifang:

> How does joy come? Where is it from?
> Like fireflies flying in the dreamy shades of trees?
> Like the fragrance from the petals of the roses?
> When it comes, is there a jingling ringing from its feet?

Joy is a kind of emotion, but here it is expressed as an object. Are not these (floral scents in the air, crisp ringtones, flying fireflies) vital images themselves a kind of joy?

In the style as represented by "Joy," *Xing* as a means of emotion elicitation is hidden and obscured. However, it is historical progress that the pattern of poetry expressions turned from explicit to implicit and from artificial to natural in terms of the poetry spirit development.

In line with the tendency of Chinese new poetry to subdue the employment of *Xing*, the heated discussion of *Xing* in modern Chinese poetry also faded after the mid-1930s. During the 1940s, when Zhu Guangqian established his more modern poetic system, *Xing* had retreated to a rather secondary position. In my opinion, this is precisely the fact that *Xing* has completed its generating mission to Chinese new poetry and entered a state of harmony with other artistic expressions.

The Creative Subjectivity Mechanism of Modern Poets

Xing's significance in generating Chinese modern poetry could also be shown through its influence on the creative subjectivity mechanism of Chinese modern poets. This influence is mainly reflected in the poet's personality cultivation and the writing mood.

The poets' personality cultivation is an important foundation of the creative subjectivity mechanism. Of course, in this respect, we cannot ignore the influence of Western romanticism and symbolic poetics on Chinese poets. For example, Guo Moruo proposed, "Only a person with a quite perfect personality could become a true poet."[9] Mu Mutian and others also repeated the concept of "pure poetry" of French Symbolism. However, it should be pointed out that such inward exploration of self or subconsciousness by Western modern poetics has not become the main target of the modern Chinese poet's personality cultivation. Even those who elaborate on the Western poetic personality are equally fascinated by the *Xingfa* personality (naturalized personality) of Chinese traditional poetics, and they show a strong preference for this naturalized personality. Guo Moruo quite appreciated Zong Baihua's "heart and objects resonance theory." Mu Mutian said, "Emotions and feelings cannot be separated from the reality of life. They are evoked by the objective reality."[10] Finally, we must "overcome our individualistic sentimentalism completely."[11]

The basic idea of *Xingfa* personality means the poet emphasizes the rhythm of his emotions in the objective world, constantly seeks to return to his inner world, and finally realizes the harmony between the two. In this way, the naturalized personality which would abandon the unrefined and maintain the essence and purification could be formed.

Several poetics articles published in *The Journal of the Young China Association* in 1920 laid the basic idea of the Chinese new poets' personality cultivation. Zong Baihua's "New Poetry Talk" believes that besides "reading for truth," two kinds of activities are the most important to develop the "poet personality." The first is acting in nature, which is a premise; the second is acting in society.[12] Kang Baiqing said in "My Views of the New Poetry" that there are three things that can be done to cultivate personality: acting in nature, acting in society, and always appreciating art.[13] The opinions of these two are similar, with both considering nature particularly important. As for the important objective conditions of social phenomena, they are related to the new changes in the living environment of modern people (of course, the ancients also attach importance to social phenomena). Both these two opinions highlight the ontological meaning of external objects. Reading for truth and appreciating the art are also keys to personal experience and return to the inner emotional rhythms. The simultaneous operation of the two is the foundation of *Xingfa*, that is, "the reflections on external objects would lead to internal thoughts and when the thoughts could not be suppressed, they have to be delivered—this is called *Xing*" (Jia Dao, *Ernan Mizhi*, a literary theory work).

In modern Chinese poetry theories, many discussions about the poet's personality cultivation could be found and the subjective and objective conditions described here are quite representative. Liang Zongdai believes "the poet is a dual observer. He should examine himself on the one hand and the external world on the other."[14] Zhang Xiuzhong, whose poetry review *Past, Present, and Future of China's New Poetry Community* was considered the first new poetry history in modern Chinese literature history, believes the poet's cultivation includes "studying the secrets of the universe and acting in nature; seeing the truth of human nature and acting in society and appreciation of art."[15] It is worth mentioning that some modern poetic theories use the terminology of Western modern literary thoughts more frequently. Yet, from a broader or more fundamental level, they are almost always the "personality model" projection required by *Xing*. The poetry theories influenced by the Soviet proletariat literature and art view are a case in point. For example, during the 1940s, Zang Kejia pointed out that poets must integrate with objective things when they live their life among the masses: "The richer the life, the more changes it has, the more inspirations one could get and with higher frequency."[16]

When a naturalized personality, a pure selfless mind communicates with the objective world, the finest and slightest information will surge, and poetic ideas will begin to brew and start to generate. This is the basic state of mind in poetry writing. Here, the naturalized personality still needs to continue to maintain the "naturalization" state of convergence and observe the life charm of external objects calmly and humbly. At this time, a too-sharp personality will destroy the integrity of external objects; excessive and too much enthusiasm will obscure the poet's eyes and ears. "When one is preparing to write a poem, one must concentrate. When observing the external things, he will express it with his heart" (*Wen Jing Mi Fu Lun, A Collection of Poetic Theories*). Kang Baiqing believes the first step in new poetry writing is to explore unintentionally in the universe.[17] Bing Xin believes "a calm heart can create a deeper world in any environment" (*Myriad Stars: 57*). Lin Huiyin's "inspiration" can only be produced in this calmness: "It is you, it is flowers, dreams, passed here, / at this moment, wrapping me like the breeze; / telling the nests in the overlapping mountains; / the slow flowing of the clear spring turned into the wild river" ("Inspiration"). Zong Baihua described his creative mood of *Flowing Clouds* in a delicate, vivid way:

> I felt the leisurely walks at dusk, peaceful meditation on starry nights, and the loneliness in the crowds. I often seemed to hear some unnamed tones in my ears, which

can't be caught; yet, they were quickly forming. It was often in the night when I lay on the bed and turned off the lights, my sleepless heart became excited and I felt the breathing of the metropolis resting outside my window. I paused to breathe in a balanced rhythm, like a sea of flat waves, a cold moon gazing at this dynamic, quiet world. I cannot help but have many distant thoughts rushing into my heart, which seemed sad, but also seemed joyous. It seemed understanding, but also seemed obscure. An infinite sense of coldness was mixed with an infinite sense of love. It seemed a deep, mysterious, dark passage in the ground was tunneled to connect this faint heart, the distant nature, and the vast majority of human beings. The most intimate contact with nature and life in absolute silence was obtained. Most of the poems in *Flowing Clouds* were written in such moods.[18]

In this kind of personality cultivation and creative state of mind, "the curtain between the world and us has been revealed forever. Like going back to our hometown, we have restored the universal and complete scenes of the universe, or we can say that we returned to the bottom of the universe or back into its arms. We not only encountered the drunkenness of lightning and dreams but the reality that we experienced at any time and anywhere." "A thread of sunshine, a flying flower, the slightest vibration of the air, and the immense amount of significant or trivial things and phenomena are always affecting our spiritual life and reminding us of our relationship with the universe."[19]

Some new poetry works emerged in such a state of mind. The meaning of *Xing* is worthy of our attention from the generation of poetry to its production.

Xing and the Symbol Technique

Interestingly, the historical encounter between Chinese modern poetry and *Xing* should be credited to Western poetics to some extent. In 1926, Zhou Zuoren first associated *Xing* with the symbol technique; thus, providing a very valuable theoretical beginning for the modern poetry movement. Basic ideas of Chinese classical poetry have been interpreted in line with the trends of the world. Foreign poetics theory has finally melted with the local cultures. Therefore, Chinese modern poets can return to the artistic world of *Xing* through the decent modern passage of symbols.

In today's view, such a Chinese-Western fusion failed to avoid Zhou Zuoren's misunderstanding.

There is a striking similarity between *Xing* and the symbol technique in terms of expressing abstract thoughts and feelings with concrete images.

However, if we introduce a profound background of national cultures, then their respective differences cannot be ignored.

Xing was born from the primitive religions of China, but its maturity benefited from the traditional philosophy of "humane culture" that dispelled this religious spirit. Therefore, the essence of Xing is not about the religious obsession, but the subtle experiences of the poets returning to the state of "integration of Heaven and Man." In the Chinese-style humane culture philosophy, emotion is not limited to human beings, but a natural life phenomenon that prevails in the universe. "The emotional expressions of anger, sorrow, happiness, and joy have always been in correspondence with the seasonal changes of coldness and warmth, winter and summer" (*Chunqiu Fanlu*). The use of symbols can also be traced to primitive religions but matured in the era of religious theology during the Middle Ages. Symbols are essentially poets' perceptions and suggestions of the metaphysical divine world. As Charles Baudelaire, a Symbolism pioneer said, it is because of poetry, also through poetry ... that the soul glimpses the glory behind the grave.[20]

The objects and images for Xing are self-contained and complete. In Chinese philosophy, "one" (wholeness) is the original, most ideal destination. Objects for symbols are more fragmented and only unified in the poet's religious concepts. While the objects of Xing can communicate with the poet's soul with independent meanings, symbolic images, on the other hand, have no such independence. They are purely products of the poet's subjective will and religious beliefs. In Western poetics, symbols are simply labeled as signs and substitutes for logical representations.[21]

As part of poetry, the production of Xing, symbols, and their basic characteristics are different. As mentioned previously, the initiation of Xing must be imaginary, remain calm, and destroy the mysterious concepts to observe the world with peace and tranquility, while symbolic thinking is full of excitement and religious obsession. Baudelaire believes "the study of beauty is a duel in which the artist cries with terror before being defeated."[22] Richard Eberhart, an American poet in the 20th century, also commented in Platonic language that poetry is divine and the process of poetry writing is ultimately mysterious, involving the whole body's impulses by some kind of God-given power.[23]

In line with this, the art of Xing and the art of symbol use are not the same in their requirements for poets. We already know the requirements for Xing are summarized as respect for objects and tempering of subjects, while the artistic requirements for symbol use are related to consistent advocacy of

Western poetics to worship the self and strengthen the poet's subjectivity with imagination as the requirement by poets for the symbolized art. As Arthur Rimbaud said, the poet is a voyant and the spiritual force can only be sensed by a chosen few. His masterpiece "The Drunken Boat" is a wonderful depiction of the sea, which he has never seen.

For Chinese modern poets, these profound cultural differences between Xing and the symbol technique seem ignored. The anxiety due to the impact of the Western poetry trends and the urgency of developing Chinese modern new poetry revealed the basic mentality that permeated Chinese modern poetry. In many cases, the revival of culture seems more deeply rooted and practical than the transformation of culture. As a result, the Xing of Chinese traditional poetics finally withstood the impact of Symbolism and firmly rooted in the new Chinese poetry.

Bi[24] and Rhetoric Devices of Modern Chinese New Poetry

> Without metaphors, there would be no poetry.
>
> —*Book of Rites*

Rhetoric is an art that presents ideas in a special way.[25] The independence of literary works is shown as the independence of rhetoric, that is, the independence of language operation. The artistic pursuit of modern Chinese new poetry also lies in its rhetorical pursuit.

It is beyond the scope of this book to analyze the rhetorical characteristics of the new poetry in detail. I only choose a typical strategy in the rhetoric of poetry—the metaphor to examine—and this kind of investigation is not entirely from the perspective of linguistics, but from the perspective of culture or the so-called "cultural rhetoric."

Distant Metaphor and Near Metaphor

The metaphorical art of modern Chinese new poetry experienced a process of gradual maturity. In the early Chinese vernacular new poetry, metaphors were quite scarce. For example, *Selected Vernacular Poems*, published by the Shanghai Chongwen Bureau in 1920, is the first new poetry collection. In the scenery writing category of this book, only about one-fourth of the poets used metaphors. One-fifth of the emotion-themed writing and less than one-tenth of thought-based poems used metaphors. It is even less for the realism school, where almost no real metaphor can be found. The few metaphors used in the book are mostly simple and sketchy. For example, snow is described as "that white sugar-like thing," "like cotton," and "like flour." When writing about Lunar New Year's Eve, it is written as "the taste is deep, just like sugar." Only after the formation of the Chinese Lakeside School (Wang Jingzhi, Feng Xuefeng, etc.), and the publication of Bing Xin's *Myriad Stars* and *Spring Water*, which indicated the poetry movement, did metaphors gradually increase. Guo Moruo's poetry writing fully mobilized the power of metaphors, which often produced an amazingly overwhelming experience. Let's take a look at some of the well-known pieces in *The Goddesses*. One-third of the sentences in "Phoenix Nirvana," and "Bathing in the Sea" used metaphors; Metaphors were used in 3/5 of the sentences in "Earth, My Mother," and "New Yangguan Trio." And there are more than 10 metaphors in the poems of "Sunrise" and "A View on the Mountain Top" with a total of 16 sentences. At this point, the metaphor art of Chinese new poetry started to form.

The metaphors in *The Goddesses*, *Myriad Stars*, and *Spring Water* signified the maturity of Chinese new poetry. However, we believe their respective characteristics are very different. The metaphor style in *The Goddesses* impresses readers with its rich imagination, evoking and inciting the reader's thoughts in a distant connection, such as "I am the *Tiangou* (Heaven Dog)," my head is "like the crematorium stove," Beethoven's "high-profile white-collar is like snow-covered mountain peppers," etc. The following are typical metaphors in works such as *Myriad Stars* and *Spring Water*: "We are all babies of nature / lying in the cradle of the universe" (*Myriad Stars*). Such rhetoric does not impress us with its weirdness. Instead, it is soft and quiet, and it uses imagination to properly resolve the sharpness and rhetoric of imagination. The words are united with the context. It seems a calm depiction of the truth of our existence. For example, are we not the babies of the universe? These do not seem to be technical metaphors. Borrowing the term used by Zhu Ziqing, we can refer to the metaphors of *The Goddesses* as Distant Metaphors and the metaphors of *Myriad Stars* and *Spring Water* as Near Metaphors. Zhu Ziqing once said, "The so-called distant and near does not refer to the metaphorical material, but refers to the metaphorical method."[26] "Distant" is to see the similarities among those that ordinary people would think differently. The poets discovered new relationships between objects and used the most economical method to weave this relationship into poetry. "Near" pays attention to shortening the distance between objects and paying attention to the connection between objects.

Distant Metaphors are often surprising and thought-provoking, while Near Metaphors are often more approachable. They are fresh but not peculiar, and we do not need to rack our brains to crack them!

Zhu Ziqing put forward the term Distant Metaphor when summing up the artistic characteristics of symbolic poetry. Not all symbolic poets have chosen this metaphorical mode. Li Jinfa wrote mosquitoes, "screaming along my innocent ears, / just like the wild wind roaring" ("Abandoned Woman"), "My loving heart ... [is like] the sounds of the remaining winter on the plains" ("Love and Hate"), Hu Yepin stated, "the sea tide is like the earth's bandits" ("Nightmare"). These are Distant Metaphors. But Mu Mutian wrote his sister's "teardrops are the most beautiful new wine" ("Teardrops"), the memory of the past is "the dust in the dream" ("String"). Feng Naichao wrote, "The church is as bright as the kingdom of heaven" ("Andante at the End of the Year"). These are examples of Near Metaphors. On the whole, it seems easier to win the reader's approval in modern Chinese poetry with Near Metaphors, so they are used more frequently. From the Crescent Moon School to the Symbolist School to the Modernist School, modern Chinese new poetry constantly improved and developed the Near Metaphor approach adopted by Bing Xin. Especially in modern poetry works, metaphors are often intertwined with the emotions derived from the scenes and the depictions of objective scenes, hiding their subjective intentions, such as Dai Wangshu's "My Memory," He Qifang's "The Moon," and Bian Zhilin's "The Round Treasure Box." Sometimes, there are no specific words indicating the metaphor, but the emotions or scenes of the entire poem constitute a huge metaphor, such as Bian Zhilin's "Organization of Distance."

The special favor toward Near Metaphors of the new poetry is consistent with the rhetorical tradition of Chinese classical poetry. As early as in the *Analects of Confucius*, the Near Metaphor is synonymous with metaphors. "The use of a metaphor easily connected is the best strategy." The metaphors of Chinese classical poetry are mainly a kind of Near Metaphors. "There are beauties in the South, whose complexions are like peach flowers" (Cao Zhi, "Miscellaneous Poetry"). "Life is rootless, floating like dust in the fields" (Tao Qian, "Miscellaneous Poetry"), "Red Flowers are easy to fall like your love, the water is flowing infinitely like my sorrow" (Liu Yuxi, "Zhuzhi Ci"), "How much my sorrow has increased if you ask?" Just like the Yangzi River water flowing eastward (Li Yu, "Yu Meiren"). The reason why these metaphors are taken as Near Metaphors is because of the short distance between the tenor and vehicle, either within the scope of the poet's lyrical ambitions or in the poet's habitual thinking logic. With the basic comprehension and cultural understanding of a Chinese reader, it is not difficult to quickly grasp their meaning. Liu Xie summed up this metaphor strategy as "right on target." He said, "While there are many kinds of metaphors, the most valuable is the appropriate one. If you described a tiger and others thought of lions, then it would be redundant" (Liu Xie, *Wenxin Diaolong*). It seems that Distant Metaphors are opposed by Chinese poetics.

Why does the metaphor choice of modern Chinese new poetry coincide with that of Chinese classical poetry? Maybe we could seek answers from the perspective of cultural rhetoric.

As a rhetoric, the metaphor is, of course, a kind of "special language technique," which fully expresses the subjectivity and will of the poets. However, literary works achieve the expected effect through special language means; yet, they could not break away from core language.[27] A metaphor is a specific speech act and cannot be separated from the deep structure of the language. All Chinese modern poets received their early education through the "superstable" Chinese language system. This creates a deep-rooted language core in their hearts and their words of individualized creation must be subject to the restrictions of this core. The core provides the language library of art and the possibility of flexibility. Particularly for poetry, there is no essential difference between the vernacular and classical Chinese in its internal language structure, such as phonological, lexical, syntactic, textual structure, and so on. The shared deep structure of language is an important basis for modern Chinese new poetry to reproduce the rhetoric of classical poetry.

The Crescent, Symbolist, and Modernist poets generally have rich, traditional, cultural literacy, while poets like He Qifang, Bian Zhilin, Dai Wangshu, Sun Dayu, and others made in-depth rhetorical studies on Chinese. Thus, they laid a cultural rhetorical foundation for the survival and development of the metaphor in modern Chinese poetry.

Two Features of Near Metaphor

There are two main characteristics of Near Metaphor in modern Chinese new poetry which show distinct national cultural qualities.

First, the metaphors of modern Chinese new poetry pay much attention to contextualization, which means the metaphors in the poems notice each other and form a scene of internal harmony. Some are the coordination between several metaphors, such as Xu Zhimo's "Laments": "I also wish my poems to be like water flow, / I also wish my heart to be like fish in the pond." These two metaphors together remind the well-known Chinese phrase: "The fish gets into the water." Another example is He Qifang's "Joy":

> Tell me, what color is joy?
> Like the wings of a white dove? The red beak of a parrot?
> What is the sound of joy? Like a reed flute?
> Or from the rustling sounds of the pine trees to the babbling flowing water?

The wings of the white dove, the red beak of the parrot, the sound of the reed flutter, the rustling sounds of the pine trees, and the babbling of water flowing, isn't such context itself full of joy? Sometimes, the metaphors merge with other objects in the poem, such as Lin Huiyin's "Still": "You stretch like a lake from the clear sky / white clouds are like a cool valley stream, crystal-clear / please allow me to trace your origin: /but I still hold all kinds of suspicions / to each reflection of you!" The images, such as the lake, the cool valley stream, and the imaginary objects in the poem, such as the origin of the spring, reflections, and the shadows jointly build an open, pure scene. Another example is the songs of the spring birds in "Spring Birds" by Zang Kejia. "Like the hands of many goddesses/press together the keys of life. /Enchanting sounds flow / from the clouds of green trees, / from the sea of blue sky. /Joined a pool of lively freedom."

In these scenes, the metaphors of certain parts are polished without any traces. As deliberate rhetoric, the metaphors properly soften the edge of the subject's will, while expressing itself.

The contextualization of modern Chinese poetry metaphors reflects the rhetorical concept inherent in Chinese culture. *Laozi* begins with his point: "Tao that can be described is not universal and eternal Tao. Name that can be named is not universal and eternal Name." That is to say, people simply cannot understand nor are they able to use language to convey the ultimate mystery of the universe. "He who knows doesn't speak, he who speaks doesn't know." In this way, it is a wise choice to maintain the unnamed state of things. Non-interpretative, non-subjective will is the main feature of the Chinese poetry language. Metaphor is a kind of intentional discourse, but in the practice of Chinese poetry, it is extremely necessary to dispel its intentionality. Therefore, the metaphor is often integrated with the mountains and rivers or context. With the natural power of the mountains and rivers, human rhetoric seems to approach the closest to Tao.

Compared with the metaphorical model of modern Western poetry, modern Chinese poetry shows national characteristics more clearly. Western poets have no intention of relying on mountains and rivers to express their understanding of the meaning of the world. Their metaphors never return to the original state of the world in contextualization, whether it is the explicit simile of romanticism or the implicit metaphor of modern poetry. This rhetoric exists only as a kind of technique chosen by the poet's subjective will. The poet's own will is always the unspeakable supreme. Wordsworth said, "Thy soul was like a Star, and dwelt apart: /Thou hadst a voice whose sound was like the sea" ("London, 1802"). Paul Verlaine said, "A cradle, I, / Rocked in a grave: / Speak low, pass by, / Silence I crave!" ("Sleep, Darksome, Deep") Objects, such as the spirit of the people and the distant stars, "I" and the cradle, are far separated and it is difficult to unite in a certain natural environment. Then, what is it that connects them? It is the subjective feelings and thoughts of people. Through his thinking, Western poets could expand without reserving the distance between the tenor and the vehicle. It is almost impossible for the metaphor to return to the natural state of the "tenor" of the world. The metaphor is just a technique.

We noticed modern Chinese poets are quite clear about our metaphorical tradition. For example, Qian Zhongshu proposed—if metaphors in the reasoning style are only a tool and could be called "signs," metaphors in the lyrics, in contrast, could not. Those in the lyric poems should be called "icons." He believes in the argumentative writings, "When the reasoning is clear, then metaphors are not necessary or even they could be discarded." That is to say, metaphors can finally be abandoned, just like giving away the boat when upon the shore. But in the lyric poems, the metaphor is an organic component. "A poem sends its message with metaphors. There are messages with the metaphors and if the metaphors were discarded then the poems would lose their meanings."[28] This kind of understanding is indeed different from Western poetics. For example, the new critic master, I. A. Richards, described metaphors accurately as the boat that arrived at the other side of truth. For Richards, external objects have no meaning at all; it is us who gives them meaning. People exist before objects and language exists before reality.

Second, the metaphor of modern Chinese new poetry embodied cultural inheritance to a certain degree, that is to say, it accepts the prototype metaphor of Chinese classical poetry. In the early new poetry, only several metaphors are almost directly transferred from the metaphors of classical poetry, such as calling the snow "flowers" and "cotton," and the sky "sapphire" and so on. For the mature modern new poetry, the meanings of its metaphors are from Chinese classical poetry, despite its modern discourse, such as Xu

Zhimo's famous metaphor: "The most gentleness of the bow, / like the shyness of a water lotus flower that cannot withstand the cool breeze." Connecting women's gestures with lotus flowers is a typical discourse of Chinese poetry. For example, the poet Guo Zhen of the Tang Dynasty wrote in the poem "Lotus Flower," "The fragrant face is full of expressions. Is there anything in the world that is as graceful? Princess Xiang visited the pond after the rain, the lotus leaves are like jade dishes with crystals rolling." The lilac in Dai Wangshu's "A Lane in the Rain" makes people think of Li Jing's verse: "The Green Bird does not carry the letter from beyond the clouds, and only the lonely lilac lost in the misty rain" ("Huan Xi Sha"). In his poem "The Letters," Bian Zhilin compared the letter to "the fish swimming through the Yellow Sea, the geese flying over from Siberia," which is naturally a modern variant of the "Fish Goose as Messengers" in ancient Chinese poems. Also, Wen Yiduo, "forget her, like a flower that has been forgotten," Shen Congwen's love poem, "You are a willow twig," Shao Xunmei compared women to "snakes." Here the flowers, willows, and snakes all have well-known archetypes of meaning in classic Chinese poetry. The common metaphor prototypes in the new poems also include symbols of a certain life situation: dreams, geese, fireflies, autumn leaves, morning fog, drifting boats, and the moon's cycling and the symbols of some life pursuit—fish, silkworms, free flowing clouds, and water, moths running into a fire, etc.

Historical inheritance strengthens the metaphor's function as an aggregation of words. It brings isolated words into the vast history and culture and provides new meaning. Thus, the individual behavior of a metaphor once again melted its edge and continued its contextualization process in the historical space.

Historical inheritance and the contextualization of the metaphor complement each other.

Is the metaphor of Western poetry also historically inherited? Maybe, because we have found the prototype metaphor from the Bible or other myths from the modern poetry of T. S. Eliot and others. Still, looking at the tradition of Western poetry, I believe the historical exploitation of the metaphor is originally a way of acculturation between man and the world. On the whole, Western poets do not feel much interest in this acculturation. Therefore, they are not keen on borrowing historical forms of metaphors, and their subjective initiative is always the most important. Although Eliot used large numbers of myths and legends in *The Waste Land,* many of the allusions and metaphors in anthropology, philosophy, and literary works do not mean he intends to entrust his peace of mind to history. On the contrary, the basic spirit is Eliot's deep thinking about the complex relationship between history and the reality of mankind. Therefore, I believe that Roger Fowler's idea could be representative of the Western poetry community. That is, metaphor is crucial in a language not only because of its importance as a literary technique but also because of its feature of being *particularly elusive and changeable*.[29]

Variations of Tradition

With the above analysis, we might have the impression the metaphor of modern Chinese new poetry seems purely a simple reappearance of the classical rhetoric of classical poetry. It is not the case. After all, modern Chinese poetry is the product of the 20th-century context. Therefore, it must face and respond to China's turmoil and drastic changes during the 20th century. As part of the discourse in a changing era, rhetoric would also have to adjust as appropriate to its traditions. When the "tenor" of the world was turbulent, could the "vehicle" still hold on to that silence? When the machines, guns, and survival competitions of the industrial age occupied the poets' life, could they rely on only a few fallen flower petals and a few branches of willow to reflect themselves? When the 20th century became gloomier and more complex, discussions on fallen flowers and willow trees were too powerless and simple to perform the tasks.

Compared with Chinese classical poetry, the art of metaphor in Chinese new poetry has at least three new changes. The first is to provide historical metaphors with new and diverse connotations. For example, Zang Kejia wrote, "Disasters are the star clusters of the sky" ("Life"). The stars in the sky are mostly bright and shining, but here they are full of misfortunes. For another example, Yin Fu wrote, "The silent chimney;" "She is standing strong, as strong as a fairy" ("Our Poetry: Silent Chimney"). It should be the experience of modern people that the gentle, elegant fairy could be so strong and determined. More examples: Shao Xunmei, "I have sinned flowers" ("Sin Like Flowers"). Yuan Kejia wrote, "Refugees, Like the land under your feet, you are the necessarily superfluous" ("Refugees"). Why are flowers "sinful"? How does land become "necessarily superfluous"? These metaphors would not work in traditional poetry.

The second is to find a new relationship between objects in the metaphors. The distance between the tenor and the vehicle is widened, which means that some Distant Metaphors are produced. Besides Guo Moruo and

Li Jinfa, other poets sometimes chose these kinds of metaphors. For example, Wen Yiduo wrote, "Hometown is a thief" ("You See"). Chen Mengjia wrote, "He is still solemn like autumn" ("White Russian Old Man"). Ke Zhongping wrote, "Poverty is like an old man in the ancient times /with no knife and axe" ("This Empty Heart"). Hang Yuehe wrote that urban people are "like fermented sewage" ("Resurrection of the Land"). Du Yunxie wrote, "The fallen leaves are like a serious artist" ("Fallen Leaves"). Hu Feng wrote that the weather "is lying like a dead snake" ("Spring on the Ruins").

Third, there are some non-physical metaphors. The physical tangibility of a metaphor is a distinctive feature of Chinese traditional poetry. An ancient definition of metaphor is "whether the borrowed object could be exemplified" (Wang Fu, *Qian Fu Lun*). "To compare one object with another" (Zhu Xi, *History of Poetry*). Objects with specific physical characteristics are often used by Chinese poets as poetic descriptions, such as using strong bamboo knots to indicate the fortitude of the human will. "People sympathize the thin knots of the bamboo, the bamboo is determined to grow higher and stronger as it matures" (Wang Anshi, "Hymn to Bamboo with my Brother at the Minjun Pavilion of Huazang Temple"). Pine trees are frequently used to indicate the strength of older people. "Old pine tree cuddled the new green, the secluded flowers blossomed in the late spring" (Gu Yanwu, "Mountain Songshan"). Fragrant plum blossoms are used to signify noble gentlemanship, "Not angling for compliments, I would be content that my integrity fills the universe" (Wang Wei, "Inked Plum Blossom").

In addition to specific objects, modern Chinese poetry uses some abstract concepts from time to time. Some metaphors are rational products without emotional characteristics. For example, "what we expect is only one promise / but only the void let us know that we are still / *the ancestors of human beings before the arrival of happiness*" (Mu Dan, "This Era"). "The peaceful wings of the returned swallows / *like the fable of life*" (Li Jinfa, "The Fall of the Night"). Some metaphors are infiltrated with reasoning along its perceptual depictions, such as "a small cluster of huts / *standing like the darkness of life*" (Mudan, "The Deserted Village"). "Life is / *the smile on / Death lips*" (Li Jinfa, "Thoughts"). "Those innocent eyes … *just like an ignorant indifferent green field*" (Zheng Min, "Little Painter"). This type of metaphor reminds us of the tradition of Western poetry. In Western poetics, the metaphor is a rather broad concept and does not necessarily go with specific objects. Shakespeare's famous saying "Ripeness is all" has always been regarded as a typical metaphor because Western philosophers believe

... every language already contains a mass of metaphors. They arise from the fact that a word that originally signifies only something sensuous is carried over into the spiritual sphere. Fassen, begreifen, and many words, to speak generally, which relate to knowing, have in respect of their literal meaning a purely sensuous content, which then is lost and exchanged for spiritual meaning, the original sense being sensuous, the second spiritual.[30]

So, does this mean the new changes in the modern Chinese new poetry metaphor have nothing to do with the national cultural tradition of China?

Of course not. I believe this "relationship" could be shown from at least two aspects.

First, the traditional Chinese Near Metaphor has a significant restrictive effect on such new changes, inhibiting and prescribing its existence. Therefore, from the perspective of history, the traditional model of metaphors still dominates. Although variation is fresh and beautiful, it is more in line with the trend of the 20th century but has limited influence in the longer term. It did not change the rhetoric of Chinese new poetry as a whole. Even Guo Moruo, who started a new generation of poetic style and made many contributions to the modern variation of the new poetry metaphor model, emphasized later that "while being influenced by foreign literature, the new poetry has not abandoned the tradition of Chinese poetry."[31]

In particular, the establishment of metaphors of non-physical tangibility, or Distant Metaphors, implied the emergence of a series of abstract concepts and a more logical tendency of language activities. This is far from the traditional Chinese figurative model. The strengthening of the logic of poetry language inevitably re-assembled Chinese poetry from lexical, syntactic to textual aspects. Thus, this new change was subject to the greatest resistance. The Chinese tradition did not seem to encourage such rhetorical patterns, so nearly 40 years later, even Mu Dan, who insisted on the most abstract lyrics, was also confused about the new poetry: "In general, I don't feel poetic about my works, I mean, not the traditional poetic sense. This leads to doubts about myself sometimes. I feel what I wrote is abstract and boring; sometimes I think this is what I want ..."[32]

Second, we could also analyze the internal relationship between variation and stability at the level of cultural rhetoric. The deep structure of the national language is also an important basis for new changes in speech. The rhetoric being an intentional discourse, its variation is closely related to the Chinese language and Chinese culture in its variation possibility, depth, and direction. In other words, it is the result of the deep structure transformation of the Chinese language. Variation and stability are interdependent, and tradition dominates the adjustment of tradition.

For example, when we say "new and diverse connotations should be given to historical metaphors," is this also related to the relative flexibility in classical poetry metaphors? Metaphor in human culture has roughly three categories: one is the religious metaphor, such as the various metaphors in the Bible, which are mysterious and rigid. The second is the metaphor of Western modern poetry, which breaks all the rules. As purely the result of the subjective mind of the poets, they are free and difficult to grasp. The third is what we call the Near Metaphor of Chinese classical poetry, which has different characteristics from the previous two. It is not unpredictable nor purely subjective, and with our intuition, we can grasp its intrinsic idea. "People sympathize the thin knots of the upright bamboo, the bamboo is determined to grow higher and stronger as it matures." Wang Anshi used bamboo to allude himself to say that he was born to be upright and he became more resolute as he aged. Without any explanation, we can accurately comprehend this. At the same time, this kind of metaphor is not rigid. There is relative flexibility. This allows us to make a new understanding from a specific perspective within a certain range. For example, Wang Anshi gave the bamboo an upright character and implied his personality was just like the bamboo. However, another poet, Du Fu, said, "The new pine tree hates not to be a thousand feet high, while the evil bamboo should be cleansed by tens of thousands" ("Written on the Way to Chengdu Cottage, First Sent to Yan Zhenggong"). Du Fu used bamboo to refer to the power that hindered life and described it as "evil." By the time of the Qing Dynasty, Zheng Xie (also known as Zheng Banqiao, an artist best known for his paintings of bamboo) wrote bamboo as an example of supporting each other. "The new bamboo could grow higher than the old, Indebted to the old for their full support" ("New Bamboo").

For another example, the traditional Chinese Near Metaphor has quietly influenced the Distant Metaphor in modern poetry. Therefore, compared with the metaphor of Western poetry, the metaphor of Chinese new poetry is still "near," although it might sound distant. For instance, Li Jinfa wrote, "My soul is the bell of the wilderness"; Hu Yepin wrote, "I am like a wounded beast"; Peng Zi said a woman's long hair is "like a lion's mane." These metaphors, at first glance, are quite fresh, but they are not particularly surprising if we think further because they are still based on some kind of recognition of nature, and are generally the "original" without subjective and excessive distortion. Although modern and contemporary Western poetry is also regarded as models by Chinese poets, how Western poets reconstruct metaphors after destruction is unacceptable for them from the point of view of the practice. Western philosophers once said the connection between the tenor and the vehicle belongs to a kind of "logic of logical aberrations." The truth of poetry comes from the collision of images rather than their collusion. For most modern Chinese poets, these methods of vehicles are still too distant.

The Tradition of *Bi-Xing* and Objectification of Modern Chinese New Poetry

Beholding the world makes me think.
—Lu Ji, Wen Fu (*The Art of Writing*)

Observing modern Chinese poetry from the views of generating and rhetoric, we see the important influence of classical poetic ideals. *Xing* and *Bi* are traditions we cannot abandon. Behind *Xing* and *Bi*, we find a unified existence—"contextualized objects." *Xing* and *Bi* strived to operate the art of thinking in the context of objects. "Using objects to express one's feelings is called *Bi*, which means the feelings are transmitted to the objects. *Xing* is the sight of objects stimulated by these feelings" (Hu Yin, *Fei Ran Collection*, citing Li Zhongmeng). "*Bi* means comparisons with objects, while *Xing* means using objects to start" (Zheng Xuan, *Zhou Li* quoted Zheng Zhong's *Collection*). "*Bi* took other objects as a comparison, *Xing* used objects to start" (Zhu Xi, *Chu Ci Notes*). Poetry does not generate purely subjective imagination but is the result of the interactions between the subjects and the objects. When objects arouse the sentiments of the poets and rhetoric plays down the subjective intentions, Near Metaphor is created in a peaceful and intimate atmosphere. I believe that this is an important aspect of the Chinese poetry culture: objectification. In classical poetics, *Xing* and *Bi* often co-occur (*Bi-Xing*) to describe the artistic characteristics of poetry, and the basis is they both reflect the objectification pursuit in Chinese poetry.

Objectification Analysis

I regard objectification as an important characteristic of the Chinese poetry culture, which needs some clarification because our traditional interpretations generally follow the old sayings of "thought expression" or "emotion expression" and recognize Chinese poetry as expressions of thoughts or emotions.

I believe this is extremely unfavorable for us to find a solution to the goal of national identity. It fails to help us understand Chinese classical poetry and confuses the two cultural conflicts in the development of modern Chinese poetry, which hinders people's observation and inquiry today.

I believe both "thought expression" as described in *Shangshu* in the pre-Qin Dynasty (221–207 BC) and "emotion expression" as described by Lu Ji in the Western Jin Dynasty (266–316) are ultimate judgments of art. Yet, under the influence of the traditional "unity of yin and yang" thinking mode, they are often extended to all areas of Chinese classical poetry interpretation without scrutiny. This could easily make people miss the core of the problem. In particular, when we talk about cultural characteristics in the sense of comparative cultures and comparative poetics, which is quite different from discussing what is poetry and where poetry comes from in the ultimate sense (although in the creative process, similar issues are mentioned from time-to-time. After all, the meaning and focus are different). In this way, if we insist the thinking process of classical poetry should be limited to thought expression or emotional expression, obscurity is inevitable. I would argue from the following four aspects:

1. With the development of Chinese classical poetry art, the interpretation of poetry writing by Chinese classical poets also experienced the process of gradual development and increased accuracy. Chinese classical poetry matured during the Wei and Jin dynasties to the Tang and Song dynasties, while "thought expression" is the theory of the primary stage of Chinese poetry, and "expressing of one's emotions" in the early Western Jin Dynasty cannot be said to include a comprehensive review for the heyday of this art. We have no reason to emphasize this conclusion and disregard the many poetic theories after the Wei and Jin dynasties.

2. An examination of Chinese classical poetry shows thoughts or emotions are not the end point of poetics elaboration, nor are they the only concepts. Others, such as "intentions," "reasoning," "delight," etc., are also under discussion. A comprehensive examination of Chinese classical poetry theories would show one frequent generalization often used is "objects." According to *Wenxin Diaolong* (*The Literary Mind and the Carving of Dragons*), "People have seven emotions and they use objects to express them" ("Ming Poetry"). "When the objects are moving, so is the heart" ("External World"). These refer to the poetry conception from the observations of the external world. Zhuangzi said,

"I am at the beginning of the heart" (*Zhuangzi*), Zhong Rong "create images by describing objects vividly and write about objects with rich emotions" ("*Poetry* Preface"). These are the descriptions of the trajectory of poetry writing. "Viewing objects as they are" ("*Yichuan Jirang Collection* Preface"). "Everything returns to its original state" (Guo Xiang, *Annotation of Zhuangzi*). These show the perfection of poetry writing.

3. From the historical point of view, it is influenced by Western romantic poetics that "thought expression" and "emotion expression" were picked out in modern times as art ontology. However, it is not the Chinese poetry tradition that emphasizes the poet's subjectivity. In the original "thought expression" or "emotion expression," thoughts and emotions do not have such a highly respected status. According to the *Book of Rites* which preferred the "thought expression," "the human mind is stimulated by the external world." The nature of emotions is to "express one's emotions based on the changes of seasons and start to conceive when beholding the things in the world as Lu Ji wrote in *Wen Fu* (*The Art of Writing*). One might become sentimental over the fallen leaves in the solemn autumn and overjoyed when they become tender twigs in full spring." From these expressions we can see thoughts and emotions are not independent and self-sufficient. To a large extent (or even fundamentally), their development depends upon external objects.

4. If thought expression and emotion expression have certain meanings when describing the poet's subjective world, then they could not be used to accurately explain the cultural characteristics of poetry. As we all know, in traditional Chinese culture, the creative activities of poetry have been endowed with strong cultural, and philosophical meanings. Confucius said, "Pursue goodness with poetry, establish oneself in ritual, and cultivate personality in music." Liu Xie, author of *Wenxin Diaolong* (*The Literary Mind and the Carving of Dragons*) argued for "the experience of external and internal integration" of poetry from Zhuangzi's *Easy Travel*. Yan Yu put forward that "poetry writing is similar to Zen." The conception of poetry is considered as the process of experiencing the world by Confucianism, Daoism, and Buddhism. However, in simple thoughts and emotional elaborations, we do not see such philosophical ideas.

Based on the understanding above, we described a way of thinking in Chinese classical poetry from the perspective of cultural studies as objectification. Self-identification in objects is the overall spirit of ancient Chinese philosophy. Confucianism considers social ethics as objects; Daoism and Buddhism consider natural existence as objects. As poetry conveys this philosophical spirit, its most striking characteristics are to deny that man is the master and essence of the world, and strive to seek spiritual harmony in the rhythm of external objects. In the ideal world of poetry, personal emotions have been banned, self-awareness annihilated (no self, pure silence). When people return to the embrace of the objective world, they become an organic component of the objective world and return to equal status with mountains, rivers, birds, and beasts as part of the objectification. Poetry freely presents the original state and rhyme of the world that the objectified self can feel. These are the basic cultural characteristics of Chinese classical poetry art. It does not deny emotions or thoughts, but it treats them as the result of the interactions between humans and the external world. It is also keen to imitate the world, but it shows the ingenuity of life through the mechanized appearance of imitation. The poet abandons the mentality of supremacy, rejecting me-only emotional expressions, turning to experience the world, and turning to catch the slightest feelings stimulated by the external world to the soul. At such times, the poet seems to have changed. He is self-forgotten and transforms into an emptiness. He would sense his existence through the existence of the objects. The object is me, I am the object. The object is objectified in my heart, and my heart is objectified in the object. This is the so-called objectification. The ideal of objectified art is not the excitement of personal emotions, nor the mystery of subjective critical thinking, but the equality of objects, the harmony of objects and people, and the "natural equal status of objects." In other words, this is a physical world where everything is in place and harmony. We call it artistic conception. The Chinese ancients described the beauty of artistic conception once and again and said it is "like the sounds in the air, the color of appearances, the moon in the water, the image in the mirror, and limitless meanings with limited words" (Yan Yu, *Canglang Shihua*). In the artistic conception, the words of scenery are also the words of emotions, the words of these emotions can be applied to the scenery; realism is also ideal and the ideals are also realistic (Wang Guowei, *Renjian Cihua*). It is difficult to find artificial traces, such as, "When an antelope hanged its horns on a tree, no trace can be found" of the world created (Yan Yu, *Canglang Shihua*). In short, artistic conception is the most complete, objectified world.

The idea of artistic conception gradually became perfect during the long process from Wei, Jin to Tang and Song dynasties. That is to say, the objectified spirit of Chinese classical poetry is most fully embodied in the poetry of the Wei, Jin, Tang, and Song dynasties. For example, "An idle man hears cassia-blossoms fall / A tranquil night brings peace to a spring hill; / A moonrise surprises a nightingale, / That twitters randomly in the spring dale." "The split in the Tianmen Mountains allows the Chu River to flow, / The blue waters running east turns to eddies here. / Green cliffs on both sides gradually unfold themselves. / After a solitary sail is coming from where the sun sheds its light." "Clouds veil emerald sky, / Leaves strewn in yellow dye. / Waves rise in autumn hue. / And blend with mist cold and green in view. / Hills steeped in slanting sunlight, sky and waves seem one; / Unfeeling grass grows sweet beyond the setting sun." These are, respectively, written by Wang Wei, "Birds Singing in the Valley"; Li Bai, "Viewing the Tianmen Mountains"; and Fan Zhongyan, "Cold Smoke Lingers." These verses vividly reflect the pursuit of objectification, which means subjective and objective integration in Chinese poetry. They are still popular today.

Of course, the positioning of any concept can only be analyzed at the most typical, representative level. Our analysis of the objectification pursuit of Chinese poetry is mainly focused on the level of man and nature because it is precisely in the observation and expression of nature that Chinese poetry is different from Western poetry. However, I believe the analysis at this level does not narrow the applicability of this concept. For Chinese poetry of social subjects, the objectified way of thinking also applies.

A remarkable characteristic of classical Chinese poetry works with social subjects is that such poems generally do not describe the social phenomenon purely and objectively. Instead, they connect the self and society as much as possible. Rather than a condescending rational examiner, the self is a conscious bearer of social history. External social reality would become the poet's moral mission, which would be expressed through recognition of a certain social role, not just based on individual intelligence. Isn't this similar to the "perception of the external world led to the emotions of the internal mind"?

> If I offer myself to the battlefield, could I still claim life as precious? If I give up taking care of my parents, could I be expected to care for my wife and children? When my name is on the list of the Cavaliers, I am not allowed to consider individual interests. I would rather die for the country and death to me is like returning home. (Cao Zhi, "White Horse")

A message to his majesty of the Nine Heavens in the morning, I was demoted to Chaoyang thousands of miles away in the evening. I would like to reform for His Majesty and would not spare my remaining years. The clouds are hanging in the Qin Range and the horses refused to continue the journey facing the mountain-covered Languan. I am clear about your kindness, coming thus far to see me off. Please collect my bones after my death and bury them along the Zhang River. (Han Yu, "To my Grand-nephew Xiang on Demotion to Languan")

The young and vigorous Cao Zhi was very passionate, and Han Yu, who was in his sixties, was depressed and sad. However, their poems do not further continue along these two moods, showing the complexity of the individual spiritual world, but the rendering of the relationship between personality and moral missions. Therefore, the emotions in the poems, both high and low, belong to ethical emotions, indicating recognition of social roles and social missions. Here, do the poets still need "socialization" (i.e., objectification) first? Isn't the world of poetry a world in which human and social morality are mutually integrated (that is, objectification)?

Objectification of Modern Chinese New Poetry

Just as the tradition of *Bi-Xing* has a wide influence on modern Chinese poetry, objectification as the basic cultural spirit of Chinese poetry also fully demonstrates its existence in modern times.

The objectification characteristics of modern Chinese new poetry can be found in many aspects. *Bi-Xing* is proof of the objectified spirit.

The significance of *Xing* in poetics lies in "generation." The significance of *Bi* in poetics lies in "rhetoric." In terms of the objectification pursuit in poetry writing, *Xing* is the preparation for the pursuit of objectification. It is an important part of the actualization of objectification. *Bi* is the self-improvement of objectified art.

It is still only a concept of human beings to define the natural state of the world as harmonious. Hence, the "unity of heaven and man." The poet is guided from experiencing the external world to objectification, which further leads to forgetting oneself and the world. For instance, if we follow the path of Western evolution, isn't it possible we identify the natural state of the world as competitive? What is the meaning of the objectification pursuit for Chinese poets in the 20th century? It means the widening divergence between ideas and reality. In the 20th century, Chinese poets were often paranoid about the rights of "I," the position of "I," and the will of "I," due to the change in the living environment and the requirements for survival and development. Thus, even though the harmony of the classical era appeared as mentioned by Ferdinand C. S. Schiller; it ceased to exist at that time. Poets turned from simple to sentimental, and the influx of personal emotions is inevitable. In such divergence, how to redeem modern people with emotions and desires into the aesthetic state of objectification mind became a tough issue for Chinese new poetry. Since then, the rediscovery of the poetic value of *Xing* became the first step, an indispensable step, in the objectification of Chinese new poetry.

Xing personality cultivation and aesthetic expectations are a kind of "preparation activities" for creative subjects, which form the vision and style of poems. Between the green mountains and clear waters of nature, the calmness of the heart is used to sense the slight natural life rhythms. The involuntary anxieties of the individual would disappear. Zong Baihua stated well in "Poetry":

Ah,
Where does the poem come from?
Within the drizzle,
that beat on the sound of the falling flowers!
From the breeze,
where the sounds of running streams float!
At the far end of the blue sky,
where the lonely star is tumbledown!

The rain falling on fallen flowers, flowing water singing, and star lights twinkling—these are the natural environment for Chinese poets to cultivate their spirits. It is the atmosphere they have been waiting for their poetic stimulation.

It is worth noting that personality cultivation in nature is only one means of personal cultivation. Modern people do not always have the opportunity to enjoy the scenery and forget everything else. They often find themselves in an independent state of facing the dangerous world. At this time, how do they proceed with their cultivation and expectations? Modern Chinese poets mobilized the power of rationality for self-temperance in line with the characteristics of modern cultural development. From the Crescent Moon School, the Symbolist School to the Modernist School, as the Chinese new poetry matured in art, some poets, who focused on art exploration, consciously used rational means to control their subjective desires and restrict their indulgence within the moderate scope. They tried to find direction for the "no self" modern poetry in theory development. Crescent poets, Modernist poets, and some Symbolist poets (such as Mu Mutian, Feng Naichao, etc.) expressed varying degrees of interest in Western Barnesian "restricting emotions with reason." Of course, Barnesianism is a merely borrowed term. The idea of intuitive rationality in Western poetics did not dominate the minds of Xu Zhimo, Dai Wangshu, and He Qifang. Chinese poets never absolutely suppress emotions, but just release emotions through the power of reason, acquire peace by feeling the world and thoughts, and write the slightest changes in the physical world. This is the solution. Therefore, Shi Ling believes the Crescent Moon School "established an indispensable bridge between old poetry and new poetry."[33] When talking about modern Chinese poetry, Sun Zuoyun also emphasized, "the poetry of the East is based on nature."[34] Some poems are originally self-presentation, but the artistic conception created is completely a self-forgotten objectified world. For example, the following is a Modernist poet's poem about love:

> The lotus flower sleeps quietly in the dream of emerald leaves.
> Its fragrant breath is like the flaming golden wings of fireflies.
> Flying along the lakeside, flying in the misty grass,
> Falling on your knees softly covered by your skirt.
>
> —He Qifang, "A Summer Night"

Only the sentiments and colors are left in this kind of love. It seems the moods, thoughts, and personalities of the two in love were irrelevant. If we talk about the subjectivity of emotions, it is better to use such gentle sentiments. It is restrained; yet, not rigid, maintaining an elated spirit.

We have mentioned the Near Metaphor of modern Chinese poetry pays more attention to the contextualization and inheritance of metaphors, which, coincide with the idea of objectified poetry and maintain the original state of the world. Contextualized metaphors and inherited metaphors have their silent operations, without interpretations from poets. All the desires and emotions of our subjective world must converge. First, we must objectify, then talk about harmony with this objectified environment. In some simple poems, the original effect of objectification is more pronounced:

> We'd like to listen to the whispering dew on the green weeds,
> We'd like to listen to the trail of the breeze on the geese-yellow rice waves.
>
> We'd like to listen to the fluffy, white, translucent clouds which gently fly up,
> We'd like to listen to the flowing songs of the winding and shallow channels.
>
> We'd like to listen to the bells' leisurely echoing from the far temple,
> We'd like to listen to the whirling, cooking smoke rings on the thatched roofs.
>
> —Mu Mutian, "After the Rain"

In this after-the-rain world, weeds, breeze, rice waves, translucent clouds, streams, bells, and cooking smoke constitute a picture not forgotten. "We'd like to listen" is a human desire but this desire is fully reduced. It is fluttering, thin, and optional. Then, the world is peaceful and everything is natural.

The emergence of a large number of social subjects is a distinctive characteristic of modern Chinese poetry. Social reality has become a very important subject of Chinese modern poets, as can be seen from the early vernacular new poems, such as "A Layer of Paper Apart," "Rickshaw Man," and "Selling Cloth Song" to "Long Night" by Pu Feng, "Summer in the Countryside" by Wang Yaping, "To the Fighters" by Tian Jian, and "To Comrades" by He Zhongping. These poems became more important because of social unrest and national crisis during the 1930s and 1940s in China. In the following chapters, we will see the poetic factors that act on this type of poetry were indeed quite complicated. However, here I want to emphasize the quite obvious influence of the traditional Chinese objectification. That is, like Chinese classical poets, a considerable number of poets still did not intend to show the power of self in social activities. They consciously integrated individuals with groups, integrated themselves with society, and when they revealed social reality, they evaded the joys and sorrows of "little I." They consciously based their thoughts and emotions on "big I." The "self" disappeared within the objects: "The workers are happy—/ rich man is crying—/ Rich man—rich man—don't cry,—/ I feed the pigs and sheep, you eat meat; you eat rice, and I eat porridge" (Shen Xuanlu, "Rich Man's Cry"). This is the workers' emotions. Their emotional tides merged into the ocean of national emotions: "I want to consolidate hundreds of millions of iron hands. / Our iron hands need to resist the enemy, / our iron hands need to fight!" (Pu Feng, "I Meet Mad Wind and Rainstorms") They always reminded themselves and their comrades to give up their independence and devote themselves to the moral obligations of society:

> But don't cherish your enthusiasm too much
> when you should cry, and laugh
> you have to be happy with everyone
> or shed tears together ... Please don't forget the human suffering and disaster
> when your intimate brothers
> fight for our happiness tomorrow
> can you sleep with your wife close by and warmed with the stove fire?
> —Li Yang, "To the Poet"

A large part of these poems also has notable characteristics, that is, the group "we" rather than the individual "I" is used as the lyrical protagonist. Just as the declaration of the Chinese Poetry Association: "We want to make our poetry popular songs, / we have become a member of the public" (*New Poetry*). Shelley cursed Bonaparte, as "a most unambitious slave." Byron wrote, "When a man hath no freedom to fight for at home, Let him combat for that of his neighbours," Whitman called, "Come, I will make the continent indissoluble, I will make the most splendid race the sun ever shone upon." It is easy for us to see the differences between Chinese and Western poetry in social subjects. Even if Western poetry expresses the social morality of the individuals, it is the realization of self-power, a kind of personal creation, and the subject is unwilling to accept "just being a member of the masses."

The Rival Growth of Subjectivity and Objectification

> We revert to sense only to find food for a reason,
> We destroy conventions, only to construct ideals
> —George Santayana, "The Elements and Function of Poetry"

The exploration of the objectified roots of Chinese modern poetry from *Bi* and *Xing* does not mean modern Chinese poetry is the natural extension of Chinese classical poetry or the offspring of the classical poetic spirit. As we have already mentioned previously, the motivation for new poetry writing came from Western poetry and poetics whose influence must not be underestimated. This is the premise of our understanding. Without this, we could not hold the truth of its development. I believe in the continuous influence of Western poetry and Western poetics on Chinese new poetry. The question is how we should re-recognize the specific characteristics of this influence and how it intertwines, resists, and integrates with the ideals of traditional Chinese poetry. What kind of impact do these interactions have in the history of modern Chinese new poetry?

I think the cultural characteristics of Western poetry lie in its subjectivity, which, together with objectification, presented a rival relationship of growth and decline in the history of modern Chinese poetry.

Subjectivity Analysis

Subjectivity is defined as corresponding to objectification.

Plato, the founder of Western literary thought, described his poetry theory very contradictorily. He used the ration whip to drive the poets out of "the

Republic," but he affectionately described the fanatical poetry thinking. "... the Muses; which taking hold of a delicate and virgin soul, and there inspiring frenzy, awakens lyrical and all other numbers ..."[35] Plato is self-contradictory, but we also see both aspects of the contradiction as mentioned. One concept is emphasized: poetry is not a response to the objective world, but an expression of certain transcendental ideas, either rational or the will of god. Ration naturally is the product of the enhancement of self-consciousness, and even the so-called god's will often must be expressed by the individual's will. Therefore, this contradiction can always be unified, and finally constitutes the earliest basis for the poet to pursue will. The poet's subjectivity runs through the entire process of Western poetry development. From ancient Greece to the 18th century, the history of Western poetry is a history dominated by the subjectivity thinking mode. Medieval theology undoubtedly also highlights the role of will in the form of allegiance to god. In this concept, closeness to the objective world is the blasphemy of god. The sentimentalism of the late 18th century and the romanticism of the 19th century seems to open a door to nature, but nature is still nature and Western poetry has no intention of giving up its individualism and returning to nature or even objectification. They "had to justify its role in the order of things, for, as Kant (following Plato) would say, pure perception of phenomena is not sufficient; real knowledge consists of the poet's faculty of imagination to see into the essence of the ontological world, to move beyond the physical to the abstract metaphysical world."[36] The basic characteristics of romantic poetry are the poet's constant interpretations and observations of objective nature, constantly asking why they exist. Here subjectivity remains a dominant position. The modern West, in line with the philosophical series of anti-traditional concepts, pioneered the new field of poetry with symbolism. According to Charles Olson and Robert Creeley, "The objects which occur at any given moment of composition ... are, can be, must be treated exactly as they do occur therein and not by any idea or preoccupations from outside the poem ..."[37] However, all these original objects are not the original state of objective things, but those that have been processed by the poet's subjectivity. E. Pound defines imagery as follows: "Imagery is not an image-like reproduction, but ... that which presents an intellectual and emotional complex in an instant of time." As a display of the "complex experience of reason and feelings," modern poetry is still characterized by its subjectivity characteristics. Self-awareness did not annihilate Eliot's "non-personalization," but it reshaped image through such an unprecedented language revolution.

In summary, affirmation and emphasis on the subjective will of the poet have always been maintained in the West from poetic theory to practice. In their view, the will of the poet's subjectivity is higher than everything else, and the objective objects are the objects to be manipulated, denied, or transcended. Poetry should become a poet's self-declaration and understanding of the world; the world of art is a world produced with the immersion of self-consciousness. Poets should focus on the humanization of nature rather than the objectification of the self. All these are the subjectivity characteristics of Western poetry.

Subjectivity Trend of Modern Chinese New Poetry

We should also pay attention to the subjectivity trend of modern Chinese new poetry. The large-scale translation and introduction of Western poetry, the reference to the grammatical norms of Indo-European languages, the introduction of loan words, and the irresistible "Western learning" that existed behind these literary phenomena constantly introduce exotic cultural concepts to Chinese poets and provided new art samples. This is the social and cultural foundation for the subjectivity of Western poetry shift to China.

Briefly, the subjectivity trend of modern Chinese new poetry can be found in the following aspects.

First, pure personal emotions began to become the targets of some poems. In terms of theory, many poets preached "self-expression" of poetry, such as "poetry is the self with personality—the sum of the individual's mind—a kind of unconditional and limited performance in language"[38]; "literary art is a product of self-expression"; "lyric poetry is the direct writing of emotions."[39] In terms of practice, there is Guo Moruo's self-expansion in *the Tiangou* style. There is a firm belief in Yin Fu's *Let the Dead Die* and there is also the passion of Ai Qing's *Dayanhe*. Modern Chinese new poetry's tracking of the inner feelings of the self also established its deep connection with Western romanticism. Although more complete romanticism only had a glimpse in *The Goddesses* in the May Fourth Movement, the different sides of this trend were displayed during the history of modern Chinese poetry. In early revolutionary poetry, we witnessed the dominance of individual willpower. We experienced the style of subjective fighting spirit in the July School poetry. And we found the tenacity of life pursuit in the writings of the Nine Leaves poets.

Second, more abstract ideas appeared in some poetry works. For example, Liu Dabai once wrote about the evolutionary law of "elimination" in a vivid way ("Here Comes Elimination"). Rao Mengkan hawked his own "soul along the street" ("Hawking"). Wen Yiduo praised highly the "national consciousness in the depths of the soul" ("An Idea"). Li Jinfa vividly expressed the "two psychological categories of hope and mercy" ("Hope and Mercy"). Hang Yuehe detailed the "historical significance of human myth" ("Myth"). Mu Dan dissected the "complex relationship between historical tradition and real life" ("Fissure").

The attention to abstract ideas is the inevitable result of the poet's increasing discernment when tackling the world with the exploration of subjectivity and questioning life. It breaks through the art model of poetry which emphasizes the integration of humans, nature, and emotions going along with objects. It provides a new and different "anti-traditional" way of thinking for modern Chinese poetry. The Nine Leaves poets in the 1940s had a clear "anti-traditional" intention. For example, Mu Dan repeatedly said, "the influence of traditional poetry would be detrimental for new poem writing,"[40] and his writing is "nearly abstract, metaphorical lyrics."[41]

Third, the objective world became the manipulation target of the subjects. This is the inevitable result of tracking inner emotions and expressing abstract ideas. In modern Chinese new poetry, there are three ways to regulate the objective world:

One is to reduce the objective images and directly present subjective consciousness. Such examples include the early vernacular new poetry, *The Goddesses* by Guo Moruo, early works by Xu Zhimo and some of the poems from the Crescent Moon School, some works of the early revolutionary poetry, the Chinese Poetry Society, and some works by Zang Kejia and Ai Qing.

The second is the subject's intervention in the objective world. For example, the Metropolitan Paris as presented by Ai Qing:

Paris
You are strong!
The magnetic force of your flames
Attracts the people
Of all ethnicities from the world
Taking risks
To run to you
To love you to kiss you.
Or hate you to the bones!
—You do not know
From that remote countryside I
Ran,
Towards you

Stretched out my trembling arms
And spurred me
Until I am deeply in pain!
—"Paris"

In his presentation of Paris, the poet demonstrated complex emotions and evaluations unique to youth from the East. This poem is the result of the fierce collision between the objective world of Paris and the subjective will of the poet. Without the intervention of the subjective will, it is impossible to make a new comment on Paris. The introduction and interpretation of Western poetics made Chinese new poetry transcend the obstacles of the native form of external objects and opened up a broad space for subjectivity. Similar works include "The Sun" by Wen Yiduo, "Life" by Pu Feng, "Forest" by Tian Jian, "Golden Rice Bunch" by Zheng Min, "Flag" by Mu Dan, and so on.

The third is the objects are completely products of the poet's subjective imagination. Such as Guo Moruo's "Phoenix" ("Phoenix Nirvana"), "Tiangou (heavenly dog)" ("Tiangou"), Xu Zhimo's blind horse ("To Find a Star"), Wen Yiduo's female ghost ("Night Song"), Dai Wangshu's body of the motherland ("I Use the Broken Palm"), Mu Dan's beast ("The Beast"), and so on.

The fourth is new patterns of poetry expressions are chosen and established. Inspirations were found especially in novels and dramas and applied to new poetry writing. Among them, the most widely used and successful is the "dramatic talk," that is, the monologue or dialogue of poetry simulated drama, showing the poet's consciousness from new aspects. "What is Your Surname" written by Shen Xuanlu during the May Fourth Movement was one of the earliest poems with dialogues of drama. Through the dialogue between the poet and "him" on the surname, it unearthed the concept of inequality between men and women in the surname culture. Wen Yiduo's "Tian'anmen" adopted a monologue to express the white terror of the reactionary authorities to suppress the student movement through the language of a rickshaw driver. The driver's unique vulgar monologue reflected the civic values and complex social effects produced by this historical event are displayed incisively and intriguingly. Bian Zhilin's "What to Do" is a dialogue between the poet "and a person in the dusk." The dialogue comes down to "What do you want to do?" "Where to go?" The poet has no answers and neither does the other person. The helplessness of life is very thought-provoking.

The application of drama dialogues is closely related to Western romantic poetry in terms of its poetic origin. Once an important art form of Western romantic poetry during the 19th century, drama dialogues enabled the narrator to stand in a relatively detached position and present the complexity of human existence through conflicts caused by the different attitudes of the speaker and the listener to a certain event. If we consider dialogue as the way people exist in the world, then the philosophical significance of this pattern of expression becomes even more apparent. All the complex art choices in this category are subjectivity efforts.

Rival Growth of Subjectivity and Objectification

Objectification is the root of modern Chinese poetry and subjectivity is the inevitable trend when Western thoughts spread to the East. During the Chinese New Poetry Movement, these two cultures intertwined with each other, contradicting each other, growing together, forming the complexity of the cultural characteristics of modern Chinese poetry. In this process, neither subjectivity nor objectification can fully display their inherent value orientation. They consume and weaken each other in the collision, and the similarity between the two sides leads to their interesting integration.

The sharpness of subjectivity is constantly offset and dimmed by the need for objectification, losing the possibility of further advancement to the deep system of Western poetics. We have seen although modern Chinese new poetry focused on purely individual emotions like never before, and even expressed subjective ideas of abstract forms, these attentions, and performances are ultimately displayed only on a relatively shallow surface. In general, the depiction is mostly sketchy without really digging into the depth of subjectivity. Thus, neither the changes in personal emotions nor the abstract forms of thought can become connected with the world of the deepest life. The meaning of life has never been challenged or re-evaluated (obviously, Confucianism behind Chinese poetics and the Taoist view of life block this way of thinking). Chinese new poetry accepts the influence of subjectivity. Some expressed the pains of life, but mostly with the sentimentality of real life, such as Hu Yepin's "Just as Death Follows Right Behind." A self-image outlined without deep introspection, such as Li Jinfa's "My Self-Portrait." Subjective imagination is depicted, but still as a reflection of real emotions, such as Wang Duqing's "Lamentation," and Dai Wangshu's "A Lane in the Rain." Writing of the ultimate ideal of life, but appearing empty and light, such as Yuan Bo's "The Ship of Truth."

The pursuit of subjectivity is also fragmented and lacks coherence in surging the objectification ideal. Subjectivity has not been able to create a strong pervasive influence in the history of Chinese new poetry. It is also difficult for us to find many persistent explorers, although many aspects of the subjectivity way of thinking are displayed by different poets in different ways. For instance, some early poems, some revolutionary realism poems, and most of the Nine Leaves poetry embodies the emphasis on abstract ideas. Guo Moruo's *The Goddesses* and some of the early revolutionary poems of Jiang Guangci, Yin Fu, and others favored emotions. In general, their significance in the history of new poetry is mainly to open a path to tradition, but in some specific works, still, the traces of subjectivity could be discovered from time to time. *Zhimo's Poems* and *Red Candle* were once popular, leaving behind the burning of the inner emotions of the self. Even during the "dead water" period of self-restraint, Wen Yiduo did not relinquish the tenacious willpower of the individual, which is rare in the history of new poetry. Other poets, such as Li Jinfa's psychological imbalances, caused him to occasionally turn to subjectivity. Dai Wangshu's later writings went "towards reality" moving toward a new awareness of personal emotions.

At the same time, although objectification is a profound cultural pursuit of Chinese new poetry, it is unlikely to maintain its complete form with the impact of the subjectivity from Western poetry. The pursuit of objectification is not as free as it is in the history of Chinese classical poetry. Corresponding to fragmentation and lack of coherence of the subjectivity trend, the pursuit of objectification of Chinese new poetry is also not so determinant. On the whole, it is interfered with by the long-lasting Western romantic poetry that entered Chinese poetry. In the specific practice of poem writing, the chaotic modern living environment constantly reminded poets that the poetic ideal of "observing objects through objects" had faded. To adapt to the needs of the changing times, the specific means of poetic objectified thinking had to be adjusted constantly. For example, under the influence of romantic poetry aesthetics, the writing practices of Guo Moruo, Ai Qing, Mu Dan, and others were no longer simply "writing about the ideals through means of objectification"; instead, a strong taste of self-expression could be found in their works.

Integration of modern Chinese poetry's objectification and subjectivity has always been ideal for many people. If the fusion is successful, it would give great comfort and encouragement to those who are still hanging on the road to cultural conflicts. However, how complicated it would be to reach the fusion of cultures? For us who are wrapped by cultures, it may be a trap that is extremely difficult to overcome, to clearly distinguish the similarities, differences, and ties between them! Of course, I cannot pronounce that "immersed in the culture" is equal to "being trapped," but without any doubt, there is a huge gap between this subjective desire and harsh reality. As a result, the so-called fusion of the two cultures based on similarity would inevitably lead to various misreadings.

The Chinese modern poets attempted to integrate the cultural pursuits of Chinese and Western poetry under the context of misreading.

This integration was conducted in two directions. As we mentioned earlier, the symbol and *Xing* were once discussed together by modern Chinese poets. This represented the most important way of cultural integration of modern Chinese poetry, that is, a connection was bridged between the ideals of Chinese classical poetry and the Western path of subjectivity. Some modern Chinese poets (especially Symbolist and Modernist poets) believed the poetic choices of Western symbolism are similar to those of Chinese classical poetry. Thus, a fully developed integration in the history of modern Chinese new poetry began in the mid-1920s until the end of the 1930s. In the following discussion, we will analyze the impact of this movement on the history of poetry and the individual writers. All in all, this integration connected the typical form of objectification with the variant form of subjectivity.

In addition, there is another way of connection we often ignore, that is, the interconnection of the primary form or variant form of objectification with the typical form of subjectivity.

We summarize the national cultural characteristics of Chinese classical poetry as objectification to distinguish it from Western poetry. But, at the same time, it should be noted that Chinese classical poetry itself is also diverse in various forms. It also had various historical stages of occurrence, development, maturity, and variations. The typical form of objectification mainly appeared in the mature period of Chinese classical poetry, that is, from the poetry of the Wei and Jin dynasties to poetry and *Ci* of the Tang and Song dynasties. Some poems before this, such as Qu Yuan's *Li Sao*, belong to the "primary form," and later Song poems belong to the "variant form." In addition, there are also folk forms different from the above-mentioned literati creations. They are represented by classical folk songs. In these respects, poetry with a lesser degree of objectification is slightly similar to the subjectivity in the West. For example, *Qu Sao* (*Li Sao*) also highlights the poet's self to a certain extent, showing people's manipulation of the objective environment. Poetry in Song Dynasty leaves some traces of rational thinking. When the Chinese classical poetry tradition is presented as a whole to Chinese modern poets, it is not surprising there will be a choice of cultural integration. Chinese modern poets can use less formalized poetry as their inner support to accept the Western poetry culture. For example, some early vernacular poets simultaneously favored poetry of the Song Dynasty and Western poetry. Guo Moruo connected *Qu Sao* and Western romanticism. Some left-wing poets associated Western proletarian poetry with folk songs.

Therefore, what new problems does such a fusion lead to? I believe all the integrations between China and the West have complicated effects on the cultural characteristics of modern Chinese poetry. They inspire us that it is insufficient to know Chinese new poetry only in the comparison of the typical forms of Chinese and Western poetry. It is necessary for us to further explore the history of Chinese classical poetry, go deep into the history of modern Chinese poetry, and observe more closely what roles these historical forms have played and how these historical forms are related to the Western poetry culture. This brings us to the next chapter.

Notes

1 *Moruo's Collected Works*, vol. 10, 203.
2 Liang Shiqiu, "The Style of New Poetry and Others," *Shi Kan* (*Poetry Periodical*), no. 1 (Jan. 1931).
3 Bian Zhilin, "Preface to *Dai Wangshu's Poetry Anthology*," in *People and Poetry: Retrospect and Prospect*, 63–64.
4 Zhao Peilin, *The Origin of Xing* (China Social Sciences Press, 1987), 184.
5 Shi Ling, "The Crescent School Poetry," *Literature* 8, no. 1 (Jan. 1937).
6 Yu Guanying, "Two Issues of New Poetry," *Literature Monthly* 2, no. 3 (Feb. 1932). But Yu Guanying also said: "the early poems were influenced by the traditional poems while the later poems were influenced by the western poems." I can't agree with that.
7 Xu Zhimo, "A Night at Florence, Preface," in *A Night at Florence* (New Moon Bookstore, 1927).
8 Zhou Zuoren, "Preface to *Yangbian Ji* (Spurring Collection)," *Yu Si*, no. 82.
9 Guo Moruo, "Literary Theories: On Poetry," in *Moruo's Collected Works*, vol. 10, 201.
10 Mu Mutian, "Poetry and Reality," in *Plainness Collection* (Xinzhong Publishing House, 1936).
11 Mu Mutian, "Epic Issues in the Establishment of National Revolution," *Literary Front* 3, no. 5 (June 1939).
12 Zong Baihua, "A Brief Talk on New Poetry," *The Journal of the Young China Association* 1, no. 8 (Feb. 1920).
13 Kang Baiqing, "My View on New Poetry," *The Journal of the Young China Association* 1, no. 9 (Mar. 1920).
14 Liang Zongdai, "On Poetry," *The Human World*, no. 15 (Nov. 1934).

15 Zhang Xiuzhong, *Past, Present and Future of China's New Poetry Community* (Haiyin Publishing House, 1929).
16 See Zang Kejia's "Another Talk on New Poetry," *Wenchao Monthly* 3, no. 6 (Oct. 1947); "On Inspiration," *Literary Journal* 6, no. 6 (Oct. 1942).
17 Kang Baiqing, "My View on New Poetry," *The Journal of the Young China Association* 1, no. 9 (Feb. 1920).
18 Zong Baihua, "Poetry and I," in *Aesthetics and Artistic Conception* (People's Publishing House, 1987), 177.
19 Liang Zongdai, "Symbolism," *Literature Quarterly*, no. 2 (April 1934).
20 Charles Baudelaire, "Further Notes of Edgar Poe," in *Selected Writings on Art and Literature* (Penguin Classics) Mass Market Paperback—June 1, 1993.
21 Kant, quoted from Roger Fowler, *A Dictionary of Modern Critical Terms*.
22 Charles Baudelaire, "Further Notes of Edgar Poe."
23 Richard Eberhart, "How I Write Poetry," in *Poets to Poetry* (Joint Publishing, 1989), 35. (Penmaen Press; 1st edition, 1975).
24 *Bi*, literally "compare," a rhetoric device roughly meaning "simile or metaphor."
25 Roger Fowler, *A Dictionary of Modern Critical Terms* (Routledge Kegan & Paul, 1987).
26 Zhu Ziqing, "Progress of New Poetry," in *Miscellaneous on New Poetry* (Joint Publishing, 1984), 8.
27 Raymond Chapman, *Linguistics and Literature* (Edward Arnold; 1st edition, 1973).
28 Qian Zhongshu, "Book of Change, An Authorized Version," in *Limited Views*, vol. 1 (Zhonghua Book Company, 1979), 12.
29 Roger Fowler, *A Dictionary of Modern Critical Terms* (Routledge Kegan & Paul, 1987). Emphasis by author.
30 G. W. F. Hegel, *Hegel's Aesthetics: Lectures on Fine Art*, vol. 1, trans. T. M. Knox (Oxford University Press, 1975), 404.
31 Guo Moruo, "On Poetry," in *Moruo's Collected Works*, vol. 17, 266.
32 Quoted from Lan Dizhi, "On the Evolution and Characteristics of Mu Dan's Poetry," in *The Traditional and Unconventional* (Zhejiang Literature and Art Publishing House, 1988), 315.
33 Shi Ling, "The Crescent School Poetry," *Literature* 8, no. 1 (Jan. 1937).
34 Sun Zuoyun, "On Modernist Poetry," *Tsinghua Weekly* 43, no. 1 (May 1935).
35 Plato, *Phaedrus*, http://classics.mit.edu/Plato/phaedrus.html.
36 Wai-Lim Yip, "Aesthetic Consciousness of Landscape in Chinese and Anglo-American Poetry," in *Diffusion of Distances: Dialogues Between Chinese and Western Poetics* (University of California Press, 1993), 123.
37 Wai-Lim Yip, "Syntax and Horizon of Representation in Classical Chinese and Modern American Poetry," in *Diffusion of Distances: Dialogues Between Chinese and Western Poetics* (University of California Press, 1993), 50.
38 Yu Pingbo, "Freedom and Universality of Poetry," *Literature* 8, no. 1 (Jan. 1937).
39 Guo Moruo, "On Rhythm," in *Moruo's Collected Works*, vol. 10, 225.
40 Quoted from Zhou Jueliang, "Mu Dan's Poetry and Translated Poetry," in *A Nation Has Risen* (Jiangsu People's Publishing House, 1987), 20.
41 Tang Shi, "Remembering the Poet Mu Dan," see *A Nation Has Risen*, 153.

· 2 ·
HISTORICAL FORMS OF MODERN CHINESE NEW POETRY

In this chapter, we continue to analyze the historical forms of modern Chinese poetry from the perspective of traditional poetry of China.

The so-called "tradition" has never been a single piece. Rather, it should be a comprehensive organism composed of many different cultural forms. With their irreplaceable characteristics these cultural forms subordinate to a certain period of historical development. They shared some common cultural inclinations which form an organic system while the differences indicate the richness of the system.

I believe there are four major forms of noteworthy Chinese traditional poetry culture, which also have the greatest influence on Chinese modern poetry: (1) free forms represented by *Qu Sao* (works of Qu Yuan, 340–278 BC, a well-known poet of Chu State during the Warring States Period); (2) conscious forms represented by the poetry of the Wei, Jin, and Tang dynasties and *Ci* of the Song Dynasty; (3) "anti-traditional" forms represented by the poetry of the Song Dynasty; and (4) ballad styles represented by the *Airs of the States* and *Yuefu*.

Next, we will discuss the cultural significance of these four forms in modern Chinese poetry.

Qu Sao and Free Forms of Modern Chinese New Poetry

> This river, although half-dried, is still called Miluo.
> The people here are the same as they were at the very beginning;
> —Zhu Xiang, "The Sonnet: Italian Style (Twenty-one)"

"A refuge to outlive the longest night"

According to China's tradition for school starters, *Qu Sao*[1] may rank behind the *Three Character Classics, Hundred Family Names, Thousands of Poems, Four Books,* and *Five Classics,* but it is one of the most important literary enlightenment books. Among modern Chinese poets, no one knows anything about the works of Qu Yuan, such as *Li Sao*, "Jiu Ge," "Jiu Zhang," and "Tian Wen," especially those who were from well-educated families and received a formal education. Many poets were so familiar with *Qu Sao* that they could quote freely from it. Guo Moruo said: "You don't need to be a poet or writer to worship Qu Yuan. There is no Chinese who does not worship Qu Yuan."[2]

Images and allusions from *Qu Sao* are frequently found in the poems of Chinese modern poets. There are innumerable literary theories, social comments, essays, letters, etc., about the arguments of Qu Yuan and *Qu Sao*. Guo Moruo said with deep affection: "Qu Zi (Qu Yuan) is my teacher, what a pity he killed himself!"[3] Zhu Xiang admired Qu Yuan and *Qu Sao*, calling it "the source of 'greatness'."[4] Li Jinfa argued *Li Sao* is "the collection of the essence of Chinese poetry."[5] Yu Pingbo praised Zhu Ziqing's lyrical long poem, "Destruction," "full of turns and emotions ... deep and mellow ... gentle, beautiful and heartrending ... .Only the *Li Sao* of Qu Zi (Qu Yuan) could compete with it."[6] When talking about his friend, Yang Hui's "anger venting" work "Qu Yuan," Feng Zhi appreciated it so much that he "read it all at once" and urged Yang Hui to revise and publish it as soon as possible.[7] Bian Zhilin also used the verse, "I would never regret; even I die nine times" in *Li Sao* to sum up the life pursuit of his friend, Liang Zongdai.[8] Dai Wangshu is the pseudonym of the modern poet, Dai Chao'an. The word "Wangshu" is taken from *Li Sao*: "In the front Wangshu (God of Moon) is driving and in the back Feilian (God of Wind) is following." We have a glimpse of the weight of Qu Yuan and his poetry in the minds of modern Chinese poets by quoting these few examples. Qu Yuan's poetry is the mentor and model of life and art, the most active life gene, and the highest magnificence in the deepest consciousness of the Chinese people.

This is not difficult to explain from the perspective of archetypal criticism. Although modern Chinese poetry is a rebel against classical poetry, very different from traditional Chinese poetry in terms of aesthetics, syntactic forms, metrical rhymes, etc., which reflect the differences between the more important social and cultural attributes, the elements of traditional poetry culture are extraordinarily rich in the spiritual structure of the modern intellectuals in China. And, the "pre-emptive" auxiliary cushion formed a thick layer at the bottom of the intellectual system, any external elements, and the shock of social and cultural changes can only be infiltrated from the outside to the inside, from shallow to deep. At the same time, along with a long process of infiltration, the traditional poetry culture character of the "original" is gradually blending with the poets' self-basic pursuit of life, and exerting a subtle influence on the Chinese poets' outlook on life, world, and art. In a certain sense, traditional poetry images even became symbols corresponding to various real feelings. When Chinese modern poets are faced with real scenes and a need to use symbolic art to show these complex feelings, the imagery, conception, and personality of traditional Chinese poetry would burst out, often more intimate and more appropriate than the images of foreign poetry. As C. G. Jung said,

> Whoever speaks in primordial images speaks with a thousand voices; he enthralls and overpowers, while at the same time, he lifts the idea he is seeking to express out of the occasional and the transitory into the realm of the ever-enduring. He transmutes our destiny into the destiny of mankind and evokes in us all those beneficent forces that ever and anon have enabled humanity to find a refuge from every peril and to outlive the longest night.[9]

Qu Yuan and *Qu Sao* fall into such "primordial images" categories. However, what is the difference between *Qu Sao* in comparison with other "primordial images" as an unconscious tradition? In other words, what special historical and cultural roots exist in its modern representation?

I believe the similarity between Chinese modern poets and Qu Yuan in the cultural mentality is an important reason for the spirit of *Qu Sao* and the images of *Qu Sao*.

Qu Yuan was faced with the historical reality that the country was weak and the king was failing. He, a master of state governance and speech delivery, was trapped by others. The sorrow of the sudden loss of individual values echoed in his heart. He grieved, worried, and even had doubts about his inherent value system, but still was "deeply concerned about the Chu State, about the king, and hoped to return to serve." Similar cultural backgrounds and mentalities appeared in Chinese history many times. The cyclical turmoil of the "super-stable" systems caused our poets to fall into this ancient nightmare repeatedly. Therefore, Qu Yuan, who was self-respecting and proud, always made people feel excited. His spirit evoked the dragon and phoenix, and conjured the sun and the moon, his anger venting his fascinating imagination, and his grand, extravagantly elegant rhetoric—all these repeatedly touched people's hearts, shocked them, showed them a free scene of personal spiritual and artistic pursuits, and became the gracious strength for them to enjoy a short, free time and to "outlive the longest night."

Living in a modern Chinese turbulent society with the invasion of foreign powers, Chinese intellectuals tried to find salvation with dark clouds of national peril hanging over them. This was similar to Qu Yuan's era. The foreign concepts of liberal democracy in the West strengthened the Chinese poets' consciousness and stimulated their self-realization desires. However, it also brought deeper experiences of loss and frustration. The more individualized, the more self-growth developed into loneliness and isolation, and the more one felt the pain of not being recognized and serving the country. As far as this psychological fact is concerned, the similarity between modern poets and Qu Yuan in the cultural roots was strengthened rather than decreased when compared with the entire Chinese feudal society. It is precisely because most modern Chinese poets of all kinds of genres shared a similar living experience to Qu Yuan that *Qu Sao* impacted many Chinese modern poets and became a more widespread "prototype" phenomenon.

Free *Qu Sao* Style in Modern Chinese New Poetry

The salvation of the Chinese future, the concern about the country and the people, the will of self-realization and individual development, and the art of free expression are the archetypes contributed by *Qu Sao* to modern Chinese poets. During the mature period of China's feudal era, *Qu Sao*'s freedom inspiration to Chinese poets is still short-lived and limited in the generally strict hierarchical order. In the increasingly sleek and narrow language framework, even the emotions of "cultivating oneself and managing well one's family and country" have been included in the limited way of expressions. If this was the case, then, Chinese modern poets have more free possibilities in both self and art. The free form of *Qu Sao* brought its unique free character to modern Chinese poetry.

First, Qu Yuan's spirit of "deep concern for people's livelihood" and "serving the government" was strengthened, becoming one of the important foundations of social discernment by Chinese modern poets who strived for the country's survival and salvation. For example, Zhu Xiang's "Calling the Spirits of the Dead," Tian Jian's "To the Fighters," Huang Yaomian's "Huanghuagang's Autumn Wind and Night Rain," Cai Mengwei's "The Sacrifice," and Cai Qijiao's "Close Fight" easily remind us of Qu Yuan's *Guo Shang*, a eulogy to the soldiers died for the state. There are a series of similarities between them—all of these are sorrowful praises to the national heroes, narrated from the tragic scenes of life and death, filled with the blood of killing, and the poets were full of intense and passionate national sentiment and magnificent emotional development. Tian Jian said the long poem, "To the Fighters," is a calling, "calling the motherland and myself, accompanied by the call of the nation, step forward together, with my hopes pinned on the people."[10] These poems called for people to "Keep fighting, / Victory / or death." They think "the warriors' cemetery / will be warmer than the slaves' country /Be warm / Be bright." These could easily be associated with impassioned Qu Yuan. "Being sincere and brave, I would fight for my country, my strength would not be tempted. Even when I am dead, I would become a ghost serving the country." The praise of heroism in *Guo Shang* became the precursor of the national emotions of later generations. The Chinese devotion to the nation and the pursuit of facing death fearlessly seemed to consciously and unconsciously identify with *Guo Shang*. As it is said: "When in the fight, I would be brave. When dying, I would die heroically. I would be determined to face death. These would not only comfort the souls of the dead but also be encouraging to the morale of the whole nation."[11]

Tian Jian once recalled the exciting scenes of the Dragon Boat Race (to commemorate Qu Yuan) in his hometown. He said: "Oh, the name of Qu Yuan, a patriotic poet, has been passed down to the present, and has not been forgotten by the villagers. It touches my heart from time to time."[12] Tian Jian was not the only one touched by Qu Yuan. During the proletarian revolution in the 1930s and the War of Resistance against Japanese Aggression in the 1930s and 1940s, people were filled with a heroic spirit of a sense of righteousness and dying for the country. People's emotions were extremely urgent, and *Qu Sao* rightly provided people with an exciting poetic beauty model of these aspects. In the early proletarian poetry—works of the Chinese Poetry

Association and poems of other anti-war themes in the 1940s, we find such a universal poetic beauty model: a distinct moral mission, political pursuit, and strong combination of personal emotions, the sorrow of the people and the pride for one's country and rage of invasion. "May 1st Song" by Yin Fu is an example:

> Today, / we must hold the red flag high, / today, / we have to prepare for war! / Fear nothing of the iron tanks and guns, / our great team is the Great Wall, / Fear nothing of the killing, shooting, imprisonment, / the blood of our youth will never run out!

The magnificent ideal of modern democracy was stirring in the blood of "us." The following is another piece, "Heilongjiang, My Hometown" by Gao Lan:

> My brothers and my parents, / my hometown where I grew up, / although /it is still covered by ice and snow, / the mountains high and rivers long /30 million people became slaves like animals. /My snowy hometown became hell and far from paradise!" "The fate of the slaves, / the shackles of the slaves, / all delivered to the resistance! /They would bleed, / they would die!

The sorrow and hatred of displacement were found in these poems. Of course, due to the uniqueness of the subject matter, it seems difficult to find many allusions and words directly from *Qu Sao* in these verses. However, in a broader space of historical cultures where modern poets expressed this group's freedom, clearly the universal poetry model is there. The long-distance communication between ancient and modern poetry is faintly discernible between the "May 1st Song" and *Guo Shang*, between "Heilongjiang, My Hometown" and "Mourning Ying." In fact, from the perspective of Chinese poetry history, the influence of *Qu Sao* as allusions and vocabulary on the poetry of future generations is certainly one aspect, but it is more important the spiritual extension of its "deep concern for people's livelihoods" and "serving the government" became the concern of the Chinese poets toward their homeland. This evolved into loyal, national emotions of famous poets in Chinese histories, such as Du Fu (712–770, Chinese poet, considered by many literary critics to be the greatest of all time), Lu You (1125–1210, one of the most important and prolific Chinese writers of the Southern Song dynasty), Yue Fei (1103–1142, one of China's greatest generals and national heroes), Wen Tianxiang (1236–1282, Chinese statesman, poet), etc. It naturally was inherited by modern Chinese poetry.

The individual freedom contained in *Qu Sao*, as an independent form of poetry, may be more worthy of our attention.

Compared with Chinese poetry during the mature period (Wei Jin, Tang, and Song dynasties), *Qu Sao* affirmed more individual personality and self, which became an important foundation for modern Chinese poets to echo Western individualism.

The introduction of Western romantic poetry is not contradictory to reviving *Qu Sao*'s spirit for Guo Moruo. In *Studies on Qu Yuan*, he evaluated Qu Yuan. "[Qu Yuan] revolutionized poetry. He accepted the influence of the trends of the times. He had sensitive perceptions, superb talent, and sincere efforts. His literary revolution is truly an overwhelming victory. He lineated an era."[13] In the article "Poetry Writing," Guo Moruo was quite "romantic":

> The classical Chinese language created by Qu Yuan and the classical Chinese are the vernaculars of the Spring and Autumn Period (770–476 BC) and the Warring States Period (475–221 BC). During the era two thousand years ago, there was once a May Fourth Movement, Qu Yuan was the leading figure of this movement.

Qu Sao should be the leader of the "May Fourth" new literature two thousand years ago! What is more interesting is the similarity between Guo Moruo's evaluation of *Qu Sao* and the present people's evaluation of his work, *The Goddesses*! This seems to show that Guo Moruo had consciously and unconsciously connected himself with Qu Yuan, paralleling *The Goddesses* and *Qu Sao*. In the self-expression of *The Goddesses*, the images of *Qu Sao*, the emotions of *Qu Sao*, and the personality ideal of *Qu Sao* are alluded to from time to time. The climax of the poem drama, *The Rebirth of the Goddess*, uses the verse "Thousands of Arrows Shoot the Sirius, similar to the verse" in "Nine Songs" by Qu Yuan ("Long Arrows Shoot the Sirius"). "Phoenix Nirvana ·Songs of Phoenix" reminded readers of "Tian Wen" of Qu Yuan:

> The universe, the universe, / Why do you exist? / Where have you come from? / Where are you sitting? / Are you a finite air ball? / You are an infinite piece, / If you are the finite big air ball, / Where does the space that embraces you come from?[14]

The poems or poetic dramas in "Against the Electric Lights" and "Xiang Lei (Suicide of Qu Yuan)" showed the pride and loneliness of Qu Yuan's style.

"The world is turbid while I am sober," and "I would search my ideal up and down." This is roughly the basic summary of the individual freedom of *Qu Sao*. The former sentence shows the poet's inner world and his personality; the latter sentence shows his realistic pursuit. These two aspects of the individual spirit are found in modern Chinese poetry.

For example, Cheng Fangwu, a member of the Creation Society, wrote a poem: "I was born like a meteor, / I don't know where to go." Another member Zhou Quanping called himself a "white lamb" who was lost in the "thousands of bizarre paths" on which there was a "stinky smell of copper coins," "cold-blooded powers," "ruthless and unreasonable ethics," and "hidden hermits," but "I do not think of removing my responsibility! / I have no fear of death! / I don't want to give up my conscience!" Still, another member Ma Renyin wrote "sorrowful songs": "harboring resentment / negative melancholy / I, drinking my sweat / lonely, walked the vast desert/walking across long cold time." "But I don't shudder / don't sink and play with loneliness / I still move forward tenaciously."[15] From the 1920s to the 1940s, there were quite a few "songs of the wanderers" in modern Chinese poetry. But generally, they showed such characteristics: (1) no beginning nor end of wandering; (2) the wanderers' melancholy and loneliness; and (3) the tough, tenacious, or self-innocent experience of the wanderers. This is the basic feature of *Qu Sao*'s freedom. These poems could easily remind us of the charm of *Li Sao*.

Since the May Fourth Movement, the spirit of individuality and self-expansion from Western poetry did not disappear in Chinese poetry (although there were some fluctuations). When Chinese poets need to look for evidence from their traditional education and culture, the brilliance of *Qu Sao* naturally emerged. As an early form of Chinese poetry, it is significantly different from the classical poetry of the mature period in that it was not captured by the "virtual world" of the "unity of Heaven and Man" in later generations. The idea of self-individuality was not completely resolved and eroded. In this way, when Chinese poets approached Western romantic poetics and built Chinese new poetry with the encouragement of *Qu Sao* to realize the rebellion against Chinese traditional poetry, it was using the original power of Chinese poetry to adjust itself. Guo Moruo said he would use the spirit of the pre-Qin freedom. He understood the resistance of the "religious, superstitious, and other-disciplined" feudal culture. The freedom of *Qu Sao* in the pre-Qin Dynasty became a conscious flag against the poetry of the Jin and Tang dynasties.

This not only applied to the essence of consciousness and the pursuit of aesthetics. Free forms of Chinese modern poetry also benefited from *Qu Sao*. When Zhang Wojun, the pioneer of the Taiwan New Literature Movement, talked about his new poetry theory in 1925, he said:

> Since the *Book of Poetry*, the forms of *Li Sao* and *Yuefu* of the Han and Wei dynasties were not restricted by fixed forms. Metrical poems and quatrain-style poems began

during the Six Dynasties. By the Tang Dynasty, these were fully developed, meaning the bondage was complete.[16]

Of course, some poets, such as Zhu Xiang, also praised *Qu Sao* from the perspective of rhyme, but a serious analysis showed in Zhu Xiang's metrical poetry, works influenced by *Qu Sao* (such as "Calling the Spirits of the Dead") were still the most free and natural. Other relatively strict modern metrical poems were mainly under the influence of the poetry of the Wei, Jin, Tang, and *Ci* of Song dynasties. It preserved "the soul of the rhythm of Chinese traditional verses."[17] Therefore, we could argue that *Qu Sao*'s archetype supports the "liberalization" of the Chinese new poetry language form in different aspects and different ways.

Freedom Comparison in Chinese and Western Contexts

The definition of any concept must rely on specific domains. When we refer to the influence of *Qu Sao* on Chinese modern poetry as "freedom," it is likely this concept might be confused with some conceptual categories of modern civilization. The most important feature of Chinese modern culture is the introduction of democracy and freedom from the West (at least in theory). According to our general understanding, freedom is an important concept of Western culture. So, free forms within the Chinese poetry tradition should be a freedom different from the freedom of Western culture. If so, what kind of relationships does the freedom of these two cultures have? What kind of differences are there? Connections and differences will help us further understand the characteristics of the time and national characteristics of the Chinese new poetry spirit.

The freedom spirit of Western culture shows its existence in modern China through Western poetry. Romantic poetry mainly expresses the individual freedom of Western culture, and proletarian poetry expresses group freedom.

The freedom of *Qu Sao* provides the base for the import of the Western poetry spirit. At the same time, the free spirit of Western poetry influences people's ideas about *Qu Sao*; thus, determining the actual composition of free forms of Chinese new poetry.

In *Qu Sao*, group freedom ("deep concern for people's livelihood" and "serving the government") and individual freedom ("when one is rooted, it is difficult to migrate," "being alone and deaf to others") are interdependent. Qu Yuan's group freedom is an important part of his freedom, and individual freedom is an important condition for realizing group freedom. However, in the free forms of modern Chinese poetry, group freedom is separated from individual freedom. They contradict and attack each other. The left-wing revolutionary poets and the Crescent poets fought each other. When writing his poem collections *Qian Mao* and *Restoration*, Guo Moruo vowed to break with previous individualism. Why? I think it is caused by the fierce bombardment of the Western poetry freedom concept on new poetry. And, the two liberal concepts (individual and group) in the West were imported by different poets. The adoption of just one aspect of the liberal concept led to the deviation. Eventually, the opposition of each other was developed. The "May Fourth" anti-feudal enlightenment and the romantic poetry adapted to it strengthened the individual's freedom and suspended the group's freedom. Later, as history proceeded, the urgency of nation salvation and the proletarian literature from the Soviet Union reinforced group freedom, and "suspended" individual freedom at the same time.

These can be described as the era characteristics of free forms of Chinese new poetry, the joint effect of *Qu Sao*'s archetype and Western poetics.

However, the connection between *Qu Sao*'s archetype and Western poetics is by no means seamless. After all, they belong to two cultural backgrounds. It is difficult for Chinese poetry borne within the Chinese culture to establish Western-style freedom. Compared with Byron and Shelley's magnificent reconstruction of the world, Mayakovski's futurism, group freedom is too realistic and specific:

> The field needs to
> Produce wheat
>
> The field needs to
> Produce millet;
>
> These would be taken,
> As
> Weapons of protracted war.
>
> —Tian Jian, "More"

We know Qu Yuan's group freedom has clear, realistic implications. Qu Yuan repeatedly proposed to King Huai (est. 355–296 BC) of Chu State to strengthen the government system and invite the capable to work for him. "I once had your trust to work for your majesty. I worked hard for the people with the credit of the ancestors and I interpreted the laws fairly to eradicate people's doubts" ("Jiu Zhang"). He also lamented the fall of the capital: "The

King's caprice led to the misery and turmoil of his subjects who were dislocated in an early, chilly spring to the east, with the loved ones separated and suffering" ("Jiu Zhang").

Like *Qu Sao*, other modern Chinese poems pursuing "individual freedom" did not intend to introduce freedom on the level of life's ontology, nor to challenge the world by the encouragement of freedom or challenge itself. In modern Chinese poetry, we rarely see such a touching scene of overcoming a distressing destiny:

> A glorious people vibrated again
> The lightning of the nations: Liberty
> From heart-to-heart, from tower-to-tower, o'er Spain,
> Scattering contagious fire into the sky,
> Gleamed. My soul spurned the chains of its dismay,
> And in the rapid plumes of song
> Clothed itself, sublime and strong;
> As a young eagle soars the morning clouds among,
> ......
>
> —Percy Bysshe Shelley, "Ode to Liberty"

Shelley allowed his thoughts and emotions to fly freely and completely as if there was no objective force to hold them. Guo Moruo's "Tiangou" seemed to be also free, but after careful analysis, the psychological process of "Tiangou" from engulfing the universe to consuming the self is no more the self-expression of the romanticist's confidence than the poet's self-expression. He was confused because of some kind of invisible power interference. What is freedom and how to pursue it? Finally, the poet can only repeatedly declare: "I am me!" The emptiness is faintly visible.

The freedom of *Qu Sao* is realistic without metaphysical erosion. It is orderly and quite different from a thorough self-expansion and radical rebellion. Then, it is likely to gradually flow to a new tendency: carefreeness, which is a kind of variant of freedom. It is unrestrained, unattached, romantic, and realistic, both comfortable and gentle. For example, the Crescent poet, Zhu Xiang, admired Qu Yuan so much that Qu Yuan's name was almost engraved into his life. He even ended his life in the way Qu Yuan did. The freedom Zhu Xiang understood and enjoyed was like the red leaves that fluttered with the waves, wandering around, roaming everywhere, and "crossing the river," he said to Qu Yuan, his mentor in life:

> I was born into the place where you were born.
> I am a red leaf, a ship without steering,

With the guide of autumn water and wind, I roamed.
—"The Sonnet, Italian Style (Twenty-one)"

When freedom is transformed into carefreeness, it actually could communicate the mature form of Chinese classical poetry of the Wei, Jin, Tang, and Song dynasties. If the freedom of *Qu Sao* style and the freedom of Western poetry is seemingly similar, then it was different from the ideal during the Wei, Jin, Tang, and Song dynasties in China.

We have said objectification is a cultural feature of Chinese classical poetry. This is the objectification of oneself, the transformation of oneself into objects, the harmony of oneself and objects, and the unity of nature and man. The so-called objects usually refer to nature but also include society (and various moral norms of society). Harmony is the rapport between man and nature, and the cooperation between man and society. The Confucianism of Heaven and Man is to unite the harmony of these two forms. This unification further promotes the perfection of Chinese poetry objectification ideal.

The free *Qu Sao* is only the beginning of Chinese poetry. It is less objectified compared to the conscious forms of the Wei, Jin, and Tang dynasties' poetry and the Song Dynasty's *Ci* (lyrics). However, I believe the difference between "free" and "conscious" forms is relative. For example, as mentioned previously, *Qu Sao*'s freedom and group freedom are united as one, which echoes the Confucian unity of Heaven and Man. There is no insurmountable gap between Qu Yuan and the Confucians of the Han Dynasty, between *Qu Sao* and the poetry of Wei, Jin, and Tang dynasties, and *Ci* of the Song Dynasty. With a tendency for harmony, Chinese poetry development has its continuity. This connection is recognized by modern Chinese poets. For example, the most rebellious Guo Moruo commented on *Qu Sao*:

> It describes the surreal situation from the position of art, but spiritually, it shows extreme loyalty and patriotism. Qu Yuan's work generally lacks the utopia atmosphere and isolation from reality as described by Laozi and Zhuangzi. However, "Distant Travel" by Qu Yuan is in line with the works of Laozi and Zhuangzi spiritually.[18]

Guo Moruo found *Qu Sao* also has more or less the elements of Confucianism and Taoism. This is interesting. It should be noted the "consciousness" of the poetry of the Wei, Jin, Tang, and Song dynasties is the result of the respective development and mutual influence of Confucianism and Taoism.

The freedom of *Qu Sao*'s style presents a tendency to extend and evolve to the "consciousness" style of the Jin and Tang dynasties. This trend also exists in modern Chinese poetry.

We noticed that free forms of the new poetry which are closely related to the spirit of *Qu Sao* showed their questioning and dissatisfaction with the Jin and Tang poetry at its birth and initial development. But overall, it is still quite tolerant and even quite respectful toward the poetry of the Jin and Tang dynasties. During his life, Guo Moruo constantly vacillated between the archetypes of *Qu Sao* and the archetypes of the Jin and Tang dynasties: "Which of the two poets (Qu Yuan and Tao Yuanming—the note of the author) would I favor more? It is very difficult for me to decide."[19] Zhu Xiang has never abandoned other classical poetry despite his devotion to Qu Yuan. Many of his works show a strong Tang and Song dynasties' influence. Su Xuelin, an expert in traditional poetry, points out that the primary characteristic of Zhu Xiang's poetry is his skills to integrate with classical poetry. For the vast majority of Chinese poets, *Qu Sao* has no special contradiction with other forms of Chinese classical poetry. They are all models to learn from. It is meaningful that the Chinese new poetry with free forms seems not so confident in the freedom pursued. They were eager to acquire the support of the prototypes of other Chinese poetry.

Poetry of the Wei, Jin, and Tang Dynasties, *Ci* of the Song Dynasty, and Conscious Forms of Modern Chinese New Poetry

> The sun is infinite, the space is infinite,
> We are just ignorant and transient tiny mayflies and frogs in wells.
> —Dai Wangshu, "To Kemu"

"Consciousness" is a clear understanding of the mind. The consciousness in poetry is to have a clear understanding of poetry as art and the writing completed on the artistic track of poetry. If we say free forms of Chinese poetry are mainly concerned with the expressions of personal emotions, and consider less the prescriptive nature of poetry, its emotional characteristics, and stylistic features, then the poetry of conscious forms always grasps the key of art and strives to make a poem more of a poem. Sometimes, we also call this pursuit "art for art's sake."

In the history of Chinese poetry, *Qu Sao*'s freedom is only a short-lived glory. It is the poetry of the Wei, Jin, and Tang dynasties and *Ci* of the Song Dynasty that have a stronger impact. We have noticed when modern Chinese poetry also embarked on the road of art for art's sake, the charm of poetry of the Wei, Jin, Tang dynasties, and *Ci* of the Song Dynasty appeared.

Towards Pure Poetry

Art for art's sake appeared in modern Chinese new poetry during the 1920s and 1930s and was represented by the works of the Crescent Moon School, the Symbolist School, and the Modernist School.

Compared with the anti-feudal freedom of the May Fourth poetry, the social mission of poetry during the 1940s included distinct political utilitarian purposes of the revolutionary poetry of the same period. The Crescent, the Symbolist, and the Modernist poets explored the art rules of "the poem noumenon." They paid more attention to the inner qualities of poetry and placed the corresponding social and historical responsibility at a distance. They were obsessed with the scoring of poetry language and rhythm, and reconstructed poetry on a new level to open an art path leading to "pure poetry." Moreover, these poetic pursuits led to a sober consciousness and they used their practice to improve the situation. Even though later generations made different accusations of the process, their great enthusiasm cannot be denied. Xu Zhimo said, "It is necessary to make the new poetry writing a serious matter."[20] Liang Shiqiu analyzed from the perspective of history that attention is paid to the "vernacular," not the "poetry" during the earliest years of the new poetry movement. Efforts were made to get rid of the barriers of traditional poetry instead of building the foundation of new poetry. Thus, he considered the Poetry Column in the *Morning News* written by Xu Zhimo and Wen Yiduo a memorable new poetry movement journal. "I thought this was the first time a group of people gathered to experiment with sincerity about new poems."[21] Li Jinfa, a Symbolist poet, said: "Art is a world that is not in harmony with morality and society. The only purpose of art is to create beauty. The only work of an artist is to faithfully express one's world."[22] Mu Mutian linked poetry and "deep big top life."[23] Wang Duqing "worked hard to complete the art" to "be an aesthetic poet," and he also quoted Zheng Boqi as saying "the crystal beads rolling on the white jade plate" is "the highest art."[24] Modernist poets pushed the "pure poetry" movement of modern China to its peak. The days when Modernist poets were active are often referred to as the "golden period," "rapid development period," and "mature period" of the development of China's "pure literature," since the May Fourth Movement.[25] The editors of *Modernity* had a clear attitude: "The poems in *Modernity* are poems."

Chinese new poetry moved along the path of consciousness from the Crescent Moon School to the Symbolist School to the Modernist School. This reminds us of the Western poetry influence. Most modern Chinese poetry movements are closely related to the ups and downs of Western poetry. Liang Shiqiu, the theoretical authority of the Crescent Moon School, said: "I thought we must now blatantly imitate foreign poetry" (Liang Shiqiu: "The Style of New Poetry and Others," published in the first issue of *Shi Kan*— or *Poetry Journal* in January 1931). Western romanticism, aestheticism, and symbolism left a distinct imprint on the Crescent, Symbolist, and Modernist schools in China. Among them, the aesthetic Parnassianism runs through. Parnassianism opposes "sentimentality" and the proliferation of emotions, and advocates rational temperance, skillful art forms, and exquisite poetry. This poetic pursuit is related to the unique features of the Crescent Moon School poetry and continues to influence Modernist poets through the Crescent Moon School.[26] Symbolic poets, such as Mu Mutian and Feng Naichao, were fascinated by Parnassianism.[27] The poems of Parnassianism pioneer Alfred de Vigny were about the passionate love of Mu Mutian. Feng Naichao loved all about "the Parnassian."[28]

The pursuit of "pure poetry" in modern Chinese poetry from the Crescent to the Modernist School is always closely related to the Parnassian spirit, which is quite different from the development track of Western modern poetry. In the "artistic consciousness" of Western mentors of the Chinese new poetry, Parnassianism and symbolism appear to be in a state of mutual confrontation and opposition. As rebels against Parnassianism, Paul Verlaine, and Stéphane Mallarmé are reunited under symbolism because of their strong dissatisfaction with "no self," "personality elimination," and "emotionlessness." According to Mallarmé, the Parnassian poets are indeed loyal servants of poetry who even dedicate their personalities to poetry. However, it is unprecedented for the younger generation of poets, who directly obtain creative impulses from music.[29] Modernist poets also discarded the adorned Victorian decoration and showed their genuine passions. In their search for art, Symbolist and Modernist poets took completely different paths from Parnassianism. In China, while the modern new poetry created by the Crescent to the Modernist School had their distinctive characteristics, these different schools agreed on the emotional detachment idea of Parnassianism.

Does this mean the "consciousness" as modern Chinese poets understand it is inherently different from Western poetics, although they seem similar? The question is, why do modern Chinese poets favor the temperance and skills of Parnassianism strongly? The answer can be found in Chinese classical poetics. The important symbol of Chinese classical poetry maturity from the Wei, Jin to Tang, and Song dynasties is the modification of poetic emotions and the polishing of forms. Compared with the free expressions of the *Qu Sao* era, the poetry of the Wei, Jin, and Tang dynasties, and *Ci* of the Song Dynasty are naturally temperate and skillful.

Poetry of the Wei, Jin, and Tang dynasties and *Ci* of the Song Dynasty are the classical prototypes of the "conscious" forms of Chinese poetry, which, since its early stages, is no longer satisfied with "helping improve morals and becoming educated." Rhetoric, antithetical parallelism, and rhythm gradually gained attention. The ideal of "the unity of heaven and man" became clearer. This is the art exploration process of Chinese classical poetry from the Wei to Tang and Song dynasties. The poetry of the Wei, Jin, and Southern and Northern dynasties can be considered the foundation of the consciousness of art. The poetry of the Tang Dynasty can be considered the maturity period. The poetry of the late Tang and Five Dynasties can be considered the sublimation period.[30] During the Tang Dynasty and the Song Dynasty Chinese poets seem to have found the best forms of expressing the Chinese cultural spirit, conveying the exquisite feelings of poets in a refined, skillful language.

During his late years, He Qifang wrote a poem entitled "Recalling the Past," which vividly described the meaning of the conscious forms of Chinese classical poetry to modern poets:

> Recalling the night when I read in a ramshackle house, the Tang poems accompanied by a lonely light, the pine tree wind waves almost toppled the house, and the birds were singing a sorrowful tune. I suddenly feel the magnificent natural beauty and my heart is not withered with such company. I didn't understand the meaning of such poems as a child, but the seeds grown long before in winter now awaken in spring.

It is the poetry during the Wei, Jin, Tang, and *Ci* in Song dynasties that opened the young hearts of Chinese poets for the first time, instilling wonderful rhythm of life into their simple souls, evoking their potential poetry interests, and bringing them into a brand new kingdom of art. The beautiful descriptions, such as flowers in mirrors and moon reflected in water have been planted like seeds, which would not disappear with the wind. They inhabit the poets' hearts and receive sunshine and rain in the coming years to find the time to break through. During the May Fourth Movement when the new and traditional poetry were still in sharp opposition, traditional poetry was suffocating the new budding poetry. Modern poets couldn't cherish history without any scruples, but once the new poetry gains a basic foothold, the situation became different. The distant traditional poetry and the latest Western poetry seemed to have become equal—each with its advantages. Especially as descendants of Chinese culture, people are always more emotionally acquainted with traditional poetry. The prototype, the cultural seeds buried in winter finally recovered and started to grow day and night. In turn, people would naturally understand, recognize, and accept foreign poetry culture in a traditional way. Therefore, the calmness and objectivity of Parnassianism integrated with the "sorrowful but not hurting, carefree with temperance" Chinese classical poetry and rooted in generations of poets. The "art for art's sake" of the Crescent Moon School, the Symbolist School, and the Modernist School is a fusion of Chinese and Western cultures. Western poetry culture was accommodated on the foundation of the poetry forms of China's mature period. Shi Ling was right when he said the merits of the Crescent Moon School is that "it established an indispensable bridge between old and new poetry."[31] Mu Mutian and Feng Naichao discussed heatedly "the national colors we advocate."[32] Bian Zhilin summarized after the vernacular new poetry gained a solid foothold, it "intentionally connected with the Chinese poetry tradition to take advantage of the artistic legacy that has been passed through years of continuous genre changes."[33] Feng Wenbing further noted clearly that the new poetry should be the development of schools of poets, such as Wen Tingyun (c. 812–866) and Li Shangyin (c. 813–858).[34] Even Li Jinfa, who was relatively weak in classical literature, said in the *Self Introduction* of *The Diner and the Fierce Year* he would like to communicate or reconcile the "fundamentals" between Chinese classical poetry and Western poetry.[35]

To put it briefly, Crescent Moon School, Symbolist School, and Modernist School, which pursued artistic consciousness, were not so many representatives of the trend of Western modern poetry as typical examples of Chinese poets returning to tradition; they did not so much consciously practice the artistic ideals from Parnassianism to modernism as they consciously raised the inheritance of tradition. The "pure poetry" pursuit is to enter a world of the purer classical art world.

Life and Art

In what ways do conscious forms of modern Chinese poetry inherit the ideals of poetry in Wei, Jin, Tang, and *Ci* in Song dynasties? In other words, what kind of influence does poetry in Wei, Jin, Tang, and *Ci* in the Song dynasties, as an art paradigm, have on modern Chinese poetry?

As mentioned previously, temperance and skills are the deep impressions of the poetry of the Wei, Jin, Tang dynasties, and *Ci* of the Song Dynasty on the modern poets. This impression determines the intimacy of Chinese modern poets toward Parnassianism. This is only a superficial influence of poetry of the Wei, Jin, Tang dynasties, and *Ci* of the Song Dynasty. In my opinion, a more substantial influence can be found in two aspects, namely the poet's attitude toward life in poetry and their understanding of the forms of poetry art.

Qu Sao focuses on the emergence of the self and the extension of the individual. "I" was surrounded by the world which is at "my" call at any time. Such "freedom" still can be found in the poetry of the Wei, Jin, Tang dynasties, and *Ci* of the Song Dynasty, such as Li Bai, "Da Peng, the bird, rose with the wind, and he was able to fly up to tens of thousands miles high, ... with three cups of wine, the Five Mountains in China look light to me." Though, poetry in Wei, Jin, Tang, and *Ci* in the Song dynasties is not intensifying and advances the spirit of *Qu Sao* on the whole. It is to express the "self" in another direction and show the poets' attitudes toward life. The individual-centered freedom of *Qu Sao* is gradually dispelled on the "consciousness" path of Chinese poetry, and replaced by the acceptance and accommodation of the objective world. If the life in *Qu Sao* is completed by the individual's search and strife, then the life in the poetry of Wei, Jin, Tang, and *Ci* in the Song dynasties is completed by the individual's constant recognition of the objective environment.

However, the generous and sad themes expressed in Jian'an (196–220) poetry were no longer the extension of self in Qu Yuan's style, but the "autumn wind is bleak and the weather is turning cold, the dew off the grass turned into frost ... the mountain could never be too high, the water could never be too deep."[36] That is to say, the poet's attitudes toward life are related to his attitudes toward the objective world. The value of the external object has attracted the attention of poets. From the Zhengshi Era (240–249) with Ji Kang and Ruan Ji as its leading poets to the Eastern Jin Dynasty (317–420), poems became more emotion-detached. However, this kind of "rationality" was not purely personal criticism or discussions, but Buddhism and metaphysical talks. Buddhism and Taoism are precisely the softening and dilution of the individual's will of life; the remarkable feature of poetry during the Qiliang Era (479–557) is the poetic descriptions of daily life. Harmonious landscapes between life and nature through the enjoyment of wind, snow, flowers, and grass frequented the poems during the Qiliang Era. Poetry in the early Tang Dynasty is a summary of life consciousness from Jian'an to the Qiliang Era. Poetry at the peak of the Tang Dynasty liberated people from the embrace of nature. "When you go with the waves, you will always find the bright moon in the spring river!" "As if the spring breeze came, thousands of pears trees bloomed."[37] At this point, a view of life in Chinese poetry, drastically different from *Qu Sao*, is established. The poetry of the late Tang and Five Dynasties and the Song Dynasty (mainly the *Man-Ci*, a kind of longer slower verses) did not have the grandness of the Tang Dynasty. Instead, their implicit sentimentality and singer-songs seemed more suitable for the will of shrinking subjectivity, which made it more convenient for the people to interact with the world, and the individuals integrated with the warm natural environment. Therefore, the poetry of this period is the sublimation of the "consciousness" conception. The term that sums up this attitude of life is "*Yi-Jing*" (an aesthetic pursuit that literally means "atmosphere" which refers to a kind of artistic conception), which was first proposed by Wang Changling of the Tang Dynasty. However, a more detailed interpretation did not appear until the mid-Tang Dynasty when Jiao Ran advocated the selection of *Jing* by putting forward "the source of the poems are from the *Jing*." Sikong Tu, of the late Tang Dynasty, tried to detail the "tastes" in the *Jing* and Yan Yu of the Southern Song Dynasty reflected by the poems from the Buddhist perspective and emphasized the *Jing* of poetry is like "the sounds in the air, the colors in the appearances, the moon in the water, and the images in the mirror. There is a limit to words, but no limits to meaning potentials" (Yan Yu, *Canglang Shihua, Poetics of the Blue Wave*).

We could understand *Jing* from different perspectives, such as the integration of emotions and the objective world, the unification of the world and ourselves, and the objectification of the inner emotions and the objective world. Yet, from our standpoint, it can be said that the maximum accommodation of individual life to the natural world is the dilution of the individuality of life until it can be easily connected with the order of nature without any difficulty.

In short, from Wei, Jin to Song dynasties, Chinese classical poetry moving to "consciousness" is attempting to explore a different attitude toward life from the spirit of *Qu Sao* despite their different styles and achievements. Their exploration was completed from all angles, but it also invariably indicated a direction; that is, how to release life experiences of the self in close connection with the objective world. The poetics of the Wei, Jin, and Tang dynasties and the Song Dynasty represent the highest of the "objectification" spirit of Chinese poetry in terms of consciousness.

The conscious forms of poetry of the Wei, Jin, and Tang dynasties, and *Ci* of the Song Dynasty is the main task of modern education for beginners. Their attitude toward life and the ideal of "artistic conception" expressing this attitude has undoubtedly become some kind of "precedents" in the poetic writing of Chinese modern poets.

During the May Fourth Era, the artistic conception aroused the interest of Chinese poets. The ideal artistic conception gradually became the conscious pursuit of Chinese new poetry development. In 1919, Hu Shih praised the poetic mood of Wen Tingyun and Jiang Baishi in his *On New Poetry*. In the second year, Zong Baihua defined the poem as: "*Using beautiful words—painting-like words with rhythm to express the artistic conception of the human beings' emotions.*" He further elaborated that "the artistic conception of poetry" is the "intuitive inspiration caused by the mysterious interaction between the poet's soul and nature."[38] This is a modern description of the artistic experience of the poetry of Wei, Jin, Tang, and *Ci* in the Song dynasties. Interestingly, around the time when Zong Baihua recommended artistic conception or shortly after, Wen Yiduo and Xu Zhimo, two later Crescent poets emerged. Of course, we cannot say these poets, who pursued "artistic consciousness," were under the inspiration of Zong Baihua's poetics, but we can at least think it is from the time modern poets had a profound understanding of the aesthetic connotation of the "artistic consciousness of Chinese classical poetry," which is the cultural psychological foundation for the Chinese new poetry to move to consciousness.

As mentioned in the previous section, the Crescent poets advocated the rhetoric of reason and opposed romantic sentimentality. Wen Yiduo was "cold" and Zhu Xiang was "stable." Xu Zhimo used the pseudonym, "Shi Zhe" (Poetic Philosopher), in the early days. What is interesting is in the minds of ordinary readers, the Crescent Moon School poetry is still lyrical or even sentimental. What does this mean? I believe this is a vivid demonstration of the national characteristics of the Crescent Moon School poetics: they are both rationally emotional and emotionally rational. The key point is the emotions they wanted to refrain from are the free release of individual life (such as Guo Moruo), rather than the vibration of the spirit. The rationality they are inclined to admire is also some kind of norm of self-restraint, not philosophical thoughts. Then, some emotions and some rationality could coexist in the harmonious form of the self and the objective world. We notice "the flashing of the stars, the vibration of the dew on the blades of grass, the shaking of the flowers in the breeze, the changes of the clouds during the thunderstorms, the turbulence of the waves in the sea." These are the expressive objects of the Crescent poets.[39] Integrated individual life into these objective natural scenes, they were not interested in the actual development of individual life—"articles and political theories." They "took pleasure in landscapes, tombs, the pine trees under the stars,"[40] and enjoyed in the "artistic conception" of beauty.

Fei Ming, a Modernist poet, said: "Modernism is the development of Wen Tingyun and Li Shangyin."[41] Indeed, it is easy to associate the Modernist poetry of the 1930s with the poems of the late Tang and Five Dynasties, both being confused, sentimental, beautiful, and full of feminine gentleness and warmth. Among them, the most noticeable is their view of life. Bian Zhilin said the Modernists "consciously connect to the long-term tradition of Chinese poetry without hesitations," which means the life attitude of classical poetry will be discerningly inherited. The important principle of Modernist poetry is "detachment." "When you were beyond yourself, you tried to restrain yourself, as if you would like to be a 'cold-blooded animal.'"[42] Comparing Modernist poetry and Guo Moruo's The Goddesses, we see that Modernists do not fully expose their own emotions nor release their inner emotions, nor become lyrical high above the objects. Modernists attempt to pin themselves on objective images and imply subjectivity with objectivity to search the communication, cooperation, and supplements in between. In the past, critics thought the "detachment" of Modernist poetry was the result of Western symbolism, especially the influence of later Symbolism. Indeed, compared with romantic poetry, late Symbolism emphasizes "emotional exile" and "non-personalization." However, we have never forgotten the fact that behind all those "detachments," strong hearts are beating. T. S. Eliot said it well:

> Poetry is not a turning loose of emotion, but an escape from emotion it is not the expression of personality, but an escape from personality. But, of course, only those who have personality and emotions know what it means to want to escape from these things.[43]

Essentially, emotional escape and personality escape are precisely the important ways for poets to avoid being polluted by dirty, trivial phenomena to achieve new affirmation through negation. "The progress of an artist is a continual self-sacrifice, a continual extinction of personality."[44] For the Western poetic tradition, "detachment" can only be a means, a process, not an end. When we read self-reports and works of Chinese Modernist poets, we see most were not interested in Western symbolism. They had seen the ideals of Chinese classical poetry from Western Symbolism. Specifically, they saw the perfect artist's conception of the poems of the late Tang and Five Dynasties from the "detachment." This is to say, the Chinese-style attitude of life is the real power to incite their emotions. Dai Wangshu's melancholy does not point to the noumenon of life, but more like Li Shangyin's "In the morning's bronze mirror, you worry about the change in your hair," or "the sunset is magnificent; yet, it also precluded the approach of dusk." He Qifang wove his dreams to the images of "beauties and fragrant flowers." Bian Zhilin, who calmly implemented the "organization of distance," said, "the 'I' in the poem can also be exchanged with you or him (her)."[45] I think this statement is applicable to many Modernist poems. The life form of the self can be replaced by you and him or her. This is the poet's conscious self-dissolution, which ends the individual's desire to raise poetry into classical artistic consciousness.

Another sign of the poetry consciousness in the Wei, Jin, Tang, and *Ci* in Song dynasties is the emergence of poetic form awareness. Judging from the law of literary development, the style maturity often lies in its conscious exploration of forms. We say *Qu Sao* is free rather than conscious, which means no clear formal awareness exists during that time. Chinese classical poetry began to explore rhetoric, antithetical parallelism, allusion use, and rhythm comprehensively during the Wei, Jin, Southern, and Northern dynasties. Cao Pi and Cao Zhi, two important poets during the Jian'an Era (196–220) opposed their predecessors and began to include florid rhetoric in the poems. Cao Zhi used antithetical parallelism. "Poetry should be beautiful" is Cao Pi's generalization of the pursuit of this language style (*Dianlun, Lun Wen*). During the Taikang Era (280–289), "antithetical parallelism became popular." Lu Ji (261–303) a famous poet and critic, is known for his focus on word mining. In his work, *Wenfu* (*The Art of Writing*), Lu Ji discussed profusely the choices of words and sentences, a result of his painstaking performance in poetry practice; Yan Yanzhi, a poet during the Southern Song Dynasty (420–479) favored the antithetical parallelism and the allusions, a transition from the ancient Chinese writing (before the Wei and Jin dynasties) into early modern writings (the metrical poems from the Tang Dynasty).[46] The study of rhythm law is the most important activity in all these forms of exploration. The rhythm started during the Three Kingdoms Era (220–280). Through the attempts of literati in the past dynasties to the Yongming Era (483–493) of the Qi Dynasty, the discussion of the "four tones and eight rhythm problems" by Shen Yue means great achievements had been made, indicating the historical turning point of Chinese classical poetry, the so-called "the end of the ancient law and the beginning of the metrical law" (Lu Shiyong, *A Brief Introduction of Poetry*). The poetry of Tang summed up the formal study of the Wei, Jin, and Southern and Northern dynasties and took it to the next level. It fully absorbed the vocabulary, antithetical parallelism, and use of allusions, a harmony of sound laws, extended from "in one phrase" and "in two sentences" during the Qi Liang Era to the whole poem, and avoided the disadvantages of rhythmic issues. Finally, the stylistic norms of poetry were established. The evolution of poetry to Ci in the following seems to be the continual development of this kind of "formal awareness" under new historical conditions.

May Fourth poetry in China was influenced by Hu Shih's concept of "poem writing as prose writing," with the tendency of favoring ideas over wording. The most prominent feature of the Crescent Moon School is to "legislate" the forms for new poetry. Thus, it is called "Metrical Poetry School" in the new poetry. Wen Yiduo's "Three Beauties" theory represents the careful design of the Crescent Moon School poets in diction choice (painting beauty), sentence making (architectural beauty), and rhythm. It is particularly worth mentioning that the ultimate idea of "three beauties" to be achieved—"harmonious order" is precisely from Wen Yiduo's in-depth study of Chinese classical poetry. In his article, *The Study of the Rhythm of Metrical Poems*, Wen Yiduo noted:

> The work of lyricism should be neat, ... the art of harmonious order should be the norm, to frustrate its tempers, to sharpen its edges and corners, to harmonize its rhythm, and then it might start in a rush but would become moderate, to flow without stagnation, and a pleasant sentiment would be created .... The lyrical works should be refined and strict .... The poems should employ the use of rhythms, just like paintings would employ the use of colors and lines.

He also believes: "The greatest trait of Chinese art is harmony and orderly, which are particularly prominent in architecture and poetry."[47] The Symbolist School was also dissatisfied with the "roughness" found in early new poetry. They even claimed Hu Shih was the biggest sinner in the new poetry movement in China. Inspired by the "pure poetry" theory of French Symbolism, the Symbolist School advocated that poetry must combine the beauty of forms and the beauty of music.[48] Emotions and strengths should be combined with sounds and colors to become poetry.[49] These terms also seem to be the "transplantation" of the French symbolic poets, Paul Verlaine and Jean Nicolas Arthur Rambo, but it is obvious that as long as the poems are of Chinese creation, their forms, rhythms, and colors would inevitably be presented through the selection of Chinese words and sentences. The characteristics of the Chinese language are still the foundation for the forms, sounds, and shades of colors. In this sense, it is impossible for the poetry of the Wei, Jin, Tang, and *Ci* of Song dynasties not to work as perfect models of the Chinese form and provide guidance. For example, Mu Mutian thinks Li Bai's poems fall into what he calls "pure poetry." To strengthen the suggestiveness of poetry, Mu Mutian advocates abolishing punctuation, because it "constrained the rhythm and the thoughts of poetry," and thus is harmful to the melody.[50] There is no punctuation in Chinese classical poetry. On the relationship between poetry and rhythm, Modernist poets have different opinions. On the one hand, the works of many poets, such as Fei Ming, Chen Jiangfan, He Jin, Hou Ruhua, Jin Kemu, Li Baifeng, Li Guangtian, and Li Xinruo, are free and seldom touched upon the issue of form. Dai Wangshu seems liberalized from the beginning of "My Memory." But, on the other hand, some of the most famous Modernist poets, such as He Qifang, Bian Zhilin, and Lin Geng, always paid close attention to the forms of poetry. They never stopped experimenting. From their respective expressions, it is clear they were consciously continuing the thinking of the Crescent poets, such as Wen Yiduo, and they pushed the issue further. This means the forms of Chinese new poetry had been frequently paying "conscious" attention to the poetry tradition of the Wei, Jin, Tang, and Song dynasties.

Challenges

The life attitudes and artistic ideals of the poetry of the Wei, Jin, Tang, and *Ci* of Song dynasties continue to exist in the artistic consciousness of modern poetry, but with external invasion at any time. Facing the completely heterogeneous challenge of Western poetry, they lost all the self-sufficiency and stability in history. In the uproar of modern existence, they had to be vacillating, even to hide. They were more like desires intended to be fulfilled, a beautiful and erratic dream because it was difficult for Chinese modern poets to strictly follow the patterns of poetry of the Wei, Jin, Tang, and Song dynasties to achieve their artistic creation.

The influence of Western poetry culture cannot be ignored. Indeed, the Crescent Moon School, the Symbolist School, and the Modernist School seem to have returned to their classical traditions during the process of learning Western modern poetry. Western poetry always encouraged them to focus more on the inheritance of traditional poetic styles when they "fall in love at first sight," but it should not be overlooked that Western poetry (including Parnassianism, Symbolism, etc.) belongs to another cultural system. When Western modern poetry was incorporated into the Chinese poetry system, it could not be assimilated in a short time. As a symbol of Western poetic culture, it would also persistently disseminate information and spread its influence. This extraterritorial information combined with the Chinese modern era atmosphere (breaking closed, turbulent, and awkward living environment based on extensive world relations) set the obstacles for the growth of Chinese traditional poetry during modern times, disturbing or even destroying the classical "objectification" conception developed earlier.

Is it true the harmonious attitude of life can dissolve the willpower of modern people? I think it is difficult. Wen Yiduo's poetry writing presents such contradictions from time to time. On the one hand, he tried to bridge the traditional aesthetic ideals; on the other hand, there is a series of doubts and confusions, as shown in "Red Candle," "Rainy Night," "Sleep," "Spring Light," "Quiet Night," etc., Wen Yiduo was both inspired by the tenacious life consciousness from the West and had keen, sincere feelings toward society. The collision of multiple poetic culture concepts made it difficult to balance and Wen Yiduo gave up poetry writing.

Other poets, although also fascinated by the objective atmosphere of the poetry of the late Tang and Song dynasties, did not always seem to "forget everything," and their modern artistic conception is not always gentle and harmonious. For the self, Dai Wangshu imagined from time to time, "The best way of being a human being is all ignorant, / it is best not to ask for a solution, just look at it, look at the sky, watch the stars, watch the moon, and watch the sun." But suddenly, he can't restrain the impulse of life:

> Or I will become a strange comet,
> I want to stop in space or move in the space as I will,
> No one can calculate my trajectory, or understand what I am doing
> then I knock the sun into broken fire pieces and smash the earth into mud.
> —"To Kemu"

Dai Wangshu still can't reach the "forget me"! Bian Zhilin's "West Chang'an Street" seems to strive to render the unique lightness and tranquility of ancient Beijing, and solidify life in an ancient serenity, but the lines are leaping out of the images of the turbulent era, such as the cavalry, the command, the gunshots, and finally, the impulse to hold back life: "Friends, let's not imitate what the elderly are doing, / let's talk about it . . ." Thus, the artistic conception of the integration of self and the external world was disintegrated.

Since some Chinese poets, including the Modernists, have instinctively found the instability of traditional artistic ideas in modern society, then the goal set by this "artistic consciousness" cannot but be said to face a crisis. In the later stage of Modernist poetry writing, the ambiguity of art finally came. Many Modernist poets found it hard for them to produce good works. This shows modern life can no longer provide nourishment for their art that is too "pure." The "artistic consciousness" of Chinese new poetry should also be freed from the traditional "consciousness" mode, and it should be separated from the "pureness" that traditional Chinese language and traditional aesthetics hold, opening a new path, as Ke Ke advocated at the time. "Poetry is rigid because it is too civilized, there must be savage, vigorous efforts to resist the pressure of these thousands of years of tradition and burden."[51]

Responding to this appeal are the Nine Leaves School and July School of the 1940s, whose new artistic ideals are "anti-tradition" and to transcend "purity." The emergence of the Nine Leaves School and July School marks the end of "conscious" forms of Chinese new poetry in pursuit of "art for art's sake."

Poetry of the Song Dynasty and the Anti-traditional Tendency of Modern Chinese New Poetry

> Where should the poetry revolution begin? Poetry should be written like prose.
> —Hu Shih, "A Response to Shuyong's Poem"[52]

"Anti-tradition" is one of the basic trends of modern Chinese new poetry. The early vernacular new poetry can be described as rebels against the fading Chinese classical poetry traditions. The revolutionary poetry of the late 1920s and 1930s also launched harsh criticism of Chinese romantic traditions in the early 1920s. The rebellion of the Nine Leaves poets and the July poets in the 1940s was particularly strong against the so-called "sentimental remnants" of the 1920s and 1930s. Chinese modern new poetry has always been accompanied by the anti-traditional call from its birth to its maturity.

The anti-tradition of Chinese new poetry often relied on the power of foreign cultures. For example, Hu Shih's first attempt was an "experiment" inspired by the Anglo-American Imagery School; the revolutionary poetry inspired by the world of proletarian literature; the Nine Leaves and July Schools inspired by 20th-century poetry styles or Western romanticism, such as those of W. B. Yeats and T.S. Elliot. We fully agree that without the inspiration and encouragement of foreign cultures, the "anti-tradition" of modern Chinese poetry would have been impossible. However, as one of the components of the Chinese language and culture, Chinese new poetry, after all its deviations from traditions, is still accomplished within the traditions by eliminating some traditions and combining other traditions; thus, continuing to form a new tradition. The stimulation and influence of foreign culture were ultimately demonstrated through the cultivation and acceptance of traditional language and traditional mentality. In this sense, "anti-tradition" is never equal to the simple collision and conflict between two cultures. Its essence is the rediscovery, re-recognition, and restructure of traditions. Of course, foreign cultures also influence specific ways and depth of such discoveries, recognition, and structures.

Therefore, to analyze deeply the anti-traditional trend of modern Chinese poetry, I believe we should go beyond just focusing on the connections with foreign poetry by further exploring the internal roots of these rebellions, summarizing how they were completed, the direction our traditional poetic culture has been steered, and the extent it had been preserved. Anti-tradition needs new national culture criticism.

Poetry of the Song Dynasty: A Cultural Prototype of Anti-traditional Poetry

Can the anti-tradition of modern Chinese poetry be supported by the spirit of Chinese classical poetry? Or, are there cultural prototypes of self-denial and self-reversal in the tradition formed by the development of Chinese classical poetry for thousands of years? These are the starting points of our research because Chinese new poetry would lose its basic foundation and the basic psychological endurance required by "rebellion" without such prototypes.

I believe the poetry of the Song Dynasty is an anti-tradition prototype that exists in Chinese traditions.

Chinese classical poetry developed and matured in the cultural background of China's great unity. As Chinese culture grew finer, more diversified, and matured, Chinese classical poetry also shifted from the freedom style of the pre-Qin Dynasty to the consciousness style of the Jin and Tang dynasties. This turn means the gradual weakening and decrease of individual freedom, as well as the purity and perfection of self-objectification and the highest harmony between man and nature. Especially during the late Tang and Five Dynasties and the two Song dynasties, the poetics of this great unity was pushed to the peak from the two aspects of life pursuit and art forms. Of course, all these artistic achievements were realized in the cultural background of great unity. If the social culture did not have a self-denying trend after a high degree of maturity, or the poet's personality continued to subside and its objectified artistic conception failed to have more complicated changes, maturity would lead to a profound crisis. The late Tang and Five Dynasties and the two Song dynasties (especially the *Man-Ci*) eventually broke into a desperate situation of emptiness and frivolity. Poetry of the Wei, Jin, and Tang dynasties and *Ci* of the Song Dynasty represented the typical forms of Chinese classical poetry tradition, including its prosperity and crisis.

Quite different from the aesthetic art pursuit of the poetry of the Jin and Tang dynasties and *Ci* (*Man-Ci* being the mainstream) of the Song Dynasty, the poetry of the Song Dynasty consciously took a turn and blazed a new antitraditional path. Two talented poets during the Song Dynasty, Su Shi and Huang Tingjian, greatly changed the style since the Tang Dynasty and drew a distinctive line between the poetry of the Tang and Song dynasties. I think the characteristics of the new changes in the poetry of the Song Dynasty can be understood from the following aspects.

Politically Strong Moral Values. This is a unique discourse of the late feudal social ideology. The Tang Dynasty (618–907) can be described as a prosperous period in the early Chinese feudal society. The flourishing national trend brewed open-minded politics. Poetry, as an ideological artistic discourse, also presented an open political mind with greater inclusiveness: "amounting high between the spectacular heaven and earth." One could be free to become an official or hermit, seeking promotions or enjoying relaxation. Attention to personal cultivation or national contributions was chosen by people according to their will. During the late period of the Song Dynasty (960–1279), however, the Chinese feudal society was losing its advantages of the bureaucratic system and poverty increased. After the establishment of the Southern Song Dynasty (1127–1279), the country was divided because of the invasion of Northern China. The Central Plains had new rulers with a huge social crisis. Before the introduction of a new political culture, people seemed more willing to maintain the dominance of Confucianism and Taoism, hoping to turn the tide by strengthening Confucian political ethics. Many poets, such as Ouyang Xiu, Wang Anshi, Su Shi, Huang Tingjian, and others, experienced the ups and downs of the officialdom. They closely linked literary activities with political activities by focusing more on the moral and practical functions of poetry, integrating preaching elements. They criticized the style of the late Tang and Five Dynasties, which deviated from the track of Confucianism. Du Fu's "Following Confucianism and fulfilling the official responsibilities" became a motto of life and art for the poets of the Song Dynasty. "Zi Mei's

(Du Fu's) collection opened the poetry world" (Wang Yucheng's "A Letter to Zhongxian"). His political ideal of "benevolent governance and love for the people" and a deep sense of social responsibility had a huge impact on the poets of the Song Dynasty.

Culturally Distinctive Rationality. The multicultural system of Confucianism, Buddhism, and Taoism was intertwined with each other during the Song Dynasty. Neo-confucianism's approach to life and morality was endowed with the philosophical features of Buddhism and Taoism, which greatly influenced people's way of thinking. From Qingli (1041–1048) to the Yuanyou (1086–1094) Era, rational thoughts that stressed practicality evolved into conscious rational reflections after the failure of political reforms, focusing on mind cultivation and inquiry into the principles of the world. This is also reflected in poetry writing. If the traditions of the Tang Dynasty are described as flourishing, full of enthusiasm, full of youth, and vitality, then the poetry of the Song Dynasty has entered a stage of reflection in history with a tendency toward meditation. Poetry during this period does not just show realistic pictures. Instead, it explores and thinks about life instead of just describing life as a means of personal development. Poets from the Song Dynasty tended to mediate the world and believed one can see all the principles within one thing, revealing a wise philosophical style. For example, even when Su Shi was enjoying the scenery in the mountains and rivers, he still did not forget the rational enlightenment: "Of Mountain Lu, we cannot make out the true face, For we are lost in the heart of the very place" ("Written on the Wall at West Forest Temple").

The Vicissitude Experience of Life. With the loss of the internal vitality of China's feudal society system in its late period, it was difficult to overcome the conflicts accumulated over a long period. There were no solutions. In a highly rigid political order, under the pressure of internal and external turbulence, intellectuals had lost their enterprising confidence and ability and were more subjected to an unpredictable destiny. The orthodox concepts of politics pushed more people into an increasingly embarrassing situation of ideal and reality separation, deepening the tragic experience of life as a dream. The poetry style of the Tang Dynasty is bright and happy, even when it is sad. It usually is the juvenile-style ethereal sentiment. Poetry during the Song Dynasty, in contrast, was sadder, heavier, and more thoughtful. For instance, Su Shi sighed, "Living such a wretched life and suddenly half my life is gone" ("Nephew Anjie's Night Visit from Far II"). Huang Tingjian wrote: "You studied so hard while living poor and your hair must have gone white, Across the river I heard monkeys howling in the distant forests" ("To Huang Jifu"). Chen Shidao: "The fallen flowers are gone with the wind, and all the joys are transient with a blink of the eye" ("Summer Reflections"). Some critics accurately argued that behind the mundane "old world" after the peak of the poetry of the Song Dynasty, "there is a kind of bleakness and depression in the world with no songs to sing."[53]

Artistical Spirit of Innovation. With a series of changes in political outlook, life outlook, and cultural outlook, the art of poetry of the Song Dynasty was established on a new historical level. Compared with the poetry traditions of the Jin and Tang dynasties, the Song Dynasty was filled with a strong spirit of innovation. During the Song Dynasty, the literary communities took "poetry and innovation" as their slogan. Huang Tingjian wrote, "If you follow others, you will end as a follower. In writing, it would be taboo to follow others" (*Poetics by Tiaoxi Yuyin*). Various summaries had been made regarding the various characteristics of the Song Dynasty reform to the Tang Dynasty style, such as:

> Where the Tang Dynasty style was heroic, the Song Dynasty style would be secluded; where the Tang Dynasty style was rough, the Song Dynasty made it more delicate; where the Tang Dynasty style was smooth, the Song Dynasty made it circumvent; where the Tang Dynasty made it easy, the Song Dynasty made it difficult; where the Tang Dynasty used decorations, the Song Dynasty used plain language; where the Tang Dynasty described plainly, the Song Dynasty tried to write lengthy; where the Tang Dynasty was outspoken and direct, the Song Dynasty was implicit. The Tang Dynasty style focused on content words, while the Song Dynasty emphasized link words. (Chen Xiangyao, *Notes of Poetry of the Song Dynasty*)

Among these various generalizations, I think the most important is the so-called "prose as poetry"; that is, breaking aesthetic norms of the Jin and Tang dynasties, including integration of human and the external world and implicitness, opposing traditional ways of creating a "pure poetry" world. Poetry was written in a prose style; narrative and argumentative statements were widely used. At the same time traditional language which intends to leave room for the readers to reflect was abandoned, the difficult expressions of the words themselves were deliberately highlighted; long, difficult sentences were made; unusual rhymes were employed; allusions were pursued; and "pointing to stone and turning into gold," "rebirth," and "transform the decayed into the magic" were stressed.

Inconsistent with the tradition of the Jin and Tang dynasties, these thoughts and artistic pursuits of the poetry of the Song Dynasty belong to another world. If we further summarize from the perspective of cultural philosophy and expand the potential cultural orientation of these thoughts and arts, then we can see the profound differences between the poetry of the Song Dynasty from the tradition of the Jin and Tang dynasties. The compatibility of Confucianism, Buddhism, and Taoism in political concepts, the enjoyment of life in life's outlook, the perceptual thinking of cultural concepts, and the pursuit of pure poetry in artistic concepts all made it easier for the poetry of Jin and Tang dynasties to dilute the "self" and realize the artistic conception of objectification; thus, radiated the most national light in the history of world poetry. Poetry of the Song Dynasty poetry with its various tendencies expanded the individual's willpower and the radiation of personal thoughts to express personal feelings, brought the self from the tangible and accessible objective world, and searched for language in the creation of human culture. As a result, the objectified artistic conception encountered difficulties and faced a crisis.

If we admit the objectified ideal of the poetry of the Jin and Tang dynasties represents the most typical form of Chinese classical poetry, then some deviations from this by the poetry of the Song Dynasty reflected a very rare "anti-traditional" power in Chinese classical poetry. Poetry of the Song Dynasty is an anti-traditional cultural prototype that exists in traditions.

Anti-traditional Chinese New Poetry

From the moment when modern poetry was born against traditional poetry, this implied the possibility of establishing an inextricable connection with the "anti-traditional" poetry of the Song Dynasty, which, as an anti-traditional cultural prototype, is likely resurrected in a certain climate, regardless of the specific forms it might take.

Not all Chinese classical poetry serves as truly historical pressure on modern Chinese poetry. Declining Chinese poetry of the Ming and Qing dynasties is unlikely to become a stumbling block to the development of Chinese new poetry, because, at this time, the bleakness of traditional art proved the necessity of pioneering and provided Chinese poets with great self-confidence and a sense of superiority. The great deterrent to the art of the young and nascent is the peak period of classical art, the era of infinite charm in its various aspects of thought and art, where its existence and glory would contrast the weakness and roughness of the emerging force. As mentioned previously, the typical form of Chinese classical poetry tradition is the poetry of the Jin and Tang dynasties. Therefore, the "traditional" elements that form a historical confrontation with modern Chinese new poetry are present during the Jin and Tang dynasties. To remove the restraints of classical poetry and establish a new aesthetic ideal of the spirit of the times, Chinese new poetry would inevitably need to break through the traditional art model of the Jin and Tang dynasties, including the objectification of self, harmony between man and nature, and so on. With such a background, the poetry of the Song Dynasty provided a poetic orientation for modern poetry.

At the same time, in Western poetry, the external origin of modern Chinese new poetry, the artistic ideals of being non-intentional and non-objectified, pursuing poets' unfailing willpower with a strong subjectivity to feel and evaluate the world are the most specific and distinctively distinguished features from traditional Chinese poetry. As a result, the poetry of the Song Dynasty was similar, to a certain degree, to the ideals of foreign poetry, which produced a sense of familiarity and amiability.

All of these set foundations for the resurrection of the poetry of the Song Dynasty as a cultural archetype during modern times, for the recognition of the "anti-traditionalism" of new poetry for its artistic trend, and the local transplantation of foreign poetics.

I once emphasized the emergence of May Fourth poetry is closely related to the introduction and translation of Western poetry. Hu Shih's pioneering "May Wind" is a translation work of Western style. Crescent Moon School was the first group of modern Chinese poets, who actively accepted the influence of classical poetry.[54]

But does this mean the early vernacular poets have nothing to do with the Chinese classical poetry tradition? Of course not. While there is a huge typical gap between the early vernacular new poetry and Chinese poetry's "objectified" ideal, we cannot claim they can freely break away from the whole classical poetry tradition, nor could we claim their attempt was completed in the absence of any inner support. Some vernacular poets of the time consciously searched for genes of change from the evolution of Chinese classical poetry. They believed the evolution of Chinese poetry is from refrainment to openness, from bondage to freedom, and the vernacular appeared in the Song and Yuan dynasties. Hu Shih said,

> There is no such thing as a mystery about the trend in the history of Chinese poetry from the poetry of the Tang Dynasty to the poetry of the Song Dynasty. The poetry is closer to prose and the vernacular.... The great contribution of the poets of the Song Dynasty was they broke the restraint of the rhyme, since the Six Dynasties (222–589) and tried to write poetry close to the spoken language.

Hu Shih noted clearly: "My thoughts at this time were quite influenced by my reading of the poetry of the Song Dynasty."[55] Although we cannot say that all anti-traditional modern poets have accepted this theory, even Hu Shih's thoughts incurred many criticisms from those who continued to advocate "pure poetry," they are very profound and typical of the cultural mentality of a pioneer at the beginning of this new era. At the transitioning point, national cultural mentalities would reveal themselves when faced with difficult times. It was not yet decorated or not necessarily to be decorated by the times. I believe Hu Shih sought the future from history and drew nourishment from tradition. This shows the long-standing "reviving the past and learning the principles" mentality of Chinese literati. Due to the urgency of developing new literature and the difficulty of writing vernacular poems, Hu Shih had to stress his "literary history of vernacular literature" to prove the legitimacy of his attempts. After this, poets crossed the historical turning point and felt the support of history. Hence, this ethnic mentality sank to a deeper level. However, the prototype is a prototype after all. In the specific atmosphere of the Chinese language and culture, its resurrection is the inevitable result of art history with far-reaching significance.

"Writing poems like prose" is Hu Shih's most intuitive, simple interpretation of the poetry of the Song Dynasty, and also affects his anti-tradition poem writing as well as other early vernacular poets. If we analyze the question by connecting it to the broad background of world poetry, we must admit the stylistic relationship between poetry and literature is quite complicated. Compared to Classicism, Romanticism is pure and prose-like, and the rules of poetry are looser. Compared with Romanticism, Symbolism is "pure poetry" and musical. Anti-tradition is not necessarily "writing poems like prose." However, in the history of modern Chinese poetry, the anti-traditional poetry style generally tended to explore the new changes in poetry from the literature style and introduce narrative elements into poetry writing. Ke Ke suggested prose poems, narrative poems, and drama poems are particularly noteworthy new trends in modern poetry.[56] Mao Dun said: "From lyricism to narrative ... can be said to be the re-liberation and re-revolution of new poetry."[57] Ai Qing proposed, "It is an improvement from the appreciation of rhymes to the appreciation of prose."[58] Although Yuan Kejia, a Nine Leaves poet, disagreed with the idea of the prose trend, he also believed "modern poets attach great importance to the application of everyday language and rhythm of speech."[59] We can't claim these poetic orientations are all derived from poetry of the Song Dynasty, yet at least ancient and modern poetry came together in the choice of "writing poems like prose," which reminds us that we must pay attention to the intangible role played by the prototype of the poetry of the Song Dynasty.

Rationalization is also a feature of the anti-traditional trend of modern Chinese new poetry.

> In the early days of the new poetry, reasoning is one of the main issues. The founder of New Poetry, Mr. Hu Shih, advocated poetry and reasoning. In An Experimental Collection, there seems quite a number of this kind of poetry. Mr. Yu Pingbo also loved to put principles in his poems; Mr. Hu commented on his poems, saying he wanted to be a philosopher.[60]

After the War of Resistance against Japanese Aggression, new poetry inclined more toward rationalization. Lü Yuan, a poet of the July School, said in one poem, "People must find the light of reason through poetry" ("Poetry and Truth"). Yuan Kejia, a Nine Leaves poet, also stressed: "Good poems often contain abstract ideas."[61]

A strong sense of social responsibility is an important life attitude throughout all these anti-traditional works. The early vernacular poems by Hu Shih, Shen Yinmo, Liu Bannong, Liu Dabai, and others are filled with strong humanitarian spirits. They represent "painful situations across poor society of that time, such as male and female workers in factories, rickshaw drivers, farmers in the inner land, and retailers and small shops across the country."[62] Jiang Guangci and Yin Fu committed themselves to becoming "the singers of the East Asian revolution."[63] The Chinese Poetry Association declared to "break this dark world."[64] The enthusiasm of the left-wing revolution undoubtedly strengthened the poets' desires to intervene in society, and the full-scale invasion by the Japanese during the War of Resistance against Japanese Aggression in 1937 pushed more poets to the solemn theme of national survival. Tian Jian recorded the struggle through verses such as "burning," "rough," and "anger." Ai Qing "praised freedom and democracy with the highest enthusiasm."[65] The Nine Leaves poets also believed, "If today's poet still thinks of removing the influence of political life, he will not only be trapped in the illusory prayers just like a fish out of water but will face the threat of suffocation, which will follow."[66] There might be various anti-traditional forms in modern Chinese new poetry in their pursuit of specific poetics. Yet, modern Chinese poetry showed a striking similarity on the point of shouldering social morality and national responsibility. I believe, in addition to looking for explanations from specific times, the "principle" concept of the poetry of the Song Dynasty played a potential role. It is easy to find the opposite of all the anti-traditional tendencies in Chinese new poetry is the "emotion and scenery" integration of those sentimental to their environment or personal experiences. Hu Shih was greatly dissatisfied with the grandiloquent and oversentimental style of poetry of the time.[67] The Crescent poets and the Modernists, who were absorbed in love affairs and sentiments, were the targets of the left-wing critics. Yuan Kejia contrasted Xu Zhimo's traditionalism with Mu Dan's anti-traditionalism. He commented that Xu's poems were "the result of heavy lyric atmosphere ... strong feelings and gorgeous imageries," while Mu Dan's poems were "strongly focused without caring much of the atmosphere." As modern people, "we naturally have reasons to prefer Mu Dan's poetry."[68] These confrontations remind us of the criticism of poetry of the Song Dynasty to the poetry of the late Tang and Five Dynasties.

Limitations, Transformation, and Transcendence

Starting with the overall pursuit of "anti-tradition" in modern Chinese poetry above, we examined its direct or indirect connection with the poetry of the Song Dynasty. It should be clear that the anti-tradition forms of Modern Chinese poetry still maintain many independent characteristics. There are differences between the anti-tradition pioneers, such as Hu Shih, Shen Yinmo, Liu Bannong, and others, the anti-tradition of the left-wing revolutionary poets, and the anti-tradition of the July School and the Nine Leaves School. This distinguishes modern poetry history benefited from the poetry of the Song Dynasty from the history of Chinese classical poetry. Poetry of the Song Dynasty as the most unique anti-Jin-Tang model has become a typical example of anti-tradition. Since then, the anti-tradition identified with the ideals of the poetry of the Song Dynasty, so all differences between reviving the orthodox of the Jin and Tang dynasties, and the transformation of the orthodox of the Jin and Tang dynasties are demonstrated as differences between the "Poetry School of Tang Dynasty" and the "Poetry School of Song Dynasty." The dispute between the Tang and Song dynasties exemplified the development of the whole Chinese poetry from the end of the Southern Song Dynasty to the late Qing Dynasty. Before the introduction of the more influential foreign poetry culture, Chinese poets could only make such choices. However, China's modern new poetry is different. Its emergence, development, and maturity are related to the continuous impact of Western poetry. From the beginning to the end, it is placed in the vast wilderness of Chinese and Western cultural interactions, and influenced by various factors. Moreover, for the modern vernacular new poetry, "tradition" actually refers to the whole classical poetry from the pre-Qin Dynasty to the late Qing Dynasty, and also includes poetry of the Song Dynasty. Various artistic forms of classical poetry have a potential prototype power for modern people. While opposing the traditions of the Jin and Tang dynasties, it is possible to return to this tradition unconsciously. All of these complex confluences of Chinese and Western poetics bring complexity to the anti-traditional choice of modern poets. In this way, the artistic ideals that also agree with the prototype of the poetry of the Song Dynasty have produced three quite different practical methods. First, the semantics of the prototype is followed, and new literature in the cultural context provided by the prototype is constructed. Second, some of the inspirations of the prototype are retained but merged with other poetic pursuits. Third, a long-distance historical connection with the prototype is maintained, while at the same time freely borrowing the power of the times to make a new assembly of "history" with fresh blood coming in. I call these three modes of practice, respectively, the limitations, transformation, and transcendence of the Song Dynasty poetry prototype.

Early vernacular new poems show more of the cultural characteristics of poetry of the Song Dynasty, such as social morality, rational thinking, and prose as poetry. This is mainly rooted in the conscious identity of poets, such as Hu Shih, who also accepted the influence of other traditional poets. For example, Hu Shih advocated the specificity of poetry, emphasized fully affecting the feelings of the readers, and opposed the abstract practice, which seemed to match the artistic ideas of the Jin and Tang dynasties' poetry.[69] Hu Shih, Liu Bannong, Liu Dabai, and others also explored the issue of the ballad tendency of poetry in theory or practice, which is also inconsistent with the scholarly tendency of the poetry of the Song Dynasty. However, these heterogeneous poets did not fundamentally change the characteristics of the early vernacular new poetry which showed the influence of poetry of the Song Dynasty. The artistic pursuit of the Jin and Tang dynasties is only the imagined pursuit of Hu Shih, and the overall feature of his poetry is prose as poetry, with abstraction and rationality dominating. These caused criticism later. The ballad tendency also failed to waver the perseverance of that generation of poets against the Jin and Tang dynasties. To some extent, the narration tone of the songs was also supported by the poetry of the Song Dynasty's prose tendency characteristics.[70] For example, in Liu Dabai's "The Landlord Comes":

> You have toiled for the whole year,
> The landlord is here claiming all as the debt.

The big heavy buckets are full on the scale,
Extra is grabbed but still accused not enough.
A chicken has to be borrowed from me, too,
I could give it to you and don't mention it anymore!

This kind of Bai Juyi poetry style, known as the villagers' language, is also a model for the poets of the Song Dynasty to rebel against the artistic pursuit of the Jin and Tang dynasties. Wang Yucheng wrote: "We plant on the northern hill and we plant on the southern hill, we would not leave any places unplanted when we are helping each other" ("She Tian Tune"), Su Shunqin wrote "eight or nine out of ten died, the corpses unattended along the roadside" ("In Commemoration of Cheng Yongshu in the South of the City"), Fan Chengda wrote: "Now I have a third daughter to be sold and I'm not afraid of renting collection next year!" ("After the Renting Collection") From these aspects, I think the early vernacular new poetry practiced the anti-tradition of the poetry of the Song Dynasty, but it is also bound by this ideal and belongs to what I call the practice of "limitation."

Some characteristics of the anti-tradition of left-wing revolutionary poetry (including early revolutionary poetry and Chinese Poetry Association) are similar to those of poetry of the Song Dynasty, such as the distinctive social responsibility, narrative elements, and narrative tone, etc. However, the rationalism of poetry of the Song Dynasty did not appear in left-wing revolutionary poetry. On the contrary, emotions were raised to a fairly high position by poets, such as Jiang Guangci, Yin Fu, and Pu Feng. In the 1930s, Mu Mutian believed the poet must "hold the feelings of the progress of the times."[71] When talking about the contribution of the poet, Wen Liu, Pu Feng commented "It is especially important that the poet *responds to the reality with fury*, and he curses, applauds and sings."[72] Yin Fu believed "we are on the pillow of the volcano that will burst, and the mouth of the volcano will eject deep red fire" ("The Heart of the Earth"). This important change is due to the convergence of Western romanticism and the proletarian poetry of the Soviet Union (both of which are similar in the point of highlighting the emotional characteristics of poetry). Although left-wing revolutionary poetry once rejected romanticism, it finally embraced strong emotions by encouraging "revolutionary romanticism." Passion replaced the rational elements of poetry of the Song Dynasty, and the Western romanticism and the proletarian poetry of the Soviet Union further transformed the Chinese-style national sorrow and made it go beyond the narrow framework of "benevolent government and love for the people" and fight for the new century:

Like the Yellow River that breaks the banks,
Who has the power to stop it?
Waves like the ocean
The raging is our team.

—Pu Feng, "Liu Yue Liu Huo" (June Flames)

The integration of social mission and emotions also urged the left-wing revolutionary poetry to accept the influence of *Qu Sao* in the "inner beauty and abilities." Compared with the integration of self and the world of Jin and Tang dynasties' poetry and the rationalism of poetry of the Song Dynasty, *Qu Sao*'s prototype offers an enchanting freedom.[73] The spirit of various poets in ancient and modern China, and foreign countries has transformed the inherent model of China's anti-tradition. The left-wing revolutionary poetry finalized the practice of "transformation" of this anti-tradition prototype.

The writings of the July School, the Nine Leaves School and poets like Ai Qing showcased the "transcendence" practice of the prototype of the poetry of the Song Dynasty. In a series of anti-traditional trends, to some extent, they are similar to the poetry of the Song Dynasty taking long-distance cultural connections. They all had a social consciousness and used it as one of the anti-traditional signs; but, they did not use the external social consciousness to replace the personality itself, but strived to find a combination between these two. The Nine Leaves poets believed affirmation of the parallel and close connection between poetry and politics did not mean poetry is a weapon of politics or propaganda.[74] They opposed the instrumentality and combativeness of one-sided, over-confidence in the literature.[75] The July School put forward the "subjective spirit." Ai Qing connected the promotional function of poetry and the fermentation and brewing of personal emotions. These poets showed different levels of rational spirit, but led rationality to a richer, deeper level, and integrated it with other spiritual elements of humans. Tang Shi, a Nine Leaves poet, admired the idea of turning "deep thought into a fresh spiritual style and emotional cost" and "thinking everything with the senses of the body and the "sensuality" of life."[76] Yuan Kejia concluded poetry must have imaginary logic besides rational concept logic. The July School poet, Hu Feng, believed the correctness of theory is something produced earlier than poetry, and poetry can only use correct theory to write the poets' "feeling about the emotion of struggle."[77] He firmly opposed poetry as the visualization of abstract ideas.[78] Ai Qing valued the association, imagination, and image thinking of poetry. All these poets advocated vernacular, narrative, and "speaking rhythm" of poetry, but they did not stop at the desire to accommodate prose discourse. In

Hu Feng's opinion, the language of poetry "must be in an unconstrained form to express the emotions of the author freely."[79] Ai Qing also expressed similar ideas: "Choose to be naked, rather than let the clothes that do not fit to suffocate your breath."[80] This shows they pay more attention to the deeper reasons for choosing "writing prose as poetry." Compared with the poets of the Song Dynasty, they have a clear modern consciousness. For the Nine Leaves poets, everyday language and rhythm of speech is by no means deliberate, new language skills. Its literary value lies in "its variation, flexibility, fresh, vivid words and rhythms, which can appropriately and effectively express the singularity of modern poets' feelings, the dramatic change of thoughts as a tool for creating the most conscious activities."[81] At the same time, "the folk language and everyday language are rich, flexible, full of changes, lively and closely related to life, full of dramatic sense, not because they are only used by the people or everyday conversation."[82] The rhythm of speech does not mean to confuse the boundaries between poetry and other literature. Poetry is still poetry. The Nine Leaves poets were deeply influenced by 20th-century Western poetry, trying to distinguish the "language of poetry" from the "scientific language." Thus, after canceling the negation of poetry as "writing prose as poetry," this drives the problem to a deeper level.

In addition, in this series of anti-tradition choices during the 1940s, the vicissitudes of life and the awareness of suffering were also highlighted and regarded as the deepest, most tenacious willpower of poetry. In the early days of vernacular new poetry in China and in the "old style" that grew stronger during the 1920s and 1930s, vicissitudes of life and suffering were seldom considered. The "teenager sentiment" of the Crescent, the Symbolist, and the Modernist schools lacked more grandeur in a broader view of life. The "anti-traditional" left-wing revolutionary poets advocated revolutionary optimism as their responsibility, which ignored the truth of existence from different angles. In contrast to previous forms of new poetry (including the anti-traditional new poetry forms), the anti-traditional poems of the 1940s were full of serious thoughts about life and detailed the suffering and vicissitudes of life. The boldness, frankness, and sorrow in the poetic descriptions of life were breathtaking. The July School poets "compressed" and "condensed" the painful observations of the disastrous reality of the national war. Ai Qing read about society and life with Baudelaire-style melancholy, and the Nine Leaves poets repeatedly wrote the rich painful tradition of a nation with a long history at the modern turning point. For example, Mu Dan delicately drew some contradictions in life:

> Tell us to be peaceful, but then we must kill,
> And that we hate, yet we must first rejoice.
> Knowing "human" is not enough, we learn
> Methods to destroy it, arranged into a mechanical formation,
> Intellectual strength creeps like a group of beasts.
>
> —"Departure"

Such "rich pain" not only is rare in the anti-tradition choice in modern China, but it also expanded its meaning in comparison with the vicissitudes of the poetry of the Song Dynasty, which is richer than traditional poetry, yet "not far from ancient times," and did not accept the impact of other new cultural trends. So, from a deeper level, there is still no escape from the specific cultural mentality of classical poets. Their vicissitudes of life mostly came from the narrow ambiguity of "time is not waiting for me" and "life as a dream." They lacked the cosmic awareness that raised personal pain or suffering to the national and even humankind level. They also did not intend to analyze more deeply and painfully. It is even harder to see the courage to resist despair and darkness; on the contrary, it is often embellished with several intelligent touches of humor in the narrative of life's suffering, which makes people forget the painful pressures while focusing on the appreciation. This is the so-called taste of ration.

> Looking at the moon in the sky, I am on the ground, my shadows walked with me, and when I stop it stops too. I don't know if I and the shadows are the same or separate. The moon draws my shadow. Could I write myself?
> —Yang Wanli, "Pondering in a Summer Moon Night"

It is the style of Zen that some kind of enjoyment was drawn from pain. It is indeed fascinating, but the deep meaning of pain was heavily lost. The anti-traditional new poetry of the 1940s greatly surpassed its cultural archetypes. It was rarely pretentiously or cheated itself to disguise the unchangeable facts of life. It touched the suffering and deconstructed this suffering. All other life choices, social choices, and artistic choices are closely cast on this level with consideration of the suffering of life as an important foundation of subjective consciousness. From this point of view, the anti-traditional new poems around the 1940s not only gave poetry's prototype more powerful ideas in the choice of poetics but also fundamentally transformed the poets' subjective consciousness.

Western poetry in the 20th century played a crucial role in the practice of anti-traditional choices surpassing the poetry of the Song Dynasty around the 1940s. The strong pulse of poetry development from the 19th century to the 20th century could be felt from their respective emphasis on intrinsic emotional factors, the emergence of human willpower, the exploration of the fascinating stylistic features of the poems, and the deep reflection on the suffering of individuals or the world. Most of the poets, inspired by Western poetry, opened their eyes for the first time and opened their minds. Without the support of Western poetry, there would be no Mu Dan, no Nine Leaves poets, and no Ai Qing, Tian Jian, or Hu Feng. Poetry of the Song Dynasty set a far-reaching example for anti-tradition, while the Western poetry style of the 19th and 20th centuries provided timely, realistic support. Similar orientations of Song poetry and Western poetry guided the direction of anti-tradition. Western poetry enriched this choice with richer, more contemporary ideas. From the analysis here, I believe the anti-tradition choices around the 1940s are distinctive from the new "Chinese and Western poetic fusion" found during the 1930s. The result of the fusion is that modern poetry is neither limited by the prototype of Chinese classical poetics (because it absorbed a lot of new connotations of foreign poetry), nor easily captured by Western poetics (because it clarified the basic direction of anti-tradition from the inspirations of the poetry of the Song Dynasty). These poems are both Chinese and modern, both national and transcend all classical traditions. As long as modern Chinese poetry continues to infiltrate the atmosphere of Chinese language and culture, live in the long river of Chinese culture, and are still modern "traditional people," then the anti-traditional practices of this era can be described as the most successful examples. This has left many valuable experiences for the healthy development of Chinese new poetry and a truly modern Chinese-Western integration.

Airs of the States, *Yuefu*, and Ballad Tendency of Modern Chinese New Poetry

If we wish to make our poetry popular songs,
We should become one of the populace.
—Chinese Poetry Association, "First Issue Declaration," *New Poetry*

Modern Chinese poets show a broad, lasting interest in folk songs and ballads, and "ballad fever" emerged almost at the same time as the May Fourth Movement. The Peking University Ballads Research Association, established in December 1920, was one of the earliest public organizations during May

Fourth New Culture Movement. Its initiators and participants included the earliest vernacular poets in China, such as Liu Bannong, Shen Yinmo, Qian Xuantong, Shen Shishi, Zhou Zuoren, etc. The *Ballad Weekly*, sponsored by it and started in December 1922, is also the earliest in the history of modern Chinese culture and lasted the longest (stopped in June 1937). It is one of the most influential journals, with many famous poets or poet-critics, such as Hu Shih, Zhu Ziqing, Zhu Guangqian, and Zhong Jingwen participating in its editorial work or writing key articles. The influence of ballads is displayed in the works of many poets, such as Liu Bannong, Liu Dabai, Shen Xuanlu, Pu Feng, Ren Jun, Tian Jian, Ke Zhongping, Ruan Zhangjing, Ma Fantuo, Li Ji, and He Jingzhi. Even Xu Zhimo, Wen Yiduo, Zhu Xiang, Dai Wangshu, and other "loyal art representatives" also once wrote modern folk songs. If we include the fragmented comments of ballads, then almost all modern poets were fascinated by this ancient, yet often renewed folk art form. Ballad tendency is one of the most worthy creative trends of modern Chinese poetry.

What we need to do is to answer the following questions: What kind of social cultural or psychological power drove the Chinese modern new poetry to ballads? What kind of cultural significance does the ballad tendency of Chinese new poetry have? What is its status in the history of literature? What is the relationship between this kind of poetry and other modern Chinese poetry?

Ballad Tendency of Modern Chinese New Poetry

Ballad tendency, as a general trend of modern Chinese new poetry, is reflected more specifically during three major poetry periods from the May Fourth era in 1919 to the 1940s.

The first period was the May Fourth era, represented by the creation of the early vernacular poets Liu Bannong, Liu Dabai, and others. Since 1918, Liu Bannong, Shen Yinmo, and others jointly advocated the collection of folk songs. Liu Bannong collected and published folk songs from his hometown, Jiangyin, a county in Jiangsu Province of China. In 1920 and 1921, he used Jiangyin dialects to write more than 20 pieces of "four-sentence folk songs" and because he compiled the *Wafu Ji (Commons' Collection)*, he was called "the first person who wrote poetry with dialects."[83] "Wafu," the opposite of "Yellow Bells" which are connected with official occasions, represents plain folk language. *Yangbian Ji (Spurring Collection)*, which was published shortly thereafter, included many modern folk songs. Liu Dabai's poems, such as "Selling Cloth" and "Here Comes the Landlord," also directly imitated the style of folk songs. Some think "during the May Fourth Movement, when the new poetry movement in China just started, only him (referring to Liu Bannong—author) and Liu Dabai intentionally wrote folk song style poems."[84]

The second period was during the early 1930s, represented by the left-wing revolutionary poets of the Chinese Poetry Association. The "First Issue Declaration" of *New Poetry* by the Chinese Poetry Association's official publication declares: "We must use the common sayings, / put the contradictions into the folk songs, / we want to make our poetry popular songs / we have also become one of the public." Chinese Poetry Association focused on both imitated creation and collection of folk songs and ballads and conducted theoretical research. They hoped to "transfer the ideas to future poetry through popular folk songs, local tune forms, adopting their strength of popularity and easy reading."[85] Pu Feng, an active member of the Chinese Poetry Association, is considered the first person to attempt to learn from folk songs and the greatest contributor with far-reaching influence. His works were highly recognized by Mao Dun and other great literary minds.[86]

The third period was from the mid to late 1930s to the 1940s around the victory of the War of Resistance against Japanese Aggression. The national salvation campaign by the Chinese people greatly shortened the psychological distance between poets and ordinary people, and folk songs and ballads became the most convenient, influential voice of the times. Tian Jian and Ke Zhongping paid great attention to absorbing the language strengths of folk songs. Li Ji found the inspiration for art from *Xintianyou*, a kind of local melody in northern Shaanxi Province. Ruan Zhangjing was enchanted by the "Zhanghe Xiaoqu" and Ma Fantuo was inspired by the folk songs of Wu, now roughly the Jiangsu Province. Well-known poets in the liberated areas, such as He Jingzhi, Xiao San, Wei Wei, Chen Hui, Lin Shan, and many unknown poets presented a powerful creation of folk songs.

In these three poetry movements, the second and particularly the third were large in scale, leaving rich experiences in poetry history. Many of the characteristics of Chinese ballad poetry and art are more fully presented in these two periods. We often find the most fundamental explanation for the reasons for the ballad tendency of Chinese new poetry in these two trends.

The two major poetry trends of the two periods have been promoted by two forces: the world's proletarian literary concepts and the national unity of resisting the Japanese invasion. Relatively speaking, Chinese poetry in the early 1930s benefited mainly from the first force, and the other poets who supported the War of Resistance against Japanese Aggression in the mid-1930s and the 1940s took advantage of the second force. The world's proletarian literature derived from the public at the very beginning. The early proletarian writers, including the British charter poets, the French DuPont, the Paris Commune poets, etc., were themselves workers, and literary and poetry writing were part of the mass revolutionary activities. The proletarian literature of the Soviet Union was consciously regarded as a revolutionary tool for educating the people and serving the people. Lenin repeatedly stressed that literature should serve "millions of working people" and that "art belongs to the people." Proletarian literature must be "understood and loved by the working masses. It must combine the feelings, thoughts, and will of these people and improve them."[87] These claims were introduced into China as authoritative arguments during the late 1920s and were considered "the basis for the theory of popularization of the popular literature."[88] The Chinese Poetry Association came into being during the trend of proletariat literature popularization. Ballads are the poems of the populace. The concept of popularization from the proletarian literature of the Soviet Union continued to have an impact on the poets of the 1930s and 1940s who supported the Chinese resistance of Japanese invasion. However, I believe for these poets, the popularization theory of proletarian literature was not so important. It was the distressful reality that disturbed their souls. It was the common historical destiny of a nation that brought together common themes from all walks of life. A ballad is the voice of the "noble" poets and the popular public. The pain and anger of the masses were also the pain and anger of the poets, and the folk songs by the poets came from the mouths of the masses. "Speech at the Yan'an Forum on Literature and Art," a summary of the spirit of this era, argued, what literary art pursues should not be the eloquent effect of theoretical logic, but the plain and simple emotional appeal:

> If you put your qualifications high above the people and act like a "hero"—the more you want to sell this, the less the people will buy. You want people to know you. You must be with the people. You must make up your mind, even after a long period or even with pain.[89]

This is the lesson from every poet who supported the resistance against the Japanese invasion during the national survival crisis. Mao Zedong's *Speech* and the vigorous development of ballad writing activities afterward are the results of reasonable development of this period. If we say the ballad trend of Chinese poetry in the early 1920s is mainly rooted in the inspirations of foreign theories, then the pursuit of the ballads of the poets who supported the War of Resistance against Japanese Aggression is the inevitable development of the spirits of the times.

Historical Foundation of Ballad Tendency of Chinese New Poetry

So far, have we fully explained the social and cultural origins of the new Chinese poetry? I am afraid not. Because the above explanations are only achieved at the most superficial level. Only the external environmental factors of this poetic orientation were resolved, and some deeper questions were not answered. For example, whether there is a unified level of environmental power between "foreign culture" and the "development of the times"? How are the three major poetry movements connected? Whether the main trends and the individual ballads have a common psychological basis? We did not fully consider some similar poetic orientations in ancient and modern China and foreign countries, and cross-reference them. In particular, we ignored the historical fact that the ballad tendency is also an important trend in Chinese classical poetry. As a constituent element of the Chinese cultural system, Chinese new poetry cannot cut off its close connection with Chinese classical poetry. The power of the prototype would not be affected by any individual subjective desire. The ballad tendency of Chinese new poetry is not simply the product of foreign culture and the development of the times, it should have a deeper historical origin.

Then, in the long river of national culture, what kind of historical background is the ballad tendency of poetry? What is the cultural significance of the ballad trends of Chinese classical poetry? Why do they happen and why will they continue? This should be discussed from the overall characteristics of Chinese classical poetry culture.

We have mentioned "objectification" is the cultural characteristic of Chinese classical poetry, where "the artistic conception" is the highest artistic ideal. The so-called "artistic conception" is "not following others' poetics, not overly decorating one's language . . . but focusing on the main theme and working towards the natural use of language, which is traceless, like the antelope hanging by its horns . . . . Just like the sounds of the air, the color of the appearance, the moon in the water, the image in the mirror, words are limited, but the meanings are endless" (Yan Yu, *Canglang Shihua*). Also "Just like the beautiful jade would send out a foggy smoke, which could be observed from afar but cannot catch it close" (Sikong Tu, *Letters to Jipu*, quoted by Dai Shulun). "I asked the flowers in tears and the flowers remained silent, chaotic red pedals flew over the swing … Cold waves rippled to rise, white birds leisurely dived … The fish jumping on the water in the drizzle and swallows flying in the breeze."[90] These verses, repeatedly discussed by poetry theorists, are typical examples of Chinese artistic conceptions. According to this idea, poets should dissolve the self in objective objects, which could also be adjusted and arranged to maintain the original state as much as possible. At the same time, words are refined to fully mobilize the pictographic functions of the Chinese characters. All these "poetic arts" require poets to have high cultural accomplishments, very sensitive intuition, and very sophisticated language and writing skills. Therefore, objectively, Chinese classical poetry embarked on a highly "literate," and "aristocratic" road. Perhaps the literati have the taste of the literati, and the nobles have the elegance of the aristocracy. However, it is undeniable that both the "literati" and the "aristocratic" can easily fall into a narrow, dry, and even artificial situation. For example, the late Tang and Five Dynasties' poetry created a perfect artistic conception of Chinese poetry. Yet, this "artistic conception" is precisely narrow, and the language of poetry is affectionate, due to its excessive deliberation. Poetry of the Song Dynasty represents some self-denial tendencies in Chinese classical poetry, but the anti-tradition of the poetry of the Song Dynasty was conducted in the communities of literati and the aristocracy, which means it might still fall into barrenness. Then, with all these disadvantageous restrictions, how can Chinese classical poetry continue to develop for thousands of years? In the long history, why can Chinese poets continue to keep up with the ideal of artistic conception? What is the lubricating balance between the crystal ideal and the barrenness of reality? I think the secret is that folk song art, based on the *Airs of the States* and *Yuefu* prototype, thrived among the general masses. It is a simple, natural form of poetry completely non-literate and non-aristocratic, and constantly brings new stimulation to Chinese poets, prompting them to temporarily leave their orthodox tracks, extracting rich nutrients, and slightly rectifying excessively distorted orthodox poetry by the vitality of folk art; thus, maintaining the historical movement of Chinese poetry.

Ballads are originally the root of poetry. Ballads in Chinese poetry can be traced to the "Yo-he-ho" School, dating back to the legendary *Songs of the Yellow Emperor*. However, the ones that have complete forms and produce a substantial impact on future generations are the *Airs of the States* of the pre-Qin and the ancient *Yuefu* of the Han and Wei dynasties (which I collectively referred to as *Yuefu*). Although the latter inherits the essence of the former in a certain sense, in the minds of future generations of poets, they both are placed in the primary position. Therefore, I listed *Yuefu* and the *Airs of the States* as the prototype forms of the ballad trend in the history of Chinese poetry. The *Airs of the States* preserved the earliest and most complete oral creation of the people of the Zhou Dynasty (1046–256 BC) with strong folk characteristics. Because it belongs to the important part of "teaching through poetry," it was highly respected by poets in the past. *Yuefu* were ballads especially collected and recorded by the Han and Wei dynasties' music institutions, with a comparable scale to the *Airs of the States*. Although *Yuefu* did not achieve an overall reputation like the *Airs of the States*, and even was rejected during a certain period, *Yuefu* is still deeply rooted in the hearts of the people. In addition, because it did not have a sacred position of poetry teaching, it made the poets of future generations feel more intimate. Therefore, many poetry movements directly used *Yuefu* as the slogan and banner. It became a special kind of poetry genre. The poets of later generations followed the example of *Yuefu* of the Han and Wei dynasties. Both developed at the beginning of Chinese poetry, the *Airs of the States* and *Yuefu* were simple and natural, without ill-conceived genres of the literati who were old-fashioned and deliberate. They are filled with vitality backed by the rich soil. Ever since, when Chinese classical poetry lost its way because of maturity, arrogant because of "perfection," and affectionate because of "being noble," there were always some poets who tried to make a breakthrough and find another way out, such as introducing vibrant ballads into the lifeless poetry. They used the poetic standards of the *Airs of the States* and *Yuefu* to attack the literary "orthodox." For example, Bai Juyi used the "*Feng Ya*" and "*Bi Xing*" as weapons to reverse sentimentality toward objects like snow or flowers, and advocated the so-called new *Yuefu* Movement. Later generations of poets also have their works in the *Yuefu* style. For instance, the "poetry revolution" at the end of the Qing Dynasty put forward the "rejuvenation of the *Bi* and *Xing*" and advocated to adopt "the theories of *Li Sao* and *Yuefu*."[91] The characteristics of the *Airs of the States* and *Yuefu* in various aspects of thought and art bring rich enlightenment to the "orthodox" literati poetry writing and often promote the evolution of poetry during an era. This happened with the development of five-character poetry, the maturity of the Tang Dynasty's poetry, and from poetry to *Ci*, from *Ci* to drama.

The adjustment of folk songs promoted the development of Chinese classical poetry from time to time, helping tide over the difficulties and turn into a new round after a crisis. Following this law, the new changes during the May Fourth era also "followed the rules." Mr. Zhu Ziqing once pointed out: "According to the poetry development path, the new poetry should be from folk songs ... But the new poetry did not borrow from folk songs, due to the impact of foreign countries."[92] Indeed, it was as Mr. Zhu Ziqing described the impact of Western poetry largely replaced the inherent status of the folk songs. Without the enlightenment of Western poetry, the series of magnificent movements in the history of Chinese new poetry would not happen. However, I believe what needs further added is from the history of Chinese new poetry development, the spirit of folk songs embodied in the *Airs of the States* and *Yuefu* still flows silently and shows its value in various new ways, because modern Chinese poetry is essentially the suspicion and rebellion of the aesthetic ideals of Chinese classical poetry. It is also a reaction to rigid, distorted "literati" and "aristocratic" characters. As Yu Pingbo commented, poetry should still return to the simple, revealing the original features of poems from heavy makeup. The empire of poetry should be overthrown and the republic of poetry should be restored.

Opposing the aristocratic tendency of literature and vigorously advocating "civilian literature" is one of the most important features of the May Fourth new literary movement.

> The aristocratic literature lost independence and self-esteem with the accumulation of affectionate descriptions; the classic literature with its exaggerations and lengthy style had lost the functions of emotional expression and truth-telling. That non-fictional literature was difficult to read and they thought they were writing for the famous mountains while most would remain useless.[93]

In this trend of thought, the *Airs of the States* and *Yuefu* were almost taken for granted as poetry and became the object of favor of some poets. Liu Bannong, an active member of the first movement of the ballad trend of new poetry, praised: "The *Airs of the States* are the most authentic poems in China because they described accurately all kinds of people, such as hermits, soldiers, girls, and unhappy wives."[94] Zhou Zuoren also said: "If we could revise some critiques of the *Book of Songs* and read the *Airs of the States* as ancient folk songs, it must be very effective in the current study of folk songs or the writing of new poems."[95] The ballad trend of the May Fourth era inherited the self-repairing method of Chinese classical poetry and revived the spirit of the *Airs of the States* and *Yuefu* against the traditional stagnation and dullness. Shen Yinmo's debut, "Rickshaw Drivers," implied the influence of the ancient *Yuefu*. Shen

Xuan's "Prison" and "Employment Agency" employed four-Chinese characters and five-Chinese characters style, which is quite similar to the *Book of Songs*. Poems, such as "Farmers," "Countryman," "A Farmer's House," "A Night Tour in Shanghai," "The Happy Workers," and "Working Hard" showed the legacy of the New *Yuefu*.[96] Poems in Liu Dabai's "Selling the Cloth" reminded people of "the *Airs of States* in *Book of Songs*, the *Han Wei Yuefu* poems, and the new folk songs advocated by Bai Juyi and other ancient folk songs."[97] Liu Bannong directly drew from the folk songs collected from his hometown. The act followed the folk song collection tradition in China.

Then, how about the second and third waves of the ballad tendency of Chinese new poetry? Did the introduction of foreign culture and the impetus of the development of the times deviate from the inherent track of Chinese poetry? Does this mean the anti-aristocratic and anti-literate adjustments and revisions represented by the *Airs of the States* and *Yuefu* cease to exist? I think this is not the case. As early as the May Fourth era, the rejuvenation of the *Airs of the States* and *Yuefu*, the input of foreign culture, and experiencing the atmosphere of the times were all linked together. These factors promoted each other. For example, Liu Bannong was an active member of the May Fourth literary revolution who was "lively, brave, and fought hard for the literary course."[98] At the same time, he was actively committed to the translation and introduction of foreign folk songs. He published more than 20 translated poems only during the *New Youth*, among which, "La Marseillaise" and "Song of the Shirt" are some of his famous works. This integration of Chinese and foreign poetry cultures runs throughout the history of the new poetry development. During the 1930s when vigorously promoted, the theory of proletarian literature by the Chinese Poetry Association continued to fight against classical poetry and the new "aristocratic" tendency revealed in the development of Chinese new poetry in the 1920s. Pu Feng, Ren Jun, and Mu Mutian criticized or reflected the "pure poetry" of the classical traditions inherited by the Crescent Moon School, the Symbolist School, and the Modernist School, and considered "the sorrow of the obsolete aristocratic landlord's bureaucratic class." It is "a kind of affectionate emotion at the end of the century."[99] Pu Feng also praised the poet Wen Liu, who "never assumes a noble position" to condescend to the lower class, "but he sings his pain and future as a part of the above-mentioned people."[100] Wang Duqing also pointed out in 1934: "I think the recent poetry has returned to the feudal era. Now, we need poetry for the masses, poetry for society. Because this kind of poetry is the fire that can destroy the feudal chains."[101] Similar thoughts could be found in the poets who supported the War of Resistance against Japanese Aggression. According to the understanding at that time, since the May Fourth Movement, poetry that was greatly influenced by tradition and pursued the artistic conception of the Jin and Tang dynasties belonged to the petty bourgeois individualism, and was not beneficial to the War of Resistance against Japanese Aggression. Mao Zedong's "Speech" accurately revealed the essence of the "popularization" movement of this period. It is necessary to promptly remove the shortcomings of the May Fourth New Cultural Movement (the aristocratic consciousness separated from the masses of the people) and oppose "the tendency of quoting Greece all the time." Chinese literature must return to the most common folks in China. It is not to "transform" the public but to strive to "be transformed" by the public. "Improvement should be emphasized, but it could not be conducted in a one-sided manner and overdone. That's wrong ... Only when all revolutionary writers and artists regard themselves as loyal spokespersons of the masses could their work make sense."[102] Compared with the "popularization" of the early 1930s, what was completed during 1937–1945 was more down-to-earth. Although Mao Zedong, the supreme authority of this trend of thought, continued to use the "imported" Marxist-Leninist terms, its true meaning is entirely "Chinese style." As Mao Zedong said: "We should discuss the issue based on reality, not based on the definition."[103]

It must be noted that the second and third waves of the ballad tendency of Chinese new poetry are not like the first wave of the early May Fourth Movement, which directly took the slogan of the rejuvenation of the *Airs of the States* and *Yuefu*. What interested them was the various folk songs circulated among the general public. Therefore, they mainly searched for simplicity and freshness from the general masses rather than from ancient books. Then, what is the relationship between classical tradition and folk art? How did people during this time deal with this relationship in their writing practice? Specifically, does this mean classical songs, based on the *Airs of the States* and *Yuefu*, lost their practical significance? We can observe this through a discussion around the 1940s. This is the famous "discussion of the issue of national forms" in the history of literature. There are three types of opinions: (1) Xiang Linbing as the representative, believed the classical tradition ("old forms") is consistent with folk art ("folk forms") and advocated "new wine in an old bottle." That is, the new literature creation should fully inherit the national heritage; the old forms should be the only way to popularize.[104] (2) Ge Yihong and Hu Feng, who opposed more resolutely old forms, and believed the new literature should mainly be "transplanted" from the "world progressive literature and art." The old forms adapted themselves to the "lower" level of knowledge of the "general masses." Using the old forms means "lowering the standards."[105] (3) Guo Moruo, Mao Dun, and others in the Kuomintang area and the writers in the Liberated Areas. They generally held a dialectical view of "unification of contradictions," which means the old forms must be used, but should be transformed, and the value of utilization and transformation is the requirement of the contemporary public. In other words, there are differences and similarities between the old forms and the folk forms.[106] These three types of opinions are very different, but when combined, I think they show consistency in an important link—they recognize the close relationship between classical traditions ("old forms") and folk art ("folk forms") to varying degrees. Xiang Linbing used this connection in a positive sense. Ge Yihong and Hu Feng discussed this connection in a negative sense. The third type of writer recognized this connection in the sense of contradictory unity. From here, we can see the intrinsic connections between folk art and classical tradition are both an objective fact in the development of Chinese literature and a psychological fact of modern Chinese writers. The latter has far-reaching significance. When modern Chinese poets explore the simplicity and freshness of modern folk songs in such "psychological facts," they cannot reject the classical tradition from the depth of consciousness. Therefore, classical folk songs, classical traditions, modern folk songs, and modern poets constitute a logical, cultural chain connected. The original forms of the *Airs of the States* and *Yuefu* as the prototype of classical folk songs would inevitably penetrate modern folk songs and modern poems.

The non-aristocratic and non-literate orientations of the *Airs of the States* and *Yuefu* continue to be the conscious pursuit of folk song tendency of Chinese new poetry. Moreover, this pursuit is more conscious than at any time in history. More thoroughly, as a cultural spirit, the *Airs of the States* and *Yuefu* are not only inherited but carried forward unprecedentedly. What's more interesting is that the movements of discovering, rewarding, and cultivating the folk song singers of the masses were very popular during the 1930s and 1940s, and they were even more spectacular in the Liberated Areas. From the Communist Party and government leaders to senior intellectuals to ordinary workers and peasants, they collected, sorted, and organized literary and artistic movements spontaneously. Folk songs of the masses were elevated to the great cause of the national democratic struggle. Isn't this the poem collection activity during the era of the *Airs of the States* and *Yuefu*? The difference is the poets not only actively collected poems but also strived to sink into an ordinary member of folk life. These poets strived to minimize the boundaries between "literati" and "folk" and write with real-life experiences with the masses.

Other modern Chinese poets were not completely involved in these three waves. Even to some extent, these poets still stood on the opposite side and continued to promote the "purification" of modern poetry. However, it is also impossible to evade the fact that the independent character of modern Chinese poetry lies precisely in its transcendence of the Chinese classical poetry tradition and the deconstruction of the "artistic conception." This is an objective historical mission shouldered by every modern poet. They have no other choice. In this way, what we have mentioned before occurred—almost all modern poets have different degrees of interest in this ancient, yet, new folk art, even Xu Zhimo, Wen Yiduo, Zhu Xiang, and Dai Wangshu, because one still had to live in reality, and poets cannot turn a blind eye to the embarrassing reality of Chinese poetry despite the advocacy of "art for art's sake." For example, the whole harmony of style is originally a genre of the Crescent Moon School's poetry, but Zhu Xiang believed it is necessary for the new poetry to "make variations in language,"[107] so it must learn from the ancient folk songs of "free metaphors and balanced syntactic structures."[108] During the War of Resistance against Japanese Aggression, Dai Wangshu also wrote four ballads in support of the resistance against Japanese aggression.[109]

Features of Ballad Tendency of Chinese New Poetry

What are the characteristics of the poetry of the *Airs of the States* and *Yuefu* styles? What are their specific effects on the ballad tendency of modern Chinese poetry?

I think it can be understood from five aspects. First, searching for truth becomes the basic principle of poetry writing. In the Chinese classical poetry system, the *Airs of the States* and *Yuefu* appear as sincere, rather than fake and artificial poetry writing. Whether it is farm work, war of soldiers, or love and marriage, they are written as is. The authors of folk art had not been completely immersed in the feudal scholars' culture. They maintained a certain distance from the orthodox cultural spirit and aesthetic taste. A series of artistic ideals that have a long tradition in the history of Chinese poetry, such as implicitness and indirectness, objectification, and harmony between man and nature are also very attractive artistic conceptions, but it is undeniable that within such artistic conceptions, the individual, self-realistic reality of the truth was diluted, concealed, and forgotten. All poets of different encounters, different emotions, and different destinies were melted into the same static harmony. Of course, this cannot be said to be the true meaning of art.

The truth of art pursues the highlighting of the self-realization of individual life, while the artistic conception of Chinese classical poetry is blurring it. Therefore, Lu Xun said traditional Chinese literature and art is a literary art of "squatting and deceiving." Liu Bannong said:

> These poets were fame-chasers but pretended to write poems of the mountain hermits. It is obvious they had no skills, but they liked to complain as if the world had harmed them. It is clear they were in their heyday, but they wrote as if they were old and wretched. It is obvious they had weak feelings, but they tended to write sentimental "nostalgic" or "farewell" poems. It is obvious they were still human, but they preferred to write as if they had become Buddha. They babbled mysterious and incomprehensible words and they spoiled poetry and Buddhist hymns.[110]

It is in the opposite direction of traditional literati poetry that Liu Bannong and other Chinese modern poets endeavor to affirm the truth of the *Airs of the States* and *Yuefu*, and used them as the basic principle for their writing. Liu Bannong praised the *Airs of the States* as "the truest poetry in China" and summed up his own experience in folk song writing: "If we want to speak for someone, we must use the true language and tone of that person; otherwise, it would be ultimately only our own words."[111] After thoroughly studying folk songs, Zhou Zuoren proposed that sincerity and integrity in the songs can be used as a reference for new poem writing.[112] Pu Feng actively participated in the "popularization" movement of poetry and learned from folk songs. He said: "There are no real poems without real-life experience. Our beautiful national defense poetry is not in the anti-enemy cry of an empty consciousness, it was created based on true anti-enemy life and its observations, experiences, and reflections."[113] Tian Jian made his self-evaluation: "No lies / the honest soul / dissected on the paper . . . ."[114]

Second, grievances and resistance are the main themes. When expressing the reality of survival sincerely and frankly, one's true feelings are included. In the hierarchical order of the feudal traditional society, both the general public and the intellectuals who were known as "advocating excellence" were inevitably in a position of being squeezed, exploited, and bound. Therefore, grievances and resistance became one of the most important emotions expressed in poetry. "July," "Wood Logging," "Huge Mice," "It's Getting Dark," and "Drumming" in the *Airs of the States*, "A Sick Woman's Will" and "Being a Soldier at Fifteen" in *Han Yuefu* showed the pains and sufferings of the laborers. "The Faithless Man" and "Gu Feng" in the *Airs of the States* and "A White Head's Song" and "Reflections" in *Han Yuefu* express the resentment of unfortunate women. The themes and emotions of the *Airs of the States* and *Yuefu* have been well inherited in modern poetry. Liu Bannong's ballad poetry has always been known for its exposure and criticism. His self-reported intentions of the *Wafu Ji* is: "To test whether I could try my best to show part of the commoners' voices who had suffered insults and contempt for thousands of years and lived the bottom of the hell without an opportunity to speak."[115] Liu Dabai used the tone of farmers to accuse the landlord of exploiting the peasants: "the working-hard people must suffer from hunger, the idle is enjoying their food, and is there any justice in the world? How fierce the landlord is, / who robs at broad daylight like a real robber!" ("Here Comes the Landlord") Shen Xuanlu often scorned the exploiters: "Rich man—rich man—don't cry—/ I feed the pigs and sheep and you eat the meat; you eat rice and I eat porridge" ("The Rich Man is Crying"). The waves of fury and resistance against the Japanese invasion further involved almost all the poets. Tian Jian called: "Shoot, Northeast people" ("Songhua River"). His "Chinese pastoral songs" are all "burning," "rough," and "furious."[116] Li Ji sang the high-pitched *Xintianyou*: "While we are tired in body, we are happy and our revolutionary hearts are vigorously beating .... If the revolution succeeded, I would succeed, and I would not live long if there were no revolution" ("Wang Gui and Li Xiangxiang"). Yuan Shuipai hymned folk songs to satire Kuomintang's ruling: "The world has been turned upside down, / 10,000 yuan note is worth nothing, / the call to peace led to blood-shed, / those who protect the human rights ended up in prisons" ("The World is Upside Down").

Third, poetry focuses on the narrative of specific behaviors and specific events. This is the unique artistic technique of ballad poetry, different from especially purely literary works. Between concrete things and abstract feelings, it focuses more on the concrete; between indirect lyrics and direct narratives, it focuses more on narrations. Many chapters in the *Airs of the States* describe specific things, highlighting one aspect of life or personal characteristic, focusing more on narration, such as "July," "Yellow Bird," "Climbing up the Hill," and so on. "July" depicted the process of one-year labor so accurately that Fang Yurun commented: "What "July" described in all aspects of agriculture which one could not write as intimate and precise unless one has been working in the field for many years and knowing everything about it" (*The Origin of Book of Songs*). Ban Gu (32–92) of the Han Dynasty, the author of the *Book of Han*, summarizes the characteristics of *Yuefu* folk songs as "one felt deeply about the sorrow and happiness and they were written with a right cause." The narration of *Han Yuefu* is more prominent than the *Airs of the States*. The storytelling and drama of these folk songs are greatly enhanced. Many works focus on a central event, and there are certain characters and relatively complete plots. For example, "Mulberry by the Roadside" and "Runaway from East Gate." Traditionally, there is no primitive epic in Chinese poetry. Instead, classical narrative poetry evolved from folk songs and ballads. It is in the folk songs of *Han Yuefu* that Chinese narrative poetry turned mature. "The Bride of Jiao Zhongqing" is an important symbol of its maturity. These artistic features constitute the main trend of modern Chinese new poetry. The works of Liu Bannong, Liu Dabai, Shen Xuanlu, and others focused on the so-called sketchy technique, which specifically depicts the images of the lower class and the "real scenes" of production and life. These works were criticized as shallow and explicit because of their lack of "food for thought"[117] after reading. However, this is the artistic essence of folk poetry. During the 1930s and 1940s, in addition to continuing to influence the Chinese Poetry Association and the artistic expressions of the poets who supported the War of Resistance against Japanese Aggression, folk song tradition also brought a very important poetic phenomenon in the history of Chinese new poetry—the narrative poems, especially the rapid increase of the long narrative poems. It became a fascinating phenomenon. Popular works during this period include "The Cart Driver's Story" by Tian Jian, "Wang Gui and Li Xiangxiang" by Li Ji, "Zhang River Water" by Ruan Zhangjing, "Not to Die Yet" by Zhang Zhimin, "Zhao Qiaoer" by Li Bing, etc. If we expand the issue and take a look at the "narrative" phenomenon in the history of modern Chinese poetry, we will say poets, such as Zhu Xiang, Zang Kejia, and He Qifang, who paid great attention to "literati color" also created works with narrative components. It is worth mentioning when they wrote these works, they all turned to folk songs for inspiration. Zhu Xiang advocated new poetry should learn from ancient folk songs. Zang Kejia believed "many folk songs with local dialect could be integrated into poetry."[118] The traditional origin of Chinese modern narrative poetry is not in *Qu Sao*, not in the "pure art"—the poetry of the Tang Dynasty and *Ci* of Song Dynasty—nor in the rational poetry of the Song Dynasty. It is closer to folk art as demonstrated in the *Airs of the States* and *Yuefu*.

Fourth, the language is simple and plain, and a large number of spoken words are used. Compared with the pure literary poetry later, the *Airs of the States* and *Yuefu* are less refined, and its words are direct, and commonly used in terms of linguistic features. They were mainly spoken by the masses.

Generally, refined words were rarely chosen. It does not deliberately revise or polish the lyrics; it tries its best to express the true nature of the events or behaviors in the true language. Hu Yinglin said it well: "The folk songs of *Han Yuefu* are natural products of the masses and there are very few decorations" (*Poetry*). Undoubtedly, the modern ballad new poetry carried forward this tradition. In a period, Liu Bannong and others first invested in the exploration and application of the dialects and local language. His "Children's Songs" imitated the tones of children. "Nini Qu" and "Bread and Salt" are similar to the spoken words of Beijing laborers. The folk songs in the *Wafu Ji* are full of proverbs from the Jiangyin dialect. Although there are different opinions in the history of modern Chinese poetry about whether dialects can be used in poetry, a very broad consensus was reached on the colloquial and simple use of language. Pu Feng's language standard is "the literate person can understand it, and the illiterate person can understand it as well."[119] Li Ji was stunned by the "simple and profound poetry" as demonstrated in *Xintianyou*, a Shaanxi dialect melody.[120] Even Zang Kejia, not a great fan of the ballad, was greatly influenced. He reflected in 1947: "After working very hard refining my language skills for 15 years, I realized the beauty of simplicity."

Fifth, free, relaxed, and rich in rhythm's musical effect. The requirements of the *Airs of the States* and *Yuefu* on the musicality of poetry are not as strict as later poems of the traditional style. The *Airs of the States* is mostly from nature and is natural. During this time, there were no strict metrical requirements, and the rhyme was free and loose. Almost a variety of metrics are included—rhymes in each sentence, rhymes in every other sentence, rhymes in odd-numbered sentences, rhymes in even-numbered sentences; rhymes in the first sentence, and rhymes in the even number of the sentences after the third sentence; the first, second, and fourth sentences use rhyme, and the third sentence does not; some use one rhyme to the end, others changed the rhyme in the middle; there are both the ending rhyme and the rhyme in the middle of the sentences. The *Yuefu* of the Han and Wei dynasties inherited the free rhyme of the *Airs of the States* and still did not pay much attention to the change of flat-fall tones. However, in the free and relaxed form of music, the *Airs of the States* and *Yuefu* pursued a strong sense of rhythm, trying to impress people with the special effects of the rhythms of music, inciting the reader's emotions. One of the important means of constructing this musical effect is the so-called "re-chanting." Sections of the *Airs of the States* (that is, a paragraph on the tone) had mostly the same number of characters, only a few words would be replaced in the next; thus, creating quite a sense of musical re-chanting. The *Yuefu* is mainly based on the repetition of words or sentences, such as "From now on, please do not miss me, (if you) miss me, I would break up with you!" ("Reflection") "The fish are playing east of the lotus leaves; the fish are playing west of the lotus leaves; the fish are playing south of the lotus leaves; the fish are playing north of the lotus leaves" ("Jiangnan"). These poetic features are visible in modern times. Liu Bannong believes: "The stricter the poetic rules, the fewer kinds of poetry would be produced, the more the bondage of the poetry, the poetry could never be fully developed."[121] To break through the traditional poetic constraints, Liu Bannong advocated destroying the old rhymes and recreating new rhymes for new kinds of poems, including inventing or borrowing from other cultures and adding no rhymed poems in addition to the rhymed ones. Here, the rhyme of folk songs drew the modern poets' attention. Pu Feng summed up the form of folk songs into ten items, of which the fifth and tenth items belong to the musical component: "there is a natural rhyme, there is a rhyme," "the overlapping sentences—this is also one of the very common forms of folk songs. There are some conveniences in the chorus, and sometimes, in terms of the idea itself, it can often be aggravated by repetition."[122] Modern Chinese ballad new poetry used natural rhythms. Besides those without rhymes, others rhymed using flexible, changeable methods. The poems are free to change rhymes. The number and manner of rhyming in one paragraph could be different, or only two sentences rhymed, or all the sentences rhymed. Within one poem, the parts with no rhyme are compatible with the parts that rhymed. The "overlapping" between words and sentences and paragraphs are also used from time to time as an important means of "enhancing power" and "moving the readers more profoundly" in modern poetry. For example, "Zhang River Water" by Yuan Zhangjing repeats several times "Zhang River Water, Ninety-nine turns," "peach flowers area, poplar, and willow trees," reminding us of the specific regional concepts and strengthening the reader's rural impressions.

Freedom, Consciousness, Anti-tradition, and Ballad Tendency

The artistic pursuit of modern Chinese new poetry has been influenced by various, distinctive Chinese and Western poetry thoughts, which constitute diverse, formal features of modern Chinese poetry. From the traditional poetry culture perspective, we can divide modern poetry into "free" forms of *Qu Sao* according to its influence, "conscious" forms of the poetry of the Wei, Jin, and Tang dynasties, and *Ci* of the Song Dynasty, the anti-traditional trend of the poetry of the Song Dynasty, and the trend of ballads based on the *Airs of the States* and *Yuefu*. In these rich, complex patterns, what kind of position does the Chinese new ballad poetry occupy? What is the relationship between this form and other forms?

First, there are differences between Chinese new ballad poetry and other forms because of its unique folk song elements. "Freedom," "consciousness" and the so-called "anti-tradition" are, in their essence, typical literati creations. "Free" poems expressed the unyielding resistance of modern Chinese poets. The poets either highlighted and strengthened their will, and subjective feelings, or shouldered the national responsibility with the worries unique to the Chinese poets in the 20th century. Just like the traditional prototype *Qu Sao*, the mentality of the intellectuals was "endowed by heaven this responsibility, and the intellectual dignity and moral principles peculiar to them" determined that poetry of this kind would not be plain and simple. "Slang words" could not be applied everywhere. Anti-tradition showed some doubts and rebellion of Chinese poets about the ideals of Chinese poetry during its heyday, which was mainly completed within the literati communities. For example, the poetry of the Song Dynasty had inextricable relations with *New Yuefu* and other folk songs, but this "relationship" did not change its inherent literati-style taste. Rational thinking and the vicissitudes of life processes could not be completed by simple folk art. The highest anti-tradition achievement of Chinese new poetry should be credited to the Nine Leaves School, which continued to explore poetry in the context of literati culture. Its theoretical authority Yuan Kejia criticized sharply the poets' "superstition" for folk language. He argued

> folk language often has a strong local color, especially in China where the local languages are extremely diverse and uncoordinated. In this case, if the dialects of all places are used without constraint, there would be no national literature, but only separate local literature. Even if we take the national language as the standard, there is still a large maneuver between the spoken and the literature national language.[123]

Only the literati could freely make choices and make refinements to the language between "speaking" and "literature." The new poetry of "conscious" forms represented the ultimate literati of Chinese poetry. Its closure and polishing of poets' personalities, the fine purification of poetry language, and the maintenance of the "aristocratic" status of poetry have repeatedly expressed the poets' knowledge possession and cultivation. This form is the closest to the typical paradigm of classical poetry in the Jin and Tang dynasties' poetry, and it is also the most affected. Therefore, as a rebel against the ideal model of Chinese poetry, "conscious" forms are the most direct and important opposite of the new poetry. Whether it was Xu Zhimo of the Crescent Moon School or Wang Duqing of the Symbolist School or Dai Wangshu and He Qifang of the Modernist School, obviously they did not need those simplified, direct, or explicit ways of expression. They were more accustomed to building and becoming intoxicated with all kinds of soft dreams, against the unscrupulous exposure, criticism, and excessive expressions of personal anger. They preferred euphemistic lyrics, the intentional cues, and avoided blunt narratives. Language deliberation and polishing are their important jobs. In these respects, the ballad new poems were sharply opposed to the new poems of the "conscious" forms. It could be assumed this state of opposition offered the ballad new poems with the irreplaceable value of independence.

However, the Chinese ballad new poetry is not incompatible with "free" forms and "anti-traditional" trends, because they took the nutrition from the literati and the general masses, respectively, but they have reached a consensus on the deviation from the prototype of Jin and Tang poetry. The "freedom" of personality is different from the "consciousness" of pure poetry. Anti-tradition is the revolution against the model during the Jin and Tang dynasties. Ballad tendency injected new vitality into the rigidity of the literati. In the history of modern new poetry, the common divergence and common direction choices make these three poetry forms possible to support and cooperate in the development process to realize the innovation and development of the "orthodox" poetry tradition. In this sense, the ballad tendency, "freedom" and "anti-tradition" will not form deep contradictions and conflicts. On the contrary, from time to time, they would influence each other and learn from each other. For example, at the moment of a national crisis, the Qu Yuan personality of the "freedom" prototype, the moral concept of the "anti-traditional" prototype, and the grievances from the "ballad tendency" prototype were closely combined to jointly create a crisis awareness of modern Chinese poets. The early vernacular poets, poets of Chinese poetry in the 1930s, and the more intellectual poets represented by Tian Jian in the 1940s were also influenced by the anti-traditional prototype or the prototype of "freedom." Thus, from the perspective of modern poets, it is not so easy to divide the poetry forms mechanically. A poet living in a modern environment experiences rich information from the whole tradition. The traditional prototypes are assembled and re-assembled in their hearts. From the perspective of modern Chinese new poetry, the poem forms showed great ambiguity.

Many modern new poems comprehensively represent the characteristics of traditional poetry prototypes. However, to analyze the modern functions of traditional prototypes more clearly and accurately today, we must work hard to separate them, treat them differently, and discuss them separately, with a view to refined discoveries.

The same complexity is also partially reflected in the relationship between "ballad tendency" and "consciousness." In the traditional prototype of modern Chinese poetry, while the "ballad tendency" adjusted the withering of "conscious" forms, it never subverted and destroyed the "literati" tradition. It never took over the aesthetics of "orthodox" poetry. Instead, traditional "literati" people can always draw nutrition from folk art, and, in turn, continue to push the "literati" creation toward a more refined, sophisticated direction. This applied from four-Chinese characters style poems to five-Chinese characters style poems, the maturity of modern metrical poetry, and the change from poetry to *Ci*. In this way, folk songs, in their essence, are inevitably in the position of being marginal. Out of unconscious fascination with the ideals of Chinese poetics, modern Chinese poets who emphasize the *Airs of the States* and *Yuefu* did not seem to have abandoned the artistic tradition because of their existence. Compared with the traditional poetry phenomenon, the trend of the ballad may be more stable and persistent. The attack on the classical "conscious" paradigm was the choice of these poets, but on the whole, this criticism did not leave deep marks in the future. The folk view of life and art is not consciously and completely summarized by modern poets; thus, creating a century-old poetic transition by rising to a new historical level. Writings of the literati had never been urged by folk songs to achieve self-denial and rise spirally. They remained the same, only temporarily concealing their stubbornness, with folk songs providing a special refreshing relief, alleviating their writings from withering due to rigidity. Setting history aside, Chinese poets are still fascinated by the poetry of the Jin and Tang dynasties. The Crescent, the Symbolist, and the Modernist schools continued to exert their influence. When this limited, new, fresh sense of folk songs dissipated later, Chinese poets and readers first sought and selected Xu Zhimo, Wang Duqing, Dai Wangshu, He Qifang, and Bian Zhilin, as well as the traditional prototypes of this type of poems. The history of Chinese new poetry throughout the 20th century is intertwined with the complex changes and cycles of "ballads" and "consciousness."

We see folk songs played an important role in the development of Western modern poetry. To oppose classical rules and regulations, Western romanticism in the 19th century proposed to return to nature and simplicity. The pastoralism of the patriarchal rural areas attracted great interest of the romantic poets. Most of the romantic poetry movements in European countries began with the collection of folk songs. Brentano and Arnim of Heidelberg, Germany, published folk song collections *Des knaben wander horn* from 1805 to 1808—a symbol of the integration of Western romanticism and folk songs. H. Heine, S. T. Coleridge, R. Southey, M. Lermontov, S. Petöfi, A. Mickiewicz, and others wrote ballads. Generally speaking, the simple, frank, freely changing forms of folk songs finally replaced the elegance and strict norms of classicalism, pushing Western poetry into a new historical era.

These different results of the ballad movement between Chinese and Western modern poetry stem from the differences in the cultural structures. During the Western classicism era, literati poetry and folk songs were two complete confrontational forces. The prosperity of classicism was the result of purely rational rules. Correspondingly, folk songs were lowered to the unfortunate fate of exclusion. The Romanticism movement mobilized the new artistic functions of folk songs and expelled classicism. The dualistic development of the dual structures made the negation of Western poetry very sound and gained tremendous development. In contrast, the "literati" of Chinese poetry did not completely reject the folk songs. Instead, it drew from folk songs constantly. This is a monolithic poetic culture structure that contains some complexities where folk songs are allowed to survive and develop. Only under this system, its inner energy is constantly dissipated. Finally, it is not sufficiently powerful to overturn the trend, guiding Chinese new poetry to challenge itself and move forward spirally.

Self-adjustment and balance are the value of the ballad tendency of modern Chinese poetry. It does not and cannot become an unprecedented trend to present a new world for us.

Notes

1 *Qu Sao*, refers to works or the literary style by Qu Yuan, a famous poet during the Warring States Period (475–221 BC).
2 Guo Moruo, "Pu Jian Collection," in *A Textual Research on Qu Yuan*, vol. 12, 93.
3 Guo Moruo, "Painting Inscriptions," in *Pu Jian, Past and Present* (Haiyan Bookstore, 1949).
4 Zhu Xiang, *The Sonnet, Italian Style (Twenty-one)*.
5 Li Jinfa, "Preface to *Lu Sen's Treatment*."
6 Yu Pingbo, "Thoughts on Destruction," *Novel Monthly* 14, no. 8 (Aug. 1923).

7 Selected Correspondence of Chenzhong Society, *Historical Materials of New Literature*, no. 3 (1987).
8 Bian Zhilin, "How the World Changes: In Memory of Liang Zongdai," *Historical Materials of New Literature*, no. 1 (1990).
9 Carl Gustav Jung, "On the Relation of Analytical Psychology to Poetry," in *Collected Works of C.G. Jung*, vol. 15 (Princeton University Press, 1966). https://doi.org/10.1515/9781400850884.65.
10 Tian Jian, "To the Fighters: The Last Page," in *To the Fighters* (Guilin Nantian Press, 1st edition, 1943).
11 Lin Yunming, quoted from Liu Yuqing's *Plain Literature* (Beiyue Literature and Art Publishing House, 1988), 207.
12 Self-narration of Tian Jian, *Historical Materials of New Literature*, no. 2, 1984.
13 *Moruo's Collected Works*, vol. 12, 394.
14 From *Tian Wen*, "At the very beginning, who preached the doctrine? When the world still did not form, let alone humans, how to examine its origin? How could we know the one who preached the doctrine?"
15 Please refer to Cheng Fangwu's *Vagrant Preface Poem*, Zhou Quanping's *Lost Lamb*, and Ma Renyin's *Ascetic Songs*.
16 Zhang Wojun, "The Liberation of Poetic Style," *Taiwan People's Daily* 3, no. 7–9 (Mar. 1, 21, 1925).
17 Shen Congwen, "On Zhu Xiang's Poetry," *Literature and Art Monthly* 2, no. 1.
18 Guo Moruo, "Pu Jian Collection, Qu Yuan's Art and Thoughts," in *Moruo's Collected Works*, vol. 12, 111.
19 Guo Moruo, "Painting Inscriptions, Past and Present," in *Moruo's Collected Works*, vol. 12, 235.
20 Xu Zhimo, "Preface to Poetry Magazine," *Morning Post Supplement Shi-Juan*, no. 1 (April 1926).
21 Liang Shiqiu, "The Style of New Poetry and Others," *Shi-Kan* (*Poetry Journal*), no. 1 (Jan. 1931).
22 Hua Lin (Li Jinfa), "Fire," *Aesthetic Education*, no. 1 (1928).
23 Mu Mutian, "On Poetry—A Letter to Moruo," *Creation Monthly* 1, no. 1 (Mar. 1926).
24 Wang Duqing, "On Poetry Again—to Mutian and Boqi," *Creation Monthly* 1, no. 1 (Mar. 1926).
25 See Wu Benxing, "Insider's Perspective," *Xiaoya*, no. 3 (Oct. 1936); Louis, "Autobiography at Thirty," in *Thirty Years Collection* (Poetry Territory Publishing House, 1945).
26 Refer to my article: "Barnesianism and Modern Chinese Poetry," *Zhongzhou Academic Journal*, no. 2 (1990).
27 Mu Mutian, "A Review of My Poetic Writing," *Modern Times* 4, no. 4 (Feb. 1934).
28 Feng Naichao, "My Literary Life," *Popular Literature and Art* 2, no. 6 (June 1930), and "Parnassian" sometimes is translated into "*Gao Dao*" in Chinese.
29 Stéphane Mallarmé, *OEuvres complètes*. Ed. Henri Mondor and G. Jean-Aubry (Paris: Bibliothèque de la léiade, Gallimard, 1945).
30 I distinguish Song *Ci* from Song poetry. In terms of creating emotional atmosphere, embellishing artistic conception and exploring rhythm, Song *Ci* is closer to Tang poetry, while Song poetry explored a new way. See Section 3, Chapter 2 of this book.

31 Shi Ling, "The Crescent School Poetry," *Literature* 8, no. 1 (Jan. 1937).
32 Mu Mutian, "On Poetry—A Letter to Moruo," *Creation Monthly* 1, no. 1 (Mar. 1926).
33 Bian Zhilin, "Preface to Dai Wangshu's Poetry Anthology," in *People and Poetry: Retrospect and Prospect*, 64.
34 Feng Wenbing (Fei Ming): *On New Poetry, Nine, Cao'er* (People's Literature Publishing House, 1984).
35 Li Jinfa, *The Diner and the Fierce Year* (Beixin Publishing House, 1927).
36 See Cao Pi's *A Song from Yan* and Cao Cao's *A Short Song Ballad*.
37 See Zhang Ruoxu's *Moonlight Night on the Spring River* and Cen Shen's *Song of White Snow on Secretary Wu's Return to Capital*.
38 Zong Baihua, "A Brief Talk on New Poetry," *Youth China* 1, no. 8 (Feb. 1920).
39 Xu Zhimo, "Self Reflection," *Morning Post Supplement* (April 1926).
40 See Chen Mengjia, Fang Lingru's *Letter* and Chen Mengjia's "Preface to *Mengjia's Poems*."
41 Feng Wenbing (Fei Ming): *On New Poetry*.
42 Bian Zhilin, "Preface to *Diao Chong Ji Li*," *Diao Chong Ji Li* (*Anthology of Bian Zhilin's Poems*) (People's Literature Publishing House, 1984), 1.
43 T. S. Eliot, "Tradition and the Individual Talent," *Perspecta* 19 (1982): 36–42.
44 T. S. Eliot, "Tradition and Individual Talent," 36–42.
45 Bian Zhilin, "*Diao Chong Ji Li*, Self-Preface," in *Diao Chong Ji Li* (*Anthology of Bian Zhilin's Poems*), 3.
46 Fan Wenlan, *General History of China* (2) (People's Publishing House, 1978), 523.
47 Wen Yiduo, "A Study on Metrical Poetry," in *Complete Works of Wen Yiduo*, vol. 10 (Hubei People's Publishing House, 1993), 156, 157, 159.
48 Mu Mutian, "On Poetry—A Letter to Moruo," *Creation Monthly* 1, no. 1 (Mar. 1926).
49 Wang Duqing, "On Poetry Again—to Mutian and Boqi," *Creation Monthly* 1, no. 1 (Mar. 1926).
50 Mu Mutian, "On Poetry—A Letter to Moruo," *Creation Monthly* 1, no. 1 (Mar. 1926).
51 Ke Ke, "Essays on New Poetry," *New Poetry* 2, no. 4 (Jan. 1937).
52 The full name of the poem is *A Playful Response to Shuyong's Poem, but Sent to Friends of Qi City*.
53 Zhang Yi, "The Pursuit of Philosophical Reasoning and Plain Beauties," *Nankai Journal*, no. 2 (1992).
54 See Chapter 1, Section 1.
55 Hu Shih, "Forced Rebellion," in *Collection of Theory Development, China's New Literature Series*, 8.
56 Ke Ke, "On the New Approach of Chinese New Poetry," *New Poetry*, no. 4 (Jan. 1937).
57 Mao Dun, "The Future of Narrative Poetry," *Literature* 8, no. 2 (Feb. 1937).
58 Ai Qing, "Prose Beauty of Poetry," in *On Poetry* (People's Literature Publishing House, 1980).
59 Yuan Kejia, "New Poetry Modernization," *Tianjin: Ta Kung Pao Weekly Literature and Art* (Mar. 30, 1947).
60 Zhu Ziqing, "Poetry and Philosophy," in *Miscellaneous on New Poetry*, 23.
61 Yuan Kejia, "Poetry and Meaning," *Journal of Literature* 2, no. 6 (1947).
62 Hu Shih, "Forced Rebellion," in *Collection of Theory Development, China's New Literature Series*, 136.

63 Jiang Guangci, "Preface to *New Dreams.*"
64 Yang Sao, *Stories of the Country.*
65 Ai Qing, "For Victory," *Literature and Art during the War of Resistance against Japanese Aggression* 7, no. 1 (Jan. 1941).
66 Yuan Kejia, "New Poetry Modernization," *Tianjin: Ta Kung Pao Weekly Literature and Art* (Mar. 30, 1947).
67 Hu Shih, "A Letter to Chen Duxiu," quoted from *Zhu Kuan's May Fourth History of New Poetry* (Shaanxi Normal University Press, 1987), 132.
68 Yuan Kejia, "Poetry and Democracy," *Tianjin: Ta Kung Pao Weekly Literature and Art* (Oct. 30, 1948).
69 Hu Shih, "On New Poetry," in *Collection of Theory Development, China's New Literature Series,* 309.
70 See the next section of this chapter.
71 Mu Mutian, "Themes and Subjects in Poem Writing," in *How to Learn Poetry* (Life Bookstore, 1st edition, 1938).
72 Pu Feng, *The Study of Several Poets · Wen Liu's Poems,* Modern Chinese Poetry Community (Poetry Publishing House, 1938), emphasis by the original text.
73 See section I of this chapter.
74 Yuan Kejia, "New Poetry Modernization," *Tianjin: Ta Kung Pao Weekly Literature and Art* (Mar. 30, 1947).
75 Yuan Kejia, "Human Literature and People's Literature," *Tianjin: Ta Kung Pao Weekly Literature and Art* (July 6, 1947).
76 Tang Shi, *Flying Song: Postscript* (Pingyuan Publishing, 1950).
77 Hu Feng, "A Brief Review of Poems since the War," in *Complete Works of Hu Feng's Poems* (Zhejiang Literature and Art Publishing House, 1992), 615.
78 Hu Feng, "On the Visualization of Poetry," in *Complete Works of Hu Feng's Poems,* 649.
79 Hu Feng, "A Brief Review of Poems since the War," in *Complete Works of Hu Feng's Poems,* 616.
80 Ai Qing, *On Poetry.*
81 Yuan Kejia, "New Poetry Modernization," in *On Modernization of New Poetry* (Joint Publishing Company, 1988), 7.
82 Yuan Kejia, "Myth of Poetry," *Journal of Literature* 1, no. 11 (1947).
83 Qumen, "Compliments to Mr. Bannong after Reading the *Wafu Ji,*" *Beixin Weekly,* no. 9 (Oct. 1926).
84 Pan Songde, "Liu Bannong's Poetics," in *40 Modern Chinese Poetics* (Chongqing Press, 1991), 57.
85 "Our Words," in *New Poetry* 2, no. 1.
86 Mao Dun, "Essays on Literature and Art," *Literature and Art Pioneers* 2, no. 3 (Feb. 1943).
87 *Lenin on Literature and Art,* vol. 2, 912, 916.
88 Lin Boxiu (Du Guoxiang), "Several Issues about Literature and Art to be Settled Urgently in 1929," *Haifeng Weekly,* no. 12 (Mar. 1929).
89 Mao Zedong, "Speech at the Yan'an Forum on Literature and Art," in *Selected Works of Mao Zedong,* vol. 3 (People's Publishing House, 1966), 808.

90 See Ouyang Xiu's *Dielianhua* (Butterflies in love with Flowers), *Secluded Garden Courtyards*, Yuan Haowen's *Farewell at Yingting Pavilion*, and Du Fu's *Two Poems on the Leisure Pavilion*.
91 Huang Zunxian, "Self Preface to *Renjinglu Poetry*."
92 Zhu Ziqing, "True Poetry," in *Miscellaneous on New Poetry*, 86–87.
93 Chen Duxiu, "On Literary Revolution," in *China's New Literature Series, Collection of Theory Development*, 46.
94 Liu Bannong, "Spiritual Innovation of Poetry and Novels," *New Youth* 3, no. 5 (July 1917).
95 Zhou Zuoren, "Ancient Literature," in *My Garden; Books on Rainy Days, Zexie Collection* (Yuelu Publishing House, 1987), 22.
96 Zhu Kuan, *May Fourth History of New Poetry*, 314, 299.
97 Zhu Kuan, *May Fourth History of New Poetry*, 314, 299.
98 Lu Xun, "Qijieting Essays, in Memory of Mr. Liu Bannong," in *Complete Works of Lu Xun*, vol. 6 (People's Literature Publishing House, 1981), 71.
99 See Pu Feng, "A Bird's-eye view of Chinese Poetry from May Fourth to Present," *Poetry Quarterly* 1, no. 1–2 (Dec. 1934–Mar. 1935); Ren Jun, *On the Approach of New Poetry, New Poetry talks* (New China Press, 1946).
100 Pu Feng, *The Study of Several Poets · Wen Liu's Poems*, Modern Chinese Poetry Community.
101 "A Letter from Mr. Wang Duqing," *Journal of Poetry*, no. 2 (Mar. 1931).
102 Mao, "Speech at the Yan'an Forum on Literature and Art," 816, 821.
103 Mao, "Speech at the Yan'an Forum on Literature and Art."
104 See Xiang Linbing, "An Explanation of 'New Wine in Old Bottle'" and "Another Response to the Skeptics of 'New Wine in Old Bottle,'" in *Popular Reading Materials Collection*.
105 See Ge Yihong, *Is the Central Source of National Forms in the so-called "Folk Forms?"* (1940); Hu Feng, *On the Issue of National Forms* (1941).
106 See Guo Moruo's *National Forms Discussion*; Mao Dun, *Correspondence on National Forms* (1940), etc.
107 Zhu Xiang, "The Generation of Poetry," in *Appendix to Informal Literary Discussions* (Beixin Publishing House, 1934).
108 Zhu Xiang, "Ancient Folk Songs," in *Zhong Shu Ji* (Beixin Publishing House, 1934).
109 See Zheng Zekui and Wang Wenbin, Dai Wangshu during the War of Resistance against Japanese Aggression, *Research on the Literature and Art during the War of Resistance against Japanese Aggression*, no. 4 (1986).
110 Liu Bannong, "Spiritual Innovation of Poetry and Novels," *New Youth* 3, no. 5 (July 1917), emphasis by the original text.
111 Liu Bannong, "Wafu Ji, A Self-Introduction," in *Wafu Ji* (Beixin Publishing House, 1926).
112 Zhou Zuoren, "Ballads," in *My Garden; Books on Rainy Days, Zexie Collection*, 36.
113 Pu Feng, *Speeches on the Poetry about the War of Resistance against Japanese Aggression* (Poetry Publishing House, 1938).
114 Tian Jian, *How I Write Poetry* (Preface).
115 Liu Bannong, "Wafu Ji, A Self-Introduction."
116 Tian Jian, "Chinese Pastoral Poetry," in *My Poetry* (postscript).
117 Zhou Zuoren, "Preface to *Yangbianji*," *Yusi*, no. 82.

118 Zang Kejia, "On New Poetry," *Literature* 3, no. 1 (1934).
119 Pu Feng, *Speeches on the Poetry about the War of Resistance against Japanese Aggression*.
120 Li Ji, *How Did I Learn Folk Songs*.
121 Liu Bannong, "My View on Literary Reform," *New Youth* 3, no. 3 (May 1917).
122 Pu Feng, "Reexamining the Popularization of Poetry," in *Speeches on the Poetry about the War of Resistance against Japanese Aggression*.
123 Yuan Kejia, "Myth of Poetry," *Journal of Literature* 2, no. 11 (1947).

· 3 ·
TRADITIONAL CULTURE AND TEXT STRUCTURES OF MODERN CHINESE NEW POETRY

The life of literature not only lies in its unique pursuit of ideas but also directly condenses in its distinctive forms—text structures. The structure of poetry can be analyzed from the grammatical system which is composed of diction, sentences, and cohesive devices, and the metrical system which is composed of rhythms, rhymes, and tones.

"Discernment" and "Forgetting": The Literary Pursuit of Modern Chinese New Poetry

> The best poem should have the best
> Textural structure, the best syntax . . .
> —Li Guangtian, "On the Ideas and Forms of New Poetry"

An examination of modern new poetry grammar is inevitably related to the study of modern Chinese lexical, syntactic, and textual structures. In the modern transformation process of Chinese literary thoughts and pursuit of language patterns, literary thought change seems more obvious, while the underlying language model (including lexical, syntactic, and textual structures) remains more stable. Discussions of "the best textual structures, the best syntax" by modern Chinese poets are mostly completed within the Chinese language system. It is often difficult to make strict distinctions between ancient and modern Chinese language. Therefore, Chinese classical poetry's grammatical achievements could offer inspiration to Chinese modern poets. Now, let's return and look at the language used in Chinese classical poetry.

"Discernment" and "Forgetting" Cycling

When examining the grammatical pursuit of Chinese classical poetry, we find two kinds of linguistic structures. The first structure is devoted to clarity and accuracy of words' meanings, and the logic of sentences and texts. The second structure is intentional vagueness of the connotations and extensions of words, free and random sentences with no fixed rules, most sentences being "parallel," non-logical, and non-causal. In the former, language tracks subjective thinking and shows a "clear discernment" function of words. The latter maintains a distance between words and subjective thinking. Its narrative does not intend to reveal its theme directly; the grammatical rules that combine words into sentences, and sentences into passages are not considered important. Strict, orderly language rules seem to become flexible, even forgotten. I summarized these two grammatical pursuits in the interpretation of Chinese classical poetics as "Clear Discernment" and "Forgetting the Language,"[1] abbreviated as "Discernment" and "Forgetting."

It should be said that both "Discernment" and "Forgetting" of language are indispensable for poetry writing. However, in general, "Clear Discernment" and "Forgetting the Language" are two alternative grammatical pursuit cycles in the history of Chinese classical poetry. Generally speaking, Chinese ancient poems before the Tang Dynasty can be categorized as "Clear Discernment," while the poems of the Tang Dynasty and *Ci* of the Song Dynasty are categorized as "Forgetting the Language" and the poems of the Song Dynasty as "Clear Discernment" again. Poems since the Song Dynasty went cyclic, just like flowers bloom and wither periodically. (Ye Xie, *Origin of Poetry*)

From Qu Yuan's time to the Wei and Jin dynasties, words used in Chinese poetry generally have accurate meanings, explicit, and simple. Flexible use of word classes and ambiguity is relatively rare in poetry. For example, *Qu Sao* is famous for its unusually rich, imaginative rhetoric, but this rhetoric also contains clear political and moral significance, and the expression of "inner beauty" and "cultivation" will not produce much ambiguity. In terms of sentence structure, most poems contain main categories of parts of speech, such as nouns, verbs, adjectives, relation conjunctions, etc., and follow the rules of "subjective-predicate-object," which is complete and orderly. For example, In *Nineteen Ancient Poems*, "The floating clouds blocked the daylight," "There are high-rise buildings in the Northwest," "The guests are from afar," and "We were born into the world, and suddenly we became travelers who went far," etc. For the entire poem, the sentences are mostly composed in two ways: (1) time sequence and (2) causal relations. The former, such as one of Wang Can's "Seven Mourning Poems":

> The capital Chang'an is in turmoil, the warlords are fighting against all. I have to abandon my hometown, a central town, and leave for Jingzhou, a remote area not yet affected. My relatives are sad and my friends are dismayed. What do I see on my way out? White bones on the grounds. A hungry mother along the way, deserted her child in the grass. She turned her head and heard the wailing. She sobbed but did not return: "I don't know when I will die. How could I still take it with me?" I left immediately when hearing this, overwhelmed by what she said. When I came to the highland of Baling, I looked back at Chang'an. I suddenly understood the author of Xia Quan, who called for a wise emperor. I sighed and felt even further the pain.

The latter example "Turn the Carriage and Trudge along the Long Journey" from *Nineteen Ancient Poems*:

> Start the carriage and trudge along the long journey, with an unknown destination. Looking around, I could see no end. Only the spring breeze greened the grass. The scenery has changed beyond recognition. How could a person not get old? Every being has its life cycle and one has to establish myself in his due time. Life has its limits and we could not be immortal like stones. In a transient moment, our life is gone and only a good reputation is the real treasure to leave behind.

The characteristics of these words, sentences, and the text itself achieve clarity, smoothness, and fluidity as a whole.

From "landscape poetry" and "objects eulogy poetry" of the Southern and Northern dynasties to the poetry of the Tang Dynasty and *Ci* of the Song Dynasty, it is another new grammatical pursuit that gradually becomes mature. Here, the diction of poetry is endowed with richer, more complex meanings. This poetry covers both culture and nature. It not only has the symbolic meaning of history but also maintains the freshness of feeling about nature for the first time. In the rich localities of humanistic tradition and objective nature, the diction loses a fixed one-to-one correspondence, giving people multi-faceted, multi-directional associations, such as the word "*Yang-liu*" (literally means poplar and willow trees) giving people a feeling of lightness and elegance, while at the same time, it has the cultural connotation of love between man and woman. For example, Liu Yuxi wrote, "The willows are green, the river smoothly flows; Singing over there on the waters is the lad I love" ("A Love Song, One"), Liu Yong, "The riverbank lined with willows, the moon sinking, and the dawn rising on a breeze" ("Chill, Shrill, To the Tune of Yulinling"). In these verses, a bright, pleasant environment, and the tenderness and sweetness of heart are intertwined, which greatly enriches the aesthetic information of the words. Numerous similar examples could be found, such as *chun-cao* (literally, grass in spring, associated with "parting"), the lingering cuckoo (associated with "missing home"), and so on. Occasionally, some poems deliberately create ambiguity, which is thought-provoking, such as "A Moon Song on Emei Mountain" by Li Bai, "The moon of the Emei Mountain is half-round, shadowing into the Pingjiang River. I traveled to the Three Gorges at night on this clear water. I miss you, but can't see you and now I left for Yuzhou." There are different opinions about whether the "you" refers to a friend or the "moon" in the poem.

The attributes of words are flexible and interchangeable. Some basic attributes of Chinese, such as verbs, have no distinctions in gender, numbers, and case, and verbs have no tenses and aspects, and so on. These features are displayed in the poetry of the Tang Dynasty and *Ci* of the Song Dynasty. Nouns, verbs, and adjectives are used interchangeably with other classes. For example, in this sentence "*wei cheng zhao yu yi qing chen* (no dust is raised on the road wet with morning rain)," *yi* (wet), an adjective, is used as a verb here (Wang Wei, "A Farewell Song"). In "*dong bian ri chu xi bian yu* (the sun arises in the east and it rains in the west)," the noun *yu* (rain) is used as a verb (Liu Yuxi, "A Love Song, One"). In "*xi lou wang yue ji hui yuan* (Looking at the moon on the West Building and wondering when it will be full again)," the adjective *yuan* (round, full) is used as a verb (Wei Yingwu, "A Letter to Li Dan, Yuan Xi"). The way to form sentences is even freer and more casual. The subjective-predicate-objective order in classical poetry underwent fundamental changes. It is sometimes difficult to distinguish the subject from the object in the original, such as "*ren xian gui hua luo, ye jing chun shan kong* (In quiet hear how bay-flowers fall to the ground—The vernal hills at night are void around!)" (Wang Wei, "The Warble Raven"). Some verses are even composed of a series of nouns and there are no grammatical connections in the original, such as "*ji sheng mao dian yue, ren ji ban qiao shuang*" (Cocks crow, small inn, and the moon. Footprints, boards of bridge, and the frost) (Wen Tingyun, "Early Departure at Shang Mountain"). The time or cause-and-effect relationship between the sentences is greatly blurred, replaced by harmony based on the correspondence of words. The similarity part of speech, the contrast of sentences in semantics, and the consistency of internal structure—all these determine the relationship between these lines of poetry cannot be linearly developed, but juxtaposed and nonlinear. The grammatical features of these words, sentences, and texts dissolve the rigor and logic of grammar at different levels, allowing poetry to float in a vague and obscure space.

Poetry of the Song Dynasty showed its differences from the poetry of the Tang Dynasty and Ci of the Song Dynasty in a series of grammatical pursuits. It reincorporated words, sentences, and texts into the ups and downs of the thinking flow. The idea that poetry writing should focus on language, the writers' talents, and argumentation (Yan Yu, *Canglang Shihua*) give poetry language a subjective taste. The idea of "turning decadence into magic" makes the connotation of words fresh and clear. The argumentation method also made the combination of words follow strict grammatical rules. The logical connection effect between sentences is explicit. Compared with the poetry of the Tang Dynasty and Ci of the Song Dynasty that emphasize feelings of implication, the language of poetry of the Song Dynasty naturally appears direct, weak, and even obscure. For example, Huang Tingjian's response poem to Su Shi: "My poems are like insignificant writings of Cao and Kuai, shallow and cannot be real states, your poems are like the powerful state of Chu, which could accommodate five lakes and three rivers."[2] However, being direct, weak, and obscure is also the inevitable consequence of "Clear Discernment." At this point, the grammatical pursuit of "Discernment" and "Forgetting" in Chinese classical poetry seems to have completed a historical cycle. "Since the Song Dynasty, the Yuan, the Ming, and the Qing dynasties produced large numbers of talented poets; yet, the scope of their works did not go beyond those delimited during the Tang and Song dynasties. They belong to either of them."[3] In a certain sense, poetry is divided into types of Tang Dynasty style and types of Song Dynasty style with the cycle of "Discernment" and "Forgetting." Roughly, this cycling is the grammatical pursuits of Chinese classical poetry.

We notice the grammatical pursuits of modern Chinese poetry also showed features of "Discernment" and "Forgetting."

The grammatical pursuit of the early vernacular new poetry stressed "Discernment." Hu Shih said the "poetry revolution" must complete three things, the second is to "follow the grammar."[4] He highlighted the inherent norms of the language itself, which, of course, means "Discernment" rather than "Forgetting." Hu Shih especially valued language with a strong narrative and clear grammar, "Where does the revolution of the poetry begin? Poetry must be written as prose." Many of the poems in his work, An Experimental Collection, are clear in semantics and have clear syntactic structures. They are more logically like proses in different lines: "I am getting up early in the morning, / Crowing on the corner of people's roofs. / People hate me, saying I am not auspicious: --/ I can't sing gently just to please others!" ("Old Crow") Similar grammatical pursuits are also prominent in other poets' works, such as Yu Pingbo's "Spring Water Boat," "I just walked forward: / I have been missing it in my heart, and now I am looking with my eyes; / appreciating the good taste of spring." Liu Bannong's "A Piece of Paper Apart": "A beggar is lying outside the house, / He clenched his teeth, yelling at the north wind: 'Death'!" Kang Baiqing's "Outside the Town," "I haven't been here for a long time, / some grass grew sparsely; / but still the green barely covered the dried." Zhou Zuoren's "Painter," "Unfortunately I am not a painter, / I can't write with brushes, / write a lot of scenes."

Since the late May Fourth era, modern Chinese poetry gradually decreased its efforts to trace complex thinking. The vague poetic and holistic feelings gradually attracted people's interest. Therefore, the grammatical pursuit of "Forgetting the Language" began to appear. In Bing Xin's *Myriad Stars*, *Spring Water*, and Zong Baihua's *Flowing Clouds*, the sturdy structure of modern Chinese was softened for the first time. *Myriad Stars: 138:* "Summer night, / cool breeze arose! / The orchid breath on the collar / around the depths of the dream." Words such as night, breeze, orchid, and dream seem to have surpassed the restraints of logical chains of cause and effect, and this transcendence provides with them a wealth of aesthetic information. After the mid-1920s, the Crescent and Symbolist poets further "forgot" the rigor of grammar, so the meaning of the words, the structure of the sentences, and the logic of the texts are in an erratic state of looseness.

For example, in Xu Zhimo's famous lines of "Farewell to Cambridge": "Quiet is the flute of departure, silent is Cambridge's tonight." Here, word classes deviated from the norm. They are declarative sentences; yet, they lack clear, logical meanings. This violent violation structure of language rules indicates the poet had no intention to distinguish the complexity and contradiction of his thoughts, but appealed to readers with full emotional tones. Looking at the entire poem, "Farewell to Cambridge," the words of quietness, separation, and silence matched with the reluctance to leave, formed a harmonious unity. The amount of information released by single words is "poetic" itself. Strict grammar rules and phrases would not be inconsistent with the lyrics of the whole poem.

Similar sentences could also be found in Lin Huiyin's "I Wish": "But hold the sad flag, / to meet the unsettled melancholy; / at dusk, the deep night, walking tiptoed, / all empty, no gentleness." Rao Mengkan's "Melancholy": "A thousand calls went in vain, / only empty mountains echoed your answer. / It is dusky in a blink of an eye, /Melancholy is permeating the world." Wang Duqing's "Beside Dante's Tomb": "That time is a charming fragrant flower, / I use it to present to your beautiful cheeks; / that time is a glass of intoxicating wine, / I use it to supply to your loving lips . . ." Feng Naichao's "Now," "I heard in the breeze / an old tune from a broken musical instrument—creaking / a dry river bed / tightly holding the silent void." These verses also exhibit a rather striking grammatical feature. Often the previous sentence is independent of the latter, that is, they are non-time and non-causal. Their connection depends entirely on the overall "artistic conception" of the whole poem and the reader's intentionality beyond time and space, which might remind us of the contrasting relationship between the two neighboring lines in the metrical poetry.

"Forgetting the Language" reached a level of perfection in Modernist poetry in the 1930s. Dai Wangshu regarded poetry as a kind of indirect expression. Bian Zhilin stated he was afraid of revealing his emotions. The "I" in his early lyric poetry can also be replaced by "you" or "he (she)."[5] He Qifang dodged the chain of language, "crossing the river without giving us a bridge."[6] From the point of view of grammatical pursuit, this can be understood as the poet consciously subverting grammatical rules, pursuing the ambiguity of words and the non-logic of sentence connections.

According to Fei Ming's analogy, poetry is loose sand and each grain of sand is a jewel, but it is difficult to thread them.[7] Compared with the Crescent Moon School and the Symbolist School, Modernist School poetry is better at refining words "tied together." Through the reference to the traditional language, through the "forgetting" of the part of speech, and the "omission" and adjustment of the sentences and passages, Modernist poetry creates an "artistic conception" ideal similar to the poetry of the Tang Dynasty and *Ci* of the Song Dynasty. Sometimes, these poems continue to use conjunctions and adverbs with distinct logic in Chinese, but they ingeniously dissolve the logical factors in them just right, creating a mellow, harmonious situation after transcending the rules of language. For example, Bian Zhilin's "Issues with Migrating Birds":

> Three or four paper eagles, paper swallows, paper roosters up in the sky / flying in the sky –Are they there to meet the wild geese coming from the south in the sky? / And am I the children's toys? / I will borrow from the library *Issues with Migrating Birds*.

During the 1940s, Chinese new poetry generally turned to "Clear Discernment." The "new poetry modernization" promoted by the Nine Leaves poets emphasized the exploration of language potential, focusing on "how to communicate the greatest number of experiences properly and effectively among the innate limitations of various art media."[8] The multi-level conflicts of language, as well as the dialectical development and spiral advancement in contradictions and conflicts, became the basic grammatical features of Nine Leaves poems. Ai Qing and the July School poets also advocated language should be "bright and unambiguous"; "complete the theme of one's choice with all the strength."[9] Many other anti-war poems have clear meanings, words from similar classes, clear sentence structure and clear logic, and a sense of mobility and obvious propulsion of the entire poem. For example, Cai Qijiao's "A Blizzard Night":

> Wind! Are you going to defeat the enemy or destroy our own home? / Snow! Are you going to breed a good year or bring disaster? / The cold is becoming thin, the night is coming to an end, / China! You stand up in victory!

Huang Ningying's "The Story of Tears": "I want to write a poem / To sum up the story of my tears in recent years / because days like that / will be the past soon, very soon." Yan Chen's "Farewell," "You are gone, / what you cannot bring/is the land you toiled, / is your spinning wheel, / many of your meaningful times." In this respect, the Nine Leaves poet, Mu Dan, made it explicit that "poems must express deeper thoughts without fail."[10] The verses he wrote have a shade of "Clear Discernment": "Although they are dead now. / Although they have never lived, / have left an immortal memory, / when we beg our own life, / in the formation of our dust" ("Rat Burrows"). The poet Zheng Min thinks Mu Dan's poems are twisted, with multi-sections, and fully loaded to almost overloaded in terms of grammatical features.[11]

Therefore, the cycling of "Clear Discernment" and "Forgetting the Language" is the common grammatical pursuit of Chinese classical and modern poetry.

Two Modes of Thinking Under Two Kinds of Poem Rules

Language is the symbol of human understanding and interpreting the world. People rely on language to define everything in nature, use language to communicate with others, and spread ideas. In turn, people accumulate their own historical and cultural achievements. Correspondingly, language is also associated with the most fundamental worldview and the most basic way of thinking. From this perspective, the so-called grammar reflects people's use of their thinking to understand and imitate the world's overall structure and principles of change. Behind the pursuit of the two grammars of Chinese poetry, "Clear Discernment" and "Forgetting the Language," the twofold thinking of Chinese poets are revealed: value judgment and the pursuit of subjective and objective unity.

Imagine the world is pure and natural before the emergence of human beings and meaning. There is no hierarchy, no order, no change, and development, and everything is in the "virtual world." In the future, people stand out from nature and gradually become masters of the world. At this time, people should conquer the world, transform the world, and constantly reinterpret the world's cultural activities following their own subjective will. What is associated with these cultural activities is a value judgment. People seek and establish one value after another, and use this value standard to understand the world and judge life. Under the value judgment, the objective world shows a hierarchy, order, change, and development. The value judgment of the Chinese people has spurred the literary pursuit of "Clear Discernment" in poetry works.

The grammatical pursuit of the "Clear Discernment" style in Chinese classical poetry always appears during the times when Chinese poets try to show their "cultural style." "Culture" exists with its distinction from "naturalization," which is the result of people creating the world according to self-consciousness. This so-called "cultural style" is to show the existence of its intelligence, highlighting the temperament and individuality of an unwillingness to succumb to historical habits.

Generally, the birth and growth of classical poetry is a process of continuous innovation and transcendence of folk collective creation. In such a process, the "cultural style" of poetry is constantly affirmed and strengthened, while the poetry of the Song Dynasty set "innovation" as its banner, trying to express its education and knowledge and prove how its cultural level is different from its predecessors.

May Fourth era as well as the 1930s and 1940s witnessed turbulent periods of Chinese culture. On the one hand, the conflict between the old and new cultures formed the turmoil. On the other hand, the national culture started to transform because of these wars. During such time, "value reset" is an inevitable choice for the Chinese. The new Chinese poetry born against this historical background is bound to be filled with self-oriented value judgment; thus, a "Clear Discernment" of grammatical pursuit follows. Of course, as explained in the previous chapter, the May Fourth era new poetry and the Nine Leaves July School poetry and other anti-war poetry accepted the influence of Song Dynasty poetry to varying degrees. Therefore, the development of history and the prototype of culture also provided a common foundation for the literary pursuit of Chinese new poetry.

At the same time, we noticed the fact that although we are trying to break free from nature and judge the world as a master, we are still a member of nature and belong to the world. For us who exist in the form of individual life, the grandeur of the universe is always boundless and endless, while the human being is ultimately small and short-lived. Therefore, people cannot master in essence the world and interpret the world accurately. After every logical explanation, we have new, more confusion. Distinctly, the original or complete world landscape shows some divisions and ruins due to our interpretation. The level and order assumed by our subjective are not inherent in the world, and there is an embarrassing dislocation between our judgment and the original nature of the world. In such a situation, Chinese philosophy is different from Western philosophy, which tries to "reinvigorate the system" to strengthen individual independence. From the very beginning, Chinese philosophy keenly felt the complicated relationships between man and the world and worked hard to explore the path of reconciliation. Laozi advocated to "return to the state of a baby" (*Tao Te Ching*), and Zhuangzi adored the "primitive man" when the world is in its intact state (*Zhuangzi, Qiwu Lun, or The Adjustment of Controversies*). The innocence of children and the primitives are what Chinese philosophy considered as the unity of oneself and others, chaotic, and all things connecting with neither thinking nor logic.

This way of thinking is quite different from value judgment. What it needs is not all kinds of ideas of self-assertion nor use these concepts and thoughts as standards to dissect the universe. On the contrary, it tries to restore the most primitive and authentic state of life in the world. The mind should subordinate to the pulse of the objective world, attach to it, and be assimilated by nature. Human thinking is by no means unconstrained, charging in all directions and doing whatever one wants, but it should go with nature. In the aesthetic pursuit of poetry, it is expressed as the artistic ideal of "objectification." In the grammatical pursuit of poetry, it is expressed as "Forgetting the Language." That is, the logic of the linguistic structure is blurred, or "forgotten." "Specific references, meanings or positioning and timing elements are eliminated or reduced to a minimum."[12] That is, the traces of "culture" should be dispelled as much as possible. Multi-meaning, multi-directional words should simulate the unnamed natural world. "Tao that can be described is not universal and eternal Tao. Name that can be named is not universal and eternal Name" (*Tao Te Ching*). The Great Tao is silent but as soon as one appeals to literature, words must be employed, then, what should one do? I have something to say, but now I forget it. This is the most unique idea that Chinese poets contribute to the history of world poetry.

The pursuit of "Forgetting the Language" in Chinese classical poetry emerged in the times of highly mature traditional poetry culture—particularly typical in the poetry of the Tang Dynasty and *Ci* of the Song Dynasty. This is an interesting reality. On the one hand, it appeared in the highly developed, mature poetry culture. On the other hand, it is the effort to subside the culture. This is very normal. The highly developed and mature Chinese poetry culture is closely related to the philosophical thoughts of Taoism and Buddhism, which offset the culture of human beings in different senses. Certain forms of disintegration of the three-dimensionality of human beings in culture are a distinctive feature of Chinese traditional culture. Here, the literati character of Chinese poetry does not mean the development of culture, and the appreciation and promotion of cultural creation activities. Its orientation may be exactly the opposite. Therefore, the "cultural pursuit" is relatively more popular in the times when Chinese poetry tended to be mature; yet, not mature or in the transition period when prosperity peaked to a decline.

The pursuit of "Forgetting the Language" in modern Chinese new poetry is driven by two forces. The first is the inheritance of modern poets to the poetry of the Wei, Jin, and Tang dynasties and *Ci* of the Song Dynasty. Starting from Bing Xin, through the Crescent, Symbolist to the Modernist School, this inheritance requirement became more and more intense, and rose to conscious awareness. In the previous chapter, I detailed an explanation. Here, what I want to emphasize is the linguistic concept of traditional Chinese philosophy, which plays a direct role in terms of grammatical features. For example, judgmental thinking drove Hu Shih to choose "Clear Discernment." In his view, language should completely succumb to the subjective will of humans. "One should say what one wants to say and say it as how it should be said."[13] The poems produced by this logic should be good. However, this changed in Bing Xin's poems: "Truth, / in the silence of the babies, / not in the debate of the wise men" (*Myriad Stars*). So, "Poets! / Silence; / those who cannot write, / is beautiful" (*Myriad Stars*). "Babies, / are great poets, / in their incomplete speech, / come the most complete verses" (*Myriad Stars*). Indeed, since then, Chinese modern poets had begun to construct those "incomplete speech" to seek the "most complete" cosmic truth. That is "the knowers do not speak out, and the speakers do not know" (*Tao Te Ching*). "Only when one is extremely serene could one enjoy the slightest beauty of nature" (Sikong Tu). "Do not walk after other's poetics and do not damage the atmosphere with decorated words" (Yan Yu).

The second is the ultra-stability of the depth model of the Chinese language. Modern Chinese vernacular has undergone major changes compared with classical Chinese, including being closer to modern spoken language, increased foreign loan words introduced, and an emulation of Western languages by adding a series of prepositions and conjunctions to enhance the logic of semantics, etc. However, for poetic language, these ancient and modern differences are far from substantive. Relatively speaking, the rigidity of classical Chinese is more expressed in classical prose. The modern Chinese language used in modern new poetry is very similar to ancient Chinese in terms of lexical and syntactic structures, for example, the symbolic imagery features of words, the ambiguity of word meanings, the flexibility of word classes, the randomness of group words and sentences, the conciseness of language, "expressiveness is enough" with little stratified tracking of twists and turns. The super-stableness existence of the Chinese language provides the most solid foundation for today's people to achieve similar philosophical thinking. It is easy for Chinese modern poets to understand the original state of the world according to the symbolic characteristics of the Chinese language. The strategy of "Forgetting the Language" highlights the imagery and flexibility of Chinese, and ultimately represents the obscurity and ambiguity of the world itself.

Between "Discernment" and "Forgetting"

In summary, due to the influence of classical poetry tradition, we see the stability of the Chinese language and the basic philosophical thinking related to it. The grammatical features of modern Chinese poetry are prominently expressed as the two cyclical factors of "Discernment" and "Forgetting." However, the evolutionary trend of modern culture cannot be ignored. Due to the development of modern culture, some new features of the existence and cycle of these two factors have also appeared, which deserve our analysis.

First, the introduction of Western poetry culture offered an unprecedented promotion for the "Clear Discernment" pursuit of new poetry.

If Chinese and Western poetry cultures are compared, the grammatical pursuit of Western poetry falls into the category of "Clear Discernment." Western languages have long embarked on the path of alphabetic abstract thinking. This kind of pursuit has been elaborated by Plato and Aristotle back to ancient Greek times, and its influence continues with modern symbolism poetry. Compared with the "Discernment" and "Forgetting" of Chinese classical poetry, the explicit pursuit of Western poetry culture is extraordinarily simple and consistent. Judging from historical facts, the relationship between "Discernment" and "Forgetting" of Chinese classical poetry is transitional from each other. There is much interweaving and intertwining. In the development process of the language, Chinese retains the main features of the primary stage (ideographic, pictographic).[14] Therefore, the anti-logical meaning of the "Forgetting" grammatical pursuit is the highest model of Chinese language art. The development that influences the pursuit of "Clear Discernment" not only determines the inevitability of the transition from ancient poetry to metrical-style poetry but also limits the anti-traditional efforts of the poetry of the Song Dynasty. The "Clear Discernment" poetry of the Song Dynasty also accommodates certain factors of "Forgetting the Language" since the prosperous Tang Dynasty, such as the multiple cultural connotations of the words (allusions), the balance of sentences and passages, the sense of harmony, and their corresponding "jumbo" effects.

In the history of Chinese poetry, Chinese modern poetry undoubtedly has the most awareness of "Clear Discernment." More importantly, because of the new blood of the Western-style "Clear Discernment" spirit, the pursuit of the "Discernment" grammar of Chinese new poetry also obtained a certain degree of independent character—it is trying to search for the deeper philosophical foundation on the one hand. On the other hand, it consciously reflected and criticized the "Forgetting the Language" of traditional Chinese poetry. The "Forgetting" factor in the "Clear Discernment" form of modern Chinese new poetry had been reduced to the minimum degree in the history of Chinese literature. The daily oral language flooded into poetry on a large scale. It is bright, clear, and fresh, and impacts the inherent cultural connotation meaning of the words. The translation and introduction of the logical language of Western literature also forced Chinese poetry to create a large number of new, logical, clear vocabulary. The significant increase in conjunctions and prepositions made sentences develop a distinct sense of hierarchy and procedural sense and strengthened the linear advancement effect of semantics.

Associated with the above-mentioned changes in the language is the transformation of the way of thinking. In the enormous cultural crisis and cultural conflicts in modern China, Chinese literati communities worked hard to remove traditional pressure and find new values and new rational thinking. Therefore, in modern China, a discussion of values and value judgments was always popular with people. This kind of thinking had a great impact on modern Chinese poets of different schools. For example, when Chinese poets need to fully and clearly explain their values, to have a leveled and logical protest and rebuttal, and express themselves, free style, propelled sentences of varied lengths and unevenness were born. This completely disintegrated the homogeneity and juxtaposition of traditional poetry. To track the subjective will, some sentences were stretched to a great extent, like wheels running ahead, which produced a large amount of information and strict logic, offering great appeal. In the history of modern Chinese poetry, such sentences have appeared in many poets of various genres, such as Hu Shih's "See Shu Yong off to Sichuan," "It has been a long time since we met last time, and now I will send you back again. It is too hasty! Thanks to God's will, you could stay for two more days, so that I can write a poem and send it as a gift." Shen Yimo's "Rickshaw Driver," "Go out and hire a rickshaw. There are many pedestrians on the street; / There are many rickshaws and horses, I don't know what they are busy with?" Guo Moruo's "A Call on the Edge of the Earth," "Countless white clouds are raging in the air, / ah! A magnificent view of the Arctic Ocean! / The infinite Pacific lifts his whole body to push the earth down." Wen Yiduo's "Li Bai's Death," "He turned over and jumped into the pool, and he hugged her. /She has disappeared. He cried in greater panic, but he didn't know that he couldn't speak out!" Dai Wangshu's "Broken Fingers," "His words are soothing, calm, like a sigh, / and his eyes seem to contain tears, although he wears a smile." Mu Dan's "The Song of Roses," "I grew up in the landscape of ancient poetry, our sun is too old. / There is no sudden change of airflow, no reversal of mountains and seas, people die in monotonous fatigue." Ai Qing's "Dayanhe," "I stared at the tablet above the door of the house, which reads "Family Happiness," I don't know the words / I touched the silk and shell buttons of the new clothes." Cai Qijiao's "Close Fight," "In the second year, a mountain eagle came to the blood-soaked warfield, / it looked around, hovered, to perch on the tomb of heroes."

In the strong cultural background of the "Discernment" spirit, a series of new features also appeared in the grammatical pursuit of "Forgetting the Language." The "Forgetting" grammar of Chinese classical poetry has rich expressions in terms of words, phrases, and sentences. Every subtle linguistic structural unit tries to maintain ambiguity and juxtaposition to adapt to the implied meaning in poetry aesthetics. The "Forgetting" grammatical pursuit of modern Chinese poetry also tries to work in every subtle linguistic unit, but, it is not always successful because of the transformation of ways of thinking and the language. The "Forgetting" of modern poetry often needs additional remedies.

From the perspective of words, spoken and colloquial vocabularies were widely used. Their unique shallowness replaced the multiple meanings and ambiguity inherent in traditional vocabulary. Some words with rich historical connotations became language tributaries, like isolated islands, which attracted attention. The use of multiple meanings of words also brought a more noticeable deliberateness, not as natural and appropriate as classical poetry. For example, in Bian Zhilin's "The Letters," "The man in green (postman) is pushing the familiar doorbell/click on the heart of the house owner: / Is it a fish swimming through the Yellow Sea? / Is it a goose flying over Siberia?" Every Chinese would conclude the fish and the flying goose are messengers. At the same time, the poet skillfully borrowed the meaning of the old saying "Fish and the flying goose as messengers" in Chinese culture. The connotation of these two words was expanded. However, compared with classical poetry, Bian Zhilin hid the fish and the flying goose, to attract attention. It does leave a deep impression on readers; yet, artificial traces are inevitable.

Similarly, the narrative and social communicative functions of vernacular colloquialism make it necessary to follow strict grammatical norms. During modern times, the words that completely transcend their part of speech can no longer meet the requirements of the development of the times. It is difficult for word arrangement in verses, such as "Cocks crow, small inn, and the moon. Footprints, boards of a bridge and the frost" and "a withered vine, an old tree, a crow, twilight" to display the "new" feature of new poetry. Then, how can modern Chinese poetry realize the freedom of words? I think the main method is to mobilize the freedom of individual words in a pattern with clear sentence structure and clear basic logic. The use of a few word class shifts or the unexpected combination of them could offer a rich association, and break away the chain of daily grammar.

The former, such as "Your pleasure is unblocked *carefree*" (Xu Zhimo, "Cloud Tour," adjective as a noun). "Sighs like *slim*" (Lin Huiyin, "Don't Throw Away," adjective as a noun). "Your sweet eyes *bright* in the dark" (Hu Yepin, "Farewell to Manjia," adjective as a verb). "Five hundred miles of water *waved*" (Hu Yepin, "On the Dongting Lake," adjective as a verb). "My sorrows with the grass *green* the end of the world" (Bian Zhilin, "Rain and Me," adjective as a verb). "The window is waiting for your *lean*" (Bian Zhilin, "Untitled II," verb as a noun). "After the spring and summer, I am secretly *withering*" (He Qifang, "Seasonal Disease," adjective as a verb). "Autumn *dreams* in the eyes of a shepherdess" (He Qifang, "Autumn (2)," noun as a verb). The latter is like "I want to *climb the moonlight*" (Xu Zhimo, "In the Mountains"). "*Blowing off* the Sun, Moon, and *Stars* of the Day" (Sun Dayu, "A Reed Flute"). "Telling the *days the overlapping* mountainous nests" (Lin Huiyin, "Inspiration"). "*New Year is waiting* outside the window" (Lin Huiyin, "Memory"). "*I am solidified* like a stone on the shore" (Chen Mengjia, "Hail"). "*The ancient bell drifts* into the sea" (Mu Mutian, "Pale Bell Sounds"). "Pick the teardrops of yours" (Feng Naichao, "In the Moonlight"). "A faint *breeze crawled* into my hair" (Peng Zi, "In the Apple Forest"). "A *wondering* quiet fishing boat" (Hu Yepin, "On the Dongting Lake"). "You *decorate the dreams* of others" (Bian Zhilin, "Fragment"). "On the moonlight night, let me guess where you are / must be *a lonely train station*" (Bian Zhilin, "The Letters"). "I *took a sip of fogginess* on the street" (Bian Zhilin, "Record"). "Others are happy, while *I was depressed and lonely*" (Chang Bai, "Looking at the Light"). "Remote, *lonely whimper*" (Dai Wangshu, "Impression"). "The air through the cool dew, like *my sighing eyes*" (He Qifang, "Seasonal Disease").

Modern Chinese new poetry also has multi-directional and multi-faceted creation about the "Forgetting the Language" approach of sentences and text structures. Pursuing a parallel effect between sentences is the dominant structure of Chinese classical poetry continued in modern Chinese poetry. For example, "I also want my poems to flow like clear water, / I also want my heart to leisurely go like fish in a pool" (Xu Zhimo, "Moaning"). "Telling the days the overlapping mountainous nests; / the clear spring water flowing into the wild river; / secluded forest dotted with fresh fragrant flowers, / fine incense is often accompanied by a round moon in the sky" (Lin Huiyin, "Inspiration"). "Sorrow wears beautiful clothes dancing gently and neatly in the vast hall/ dusk quietly crossed the tip of the leaf and quietly broke into the dust of the empty silence" (Feng Naichao, "Sorrow"). "The mud across the river was sent to your beam, / the spring water across the courtyard was poured into your cup, / overseas luxury goods were brought to your chest: / I want to study the history of transportation" (Bian Zhilin, "Tears across the River"). "The flowers blooming in the remote valley are the most fragrant. / The unrecognized dew is the brightest. / I said that you are happy, little Lingling, /The stream that had not seen human's shadow is the brightest" (He Qifang, "Garland").

However, it is particularly worthy of our attention that modern Chinese poetry is less likely to be simple as classical poetry because of the limited multi-meaning, ambiguity of a series of words and sentences. That is, a simple sentence cannot fully convey the semantic meaning of various levels and logic. Therefore, a concentrated literary meaning of modern poetry often needs to be distributed in several lines of sentences. For example, "If I were a snowflake, /Dancing and skiing in the air, / I must recognize my direction—/ fly, fly, fly,—/ My direction on the ground" (Xu Zhimo, "Snow's Happiness"). Here, the "if" clause is explained with five lines. Another example is "there are two kinds of voices in the ancient town, / the same loneliness. / During daytime it is the fortune telling gong, / at night it is the drum" (Bian Zhilin, "The Dream of the Ancient Town"). "I don't understand why others give those stars / some names they do not need, / they are free to swim in space, without any worries, / they do not understand us, do not ask for being known" (Dai Wangshu, "To Kemu"). Here, the meaning does not dwell in the adjacent two sentences, but the juxtaposition of meaning is realized through probably two semantic groups (which might consist of several clauses) or even two paragraphs.

The juxtaposition of semantic groups and paragraphs can be said to be the "Forgetting the Language" method commonly used in Chinese modern poetry.

The modern Chinese language has complicated meanings and varied sentence structures, which adds difficulty to the juxtaposition. It can no longer rely on the extremely regular forms and strict fall and flat tone correspondence of classical poetry rhythm to imply a mutual relationship. So, what means could it rely on to remedy this? Modern poets adopted the way of properly repeating certain words in a sentence (or a semantic group or a paragraph; more words at the beginning are repeated), resulting in a similar pattern of linguistic structures to imply an intrinsic link between them. For instance: the juxtaposition of sentences: "A glimpse of the mind/woven into the slender lines of the rain thread/ woven into the drizzling shadow /woven into the shreds of the flickering smoke fiber" (Mu Mutian, "Rain Thread"). The juxtaposition of semantic groups:

> I dreamed of wandering into the remote valley last night, /I heard the cuckoo crying blood in the lily bushes, / I dreamed of climbing to the mountain peak last night, /I saw a drop of tear of light falling from the sky. (Xu Zhimo, "Condolences on Mansfield")

The juxtaposition of paragraphs, for example, Xu Zhimo's "No. 7 Shihu Hutong" consists of four sections. Each section begins with "My little garden, sometimes ..." Another poem "I don't know which direction the wind is blowing" has a total of six paragraphs, with four sentences in each paragraph. The first three sentences are the same: "I don't know which direction the wind / is blowing—/ I am in a dream." Among the five paragraphs in Dai Wangshu's "Don't Be So Love-sick," there are three paragraphs repeated, "Don't be so love-sick / hang down your sad head."

In the grammatical history of Chinese poetry, the relationship between "Discernment" and "Forgetting" developed into a spiral cycle. If we say Chinese classical poetry takes "Forgetting" as the highest ideal and uses it to block the development of "Discernment," then Chinese modern new poetry enters a complex era of the contradiction between "Discernment" and "Forgetting." Moreover, "Discernment" has restricted the development of "Forgetting"—a new feature pursued by modern poetry grammar.

Harmony and Dissonance: Metrical Features of Modern Chinese New Poetry

> The fine melody of classical poems, *Cis* and *Qus*
> Could be easily understood and adopted by us;
> —Zhu Ziqing, "Preface to *The Winter Night*"

Metrics are the internal life and the external symbol of poetry. Among the textual structures of all literary varieties, it seems only poetry is so deeply embedded in the rhythmic factors. If there is no rhythm, there is no poetry. This is true both in the past and the present, domestically and internationally, in rhythm or free style.

At the same time, metrics and rhythms are directly connected with the attributes of the language of specific countries. Different languages produce poems with different rhythms. Different nationalities have their own irreplaceable rules of poetry. According to Madame de Staël, a French-Swiss woman of letters and historian during the French Revolution, learning a language of poetics is more in-depth into the spiritual world of the country than learning anything else, because it belongs to the finest category of national character beyond language descriptions.[15]

Harmony and Dissonance

The metrical issues of poetry generally include rhythm, rhyme, and tones. We will naturally divide modern Chinese new poetry into two parts from the phonological perspective—rhymed verses and free verses. This new poetry of the metrical style continued from the May Fourth Movement to the 1940s. Lu Zhiwei, Wen Yiduo, Sun Dayu, Lin Geng, Feng Zhi, Yan Zhilin, and He Qifang contributed through their theoretical research or practice and achieved remarkable results. Among them, the greatest contributor is the Crescent Moon School represented by Wen Yiduo, Xu Zhimo, Zhu Xiang, and others. The metrical-style poets have a deep understanding of the rhythms, rhymes, and tones of Chinese, and applied them to their practice. These new metrical verses are devoted to the balance of rhythm, the regularity of rhymes, and the harmony of tones. The new poetry of free style shows more randomness and freedom in the processing of rhythm, rhymes, and tones. Generally speaking, the regularity of rhythm, rhymes, and the harmony of tones are not the criteria it must follow. From the violent *The Goddesses* of the May Fourth Era to the Modernists who surpassed the Crescent Moon School, and the writing of most poets in the 1940s, we can see free-style poetry is often full of pioneering spirits, consistent with the pace of development of the times. And free-style poetry seems to ignore the metrics pursuit of classical poetry.

However, it is insufficient to discuss the rhythms of modern Chinese poetry only through the distinction between metrical style and free style. A Chinese poet who grew up under the nurturing of Chinese culture could be said to be innate to the rules of the Chinese language. The charm of Chinese rhythm has undoubtedly become part of his unconscious feeling. This could not be explained by rational consciousness. For modern Chinese poets, the understanding and application of metrical rules are complex. We cannot claim that metrical-style poets knew the rules and free-style poets did not. Metrical-style poets did not refuse to write free-style poems. For example, Wen Yiduo wrote many free-style pieces in the collection of *Red Candle*. Zhu Xiang also wrote free-style poems, such as "Late Plowing," "Spring," and "Early Spring Rain in the North" in his poem collection, *Summer*. Free-style poets also wrote works that scrutinize rhythms, such as some works by Dai Wangshu during the early and late stages of his writing career. Even Guo Moruo, a poet who pursued extreme free style, also wrote metrical-style poems, such as "Seduction of Death," "Venus," "The Street on the Sky" and so on.[16] There are some crucial questions here. Does free-style poetry no longer need rhythm? Is it completely free? Is there no rhythm rule? The answer is obviously "no" as the development of poetry history shows. Although free-style poetry does not have a fixed rhythm, it does pay attention to tempo and rhythm, only with different and varied rhythms. Rhythm is precisely one of the most essential stylistic features of poetry, an important mark that distinguishes it from prose. Therefore, for many modern poets, it is not difficult to find metrics a factor that must be considered in poem writing. The boundary between metrics and freedom is obscure. Feng Zhi, Bian Zhilin, He Qifang, Lin Geng, and others should all be classified as free-style poets, if we try to classify them by their schools. However, what is interesting is they explored some important aspects of the rhythm of modern new poetry in theory or practice. Ai Qing, Zang Kejia, and other free-style poets during the 1930s and 1940s also attach such great importance to rhythm and rhyme that some critics describe their poems as using a "semi-free style."[17]

So, how do we understand this kind of convergence and differences in the metrical pursuit of modern Chinese poetry?

I believe since the rhythmic laws of Chinese culture have been widely submerged in the hearts of Chinese poets and have become part of their collective unconsciousness, their understanding of the metrics of poetry cannot be a simple question of choice. The differences should be based on different understandings of the poetry metrics development, which have different levels of connections with the characteristics of Chinese metrics. Rhythm rules form a rich, cultural tradition as a collective unconsciousness in the long history of Chinese poetry. Therefore, modern Chinese poets' awareness of Chinese metrics and the varied ideas of rhythm development, are inevitably related to certain historical and cultural prototypes.

Reviewing the metrical history of Chinese poetry and analyzing the metrical awareness of Chinese classical poetry provide a window to a better understanding of the metrical pursuit of Chinese new poetry.

For Chinese classical poetry, the rhythm and meter are not issues of whether they are needed, but how to use and develop them. This involves the unique metrical awareness of Chinese classical poets, which involves the musical concepts of Chinese traditional culture. There are two pursuits of classical metrics that deserve our attention: "Harmony" and "Dissonance."

"Harmony" is the ultimate rhythm pursuit of Chinese classical poetry. It is rooted in the musical ideal of "eight-tone harmony" in China. According to *Shangshu*, "Poetry is used to express our thoughts, songs are the words being sung, tones are designed based on the sounds, and metrics are used to harmonize these sounds. When the eight tones harmonize, there is nothing that can compete." Harmony is based on the study of Chinese language vocabulary and coordination of the rise and fall of tones, making them fit properly, unrestrained, and pleasant. According to Shen Yue,

Different colors could be made harmonious. Different musical instruments could be made harmonious. Black is used to define the general color and tuner is used to define the tone. Every element should be placed properly. Different sounds should be varied, and high and low-pitch sounds should be balanced and checked. If there is an unstressed sound earlier, then there some stressed sounds should follow. Within one line of the five-character poems, the metrics should be different. For two lines, the stressed and unstressed sounds should vary. Only after one easily reaches such a level can one begin to write. (Shen Yue, *Book of Song Dynasty*)

Generally speaking, the development of Chinese classical poetry before maturity is a constantly moving process toward metrical harmonization. Before the Eastern Han Dynasty, Chinese poetry was closely related to music. The *Book of Songs* is a collection of poems (songs) of harmonious music. The *Yuefu* poems are songs of harmonious music. The five- or seven-character poems by the literati after the Eastern Han Dynasty grew independent from music and urged poets to search for harmony in the language itself. This exploration began with its foundation during the Qi Liang periods and reached its peak by the Tang Dynasty. Chinese classical poetry of the eight-tone concert is called metrical poetry. In terms of the tone, rhyme, and rhythm of the language, modern metrical verses were cultivated and scrutinized in many aspects. These constituted the main connotation of the metrical tradition of Chinese classical poetry: the *Ping* (flat or level) and *Ze* (fall or downward) sounds of the poems must balance with each other (usually two-flat sounds followed by two fall sounds), the upper and lower lines have opposite tones, the tones of the two stanzas are connected and go spiral, creating a melody that echoes back and forth, high and low fluctuations that are neatly-cut and stable. A large number of rhyming rules are applied. There is one rhyme at the end and no similar rhyme is allowed. There are also rules for specific rhymes and rhymes in even numbers of lines. "As a result, the syllables with the same phonemes are always present at the joint points of the network, which can create an aesthetically pleasing tone effect."[18]

Sentence rhythm is achieved through the "pauses" between phonemic groups. A phonemic group is composed of Chinese characters, forming a one-character group, two-character group, and three-character group, etc. And, the number of pauses and the structure of the poems are consistent. A five-character poem would be a combination of a two-character group and a three-character group, which is △△-△△△ (alternatively, △△-△△-△), and the seven-character poem would be two two-character groups plus a three-character group: △△-△△-△△△ (alternatively, △△-△△-△△-△).

Because there is one sound for one Chinese character, the pauses would be regular with the same number of characters. After metrical poetry, there are *Ci*s and *Qu*s, which broke through the constraints of the same number of characters for one line. This created a combination of flexible and changeable long and short lines. However, because *Ci* and *Qu* are the lyrics that accompany the music, they matched metrical poetry in terms of metrical rules. The rhythm tradition of metrical verses had a great influence on *Ci*s which went a step further and established a series of stricter rules to maintain metrical harmony in the varied sentences. *Ci and Qu*s accept the tone flow rule of metrical verses that the flat and fall tones would contrast each other. They divided the flat and fall tones into more subcategories.

Besides requirements about the flat-fall tone rule, *Ci*s also has requirements about four tones. *Qu*s also distinguish between the flat and fall tones and have particularly strict requirements for the last sentence and the last rhyme character. The rhyming of *Ci and Qu* is also determined by their respective "tonality" (kinds of *Ci* and *Qu* genres). Whether rhymes can be changed, the positions of rhythm, whether they can be rhymed through, etc. are all based on this. "Tonality" also largely determines the structure of phonemic groups and the rhythm pattern of the internal sentences, which could be stricter than metrical poetry. In Chinese classical poetry, the rigor of the rhythm rules indicates the difficulty of phonological considerations. Indeed, it is a great challenge for all generations of literati to eliminate the differences and conflicts in sounds so they can cooperate without gaps and obstruction. They could be expressed smoothly and properly, creating the rhythm for the "artistic conception" of Chinese poetry!

At the same time, as explained in previous sections, the artistic conception of the poetry of the Tang Dynasty and *Ci* of the Song Dynasty does not fully represent the aesthetic propensity of Chinese poetry. Along the way of the "conscious" path, there had been the voice of freedom and a call for antitradition with the trend turning to folklore. This trend is reflected in the literary pursuit of poetry, which is the inclusion of "Clear Discernment" in "Forgetting the Language." When this is reflected in the metrical pursuit of the poetry, it is the inclusion of "Dissonance" within "Harmony."

What is "Dissonance (*Ao Qiao*)"? As the name implies, it could not be pronounced easily and thus sounded awkward. To be honest, both the evolution of the objective world and the movement of subjective thinking have their complexities. The artistic conception of the unity of heaven and mankind, and the seamless rhythm are just human beings' imagination. The harmony of man-made sounds, regardless of how close it is to nature, is only a partition of human's free thoughts. Only human intrusion was reduced to the minimum. That is to say, in terms of tracking free thoughts—the essence of poetry—it is completely normal the rhythm deviates from the level of mellow smoothness to some extent. And, this kind of deviation probably made it possible for new metrical rules to become acceptable, which promote the metrical development of poetry along with its self-denial. From time to time, Chinese classical poetry would go against the norm of Harmony and convey some unharmonious feelings, "some dissonance between man and nature" or a signal of innovation. "*Qiao*" means sturdy and powerful. Although such metrical pursuits are neither coherent nor thorough, their existence, showed the possibility that Chinese poets use Chinese to make multi-directional choices in metrical art. According to the Harmony standard of metrical poetry, the sounds of dissonance can be heard everywhere in the history of Chinese poetry before the Tang Dynasty. Shen Yue distinguished the four tones and analyzed eight defects. This showed that Chinese poetry did not distinguish the four tones before its maturity. Therefore, the eight defects identified by She Yue were prevalent due to a laissez-faire attitude. What is important is after the rules for writing the poems dissipated, many Chinese poets still had a strong interest in the rhyme of Dissonance. They imitated the styles of ancient poetry and went against the rhythms required by metrical poetry, creating disharmonious sentences that violated flat-fall tone rules. The poets did not follow the rules of consistency and balance but tried to be crude and avoid any refinement. During the Tang Dynasty, great poets, such as Li Bai, Du Fu, Li Shangyin, Han Yu, and others, all produced such works. During the Song Dynasty, such metrical pursuits received full attention, especially through the practice of the Jiangxi Poetry School represented by Huang Tingjian. Naturally, with dissonance, you must try to "remedy" it by adjusting other language resources. However, in my opinion, such "salvation" is based on a conscious "Dissonance" first. It is impossible to remove its original intention of going against the rules to seek innovation just because it should be "remedied."

The historical continuity of Chinese phonetic features is a bridge between past and modern Chinese poetry. It is through this bridge the poetic concepts of Chinese classical poetry and the philosophical thought behind it flowed to modern poetry. Harmony and Dissonance can be said to be the genes of all modern Chinese poetry rhythm art, regardless of which genre they belong to.

These two artistic trends affected Chinese new poetry to a different extent and scope. Generally speaking, this difference mainly depends upon the following two facts. First, the two philosophical thoughts behind Harmony and Dissonance are, respectively, the harmony between humans and heaven, and the spirit of freedom, which had different positions in Chinese modern poetry. Second, as an aesthetic summary of rhythm, Harmony and Dissonance are specifically expressed in practical skills, such as rhythm, rhymes, and tones, which had different effects in modern Chinese and had differences in terms of accepting the foreign language influence. Recipients have different priorities in terms of their needs. Ever since, when we combine different rhythms, rhymes, and tones of quality and quantity from different philosophical consciousness to become "concordant" or "disharmonious," we leave prints of different degrees and different ranges in the history of poetry.

Harmony Pursuit of Modern Chinese New Poetry

From the perspective of modern Chinese poetry's overall development, the traditional rhythm of Harmony has a profound influence. Traditional harmony between humans and heaven is still appealing to Chinese poets. Harmony requirements of rhythm, rhyming, and tones also gained more recognition.

In the harmony pursuit of Chinese classical poetry, rhythm, rhymes, and tones play different roles, with rhythm in the central position. From the *Book of Songs* and *Chu Ci* to ancient poems and metrical verses, the tone of phrases and characters, and the rhythm of sentences vary, but the trend for maintaining harmony of rhythm (syllable) is consistent.

The flat-fall tone rule is not required for ancient Chinese poetry, which has free rhyme and regular pauses. Generally, there are two-flat and two fall tones for the four-character poems, two-flat tones followed by three fall tones for five-character poems, and four-flat tones and three fall tones for seven-character poems. Strict rules for the neat structure of metrical poetry are the epitome of the rhythm art development in Chinese poetry. The sentences of *Ci* vary in length, which seems to make it very difficult to achieve neatness between sentences. This is not the case, however. Although a *Ci* can cover a variety of sentence patterns from one character to 11 characters, the rhythm formed may be very different. Yet, the typical form of *Ci* (the symmetrical structure of the upper and lower pieces) provides a new means for the symmetry of sounds. Here, each sentence with a nonmetrical style has the same tone structure, but there is a consistency in the number of sounds between the two sentences corresponding to the upper part. So, among the free movement of the surface text, a special inner correspondence and unity are achieved. *It can be said that through close study, acculturation, and popularization of Chinese classical poetry, the rhythm of sounds penetrated the hearts of all Chinese language speakers, becoming a kind of unconscious expectation of language and an important melody aesthetic need for Chinese poets.*

For many modern Chinese poets, the restraints of classical poetry as a form of metrics mainly refer to its rigid flat and fall patterns and rhyming, rather than its regular inner rhythm (syllables)—the latter seemed considered as the stylistic features inherent in poetry, a "self-evident truth" under the collision of Chinese and Western poetic concepts. The earliest vernacular poetry experimenter, Hu Shih, attacked the flat and fall patterns and rhyming of traditional poetry and advocated for the liberation of poetry, but he still regarded the beautiful harmony of the syllables as necessary formal features of new poetry. In *On New Poetry*, Hu Shih used a special section to discuss the syllable problem of new poems. He argued that the syllable rhythm relied on "two important elements: one is the natural rhythm of tones, the other is the natural harmony of the characters in each sentence . . . . The internal structure of words and phrases should be studied before they can be harmonious like natural syllables."[19] Of course, Hu Shih's so-called syllables are a more general concept, including tones (*Ping*—flat tone patterns in Chinese or *Ze*, fall tone patterns in Chinese), rhymes, etc. Yet, how can the natural syllables of the new poems be made harmonious? Hu Shih did not elaborate and the poem syllables listed in his texts are not so harmonious. But, as a pioneer, he did raise the issue of syllables, which shows an important message—modern Chinese poets do not reject the ideal of rhythm and harmony in their antitradition movements. Many early vernacular poets held similar ideas though without much specific discussion. Yu Pingbo believed the new poetry's "syllables should be harmonious, and those who make vernacular poems do not have to study all the traditional metrics, but should have some knowledge on the changes of tones and rhyming."[20] Zhu Zhixin also held similar opinions, "It is very dangerous that many people who write new poems don't understand the flat and fall tone rules of new poems. This might lead to the bankruptcy of poetry."[21] Lu Zhiwei is the first to have a conscious, clear understanding of the harmonious meaning of rhythm in modern poetry. He broke the routine of using the flat and fall tone rhythm by borrowing the iambic rules in Western poetry. For the first time, Lu Zhiwei identified the rhythm of modern new poetry as the stress and length of the sounds and distinguished the difference between "natural spoken rhythm" and "rhythm" (for Hu Shih, the so-called "natural harmony" of sounds is a rather ambiguous formulation, reflecting awkwardness of the generation who falls between the traditional and anti-traditional). He clearly stated, "Only natural sounds with rhythms could be called poems."[22] The inspiration Lu Zhiwei acquired from the rhythm of Western poetry is consistent with rhythm operations of Chinese classical poetry, often ignored by the early vernacular poets so that the tones of the word (*Ping*—flat tone patterns or *Ze*, fall tone patterns) are often mixed with the pauses (syllables).

The Crescent Moon School, which continued to develop along the direction of Lu Zhiwei, clearly became more aware of the relationships between rhythm and harmony ideals in classical poetry. Wen Yiduo never concealed his opinion of the relationship between rhythm and Chinese poetry. He praised "a metrical poem is a tool for lyricism, which should be related to the accurate diction choices. Thus, no redundant words nor no lengthy expressions should be allowed. The rhythmic patterns would make the meanings richer."[23] The Crescent poets paid special attention to the syllables of poetry. For instance, Wen Yiduo thought the most important "form of poetry is syllables."[24] Xu Zhimo said, "The life of poetry is in its inner syllables." He proposed the most important for poem writing should be centered on syllables.[25] Rao Mengkan, Zhu Xiang, and others held similar arguments. Wen Yiduo made great efforts in promoting the perfection of the new poetry syllables. He believed the perfect center of syllables is artificial participation, tempering, and retouching. "The so-called "natural syllables" is at best the syllables of prose . . . which are not, of course, as perfect as the syllables of poetry." He specifically summarized on the technical level that the means of harmony (sounding scale, that is, pauses) should be made possible when the total number of syllables for each line is equal, and the number of words of the syllable consistent.[26] Wen Yiduo's music beauty and architectural beauty of his so-called "Three Beauties" are associated with the harmony of syllables. Some of the popular works of the Crescent Moon School poets have such rhythm patterns, such as Wen Yiduo's "Dead Water." It has four pauses per sentence, each sentence with three two-character clusters and one three-character cluster in original Chinese:

Zhe shi—yi gou-jue wang de—si hui,
Qing feng—chui bu qi—ban dian—yilun.
(This is—a ditch—desperate—stagnant water,
Breeze—cannot bring—even the smallest—ripples.)

Another example is Zhu Xiang's "Bury Me," which pauses three times for each sentence and each sentence is a combination of one three-character cluster and two two-character clusters:

Zang wo zai—he hua—chi nei,
Er, bian you—shui yin—tuo sheng,
(Bury me—in the—lotus pond,
Water earthworms—are singing—along the ears,)

Another example is Sun Dayu's "A Reed Flute," which paused four times for each sentence. Each sentence has two three-character clusters and two two-character clusters:

Zi cong—wo you le—zhe yi zhi—zhu di,
Zong shi—zuo shou zhe—huang hun—kan tian ming.
(Since—I have—this—reed flute,
Always—sitting and waiting—in twilight—to see the coming of the dawn.)

However, strictly speaking, the requirement of a total equal number of sounds in each sentence and a completely consistent number of words in each group are strict and nearly demanding. Compared with ancient Chinese, the meaning of modern Chinese is complicated, and the two-tone, three-tone, and four-tone phrases increase sharply. It is difficult to use modern vocabulary to express the complex emotions of modern people and to completely follow the syllable rules of classical poetry. Xu Zhimo said, "Because of the increase of polysyllabic words in modern Chinese, it is often necessary to have several sounds to represent one image or concept, which makes it difficult for Chinese modern poetry to have equal numbers of sounds per line."[27] Thus, in the works of Xu Zhimo and others, the harmony of syllables is built from time to time in another variation, a flexible adaptation of the uniqueness of modern Chinese. Its national culture prototype could be traced to the syllable processing of words. There are several such "alternatives" generally.

1. In terms of the internal composition of the sound groups, due to the lengthening of modern Chinese words and the faster recital flow, classical poetry grouped in one-character clusters, and two-character clusters are excessively fragmented (the three-character cluster of classical poetry can also be considered as a one-character cluster combined with a two-character cluster). So, it is necessary to expand the composition of the number of characters within one cluster. Within one sentence, it is possible to use four or five characters and even six characters as one cluster, forming a four-character cluster, a five-character cluster, and a six-character cluster. For example, *"feng ding—yu fei—mei"* (wind stopped-rain fattening-plums), *"jiang jian—bo lang—jian tian—yong"* (within river-waves-surge to sky)—all are one-character clusters or

two-character clusters in the classical poetry. In modern new poetry, there is "*men wai—zuo zhe—yi ge—chuan po yi shang de—lao nian ren*" (outside the door-seated-one-wearing torn clothes-old man); "*ruo huo lun—fei xuan yu—sha qiu zhi shang*" (as if the steamer-flying on the dunes). More three-character, four-character, and five-character clusters are used as well. When discussing this change in On New Poetry in 1919, Hu Shih called the sound groups "sections": "There are many more multi-phonetic words in the vernacular than classical Chinese, not limited to two-character clusters. So there are often three-character clusters or four- or five-character clusters for one section."

2. The relationship between neat sounds and sentences is also "adjusted." Under the premise of keeping the sentences of the whole poem sounds regular, a few sentences are allowed to change slightly. For example, Xu Zhimo's "Saying Goodbye to Cambridge Again" is based on three-paused sentences, but there are also a few two pauses such as "*kang qiao—zai hui ba* (Cambridge—See you again)."

3. There are roughly equal numbers of clusters in one sentence, but the composition of each sentence is different. The one-character cluster, the two-character cluster, the three-character cluster, and even the four-character cluster are selected according to specific conditions without harming the overall sense of harmony, due to the equal number of sound groups. For example, there are three pauses in each sentence of Lin Huiyin's "I Wish," while the composition of each sentence is different. Take the first paragraph as an example. There are one four-character, one three-character, and one two-character cluster in the first sentence. "*wo qing yuan—hua cheng—yi pian luo ye* (I would rather turn into a piece fallen leaf)." There are two four-character and one one-character clusters in the second sentence. "*Rang—feng chui yu da—dao chu piao ling* (Let-wind blows rain strike-is drifting everywhere)." There are two four-character and one one-character cluster in the third sentence. "*huo—liu yun yi duo—zai deng lan tian* (or-a flowing cloud-in the blue sky)." There are one four-character, one three-character, and one two-character cluster in the fourth sentence: "*he da di—zai mei you xie—qian lian* (and no more—connections or relations—with the earth)."

4. The composition of each sentence and the composition of the sound clusters are quite different, but in the various verses (paragraphs), the sentences at the corresponding positions are consistent; thus, forming

the responses within the poem. Similar examples are found in Xu Zhimo's "By Chance," "Sea Scenery," "I Don't Know Which Direction the Wind is Blowing"; Zhu Xiang's "Lotus Flower Picking Song," "Calling The Spirits of the Dead," "The Ever Seas," "Night Song"; Sun Dayu's "The Song of the Sea"; Lin Huiyin's "Music Heard in the Middle of the Night," "Deep Smile" and so on.

5. There are differences in the number of sound clusters and the composition of sound clusters. The correspondence between paragraphs is not obvious. The harmony of syllables mainly depends on the correspondence between the internal sentences for each paragraph. This is very technical. If used skillfully, it will be a top piece. For example, three-paused sentences "*you you de—zai shui di—zhao yao* (Sways leisurely under the water)," and two-paused sentences "*ruan ni shang de—qing xing* (The floating heart growing in the sludge)," are used in Xu Zhimo's "Farewell to Cambridge," but overall it is very well-balanced. Why? Because in one paragraph with different pauses, the first two lines and the last two lines form relatively independent, complete structures with equal sums of pauses. The structure of the sound group between the first and third, and second and fourth lines are also roughly the same, such as "*ruan ni shang de—qing xing* (The floating heart growing in the sludge)" and "*zai kang qiao de—rou bo li* (In the gentle waves of Cambridge)," "*xiang qing cao geng qing chu—man su* (To where the green grass is more verdant)" and "*zai xing hui ban lan li—fang ge* (And sing aloud in the splendor of starlight)." The syllable harmony of the Crescent Moon School poetry is noticed by later Modernist poets. In some works by Dai Wangshu, He Qifang, Bian Zhilin, Lin Geng, and Fan Cao, the influence is obvious. In the case of Dai Wangshu's "A Lane in the Rain," it is obvious these flexible strategies have been comprehensively and perfectly applied. There are three pauses as well as two pauses in the entire poem and the internal structure for each syllable group is very different. There are three main ways to achieve harmony. First, the internal number of pauses within paragraphs is kept the same as possible, such as in the second and sixth paragraphs. Second, the correspondence between paragraphs is established, such as the first and seventh paragraphs (the first and last paragraphs). Third, a correspondence between the internal sentences of the paragraphs is established, such as three pauses for the first and last lines of the third and fourth paragraphs, and two pauses in the middle four lines. In the

fifth paragraph, the pauses of the lines next to each other are consistent. There are two pauses in Lines 1–2, 5–6, and three pauses in Lines 3–4. While fully respecting the laws of modern languages and satisfying the ideas of Chinese poetics, "A Lane in the Rain" is indeed a top piece that draws from tradition and provides great inspiration for other free-style poets. It is in this sense we can say this poem truly "opened a new era for the rhythm of new poetry."[28]

Although Dai Wangshu and some Modernist poets later lost interest in the harmony pursuit of rhythms and embarked on other art paths, two other Modernists, He Qifang and Bian Zhilin, worked continuously in this direction. Without too many theoretical declarations nor particular stubbornness, their series of masterpieces continued to show the beautiful chords of free-form poetry in rhythm. In a discussion on the form issues of poetry during the 1950s, He Qifang and Bian Zhilin forwarded pioneering ideas for rhythm development, a theoretical summary of their artistic practice. He Qifang realized "a very important factor that constitutes the rhythm of ancient Chinese poetry [is] every sentence has an equal number of pauses." About the situation of Chinese new poetry, He Qifang said, "The main difference between metrical poetry and free poetry is that the rhythm law of the former is strict and neat while the law of the latter is relatively free. However, free poetry should still have a relatively distinct rhythm."[29] Both He Qifang and Bian Zhilin considered orderly pauses as one of the important attributes of modern metrical poetry, and both repeatedly emphasized poetry must conform to the rules of modern spoken language and differentiated the orderly pauses within lines from the equal number of characters within each line. Bian Zhilin also divided pauses into two types: the two-character (cluster) and the three-character (cluster). He emphasizes there should be variations between the lines, and the two-character (cluster) should correspond to the three-character (cluster). Different from the Crescent Moon School poetry, they found a better way to reconcile modern vocabulary with traditional art ideals.

Due to the continual efforts of poets, such as Wen Yiduo, Xu Zhimo, Dai Wangshu, He Qifang, and Bian Zhilin, Chinese modern new poetry has a very valuable rhythm art experience. With the development of the poetry movement and culture exchanges, all these artistic experiences have naturally become shared feelings for all Chinese poets and have become the unconsciousness of Chinese modern poetry culture. Therefore, even in those rather free verses, we can feel their harmony in rhythms from time to time. For example:

TRADITIONAL CULTURE AND TEXT STRUCTURES 163

Wo men yao ting—xu xu du lai de—yuan si de—zhong sheng
Wo men yao ting—mao wu ding shang tu zhe—yi lü yi lü de—yan si

We listen to—slow rippling sounds—of the bells—from the temple afar
We listen to—the flow of—smoke rings—out of the thatched roofs   four pauses

—Mu Mutian, "After the Rain"

Wu ya—lai le,
Chang—hei se zhi ge;

A crow—came,
Sang—a black song;   two pauses

—Lu Yishi, "Crow"

Cong yuan gu de—mu ying
Cong hei an de—nian dai
From ancient—tombs
From the dark—ages   two pauses

Cong ren lei—si wang zhi liu de—na bian
Zhen jing—chen shui de—shan mai
Ruo huo lun—fei xuan yu—sha qiu zhi shang
Tai yang—xiang wo—gun lai . . .

From the side of—the human—death stream
Shocked—the sleeping—mountains
As if the burning wheels—spin on—the sand dunes,   three pauses
The sun—coming to me—rolling . . .

—Ai Qing, "The Sun"

He liu
Yi tiao tiao
Zong heng zai—di mian
Jie xiang
Yi dao dao
Jiao cuo you—lian mian

Rivers   one pause

One after another
Vertical and horizontal—on the ground
Lanes,
One after another
Interlaced and—continued   two pauses

—Chen Jingrong, "A Group Portrait"

In addition to rhythm harmony, traditional rhyming techniques also contributed to the harmony of modern Chinese poetry. To put it simply, the rhyming of Chinese classical poetry can be said to be a deliberate arrangement of rule adherence. Although the *Book of Songs and the ancient poems before the Tang Dynasty rhyme, they are free to change, with no restriction of rules. Therefore, even if people have* summarized several models, they cannot say they are "following rules." Harmony rhyming begins with metrical-style verses, which require the rhymes to fall on flat tones. Generally, the rhymes fall on the last character of an even number line and to the end. They cannot be replaced in the middle. The rhyming of *Ci* and *Qu* seems to be flexible, but it is determined by its strict tonality. The change is just a requirement of the inherent rules. *Ci* and *Qu* are other typical forms of Chinese poetry concordance harmony.

Modern poets have different opinions about the relationships between rhymes and new poetry styles, especially during the May Fourth era, when people tried to break away from tradition, the importance of rhymes had been more generally challenged, and it was even once regarded as a chain that must be broken. However, on the whole, regular rhymes still exist in the tolerant mood of modern people. They have far-reaching influence in practice. The frequent call for metrical style strengthens its influence. I have made a preliminary statistic on several representative collections of important poems. With the "there are rules to follow" rhyming method as the standard, 65.5% of the poems are found to fit the standard in the first collection of new poems, *Classified Vernacular Poetry*. This number is 58.8% in the *Creation Society Books and Poetry Volumes* (edited by Huang Houxing), 85.4% in the *Crescent Moon School Poetry Selections* (edited by Lan Lizhi), 37.8% in the *Poetry of the Symbolist School* (edited by Sun Yushi), 27.2% in the *Modern Poetry Selections* (edited by Lan Lizhi), about 50% in the *Nine Leaves Collection*, about 10% in the *Poetry of July School* (edited by Zhou Liangpei). Naturally, such statistics are quite crude, ignoring the works of poets from other genres, but it shows two important facts at least: (1) "There are rules to follow" rhyming affects the entire Chinese modern poetry. (2) This idea is quite influential, with an average of nearly 50% fitting the standard (poems repeated in different collections are counted only once).

In such rhyme pursuit, a small part adopts one rhyme from the beginning to the end. Despite the low percentage of these poems (e.g., only about 10% in the *Crescent Moon School Poetry Selections*), it is particularly eye-catching, because the same texture of the sounds appears in the gap between the sentences, which inevitably forms a kind of neat artistic effect, which, according to Wen Yiduo, is undoubtedly directly influenced by metrical poems. In the following poem, although the old rules of flat rhyme and even rhyme (the natural requirement of modern spoken language) are abandoned, we see it grasped the core of metrical poetry (the last character in each line rhyming in the original):

> There is a phrase that is a curse,
> There is a phrase that can catch fire.
> Although not explicit for five thousand years,
> Can you guess the silence of the volcano?
> Maybe suddenly the mind is changed,
> Suddenly a blue bolt in the sky
> Boom:
> "Our China!"
>
> —Wen Yiduo, "A Phrase"

The regular rhyme change of *Ci* and *Qu* had a greater influence on modern new poetry. Of course, this rule will no longer be the "tonality" of *Ci* and *Qu*, but a series of new rules based on the basic linguistic features of modern poetry, such as rhyme in each odd or even line or a new rhyme for each stanza. On this basis, some uncommon rhymes, such as cross rhyme, overlapping rhyme, and interline rhyme (rhyme in the middle) are discovered or introduced. The cross rhyme is abab, and the overlapping rhyme is abba. The cross rhyme appeared in China's *Book of Songs* and *Flower Collection*. The rhyme of "Ding Feng Bo" (a well-known *Ci* by a famous Chinese poet, Su Shi) also contains a structure with almost abba rhyming. But they are still no typical forms of China's national poetry in the history of classical poetry. On the contrary, these two rhymes are frequently seen in Western poetry. The use of this rhyming style by Chinese modern new poetry probably is an adaptation from Western poetry. Naturally, after they become familiar, it is also an innovation to look back at their atypical rhythmic traditions. This is the case with Bian Zhilin. Rao Mengqi's "Hawking" is an example of the cross-rhythm of Chinese modern poetry, "I want to sell this soul, / with a selling sign put on the chest; / shouting from early morning to dusk, / to the ends of the street." "The Song of the Iron Horse" by Chen Mengjia is another example: "No worries, / no joy; / I am always old, / always fresh." Zhu Xiang's "Xiaochao Qu" is an example of interline rhyme: "Two torches in front of the palace gate red, / break through the darkness against the wall of the palace, the golden sparkles run over the Chinese Monuments, and over the wall wave the cypress and the pine trees." Sun Dayu's "Soul Calling" is a five-line poem, basically following the interline rhyme: "No, didn't go? I saw you / in the water along the wind / in the faint morning sun, / vehicles across the clouds, / appear and disappear without a trace." The rhyme in the line usually refers to the pause within the line and rhyme at the end of the line (rhyme in the middle), generally related to the crossline of poems, such as "the heart is swirling, a few words / you have said, like a dove flying" (Lin Huiyin, "Recall"). "We often gazing on the wall / at the morning glory seems to send a traveler's expectations / to a narrow oasis" (Zheng Min, "Poets and Children").

Modern Chinese poetry also fully borrows the rhyme of Western sonnets to build a harmony that conforms to modern language habits. The sonnet was originally folk poetry in the Provence region along the borders of Italy and France. Used by Petrarch, Dante, Spencer, and Shakespeare, among others, it occupied the most prominent position in European lyrics. Sonnets are generally divided into the first eight lines and the last six lines. The rhythm change has a variety of styles, such as the standard Petrarch style, that is abba, abba, cde, cde; the standard Shakespeare style, that is, abab, cdcd, efef, gg. It seems flexible and comfortable in the key poetry line connection, which adapts to the freedom of modern spoken language and meets the traditional psychology of Chinese poets seeking alignment and order. Therefore, to a large extent, the sonnet has become a bridge for modern Chinese poets to return to tradition through a Western style. The sonnet reminds Chinese poets of China's classical poetry tradition and a sense of intimacy. Wen Yiduo, the first person to translate sonnets into Chinese (*shang-le*), said, "The so-called metrical poems are similar to the sonnet of English poetry. It is neither too long nor too short."[30] Bian Zhilin said, "The sonnet is still vigorous in the West today. I think the seven-character metrical poetry of our country can also be used freely."[31] Tang Shi also said, "The sonnet is similar to Chinese metrical poems in terms of its regular length, the changing rhythms, and the rich colors."[32] Some theorists analyzed,

> In the 1920s, when the sonnet was imported into China, many other European metrical poems, such as the triolet, the Roundel, the ballad, the rondel, etc. were imported as well. But these styles faded quickly and did not last like the sonnet in poetry history. We believe the reason is the match between the sonnet and traditional Chinese poetry in terms of aesthetic consciousness, formal law, and rhythm.[33]

It is necessary to note the sonnets in China not only could be found in the history of new poetry but widely affected the poem writing of many, including the early vernacular poets, Zheng Boqi and Pu Xuefeng, as well as the mature period of Feng Zhi in the maturity period. Wen Yiduo, Sun Dayu, Xu Zhimo, and Zhu Xiang of the Metrical School; Li Jinfa, Mu Mutian, and Tu An who were "Liberals"; Dai Wangshu, Bian Zhilin, and He Qifang who consciously inherited traditional poetry, and Nine-Leaf poets, Mu Dan, Zheng Min, Tang Qi, Chen Jingrong, and Hang Yuehe who consciously transcended the tradition. All of these poets were affected by the sonnet style. From this, we argue regular rhymes are representative of the psychological needs of modern Chinese poets. From another aspect, sonnets express the modern vitality of the traditional Chinese rhythm harmony.

For the flat-or-fall word choice tradition of poetry, modern Chinese poets also held their own opinions. Hu Shih, Yu Pingbo, Bian Zhilin, Feng Wenbing, and others argued against "the stipulation of flat-or-fall tones." More poets did not make it clear but supported this opinion. Feng Wenbing asserted, "The musicality of the new poetry is limited in its nature."[34] The so-called "nature of the new poetry" is probably the nature of the speech determined by the vernacular of the new poetry, and the meaning of the four tones declined. Bian Zhilin also offered a more detailed analysis of this, "until now, I just think the flat-or-fall tone issue is not as important in our spoken language as it is in classical Chinese."[35]

> For example, the title of the four-character Chinese translation by the author of *Shunxi Jihua* (*Moment in Peking*, originally written in English by Lin Yutang) is pleasant to the ears as well as easy to speak. When changed into *Jinghua Yanyun*, it is not so smooth. This is because the former is fall-fall/ flat-flat in tone, and the latter is flat-flat / flat-flat in tone. On the one hand, if we change it into our vernacular, modern spoken language, both *Jinghua De Shunxi* and *Jinghua De Yanyun* are pleasing to the ear. As seen in our vernacular or oral statements, the flat or fall tone issue is not so significant.[36]

On the other hand, there is also Rao Mengkan, Zhu Xiang, Liang Zongxi, Zhu Guangqian, and other people who claimed clearly that new poetry should not abandon the flat-or-fall tones. Rao Mengkan took Zhu Xiang's "Lotus Picking Song" as an example. He showed flat-fall tones are characteristic of Chinese characters. The rhythms of Chinese characters are completely determined by them. Abandoning flat-fall tones means abandoning rhythm and rhyme.[37] Zhu Xiang believed "flat or fall tones is a precious heritage of all new poetry."[38] The disagreement of opinions again shows the dual choices of modern Chinese poets in moving toward modernity and inheriting traditions.

However, as I have repeatedly stated in the previous section, in modern China, the distance between these two choices is not as wide as we imagined and the differences in some superficial conclusions do not hinder the communication of deep consciousness. Differences in certain issues do not affect their acceptance of universally recognized theories. Moreover, the theoretical difference is one thing, and practical identification is another. For example, aside from their discussions of the sensitive old terminology of flat-fall tones, we can still find several important common trends—those who advocate the inheritance of the tradition do not emphasize the strict, rigid relationship between sentences. They gained a consensus on the basic nature of modern vernacular spoken language. Almost all those who enter modern times agree the combination of unstressed and stressed sounds constitutes the smallest pauses in their theory of modern metrics. The unstressed and stressed sounds problem corresponds to the question of the flat-fall tones of classical poetry. Concerning the basic characteristics of the Chinese language, they gained a consensus—modern Chinese poets do not lack a common language in the way of modernity and traditional inheritance.

Therefore, in actual writing, the choice of different flat-fall tones for the unstressed and stressed collocation of Chinese characters is still quite influential in the history of modern Chinese new poetry. For example, in Bian Zhilin's "The Letters," we use "—" for unstressed sounds (flat tone) and " | " for stressed sounds (fall tone):

> *Lü yi ren shu nian de an men ling*
> | ——— | — | ——
> (The postman is pressing the doorbell like an old friend.)
> *Jiu an zai yong hu de xin shang*
> | | | | | —— |
> (Right on the heart of the owner of the residence.)
> *Shi you guo huang hai lai de yu?*
> | — | — | ——
> (Is it a fish from the Yellow Sea?)
> *Shi fei guo xi bo li ya lai de yan?*
> | — | —— | | —— |
> (Is it a goose from Siberia?)

The natural randomness of modern spoken language undoubtedly broke through the taboos of classical poetry, but modern poetry also has its tone changes. Within one sentence, it is still varied with stressed and unstressed tones, creating a rhythm. The closing characters of the two neighboring lines would also intentionally or unintentionally oppose each other. "If there is a flat tone, then there is a fall tone afterward" (Shen Yue). In the verses by Feng Wenbing (Fei Ming), a flow of stressed and unstressed sounds is naturally formed, such as the following several lines in "A Letter to Zhilin":

wo xiang xie yi shou shi,
| | | | — | —
(I would write a poem,)
you ru ri, you ru yue,
— | | — | |
(Like the sun, like the moon.)
you ru wu yin,
— | | —
(Like the shadows at noon,)
you ru wu bian luo mu xiao xiao xia
— | — — | | — — |
(Like the endless trees blowing in the wind.)
wo de shi qing mei you liang ge ye zi
| — — — — | | | —
(My poem did not have two leaves.)

In the history of modern Chinese new poetry, the rise of recital poetry and its influence are important. Their appearance is related to social needs before and after the War of Resistance against Japanese Aggression, but also the inheritance and utilization of the Chinese poetry tradition. The prerequisite for the success of recital poems is to fully mobilize the audience's (reader's) hearing and resonate with it. It contains a series of exquisite digs into the poetry heritage of the Chinese language by modern poets. This is the case in rhythm and rhyming. I think its combination of different tones is also worthy of study, such as Gao Lan's "Natural Gas Fire of Artesian Well": *"zai yuan gu / zai zu guo, /san bai zhang shen de di xia, /da zi ran de jian lao, /wo men yi shen cang le ruo gan sui yue!* (In ancient times, / in the motherland, / three hundred feet deep underground, / the prison of nature, / we have been hidden for years!)"

Dissonance Features of Modern Chinese New Poetry

Similarly, modern Chinese new poetry resisted classical poetry from thought to form and established its style. This historical fact showed a distinct, free spirit of dissonance. Without freedom, it could not flourish with modern society and adopt the cultural background of forging ahead. Without dissonance, modern Chinese new poetry could not match the natural flowing form of the modern spoken language nor could it be liberated from the pressure of Chinese classical poetry in the period of great prosperity and gain space for independent development. As a result, the Dissonance pursuit, often disfavored in the classical Chinese poetry tradition, was strengthened in an unprecedented way.

As far as the rhythm of poetry is concerned, Harmony requires a relatively similar number of sounds and the syllabic structure of sentences often seeks regular, contrasting arrangements in adjacent verses to achieve overall harmony. However, Dissonance broke through this uniformity—the sentences are either long or short. The number of pauses and the structure of phrases are naturally different. In the history of Chinese classical poetry, such verses do not form strong schools or independent aesthetic camps. There are also flashes now and then, providing valuable insights to today's people. For example, in the four-character and two-pause dominant *Book of Songs*, two-character, three-character, five-character, seven-character, and eight-character pauses are interspersed. There is no single law. *Chu Ci* is also known for its freedom of change in verses. Even during the Tang and Song dynasties, in all kinds of "pseudo-ancient" models, such verses are still being written, "Alas! The height, the staggering height! The road to Shu, so steep, steeper than Heaven!" (Li Bai, "Perilous Journey to the Land of Shu") "You can't play tricks in rooster fighting like those rascals and demanding the air off your nose to blow away the rainbows" (Li Bai, "In Response to Wang Shier Drinking alone in a Cold Night") "The Hu people take horses as their homes and shooting as their tradition" (Ouyang Xiu, "In Response to Wang Hefu's 'Ming Fei Qu'") "Don't you see that Ajiao, the beauty, was confined only after several days of favor and the frustrations are the same in the past as the present?" (Wang Anshi, "Ming Fei Qu"). In modern Chinese new poetry, poems that consciously break through the restrictions can be seen everywhere. Hu Shih, who advocated the harmony of rhythm, did not understand the "truth of harmony." In his "Dove" and "Mourning to Mr. Huang Keqiang," there are several disorderly two-character, three-character, four-character, and five-character pauses. The rhythm was rarely considered in a large part of Li Jinfa's poetry. Even for the Crescent Moon School, which stressed rhythm, there are also works, such as "A Golden Light Mark" (Xu Zhimo), "See You Again," "Beginning" (Chen Mengjia), "I Love the Equator" (Fang Weide), which did not follow the rhythm laws. In the free-form poetry of the 1930s and 1940s, there are even more free changes in rhythms and rhymes.

Here, I would like to mention another special kind of metrical issue in modern Chinese new poetry. That is, it could be found some poem lines have so many characters and so many pauses that exceed the needs people inherited from traditional aesthetic psychology. What is the maximum that traditional Chinese aesthetic psychology considers proper in the number of sounds? Zhu Xiang believed there should be no more than 11 characters in each line,[39]—generally four pauses. By referring to Bian Zhilin's experience, Zhu Ziqing believed the most appropriate length of a new poem is about ten characters, up to five pauses.[40] Bian Zhilin said later, "In the Chinese new poetry rhythm, it would be natural for each line to have no more than four or four pause groups."[41] Based on this, we can say modern Chinese new poetry is generally around 10 characters per line, with four pauses, and the maximum cannot exceed 11 characters and five pauses. However, in real practice, modern Chinese new poetry often goes beyond this limit. Five pauses could often be found and there are cases with more than five pauses (here, I excluded those sentences punctuated many times and referred to by some poets as prose poems, such as Xu Zhimo's "Poison," "White Flag," "Baby," etc.). For example, Guo Moruo "has a few—small—paper eagles—in the air—flying" ("Heart Light," 14 characters, 5 pauses), "infinite—Pacific—summed up—the whole body's—strength to—to push the earth down" ("A Call on the Edge of the Earth," 21 characters, 7 pauses). Li Jinfa "bleak—cold winter—is preparing—for us—more—splendid—spring" ("Disappointment," 18 characters, 7 pauses), "the more obvious—the world's—meaninglessness—and the aimless night—the crying—of the homeless" ("West Lake Side," 20 characters, 6 pauses). Mu Mutian "We—go straight—our—heart waves—slept lonely—in the obscure—arms" ("After the Rain," 18 characters, 7 pauses), "I am willing—quietly—listen to the—brush on the shore of the sands—one after another—gently—waves" ("I Wish," 24 characters, 7 pauses). Ai Qing "after you—patched up—your sons'—thorns tore—clothes—on the mountainside" ("Dayanhe—My Nanny," 22 characters, 6 pauses). Guo Xiaochuan "My—comrade's—eyes—all flashing—deep—pride" ("Grass Shoes," 15 characters, 6 pauses). Mu Dan "I want to—rush to the station—take the train—of the 1940—to—the hottest—furnace" ("Song of Roses," 23 characters, 7 pauses). Grammatically, long sentences often show the Chinese poet's "Clear Discernment" syntactic pursuit. Rhythmically, it was a kind of conscious rhythm creation of Dissonance. This is a new development in the modern Chinese new poetry of the Dissonance tradition. When a long series of continually exhausting, tense poem lines are presented, it is hard to achieve a relaxed and mellow environment of a "harmonious symphony of all sounds."

In terms of rhyme, "Harmony" requires a poet to follow the rules, while "Dissonance" is unrestrained. This is displayed in two ways in modern Chinese new poetry. First, no rhyme. Take the poems mentioned in the previous sections as examples. Rhyme-free poems are used by the Creation Society, Symbolist, Modernist, Nine Leaves, and July schools. Forty percent of the Creation Society, 60 and 2 percent of Symbolic poetry, 70 percent of Modernist poetry, and 80 percent of the July School poetry are rhyme-free poetry. This also accounts for approximately 30 percent of early vernacular new poetry (before 1919) and about 12 percent of the Crescent Moon School poetry. Through these rough statistics, we know rhyme-free poetry is also widely used in modern Chinese new poetry, especially in free-form poetry writing.

Second, the rhyme is irregular. Different from the regular rhyme, this irregular rhyme completely depends upon the writer. Sometimes, there is rhyme, sometimes not. It may rhyme, or it may not. The generation of the rhyme was purely natural. It was not deliberately arranged or the rhyming word was sporadic. For example, there are six stanzas in "The Road to the Orchard" by the Modernist poet, Ling Jun, but only the first stanza and the sixth stanza rhyme, and the remaining stanzas were freely produced. "Autumn Song" by the Symbolist poet, Peng Zi, has a total of four stanzas and 16 sentences, with only the second and the third stanzas rhyming. Some may rhyme, but this also appeared erratic, such as "Accusation" by Mu Dan. From the perspective of specific artistic techniques, these situations are not found in Chinese classical poetry. They were the creation of modern Chinese poetry, based on modern special language, but they met the requirements of Dissonance in terms of the violation of rhyme use for "consistency."

In addition, the Chinese classical poetry metrics tradition during its maturity period concluded that using the same word at the end of the sentence is not conducive to the harmony of the entire poem. True harmony must come from the cooperation of different words (different initials). Therefore, it is also a major principle of Harmony to avoid repetition of the same word. However, in Chinese classical free poems before the maturity period, the same ending words can still be found. For example, these words and sometimes even sentences in many works of the *Book of Songs* are like this. Singing in simple repetitions is precisely an important feature of early Chinese poetry. Compared with Harmony during the mature period, isn't this a kind of Dissonance? There are many repetitions of last words in the history of modern Chinese new poetry, and some repeated content words, such as *Jiangnan* by Kang Baiqing, "The red is the maple leaves, / the yellow is the sweet potato leaves, / the vast white are fallen leaves." Some repeated function words, such as "On the Dengchang City on the Lunar Night of Sept 15" by Fu Sinian, "the moonlight is shining, / the night is silent, / the sky is empty." Some repeated the end of some sentences, such as Hu Shih's "Should," Dai Wangshu's "My Memory," and Hu Feng's "To the Coward." Others repeated all sentence endings, such as Shen Yinmo's "Moonlight Night," Liu Bannong's "Car Blanket," Guo Moruo's "Good Morning," and Du Yunxie's "Thunder." To some extent, I can say this is some kind of reinforcement of the ancient tradition that was almost discarded.

As far as the flat-fall issue is concerned, Harmony requires the up-and-down flow of the tones of the poetry, while Dissonance is not subject to this limitation. Of course, there is a special situation here. According to daily oral speech habits, the ups and downs of sentences are also a relatively natural phenomenon. Modern Chinese new poetry has adjusted the tones of the words and sounds and abandoned the traditional rigid connotations of the flat-fall norms (such as emphasizing strict antithesis and avoiding "loner flat tones"). That is to say, modern Harmony has become more tolerant in terms of the flat-fall rules. Compared with the melody of emotions, specific strict requirements are greatly reduced, which, in turn, reduce the possibility of Dissonance resistance. Therefore, in modern Chinese new poetry history, there are few disharmonious ways to oppose the coordination of stressed and unstressed sounds. At least the example of disregarding the stresses of the entire poem is almost impossible. The phenomenon of violating this law is only found in a few lines of a poem. For instance, at the end of the poem, likely, attention is not paid to the stress and unstressed match. "Everything is singing/ Everything is singing/ Are you singing? Am I singing? Is he singing? Is she singing? Is the fire singing? The singing is singing! / Only singing! / Only singing! / Singing! / Singing! / Singing!" (Guo Moruo, "Phoenix Nirvana") "You didn't learn to let go of your throat and sing: / 'Get up! Hungry and ruthless slaves! . . .' / You are not used to shouting: / 'We, Steel Bolshevik! . . .'" (Gong Mu, "Hello, Beard!")

> On a cold night in December, the wind howling across the plains of the North, / The fields of the North are bare, in the barns stored the barley and millet yield, / The year is coming to an end, the farming animals are resting, and the small river outside the village is frozen. / On the ancient road, a light flickering in the far field.
> —Mu Dan, "On a Night in December"

Both Guo and Gong's poems finished with a falling tone. Mu's poems finished with a flat tone (or unstressed tone). Of course, these are more extreme excerpts, because this way of ending was not applied to the whole poem, but this subversion of Harmony by several lines still left a deep impression. Guo and Gong's poetry are filled with a passion for active prospects, while the quiet ending of Mu's poem conveyed the dullness and stagnation of the old times. In the moment of expressing the poet's certain non-harmonious emotions or feelings, the deliberate ignorance of stresses produced very strong effects.

In addition to these above-mentioned violations, is there any connection between the Dissonance and Harmony of modern Chinese new poetry? Definitely. I think there are some connections.

The pursuit of Dissonance and the pursuit of Harmony often promote and develop each other continuously. Without the reinforcement of the Dissonance tradition and the negation of the series of rigid phonological norms of classical poetry, it is impossible to push people to familiarize themselves and study complete modern language and explore new forms of Harmony consistent with oral habits on this basis. The practice has proven the pursuit of the Harmony of modern Chinese new poetry originated after the May Fourth Revolution (Dissonance). In turn, the efforts of Harmony are always a sign of the maturity of the era. Harmony enables the revolution results to be fully utilized. In the aftermath of the revolution, a fascinating landscape is built, which is also self-consumption, while perfecting itself and accumulating energy for a new round of violations. The rhythm development history of modern Chinese poetry is a history of alternative existence of Harmony and Dissonance, which applied both to individuals as well as groups.

Behind this mutually reinforcing objective movement is some inherent unity between Harmony and Dissonance, which are not completely exclusive to each other. A poem necessarily requires a certain sense of melody, which brings some Harmony to the opposite level of the sounds. Therefore, any Dissonance contains some harmonious factors, except it seeks to reduce the uniformity of the external sounds and wrap it in the ups and downs of the emotion itself. When the impact thoughts and emotions are enough to require a break of Harmony, it does not hesitate to use the unbalanced phonetic forms as the charm of the melody, rather than compromise to keep the forms. At the same time, Harmony undoubtedly reflected the times distinctly, since they must be based on the solid foundation of the language of the times. Modern language is also a kind of variation and violation. Thus, there are certain discord factors within Harmony. This kind of unity between Dissonance and Harmony makes their influence on modern Chinese new poetry rhyme often holistic and collateral. Therefore, for modern metrical poets, there are also pure poems unconstrained or accepting the influence of the tradition of Harmony on one side and reflecting the disharmonious pursuit on the other side. Modern Chinese free-style poets do not escape from rhymes and rhythms. Rather, they are often devoted to the deliberation of coherence in a certain direction, which can be seen in the examples above. All of these contributed to the complexity of the metrical features of modern Chinese new poetry as well as difficulties in research.

Notes

1. See Han Jingtai, *Chinese Poetics and the Spirit of Traditional Culture* (Sichuan People's Publishing House, 1990).
2. Huang Tingjian, *Zizhan's Poems are Supreme though he Claimed to Imitate Tingjian, A Response to It*.
3. Qian Zhongshu, "Poetry Divided between the Tang and Song Dynasties," in *Tan Yi Lu (Notes on Literature and Art)* (Zhonghua Publishing House, 1984), 3.
4. Hu Shih, Preface to *An Experimental Collection* (People's Literature Publishing House, 1984), 148.
5. Bian Zhilin, Preface to *Diao Chong Ji Li (Anthology of Bian Zhilin's Poems)*, 3.
6. He Qifang, "Road in the Dream," in *He Qifang's Collected Works*, vol. 2, 66.
7. Refer to Feng Wenbing (Fei Ming), "Past Poetry Literature and New Poetry," in *On New Poetry*.
8. See Yuan Kejia, "Another Discussion on Modernization of New Poetry," *Tianjin: Ta Kung Pao Weekly Literature and Art* (May 18, 1947).
9. Ai Qing, "My Requirements for Poetry," in *On Poetry by Ai Qing* (Huacheng Publishing House, 1982), 38.
10. Quoted from Guo Baowei, "Letters still Exist Today, but Where to Find Poets," in *A Nation Has Risen*, 180.
11. See Zheng Min, "Poets and Contradictions," in *A Nation Has Risen*, 33.
12. Wai-Lim Yip, "Language and the Real World," in *Diffusion of Distances: Dialogues between Chinese and Western Poetics* (University of California Press, 1993), 63–99.
13. Hu Shih, "Preface to *An Experimental Collection*," 149.
14. According to Lewis Henry Morgan's *Ancient Society*, the development process of character symbols can be divided into five categories: (1) Gesture or personal symbol language; (2) Pictographic characters or ideographic symbols; (3) Pictographic characters or conventional symbols; (4) Phonetic symbols or notes for simple records; (5) Pinyin letters or written sounds.
15. See Fei Bai, "Poetry Metrics," in *Poetry Ocean (Oceanus Poeticate)* (Lijiang Publishing House, 1989), 1600.
16. According to the textual research of some critics, Guo Moruo's *Temptation of Death* (1918) is "the earliest work in the history of new poetry that meets the requirements of modern metrical pattern." See Yu Jian, "Modern Metrical Poetry (New Metrical Poetry): Past, Present and Future," *Chinese and Foreign Poetry Exchange and Research*, no. 2. (1992).

17 See Sun Yushi, *A Study of Symbolism Poetry in Early China* (Peking University Press, 1983), 25.
18 Kang Lin, Textual Structures of Chinese Classical Lyric Poetry, *Hebei Academic Journal*, no. 3 (1990).
19 Hu Shih, "On New Poetry," in *Collection of Theory Development, China's New Literature Series*, 303, 306.
20 Yu Pingbo, "Three Conditions of Vernacular Poetry," *New Youth* 6, no. 3 (Mar. 1919).
21 Zhi Xin, "The Syllables of Poetry," in *Selected Poems in Classified Vernacular*, ed. Xu Delin (People's Literature Publishing House, 1988), 17.
22 Lu Zhiwei, "The Shell of My Poems," Preface to *Crossing the River*.
23 Wen Yiduo, "A Study on Metrical Poetry," in *Complete Works of Wen Yiduo*, vol. 10, 144–145.
24 Wen Yiduo wrote to Liang Shiqiu and Xiong Foxi, *Complete Works of Wen Yiduo*, vol. 12 (April 15, 1926), 233.
25 Xu Zhimo, "Poetry Magazine Holiday," *Morning Post Supplement Shi-Juan* (June 10, 1926).
26 Wen Yiduo, "The Rhyme of Poetry," *Morning Post Supplement Shi-Juan* (May 13, 1926).
27 Quoted from Pan Songde, *Modern Chinese Poetics—Forty Contributors*, 129.
28 Ye Shengtao, The author believes only in the development of the art of Chinese new poetry syllables, can we accurately understand its message. It should be noted the "epoch-making" achievements of syllables cannot be attributed to Dai Wangshu.
29 He Qifang, "On Poetry Writing and Reading," in *Collected Works of He Qifang*, vol. 4 (People's Literature Publishing House, 1983), 454–455.
30 Wen Yiduo, "A Study on Metrical Poetry," in *Complete Works of Wen Yiduo*, vol. 10. 145.
31 Bian Zhilin, "Diao Chong Ji Li, Preface," in *Diao Chong Ji Li (Anthology of Bian Zhilin's Poems)*, 17.
32 Tang Shi, "A Journey to Beauty, Preface," in *A Journey to Beauty* (Ningxia People's Publishing House, 1984).
33 Lu Dejun, Xu Ting, "Another Discussion on the Sonnet in China," *Chinese Modern Literature Research Series*, no. 2 (1992).
34 Feng Wenbing, *On New Poetry, Nine, Cao'er*.
35 Bian Zhilin, "Humming Rhythm (chanting tone) and Speaking Rhythm (reciting tone)," in *People and Poetry: Retrospect and Prospect*, 139–140.
36 Bian Zhilin, "A New Poetry Discussion with Zhou Ce," in *People and Poetry: Retrospect and Prospect*, 163–164.
37 See Syllables of New Poetry, *Morning Post Supplement Shi-Juan* (April 22, 1926).
38 Zhu Xiang, The Generation of Poetry, *Appendix to Informal Literary Discussions*.
39 Zhu Xiang to Zhao Jingshen, *Letters of Zhu Xiang* (Tianjin Life and Literature Society, 1936), 52.
40 Zhu Ziqing, "The Form of Poetry," in *Miscellaneous New Poetry*, 104.
41 Bian Zhilin, "Thoughts on Reading Hu Qiaomu's Six Poems," in *People and Poetry: Retrospect and Prospect*, 125.

· 4 ·

INDIVIDUAL POETS IN CHINESE CULTURAL TRADITIONS

Cultural traditions are twofold. On the one hand, cultural traditions are beyond individuals and it exists in our deep thoughts of us in the form of collective unconsciousness and does not often change with our emotional changes in the real world.

On the other hand, cultural traditions are concrete and realistic, because the world is always composed of real people. Without individuals, there is no society. Cultural traditions will ultimately be undertaken, displayed, and transmitted by individuals. For individuals, cultural traditions cannot be a condescending and domineering spiritual master. An individual is always and only can represent one part of cultural traditions with inherent potential and the foundation of survival. This necessarily means another component will be discarded, and the individual's change and agility will adjust some of the traditional structures or add something.

The basis of literary creation is individuality and poetry demands an even higher individuality. The classical Chinese poetry tradition as a collective unconsciousness is beyond individuals, which is self-evident, but its existence must be carried through individualized modern poets—a historical fact. The dual combination of super-individuals and individualization is the complex relationship between Chinese poetry tradition and modern poetry. Therefore, it is not sufficient to dissect the connection between Chinese modern poets and traditions by "categories." It is necessary to go one step further and lead the problem to the individual's living experiences. We are going to see how cultural traditions produce impact; how individuals accept, use, and transform this impact; and how individuals' modern experiences specifically intersect with ancient traditions. Perhaps this can be considered a more detailed interpretation of tradition and new poetry.

For this purpose, 15 individual poets are selected. This choice does not signify their actual status in the history of Chinese new poetry (it is necessary to introduce more standards for this). It is not intended to erase the close connections between other poets and Chinese poetry traditions. These poets are chosen because they appear in several important periods already discussed. At the same time, these poets also reflect individual characteristics that cannot be fully summarized in previous chapters of their poetry pursuits. A closer study may lead to a better understanding of the issue of modern poets and traditions.

Hu Shih: Slow Flow of Two Poetry Cultures

> It is time for a writing revolution! I am ready to be a flag holder.
> —Hu Shih, "Poetry Pledge: In the Melody Qin Yuan Chun"

It is past tense to simply identify Hu Shih as a member of the "reactionary literati." Therefore, our impression seems to be led toward a new direction by the history of change. Hu Shih, a scholar with both Chinese and Western academic training, opened his mind, introduced Western poetry to China for the first time, and started a series of "Poetry Revolution" both in terms of language and thought pursuits. His translation, introduction, and imitation of Western poetry and the investigation of Chinese literature vitality seem to be the results of deep rational thinking and prudent choices. Undoubtedly, this understanding separates Hu Shih from other predecessors of the Poetry Revolution, such as Huang Zunxian, Liang Qichao, and others. These people did not match his efforts in valuing the independence of Western poetry and unprecedented cultural transplantation. However, when we attempt to establish Hu Shih's position over previous poets of the late Qing Dynasty, we should be aware not to exaggerate the consciousness of his efforts to new poetry. Hu Shih's early poetry attempt as a whole is complicated. Traditional-style poetry or works close to traditional-style poetry still account for the vast majority of his work, *An Experimental Collection*,[1] which should not be ignored. As an "intermediary" in the transitional period,[2] Hu Shih was closely connected with tradition, which also should not be ignored. It is unlikely for Hu Shih to have stood on the ruins of the century, and unscrupulously introduced exotic poetry culture to complete unprecedented new creations. Hu Shih's involvement in Chinese modern poetry is a kind of transitional exploration, which is difficult. The significance of its historical progress can only be found in terms of transition and exploration.

Between Contingency and Clear Direction

A comprehensive review of Hu Shih's participation in the May Fourth literary revolution and his *An Experimental Collection* would lead us to the conclusion that Hu Shih's involvement in Chinese modern poetry is not a well-thought-out choice. Rather, his involvement showed certain contingency and his texts had a large amount of redundancy.

From a student who copied *Revolutionary Army* at Meixi School in Shanghai and read *Evolution and Ethics* at Chengzhong School to John Dewey's student later at Columbia University in New York, Hu Shih's knowledge of democratic politics and modern philosophy gradually increased. However, all these Western advanced cultural concepts did not rapidly aggregate as a sharp weapon to break the traditional bondage, nor did the revolution of language and literature become an important part of Hu Shih's cultural pursuit from the beginning. This is different from Lu Xun's call of "the warrior of the spiritual world" as the core of cultural pursuit. Hu Shih even sharply criticized a certain young man's proposal of a radical change in the Chinese language, showing little tolerance and understanding to a peer reformer of language and culture.[3] Rather, he devoted himself to the study of Chinese culture as a knowledgeable, mature scholar, which undoubtedly showed his initial willingness to correct diversions and maintain the orthodox tradition of Chinese studies. Eventually, it seemed to be somewhat unexpected that he discovered the differences between classical Chinese and the vernacular and the gist of the living and dead languages. His change from a full supporter of tradition to a deconstructor of tradition, which laid the foundation for the later literary revolution, the transformation is somewhat dramatic and contingent, beyond the rational design of Hu Shih himself.

Hu Shih put forward his revolutionary proposition of contingent poetry in "Send Mei Guangdi to Harvard University." The mixture of Chinese and foreign nouns in the poem drew his friends' criticism. Hu Shih did not accept this criticism and righteously defended himself: "Where does the poetry revolution start? It should start from writing poetry as you write prose" ("A Response Intended for Ren Shuyong, but now for friends in Yicheng"). Thus, a small-scale unprepared academic debate started with this seemingly defensive "revolutionary declaration." If we read the defense poem again:

> I wish we would have several Newton and hundreds of Darwin. With numerous Edison, our treasury would be abundant and people would be free from want. Millions of soldiers would be trained. A general like Napoleon would be nominated, our lands would be reclaimed and borders be well-guarded. The shame China had suffered for hundred years would be eliminated in a day.

Such classical patriotism does not go beyond what is expressed in the poems at the end of the Qing Dynasty, such as "A Song for General Feng," "A Song for General Wu" by Huang Zunxian; "Four Chapters of Patriotic Songs," and "Reflections on *Lu You's Collection*" by Liang Qichao. The foreign language transliteration in Hu's poetry sometimes confused its readers. I believe this clearly shows Hu Shih's poetry revolution did not start high and he still did not have systemic "deep reform" thoughts that transcended the pioneers during the late Qing Dynasty. The academic debate caused by it is not so much as friends' criticism of Hu Shih's peculiar behaviors as the dissatisfaction toward the proposition of "writing poetry as prose" inherited from the late Qing Dynasty. The argument revealed the long-standing differences between the orthodox Chinese poetics and the unorthodox new changes (the dispute between Tang and Song dynasties). If one thought Mr. Mei Guangdi and Mr. Ren Shuyong commented exclusively on Hu Shih, it was a great misunderstanding!

The end of the poetry revolution during the late Qing Dynasty is also the starting point Hu Shih chose for himself, but he must have felt uncertain about where to go. Therefore, his choice of poetry path continued with uncertainty, leaving prints of hardworking exploration. *Staying Abroad Collection* and other early old-fashioned poems (a total of about 113 pieces) included ancient genres, metrical verses, Cis and Qus, etc. His vernacular, *An Experimental Collection*, is also like a collage, with some roughly five-character poems, such as "On the River," some roughly seven-character poems such as "Mid-Autumn Festival," some with newly filled lyrics in the traditional melody of "Qin Yuan Chun" and "Bai Zi Ling." Of course, there are also relatively pure free-style poems, such as "Dream and Poetry," "Old Crow," "Art," and so on. Here, Hu Shih's additions and deletions to the *An Experimental Collection* are also worthy of our attention. From the first edition in March 1920 to the fourth edition in October 1922, changes were made in each version, with some poems deleted, and some sentences or words changed. Hu Shih not only did it himself but also asked others to help, and he accepted the opinions of others, such as Ren Shuyong, Chen Shafei, Lu Xun, Zhou Zuoren, Yu Pingbo, Kang Baiqing, Jiang Baili, and others. By the fourth edition, over 70% of the original works had been replaced, which shows the instability of the author's poetry aesthetic standards. Initially, he did not find a relatively stable new poetry standard and was in the process of constant exploration and adjustment, which led to an interesting phenomenon of giving up the individual's pride in the originality of writing and accepting others' feedback uncritically. Such a large-scale poetry deletion activity involving many people rarely happened in the history of Chinese modern poetry. It illustrates Hu Shih's immaturity as a vernacular poet in the initial and transitional periods.

In summary, Hu Shih's initiative in Chinese modern poetry contains more incidental factors. The formation of his poetry proposition and the trend of his poetry practice were not from his comprehensive planning and thinking. Hu Shih even lacked sufficient preparation but was pushed to the forefront of history by a series of unexpected events. Of course, this may be considered as fortunate, because Hu Shih personally experienced cultural conflicts, had to argue reasonably, and had to prove his existence in poetry. For the first time, he carefully organized the language and literature thoughts that he did not have many systemic, sharp senses previously. Constantly, he adjusted and perfected himself in an orientation that resisted the traditional habits of others. Here, Hu Shih found his direction. The clarity of Hu Shih's poetry revolution and literary revolution comes from some unplanned thoughts. As shown in *An Experimental Collection*, even in his more oriented exploration, there is still a lot of confusion and ambiguity in the sense of direction and hesitation in action. These show insufficient clarity of thinking. The interaction of contingency and specific orientation leads to exploration and a historical transition.

The pursuit of Hu Shih's poetry revolution falls between contingency and clear direction.

Two Poetry Cultures: The Living and the Dead

Hu Shih formed his basic concept of poetry culture between contingency and clear direction. This position is unique compared with the sobriety and consciousness of the latecomers.

For generations of obsessive new poetry creators after the May Fourth Movement, the production of Chinese modern poetry contains very rich, contemporary messages. At the time, the development of modern Chinese society and culture had pushed its core issues to the people—the relationship between Chinese traditional and Western cultures. People believed the loss of Chinese traditional culture vitality was the fundamental root of the decline of Chinese society since modern times. During the same time, the strength of the Western world reminded the Chinese people from time to time of the long-lasting vitality of Western culture. Therefore, the discussion of China's modernization issues naturally focused on the comparison between Chinese traditional and Western cultures. Various shortcomings of Chinese traditional culture were reflected and Western culture was used as a reference to explore the future direction of Chinese culture. The discussion of Chinese and Western cultures was the most exciting and continuous historical event since modern times. After the discussion of material and institutional cultures, the discussion went deep into spirituality after the May Fourth Movement, in which literature played an important role. For modern poets and poetry theorists since the May Fourth era, their poetic ideas were directly influenced by the interactions between Chinese and Western poetry. The Crescent Moon School poets would like to be "babies from the marriage of Chinese and Western arts."[4] Modernist poets consciously connected the pure poetry proposition of Western Symbolism with the aesthetic conception of traditional Chinese poetry. The new poetry modernization pursued by the Nine Leaves' poets recombined Westernization with the Chinese tradition. Even the poets who advocated Chinese style in the Yan'an area also agreed Europeanization and nationalization should be integrated in a certain sense. "Europeanization and nationalization are not two incompatible concepts" (Zhou Yang). Of course, those who opposed Europeanization (such as Xiao San) saw the conflicts between Western poetry culture and Chinese culture, but such an idea was premised on the recognition that Chinese and Western poetry cultures influenced each other in modern China. The development of Chinese modern poetry after the May Fourth Movement constantly conveyed spiritual interactions and collisions between the two major poetry cultures.

From modern times to contemporary times, from the Pre-May Fourth era to the May Fourth era, being in such a historical transition period made it impossible for Hu Shih to fully and consciously realize the spiritual interactions and collisions between Chinese and Western cultures. The poetry movement he understood was mainly a self-evolution within the Chinese poetry system. This self-evolution occurred many times in history. Additionally, poetry was liberated and evolved many times. Qu Yuan's literature broke from the simple organization of the *Book of Songs*, "This is the first liberation." "The five- or seven-character poems after the Han Dynasty deleted meaningless ending words and became more coherent." "This is the second liberation." *Ci* created a "naturally-parametric syntactic structure." "This is the third liberation." The new poems were created, based on *Ci* and *Qu*. "This is the fourth poetic liberation." "This kind of liberation seems to be fierce at first glance when it is a natural trend, since the *Book of Songs*." "New style poetry is a natural trend of Chinese poetry."[5] Then, in the self-evolution of Chinese poetry, what are the factors of vitality and what factors tend to decline? Hu Shih repeatedly used a pair of concepts in his series of articles: the living literature and the dead literature. In Hu Shih's view, it is the living literary spirit (and its living poetry spirit) that drives the development of history. Living and death are two opposing forms of poetry culture that Hu Shih extracted from the Chinese literary system.

In 1915, Hu Shih wrote "How to Make Classical Chinese Easy to Teach," for the Chinese Student Association at Cornell University, a conference paper that can be considered the earliest foundation of Hu Shih's literary revolution, where Hu Shih proposed the concept of "living" and "dead." He argued ancient Chinese is a semi-dead language, while vernacular Chinese is a living language. Thus, "living and dead" as basic cultural values became part of Hu Shih's thoughts. Languages have a distinction between life and death, and so is literature. He commented on Ren Shuyong's four-character poem, "Thoughts on the Lake": "The words "yan (literally means 'words')" and "zai (literally means 'carry')" used in the poem are dead words." The phrase "zai xiao zai yan (literally means 'speaking while laughing')" is a "dead phrase used three thousand years ago."[6] In a parody poem response to Mei Guangdi, Hu Shih wrote: "There is no distinction between ancient and modern language, but there is a distinction between the living and the dead."[7] From such a perceptual experience, Hu Shih refined his rational understanding. Through his reflection on the history of Chinese literature development, he believed a literary history is a history of "living literature" replacing "dead literature"; the contradiction between the "living and dead" is the driving force of self-development within the literary system. He thought "The purpose of the literature revolution currently is to create a 'literature of the national language' for China—a living literature."[8]

Logically, the dead and living concepts do not necessarily fall into the Chinese literary system. They are nothing but a description of existence. However, from the perspective of Hu Shih's discussion and their main applications, they undoubtedly own a distinct nationality for the Chinese language and Chinese literature.

Starting with the Chinese language, Hu Shih first explained the specific differences between the "dead and living," which he proposed as the differences between classical Chinese and vernacular Chinese. Dead poems, whose discourse is separated from everyday oral language, lost their vitality in a written dead end, while the living poetry's discourses are rooted in everyday spoken language. Taking this as a standard, Hu Shih examined the history of Chinese classical poetry. He said: "From the *Book of Songs* to the present, Chinese literature with value and life are vernacular or near vernacular. The remaining are all lifeless antiques, like the exhibits in the museum!" "Song of Mulan," "The Bride of Jiao Zhongqing," "The Conscripting Officer at Shihao," "Song of the Conscripts" and other living literature[9] are all vernacular, while those typical "aesthetic conception" of sentimentality are precisely the dead literature with "stifled and rotten language." Hu Shih tried to liberate the language of poetry from the written engravings, which is undoubtedly contrary to the maturity of Chinese classical poetry. We know from the *Book of Songs*, *Qu Sao*, to ancient poetry and the metrical verses matured during the Tang Dynasty, the separation between formal written language, spoken language, and literature is a remarkable symbol. In this way, Hu Shih is destined to find no living model from the orthodox mature Chinese classical poetry. As his repeated examples show, living poetry exists in two stages of history—before the peak period and after the heyday. The former examples include *Airs of the States and Yue Fu* and some ancient poetry, the latter examples include the poetry of the Song Dynasty (the rational spirit of Du Fu's works is also carried forward during the Song Dynasty). Additionally, in the excavation of these "pre-orthodoxy" or "after-orthodox" classical poetry, Hu Shih further summarized their important features in grammar: using prose as poetry. That is to say, these poems break away from the attention on wording and the "pure poetry" pursuit of "literary decoration over quality," and pursue a narrative and prose style with strong logic instead. He said: "I have found the trend in the history of Chinese poetry change from the Tang Dynasty to the Song Dynasty. There is no mystery, but poetry is getting closer to prose writing."[10] In other words, the narrative and prose trends of poetry are a standard of Hu Shih's living literature, which provides a concrete meaning to the "living." Other theories, such as "metrical rules, fall-flat rules, and length could be flexible"; "writings should be substantive,"[11] etc., are the technical details for this trend. From this point of view, the verbal and narrative natures of the verses are the living literary spirit that Hu Shih derived from China's literary history of vernacular literature. This is his artistic means to counteract the part of the rigid traditions.

According to his concepts of the poetry revolution, Hu Shih distinguished between "the living and the dead" within the Chinese poetry tradition, and finally abandoned the "dead" poems of classical Chinese and created the "living" poems in vernacular Chinese. Of course, this is not to say that his poetic concepts at the time rejected external influences or failed to be inspired by foreign poetry. As known to all, during his stay at Cornell University, Hu Shih "read Western literature books extensively, which influenced him indirectly."[12] Even when he was studying in Chinese public schools, he began to translate Western poetry works and more translations were produced after he studied in the United States. He was also inspired by the American New Poetry Movement represented by the Imagery School, a fact recognized by critics.[13] However, we can't ignore the fact that Hu Shih's contact and translation of foreign poetry in foreign literature on the eve of the May Fourth Movement were quite juxtaposed. The translated poems collected in his *An Experimental Collection* and *Staying Abroad Collection* included both romantic works, such as George Gordon Byron's "The Isles of Greece," and anti-romantic imagery works, such as Sara Teasdale's "Over the Roofs"! Both Western poetry and translated Eastern poetry, such as the medieval Persian poet, Omar Khayyam's "Hope" are included. Both recognized masterpieces and second-rate writers' works, such as "Auld Robin Gray" by Scottish poet Anne Lindsay are included. From these complicated foreign works, it is difficult to see the flow of Western poetry and the true features of Western poetry culture. When Hu Shih approached and translated Western poetry, it was not his intention to fully understand Western poetry nor to understand the context of Western poetry to provide a successful guide for the development of Chinese new poetry so Chinese new poetry can track the world's advanced trends and go hand-in-hand with the West. These would not begin until the May Fourth Movement when people persistently and consciously pursued Chinese and Western cultures. But these could not be credited to Hu Shih, who was still groping for poetry and transitioning at the time. Hu Shih's main motivation in approaching and translating Western poetry was his interest in the natural vernacular. For example, he commented on "Auld Robin Gray": "The whole story is written in a female villager's words, which is very honest and outspoken. This could be considered the vernacular poem of its time."[14] Here, Hu Shih was looking for proof of his "living literature"; hence, he chose to translate several foreign poems. Therefore, these poems did not shine with his thoughts and genre characteristics, nor attract attention. Instead, they were used to make circumstantial evidence and explanation of Hu Shih's poetry concepts. Hu Shih did not establish the concept of the unity of opposites between Chinese and Western poetry cultures because of translating foreign poetry. His basic poetic concept still relied on the distinction between "the living and the dead." What he needed was to break free from the bondage of "the dead" with the encouragement of historical facts and look for a "living" space. This applied to the translation of poetry as well as the acceptance of foreign theories. Hu Shih did not intend to explore the history and future of the imagery theory. His emphasis was on the advocacy of vernacular. He did not specialize in imagery. As long as these poems met the requirements of his creation of "living literature," he would introduce them. Also, in the process of countering the increasingly rigid traditional "pure poetry" advocacy, he put forward the proposition of using prose as poetry and pursuing the poetic prose culture. For that purpose, he highly recommended the prose and rationalism works of Wordsworth, Keats, Browning, and others, whose styles were very different from the Imagery School with their systems.[15] Regarding the relationship between Western literature and the Chinese literary revolution, Hu Shih once had a debate with his friend, Mei Guangdi, who believed Hu Shih was plagiarizing "the worthless stuff from Europe and the United States to cheat the Chinese." Hu Shih defended

> ... the literary revolution that I advocate is based on the current situation of Chinese literature; *it has nothing to do with the new trend of literature in Europe and America*; sometimes I refer to the history of Western literature—only the literature history of "national languages" by European countries three or four hundred years ago, because the needs of Chinese literature today are similar to those of Europe at that time. Studying their achievements, perhaps could *make us less conservative and more courageous*.[16]

From Dead Poetry to Living Poetry

Hu Shih lived in a transitional period. His poetry revolution is between contingency and clear orientation. Hu Shih's poetry concept is based on the tradition of Chinese poetry. He was encouraged by foreign cultures to diverge from tradition. As a result, we feel the similarity between him and the Poetry Revolution generation during the late Qing Dynasty. For instance, Huang Zunxian advocated, "Write what is out of my mouth," "Revive the *Bi Xing* Style," and "Draw from *Li Sao and Yuefu*," which is in line with Hu Shih's theory of living literature. There should be no doubt that Hu Shih's poetry revolution is rooted back to the late Qing Dynasty. So, does this mean Hu Shih's poetry revolution does not exceed the level of the late Qing Dynasty, or is it just a different expression of the revolution in the poetry of the late Qing Dynasty? I think this is not the case. Living in a historical transitional period, Hu Shih's concept of poetry culture connects the late Qing Dynasty with the future. When he declared the poetic culture as "the dead and the living," he had secretly distanced himself from "creating new aesthetic conception with traditional forms." Although both intended to make some adjustments within the traditional poetry culture, "creating new aesthetic conceptions with traditional forms" advocacy during the late Qing Dynasty is excessively indecisive and timid. This is still pleading for tolerance and protection from orthodox concepts. Therefore, this concept lacked the vitality to break free and forge ahead. Hu Shih's verdict on the dead literature and the call for the living literature are more decisive, and filled with an exciting courage. Hu Shih was also influenced by the great tradition of Chinese poetry, but he seemed to take an important step, an unprecedented step toward the modern era with his full strength.

The "dead" declaration liberated Hu Shih from the most suffocating Chinese traditional barriers and his call for the "living" showed us a new field—a vivid, historical background after the transformation. Hu Shih not only separated the dead and the living in the theory of poetics but also tried to push Chinese new poetry from the dead to the living world through his experiments. This is an important contribution. *Staying Abroad Collection* and *An Experimental Collection* demonstrated vividly the process of the May Fourth poetry from the dead to the living, from the old to the new. We could say that Hu Shih offered many valuable experiences in Chinese poetry history.

As mentioned previously, the *Staying Abroad Collection*, *An Experimental Collection*, and other poems of the same period show Hu Shih's poetic standards were quite complex. He still experimented with a variety of poetic styles and needed to improve them with others' feedback, which led to continuous revisions. However, when *An Experimental Collection* was reprinted in September 1920, Hu Shih once again summarized:

I only admit fourteen pieces here would be considered as vernacular new poems, including "The Old Crow", "Auld Robert Gray", "You Don't Forget", "Over the Roofs", "Hope", "Should", "A Star", "Authority", "Optimism", "Up the Mountain", "Happy Birthday", "A Robbed Star", "Xu Yisun", and "Smile". As to the remaining, there are several readable poems and two or three readable *Ci*s, but they should not be counted as true vernacular new poems.[17]

To be fair, such comments are quite objective, which shows the author had a clearer concept of new poetry at this time. Given this, I think we will see a more in-depth and more detailed overall development process for Hu Shih. That is to say, besides confusion and hesitation, Hu Shih also showed his sensibility. During his process of exploration, the poet was becoming increasingly aware of his path toward the direction of modernity. Although these advances were uneven and often submerged in other frustrating mediocrities, after all, they showed a progress of history, a progress in the transition. Today, when we combine these tiny progressive factors, we can see more clearly they are transcending tradition and pointing to the future as a whole. The relationship between "the dead and the living" in Hu Shih's poems should be regarded as such.

Specifically, the awareness of the juxtaposition, contingency, and living transitions that originated in the background of dead literature are found in the following aspects.

The Violation of Traditional Poetry Style

If we refer to various formal benchmarks of mature, Chinese poetry as "the norms," then "the living literature" in Hu Shih's understanding is not up to the norms, either being the crude state before maturity or conscious violations of the norms after maturity. Based on these unconventional, unorthodox inheritances, Hu Shih's writing inevitably violated the norms in many aspects. Traditional poems that violated the standards are the starting point of Hu Shih's poems. Some scholars found in his 92 early traditional poems, 52 of the ancient styles were unbound by the rules for metrical poems, and only 30 are metrical poems. Among the 21 poems in the *Staying Abroad Collection*, 13 pieces belong to the ancient style and only one is a metrical poem.[18] In my opinion, if using the strict metrics, then none of the metrical poems in *An Experimental Collection* is a true metrical poem. Hu Shih consciously violated the norms, a way for him to reverse the orthodox form of Chinese poetry and refuse to enter the dead literature.

The Reconstruction of Traditional Poems

The traditional poems that violate the norms are still traditional poems. They deviate from the traditional part (mainly referring to the use of *Ping-Ze*, or the flat-fall rule), but they also agree with another part. Even these "violations" are allowed by tradition. The deviated traditional poems by Hu Shih, such as "Mid-Autumn Festival" and "On the River" do not have much more new aesthetic conception than the traditional. The "reconstruction" is different; it tries to change the rules of poetry at a more basic level, so the poems contain more new pursuits. For example, "Butterfly" has seven lines with three pauses: "also—not interested in—getting into heaven," which destroyed the order formed by the other two-paused poetry: "two yellow butterflies," "flying to the sky—as a pair," "the sky—is too lonely." If other poetry lines with a parallel pause provide a traditional harmony, then this abrupt line produces a dynamic linear upward effect. Another example is one of "Letters from Dongxiu during Sickness": "I received the letter from her. It is as short as eight lines nothing significant happened. It makes me happy." The poet tried to use modern spoken language as much as possible even to the point of joking to reach the humorous effect that is difficult to obtain in traditional poetry. Sometimes the poet also consciously used several similar words repeatedly to make the poetry distinct and prominent. The so-called implicit meaning of the tradition no longer exists, such as the "Third Letter": "Do you not love freedom? No one could understand me. I'd rather not be free, that is also freedom." Another example is "A Short Poem": "I prefer not thinking about you, so I could escape from the suffering. I ponder it again and again, and I'm willing to suffer!" Later development of new poetry shows that the clarity of outstanding thinking is the effective means of going beyond the emptiness and subtlety of tradition, when implicitness becomes a kind of requirement for all, the edges of poetry are increasingly dampened. This is the "death" of the artistic spirit; breaking the subtle implicitness is liberating poetry. It is the resurrection of the artistic spirit.

The Collage of New and Traditional Poetry

The "reconstructed" traditional poems are more dependent on the traditional poetry framework, and the "collage" is a step further. In Hu Shih's writings, there are two ways to mix the traditional and the new. First, the aesthetic pursuit of traditional poetry is expressed in new free-style poetry lines, such as "Dove":

Clouds are scattered and the sky is high, what a good late autumn! / There are a group of pigeons, playing in the air. / Looking at them in twos and threes, / looping back and forth, / all at their will- / suddenly, they turned over against the sun, their white feathers against the blue sky, / How bright!

This late autumn sketch, from the selections of intuitive imagery to the invisibility of the lyrical protagonist falls into the aesthetic pursuit of classical poetry. But the arrangement of poetry is free, despite a syllable rhythm of the lyrics in the deep structure.[19] At least it is quite free and casual from the visual perspective, which will undoubtedly give greater inspiration to the growth of new poetry in the future. The second collage is a combination of the orderly lines of traditional poetry and the free style of the new poetry. For example, in "A Red Leaf in the Snow on the Sanxi Road," the first six lines are similar to the five-character poem: "Snow covers empty mountains, I look up and you fall into my eyes! I don't know why, but my heart is overjoyed; I take you off the tree in the snow, put you in the small book." Then the following two lines are free style: "I also want to write a poem, write the reasons for my joy." The last two lines are in the form of a seven-character style: "Unexpectedly, it is difficult to write, I picked up the pen but then put it away."

The attempt at the new poems is only a small part of Hu Shih's poetry, but it tells us the new look of the new poetry from different aspects. They are the real poetry that "cannot be replaced by any classical poetry." It is their existence that provides more successful examples of Chinese poetry, which emerges from the "dead water" and embarks on a "living path." For example, "The Old Crow" symbolizes an independent attitude toward life in a personified way. "A Star Robbed" uses the relationship between black clouds and stars to insinuate the forced shutdown of the *National Gazette* in Beijing. Both describe nature but no longer have the integration of oneself and the external world. Subjective emotions are no longer kept plain. On the contrary, subjective ideas are very prominent and the natural things are completely the objects of manipulation and deportation by the poet. Here, the traditional "natural humanization" is replaced by the modern "humanized nature." "Up to the Mountain" is a demonstration of the poet's consciousness, while "An Idea" traces the ego's fleeting, unconstrained thinking, which reminded people of Guo Moruo's "Tiangou." The focus and the topics of these poems are not found in Chinese classical poetry. Hu Shih even fully affirmed the value of the individual in the confrontation between the individual and the state, and issued a discussion that would be outrageous for the ancient people: "You don't forget: / When your father was dying he only hoped the country to perish quickly: / submit to the 'Cossacks', submit to the 'Prussians', —/ either one" ("You Don't Forget"). "Start a new revolution, / make a good government: / That is the commemoration of the Double Ten!" ("Ghost Songs of the Double Ten Festival") Other poems express the emotional world of human beings, but not through objects, or the traditional routines presented in an unresolved manner, but describe the ups and downs of subjective mind as clearly as possible. Hu Shih tried new artistic pursuits for the new poetry, such as "Should," "Art," and "Being Drunk and Love." In *On New Poetry*, he specifically analyzed this artistic pursuit: "That kind of fine observations, that kind of indirect ideal could by no means be reached by the old-style poetic lyrics." He then took "Should" as an example:

> The meaning and feelings of this poem could not be delivered through traditional poetry. On top of other things, let's say the lines "he may love me, maybe he still loves me". There are several layers of meanings in this piece, which could not be delivered by the traditional style of poems.

Hu Shih's new poetry writing in the above aspects has been widely inherited and developed by other poets, who played an important role in shaping the independent character of Chinese new poetry.

It is a gradual process from the violation of the rules of traditional poetry, the reconstruction of traditional poetry, and the juxtaposition of new and traditional poetry to the new poetry attempt. There are many repetitions, hesitations, and confusions when the dead culture has a difficult dialogue with the living culture during this gradual process. The living culture continues to expand its power, while the dead culture continues to have an impact. Hu Shih's attempt was prudent, calm, and cautious. In this way, in a long process, the two poetry cultures of life and death are slowly adjusting the proportion and weight of each other. The composition of "active" factors slowly increased, while the composition of "dead" elements slowly decreased. But there has been no fierce conflict nor confrontation all along. To portray the image vividly, it seems one clear river intersected with one turbid river silently. There is no violent interaction. They flow together for a long time and change from distinctively two to one within another. All changes are quietly achieved. This is the so-called "slow flow." The concept of Hu Shih's poetry and the development of his poems clearly show two kinds of slow-flow poetry cultures.

Ahead of this long river of poetry development, there would be finally clear, broad waters, where a living culture full of vitality would replace the withered culture of death. Of course, in the process of this qualitative transformation, the involvement of Western poetry culture played an important role. Specific to poetry practice, translated poems, such as *Over the Roofs* provided an example of the maturity of Hu Shih's writing in both thought and form. However, even so, Western poetry still did not appeal to Hu Shih with an image of independent historical significance. What Hu Shih realized is not the contradiction between the Chinese poetry culture and the more magnificent, far-reaching influence of Western poetry culture. Some of the inspiration from Western poetry was incorporated into the context of fresh living literature. That is to say, the moment when Hu Shih came into contact in his unconscious world with the Chinese and Western poetry cultures, these cultures showed a scene of mutual convergence and slow flow.

Of course, Chinese and Western poetry cultures are, after all, two systems that are heterogeneous to each other. Fundamentally speaking, they cannot be as slowly and harmoniously transitioned as Hu Shih's understanding of death and life. The most substantial collisions and conflicts will eventually occur. However, before the characters of Western poetry culture grew in Hu Shih's thoughts, the pioneer stopped his experiments.

In this way, Hu Shih completed the most important transition of the Chinese new poetry conception period, but he, as a poet, has forever stayed in the transition of the two cultures.

Guo Moruo: Free and Conscious Forms of Chinese Poetry Culture

> We must restore the inherent creative spirit,
> We must study the treasures and inherit
> From our ancestors, with a view to the future.
> —Guo Moruo, "On Literature and Art—A Declaration"

With his first appearance in the May Fourth poetry community, Guo Moruo publicly announced: "he would study the treasures of ancient times and absorb the heritage of the ancestors to closely bridge the past with the future."[20] He listed the influences of Rabindranath Tagore, Walt Whitman, Johann Wolfgang von Goethe, etc., but also emphasized the enlightenment of Chinese classical poets, such as Qu Yuan, Tao Yuanming, Wang Wei, Li Bai, and Meng Haoran. Even after the foundation of the People's Republic of China in 1949, the poet insisted new poetry had not abandoned the tradition of Chinese poetry despite foreign influences.[21] Therefore, the significance of

Chinese traditional culture as a prototype is particularly noticeable in Guo Moruo's works and it transformed from unconsciousness to consciousness.

Free and Conscious Styles of Poetry

There are quite a few Chinese classical poets, whom Guo Moruo's favored and influenced him from his self-reports. When carefully examined, they seem to fall into two categories: one is the pre-Qin poets represented by Qu Yuan, and the other is poets during Jin and Tang dynasties represented by Tao Yuanming, Wang Wei, and others. Guo Moruo said: "Qu Yuan is one of my favorite writers. When I was a child, I loved to read his works."[22] He sighed with emotion in a metrical poem: "Qu is my teacher. What a pity he died so tragically!"[23] In his childhood narrative, Guo Moruo also talked about how poetry during Jin and Tang dynasties offered him great enjoyment,[24] with Tao Yuanming and Wang Wei as representatives. For example, in 1936 when Guo Moruo talked about writing *The Goddesses* and *Starry Heaven*, he said: "As for traditional poems, I like Tao Yuanming and Wang Wei best. Their poems are deeply transparent, feeling like smooth and gentle jewelry. Li Bai's poems are two-dimensionally transparent, while Tao and Wang's poems are three-dimensionally transparent."[25] The prototypes of Guo Moruo's poetry originated from Qu Yuan, Tao Yuanming, and Wang Wei.

It is worth noting these two prototype forms represent two important stages of development in the history of Chinese classical poetry: the primitive stage and the mature stage, or the stage of "freedom" and the stage of "consciousness."

The *Chu Ci* by Qu Yuan represents the "free" form of Chinese classical poetry. Its basic characteristics include: (1) Self and individual personality receive more respect. For example, magnificent personal ambition and the poet's pride in being unique are written all over *Li Sao*. In the first eight sentences (as divided by modern people), there are as many as six "I" (*zhen, wu, yu*, etc.), which is unimaginable in later generations. (2) Humans not only achieve relative independence in the objective world but also try to choose and change the objective world (nature and society). The pain of *Li Sao* contains the poet's dilemma in choosing a living environment, and the poet can also "take advantage of the ride" (*Li Sao*) and "climb to the top of the sky to pick the stars" (*Goddess of Birth*). The author chased the dragon and the phoenix, driving the sun and catching the moon, and had supreme power. (3) The poem excels in the mysterious magnificent imageries as shown in the comments by Ban Gu: "*Hong Bo Li Ya* (grandeur, beautiful, and elegant)" and Wang Yuan: "*Aoya Hong Shen* (elegant, magnificent, and deep)." (4) The whole work is rich in twists and turns, showing the dynamic beauty of changes.

The poetry of the Jin and Tang dynasties represented by Tao Yuanming and Wang Wei falls into the "conscious" form of Chinese classical poetry. Chinese poetry matured from the "freedom" style during this period, which is precisely a result of the "great unification" and "super stability" of Chinese traditional culture. This provided Chinese literati with a relatively "fair" approach compared to the pre-Qin period, but it also deprived their freedom of choice. The Chinese literati were defined as limited and weak individuals in a strict system. The features of "self" gradually disappear, are lost in society, or are dissolved in "nature." The maturity of Confucianism, Buddhism, and Taoism and the harmony between them affect the basic characteristics of the "conscious" form of Chinese poetry: (1) The dissolution of the self and the downplay of individual personality. (2) People accept the conditioning of the objective world and pursue the "harmony between man and nature." (3) Poetry pursues the "aesthetic conception" harmoniously formed, and "hidden or implicit beauty" became its new aesthetic orientation. (4) "Plainness and inaction" became typical temperaments of poetry, showing a static beauty of "far-reaching quietness." Of course, not all Jin and Tang poems are plain and peaceful, "winning by the atmosphere it created." Yet, Tao and Wang's poetic inclinations represent the most unique and far-reaching choices of Chinese poetry culture in the "conscious" period, especially in line with Guo Moruo's understanding.

Free poetry and conscious poetry provide different inspirations for Guo Moruo's prototypes from the idea to the art. Then, how did Guo Moruo view such differences? Qu Yuan's "pre-Qin freedom" was always respected by Guo Moruo, and Tao and Wang's "Jin and Tang consciousness" also fit his needs. Guo Moruo once compared Qu Yuan and Tao Yuanming, the "extremely antagonistic pair," and said: "Of these two poets, which one do I prefer? It is difficult to say. According to my recent narrative, naturally, it is more about Qu Yuan." "However … anyone who had been influenced by Laozi and Zhuangzi's thoughts, I believe, would favor Tao Yuanming and his poems … . This kind of plain poetry is the main style of Chinese poetry."[26] On another occasion, he said: "I would like the plain style. For example, Tao's poems quite fit my taste, and I like Wang Wei's poems of the Tang Dynasty. These belong to the plain style."[27] It can be seen that Guo Moruo dismissed such differences.

His cultural tolerance spirit during the May Fourth era also included tolerance for the difference itself.

The meaning of "free" and "conscious" as prototypes were determined and played a decisive role in the depth of the poet's subjective consciousness.

Cycling of Free and Conscious Forms: Guo Moruo's Poetry

Free and conscious forms of Chinese classical poetry culture are the basis for Guo Moruo to interpret and accept Western poetry, just as Zhuangzi and Wang Yangming are the basis of his recognition of Western "pantheism." The archetypal form of Chinese classical poetry culture was activated by the spirit of the times and produced its modern forms under the impact of Western poetry. These modern forms often contain more modernity and Westernization tendency, but they are still guided by the spirit of Chinese traditional culture. It is the Chinese classical poetry culture that determines what Guo Moruo chose and how to choose from the Western world.

After "Ten Years of Writing," Guo Moruo had a well-known self-reflection:

> My short process of poetry writing experienced three phases. The first phase is Tagore style before the May Fourth era. The poems written during this period were light and short, with very little achievement. The second phase is the Whitman style, which fell into the climax period of the May Fourth era. The poems written during this period were bold and crude, but it was the most memorable period of my life. The third phase is Goethe-style, during which I somehow lost the enthusiasm of the second period and became a player of the verses.[28]

Although his self-interpretation borrows images of Western poets and his division of several stages is rather complicated, once we analyze it with some of the poet's other important self-reports, especially if we delve deep into his poetic art world, it becomes clear and simple. The important reason for the multiple changes in Guo Moruo's poems can be found in the prototypes of Chinese classical poetry. The mutual growth of free form and conscious form promotes the volatility of the inner spirit of the poet. The changes are not boundless or elusive. It is either the increase of the "free" spirit or the rise of "consciousness," a spiral cycle of freedom and consciousness.

In "My Poem Writing Experience," Guo Moruo associated the plain style of Tagore with the plain styles of Tao, Wang, and others. This shows when he just set foot on the path of poetry writing, the "conscious" form of Chinese classical poetry plays a major role. This may be the enlightenment period of poetry that every modern Chinese poet can hardly avoid. Verses of the Jin and Tang dynasties are the most important part of Chinese modern poet education. In Guo Moruo's unique "creative misunderstanding," the plain style created by the modern Indian poet Rabindranath Tagore evoked his "acquaintance" sense of intimacy and encouraged him to make the "Chinese-Western integration."

During the May Fourth era, with the rise of the call for individual liberation, the flourishing of the literary revolution, and the spread of Whitman's poetry, Guo Moruo's inherent "freedom" genes grew again. During this period, what he termed "naked humanity," "dynamic cultural spirit," "compete with the environment," "self-expansion," and "rebellious spirit of despising all authority,"[29] were his understanding of the "inherent" indexes of pre-Qin culture. Qu Yuan and his *Chu Ci* were the verses of the pre-Qin culture. Therefore, Guo Moruo saw a self-projection more or less in Qu Yuan:

> Qu Yuan's *Li Sao* style and the classical Chinese texts—the equivalent of the Chinese vernacular of the Spring and Autumn Period and the Warring States Period—went through a "May Fourth Movement" two thousand years ago. Qu Yuan was a leading player in this movement.[30]

The Goddesses is the "free form" *Li Sao* style by Guo Moruo, where Guo Moruo shaped the "I" who defeated idols and advocated creation and freedom of will. He spoke in Qu Yuan's tone in "Xiang Lei": "I follow the spirit of creation. I am free to create. I freely express myself." *The Goddesses* advertises the status of "self" strongly, while the objective world is the object of "my" creation, control, and spur, and the externalization of the spirit of "I." According to "Xiang Lei": "I create dignified mountains, magnificent oceans. I create the sun, the moon, and the stars. I ride over winds and thunderstorms. Although my essence is limited to me, if allowed, it could fill the universe." "I have blood to be shed, fire to erupt. I want to gallop no matter in any respect!" In "Tiangou," "I swallowed the moon, / I swallowed the day, / I swallowed all the planets / I swallowed the whole universe." The sun in *Sunrise* became a symbol of vigorous life: "Oh, the bright lights on the front of the motorcycle! / You, the Apollo at the end of the 20th century! / Do you now ride a motorcycle?" Similar to *Qu Sao*, *The Goddesses* is colorful, full of imagery and dynamic beauty of the ups and downs, including the rushing body movements and the thought movements of dramatic changes. For example, in "Trumping on the Edge of the Earth": "The infinite Pacific lifts the power of his whole body to push the earth down. / Ah! The rolling giant waves that come to my eyes! /

Ah! Constant destruction, constant creation, constant efforts!" This is the movement of the bodies. Others such as "Phoenix Nirvana": "The universe, the universe, / Why do you exist? / Where do you come from? / Where are you sitting? / You are a finite big air ball? / Are you an infinite piece? / If you are a finite ball . . ." This is the flow of thoughts.

From 1921 to 1922, Guo Moruo returned to China many times from Japan. What he heard and witnessed destroyed his illusion of reviving the spirit of the pre-Qin culture: "Weeping for our fallen children, / weeping for our fallen culture, / weeping for our young people" (*Starry Heaven*). To relieve these deep sorrows, Guo Moruo started his *Starry Heaven* period, what he called Goethe-style writing. However, the so-called "passionate enthusiasm lost and become a player of verses" is not the true face of the wise, persistent Goethe. It is more like the second resurrection of the "conscious" prototype of Chinese poetry. Such as "After the Rain":

> The universe after the rain,
> Like a conscience washed by tears,
> Quiet and peaceful.
>
> Silver waves shining on the sea,
> The sky is painted with clouds,
> Like a lush green forest!
>
> Flat on the shore,
> Fishing boats standing in lines,
> Not a half soul seen.
>
> Two or three lights,
> Flickering on the island far away -
> Or are they the rising stars?

This could remind us of Wang Wei's "Autumn Evening in the Mountains":

> After fresh rain in the mountains bare; Autumn permeates the evening air. Among pine trees bright moonbeams peer; Over crystal stones flows water clear. Bamboos whisper of washer-maids; Lotus stirs when the fishing boat wades. Though fragrant spring may pass away, Still here's the place for you to stay.

"Freedom" is the need of Chinese poets to show their personality during social turmoil periods. "Consciousness" is the product of self-comfort during social stability periods. Interestingly, this historical law also applied to Guo Moruo, who easily raised the banner of freedom as an active, enthusiastic youth studying abroad. Yet, when he had to face the reality of a stable, silent

Chinese society, "freedom" becomes meaningless so the "consciousness" prototype quietly prevailed. But, history also offered another chance for "freedom" to Guo Moruo. After 1923, with the development of the social revolution, especially with Guo Moruo's contact and understanding of Marxist thoughts, his restrained, subconscious desire for struggle and resistance gained stronger support than before, and so came the writing of *Prelude* and *Recovery*. *Prelude* is about the revolutionary and rebellious prelude, while *Recovery* is a symbol of Guo Moruo's "resurrection" from the "deep depression" of a strong will, "to urinate in a determined attitude . . . to defecate with the power of the will" (*Recovery*). In the past, it was generally believed Guo Moruo reacted against "the deep individualistic color of the past" during the *Prelude* and *Recovery* period. He also stated clearly: "I used to be a person who respected individuality and admired freedom. However, in the past one or two years, I had learned more about the tragic society under the bottom line. I feel it is outrageous for a few people to advocate individuality and freedom in an era when most people lost their freedom involuntarily and lost their personality."[31] Despite this, as long as we carefully analyze the poetry of this period, we can easily see the poet still longed for freedom and desired to show through the "rough screaming." And when he spoke loudly and wildly as the spokesperson of all the oppressed, *The Goddesses*-style character and *The Goddesses*-style poetic pursuit are presented clearly:

> The example of revolutionary life in this vulgar language.
> I want to keep a determined attitude and the boiling will,
> What if my head is sawn off by someone?
> There are no curved bows on both sides in the world.
>
> —"Recovery"

Then, after the second resurrection of the prototype of the "freedom" of Chinese classical poetry, is the "conscious" prototype also activated once again? On the surface, works including the *Tiao Tang Collection* and *War Collection* during the War of Resistance against Japanese Aggression and the *Ode to New China*, *Tide Collection*, *Camel Collection*, and *Dongfeng Collection* after the liberation were filled with the passion for the revolution, which seemed to be far from the "plain and quiet" style of Tao and Wang. But, if we take into consideration this poet's special status during this period, especially after 1949, we can believe Guo Moruo was no longer likely to be wild and could "scream." In theory, he undoubtedly entered the "consciousness" stage. Therefore, we have to pay special attention to the fact that during this period, the most important of Guo Moruo's poetry writing is the emergence of a large number of traditional-style poems. We know Chinese classical poetry established its forms during the Jin and Tang dynasties. The typical form, the third resurrection of the "conscious" prototype, seems to be first manifested in the form of poetic art. In addition, we also noticed in Guo Moruo's traditional-style poems, such sentences are frequently seen:

> On the top of the mountain, the sun climbed to the peak. I looked down the running stream. The breeze is gentle and the river is dancing in the warm weather. The narrow paths are decorated with pine trees and the cars almost run over the rainbows. There are no clouds in the sky and the green mountains are circling. ("The Vision")
>
> Beihai once came here, said the calligraphy on the rocks. The scenery outside the cave is beautiful and the blessed land is magical in the cave. Brightened by the torch of the yacht and quenched my thirst with the veggie soup. I would like to linger longer, but time is going fast. ("A Visit to Qixingyan of Duanzhou-Bixia Cave Visit")
>
> Hibiscus flowers are blossoming right now. The lake is fully red with autumn water. We watched the fish jumping on the boats, and crabs to be cooked with wine glasses ready. The return of birds made the willow branches swing. Wild geese broke the gentle pine tree breeze. The thatched house of Goushan was still there. Yet, the master was nowhere to be seen. ("A Visit to the Former-residence of Goushan")

As a high-ranking official at that time, Guo Moruo must have been busy with government duties. It was natural he would not have the "plain" feeling. Yet, when given some leisure time, Guo Moruo enjoyed the landscape so much that the traditional cultural prototypes in his deep consciousness would emerge.

Simply put, in Guo Moruo's poetic art career, the "free" form and "conscious" form of Chinese poetry culture have been rotating and played a crucial role for him. In the preface of *Starry Heaven*, Guo Moruo once quoted Kant's famous saying: "Two things fill the mind with ever new and increasing admiration and awe, the oftener and more steadily we reflect on them: the starry heavens above me and the moral law within me." By examining Guo Moruo's creative practice, he showed the Chinese characteristics to interpret the "starry heavens" as an objective world, and interpreted personal free will and the principle of survival as "the moral law within me." The former attracted the poet to enter "consciousness," while the latter stimulated the "freedom" of the poet. Therefore, the "freedom" and "consciousness" of the prototype of Chinese poetry indeed refreshed themselves, renewed themselves, and presented feelings of surprise and magnificence all the time.

Rival Growth of Free and Conscious Forms: A Glimpse of Guo Moruo's Spiritual Structures

Now that we have made a brief review of Guo Moruo's poetic writing through the archetypal meanings of "freedom" and "consciousness," I think there are two points that should be specifically stressed:

1. The so-called "free" and "conscious" cyclical growth is just a rough description. In fact, in addition to such a regular evolution, the relationship between the two prototype forms is much more complicated. For example, both "freedom" and "consciousness" may be working in their power during the same period of writing; thus, making a quite complex impact on Guo Moruo's poetry writing.
2. It is also interesting, although Guo Moruo experienced such tortuous changes in poetry style and saw the influence of the "free" prototype and the "conscious" prototype on himself, it is obvious Guo Moruo did not realize the special status of these two poetry forms in his poetry art—their cyclical growth, and their differences and contradictions.

What conclusions can we draw from these two aspects? It is clear in Guo Moruo's spiritual structure, the relationship between "freedom" and "consciousness" is implicitly presented as a kind of mutual growth, dynamically balancing and checking each other.

First, let's review these two. "Freedom" and "consciousness" coexist during the same period of Guo Moruo's poem-writing process. However, due to their differences in ideas and the visionary world, Guo Moruo showed some confusion and disorientation in his poetic pursuits. This is the so-called "checking," especially when both prototypes attempt to show themselves within the same poem. Thus, internal conflicts are inevitably exposed. In general, "freedom" arouses the poet's self-awareness and demands "emergence" of the self, while "consciousness" strongly dissipates the self-consciousness and demands "forgetting" of the self. "Freedom" allows images and thoughts of the subject to be fully expressed in poems, while "consciousness" is repeatedly intoxicated in the world of "the Unity of Heaven and Man." "Sudden emerging" and "forgetting," "full expressions" and "intoxication" as two separate poetic art tendencies are mixed from time to time, which constitutes the unique juxtaposition feature of Guo Moruo's poetry.

For example, in "Phoenix Nirvana," the burning fire of the West Phoenix is a symbol of free will highlighted in the poem, making it fully express its feelings in a cursed world. But, when it was "reborn from the ashes," a scene of "freedom" is presented:

> One of everything, harmony.
> Everything of one, harmony.
> Harmony is you, harmony is me.
> Harmony is him, harmony is fire.
> The fire is you.
> The fire is me.
> The fire is him.
> The fire is fire.
> ...

Regardless of you and me, regardless of the self and the world, all the mountains and rivers, birds, animals, and human beings are wrapped in "harmony," which is precisely the spirit of the "conscious" prototype of Chinese poetry culture. In Chinese culture, the philosophical significance of "one" is so prominent that it is precisely the characteristics of the "three religions in one" during the Jin and Tang dynasties. Only at this time, "The Dao formulated the one (nonbeing gives birth to the oneness)" and "Sages would make this one principle as their guideline" by Laozi (*Laozi*), "My path is consistent" by Confucius (*The Analects of Confucius*), and the "emptiness" of Buddhism were interpreted by Chinese literati so freely. "Consciousness" eventually dominated "freedom." Another example is "The West Lake: in the Rain":

> It's raining so loud,
> Yet, the lake is dyed pink.
> The cloudy sky around
> Which seems to be drunk.
>
> The bathing West Lake,
> A nude beauty!
> In my body ...
> Such unspeakable shivering!
> Oh, here come a few girls who sketched,
> However, *unschoeh*.

Unschoeh (as written in the original poem) means not beautiful. Guo Moruo was originally in a "self-lost" state, "forgetting" himself, indulging in the misty scenery of the West Lake. However, his heart was not "dead," and his consciousness was still operating, so when the opposite sex appear, the desires and thoughts of the self were activated. Here, "freedom" overtook the "consciousness." Similar examples can be found in "The Drunk Song under the Plum Blossom Tree," "Night Walk," "Snowy Morning" etc.

However, we do not need to exaggerate the contradictory relationship between "freedom" and "consciousness" because despite differences, after all, they belong to the two prototypes of Chinese classical poetry culture. They have an opposite side, but there is a more unified side. The "conscious" form, however different from the "free" form, is the product of the latter's transformation. The Chinese pre-Qin poetry represented by *Qu Sao* cannot parallel with Western poetry, especially the romantic poetry of the 19th century despite its individuality and self-prominence. After all, the "freedom" of pre-Qin culture and the "consciousness" of Jin-Tang culture have their own special "Chinese characteristics."

The "freedom" of pre-Qin culture did not achieve the absolute, ontological meaning of the Western style. It is relative and related to a series of specific cultivations of individuals. These self-cultivations generally include such ideas as patriarchal ethics, the moral personality of the inner sage, teachings of the sages, the basics of personal cultivation, and the responsibility to the nation. These connotations are very obvious in *Qu Sao*. This has already given birth to the possibility of dissolving the self and achieving the unity of Nature or Heaven (*Tian*) and Man ("*Tian*" has multiple meanings. It can be nature. It can also be the heavenly principle, the national righteousness, etc.), which laid the foundation for the pursuit of poetry culture essence in the "conscious" period. Correspondingly, the "consciousness" of Jin and Tang culture did not completely abolish the "freedom" of the pre-Qin style. When it comes to personal cultivation, poets such as Tao Yuanming all valued the morality of human beings and advocated human ethics and role modeling of the previous sages without exception. Poets during Jin through Tang dynasties expressed their thoughts and feelings freely. However, they internalized more spiritual factors (natural life or national responsibility) "outside the self" into personal thoughts and emotions, and achieved "freedom" within "consciousness."

This consistency of free prototypes and conscious prototypes in the deep structure is understood and accepted by Guo Moruo naturally, and led to the characteristics of Guo Moruo's poetic pursuits of "variety along with unity" and "purity among mixture." It is what we call "there is dynamic balancing and checking each other"—a key to our deep exploration into the spirit of Guo Moruo's poetry.

Since the publication of *The Goddesses*, Guo Moruo's "freedom" pursuit was deeply influenced by the spirit of *Qu Sao*: "Freedom" is not purely individual and certainly not absolute. It always refers to national salvation. "I would not be willing to live stealthily, I would rather die like a hero. I would be willing to sacrifice my life, to save all the lives of the nation!" ("Flowers of the Brotherhood") Self does not mean chasing individual interests and happiness without hesitation. He often called himself a savior and observed the world and others from this savior's point of view. In this way, even "gangsters" became the benevolent people who dedicated themselves to society ("The Gangsters"), and the working people became the objects of pity and sympathy ("In the First Hour of the School Dropping"; "Earth, My Mother"; "Under the Leifeng Pagoda I"). Guo Moruo never explored his inner state, never made more complicated, detailed human spiritual freedom. He seldom expressed the hardships and difficulties faced by self and freedom in confrontation with the realistic world. However, these are all problems that must be solved by true modern "freedom." Guo Moruo was more accustomed to presenting "freedom" in the definition of a Chinese prototype form to "respond to" Western romantic poetry. This brings about a problem. When the poet wanted to highlight the "self" and "freedom" as the Western poets did, he appeared somewhat lacking in strength, exposing his inner weakness. "Tiagou" may be Guo Moruo's most wild, most free works, but, in my opinion, from the engulfing of the universe to the engulfing of the self, the spirit of *Tiangou* is precisely chaotic, confused, and lacks real strength. Sometimes, Guo Moruo endlessly quoted from Chinese and foreign cultures, and compiled them to express his "creative power":

> I called the Yabo of the Zhou Dynasty, / I called the scholars of Chu, / I called the poem masters of the Tang Dynasty, / I called the Ci masters of the Yuan Dynasty/ The ancient Indian poets who wrote *Vedas*! / Dante who wrote the *Divine Comedy*! / Milton who wrote *The Paradise Lost*! / Tragic Goethe who wrote *Faust*!
> —"The Creator"

But, what kind of courage does the creator have? What we see is limited. During the *Prelude* and *Recovery* period, the hollowness of freedom and resistance is even more apparent. Sometimes, even Guo Moruo felt this deeply:

> I am poetry, this is my declaration, / I belong to the proletariat; /but I think I am still weak, / I should have to burst / I am afraid that I recovered not long ago, / my temperament is not as strong as before. / I hope that one day, / I can roar like a storm.
> —"The Declaration of Poetry"

The withdrawal of self-awareness and the emptiness of the freedom spirit also determined Guo Moruo's attitude toward the objective world. We have seen although the poet often rose to the praise of life when facing the mountains and seas, and often evoked an exciting and sublime experience, he always put himself in an "infected" and "being called" position, without showing much of the fight and clash between humans and nature in the landscape of Western romantic poetry. Following this logic, when the poet's "self" and "freedom" were further weakened in practice, the objective world would naturally look majestic and terrifying, and he felt oppressed and shocked: "Ah, I am afraid to see the dark mountain shadows, / they are like giants in fairy tales! / That cannot be resisted . . ." ("The Lampstand"). Guo Moruo rose and fell in the storm of the objective world. Over time, he finally became tired and weakened: "All the way through the turbulent tide / I was rushed into the sea." "The turbid waves / have already dyed my deep heart. /When / can I recover my clarity and purity?" ("Lamentation in the Yellow Sea")

When one sighed about his weakness in the face of the objective world without stronger, tougher support, the idea of "unity of Heaven (Nature) and Man" was born. Guo Moruo once said Si Kongtu's *Poetry* was one of his favorites during his life. In the excitement of national righteousness, in the "smooth, exquisite" nature, as Si Kongtu mentioned in his *On Li's Poetry Book*, our weak hearts found the most practical, more appropriate support. As a result, Chinese poetry turned to a "conscious" form. Thus, it realized its internal transition from "freedom" to "consciousness," starting another cycle.

In the Preface of *Starry Heaven*, Guo Moruo discussed his basic concept of traditional culture.

> There is no absolute newness between heaven and earth, and there is no absolute old. All new and old are only relative, and hypothetical, and cannot be used as a criterion for value criticism. I want to borrow the skeleton structure of the ancient people and blow some life into it . . .

In poetry writing, Guo Moruo borrowed the "freedom" prototype of Chinese traditional poetry culture and "conscious" prototypes, trying to endow it with the colors of modern life. Of course, it is beyond Guo Moruo's expectations that the "ancient people" did not die rigidly nor only skeletons were left. Rather, they may have a significant impact on today's new life.

Wen Yiduo: Self-deconstruction of the Traditional, Psychological Structure

Great Wall! Let me knock you down, too,
We both are burdens, what are the pities?
—Wen Yiduo, "Lamentation at the Foot of the Great Wall"

"A Simple Chinese"

The generation and development of Chinese modern poetry can be said to be an adjustment to the traditional Chinese poetry culture. People gradually break from the constraints of traditional aesthetics and language models and look for poetry styles with modern significance. However, different poets have completely different choices about how to understand Chinese tradition and how to adjust to modernity. It is precisely the individual's choices that determine the kaleidoscopic modern Chinese new poetry—its characteristics and orientation, successes and failures.

When Hu Shih and other early vernacular poets advocated the great liberation of poetry, their attitudes and courage were unquestionable, regardless of whether they used Western poetics or another part of Chinese traditional poetics to fight the problems with tradition. Regardless of whether Guo Moruo suspected Tao Yuanming, Wang Wei, and Li Bai because of his reading of Rabindranath Tagore, Walt Whitman, and Johann Wolfgang von Goethe, undoubtedly he was excited and did not hesitate to change his direction. However, Wen Yiduo, who rose a little later than the generation of Chinese poets in the history of new poetry, is very special. The increasingly strong new cultural atmosphere did not make him feel high-spirited. On the contrary, he seemed to be more cautious, even serious, and old-fashioned than previous generations. This is very interesting in the development of Chinese new poetry. It is also unique within the Crescent Moon School.

Wen Yiduo was known for being calm, simple, and strictly self-disciplined. At Tsing Hua College (it was renamed "Tsinghua University" later), he was self-cultivated, and reflected himself three times a day, like a standard traditional Confucian scholar.[32] A series of commentaries he published in *Tsinghua Weekly* indicated Wen Yiduo was incompatible with the "Westernization" faction. "Recovering traditional ethics" was his conscious pursuit. After studying in the United States, the most important for him were his motherland, his hometown, and his loved ones on the other side of the ocean, including his wife, whom he married by his parents' orders. The autumn colors of Chicago's Jackson Park were always superimposed with the golden color of Beijing. He studied diligently and rejected entertainment for a young man. From 1925 to 1926, as a university professor, he was self-disciplined and highly respected. He provided opportunities for younger scholars. As a scholar, he was rigorous, realistic, and meticulous. As a democratic warrior, he dedicated his life to the future of the nation. He practiced traditional Confucian moral ideals of "self-respect and repaying the benevolence" and "solving the crisis and shouldering responsibilities for the country."

More importantly, Wen Yiduo, who had a strong classical temperament, maintained a distinctive Chinese character in his academic research, poetry writing, and overall cultural pursuit. He connected these creative activities with the historical mission of maintaining Chinese traditional culture. Whether in "the Americanized Tsinghua" or in the simple "Two-Month Sojourn Hut," his main study plan was based on Chinese traditional culture. When he was in the United States, he strongly advocated the "nationalism of Chinese culture" to resist the "conquest" of foreign cultures. His earliest work, "Notes of the Two-Month Sojourn Hut," is his thoughts on learning Chinese traditional culture. During the next 20 years, he devoted himself to the research and compilation of the cultural heritage of China. Wen Yiduo's fame as a poet among his classmates at Tsinghua was originally from his classic Chinese poetry writing. When vernacular poetry became popular, he was cautious and did not rush to join. From *Winter Nights Review* to "The Local Colors of *The Goddesses*," Wen Yiduo attacked the "European envy" of the May Fourth poetry community. Fairly, *The Goddesses* does not lack the pursuit of Chinese classical beauty, but in the view of Wen Yiduo, it still lacked "local colors" and was "excessively Europeanized."[33] Wen Yiduo was the first to criticize the radical thoughts of early Chinese new poetry. He first announced unambiguously: "I want to always remember I am Chinese, I want to write poems of a new style, but the new poetry of China."[34] He was immersed in the artistic world of Western poets, such as Keats, Hardy, Haussmann, Tennyson, Browning, etc., but all these foreign cultures were based on his "déjà vu" nostalgia for Chinese classical poetry. According to him, the resurrection of traditional poetics was the "baby born after the marriage of Chinese and Western art." In Wen Yiduo's poetry writing, the imagery and emotions of Chinese classical poetry continued especially the persistent, strong nationalist consciousness that had been forgotten by some modern poets. Even Zhu Ziqing praised him as "the only poet before the war who called loudly for patriotism."[35] The traditional origin of Wen Yiduo's theory of metrics is also obvious. He believed Chinese metrical poems were "the most esoteric poetry of art principles" and "regularity and harmony were the natural colors of Chinese philosophy, ethics, and art. And, poetry is the crystallization of these."[36] In his poetic theory of the "Three Beauties," the beauty of music came from his experience of the rhythm of the Chinese language. The beauty of architecture came from "the rhyme of the verse and the uniformity of the sentence."[37] The so-called beauty of painting was not what people often said, "painting within the poems," but the use of Chinese characters with their pictographic traits and perspective effects.[38]

It should be noted that the history of Chinese modern poetry has never severed its relationship with historical traditions. Among Chinese modern poets, it is not difficult to find the deep imprint of Chinese traditional culture from the attitudes of life, and academic thoughts to creative practice. These imprints can be found in those who actively develop new poetry as well as those who are once critical and oppose the development of new poetry. Guo Moruo regarded Spinoza and Tagore's pantheism as the "Unity of Heaven and Man" of Chinese traditional aesthetics and regarded the May Fourth literary revolution as the development of the Qu Yuan spirit. Xu Zhimo wrote for "spiritual" and the Symbolism poets discussed "the national colors we advocate."[39] The Modernist poets "had the intention to connect with the long tradition of Chinese poetry willingly,"[40] while during the May Fourth era, opponents of the new poetry, such as Huang Kan, Hu Xiansu, Wu Mi, Mei Guangdi, and Zhang Binglin, were defenders of the traditional poetry culture of China. Then, what independent characteristics distinguished Wen Yiduo from others in the national consciousness?

I believe this independent trait is Wen Yiduo's efforts to maintain Chinese traditional culture linked to his inner emotional needs and feelings. This made him more persistent and focused than others, and his feelings richer and purer. "He has a strong personality, strong opinions, and is full of emotions. [Wen Yiduo] always insists on what he considers as right."[41] For this spiritual feature, Wen Yiduo neatly and humorously described himself as a "Simple Chinese." In 1922, he declared emotionally: "Americanization! Enough! Enough! Material civilization! I am afraid of you, I am tired of you, please leave me! Eastern civilization! China's soul! Come back! ... Let me remain an "old, dopey man" in the East! That's the ideal life for me!" Only because he had more dedication and purity than ordinary people can he be called a "dopey man"!

Both Chinese traditional culture and Chinese traditional poetry culture have a distinctive feature, that is, they both set their visionary world in a place far from reality. The "sages" of Confucianism, the "real persons" of Taoism, the "nirvana" of Buddhism, and the "Unity of Heaven and Man" are not the true state of our real life. Therefore, in the face of survival needs, in the context of constant movement and change, Chinese traditional culture and traditional poetry culture must try to maintain their authority with only two choices: one choice is to close eyes and separate the self and the real state of existence from the changing times by refusing to feel and reject the emotional demands aroused by new feelings. This "rejection" led to their decay, which is the real "corruption." During the May Fourth era, the opponents of the new poems fell into this choice. For example, Hu Xiansu refused to recognize Shen Yinmo's "Moonlight Night" as a poem. But, if you look closely, such outdated comments can't pose too much threat to the historical development, because they have blocked themselves in a fading past. In Chinese history, the most typical one should be the second choice. This choice is not to entangle the traditional ideal itself but try to grasp the message of the changing times and construct the traditional ideals of society. This requires generations of cultural descendants to constantly adjust to traditions, while also constantly adjusting to times, so they properly eliminate the sharpest and most subversive factors in the spirit of the times; thus, realizing the traditional and modern peaceful compromise. Such a choice not only preserves the traditions perfectly but also makes the subject seem flexible. Here lies the true preservation of Chinese cultural traditions and Chinese poetry culture traditions. Guo Moruo, Xu Zhimo, and the Symbolist and Modernist poets mainly chose the second option. They were the successors of the traditional poetry culture, but at the same time, we always see they conformed to the trends of the times and quickly accepted the modern message. The Western poetry cultures that came with the new era and the Chinese classical poetry culture of their "preconditioning" complemented and explained to each other. During the process of integrating Western poetry, they successfully practiced the traditional aesthetic ideals of China. They did not need to be only focused and obsessed with traditional ideals!

Wen Yiduo also looked forward to "the marriage of Chinese and Western art" (even one of the earliest advocates of the integration of Chinese and Western poetry). He hoped his favorite Western poetry and Chinese classical poetry would complement each other, but I think this kind of state of "peaceful coexistence" is mainly a mirage because we receive the messages of regret in his words. Wen Yiduo did not possess the flexibility of Guo Moruo or Xu Zhimo's calmness, freedom, and ease. Of course, he was less carefree compared to the Symbolist and the Modernist schools. He immersed his emotions in traditional poetry ideals. It is the rhythm of the metrical poetry that Wen Yiduo relished the most. He also focused his artistic feelings on the taste and appreciation of classical poetry, lingering and reluctant to leave it. Compared with the typical way of Chinese poets to maintain tradition, indeed, this is a special, extraordinarily, "dopey" way! Of course, Wen Yiduo's "dopey," and "rigidness" is essentially different from the "corrupted Confucianism" in that Wen Yiduo had true emotions and maintained keen senses, while the decaying cultural conservatives had completely lost such a state of mind, they only maintained "the poems as relics," without the ability to accept new poems or the artistic ability to write traditional poems!

The sincerity, perseverance, richness, and purity of emotions are the poetic talents of Wen Yiduo. For a long time, such feelings and emotions were closely wrapped around the traditions of Chinese classical poetry; thus, forming the unique "dopey" poet. Wen Yiduo's spiritual pursuit of "being dopey" deeply influenced his "Red Candle" and "Dead Water," affecting his entire poetry career and even his life path.

Coexistence of Two Kinds of Poetic Ideas

The sincere, persistent, and pure "old-fashioned, dopey man" characteristics also forged the complexity of Wen Yiduo's thoughts.

The sincerity, perseverance, richness, and purity of emotions must introduce one into a real world in practice, thus, separated from those ideals forms alienated from actual life. Any true emotions and feelings would lead to reality ultimately. When Wen Yiduo connected his true feelings of emotions and purity with the aesthetics of Chinese classical poetry independent of the times, it brought instability and complexity to his thought system. The poet's original intention was to maintain the "local colors" of modern poetry and the traditional poetry culture, while his emotions and feelings directed him to devote himself to a more contemporary, realistic place. Perhaps there should not be such a distance between traditional culture and reality in the "spirit of the times" and "local colors." Yet, the new Chinese poetry born at the end of the 20th century had indeed been thrown into a gap difficult to bridge. A sincere experience necessarily means an experience of the "gap" itself. When Wen Yiduo critiqued Guo Moruo's poems with the titles of "Spirit of the Times" and "Local Colors," we see the existence of this gap in Wen Yiduo's thoughts.

On the one hand, it is faithful feelings of the spirit of the times; on the other hand, it is bitter love for local colors and national traditions. Thus, two kinds of emotional powers and two characteristic feelings were formed. When they existed in the inner world of Wen Yiduo at the same time, the contradictions between them were not sufficiently large for them to separate and disintegrate from each other. They functioned as a special way to greatly expand the poet's feeling of space and enrich his emotional needs. From 1920 to 1922, Wen Yiduo received modern education, while submerging himself in the vast Chinese, traditional culture. While listening to the call of Keats and Tennyson, he frequently reviewed Li Bai and Li Shangyin, two poets during the Tang Dynasty. At this time, Wen Yiduo did not fully realize the contradictions and conflicts between these ancient and modern cultural factors. Therefore, he produced the richly conceived *The True Self Collection*, *Red Candle*, and other early works.

I believe the implications of this richness can be interpreted in two interrelated aspects: First, the feelings of traditional poetry blend with the feelings of modern society in Wen Yiduo's works; thus, increasing the emotional potential of his poems. In the early works of Wen Yiduo, such works accounted for the largest proportion, such as "Rainy Night," "Snow," "Two-month Sojourn Hut," "Flowers Opened," "The First Chapter of Spring," "The End of Spring Chapter," "Yellow Bird," "Lonely Wild Goose," "End of the Autumn," "A Young Pine Tree," "Innocence," "Morning Sun," "Advice," "Sadness," "The Death of Li Bai," "In Memory of Chrysanthemum," "Red Candle," and so on. The majority of these poems are all kinds of feelings generated in the natural environment, except for "The Death of Li Bai," a "re-reading" of the humanities tradition. But Li Bai, as a traditional symbol, is said to be an "object" in the broad sense. These are the typical motifs of Chinese classical poetry. Wen Yiduo's true passion for Chinese classical poetry made him familiar with traditional poetry so that he consciously and unconsciously "integrated" with these historical beauty imageries. When the crystal poetic and rich images emerged in front of the poet, he would have the traditional "*Gan-Xing*" (feeling and starting up). In previous chapters, I analyzed the special "generation" meaning of *Xing* to the creation of Chinese new poetry. It can be said that a large number of poems by Wen Yiduo are "generated" in such a way. Sometimes, when Wen Yiduo wanted to express some inner emotions, he would use external objects and borrow Chinese poetry's "starting up" (*Xing*) mode. For example, to express his feelings about leaving the country, he wrote a "lonely goose" ("Lonely Wild Goose"). To dispel his loneliness and seek beauty, he invited Li Bai ("The Death of Li Bai"). However, Wen Yiduo is an excellent artist who was sensitive to feelings. After all, he was always in the same "typical" modern living environment, which would shape people and the world. When he left home to study alone, it means the kindness and harmony he was familiar with was left behind. Wen Yiduo had to rely more on himself. Whether in the Tsinghua University of China or the United States, personality, undoubtedly, is particularly important in the survival competition between each other and in the future. Willpower is undoubtedly necessary. Likewise, whether in Tsinghua or the United States, the pure, innocent natural environment of the rural areas of Xishui in Hubei Province, his hometown, ceased to exist. The busy rhythm of the metropolis destroyed the relationship between man and nature. People were separated from the natural background and looked at the misty landscape from a distance, which created new feelings.

All of Wen Yiduo's experiences brought new perspectives and new points of view to his observations. Therefore, although he still "expressed his feelings through scenery" and "expressed his thoughts through objects," the human spirit and will were more infiltrated into objects, thus often achieving the "humanization" of objects rather than the "objectification" of human beings. For example, Wen Yiduo commented on things in nature from time to time, summarizing the philosophy of life—the beautiful songs of nightingales and ugly songs of the crows are all natural; yet, the parrot "forgets his songs to learn the human language," and eventually becomes a traitor of birds. How important "innocence" is (*Innocence*)! The rainy night was horrifying and he wanted to escape into dreams, but the sober rationality reminded Wen Yiduo to face life: "Oh! It turns out that I have been disgusted by the real me. Does the fake me have no dignity" ("Rainy Night")? Nature became the externalization of the human spirit and human taste. The yellow bird was a beautiful life, "shot into the sky" ("Yellow Bird"). A little pine tree turned his neck and looked at you ("A Young Pine Tree"). The lonely goose had a letter on its feet, shouldering a solemn mission to fly "into the stinky butcher's yard" ("Lonely Wild Goose"). The bee was "like a sick monk begging for alms with his bowl from door-to-door" ("Waste Garden"). "The diligent sun is like the master of a family" ("Morning Sun"). The "luxurious autumn" was "the prodigal son of nature" ("End of the Autumn")! The poet's subjective image began to rise and emerged. They were no longer satisfied with the response from nature, and no longer had resonance as the only channel for poetry. The rich inner world of the subject is a source of poetry. "Although the strings are not ringing, the music is still there.... Even with the fall of the flower pedals / I dare not to feel disappointed, nor do I want to plant another one to replace it" ("Blossomed Flowers")! Wen Yiduo was no longer only preoccupied with the unity of Heaven (Nature) and Man, peace and harmony. Conflicts were also presented, including conflicts between various life phenomena in nature, the struggle between man and nature, such as "the wind and frost was condescending the world," "the people who trembled in the forest" were striving against nature, even the heavy snow "can't bury the blue smoke on the roof," "Ah! The blue smoke flying into the sky! / It seems to be the poet's soul going upward, / penetrating his own body and going straight to heaven" ("Snow"). The aesthetics of Wen's poetry is elevated.

Second, under the premise of not deliberately subverting the classical poetics mode and achieving the effect of "defamiliarization," Wen Yiduo also expressed some new feelings of existence that can only be produced under modern conditions. For example, Wen Yiduo felt the different human images in the state of sleeping and waking: the sleeping looked innocent and pure as the moon, while the waking mode made others feel "terrible" ("The Sleeping"). "The Lesson of Time," "Bell," and other poems described the relationship between time and life. "Encounter in the Illusion," "The Tributaries," and "National Champion" show a special kind of love: spiritual love in dreams; yet, persistent and sincere. "Volunteer" conveys sincerity and ideals that should exist in a frenzied world. This is "an unyielding youth's will." These emotions and feelings are abstract, and they do not necessarily resort to the images of nature. They mainly come from the poet's subjective conscious world, but they all have one common feature-—either they are short or they are influenced by the classical improvisation of the style. These show a certain partial feeling of Wen Yiduo, so they do not form their majestic feelings to replace the lyric mode of Chinese classical poetry.

At the same time, Wen Yiduo's modern feelings also led to some longer pieces (such as "Sword Box" and "West Bank"), and he also produced anti-improvised works (such as "The Faithful Servant of Art" and "The Soul of Red Lotus"). Yet, these poems, while depicting personal artistic ideals, personal ideals, or cultural explorations, are filled with strong traditional accents. Why? There are a large number of images or the language of classical poetry in these poems: Taiyi (name of an immortal), incense burner, swirling smoke, ancient harp, reed, mandarin ducks, sacred, monarch, cauldron, virtuous people, young phoenix, Buddha, Five-Old-Man Peak of Lushan Mountain, and frustrated intellectuals. Wen Yiduo wanted to express new feelings and create a classical atmosphere at the same time, which showed the tempting charm of traditional art.

To put it simply, when young Wen Yiduo first embarked on the road of making a living independently, the new life experience of modern society enveloped the sincere, keen poet. It can be said all of his early writings (*The True Self Collection, Red Candle*, etc.) contain a "modern message," and none is the product of pure Chinese traditional aesthetics. However, for a long time including his studying in the United States, Wen Yiduo still had a great passion for Chinese traditional poetry culture and consciously immersed himself in the aesthetic concept of classical culture, which means it is not possible for him to quickly recognize the sharp contradictions and conflicts between ancient and modern cultural forms. Therefore, his writing presented to readers the coexistence of ancient and modern Chinese and Western poetry cultures. In connection with the two aspects analyzed above, I believe these cultures can coexist precisely because the poet's understanding of these kinds of cultures was not deep; when the crisis of Chinese classical poetry culture was not shown; yet, the poet's nostalgia for it remained calm. Likewise, when the real survival problem had not appeared, any modern experience by Wen Yiduo can only be shallow, and the two facts each found are "neither too big nor too small" in his emotional world. Thus, they avoided the collision of each other under normal circumstances.

Conflicts: From Emotions to Art

With a richer experience of life, the two cultures Wen Yiduo experienced simultaneously showed sharp contradictions. On the one hand, returning to China caused him a huge shock. Ancient China and the traditional Chinese culture associated with it were not as colorful as he imagined. In the real world, it had been crippled and lost the kind of vitality described in the historical books of China. On the other hand, with the end of student life, Wen Yiduo entered the real life of China and stepped into the bitter, dull society that was consistent with the culture of sedimentation. The torment of fate was just unfolding. The former aspect spurred the poet to lament the traditional culture of China. This sincere feeling finally culminated and burned within him; the latter aspect spurred Wen Yiduo's feelings of real life to reach a considerable depth. Both young and ancient cultures were operating in his emotional world. The space occupied by their respective poetic thoughts could no longer coexist in parallel. Contradictions and oppositions were inevitable. Wen Yiduo particularly respected feelings and emotions toward poetry. He did not intend to complete any form of reconciliation nor to weaken any part of the emotions. This gave birth to "Dead Water," a "self-contradictory" strange masterpiece in the history of Chinese modern poetry.

Wen Yiduo's deep national consciousness and his deep sense of reality were tightly intertwined. Contradictions and confrontations made his emotions extraordinarily sharp and fierce. His famous pieces, such as "Dead Water," "Discovery" and "One Phrase," certainly show the poet's patriotic and nationalistic spirits, but we should see this is by no means the kind of patriotism and nationalism we are familiar with. It did not have the "Everyone will one day die; When my day comes, may my loyalty be inscribed in the pages of history" (Wen Tianxiang, "A Prisoner's Lamentation Passing by Lindingyang"). It did not show the playfulness of "The Coal in the Furnace" by Guo Moruo, nor is there any heroism like the later anti-war poems. It was not as simple as the poet's early works, such as "I am a Prisoner" and "In Memory of a Chrysanthemum." The core of Wen Yiduo's patriotic emotions was a serious sense of frustration. His patriotism suffered serious frustrations. How unique this experience was! The profound reality experience made the poet soberly aware that in this decadent real society, under the control of the Chinese "unworthy offspring," how difficult real patriotism was, and how weak and how unreal it was! He deeply felt the decay of society and culture, and was restless, yet, helpless, toward it. Maybe these are the "self-contradictory" emotions surrounded by the "death water"! So he was disappointed by this "discovery," and he suppressed himself until he couldn't bear it. Wen Yiduo broke out and finally was indignant when he wrote "One Phrase." He could not help but outpour his curse to the "dead water." "Let 'ugliness' show its 'evil' nature as early as possible."[42]

For Wen Yiduo, a sincere, persistent patriotic intellectual, defending and promoting national culture dominated his spiritual pursuit. The frustrations of the goal in reality surely affected the poet, which had a huge impact on his spiritual world, and, thus, determined the artistic characteristics differences between his "Dead Water" and previous works, such as "Red Candle."

In my opinion, the most noteworthy feature of "Dead Water" is its "contradictory" nature. This contradiction includes two aspects: first is the contrast between the theme of poetry and emotional tones. The love poems in it have no warmth needed in the love poems. Rather, they are like a cold chilling well, such as "You Swear by the Sun," "Wolf," and "Drummer." The mourning poems try to restrain personal, and emotional impulses and put on an iron heart, such as "Maybe," and "Forget Her." Second, the contradiction is presented within a poem or presented as unexpected "mutations." For example, "Laundry Songs" shows the contradiction between actions with humiliation and the unwillingness to be humiliated. "Don't Blame Me" shows the contradiction between casual speech and emotionally deep devotion. "Spring Light" shows the contradiction between natural harmony and social disharmony. "You See" shows the contradiction between the effort to remove homesickness and the failure to do so. "Heartbeat" shows the contradiction between a peaceful family and unquiet thoughts. "What Dream" shows the contradiction between two choices—survival and death. "Prayer" shows the contradiction between attachment and doubt of the Chinese soul. "Sin" shows the contradiction of the misfortune of life and the numbness of bystanders. "Tiananmen" shows the contradiction between the sacrifice of the revolution and the indifference of a weak public. Among them, the poem "Confession" is the true expression of Wen Yiduo's contradictory personality: "The firmness of white stone," the admirer of heroes, mountains, and national flags—this is the "moral gentleman" who is familiar to us and admired by the world. "Flies-like thoughts" are the dark side of human beings. The vicissitudes of Wen Yiduo's life formed a deeper understanding of the self with a richer experience of the world. In his view, humans are inherently a wonderful combination of greatness and insignificance, beauty, and wretchedness. Light and darkness are always indispensable. Here, we can see the stable, changing aspects of this "Simple Chinese." He can be so sincere and frank, and speak what others do not dare say. Indeed, he was very "outspoken." However, at the same time, he was not willing to live only as a loyal, simple, "old, dopey man," which was progress in his understanding. The collision of the changed and the unchanged parts of this "Simple Chinese" constituted the contradiction of Wen Yiduo's personality, which further formed multiple characteristics of the poet's emotions and feelings. It was difficult for him to continue his writing as a "consistent" Chinese traditional poet.

The multiple characteristics of emotions and feelings formed the "mutual exclusion" effect of Wen Yiduo's poems in terms of ideas and forms. As we all know, a writer's choice of form is always a kind of "closeness in the struggle." As a habit, as a pre-existing norm, it seems natural that language forms do not comply with the needs of individual writers, especially for poets who need to ⋯⋯ ⋯e language potential most. However, in general, after the "wrestling" of ⋯⋯ ⋯t's selection process, the texts would finally show a "harmonious" scene in which thoughts and forms are relatively coordinated, different from the general cases. Wen Yiduo did not seem to achieve such perfect harmony. In the text of "Dead Water," the language form he chose still maintained a tense relationship with the ideas as if still wrestling and not yet finished. Undoubtedly, Wen Yiduo's spiritual contradiction is the expression of his free will. It is difficult for us to determine the aesthetic ideal of "Unity of Heaven and Man" from his works. His rich imagination fled across time and space, but the language forms he chose were a strict classical style, showing well-balanced sounds, sentences, paragraphs, and even the number of words. This stereotypic language put great pressure on free thought, while active thoughts and changing images attempted to open the closed shell of forms, which is the "mutual exclusion" effect on ideas and forms. For example, in *An Idea*, "everlasting mystery," "beautiful lies," and "significance of intimacy" are all abstract ideas. "Golden light," "fire," "call," "waves," and "rhythm" are irrelevant objects, which rise and fall in the flow of Wen Yiduo's thoughts. The differences between them show the complexity of the poet's spiritual world. It is the product of the alternation of his various emotions and feelings. Finally, the poet did not enter into a stable, simple "aesthetic conception." "Five thousand years of memory" was presented as "barbarian" and "beautiful" in the feelings. This showed Wen Yiduo's love and resentment, pursuit and resistance had not been properly matched; the "anti-aesthetic pursuit" thoughts of the free movement were shackled in very rigorous forms. Each sentence is composed of four pauses, and the number of Chinese characters is roughly equal (10 or 11 Chinese characters), with two sentences having one rhyme neatly. Wen Yiduo's free thoughts tried to break the restraints of the form but met patience. Patience and shock are the "mutual exclusion" of Wen Yiduo's thoughts and art. Shen Congwen said the author of "Dead Water" was so calm about the forms that the emotions in the poems were eradicated by their organization.[43] After reading "A Phrase," Zang Kejia said: "When I read these 16 sentences, I feel it is more powerful than reading another ten groups of 16 sentences. It has an inner power."[44]

Of course, such "mutual exclusion" also makes Wen Yiduo's writing fall into a trap. His free thoughts and the classical forms were so hard to accommodate each other that he arduously worked, and repeatedly revised and may still not be satisfactory at the end. He said, "I only feel that I am a volcano that has not erupted. The fire burns me, but I have no power (that is, skill) to blow up the crust that is confining me ...."[45] Sometimes, he also felt that the strict language forms could not coordinate with "the tone of the whole poem."[46]

In the history of Chinese modern poetry, this "mutual exclusion" phenomenon in Wen Yiduo's poems is very unique. *The Goddesses* by Guo Moruo include two styles of glory and plainness. The majestic, spectacular atmosphere generally matches a liberal language, such as "Good Morning." The dim and quiet mood is also entangled in some generally harmonious and traceable chapters. In the poems following, such as "Evening Walk," Guo Moruo's multiple mindsets successfully find the support of the language. Xu Zhimo's poems are essentially a combination of modern free personality and classical aesthetic spirit, but he can just melt rightly classical aesthetics into the freedom of modern language. Just as salt melts in water, we do not feel any external pressure. Although Guo Moruo and Xu Zhimo were also very different from each other in the complicated mentality adjustment process of "tradition-modernity," they weakened various cultural pursuits in different directions and successfully practiced modern culture. The digestion and absorption of classical culture ultimately safeguarded the unity of feelings and emotions and also maintained the unity of idea pursuits and artistic choices. For some young poets Wen Yiduo favored, such as Zang Kejia, Tian Jian, Ai Qing, Mu Dan, etc., the spirit of modern freedom had completed the transformation of classical taste. At a new level of transcendence, they found modern prose-style poetry compatible with their spiritual pursuits. "Mutual exclusion" would not be an obstacle for them. In the long river of historical development, only Wen Yiduo was trapped in the crevice between cultures, so he was destined to explore and struggle.

This echoes the spirit of the "Simple Chinese" mentioned earlier. From the moment when Wen Yiduo recognized this Chinese character, he unconsciously distanced himself from the traditional typical form. But excessive honesty that never let go of every bit of his feelings led to a dangerous self-subversion, which made his cultural pursuit full of contradictions and led to the fragmentation of the traditional Chinese poetry culture. In this way, Wen Yiduo walked through the "red candle" along with his own experiences and feelings, walked into the "dead water," and gradually dismantled the traditional psychological structure he had established.

Naturally, Wen Yiduo's entire dismantling process is very meaningful historically, bringing endless inspiration to future generations, but it is somewhat cruel to Wen Yiduo. The psychological pressure and division he suffered was something many poets (such as his colleague, Xu Zhimo) never had. As a realistic person, especially as an outstanding poet, it is difficult for him to live in the "mutual exclusion" of thought and art for a long time. "I only need a clear word, like the relics of the Buddha /with the light of treasure shining, I want the whole, positive beauty" ("Miracle"). The lyrical ambition of such freedom was not completed in the end, and the new "miracle" never came, so Wen Yiduo ended his painful poetry writing. In a certain sense, the suspension of Wen Yiduo's practice of poetry is the result of the difficulty of reconstructing Chinese traditional cultural psychology after self-dismantling. Suspension is a symbol that showed the difficulties that Chinese traditional poetry cultures faced in this transition to modern society.

Xu Zhimo: Modern Reconstruction of Classical Ideals

In the gentle waves of Cambridge
I would be a water plant!

—Xu Zhimo, "Farewell to Cambridge"

Zhu Ziqing, an authority on Chinese modern new poetry criticism, once said: "Xu Zhimo and Guo Moruo are two top Chinese modern poets."[47] However, people once had quite different opinions of Xu Zhimo. In particular, what kind of pursuit occupies the most fundamental position in Xu Zhimo's miscellaneous "idea tank"? What factors constitute the uniqueness of Xu Zhimo's poetics? Is it a democratic individual? Is it the British-style petty bourgeois spirit, or the so-called "simple belief"? Is it love, freedom, and beauty? These different understandings reveal some important messages about Xu Zhimo's thoughts and artistic pursuits. Yet, it is a regret that we have not found any elements with Xu Zhimo's representative personal traits. We have not elaborated on the individual meaning of Xu Zhimo's democratic individualism, petty bourgeois interest, and "love, freedom, and beauty" as a universal cultural trend.

I believe among all of Xu Zhimo's thoughts and artistic pursuits, what is most worthy of our study is his relationship with nature, his closeness and devotion to nature, and his acceptance and experience of nature. The simplicity and harmony of nature are deeply internalized as part of his spiritual world, which intrinsically determines the artistic choice of his poetic writing. Also in affinity with nature, Xu Zhimo consciously and unconsciously realized the tradition with a tacit understanding of the spirit of Chinese poetry culture, coupled reality and history, combined individual poetry and cultural traditions, and completed the modern reconstruction of Chinese classical poetic ideals. Whether it was an affinity with nature or a tacit understanding of tradition,

Xu Zhimo made it all natural. It is the first time such a delicate, cultural restructuring strived to rebel against tradition and create its own character, which proved successful in the history of Chinese modern poetry.

A Son of Nature

Nature was very important in Xu Zhimo's life. In his childhood, he "loved to play freely in the wilderness, and loved to imagine widely looking at the clouds in the sky."[48] The childhood wish of imagined flying when ascending high and looking into the distance stayed with him for a lifetime. Xu Zhimo was fascinated by the embrace of nature that Cambridge's "deep grass and people in the distance" and "cooling water flow" scenery attracted him. The blue sky and the gentle breeze of Florence filled him with imagination. India's late autumn made him feel the warmth of spring. He left footprints on Tianmu Mountain, Xizi Lake, Beidaihe, and other famous mountains and rivers in China. He liked teaching his students in tree-lined, bird-chirped nature. He thought about the "moonlight," "sunshine," "cry of the monkeys," and "the sound of the waves" in the Tang Dynasty ("Farewell to Japan"). He called people to "return to the simplicity of nature" and "return to the natural fetal palace to re-absorb some nourishment."[49] What deserves our attention, in particular, is during several crisis moments in Xu Zhimo's life, nature healed his wounds. The gentle water waves of Cambridge washed the sorrows brought by Lin Huiyin's refusal of his courtship. The quietness of Florence solved the painful departure of Lu Xiaoman, another love of his. Logically, nature became the most important place for Xu Zhimo to feel happy. According to my rough statistics on *Xu Zhimo's Complete Poems* (published by Zhejiang Literature and Art Publishing House), almost half of the subjects in the book are of natural scenery, and other lyrics are often associated with nature.

In this sense, I label Xu Zhimo a "son of nature," who is simple, innocent, and easygoing. This label helps us understand Xu Zhimo's life and artistic pursuit more deeply, so we can distinguish him more clearly from other Chinese poets in the 1920s.

Almost all modern Chinese poets experienced close encounters with nature. For example, Guo Moruo, a poet earlier than Xu Zhimo, lingered in the mountains and rivers and wrote about his feeling about nature in more than half of *The Goddesses*.[50] Xu Zhimo's Crescent Moon School colleague Wen Yiduo thought art is "an imitation of the artwork in nature" and "the world is a natural art museum."[51] However, in comparison, Xu Zhimo's feelings are the most natural, and also the earliest among modern Chinese poets. Judging from Guo Moruo's life history, his interest in society is no less than his attachment to nature. The ups and downs of his life are closely related to the changes in his social consciousness. Both Xu Zhimo and Guo Moruo were active in their personalities, but once they entered the social field, Xu Zhimo was slow and clumsy, while Guo Moruo's lively and active personality was the same throughout all fields.[52] His enthusiasm for social affairs was even more striking. Even the feelings of nature in *The Goddesses* infiltrated the social transformation thought he understood. If Xu Zhimo is a "son of nature," then Guo Moruo is more like a "child of society." While appreciating the beauty of nature, Wen Yiduo said contradictorily, "Nature is certainly not without beauty. Natural beauty can also be found in the world, but that is accidental."[53] "Selection is the process of creating art. What is natural is not all beautiful."[54] Associated with such a conscious choice is Wen Yiduo's persistent cultural consciousness. Different from Xu Zhimo's unrequited attachment and different from Guo Moruo's strong social enthusiasm, Wen Yiduo was more inclined to think about the world and explore life on a cultural level. From the beginning, Wen Yiduo consciously placed himself in the position of comparison and conflict between the major Chinese and Western cultures. His nostalgia and homesickness, his experiments on modern metrical poetry, and his study of ancient books all indicated his sublime beliefs in promoting national culture. Therefore, the natural scenery itself was also branded with distinct cultural imprints. The "lonely goose" in his eyes was not a bird of nature, but a symbol of a son of Eastern civilization: "The screen of the light mountain and the clear water" was smeared with some "unrestrained ancient sadness."[55] Xu Zhimo threw himself into the "bright mountains and clear waters" of nature. He often forgot his surroundings, and he did not intend to feel the conflicts and pressures of various cultures. Xu Zhimo was not so hardworking during his student days and had "no real passion for scholarship."[56] He was not much interested in the cultural heritage of Chinese classics. The hometown in Wen Yiduo's thinking was a Chinese, cultural, sacred place. Xu Zhimo's hometown had beautiful scenery in Cambridge; Wen Yiduo was born to be a "son of culture," while Xu Zhimo was an inborn "son of nature."

A Soul of Nature

The closeness and dependence on nature are the foundation of Xu Zhimo's thoughts and artistic pursuits. His other spiritual trends, such as democratic individualism, British-style petty bourgeois thoughts, and "simple faith," love, freedom, and beauty, etc., are unified on this foundation.

Xu Zhimo declared: "I am an unteachable individualist."[57] He did stand on democratic individualism to understand humans' personalities, selves, emotions, dignity of personality, and even social revolution. However, what deserves our attention is Xu Zhimo's repeated writings of individuality, self, emotions, and personality are in no way subject to any extremist tendencies but are often associated with "harmony" and opposite to the "wild civilization." This is not a true Western-style democratic individualism. It is also different from Guo Moruo's Heaven's Dog-style personality in the May Fourth era. Such "harmony" obviously comes from the inspiration of nature. For example, he said in "Tagore's Visit to China": "We are really glad that Tagore comes to China because of his superb, harmonious personality, ... [who] can develop our original silted spiritual source, ... [who] can correct the modern wild escapement and abnormal behaviors."[58] Such superb harmony appears more in the natural environment. "Only you, body and spirit, beating in the same pulse with nature, undulating in the same sound waves, and enjoying yourself in the same magical universe."[59] Xu Zhimo emphasized one should try "solitude" in the embrace of nature. Perhaps this is the true meaning of his individualism: it is not the independence of real life, but the individual senses from the harmony of nature in undisturbed conditions. "Only when you embrace nature, like a naked child rushing into his mother's arms, you know the joy of the soul, the happiness of living. You know the happiness of breathing, walking and looking around, and listening carefully."[60]

The beauty pursued by Xu Zhimo is not the splendid glory of life, the beauty of power, the beauty of majesty, or the beauty of tragedy. In the vast majority of the cases, it is difficult for Xu Zhimo to "trump on the edge of the earth" as Guo Moruo did, and it is impossible to find beauty in Wen Yiduo's "dead water." His so-called beauty should be the harmonious, tranquil beauty of nature:

> On the opposite grassland, no matter how early or late, there will always be more than a dozen yellow cattle and white horses. Their hooves are submerged under the grass of the vines, eating leisurely. The crisp yellow flowers are dancing in the wind responding to the swings of their tails.[61]

He also used the same aesthetic standards to appreciate people. Xu Zhimo wrote about the British female writer, Katherine Mansfield:

As if you are facing a masterpiece of nature, whether it is the lake and the mountains washed by the autumn moon, the glory of the sunset, or the starry sky in the South Ocean ... you only think of their overall beauty, pure beauty, complete beauty, a beauty that cannot be analyzed, a beauty that can be felt but cannot be described.[62]

The "freedom" Xu Zhimo had fought for had multiple meanings: freedom of life, freedom of the soul, freedom of thought, etc. He also talked about his political ideals to defend his "freedom" and wrote reflections on his thoughts. However, from his life practice, especially art practice, "freedom" is not a challenge to the world, but it is usually a kind of free status from interference.

"Love" is regarded by Xu Zhimo as the center of life. Although people always compare it with the more inclusive "loving" spirit of Western culture, we know Xu Zhimo does not have such holiness. His love is the love of mortals. It is the love between men and women. It is the simple, secular feeling between people. Religious fraternity takes our hearts away from the earthly world, away from nature, and goes straight to heaven. The love of mortals, on the other hand, is an affinity between people. It is in harmony with beautiful nature, and the passion of love for Xu Zhimo often echoes his passion for nature.

Such pursuits of taking individual independence as a self-satisfying state of mind, recognizing beauty as harmonious and tranquil, savoring "freedom" in the journey of nostalgia, and understanding love in sympathy with nature, undoubtedly have obvious Chinese characteristics. The core of Laozi and Zhuangzi's thoughts is to experience Tao in the form of an individual. This individual must be "heart-fast," that is, to eliminate self-consciousness and dissolve the spirit of the subject. Zhuangzi's freedom is "carefree." It means "there is no change in the spirit. Even the forms change daily, and look into the ever-changing world with ease" (Guo Xiang, *Zhuangzi*). The "transformation" of beauty is "empty, unbreakable, and inseparable" (He Yisun, *Poetry*). "Love" is one of the joys of survival. There is no fundamental opposition between it and Heaven or the spirit of nature: "What is repugnant to man is repugnant to nature. What people love would be the same in Heaven" (*The Taipingjing Hejiao*). Xu Zhimo's love also contains a kind of compassionate empathy,[63] including his sympathy toward the poor. It is precisely in this condescending compassion and sympathy, we sense a strong traditional element, the Confucian empathy, the Mohist's concurrent love, and the Taoist and Buddhist's benevolence. Pu Feng once commented Xu Zhimo had "the kindness of an aristocratic landlord."[64] Although this description was harsh, it partly revealed the truth.

What deserves our attention is the Chinese characteristics pursued by Xu Zhimo are not the result of his conscious inheritance of traditional culture. Although "he was immersed in books and rituals from childhood,"[65] we see the fact he always escaped from this compulsory education. Xu Zhimo's exploration of Chinese classical poets is mainly the result of the natural development of his personality. His role as a "son of nature" excluded the possibility of his involvement in society and also excluded the possibility of self-reflection from the perspective of culture. So, Xu Zhimo became a pure poet who was completely immersed in nature. In the cultures of the world, it is obvious that only Chinese culture has the most in-depth exploration of the "aesthetic conception" of nature, and the integration of man and nature. When Xu Zhimo needed to use some cultural concepts to explain personal feelings, the "natural view" of Chinese culture almost became the only choice of this "son of nature." His talents and pursuits naturally coincide with those of Chinese classical poets.

It is precisely because Xu Zhimo's embrace of tradition is his nature instead of the result of education, he rarely realizes the necessity of advocating traditional culture. On the contrary, he repeatedly immersed himself in Western culture, especially British culture, and even won the name of "British petty bourgeois." Among modern Western countries, the British people were deeply influenced by Puritan morality. They appear more moderate and restrained, and advocate society's development in gradual progress. "British people are "free," but not fierce; conservative, but not stubborn."[66] In Xu Zhimo's eyes, Bernard Russell is a symbol of this British spirit because Russell believes human salvation should be peaceful, not violent; violence can only produce violence.[67] In terms of poetry culture, 19th-century English poetry not only highlighted the image of nature (such as the Lakeside poets) but also paid attention to refrain emotions with reasoning (such as the creation of Victorian poetry). These characteristics are related to the life and art goals of Xu Zhimo, a "son of nature." Xu Zhimo hoped to become a "British-style petty bourgeois" because the British spirit gave him strong support for the "return to nature" choice. However, Xu Zhimo, as a talented poet from the East, could not become an English gentleman. He did not possess the perseverance of the British, nor was he a religious person. In his eyes, the charm of the Utopia in the rural area of Dartington was not the idea of transformation, but the dream of "poetic life." Despite the deep influence of British civilization, he had the heart of an Eastern genius. The will to be with nature and harmony search made him accept the influence of the British spirit partially, but the "English-style petty bourgeois" is not his true soul. The soul of Xu Zhimo belongs to nature in the Chinese cultural context.

Natural Ideal

As a modern poet, Xu Zhimo followed the Chinese tradition of returning to nature without much effort. He is a natural, Chinese son, with a Chinese-style natural soul. When he expressed his feelings about life with poetry, he completed the modern reconstruction of classical ideals. This reconstruction integrates his sincerity and confession, his spirit and flesh, and is the most complete and exquisite in the history of Chinese modern poetry, with the smallest crevice. Therefore, it has special significance.

The highest ideal of Chinese classical life and artistic ideals is the harmony of objectification state: harmony with the heavens, harmony with the earth, and harmony with the virtues. This harmony often comes from the subtle experience of nature. People try to understand the rhythms of nature, adjust their own pace of life, and unite things internally and externally. From the perspective of human beings, the subject abandons intervention in the objective world and preserves the simple, complete, and self-disciplined state of the world. The subject consciousness should be "objectified." Chinese classical poetry is the artistic expression of "objectification." In this regard, Xu Zhimo was very savvy. In his poems, prose, and other writings, he repeatedly praised the basic spirit of nature as "everything is doing its best"[68] and admired the "intoxication of nature."[69] He felt natural simplicity is an ideal, an ideal of detachment from real life. In the clear nature, he experienced eternal, mysterious changes, so he decided to put aside all personal emotions and imagination. "Don't ask my hope, my melancholy." I only want to "become a dust, an invisible dust, / follow the wheels of creation, carry on, carry on . . ." ("Thank you! My heart is beating again!"). Xu Zhimo's poetry writing is a successful attempt at life objectification. Some critics divided the development of Xu Zhimo into two periods with *Zhimo's Poetry* as the first and *A Night at Florence, Fierce Tigers*, and *Travelogue* as the second.[70] Or it is divided by the passion in the early stage, and the soft, refreshing style in the second stage. Some critics divided it into three periods with *Zhimo's Poetry* as the first, *A Night at Florence* as the second, and *Fierce Tigers*, and *Travelogue* as the third to explain the change and development of Xu Zhimo's poetry style. In other words, he experienced the three stages of "hope-confidence-despair." In my opinion, Xu Zhimo's pursuit is unified and continuous throughout the analysis of "life objectification." *Zhimo's Poetry* already expressed his willingness to abandon real life and integrate into the embrace of nature. For example, "the future and the past are just slim fantasies, / not the entrance to the world of happiness" ("Thank you! My heart is beating again!"). He also said: "I want to entrust the annoying years, / I want to entrust the annoying love, / with the endless ethereal—eliminating them all" ("The Music in the Country"). Starting from here, he moved toward a reflection of the rapid life changes: "Who is responsible for this bizarre life?" He praised the greatness of "deconstruction," and took for granted "to travel the world leisurely."[71]

Indeed, *Zhimo's Poetry* does have more "warmth" and "life," as if it were real life in objectification. Later works have more "coldness" and "escapism" as if it were real life after objectification. But compared with most Chinese modern poets, Xu Zhimo's poetry pursuit is undoubtedly the most unified, with minimal changes. The reason, in addition to the short term of his own life, seems mainly that he had the most profound, complete understanding of the Chinese poetry objectification tradition. For other Chinese poets around that time, although they also indulged in the ideal of classical culture to varying degrees, the influence of other cultures produced some "impurity," resulting in conflicts between multiple poetic ideas, which further caused their greater instability in poetic orientation. For example, Guo Moruo once praised Tao Yuanming and Wang Wei's poems and wrote some "plain" works, such as "The Night Walk" and "A Night Walk in the Pine Forest" in *The Goddesses*, but Guo Moruo was also full of interest in Western romanticism and early Chinese poetics (such as *Qu Sao*), which predicted conflicts later. In "A Night Walk" and "A Night Walk in the Pine Forest," we can feel the "hard blocks" in the aesthetic conception—an immature "plainness" and coarse "objectification." Another poet, Wen Yiduo, always vacillated between affinity and detachment from Chinese classical poetry. In his poems, there is little indulgence in life and objectification. His devotion and suspicion parallel each other. Later, although the ideals of classical poetics have been carried forward once again by the Modernist poets, Dai Wangshu, He Qifang, and Bian Zhilin, who even surpassed Xu Zhimo in some aspects, their poems, in general, are insufficiently stable nor "pure." The most complete example of the reconstruction of Chinese classical ideals in modern times can only be found in Xu Zhimo's works.[72]

Xu Zhimo's poetry takes the objectification of life as its ideal aesthetic conception, which is reflected in two remarkable features in his works. First, Xu Zhimo is good at drawing specific concrete objects instead of direct lyrics.

This does not mean Xu Zhimo completely rejected straightforward expressions. The most successful poems he wrote are mostly subjective and concrete objects, such as "No. 7, Shihu Hutong" and "Farewell, No. 18," "Happy Snowflakes," "Singing Fallen Leaves," "Untitled," ("mountain explorers"), "Mountains," and so on. "Xu Zhimo pays attention to finding the most expressive scene in his poetic conception, even a detail such as a starting point. He reflects his unique experience of life with "one spot," instead of making a generalized description."[73] This is typical of Chinese classical poetry: to express one's thoughts with objects. Its significance is to attach the changeable feelings to tangible and natural objects, so abstract thought is given vivid forms, and fluid personal concepts obtain some kind of restraint and resolution. In modern times, Xu Zhimo is the first to successfully realize the personalization of personal ideas. Before early vernacular new poetry, Guo Moruo and Xu Zhimo's era, the trend of rebellion against the tradition occupied the dominant position of poetry. This trend of thought emphasizes the individual's concepts and will. Both Hu Shih and Guo Moruo chose to do so and did successfully. Most of Wen Yiduo's poems started with objects. Between the self-sufficient objects and the powerful self-will, however, Wen Yiduo seemed to pay more attention to the latter, so his images were often transformed and adjusted by the subjects. What Xu Zhimo suggested—"everything should be shown with their nature" is rarely seen in Wen Yiduo's works—where the will of individual would not be restrained and dispelled in the self-sufficient image. Instead, Wen's works would destroy the harmony and integrity of the images themselves. This is different from the tradition of Chinese poetics "express one's ideas through objects." To be precise, Wen Yiduo no longer "expressed his thoughts with objects," but tended to "create objects" and "expressed his thoughts" in the "changes of objects." The distinctive feature of Wen Yiduo's "thought expressions" is to seek a change and emphasis process. For instance, he used a red candle to convey his thoughts, which cannot be interpreted with the usual symbolic meaning of "Till burning itself out a candle goes on lighting us." "The Red Candle" sometimes agrees with this meaning, and sometimes shows its doubts. When emotions rise and fall, it is really "a mistake after another mistake, / contradictions! Conflict!" Xu Zhimo's "thoughts expression" is characterized by unity and emphasized the quiet atmosphere. Some of them chose a "fixed" lens: "The most gentleness is the moment when you lowered your head, / just like the shyness of a water lily flower in the cool breeze" ("Farewell, No. 18"). Some are full of imagery with shifted time and space, but he paid attention to the deployment. They were properly placed in a harmonious static environment, for example, in the "Mountains," there is a courtyard, pine shadow, moonlight, breeze, quiet me and you.

Naturally, living a modern life that changes dramatically, Xu Zhimo cannot refuse the flow of emotions. The 19th-century British romantic poetry he favored is also known for the straightforward expressions of personal feelings. This makes it impossible for Xu Zhimo to indulge forever in the classical atmosphere of hiding himself and only expressing his feelings indirectly. Under the conditions of modern life, how should he deal with the relationship between "love" and "object," self, and nature in the influence of Western romantic poetics? How did Xu Zhimo integrate personal ideas when he reconstructed classical ideals? I think many of Xu Zhimo's writings adopted a way of interweaving the feelings of self and natural objects, which intertwined, interpreted each other, and reflected each other. In this way, personal feelings gained some freedom and fluidity, but these free and flowing feelings have finally circumvented the self-contained abstraction. There are constraints in freedom and stability in change. Therefore, he created a style of poetry that conformed to the traditional aesthetic ideals; yet, took into consideration modern people's feelings. For example, to express the fleeting "hope" in the heart, Xu Zhimo grafted this abstract and uncertain process to the thunderstorm scene of the sky. After a while, the rain stopped and the thunder disappeared. The rainbow was brilliant, and then it was dim and the thunder rumbled. "Hope, before it could stand firm is ruined" ("News"). In this way, the original abstract and metaphysical "hope," is replaced with a concrete, sensible appearance. Readers would not wander away because of "hope" and what they are most concerned about is what it means to be "hope" in this situation. Similar poems abound in Xu Zhimo's works, such as "The breeze blows off the spring dream" ("The Breeze Blows off the Spring Dream"), "Hope, I touch gently / the trauma of your misery, / in this cold winter night / who discussed with me about the burial?" ("The Burial of Hope"). "I will send you a Leifeng tower shadow, / dense dark clouds and white clouds; / I will send you a Leifeng tower top, / The bright moon cast its shadow in the heart of the sleeping lake" ("The Leifeng Tower under the Moonlight"). "I also want my poems to flow like clear water, / I also want my heart free as the fish in the ocean" ("Moaning"). Such a way of thinking inspired Chinese Modernist poets later.

The objectified harmonious life necessarily requires harmonious, orderly language patterns, which are mainly reflected by the architectural beauty (the arrangement of lines) and the beauty of music (the rhythm setting) of poetry. We know the Crescent Moon School where Xu Zhimo was a member always insisted on "Three Beauties," a feature distinctive from the early vernacular poets and Guo Moruo. However, within the Crescent Moon School, Wen Yiduo was the active advocate of the "Three Beauties," while Xu Zhimo was not a strict follower. So, does this mean the structure and melody of Xu Zhimo's poetry is what he wanted and he could write at his free will? Absolutely not. Comparing Wen Yiduo with Xu Zhimo, we see the "strictness" of Wen Yiduo is almost sturdy and rigid. The uniformity of the poems and uniform temperament in "Dead Water" by Wen Yiduo is exactly the reasons for the contradictions with free modern will. These contradictions brought about the uniqueness of "Dead Water," but it also indicates such a language model is the chain of modern poetry! Xu Zhimo's uniqueness lies in the proper adjustment of his natural talents. In dealing with the subtle relationship between freedom and regularity (just as he adjusts the relationship between freedom consciousness and nature). Xu Zhimo abandoned all kinds of strict external form requirements and constructed a less tidy variety to obtain inner harmony. In "Poetry Holidays," Xu Zhimo argued too much attention to the metrical laws may cause formalism bias. "This is what we should guard against from time to time." Also, he said, "The soul of poetry is music, so the rhythms are extremely important. But that does not mean we have to follow the flat-fall and rhyming rules rigidly. Even the movement of our steps is a kind of rhythm."[74] "The length of the lines, the decisions of neat or irregular lines, all depend on your understanding of the volatility of rhythms."[75]

Xu Zhimo's freedom in verse lengths is different from *The Goddesses*, which tries to break away from rules. Xu's poems have rules to follow. Some poems have different numbers of characters, but they are not much different, achieving a roughly equal number of characters. For example, there are 15–17 characters in the lines of *No. 7 Shihu Hutong*, 9–12 characters in "The Leifeng Tower under the Moonlight," and 11–13 characters in "Beside the Mountain Road." Some poems have greater differences in the characters of each sentence; yet, achieve a variety of effects with the regular length change. For example, see "Covering a Few Sheets of Oil Paper": "Roaring, roaring, the wind is roaring / in the woods; / There is a woman, there is a woman, / she is sobbing alone." In many cases, the length of the poem lines is combined with the pauses of the whole poem, and the changes between the two adjacent lines or within the poem maintained the rules of branching and the division of sounds in the whole poem, such as "By Chance":

> I am—a cloud—in the sky,
> Occasionally projected in—your—heart—

You don't have to—be surprised.
Don't be—joyful—either
In the twinkling of an instant—no traces—could be found.

You and I meet at the dark sea—at night,
You have your,—and I have my,—directions;
You remember it—well,
But you'd better—forget,
The light—that shines together—at the time of the encounter!

There are two stanzas in the poem, the number of characters varies greatly (5~10), and the number of pauses is also different, but obviously, there are rules to follow. In the corresponding lines of the two stanzas, the number of pauses is the same, and the number of characters is also approximately the same. This is the so-called inner harmony, a sense of harmony in the overall sense of tolerance of local freedom. Most of Xu Zhimo's poems have his inner principles in the structure and sound pauses. (However, these principles are not fixed and need analyzed case-by-case.) This arrangement of rules and rhymes at the end of the lines indeed creates a harmonious language world without restraint and oppression for readers, which is like the free and regular nature that Xu Zhimo indulges.

The exquisite reconstruction of the traditional poetry ideal in modern society necessarily requires it to accommodate a certain amount of modern information, because successful reconstruction can only be achieved by modern poets and modern readers. Too much emphasis on the strict forms of classical poetry, on the contrary, is not helpful for the realization of traditional ideals. Therefore, Wen Yiduo's stubbornness widened the distance from tradition and eventually turned to the dismantling of tradition. Xu Zhimo's flexibility made better use of traditional culture and completed a fairly successful reproduction of traditional ideals.

Li Jinfa: Communication and Non-communication

I carried the burden of my ancestors and walk away with bound feet.
Oh, a traveler with little luggage, finally fell asleep on the roadside.
—Li Jinfa, "I Carried . . ."

How to seek new artistic resources after the break from the classical tradition of Chinese new poetry is a problem for every poet. Almost all poets pay attention to the exchange and communication of Chinese and foreign poetry, although it may still end in a beautiful void.

Interestingly, Li Jinfa, who once distanced himself from the Chinese art tradition with the title of "Poet Monster," also communicated clearly with the classical traditions of China:

> I often felt strange why the works of ancient Chinese poets were not mentioned by people now, all of whom tried to learn from the West instead. I thought this was absurd after the literature revolution. But indeed, nobody criticized it, and actually if writers had some ideas and visions, and paid some attention to these, they dare not deny or weigh against the classical poems of China. What I did was to adopt both the traditional and the West, which means I try to reconcile these two.[76]

So, what is the special effect of the communication between Chinese and foreign cultures for Li Jinfa, who distanced himself from the Chinese tradition through his Western symbolism poetry style? Or, did Li Jinfa's communication ultimately succeed or go nowhere? This in itself is an interesting topic of Chinese modern poetry.

Symbolism: Baudelaire and Mallarmé?

As one of the Symbolist pioneers of Chinese new poetry, initially, Li Jinfa was noticed through his connection with French Symbolist poetry. In his own words, he started to write poems "under the influence of Baudelaire and Verlaine."[77] With Li Jinfa's rise in Chinese poetry, people realized no one could compete with him who wailed in the long darkness, wandered along the graveyards, or groaned on the decaying bodies. No one ever talked about death, exhaustion, the anxiety that cannot be eradicated at the end of the century like him. As Sun Zuoyun pointed out: "Mr. Li's poems focused consciously on the darkest side and the most hopeless aspect of life. He was more pessimistic than others."[78] Therefore, in the 1920s, Li Jinfa was one of only a few whose poems resembled the atmosphere and style of Baudelaire and Verlaine.

However, if we say Li Jinfa is China's Baudelaire, Verlaine, or that Li Jinfa's poems represented their modern forms in China, it would be too hasty, or at least we fail to understand "another Li Jinfa" beneath these modern pains.

In spite of the atmosphere and style similar to Baudelaire and Verlaine, Li Jinfa's soul actually has something unique from the beginning. We may wish to read his "To My Self-Portrait" first:

I'd sleep with the moon on the bottom of the river
And smile at a purple patch of wood.
That's too much of a Jesuit.
Oh, how fond and tender!
Grateful to these hands and feet of mine.
Though they are not many,
Enough for my employment.
In the old days a warrior in his suit of armor
Could even wrestle with a tiger!
And me? A bit bashful.
As fervent as the blazing sun at noon,
As pallid as the crescent among clouds.
But with my own apparel, I can only visit a small corner of the world.
To be feathered? What a lot of bother!

It is still a rigid poem of Li Jinfa's usual style, but a careful examination would show that the main spirit does not seem to be Modernist. He compared himself to a Jesus disciple who wanted to save the world, but immediately consciously felt "too much." He imagined fighting the tiger like a hero, but he felt self-deprecating. "But with my own apparel, I can only visit a small corner of the world." Life is short, and even a tall man would end up with a handful of dust. A thin "modern experience" seemed to be revealed here, but Li Jinfa was still quite self-sufficient in the whole poem: "Grateful to these hands and feet of mine. Though not many, Enough for my employment." The self-confidence in the smile is quite romantic and elegant. Riding with waves, self-sufficiency and self-cultivation are typical of Chinese national traditional mentality, especially the last sentence: "To be feathered? What a lot of bother!"

In contrast, if we read Baudelaire's "The Man Who Tortures Himself," fundamental differences can be found clearly:

I am the wound and the dagger!
I am the blow and the cheek!
I am the members and the wheel,
Victim and executioner!

I'm the vampire of my own heart
—One of those utter derelicts
Condemned to eternal laughter,
But who can no longer smile!
A major criminal who has been abandoned!

Here Baudelaire did not show self-confidence and self-sufficiency. Instead, he wanted to break the state of self-sufficiency. "I am the wound," but with no intention of finding a refuge for healing. On the contrary, he has to be with the dagger! "I am the blow," but it does not fight the enemy of evil, because "I" am the evil, I blow myself ... Mankind created civilization for the emancipation and development of self; yet, once civilization was established, it became the chains and cages of man. This increasingly clear, cruel reality educated modern Westerners since Baudelaire's time. Their traditional beliefs about the eternality and stability of human beings were shattered, and they were shrouded with Schopenhauer's dilemma and pessimistic experience of loss. For them, any complacency and self-confidence were nothing but a dream of self-deception.

In this way, Baudelaire's "I" became the irony of self-deprecating "I," while Li Jinfa's "I" was a self-confident and complete "I." Despite the pains and wailing by the poet, the ideal, bright space in the depth of his soul was intact, protected from the corruption of reality. In the theme of the "end of the century," Li Jinfa still saw the beautiful aura of the new century from time to time. Although the world was as humming and annoying, making people restless, we may still "walk in the sky" and bathe in the sun ("To Fengming"). This is not, of course, the same as Baudelaire's ugly, broken world. It seems Li Jinfa's cultural tradition also did not allow him to "pierce" through the world and life. Such a verse is something Li Jinfa would not produce: "That even the Void's a traitor, that even Death tells us lies?" (Baudelaire, "The Digging Skeleton").

Facing this ugly, ill-stricken world, Baudelaire's ideal can only be found on the distant other side, only in the dim illusion: "When I open my eyes again, / see my horrible room, /When I wake up, I feel / cursed sadness and spikes in my heart." The ideal world is like an instant mirage! In contrast, Li Jinfa's ideal is realistic and solid. "Traveling to the volcano of Sicily and the desert on the ground" is not a too demanding request ("To Fengming"). The afternoon's warmth was also forthcoming: "Breaking the silence only by the spring birds on the branch /just a couple of calls, friends on the neighboring tree / also sang together, admiring this charming scenery" ("Afternoon"). The embrace of a real corner in the real world is the romantic feeling of the poet.

If we say that homelessness is the common distress of Modernists, then Li Jinfa was not without a "home," but just someone who got lost and "shouted like roamers who lost their way."

Therefore, as a seeker, a lonely hero who was temporarily frustrated, he also needed to protect his self-sufficient, confident attitude and was unlikely to have the feeling of self-disintegration.

Li Jinfa also believed: "Oh, What I love! God always knows, / but the devil beguile everything" ("Ugly"). It seemed to Li Jinfa "God is not dead." It was only Mephisto who set up "ghost walls" on the returning way of the roamers. The broken world is the devil's trick. "All these things and glamour are not created by the hand of God anymore" ("Ugly"). The world is also harmonious. "In my childhood, I was often attracted by the birds, / Oh, Living in the town of clear streams, / residents were singing against their walking sticks, / I closed my eyes to see the short bushes along the stream" ("My Autumn"). Suffering is just an accident, we still have the opportunity to lament to God ("Wailing"). Although the hope is as thin as the "morning fog," still there is hope ("Hope and Mercy").

We see Li Jinfa always believed beauty is not just an ideal in spite of the multitude of ugliness. He often called for the beauty of reality to dispel ugliness. "Alas, This urgent autumn, / urge us to have a feast of *amour*! / Go, if you do not forget your obligations, we would be friends eventually" ("The Beauty God").

At this point, we seem to be able to solve this contradiction: as a Symbolist, on the one hand, Li Jinfa was influenced by Baudelaire and Verlaine. On the other hand, he believed he would "fit more in personality" with the romantic poet Musset[79] because Musset was a "loner" who constantly searched for ideals and was constantly disappointed (this sentence can also be reversed). He had a lonely heart and often felt the distance of the individual "I" from the others in the group. Loneliness is the shared experience of romanticism and modernism, but Musset had the pride of being the sober-minded among the drunken, which is in line with Li Jinfa's "I feel I'm the only lonely one" ("Fantasy").

In spite of constant disappointments, Musset often encouraged himself: "I have decided to go high, / go to every corner of the world, / to find the slim chance of hope."[80] He continued the search. Although the road is difficult, faith still existed. "It is said that people are kind by nature, they are only eroded by the evil forces in this world. There is a similar belief that the pursuit of ideals may improve both individuals and society. In fact, all aspects of romanticism contain such ideal factors."[81] Li Jinfa, like Musset, also had such beliefs and ideals. They both belonged to the "wanderers" and "roamers" under this ideal.

In the history of Chinese modern literature, the theme of anti-feudalism and the fight for individuality has always been permeated explicitly or implicitly. The idea of romanticism is naturally rooted in the hearts of Chinese people. Although romanticism as a complete movement may be short-lived, its spirit still has potentially far-reaching effects on many writers. As quite a few researchers have pointed out, many of the Modernist literary practitioners in China choose the "modern experience" from the stand of romanticism.

Tradition as a Personality Temperament

The import of any kind of literary thought must be subject to the dual screening of the characteristics of the times and the national cultural mentality. Li Jinfa was fascinated by Western Symbolism, but the theme of the times tied him to romantic ideals. It was even more difficult to change the aesthetic mental structure of the nation.

Wailing, mourning, and groaning is Li Jinfa's usual ways of expression, "the night is crying for a long time" ("Seventeen Nights"), and "Aging skirts are crying their mourning" ("Abandoned Woman"). "The wind in the distance aroused the wailing of the oak forest" ("Enchanting Journey"). These images that break through the traditional harmonious beauty are a major contribution by Li Jinfa to Chinese modern poetry. However, going deeper, a unique national mental origin can be found. For example, from a psychological point of view, it is not a deep sorrow to cry, since at least it has specific causes of pain, including this better outlet. Those who were truly sad and desperate were unable to clarify specific reasons for suffering. They cannot find specific means to vent their pain. If they are in sorrow, it would be as if they were surrounded by enemies, but they are unable to shout for help, and their calls cannot be answered. They would be too tired to have tears. We should see for French Symbolism poetry, especially in the later stage, such sorrows and complaints as "cries" and "tears" are rare. They are images as if the souls were exposed to the air and cracking under the scorching wind. For example, Baudelaire wrote, "Over the vast gulf / Cradle me. At other times, dead calm, great mirror / Of my despair!" (Baudelaire, "Music," trans. William Aggeler).

In traditional China, the self-realization path provided to Chinese intellectuals was narrow. The dependent existence of the autocratic system formed a mentality that Chinese scholars call "the personality of the courtiers," which naturally followed a weakened and submissive mentality. Crying, mourning, and groaning are the natural displays of this kind of mentality. The same sadness and pain are very different for Li Jinfa and the French Symbolist poets.

For example, for the idea of "extinguishing one's sorrow with wine," Li Jinfa wrote, "Drinking the wine, deep into my sad body, / immediately they are turned into tears" ("Twilight"). Painful feelings need to flow out in tears, the mood is looking forward to re-stabilization. For Baudelaire, he wrote: "in our mirrored desire . . . / to my dream paradise!" ("Lover's Wine"). Being drunk would not dissolve the dream of transcendence.

For another example, both Li Jinfa and Verlaine liked to use piano images in their poems. Li Jinfa's piano sounds symbolized the idea of the self. "When the highest note is played, / it seems to indicate the happiness of life." However, there is a strong external force to attack it: "The nosy wind, / slamming through the window, / meddled with my piano, / and disturbed the perfect notes!" And the real tragedy is: "They can't understand." Here, tragedy was defined as the relationship between people. The barrier of human relations caused self-spiritual discomfort and resentment and grudges: "If I go to the wilderness, / The sounds of the piano will be suspended, or it will continue weakly" ("The Sorrow of the Piano"). And Verlaine's piano is not so much a clear idea, but rather a kind of unreasonable sigh, an inexplicable emotion: "My heart is drowned, In the slow sound, Languorous and long" ("Autumn Song"). More importantly, Verlaine made it clear that his sorrow had nothing to do with interpersonal relationships:

> It is crying without any reason
> Inside that heart that makes itself sick.
> What! No betrayal? . . .
> That mourning is unjustified.[82]

Verlaine's pain comes from his deeper thinking, and care about life and the world beyond the pressure of personal social relations: "This is most painful, / when you don't know it. /There is neither love nor hate, / I have so much pain in my heart!"

It should be noted many of the grievances of Li Jinfa's poems are related to the personal love experience. Many of his love poems give people the impression he was struggling to chase the ideal other half, but most of these pursuits were hopeless and unpredictable. He was exhausted and finally tired in the middle of life: "I carried the burden of my ancestors and walk away with bound feet. / Oh, a traveler with little luggage, finally fell asleep on the roadside" ("I Carried . . ."). Feelings of fatigue and weakness are in the same vein.

Therefore, such a poet needs a "cane": "Oh, my protector, / my magical friend, / we have forgotten the age differences and became friends" ("Cane").

Also, this love is full of "Oedipus complex": "You hold my hand, gentle like a comforting quilt, everything of mine /guidance and obedience, all in your breath" ("Untitled"). "I see you in the distance, wondering along the way

/ like a homeless animal" ("Impression"). "I hate you like the hummer under the yoke, / cannot tear the reins, / as a child resenting the mother's harshness ..." ("My Attitude towards You"). During this moment, Li Jinfa was living in Paris.

Paris, as the epitome of modern Western civilization, is summarized in Balzac's famous book, *Father Goriot*:

> On the one hand, he beheld a vision of social life in its most charming, refined forms of quick-pulsed youth, of fair, impassioned faces invested with all the charm of poetry, framed in a marvelous setting of luxury or art; and, on the other hand, he saw a somber picture, the miry verge beyond these faces, in which passion was extinct and nothing was left of the drama, but the cords and pulleys, and bare mechanism.[83]

For a young man from the ancient East with a deeply-carved traditional mind, this is a life of great contrast: impulsion and oppression, warmth and inferiority, humanity and animalism, realistic desire, and psychological burden.... All these external attractions and inner self-resistance make a weak, exhausted soul miserable. This is similar to Yu Dafu's experience in Japan. However, Yu Dafu was more "exposing" and willingly publicized himself, while Li Jinfa seemed to be more willing to cover himself.

I think the reasons for the obscurity of Li Jinfa's poems can be partially explained: they came from his shameful desire for life, and the desire to speak; yet, fearful, as if walking on thin ice, treacherous and obscure. He seemed to avoid sharp personal pains consistently.

Li Jinfa is a rare person in Chinese poetry who writes deeply about death, darkness, fear, and other deep mental activities. However, at the same time, we should also see most of these sensations only appear in some abstract generalized descriptions, once the details of life are entered, especially when it comes to personal experience, his words become hazy. For example, what kinds of thoughts does he have facing this French girl in "To Jeanne"? Is it "the emptiness of sympathy, / can't expect with the truth? Without the authority of Creator, / can't help but shine like a night firefly." "Emptiness of sympathy" is about reality. "Real" refers to "real feelings." Next, it should be "I" had no authority over the Creator, so I can't control you. "Night firefly" might suggest a girl's blinking eyes. This is a complex mentality that one does not get the love he desires; yet, he cannot restrain inner desires. The introverted shy poet would not be straightforward here, and he intentionally or unintentionally adopted the symbolist hints and omissions. If this technique is used frequently in the poems, they would naturally appear to be awkward and obscure.

For Li Jinfa, tradition does not refer to the visionary world of art, but the mentality of Chinese intellectuals, an inborn temperament he cannot change. Although he said he tried to "communicate" and "reconcile" Chinese classical and Western culture, what we find in his poetry writing is not the more sophisticated ancient art skills and qualities, but a mentality and personality model that originated from ancient times.

The communications between Chinese and foreign arts are only a preliminary idea for Li Jinfa.

Obscurity and Non-communication

Previously, we attempted to explain the language issue of Li Jinfa's poems through the traditional Chinese psychological habits of Chinese intellectuals, but this can only be applied to some poems. Implicitness in modern times is only a deep mentality of the Chinese. He cannot be shy and concealed at all times. We also need to combine his spiritual temperament with his knowledge structure and poetry cultivation to make a new comprehensive analysis.

The cultural mentality of the artist, together with his rational knowledge structure, ultimately affected his artistic decisions. As far as Li Jinfa's knowledge structure is concerned, he accepted Western romantic poetry and Symbolism poetry. As to Li Jinfa's deep cultural psychology, he also had an obvious personality temperament of traditional Chinese intellectuals. However, the artistic orientation of these aspects is inconsistent. For example, the optimistic ideal of romanticism continuously eroded the quiet thinking of "the end of the century," guiding him to face reality firmly in self-sufficiency and self-confidence. His seemingly thick, modernist consciousness was disintegrated. At the same time, traditional humane care with its long history in China transformed fundamentally the grand theme of the Western Symbolism concern to life, guiding him to confide in the grief of the human world the story and feelings that individuals feel difficult to discuss.

However, the problem is "modern experience" and "modern expression" carried by French Symbolic poetry had already formed a kind of "knowledge" that deeply impressed the Chinese students who studied there. It seems contemporary people "should" master, accept, and apply the knowledge. So, Li Jinfa cannot refuse the temptation of this era. This is a contradiction of the self quite difficult to solve: the temperament in the depths of the mind and the pursuit of rational knowledge already experienced such disharmony. Therefore, we find Li Jinfa's writings show the growth and decline of several forces. The poems are flawed, but full of charm—when he cried for the hopelessness of the ideals, the obstacles of pursuit, or the construction of his own Eden Paradise. But if we analyze it seriously, most of Li's poems at that time have nothing to do with the Symbolism acclaimed by many in the history of literature. When Li Jinfa deliberately used Symbolism as a banner and compiled modern images and colors in poetry, he often broke from the support of his spiritual depth. Thus, he often appeared to be conceptualized and abstract. If we examine them closer, we will find the inner emotions of these poems are incoherent and many "modern" flavors are attached.

For example, when the concern of the modernity of "time" becomes a transcendental idea, many forms that do not necessarily involve time issues appeared inexplicably. In his well-recognized masterpiece "Abandoned Woman," there is "the fire of the sunset can't make the boring time / turn into ashes . . ." The mood of the entire poem is still basically coherent, but the word "time" is too abrupt, too abstract, and too eye-catching. In the inexhaustible time for poems of Western modernism, all "time" is concrete, sensible, practical, and a three-dimensional object with rich implications. Li Jinfa also wrote "Temptation of Time," which is also an open topic and can be fully explored. However, after finishing reading the complete poem, one would know the poet is not clear about what time "temptation" means and how to "tempt" it. It is just a superficial touch on the topic. These kinds of light touches would not lead to a deep discussion.

Once knowledge and concepts are separated from the real feelings, there may be artificial feelings of super-feeling, which would eventually destroy the emotional atmosphere of the whole poem and cause many cancerous blocks in the blood of poetry. This can be found frequently in Li Jinfa's poems. For example, the wind and the rain are the "for what" of the world, and the spring, summer, autumn, and winter are the conceptual metaphors of the "then" of the world ("I Know the Wind and the Rain"). "I love the singing of no rhythm/ or the recitation of the verse" ("The Broken Road"), this sentence structure is unnecessarily awkward. Sometimes Li Jinfa also intended to pursue a philosophical taste, such as "the language reveals warm love everywhere / but this "Today" "Tomorrow" makes me fall into illness" ("North"). However, the philosophical sense of Western modern poetry is not demonstrated with direct concepts of philosophy. It should be fully digested by the poets and then emerge from the most realistic, true experiences of poets.

Best poems are always realized as a whole whether it is philosophical or modern. If their meaning can only be achieved by a few modern nouns (even with quotation marks to attract readers' attention), then it is sad. Everyone loves to quote Li Jinfa's famous line: "Life is /the smile/ over Death's lips." Yes, the Modernist style sentence is wonderful, but unfortunately, there is only such a solitary sentence in the "Thoughts," and it is difficult to understand how it got there. This seems to be a way of poetry for some ancient Chinese, who occasionally had a good sentence and then wrote the rest. A key sentence is very eye-catching, but if there is only one such sentence to arouse others' attention, then it is best not to stretch.

In addition, Li Jinfa's poetry competence (especially the language competence of poetry writing) also fundamentally determines the quality of his poetry. Mallarmé once said obscurity was either caused by the incompetence of readers or poets.[84] Here, the "modern" feelings of Chinese readers cannot be precisely positioned. What can be analyzed is Li Jinfa's poetry writing ability.

As a Hakka, Li Jinfa used a native language quite distant from the written Chinese poetry writing in terms of vocabulary and syntax. He must overcome this distance to combine his instinctive thinking with universal expressions. The question is, did he make it? People who were close to him continued to convey such information to us: Li Jinfa is "a Cantonese, an overseas Chinese who lived in the Southern Asian Islands, and he could not speak the Chinese language well."[85] Indeed, this was frustrating news, which hinted at some kind of failure of his writing.

Besides this, Mr. Sun Xizhen also revealed Li Jinfa was "not very good at French … He learned a little bit of miscellaneous classical Chinese, which polluted the purity of his language…. He should be credited with introducing the Symbolism but he is the culprit in corrupting the language."[86] Degrading language is undoubtedly the most serious accusation for a poet who regards language as his life. If we still have doubts about its seriousness, it is worthy of our calm thinking of the comments by the Symbolist pursuer Bian Zhilin, who concluded that Li Jinfa "has a very poor command of Chinese, not only of the vernacular but also of classical Chinese. As to French, some basic grammar sounds are foreign to him, too."[87]

Under such circumstances, Li Jinfa failed to meet his ambition to bridge Chinese and foreign poetry. It is quite difficult to achieve smooth writing of his own, not to mention to complete the higher communication.

For modern poetry, obscurity is a new aesthetic effect, but the ambiguity of aesthetic meaning is a form of complex thinking and deep feelings. It is not the same thing as the unsmooth expressions. As Valéry said in modern poetry writing, the melody should pass through without interruption. The semantic relationship always conforms to the harmonious relationship. The mutual transition of ideas seems to be more important than any single idea.[88] In a sense, the mixture of Chinese classical and vernacular language was intended to find language resources, but when this was not built on a solid language foundation, it was likely to fall into the "non-communication."

From trying to "communicate" to "non-communication," Li Jinfa provided us with profound experiences and lessons.

Dai Wangshu: *The Century of Sickness of a Chinese Soul*

> I am a unity of youth and aging,
> I have a healthy body and a sick heart.
>
> —Dai Wangshu, "Self-sketch"

In the history of Chinese modern poetry, Dai Wangshu's image contains a series of extraordinary factors waiting to be closely examined. On the one hand, he drafted the artistic outline of modernist poetry with "Poetics and Miscellaneous" and practiced the new "prose into poetry" approach with his writing; thus, breaking through the rigid patterns of the Crescent Moon School. He promoted French Symbolism poetry, which inspired the development of Chinese new poetry. He also advocated the modernity of poetry and opposed the expressions of ancient through the vernacular;[89] thus, promoting the modernization of Chinese new poetry. On the other hand, for the public, Dai Wangshu was dubbed "Yuxiang ("A Lane in the Rain") Poet," when "A Lane in the Rain" is another kind of traditional metric poem. He was very critical of the "ancient flavor" of Lin Geng and others' poems, while many of his works were still antique, such as "My Sentimentality," "Autumn Night Thoughts," "Loneliness," and the like.

Then, what is the relationship between all these classical and modern poetry cultures? How does Dai Wangshu practice Symbolism ideals in an extraordinary combination? These are the questions we should answer today.

Love and Privacy: A Sample Analysis

What was Dai Wangshu most concerned about as a poet? What was the emotion that constantly touched his feelings? These are the first questions to answer before entering the world of Dai Wangshu's poetry.

We saw the close connection between Dai Wangshu and the political revolution, the failure of the Great Revolution in 1927 which cast heavy shadows on a young man who cared about politics. We also saw the prison experience which was rare for most poets. His vows and courage, these observations, and conclusions are undoubtedly very valuable. However, we seem to neglect relatively the fact that apart from the four or five poems in *The Times of Disaster*, he did not write about politics directly. His vision is limited to the scope of personal life basically, themed on love and female images frequently.

I made statistics of the new edition of *Complete Poems of Dai Wangshu* published by Zhejiang Literature and Art Publishing House. Of all his 93 poems, nearly half are direct and indirect works of love experience (such as "My Love" and "No Sleep"). Slightly more than half seem to be broader (such as "Nostalgia," "Missing a Friend," "Self-sketch," etc.), but they also often contain love or female-related elements, such as "My Memory," "Secret Crush," "Self-sketch," all with images of women. At the center of "February" is the landscape painting about love. "Autumn" says that "I" am the one who could "best understand" "the heart of a bachelor." In short, Dai Wangshu is particularly sensitive to the feelings of romantic love, and love accounts for a considerable proportion of his life experience.

I believe emphasizing the importance of love in Dai Wangshu's poetry does not weaken his position in poetry history, nor does it erase the political consciousness he already had. On the contrary, it helps us reach the poet's emotional world, his basic ways of understanding the world, because other feelings of Dai Wangshu are usually combined with his love experiences. It is likely to start with personal love, then integrate other social experiences. His masterpiece, "A Lane in the Rain," is a case in point.

For a poet of adolescence, love is unique. In addition, Dai Wangshu was different from other poets because of his childhood disease which branded physical defects on his face, his heart as well as his future life. The mocking of peers made him feel inferior and always self-reliant. Self-improvement in the inferiority atmosphere was itself pathetic, which was also reflected in his love needs. He seemed to desire love more than others to the point of paranoia. This brought more failures; hence, too much for our poet. Dai Wangshu needed to release them in the poems!

Love as one of the main parts of life experience is itself a feature of the modernity of Dai Wangshu's poems. Because, only in modern society, in an environment where individuals have gained relative freedom, love can break through all kinds of ethical rules, and raise the emotions of people collectively and repeatedly. Dai Wangshu's love is the living emotion of modern people. As he said in "Poetics and Miscellaneous," "new poetry should have new emotions," which is different from the "ancient style" of Lin Geng and others. Along with this, the French Symbolist love poems of Verlaine, Gourmont, and others provided him with great inspiration to integrate modern Chinese and Western cultures.

It is worth noting the theme of love presents a special form in Dai Wangshu's writings. We saw Dai Wangshu wrote about love, but at the same time, he intentionally or unconsciously concealed dazzling love. He rarely let go of his voice and sang a song of love, joy, or sadness. "Privacy" is the salient feature of Dai Wangshu's love. He regarded love as a hidden part of life. He did not want to expose it without any scruples. Instead, he blurred it in his writing with a refrained release. A secret love becomes a hidden, hesitant desire. Sometimes, his realistic, dreamy boundaries were obscure, making it difficult to distinguish, such as "No Sleep": "In the quietness of the sound waves, / each shadow of love / was having a walk instantly/ in the dizzy brain." Sometimes, the image of a woman flashed in his heart and there was no way to capture it. For example, in the wilderness where fireflies flickering, he suddenly had an idea: "Like a pair of slim hands, / when I was sleeping in the past, / put a thin quilt / lightly draped over me" ("To Fireflies"). Sometimes, he simply avoided the truth of love: "I said it is the gloom of the lonely autumn, / it is the nostalgia of the distant sea. Someone asked me the reason for my distress, / I dare not say your name" ("Worry"). A very insightful critic once pointed out "From 'A Lane in the Rain,' Dai Wangshu's love description is mostly (not all) an interrelation between love emotions and political emotions, with few pure love poems."[90] I think it is also his understanding of love when he infiltrated love emotions with political emotions. Isn't it also a way of maintaining personal privacy via political interference?

According to Du Heng in the "Preface to *Wang Shu's Poem Collection*," the obscurity in Dai Wangshu's poetry was identified as "subconsciousness,"[91] which proved the inheritance relationship between Dai Wangshu and French Symbolism poetry. I do not agree with this. Of course, this does not deny the French influence on Dai Wangshu's poetry, but I feel here, Dai Wangshu showed his particularity as a Chinese poet. Dai Wangshu's subconsciousness is not the opposite of the "explicit consciousness" of social culture. On the contrary, as mentioned previously, love and politics, and individual and society may also be mutually integrated for him. Subconsciousness is not purely sexual instinct. Dai Wangshu and his friends disagreed with the "naked instinct."[92]

The subconsciousness as he understood it was love, which itself was a social emotion, a necessity of reality, and a bond of humanity. Dai Wangshu's so-called "hidden" is not because it can't be touched, but because it showed his attitude and intention to conceal. The "hidden" is concealed, hesitant, and ambiguous. It is Dai Wangshu's protection of personal privacy.

French Symbolic poetry is also full of love expressions. Baudelaire, Verlaine, Gourmont, Paul Fort, and Francis Jammes wrote masterpieces of love. Poems of love dominate the French poems translated by Dai Wangshu. However, when interpreting the love and poetry of French Symbolism, we can feel their so-called subconsciousness is the real subconsciousness, the instinctive impulse of human beings (such as in some poems by Baudelaire). The instinct is often regarded by these French poets as the foundation of their lives. When they experience life, they must first return to the ego to feel the instinctive impulses of human beings. Their "love" greatly exceeds the world of human beings and connects with the human body. Love is often a magnificent, mysterious life adventure, and obscurity is just the existence of subconsciousness. The subconscious mind is oppressed and interfered with by social rationality. It is difficult for people to accurately capture it. For example, in Gourmont's "Dead Leaves":

> When they are stepped upon, they wail like ghosts.
> They make a buzzing sound and the rustling of women's clothes.
> Simone, do you like the sound of footsteps on dead leaves?
> Come! We will be a poor dead leaf in one day,
> Come! The night has fallen and the wind has taken us.
> Simone, do you like the sound of footsteps on dead leaves?

Thus, love is mixed with life and death in a complicated way, giving people a kind of obscure experience. Dai Wangshu's love poems did not explore so deeply. In many cases, his ideas remind us of Wen Tingyun and Li Shangyin, two famous poets during the late years of the Tang Dynasty.

Too much involvement in the romantic love between a man and a woman is heavily criticized in classical Chinese poetry. Both Wen Tingyun and Li Shangyin are famous for writing about love and women. This is inevitably a little euphemistic from the perspective of orthodox poetry. However, artistic modern freedom created conditions for Dai Wangshu's unscrupulous absorption. Therefore, Wen Tingyun and Li Shangyin's "love sickness" was inherited by Dai Wangshu. "Seated, we played hook and drank warm spring wine, While we guessed at riddles, scarlet beams shimmered in the candlelight" (Li Shangyin, "Untitled II"). "In the deep spring night, missing you infinitely, those happy old days like dreams" (Wen Tingyun, "Night Drummer"). Isn't the love of temperance and distance the characteristic of Dai Wangshu? Interestingly, some of Wen Tingyun's words and Li Shangyin's poems have different degrees of obscurity characteristics. Of course, it is not that Wen and Li revealed human instinct and subconsciousness, but because some of the content of their lives was so private they did not want to be exposed.

It seems the privacy of love is a tradition of Chinese poetry.

Dai Wangshu's poetry is based on varied life experiences and is not limited to love. However, in my opinion, on the theme of love, the modernity and tradition of Dai Wangshu's poetry are exceptionally sufficient. Therefore, they are the most representative, and most worthy of a sampling analysis. Dai Wangshu's love experience is modern, and "external," but the special form he gave to love is classical and traditional. The duality of Dai Wangshu's love vividly expresses the duality of his life consciousness. This duality of life consciousness determines the duality tones of his poems.

A Sentimental and Worried Tone

I think distress is the emotional tone of Dai Wangshu's poems. On a cold day, in the cold rain, the falling leaves spread on the quiet road, and a haggard, aging poet walks alone, with eyes blank. This is the basic sentiment of Dai Wangshu's entire poems, although there is also the freshness in "Village Girl," the briskness of "February," the humor of "Triple Worshipping," and the tragic strength of "Notes on the Wall in Prison." Overall, the images throughout Dai Wangshu's poetry are still disillusionment, troubles, exhaustion, tears, bitterness, and the like from the early "Tearful Departure" to "Untitled" in 1947.

Taking distress as the emotional tone of poetry distinguished Dai Wangshu from his predecessors in terms of modern tendency. Guo Moruo rides ups and downs in the tide of emotions, and excitement is the keynote of his writing. Wen Yiduo struggles with the misplacement between history and reality, and contradiction is his keynote. Xu Zhimo is in the embrace of nature and comfort is his keynote. For Dai Wangshu, distress comes from his profound realistic experience and is the product of "modernity" in a sense.

The greatest similarity between Dai Wangshu and French Symbolism poetry is the similarity of sentiments. The huge difference between French Symbolism and romantic poetry is the former uses distress rather than optimism in its emotional expressions. If romantic poetry is filled with passion and hope for the "beginning of the century," then Symbolic poetry echoes the sorrow and depression of the "end of the century." Dai Wangshu's "Tearful Departure" depicts the pain: "a faint lamp, / drizzling rain, / a deep dark day; / a sad mood; / fully occupied my mind." Isn't this like Verlaine's poem which he translated: "There is Weeping in My Heart"—"There is weeping in my heart, / like the rain falling on the town. / What is this languor/ that pervades my heart?" Apparently, the French Symbolist poet's "mal du siècle" infected Dai Wangshu from China, who had been immersed in pain and suffering of the century for a long time, not knowing how to extricate himself. This is an important feature of Dai Wangshu, which distinguished him from his predecessors. He is also very special compared with his peers, such as Bian Zhilin and He Qifang. Among all the Chinese Modernist poets who accepted French Symbolism, Dai Wangshu walked the furthest along the road of "distress." Even during the War of Resistance against Japanese Aggression period when his poetic style was said to be open and upward, the distress element remained. Except for the works of pain and passion, such as "Notes on the Wall in Prison," "I Use the Broken Palm," and "Wish," what we see is still the lonely, bitter, and self-claimed "passerby" Dai Wangshu in "Waiting," "Over the Old House," "Gift Inside," "A Visit to Xiao Hong's Grave."

So, does Dai Wangshu fully identify with the "distress" of French Symbolism poetry? I do not think so. Just like his writing on the theme of love, within the often brand new, modern, foreign framework, the details of the excavation are entirely his own, belonging to the deep culture of his heart. He often criticized the "retro" of others in terms of topic, but he was unaware of his fascination with the classical culture in detail.

A very prominent feature of Dai Wangshu's distress is his distress is always a kind of *continual subtle melancholy*, or it could be called "sentimentality" in a more familiar term. Dai Wangshu created a sentimental tone with his tears and white-haired head images.

Distress is just an abstract general term. The substantive meanings may be quite different. French Symbolism did not seem to express such a delicate sentiment, but a kind of secluded feeling of "worries."

Dai Wangshu's sentiments are rooted in his personal life. The songs of the sparrow in the cold wind reminded him of his loneliness ("The Sparrow Singing in the Cold Wind"), and the cold encounter with his lover makes him sentimental ("My Sentimentality"). The breeze on the sea made the wanderer burst into homesickness ("The Wanderer"), and in the spring of February, he sighed the regrettable love memories ("February"). All the emotions and thoughts of French symbolic poetry have the power to penetrate reality. Baudelaire said, "The soul glimpses the glory behind the grave"[93] through poetry. Rimbaud believes the poet is a psychic. The famous saying by Mallarmé is that poetry does not create real flowers, but flowers that do not exist in any bouquet. He wants to create the so-called pure essence in the case of eliminating all the "echoes" of the specific life around us.[94] Sorrows in French Symbolism poetry are rooted in individuals' experiences of life. They do not care about the suffering of daily life. Baudelaire's "trouble" is: "I am a base that the moon hates, / there, like a regret, hatching a long worm, / always attacking my closest, intimate deceased" ("Sorrow I"). Gourmont tastes the "hard labor" of life from the rotating wheel: "They go, they cry, they spin, they die / ever since, since the beginning of the world: / people are afraid, wheels passed, wheels turned/as if they were doing an eternal hard labor" ("The Mill").[95]

Dai Wangshu's sentimentality is often mournful, weak, and branded with a distinctive female shade and aging signs. He often looks for resonance in the image of women and speaks with women's temperament, such as lamenting "my unfortunate life" ("My Unfortunate Life"). "I will choke like a stream" ("Mountain Trip"), "My pale face, my eyes red because of weeping!" ("Change Your Mind"). "My minor ailment body is weak in the early spring wind" ("Minor Ailment"). He often feels tired and aged, "Like a black aging thin cat" ("Sonnet"), "[I'm] a young old man" ("Outdated"), "[I'm] a unity of youth and aging" ("Self-sketch"). The sorrow of the French Symbolist poets is heavy and tragic. Under the surface of decadence, there is often an unyielding ambition. "The poet is like the Sovereign between the clouds, / It goes out into the storm and laughs at the archer." The melancholy at dusk is described like this: "Melancholy waltz and lazy dizziness! / The sky is sad and beautiful, like a big altar."[96]

Dai Wangshu's sentiments mainly focused on human feelings, while the French Symbolist poets' worries had been extended to the philosophical field; thus, communicating with people's philosophical and religious experiences. Dai Wangshu was sentimental for his sake, and he had no intention of chewing and thinking distress, while it was the characteristics of many French Symbolist poets to raise the distress of reality to transcendence. Dai Wangshu was not interested in those works that fly too far in the "transcendental" field. Among the French Symbolist poets, Dai Wangshu had the greatest interest in Verlaine and Gourmont because these two poets were relatively realistic, paying attention to creating an atmosphere in the feelings, especially Verlaine. "There is a general lack of Symbolism transcendental content in his poetry.

His writing is still emotional basically." According to the strict Symbolism standards, some of Verlaine's works are more romantic, filled with sentimentalism cliché.[97] In contrast, people such as Rimbaud and Mallarmé had never entered the emotional world of Dai Wangshu nor been the targets of Dai Wangshu. In this respect, Dai Wangshu's friend Du Heng had a vivid interpretation in "Preface to *Wangshu's Poem Collection*": "I can be regarded as a Symbolist, but I don't like the mystery of this group, whose works sometimes are difficult to understand." In a sense, we can also argue Dai Wangshu shared this feeling.

If we put French Symbolism aside, we find that feeling sorrow and melancholy in real life is precisely the historical feature of the poetry of the late Tang and Five Dynasties in China. Compared with the prospering peak time during the Tang Dynasty, Wen Tingyun and Li Shangyin's poems are less straightforward. They are more uniquely objective, but this does not obscure the sentimental tone. Neither Li Shangyin nor Wen Tingjun linked the subtle distress with thoughts of human life, with the feminization and aging of the mood as its distinctive features. Wen Tingyun's *Ci* is mainly based on female expressions. Li Shangyin expressed himself through the female perspective of famous beauties or wise concubines: "With toileting finished, relying on River Watching Building alone. Thousands of boats have passed, but I could not see the one with my love. The sun is setting and the water is running silently. And I, was in such a desperate sorrow in this Bai Pingzhou" (Wen Tingyun, "Dreaming of Jiangnan· II"). How could the weak soul stand the wind, rain, and snow of life? Li Shangyin "was sad to find my hair is turning grey" in his 30s ("Untitled"). Also, he sighed "The sunset is glorious indeed, only it is so close to dusk" ("Ascending the Leyou Height").

In a sense, sentimentality has become part of the Chinese poets' temperament. In the face of life's setbacks, they tend to sink into such delicate grievances and are less likely to choose metaphysical thinking. In the early 1920s, the Lakeside Poets were sentimental. Li Jinfa was also sentimental. The Crescent Moon School launched a campaign against "romantic sentimentality"; but, in fact, many Crescent Moon School poets, including Xu Zhimo, wrote in a sentimental tone from time to time. The worries of French Symbolic poetry were originally an alternative to sentimentality, but for the Chinese poet, Dai Wangshu, it was very "Chinese," where the sentimentality replaced the worries.

It could be summarized that the painful experience of life is the basic sentiment of French Symbolic poetry and the "Mal du Siècle" they had. During its gradual movement eastward with Chinese culture, some contradictions and dislocations were produced through this kind of sentiment and disease. Therefore, Dai Wangshu finally understood and expressed external influence and the requirements of the times in the Chinese way. He was infected with the Chinese-style "Mal du Siècle." Chinese and Western poetry culture seeks unity in contradictions.

Pure Poetry or Prose Poetry

The contradictions and unity in Chinese and Western poetry cultures constitute the basic characteristics of Dai Wangshu's artistic exploration.

Dai Wangshu's publication of "Poetics and Miscellaneous" in Modernity, Vol. 2, No. 1, November 1932 fully demonstrates his great attention to poetic art. His 17 pieces of poetic theories are mainly about the exploration of poetics. As noticed, these opinions were issued targeting the Crescent's positions on rhythm. The Crescent Moon School advocated architectural beauty and musical beauty centered on metrics. Dai Wangshu focused on emotions and believed musicality and orderly lines will hinder poetry or deform poetry. While the Crescent Moon School advocated the beauty of painting, Dai Wangshu argued that poetry cannot take advantage of paintings. In the history of Chinese modern poetry, the form of the Crescent Moon School represented a modern trend of classicalism, reflecting the formal ideals of Chinese traditional poetry. "Three Beauties" was originally the result of the deep understanding of Chinese metrical poetry by Wen Yiduo, a representative of the Crescent Moon School. From this background, Dai Wangshu's reaction was anti-classicalism, which represented the modernization trend of Chinese new poetry. His repeated advocacy of prose-like poems based on free emotions is more in line with modern people's rhythm of life and mentality.

However, Dai Wangshu fell into a trap in the anti-musicality proposition, because the French Symbolism poetry (especially early Symbolic poetry) that gave him great support for modernization precisely promoted musicality. Musicality is the most important form feature of Symbolism. Ellen Poe, the pioneer of Symbolism in the United States, said long ago: "Maybe in music, the soul is closest to the sacred beauty creation." Valéry said, "The long, ever-lasting power of Baudelaire's poetry is from the enrichment and peculiar clarity of his sound use."[98] Mallarmé said "What I wrote is music," and Verlaine put music in a priority status. Dai Wangshu rejected the pursuit of French Symbolism, which means his anti-traditional choices could be lonely.

With no examples as a reference, he relied on his pioneering exploration completely.

There are at least two problems worth solving: (1) If emotional flows cannot be translated into a specific rhythm of music, how should they be expressed? (2) Does the breakthrough of the metrics equal no music at all? Is there any inevitable connection between music and poetry?

Judging from the history of Dai Wangshu's poems, I do not think he solved these problems himself. Conscious rejection is one thing and the fulfillment of creative practice is another. Therefore, over time, his artistic pursuit also varied. In the early years of the "A Lane in the Rain" stage, Dai Wangshu was interested in musical beauty. Ye Shengtao praised "A Lane in the Rain" which "opened a new era for the musicality of new poetry." This does not mean Dai Wangshu rebelled against the Crescent Moon School at this moment. Instead, the harmony and uniformity advocated by the Crescent Moon School and the freedom of modern language are organically integrated, which preserves the free, flexible features of modern language, without being loose and broken. In many poems of the Crescent Moon School poet, Xu Zhimo, we can find such exploration, but "A Lane in the Rain" is more sophisticated and perfect. From the beginning of "My Memory" until 1934, Dai Wangshu seemed to be content with writing free style without rhyme, but this does not mean he would pay no attention to the rhythm of music from then on. *Wangshu's Poem Collection* deleted "A Lane in the Rain" and "In Front of the Ancient God Temple," but his rhythm variety was achieved with the help of the power of the word sounds from time to time, not relying entirely on the ups and downs of the emotion itself. For instance, "Impression," "Come to me," "The Dream Seeker" used end rhymes. Other works pay attention to the unstressed and stressed tones between the two lines. At least, compared to Guo Moruo's *The Goddesses*, Dai Wangshu's poetry should be more symmetrical. It is no wonder that some people are critical: "The so-called musicality can refer to a rhythm formed by the language to cope with the ups and downs of poetry, not necessarily referring to the rhythm of strictly regulated forms." "Even Dai Wangshu talked about this himself, isn't he still writing the rhythm that was born from the Crescent Moon School?"[99] After 1934, when writing the majority of the work in *The Times of Disaster*, Dai Wangshu resorted to metrics more heavily. So, in another "Poetics and Miscellaneous" published in 1944, he made the necessary amendments to his early concepts: he continued to oppose the rules requiring the regularity of rhythm and rhyming, but claimed he did not go against the words and the rhyme itself. They should be discarded only if they are unnecessary or interfere with poetry.

Dai Wangshu's exploration of the new musical poetry is part of the development of the "pure poetry" he wanted to complete. "Pure poetry" is the artistic ideal of French Symbolism, clearly stated by the later Symbolist poet, Valéry. This ideal evolved into the Modernist of the 1930s after the introduction and practice of the Chinese Symbolist poets, Mu Mutian and Wang Duqing, in the 1920s. Its original meanings include (1) musicality and (2) direct grievances and statements replaced by symbols and hints. Dai Wangshu abandoned musicality more on the level of consciousness. His so-called pure poetry does not include musicality: "Free poems are pure poems that do not seek support from the music of general sense."[100] Linking the sentence patterns of prose culture with pure poetry is the unique view of Dai Wangshu, separated from French Symbolism. At the same time, he is quite thorough in understanding the second layer of its meaning, and in Article 16 of his "Poetics and Miscellaneous," he said: "Emotions cannot be caught with a camera. It should be drawn with ingenious writing, which must be alive and ever-changing." The emotions of photo-taking with the camera are of course direct expressions of emotions, while the so-called ingenious writings are symbols and hints from actual writing analysis. For example, he turned "lonely" into an objective symbolic image: "The dead branches sighing in the cold wind, / the dead leaves withering away on the avenue; / The bird singing an elegy, / half is self-sorrow" ("Bird Singing in the Cold Wind"). He presented strong nostalgia: "When the hometown reed flowers blossom, the traveler's heels are covered with mud, / the sticky mud glued to the heels, and glued to the heart, /When would it be wiped off by those lovely hands?" ("Travel Thoughts"). He pinned the patriotic sentiment in such a verse: "I use the broken palm / groping this vast land: / this corner has become ashes, / that corner is covered by blood and mud" ("I Use the Broken Palm").

As we all know, using symbols and hints instead of direct lyrics and statements is the artistic means of Chinese classical poetry summed up in the long historical development. Poems by Wen Tingyun and Li Shangyin made further contributions to this development. The artistic exploration that French Symbolism advocated at the turn of the 20th century is in harmony with the tradition of Chinese classical poetry. Is this the so-called everlasting "essence of poetry" value by Dai Wangshu that the "purity" of both Eastern and Western poetry art integrated into harmony? While accepting the advanced poetics of the West, he found the essence of the classical tradition, and the extraordinary factors of the two cultures of China and the West were once again unified.

In short, Dai Wangshu's pure poetry continues to show the contradiction and unity of various cultures. Opposition to the metrics of classicism and the application of prose into poetry is his independent opinion. His insistence is not without contradictions and difficulties, and his advocacy of objective expressions is also the unification of integrating ancient and modern times connecting China and the West. Interestingly, the concepts of rebellion against traditional art rules always confused him, while the inheritance and accommodation of Chinese and Western art rules made him a success.

He Qifang: *"Jiaren Fangcao"*[101] in the Western Storm

> I will forget the coming winter of ice and snow.
> I never believe your sweet voice is a deception.
>
> —He Qifang, "Silky Dress"

We only examine the poems He Qifang wrote early in his life limited by the scope of this book. These poems refer to those written before 1949, including *Prophecy* (1931–1937), *Night Songs* (1938–1944), and other works, which represent He Qifang's unique poetic conception and establish him in the history of Chinese modern poetry. These poems have always been the focus of research, in which consensus has been achieved. For example, these poems generally express the loneliness and sorrow of the poet.[102] In terms of poetics, the author covered a variety of poetry in China and the West along the path of the integration of Chinese and Western poetics.

However, I believe the consensus reached by studies so far still lacks a more in-depth, more detailed examination. The sorrow and loneliness of Chinese and Western poetry can be said to be the universal characteristics of Modernist poetry in the 1930s, a common choice of He Qifang's peers, including Dai Wangshu, Bian Zhilin, and others. So, that being said, what is the unique feature of He Qifang?

Self-satisfaction, Self-respect, and *"Jiaren Fangcao"*

The independent characteristics of He Qifang's poetry are determined by his distinctive worldview, outlook on life, and personality. That is, he had a rather flexible mental ability, could maintain the most lasting mental balance among all kinds of loneliness, and find happiness from the balance, weaving the dream of self. He was not drained by loneliness, nor became pessimistic and desperate under the pressures of life, nor did he intend to make a serious poke of the suffering of life. On the contrary, He Qifang was always found in gentle, dewy emotions. He did not believe life would be so dark and the world would lose its true feelings. He was constantly looking for and welcoming everything with a faint smile. I call this kind of mentality self-satisfaction and self-respect.

Self-satisfaction helped He Qifang go through the "malnourished, undeveloped childhood and dark, narrow, crowded, desolate" teenage time.[103] From very young, he used "loneliness and books" to protect himself. He was enchanted by the beautiful world of Andersen's fairy tale *Little Mermaid*; he hated those "arrogant emotions and things" in college. "He created a beautiful, quiet world full of loneliness, with some lovely poems and essays,"[104] dreaming of some beautiful, gentle things. "(He Qifang) is an idealist."[105] "He locked himself in the black door, listening to his monologues, praising."[106] Cultural activities always were his best choice for self-satisfaction and self-appreciation. This kind of character remained in the *Night Songs* period at Yan'an. The memories of old friends vividly outline a gentle, innocent, self-satisfied He Qifang for us: "Sometimes, even a more qualified complaint will often make you feel that he complained because he was too happy and needed to have a change. It was not accidental, he seemed to be like this all the time."[107]

In contrast, Dai Wangshu seemed to have a lot of worries, paying special attention to his subconsciousness, which was pessimistic from time to time. "Beauty" is not his strength. Bian Zhilin was extraordinarily calm, reserved, unwilling to permeate more warmth for his imagination, and "beauty" was not what he needed.

He Qifang's self-satisfaction and self-respect led to his mental choice of the Chinese classical "*Jiaren Fangcao*." Immersed in the small world of personal spirit without the intention to fall into philosophical thoughts, He Qifang would find mutual understanding and comfort between people indispensable. For a young male writer, the warmest, most welcoming comfort naturally is women. He Qifang fancied "a dress with a corner flying in the breeze" ("Seasonal Sickness"), reveling in "the sweetness of the heart" ("Footsteps"). His "bone-deep love craving" made him almost forget the "winter with ice and snow." Women, as the non-powerful role of society, as victims of social power and order, as weak persons who have to rely on the fantasy of the individual spirit to survive in many cases, their experiences were intertwined with the lonely poet. Therefore, "*Jiaren*" (beauties) with its elusiveness was more gracious and more heart-wrenching. It brought a smoothing tacit understanding for the poet. "*Fangcao*" (precious plants) is a kind of self-analogy of He Qifang, who consciously and unconsciously shaped a self-image of purity and sincerity. He had a pair of warm hands and his songs went "sinking and high" concurrently. He flew in the air filled with white fog, with "transparent sorrow." He guarded the cold night of the tall building, the rustling trees accompanied him with silence. He felt he was "the faded flower on green branches," singing the sadness and joy of "twenty years of life."[108] To a large extent, "*Fangcao* (precious plants)" is the dream of a poet's self-indulgence, his beautiful choice of self-identity to go through a long life.

In the strict political hierarchy of China's feudal society, the exhaustion of Chinese intellectuals when they served the government, the boredom of literary men who hung on to and served the rich and powerful, and the self-enlightenment of "the entertainers" constantly forced them to fall from the center of social power and taste loneliness. Without self-satisfaction and self-respect, they might become schizophrenic and suffer from being alive. Without the warmth of "beauties" and spiritual comfort of "precious plants," where would they go to relieve their loneliness? How could they maintain their independence from the world and not yield to corruption? The tradition of the "beauties and precious plants" in Chinese poetry originated from *Qu Sao*, developed and thrived in the late Tang and Song dynasties, represented especially by Wen Tingyun and Li Shangyin. If "beauties and precious plants" in the *Qu Sao style* are burdened with resentment and send anti-social messages, then Wen and Li's style eliminated these painful tones and created more warmth, more tenderness, and became extraordinarily exquisite, beautiful, and compelling.

He Qifang's "beauties and precious plants" obviously fell into the latter category. He was not a kind of world-saving hero and did not intend to search for universal truth like Qu Yuan. His personality made him identify with the gentle, beautiful style of Wen and Li. While still attending a private elementary school, He Qifang "read the six large-scale versions of selections of the *Poetry of Tang and Song Dynasties*. He could recite many classical poems, mostly poems of the Tang Dynasty," especially the poetry represented by Wen and Li during the Late Tang and Five Dynasties.[109] Although introductory education is accidental, it contains the inevitable law of culture. It is the poet's personality that created the possibility of education, fully guaranteed the effectiveness of education, and consolidated and deepened the effects of education.

Chinese and Western Cultures, and the Modern Choice

Naturally, in modern cultural circumstances, it is difficult for He Qifang to use the tune styles of the Tang and Song dynasties to express feelings of ancient times. The poetic ideas that were seeded during his childhood will eventually find new expressions in the context of modern culture.

This seemed to determine He Qifang's unique "Chinese and Western integration" path of poetry. Until the age of 15, He Qifang's poetry focused on the purely classical. He did "not know the May Fourth Movement, nor the new culture or literature. Even vernacular writing was regarded as heresy."[110] In 1927, ZHu Shihde, a poet who taught at Wanxian Middle School and whose poems were deeply influenced by the Crescent Moon School, brought He Qifang a new style of literature for the first time—the Crescent Moon School poetry. From 1929 to 1930, when he was in Shanghai, He Qifang was once again immersed in the artistic atmosphere of the Crescent Moon School. The principal was a leader of the Crescent Moon School and there were quite some Crescent Moon School supporters among the professors. *The Crescent* magazine was popular, and young students who loved new poetry would read Xu Zhimo and Wen Yiduo's poems. The new poems fascinated He Qifang. "At that time, his favorite poets were Wen Yiduo and Xu Zhimo, whose poems were often on his lips. He could recite these good poems . . . ."[111] In the history of Chinese modern poetry, Crescent Moon School poetry is a bridge between classical and modern cultures, the East and the West. It integrates the French Barnesian restraint, rationality, and the "art for art's sake" with the Chinese tradition of emotional restraint, which provides a sense of intimacy to modern Chinese, who both learned Western poetry and valued traditional art. The choice of the Crescent Moon School gave He Qifang the initial and in my opinion, the most important, inspiration from which he found a style of modern poetry that fitted his nature and artistic trends.

Along with the foreign path of Crescent poetry, He Qifang further stepped into the "art for art's sake" world: the French Parnasse, the English Romantic poets, such as Keats and others, and the English Victorian poets represented by Tennyson and Rossetti. These Western poetry movements had a common feature, that is, the obsession with art. When faced with life-or-art choice, they were likely to sacrifice their lives and follow art, because real life was full of crises, filth, and alienation between people in the eyes of these poets: "Everyone lives a lonely life"; we are carrying "a longing like despair."[112] Art became a self-designed ivory tower. It was crystal clear, a sanctuary for people to talk about self-comfort and temporary relief. Since reality was not worthy of people's dedication and hard work, then, "art for art's sake" would be the goal! "I, closed from the tempest that shook// My window with fury impassioned, //Sat dreaming, and, safe in my nook, //Enamels and Cameos fashioned."[113] "We have to turn to poetry to interpret life for us, to console us, to sustain us."[114] It is conceivable the tendency of Western poetry to abandon reality and focus on individual artistic fantasy echoed He Qifang's "deja vu" feelings naturally. Therefore, He Qifang, deeply influenced by the ideals of Chinese classical poetry and eager to find modern discourse for this ideal, had no time to carefully analyze the essential differences in poetic choices between Chinese and Western cultures.

He Qifang continued to advance along the track of modern art and met French Symbolism through Dai Wangshu's poetry. "He had a good impression of the fine art form of the Banuss. Symbolist poets, such as Stéphane Mallarmé, Paul Verlaine, Arthur Rimbaud, etc. fascinated him the most. Paul Valéry particularly has long been his favorite poet."[115] However, He Qifang's acceptance of Symbolism did not mean abandoning the spirit of "art for art's sake" (this is different from Symbolism itself). Strictly put, he found a mostly modern, purely poetic model for all previous life-art pursuits. Because Western Symbolism is very similar to the poems of the Late Tang and Five Dynasties in China, "Qifang has been influenced by the fine poetry of the Late Tang and Five Dynasties, and now the French Symbolic poetry also fascinated him. One is ancient and Chinese. The other is foreign and modern, and the two integrated."[116] Western Symbolic poetry promoted the full maturity of He Qifang's writing and *Prophecy* is an artistic summary of this integration.

It is generally believed that *Night Songs* shows He Qifang's breakthrough since *Prophecy*. He showed a different style compared with *Prophecy* in terms of the reality of content writing, the socialization of the pursuit of thought, the clarity of sentiment, the simplicity of language, and so on. However, does this mean he completely denied his previous "beauties and precious plants" mentality and found a new art model? I think while *Night Songs* seem to be different from *Prophecy*, there are no radical differences between the two. *Night Songs* does not completely change the temperament of his self-satisfaction and self-respect. In a certain sense, it is just a transformational development of the psychological choice of "beauties and precious plants." During the *Night Songs* period, He Qifang regarded the flourishing new life of Yan'an as the habitat of his dreamed soul and regarded the fiery labor work as the ideal life form. In his writing, "culture is endowed to everyone as if offering wings ... and then we will go further and move towards a more beautiful golden world ..." ("New China's Dream"). He enthusiastically portrayed the Chinese revolutionary leaders: "He raised the Chinese people's dreams to the most beautiful, / Using the step-by-step approach in the revolution / they made the most sinister road flat" ("New China's Dream"). He also imagined Lenin was "sitting in front of the window in the morning;" "writing a letter to a comrade working in the country" and saying "*he felt lonely. He was tired. I can't help but comfort him. // Because the state of mind is nothing trivial.*" In the midst of it, He Qifang seemed to "receive the letter Lenin wrote" ("Night Songs II"). It is not difficult to see that at this moment, He Qifang was still immersed in the dreams of his life, still attempting to seek spiritual comfort and sustenance for his "loneliness" and "tiredness." All these stemming from new life, these splendid, vivid ideals of life were explained by his inclusion in the path of loneliness. In *Night Songs*, the style of social life was always associated with the fragility and instability of individuals. He strived to use these new ideals and new social life to dispel personal sentiments. Can we say these ideal forms for self-encouragement also belong to the far-flung, tortuous projections of the "beauties and precious plants" prototypes? It may be mentioned that, in the long river of Chinese classical poetry, the earliest prototypes of "beauties and precious plants" have a strong political meaning in *Qu Sao*.

Characteristics of He Qifang

So, what is He Qifang's characteristics? I think it could be summarized at least in the following aspects. The first is the miraculous combination of childishness and maturity. The youth characteristics of He Qifang's poetry are the most obvious in *Prophecy*. Here, joy is as bright as "the wings of the white doves" and as fresh as "the red mouth of the parrot." Sadness is also like "pure pearls." Both happiness and sadness are derived from the special life experience of adolescence. Most of them lack the profound macroscopic and the universe sense. But what's interesting is these young, innocent emotions have a certain "mature" shell. He Qifang has an early-maturing insight into the passage of life: "The girl in the south, I am sorry for you. / Sorrow for your pride, your youth" ("Another Parting Poem"). He also reveals the experiences of the vicissitudes of history: "I don't see the sails of the Yellow River in the setting sun, / I don't see the Sanshen Mountain on the sea . . ." ("The Ancient City"). He Qifang seems to be particularly fond of the autumn, the symbol of maturity: "Put down the sickle that saturates the rice fragrance, / use the backbaskets to hold the fat fruit of the bamboo-fenced yard. / Autumn inhabits the farmhouses" ("Autumn"). In *Night Songs*, He Qifang's immaturity shows through this innocent fragility, while maturity shows in the strong social and political ideals he defends.

Perhaps we can regard the combination of young and middle-aged culture in poetry as the common trend of Chinese Modernist poetry during the 1930s. Dai Wangshu has a famous verse: "I am a unity of youth and aging / I have a healthy body and a sick heart" ("Self-sketch"). Critics believe such a verse "is typical for Modernist poets."[117] Different poets differ greatly in how to adjust the proportion of youth and middle-aged, childishness, and maturity. Dai Wangshu embraced the exhaustion of calmness and the turmoil of adolescence at the end of the century. "Because when a girl starts to love me, / I will be afraid of it at first" ("Self-sketch"). It seems more like a hybrid of youth culture and senior culture. In poetry by Bian Zhilin, the mature, middle-aged ingredients often overwhelm the composition of the innocent youth. His love is also full of metaphysical and philosophical tones: "I am lost in the flowers / the world is empty, / because it is useful, / because it accommodates your leisure steps" ("Untitled, 5"). Only He Qifang is capable of the natural, graceful integration of innocence and maturity, youth and senior cultures. Only He Qifang is good at using the mental power of "self-satisfaction and self-respect," as much as possible to eliminate the contradictory factors of disharmony and let the young paranoid heart linger in the mature transcendental air:

> Whose is it with speaking black eyes like the shepherd's ringtones?
> Calling the tamed flock, my poor heart?
> No, I am dreaming, remembering, thinking about autumn!
> How high is the clear sky in September, how broad!
> How gently my soul will lift and fly,
> Passing through the air of white frost, like the sigh of my eyes!
> —"Seasonal Sickness"

He Qifang's fine blending of self-satisfaction and self-respect, "beauty and precious plants," childishness and maturity, emotions and ideas determined the special artistic conception of his early poems. He especially emphasized the overall effect of poetry, emphasizing the connection and match between the figurative emotions to highlight the unity sense of the overall atmosphere, the so-called "repeated cycling, singing, and emotion-delivering lyric atmosphere."[118] It is quite accurate. Mr. Luo Hanchao summarized it as "a static tone."[119] He Qifang was accustomed to melting abstract love in such a concrete, complete space:

> Dawn light is shining on the dewy pomegranate flowers. / The midday shadow is the late steps / play between the deciduous poplar and the Bodhi trees. / When the southern wind sent breezes from the water lily / the night, the wilderness is overflowing with the aroma of the scent, / because the evergreens are all over the place, and the dodder is wrapped around the tree tops. / The love of the South is falling asleep. / The sounds of flapping wings make one drowsy.
>
> —"Love"

The most radiant horizon, the purest innocent realm can only exist in the "pure nature" of the uninhabited. Human activity is the interference and destruction of the will of the "rounded" space, so when the poet was obsessed with the artistic atmosphere he created, he naturally took some fantasy of "leaving dust and abandoning the world." He was looking forward to "The flowers in the valley are the most fragrant. /The unrecognized morning dewdrops are the most shining. / The creek without the shadow of a soul is the brightest" ("The Garland").

In *Night Songs*, the subject "I" is more active, and the narrative verses are greatly increased. The emotional figurative strategies are relatively reduced, and the crystal, relaxed mood is no longer common. However, compared with mass poetry writing in the Yan'an area during the same era, He Qifang's works have a stronger literati style, often showing more interest in atmosphere and tones, still not forgetting to surround people's activities in the delicate, harmonious nature.

> The world is still full of youth everywhere.
> There are hearts open everywhere.
> Young comrades, let's go to the wildness together.
> Under the soft blue sky,
> I want to talk to you about all kinds of pure things.
>
> —"I Want to Talk about All Kinds of Pure Things"

Among his peer poets, Dai Wangshu and Bian Zhilin also attached importance to "imagery." However, Dai Wangshu sang low with a gloomy mood, instead of the crystal-clear beautiful, spotless aesthetics. There are also many turnings and turbulences in his works instead of "static tones," such as "Broken Fingers" and "Come to Me." Bian Zhilin's metaphysical whispering also leaped from the unified field of "imagery" frequently. The idea moved, crossed the sky of thought, and left "hard blocks" in his works, such as "The Tears Across the River" (or "Untitled 4"): "The river mud is on your beam, / the spring water from the neighbor is poured into your cup, / overseas luxury goods decorate your blouses: / I want to study the history of transportation."

It is not difficult to imagine the style development of He Qifang requires the scrutiny and polish of language subtleties, a style evolved from self-satisfaction, and self-respect to the "beauty and precious plants," from the youth innocence to maturity in middle age, from crystal images to the artistic conception imagery. The poet must have a superb refining ability and timely screening, selecting the most poetic language, and properly placing and adjusting it, so it can become the best adhesive for the multiple ideas, thus forming the painstaking carving of He Qifang's early language style. Because of the deliberate pursuit of sophistication, many of the poems in *Prophecy* appear delicate and rich, such as "beautiful death," "sweet mourning," "joy as my melancholy," and other complicated verses. "Each line here is like a big gemstone on a Qing Dynasty official's hat."[120] He Qifang also said, "I like the kind of tempering, the cooperation of these colors."[121] "The language of the poems in *Prophecy* is all carefully-chosen."[122] The style of *Night Songs* became plainer and more natural, but there were some constants within the change. He Qifang pursued the rich and subconscious mind of language and expressed it in another way: "I sing for the boys and girls. / I sing in the morning. / I sing hope, / I sing something that belongs to the future, / I sing the power that is growing" ("I Sing for Boys and Girls"). "Go to the choir, go to the acting, / to build the railway, to be a pilot, / go to the lab, write poetry, go skiing on the mountains, drive a boat bumping on the waves, go to the Arctic expedition, go to the tropics to collect plants, / go with a tent to sleep under the stars" ("How Broad Life Is").

Modernist poetry during the 1930s in China stressed the effect of language more or less. However, if comparing them carefully, each has its focus. The love poems represented by Dai Wangshu focused on the flow and transformation of language and paid more attention to this, such as: "You climb icebergs for nine years, / you sail the dry sea for nine years. / Then you meet that golden shell" ("The Dream Seeker"). The poetry of reason represented by Bian Zhilin focused on the wonderful contrast and cooperation of imagery. To create a dramatic effect, allusions were piled, for example: "The postman is pressing the doorbell like a friend/ touching the minds of the residents: / Are those fish that swim through the Yellow Sea? / Are the geese flying over

Siberia?" ("The Letters"). He Qifang paid more attention to the color and mood of the verses and attempted to modulate a bright, colorful, full-fledged picture: "Red leaves like palm fall from the southern trees, / Horse galloping breaks the silence of the mountains or the transparent sorrow of a bay stream" ("Seasonal Sickness"). This difference is more clearly seen after the change in the poets' respective poetic styles. For instance, Dai Wangshu's "Dawning" in 1945: "If the spring of life comes again, / the old ice is thawed, / then I will see bright smiles again, / I will hear the clear calls—these happy dreams." Still, here we see a flow of meaning. Bian Zhilin wrote "Workers on Roads and Railways" in 1938: "You have worked hard, the blood vein is through, / New China is there to rise. / One thousand trains, tens of thousands of cars / looking through your fingers." It is still a show of language imagery. Probably only He Qifang continued to use the language function of *Fu* (a style combining prose and poetry) to continue his fascination with the colors and sentiments.

The three aspects above summarized the unique pursuit of He Qifang's early poetry in thought and art, which can be called characteristics of He Qifang. In summary, we can say the so-called characteristics of He Qifang are his creation of the "from life to art" ideals based on self-satisfaction and self-respect and the "beauty and precious plants." It is an integration of his multiple poetics. Among these, though, the foundation is He Qifang's profound concept of classical poetry culture, a kind of "beauty and precious plants" consciousness that has been extended from self-satisfaction and self-respect. He Qifang chooses to combine foreign "art for art's sake" with such original thinking. He has negative feelings but does not reveal them. He avoids the tragic writing style. All his poetry is immersed in a gentle, beautiful solution. He sincerely sings and applauds for real life.

Bian Zhilin: The Sight Downstairs

> You stand on the bridge viewing the sight;
> You're beheld by the viewers from height.
>
> —Bian Zhilin, "Fragment"

Dai Wangshu, He Qifang, and Bian Zhilin are the most important Modernist poets of Chinese new poetry. While the most striking feature of the Chinese Modernists is to combine Western Symbolism poetry and the inherent poetry tradition of China to integrate Chinese and Western poetry, different poets have different personalities, and the fusion attempt is different. It is generally believed Dai Wangshu and He Qifang belong to the "sentiment advocate" in the fusion, while Bian Zhilin belongs to the "reason advocate" in the fusion. How did this difference arise? What kinds of personality prompted Bian Zhilin to move toward the choice of "reason advocate"? What is the meaning of Bian Zhilin's "reason advocate"? These are what interests us and what we will analyze in detail in the following.

A "Cold-Blooded Animal" Label

A "cold-blooded animal" is a generalization of Bian Zhilin's attitude toward his writing. He said: "I have always been writing lyric poems. While I can't always be myself, I always tend to restrain myself as if I wanted to intentionally be a 'cold-blooded animal.'"[123] I think Bian Zhilin's summary here is not just his attitude in poem writing. He intentionally or unconsciously expressed his personality. Bian Zhilin was not that kind of arrogant, show-off person. "I am always afraid of showing up and I'm happy being one in the crowd, and even more afraid of revealing my private life."[124] From the September 18 Incident in 1931 to the Yan'an trip in 1938, Bian Zhilin remained uniquely calm at every moment when he might be involved in historical torrents. "The more they bullied us with gunfire, the more I want to see what is behind them."[125] In Yan'an, "I have seen many revolutionary predecessors and heroes in public," which did not prompt him to quickly devote himself to a new life. Even in 1948, when the history of China changed dramatically, he was alone in the fog of the medieval mountain village of Cotswold, dozens of kilometers west of Oxford in England.[126] Bian Zhilin explained this is "because the direction is unknown, while I am sensitive to tiny things, I am lost with the big trend. In the face of historical events and the times, I don't know how to express my sorrows and joys."[127] Compared with Dai Wangshu and He Qifang, Bian Zhilin's trait is even more striking. Until the early years of the 1930s, Dai Wangshu also wanted to maintain the privacy of his personal life, but he did not refuse to express his joys and sorrows about his social life while He Qifang was good at wrapping himself with dreams and illusions, but dreams and fantasies were also the coats of his strong emotions. During the War of Resistance against Japanese Aggression, they both actively embraced a new way of life, more enthusiastic and more active than Bian Zhilin.

Art is a way for artists to look at people and the world, based on their personalities. The kind of artistic thoughts an artist agrees with is ultimately determined by his essential personality. On the surface, Bian Zhilin, together with Dai Wangshu and He Qifang, tended to align Western Symbolism poetry with China's inherent poetry tradition and integrate Chinese and Western poetry. Western Symbolist poets, such as Baudelaire, Verlaine, and Valéry, among others, and the poets of the Late Tang and Five Dynasties, such as Wen Tingyun and Li Shangyin, are all his favorite poets. But with careful analysis, one can find the calm, reserved Bian Zhilin is quite different from Dai Wangshu and He Qifang. The Baudelaire and Verlaine style of grief could be found in his early writings, but on the whole, the late Symbolism, represented by Yeats, Rilke, Valéry, and Eliot, was the one that contributed more to Bian Zhilin's art maturity. He also had a unique understanding of Chinese classical poetry.

The most remarkable feature of the late Symbolism, represented by Yeats, Rilke, Valéry, and Eliot, is their onlooker attitude toward life in the world when compared with earlier Symbolism poets represented by Verlaine, Mallarmé, and Rimbaud although both groups originated from Baudelaire. If early Symbolism poets prefer self-expression (which has something in common with romanticism), then later Symbolism prefer self-disappearance and like "non-personalization." If early Symbolism prefers to express self-emotion, then late Symbolism advocate "emotions exile" and pursue objective and rational observations. From the day when he chose the art of poetry, Bian Zhilin's nature did not allow him to show himself too much. For instance, in his earliest poems depicting the gray scenes of Beiping's streets, he withdrew himself from the picture even though influenced by Baudelaire and made some comments on life. Compared to Dai Wangshu's similar works (such as "Life," and "Wandering Night Songs"), Bian Zhilin was unwilling to show himself. He always wrote about others instead of depicting himself. He remained cold and calm as possible and joked from time to time. It seems natural for him to be included in the category of "Western modernism" literature during the 1920s, which is late Symbolism.[128] In the poetry texts by Bian Zhilin, the imprints of Western poetry, especially late Symbolism can be found. As critics noticed in "*Returning Home*," "Measuring Days with an Electricity Rod" is derived from the famous sentence "I have measured out my life with coffee spoons" in Eliot's "The Love Song of J. Alfred Prufrock." The line in "Going Home"—"The road to dusk is like a discouragement" can find its traces in Eliot's poem: "Streets that follow like a tedious argument / Of insidious intent / To lead you to an overwhelming question . . ." ("The Love Song of J. Alfred Prufrock"). In "Long Distance," "Several continual cicadae sound" makes people "think of the famous saying in Valéry's 'The Graveyard by the

Sea.'"129 When writing "Fish Fossil," Bian Zhilin "thinks of Éluard's 'She has the form of my hands, She has the color of my eyes.'"130 In contrast, while Dai Wangshu and He Qifang also read some post-Symbolism poetry, they understood and accepted the position of the Symbolism "self-expression" during the early stage. So, they only, in fact, partially accepted the late Symbolism and made more adaptations. For instance, for Dai Wangshu, Paul Fort "is the simplest, most glorious, most poetic poet in French Symbolism." Gourmont's poetry expresses "the subtlety of the soul."131

I also notice Bian Zhilin was deeply in love with Chinese poetry of the Late Tang and Five Dynasties. Jiang Kui, a poet of the Southern Song Dynasty was also his favorite poet. He also admired the art of Ji Kang, a poet who "played the five-string instrument, seeing friends off." He commented: "It's the most divine, graceful style of art to wave one's hands and see others off."132 These cross-era poems also share a common feature, that is, they generally deal with the feelings of life "coldly," facing reality in a light-hearted manner without describing personal emotions directly. Personal emotions are always transferred to the "third party" at a distance. Although Ji Kang's four-character poems are criticized for their "explicitness," they are mostly the direct revelation of rational criticism. They are not affectionate. His writings indicate the imminence of the Eastern Jin Dynasty's "metaphysical era" and the divergence from personal emotions. Li Shangyin's poems are known for "deep love," but his feelings are often hidden behind several abstract objects, giving people a feeling of twists and turns (especially those written during his later years). He Qifang took a fancy to Li Shangyin's deep love, while Bian Zhilin took a fancy to his hidden expressions, called "subtlety." *Hua Jian Ji* represented by Wen Tingyun's *Ci* was "mostly calm and objective . . . without explicit strong emotions and distinct personality."133 Jiang Kui's *Ci* is marked by the rational thinking style of the Jiangxi School, which Bian Zhilin imitated in his early years. Wang Guowei's *Ren Jian Ci Hua* commented that "Jiang Kui's *Ci* showed his character, but not emotions."

In a kind of detachment from a specific life modality and lifestyle, Bian Zhilin not only identified with the late Symbolism of the West but also the "metaphysics" from Ji Kang to Jiang Kui's "emotionlessness." The two Chinese and Western poetry cultures blended in this particular state of mind. Bian Zhilin observed silently, "A man with his hands crossed behind his back" was walking, holding walnuts in his hands; in the distant mountains, the monk stroked the lifeless knell during the day; "She" sat on the cliff on the beach, watching the tides rise and fall; in the stall selling sour plum soup, at the entrance of Old Wang's teahouse, in the "Passers-by Restaurant," customers talked in twos and threes aimlessly. Sometimes, "I" was also like "advertising paper stuck at the station," imagining "fishing up a round treasure box." I "want to go to the high-rise building to read *The History of Roman Decline*," but through this "I," readers only saw a cold, distant Bian Zhilin, without any idea of the ups and downs of his inner feelings. So, concerning Bian Zhilin, people were always arguing and speculating that even experts, such as Li Jianwu and Zhu Ziqing, can only interpret his poems like blind men with an elephant. Wen Yiduo simply did not understand the "Untitled."[134] What are the intended meanings of "Fragment," "Reflections on the Eve of Lunar New Year," and "White Snail Shell"?[135] Bian Zhilin continued to obstruct our thinking with such a self-report, "For most of the poems during this period (refers to 1930–1937—notes by the author) "I" can also be "you" or "he" ("she")."[136] Such a long period of controversy reminds us of Eliot's *The Waste Land* and *The Four Quartets*, as well as Li Shangyin's "The Sad Zither," which echoes "the ideas and writing techniques expressed in my vernacular new poetry coincide with quite a few places both in ancient and modern China and abroad."[137]

We can say that Bian Zhilin is like what he wrote in his poem "viewing the sight downstairs," there are others in the scenery "downstairs," and perhaps his phantom, but he always stayed up the floor, with the distance between "upstairs" and "downstairs" helped him to cool his enthusiasm.

A Cold, Detached Tone

With his inherent restraint and calmness, Bian Zhilin integrated Chinese and Western poetry cultures, but this does not mean the classical Chinese poetry tradition and the Western modern poetry trend can be blended without any contradictions. It should be noted that Chinese classical poetry and Western modern poetry have developed with two completely different philosophies. Regardless of how Western modern poetry accepts the Chinese tradition inspiration, it is the fruit of the big tree of Western culture. The substance of the two major poetry cultures in China and the West is different and produced different influences on Bian Zhilin.

The stress of individual will is the tradition in Western poetry. Symbolism in its late stage emphasizes the disappearance of self and the pursuit of "non-personalization" seems to be a denial of this tradition; however, no one can deny the fact it is precisely the modern poets who are trying to find themselves.

"Negation" is the "personality" that distinguishes them from romanticism and early Symbolism! Eliot said, "Poetry is not a turning loose of emotion, but an escape from emotion; it is not the expression of personality, but an escape from personality. But, of course, only those who have personality and emotions know what it means to want to escape from these things."[138] Essentially, the "self-destruction" and "depersonalization" of later Symbolism are painful and serious questioning of the truth of the world, the future, and humanity by poets who pursue based on their understanding. Because in their view, the reality of the self (and their emotions) has been polluted by the world, I am not me and the others are not others. Poets can only regain themselves in the process of "elimination"! Eliot argued what happened to a poet is "a continual surrender of himself as he is at the moment to something more valuable. The progress of an artist is a continual self-sacrifice, a continual removal of personality."[139] Rilke went further by saying that poems created out of solitude into the inner world are "the voice of your life."[140] The late Symbolist poets were indeed indifferent and even rejected self-specific life feelings and realistic feelings, but in a deeper sense, the indifference and rejection of trivial facts enabled them to complete a more magnificent, solemn thinking on humanity. So this "coldness" is a "frigidity" with a philosophical feature. It is "cold" and sharp, revealing many of the truths about human existence, such as the "wasteland" state of the world, the "cemetery" of the spirit of human nature, and how we are eager to sail to "Byzantine."

"Frigidity" makes people soberly aware of the many philosophical subjects that have been concealed by their predecessors: death and life, spirit and flesh, time and space, and so on.

Symbolism in its later period led Bian Zhilin into modern philosophy where he paid attention to raising the observation of reality to a new philosophical height; hence, a series of wise thoughts emerged in his poems. He reflected when seeing a child throwing a stone: "Maybe someone, / child, once pick something up / (something that you neither love nor hate) / for fun, / like a small stone, / throw it to the world" ("Throwing"). He reflected on "emptiness" because of the disappointment of love: "Epiphany falls upon me in the scent of flowers / the world is empty" ("Untitled Five"). Many of his poems come from his rational consciousness combinations, such as "Fragment," "Reflection on the Eve of Lunar New Year," "The Round Treasure Box," "Contrast," "Navigation," "Organization of Distance" and so on. In the history of Chinese modern poetry, Bian Zhilin is a poet who truly has an explicit philosophical consciousness. The influence of Western Symbolism in its later stage on this "philosophical consciousness" is obvious: "Throwing" discusses the concept of destiny, "Fragment" shows the relationship between the subject and the object, and "Water Dropping Stone" describes the experience of time, which belongs to the topic of post-Symbolic poetry. The "frigidity" of Symbolism distanced Bian Zhilin from some peer poets, such as Dai Wangshu and He Qifang, pointing to some trends in the future new poetry, and thus continued to influence the Chinese Modernist poetry of the 1940s.

However, I don't think we should exaggerate the meaning of "frigidity" of Symbolism in its late stage for Bian Zhilin because an equally obvious fact is Bian Zhilin touched on some topics of Western modern philosophy but did not intend to pursue deeper into these aspects. His wisdom sparkled and flashed at times, such as "Throwing." Bian Zhilin liked to capture some philosophical phenomena, but he did not intend to get to the bottom of it, such as "Fragment." He can often resolve the seriousness of thinking in a vague blandness, just as the emptiness view demonstrated in "Untitled Five": "Epiphany falls upon me in the scent of flowers / the world is empty, / because it is useful, / because it accommodates your steps." This peaceful mentality seems to imply that the foundation of Bian Zhilin's calmness lacked solidity and sharpness. It is very different from the "frigidity" of Western Symbolism in its late stage. His calmness focused on "quietness" and to place it more accurately, it seems to be called "calmness." Calmness means neither investing nor giving up the world when faced with world changes, and personal sorrows and joys. One would be indifferent and seemingly like nothing. One might have emotional fluctuations but could be pacified in time. As Wei Yingwu, a poet in Tang Dynasty said, "One comes from silence, and a desire to disappear into silence." Calmness mentality is more likely to remind us of Chinese classical poetry, from the detached good-bye waving gestures of Ji Kang, to the quietness of Wen Tingyun's "*wutong* (Chinese parasol) trees in the night rain," from Li Shangyin's pleasant distance in "warm jade smoke" to the Jiang Kui's quiet "chilly lights in early spring." The choices of Chinese classical poets are so detached from the human world.

Possibly, here lies an important difference between Chinese and Western poetry cultures. The "frigidity" of Western Symbolism poetry in its late period showed the grit of the poets' will to live. It changed the tradition of "lavishing emotions" in Western poetry on one level but developed the Western pursuit of "will," a fundamental "tradition" of Western poetry on another, deeper level. This tradition was born in the "idea" of the ancient Greek era, consolidated as the "reason" of the Enlightenment in the Renaissance after the reverse strengthening of medieval theology. It has been deeply embedded in the spiritual structure of Western poets and becomes a fact. The "calmness" of Chinese classical poetry reflected the life choice of Chinese poets in some way who take a step back from the disturbing social reality and turn to peace of mind in the harmony of nature. Regardless of whether it is "sending the message through objects" or complete "objectification," whether it is the natural revealing of the spirit or the deliberate self-disguise, the essence of "calmness" is the relaxation of the will of the individual and the relief of the inner life impulse. When there are no priori "ideas" to be in absolute leadership, in the cultural atmosphere in which God's authority does not exist, the "calmness" sense of reason becomes a typical example of the spiritual characteristics of Chinese classical poets.

Chinese modern culture development did not fundamentally subvert the inherent philosophical background of Chinese culture. The "calmness" of Chinese classical poetry continued to affect Chinese modern poets spiritually through various enlightenment education. What is important is in the level of consciousness of Bian Zhilin, the "coolness" of these two Chinese and Western poetry cultures has never been in the same important position. He pointed out that the Modernist poetry of the 1930s "tended to shift the focus on absorbing from the Western poetry to the focus on the inheritance of Chinese traditional poetry."[141]

It is possible to conclude the "frigidity" of Symbolic poetry in the late stage once gave him great inspiration and guided him to the maturity of art. But, in the depth of the spiritual structure, he still preferred the "calmness" in Chinese classical poetry. A calm and objective attitude determined the rational spirit of poetry writing. Bian Zhilin's calmness determined he must move toward "reason advocacy," which has distinct national characteristics and is different from the philosophical trends of Western Symbolism poetry in its late period.

The charm of the "philosophicalization" of the late period Symbolism poetry comes from the deepening of its thinking and the intricacies of thought. W. B. Yeats believes only reason can determine what the reader should think about a series of symbols. If these symbols are only emotional, then he can only look at them from the perspective of coincidence and the inevitability of the world. But, if these symbols are also rational, then he becomes a part of pure reason.[142] The charm of Bian Zhilin's poems—"being rational" comes from the wonder of their concepts. They do not overly unfold their philosophical concepts, but just put these concepts in front of the readers, making people appreciate and admire them. Symbolic poetry in its later period excels by reason, and Bian Zhilin's poems excel for their savoring in reason, which is also in line with the requirements of Chinese poetics as Yan Yu said: "Poetry writing requires special talents rather than abstract reasoning."

Bian Zhilin wrote about the movements of time and the relativity of time and space, but his wise thoughts are mainly immersed in the interests of life, rarely distracted by "thought." The meaning "something out of nothing" is infiltrated with some kind of long-cherished feelings in "White Snail Shell": "The ethereal white snail shell, you /with not a tiny dust in your world, / flowed into my hand / with a thousand kinds of feelings." The historical consciousness of "The Letters" is just the embellishment of "missing a friend": "If that is a golden point, / If my seat is the top of the mountain, / on the moon night, I have to guess where you are / It must be a quasi-lost train station. / However, I am facing a history book. /Looking at the Xianyang Ancient Trail in the sunset, / I waited for the hoofs of a galloping horse." He "wants to go to the high-rise building to read *The History of Roman Decline*," but finally awoke in the "snow" brought by the friend, and returned to reality ("Organization of Distance"). In the notes, Bian Zhilin elaborated on this "Organization of Distance": "There is a relationship between existence and consciousness. But the whole poem is not about philosophy, nor about expressing mystery, but follows the tradition of Chinese poetry to express emotions or feelings."

Any thought that transcends the actual life will necessarily point to a more perfect future. Thus, it will inevitably show suspicion, sorrow, and even negation of real life. This is the case with the late Western Symbolism poetry. Rilke saw the "final fruit" from the prosperity of autumn: "Who is lonely would be forever lonely" ("Autumn"). Eliot felt: "April is the cruelest month" (*The Wasteland*). Bian Zhilin did not intend to abstract the idea from the honey of life, then he cannot fall into the suffering of this swamp. Liu Xiwei, a critic, believed there was great sorrow in the "Fragment," but Bian Zhilin denied it. Probably the experience of the Modernist colleague Fei Ming was more accurate, who, after reading some of the cool "rational poems" by Bian Zhilin, exclaimed, "he was just naive and thinking more rather than being away from the earthly life."[143] Sometimes, Bian Zhilin does not even want to ask anything at all. He is more willing to accept freedom as expressed by the classical poems. "Let the time be water, the bed being the boat, / lying in the boat and flow with the clouds, / Not aware of being far away from the peach blossoms along the banks" (Note from "The Round Treasure Box").

On the whole, the peaceful Bian Zhilin had no intention to become a "philosophical poet." He stood on the upper floor to view the scenery, looking at it without much attention, as if he was not looking or thinking. He imagined he was a philosopher, but a philosopher who "relaxed in the spring water" and "had a nap" there ("Contrast"). Bian Zhilin showed more national cultural characteristics in the depth of the poetry spirit.

Cultural Characteristics of Bian's Poetry

The multi-faceted integration of Chinese and Western poetry culture also exists in the artistic forms of Bian Zhilin's poems.

It is generally believed Bian Zhilin's poems have three main artistic contributions: attention to typical dramatic techniques; novel and varied language; and strict and consistent rhythms with modern language habits. I think it is in these three aspects that we can see the multiple imprints of Chinese and Western cultures.

The techniques of drama and novel language can be said to be the artistic features of later Symbolism. T. S. Eliot paid special attention to expressing his own experience dramatically, either through dramatic character dialogues or dramatic scenes in which the narrator disappeared. Dramatic techniques are effective by avoiding the interference of the poet's trivial emotions, allowing readers to experience more of the true state of the world and human existence. Initiating rebellion against the referential language, creating ambiguity, and the unexpected "defamiliarization" effect of the words is the conscious pursuit of modern poets. Bian Zhilin "often tended to write dramatic situations, made dramatic monologues or dialogues, and even novelized" writings.[144] "Sour Plum Soup," "Bitter Rain," and "Spring City" all use or partly use monologues and dialogues. In "Cold Night," "A Leisure Man," "A Monk," "Long Distance," "A Piece of Ship Wreck," "Home," "Dream of the Ancient Town," "Fragment," "Lonely," there are almost no "I" as a narrator. In the works such as "The Letters," "Organization of Distance," "Reflections on the Eve of Lunar New Year," "Chiba" (Shakuhachi), and "White Snail Shell," objective and self-sufficient dramatic scenes are still maintained although there is a narrator "I." At the same time, Bian's poems are also known as obscure. There are quite big gaps and giant leaps between words and sentences. As mentioned above, even great poetry critics, such as Li Jianwu, Zhu Ziqing, and Wen Yiduo, cannot completely decipher the "secrets" of these words, not to mention other readers! However, it is not only works, such as "Fragment," "Organization of

Distance" and "Untitled," that are obscure and ambiguous, so are "Reflections on the Eve of Lunar New Year," as well as others, such as "The Letters," "White Snail Shell," "The Round Treasure Box," "Fish Fossil," and "Being Naughty." Bian's tactics of dramatic language and language leaping style benefited from the late period Symbolism.

Bian Zhilin constantly compared and explained foreign poetics and China's traditions. For example, he connected the dramatic approach with China's "aesthetic conception": "When I write lyric poems, like most Chinese classical poems, I focus on the 'aesthetic conception', often making 'dramatic lines' through the Western 'dramatic situation.'"[145] According to him, the "subtleness" caused by language breaks is also where Chinese and Western poetry "communicate" and "match" each other.[146] Indeed, the aesthetic conception of Chinese classical poetry is "things in their natural states," which opposes the interference of the subject with the objects, and maintains objectivity. "Chinese poets give paramount importance to the acting out of visual objects and events, letting those objects and events explain *themselves* by their coexisting, coextensive emergence from nature, letting the spatial tensions reflect conditions and situations rather than coercing these objects and events into some preconceived artificial order by sheer human interpretive elaboration."[147] Isn't this dramatization? Chinese classical poetry emphasizes the disintegration of the "referential" nature of language and maintains the three-dimensionality and polysemy of its original state. It is "subtle," and the language operation of Western modern poetry in the 20th century is influenced by Chinese classical poetry. However, I believe all these similarities still do not prove that the art of Chinese and Western poetry integrate. In fact, under the appearance of these superficial integrations, there is a profound spiritual separation: the dramatic approach of Western Symbolism in its late period is mainly to arouse readers' personal experiences and allow all readers to enter the living atmosphere of the poetry and think about the destiny of the world and mankind. The temporary elimination of the narrator's voice is to avoid the interference caused by the poet's narrowness, but what needs to be eliminated is only the personal narrowness, not the great will of man. On the contrary, the dramatic approach is to mobilize the willpower of many recipients. Therefore, the so-called "objective" of dramatic means is only an agent, and its ultimate point is precisely the subjectivity and will of human beings. The "aesthetic conception" of Chinese classical poetry is more than arousing the reader's personal experiences. The "aesthetic conception" is the ideal state of Chinese philosophy and Chinese culture. "Aesthetic conception" is eliminating all traces of will, allowing the subjective state to return to the objective and becoming an integral part of the objective environment. It is by no means an agent, it is the purpose itself! If the world in the drama scene is still the world of reality, with broken, disastrous objects in crisis, then the imagery within aesthetic conception is like the ideal world, where the people and the world live in harmony and peace. Similarly, the symbolic rebellion against the "referential" of language in the late Western period was not to eliminate the artificial factors in the language, but rather a way of anti-tradition. They eliminated the old "referential," but created a new "referential." Language is still constantly tracking people's thoughts. When a poet's thoughts are excessively advanced and bound by traditional grammatical rules, the poet does not hesitate to break these rules and adapt the traditional "pieces of language" to new ideas. This is exactly what T. S. Eliot and others pursued. Therefore, the novelty of the late symbolic language and the "obscurity" formed by the language leap occurred because essentially the poet's thinking went beyond the acceptance and understanding ability of his contemporary. It is the advanced effect of thought. Chinese classical poetry tries to eliminate the artificial traces of language and completely break through the limitations of grammar, at least restrictions on referential and semantics, positioning and timing should be reduced to the minimum. However, this is not to adapt to a novelty nor advanced thoughts, but to return to the "clear" state and "pre-referential" state without human-induced thoughts. This kind of processing transcends our rational consciousness and does not make us feel awkward or weird. It is fresh and natural because it adapts to our most authentic state of life in essence.

I have always felt it is inappropriate to refer to the dramatic effect of Bian Zhilin's poetry as "agents." In some works, Bian Zhilin's dramatic effects are used to provide contexts for the kind of perfect, complete scenes, suggesting his traditional understanding of the state of life is more like China's "aesthetic conception." The wilderness, the cicada singing, the sunset, the long willows, and the long distance of white heat make up the world of porters ("Long Distance"). The tides, pieces of a shipwreck, stone cliffs, sunsets, and white sails are the spaces of "her" ("A Piece of Ship Wreck"). A broken temple, cigarettes, wooden fish, vague mountains and rivers, groggy bells, this is the monk's "pale dark dream" ("A Monk"). Other works, such as "Organization of Distance," "Shakuhachi," "The Round Treasure Box" and so on, are complicated in imagery, but they are not arbitrary. They are all united by a certain kind of faint emotion and have a common orientation.

In "Organization of Distance," it is a reflection on life. It is a vague historical feeling in Shakuhachi. It is the illusion of love in "The Round Treasure Box." These drama scenes pay attention to internal connection, coherence, and cooperation, quite different from the fragmentation of post-Symbolic poetry. It is still Chinese thinking. "Chinese thinking can be said to be a kind of cyclic thinking. Thoughts diverge, but they must be returned and fall back to the original starting point,"[148] said Bian Zhilin, "I think "circle" is the most complete image, the most basic image."[149]

The leaps of Bian Zhilin's language brought some difficulties to our understanding. However, it should be noted this is due to the more realistic considerations of the poet instead of deliberately distancing himself from our thoughts. On the one hand, he was ashamed of exposing some of his hidden individual emotions (this has something in common with Dai Wangshu). On the other hand, he tried to establish the organic connection between man and the world across time and space through language freedom. Essentially, such a trans-temporal connection does not break through our tolerance for Chinese variation. It is unfamiliar and novel, but not weird. Readers would admire the use rather than become confused. The "jumping" of his words is mainly a more flexible use of part of speech and the change of usage habits of words, such as "I took a sip of the vagueness of the street" ("Record"). "Friends brought the feel of snow and five o'clock" ("Organization of Distance"). His sentence "jumping" across time and space is based on the traditional Chinese concepts of time, space, and contradictions. For example, in "Untitled Five," "I am thankful in my walk / the buttonhole is useful, / Because it is empty, / because you can pin a small flower there." He explained this jump, "There is an old saying: 'the useless is for real use.'" After the "Comfort Letters," Bian Zhilin's writing entered a new era with a new look, but remained as always in the witty "leap" of language use. For instance, in "A Coal Miner," "every day three hours are vacated to attend the lectures, / looking at the new world from the window of the texts." "The New Soldiers of the Local Armed Forces," "Beware of the full belly anger of the grenade / cannot help but engulf yourself." The sentence jumps in "All Laborers," "There is at least one chance in one hand / pushing a stinging small gear tooth. / Waiting for a new milestone in the front, / the world marked another hour."

As everyone knows, Bian Zhilin had long been committed to the exploration of Chinese modern new poetry rhythm forms. He attempted 2 lines, 3 lines, 4 lines, 5 lines, 6 lines, 8 lines, 10 lines, 14 lines, and so on with both original as well as variants. The most frequent are fourteen-lined sonnets. The metrical poems represented by sonnets have been a favorite in the history of Western poetry and their influence continued into the late Symbolism of the 20th century. Mallarmé, Valeri, Yeats, Rilke, Eliot, and others wrote metrical poetry, an encouragement undoubtedly for rhythm exploration. Bian Zhilin said the rhythm styles of some of his poems directly adopted Western poetic styles, such as *A Monk* adopted the "second- or third-class Symbolism sonnets in France during the 19th century." "White Snail Shell" adopted a complicated rhythm once used by Valéry. "Air Force Warrior" adopted the rhythm of a sonnet variant of Valéry[150] ("Le Sylphe," the author's note). In addition to the expansion of poetry style, he also carefully scrutinized the rhythm of metrics (pauses). Bian Zhilin introduced a variety of rhyming methods, such as rhyme change, implied rhyme, alternate rhyme, and poetry crossline in addition to one rhyme to the end. Judging from the numerous discussions of metrics by Bian Zhilin, his purpose was to find a style more in line with modern Chinese language habits and explore how poetry can be both smooth and natural under modern Chinese conditions. The premise of his discussion is often "the new poetry in China today, ... how to write a sonnet in Chinese," which shows Bian Zhilin's profound sensibility to the Chinese language and the confidence in accepting Western culture. The openness and development in line with the requirements of the times are also where Bian Zhilin surpassed his predecessor poet, Wen Yiduo. From the concrete practice of the metrical law, Wen Yiduo's architectural beauty and musical beauty are dull, mechanical, and conservative, while Bian Zhilin's is more flexible, free, and open.

However, we should also take note of the fact that Bian Zhilin's various flexibility and openness about poetry, rhythm, rhyming, and cross-lines are not his unscrupulous creations. Like other ideological and artistic pursuits, this reflects his conscious inheritance of the Chinese classical poetry tradition. Bian Zhilin thinks sonnets "is closest to China's seven-character metrical poetry, with the functions of starting, continuing, turning, and closing, which could also be used freely."[151] Inspired by this, he wanted to create in vernacular a new eight-line style of the Chinese seven-character poems. He also proved rhyme change, implied rhyme, alternate rhyme, and poetry crossline "already existed in ancient times" in China. As long as they no longer emphasized the flat-fall tones and no longer insist on the strict regularity of each line, the sound of the same pauses can also achieve a melody effect similar to Chinese classical poetry.[152] Therefore, we seem to witness the rhythmical style of Xu Zhimo's poetry again, which reconciled the regularity of the classical poetry rhythms with the freedom and flexibility of modern Chinese.

This is the charm of Xu's poems. Feng Wenbing once said that Bian Zhilin "completely developed Xu's style."[153] I think this has a deep meaning. At least objectively speaking, "development" does not mean complete negation, but rather affirmation, even extension, and reinforcement. The Crescent Moon School poetry represented by Xu Zhimo is a bridge between the new poetry and classical poetry as commented by Shi Ling. So, isn't this more accurate to describe Bian Zhilin? He accepts the influence of Western poetry culture, based on late Symbolism. However, these influences are always placed in the cognitive mode of Chinese classical tradition to be milled, digested, and absorbed to obtain a multi-faceted fusion of Chinese and Western poetry cultures.

Liang Zongdai: Glory of Subjectivity and Enchantment of Objectification

> We seem to have come to one
> Divergent intersection. New poetry writing
> And its future will be dependent on our
> Choices and directions to go.
>
> —Liang Zongdai, "At the Crossroads of New Poetry"

Starting from "Subjectivity"

Today, when discussing Liang Zongdai's poetry and poetic contributions, most would agree with the evaluation of "Chinese-Western integration." This is in line with Liang Zongdai's own artistic path and poetic interests, but the problem is when dissatisfaction with the early vernacular new poetry had become a mainstream discourse in Chinese poetry after the 1920s. "Chinese-Western integration" had become a "common goal" of many poets, including the Crescent Moon School, the Symbolist School, and the Modernist School. With this background, what distinguished Liang Zongdai from others? This is the question we must answer to discuss the achievements of Liang Zongdai today.

I would like to start with Liang Zongdai's poems during the early 1920s. The following poem comes from his poetry collection, *Evening Prayers*:

> When the night god came quietly and silently,
> A sweet sleep
> Is endowed to all,

Heaven, draped in a cloud of silver,
Spray the pearly dew
Quietly over the earth.
So quietly Mother Earth
In the early morning sunshine of Zhaosu,
Blossomed many beautiful, fragrant flowers
Each sends their thank-you note to the sky.

—"Night Dew"

On a night in 1923, Chinese poet Liang Zongdai wrote this quiet, serene "ode to night." The reason it can be called "Ode to Night" rather than the traditional Chinese style of "Quiet Night Thoughts" lies in the fact that Liang Zongdai here did not show us the Chinese traditional poetry in which integration of the writer and the surroundings would be found, nor the slender rhythm of the natural night led to the thoughts of the poet. "The night is quiet and everything stops its activity, Only the buzzing of the cicadas. The north wind rustled through the trees in the courtyard, and the sunset revealed the late autumn."[154] "The scenery is beautiful both at day and night, right for you and me to write poems. Looking far into the sky and my cheeks were caressed by the carefree emotions."[155] "The moon is hanging right out the window, the starry night seems to come indoors, the trees growing even greener in this spring, the cuckoo whining at night. The lonely traveler listened and suddenly heard the morning call of roosters."[156] For ancient Chinese, the night, the night's sounds, and the poet's mind are within a certain natural extension. So, for poetry conceptualization of "the sight would arouse certain feelings and express one's thoughts through something concrete," the sight and the feelings, the things and the thoughts maintain a certain "isomorphic" relationship in the harmony of each other. Liang Zongdai's "ode" outlines a peaceful, harmonious, separate world: peace and harmony are its temperament and atmosphere, and separation is its way of existence—heaven is the grace of the "night god," surrounded by the extraordinary magnificence of grace from God, the earth holds tens of thousands of lives that bear the grace of God. They look up into the sky and "thank the sky silently and respectfully." In such a world order led by "God's grace," the human self-spirit is not distorted in the original form of nature's sensuality. It is not in the harmony of the natural form to pursue the floating of self-emotion. The "ode" to God is human beings' gratitude, which also means the recognition of the "separated" world created by God: we all need to constantly get rid of the mortal world, praising and flying to the eternal magnificent heaven. Prayers and praises are noble forms of self-spirit transcendence. Prayer is called "the soul and essence of religion … the most spontaneous and personal expression of the individual …. People stretch their bodies to God in prayers. He wants to surpass Himself, doesn't want to be lonely again, nor want to let oneself be alone with Himself."[157] "The contemplative person has merged with his faith in prayers so that he can see God's Revelation or reach the beatific vision, which is at the same level as the highest level of spiritual sublimation we just said."[158] Liang Zongdai's evening prayers and ode to night are different from many Chinese symbolic poems of the same period, such as Mu Mutian's, "The Village at Misty Dusk":

>   …
> The beach behind the village
> Paddling sounds from time-to-time
> In the dense path of the willows
> Intermittent singing of late pedestrians
> The whispering water channel, quietly babbling ….
> Ringing between the grey sky and the dim plains
> Oh, my lovely hometown
> Enveloped in the misty cloudy sky

It is the landscape in the misty dusk that aroused the poet's inspiration and imaginary thoughts. Mu Mutian's "misty dusk world" is complete, and the poet's self and thoughts are also floating in the image of the world. There is no difference between "up" and "down." There is no such thing as soaring from the common to the sacred. It is closer to the "thought expression on-site" model of Chinese classical poetry.

I once summarized the spiritual pursuit of Chinese classical poetry as "objectification," to distinguish it from the "subjectivity" tradition of Western poetry.[159] Objectified poetry art does not pursue the turbulence of personal emotions, nor does it intend to indulge in subjective speculations. The ideal world is the equality of things, the harmony of objects and nature. "Expressing oneself through objects" and "viewing things through objects" are regarded as the highest art pursuit of Chinese classical poetry. In the history of Chinese modern new poetry development, with the increasing criticism of the crude defects of the early vernacular new poetry, it is an attractive choice to seek the nourishment of art from the millennial traditions of Chinese classical poetry. Therefore, from the early 1920s, the "objectified" poetry in the form of vernacular once again emerged in the writings of the Crescent Moon School and the Symbolist poets.

Liang Zongdai created "non-objectified" poetry for us in his evening prayers and ode to night because the knowledge and spiritual background of his childhood in the church school provided another equally attractive spiritual choice: It is not in harmony with nature, but he searched for meaning in the dialogue with God above nature, in the divine order led by prayer and apocalypse. The will of God runs through the universe, not nature itself. It is God's will that guides his life to complete the most fundamental transcendence. In this spiritual resource, "thing or object" is only the embodiment of "will," and "will" is the foundation of life. We enhance the "will" of the self through admiration and acceptance of God's "will." Through this process, Christian culture continues to strengthen the "subjectivity" tradition of Western art since ancient Greece. The experience of Liang Zongdai's bathing in the world of "evening prayers" allowed him to walk out of the "objectified" tradition. When night fell, he was not as gentle and sentimental in the natural tranquility as the ancient scholars. He was meditating on another "light" in the darkness of the mortal world, the "light" of the will of the Creator. "I am only looking forward with tears—/ I hope there is a faint piece of red / to the east wind of spring / which unexpectedly sends its breeze to me" ("Evening Prayers II"). "The slight leaping which made a peaceful mind/ deep praise/ the Creator's warm love" ("Prayer I"). The night sky filled with the will of the Creator was so magnificent: "Under the deep stars, / Unlimited sound waves / They are playing their silent music. / Listen! Listen silently! / The messenger of a far, wide light" ("Starry Sky"). The poet not only celebrated the transcendence of will but also began to discover the mapping of self-will in the material world: "A Canary" and "A Black Butterfly" are also like human beings to find life's companions ("Disappointment"), and the Night Owl's hooting turns into "the voice of life curse" ("Night Owl"), "Morning Birds" sang "Song of the Holy Spirit" ("Morning Birds"). Regardless of how simple these poems are, we must admit they indeed opened up another new field beyond the usual mode of Chinese classical poetry.

If you read the Western poetry that entered Liang Zongdai's vision later, we can easily find the kind of "subjectivity" of the relationship between objects and images. Verlaine interpreted the existence and significance of nature:

> The sky-blue smiles above the roof
> Its tenderest;
> A green tree rears above the roof
> Its waving crest.

> The church-bell in the windless sky
> Peaceably rings,
> A skylark soaring in the sky
> Endlessly sings.
>
> My God, my God, all life is there,
> Simple and sweet;
> The soothing bee-hive murmur there
> Comes from the street!
> —Verlaine, "The Sky-Blue Smiles above the Roof"[160]

This is a constant "upward" feeling. There is a house on the earth, the house has a roof, there is a tree on the roof, and there is a bird on the tree. On all of this, there is a quieter sky and there is God. This is the typical form of human spiritual transcendence. It is the high-level life that encourages the poet to abandon the prison-like reality and constant struggle to rise. We often think Western poetry has consciously and unconsciously approached the ideals of Chinese classical poetry since the beginning of Symbolism. The difference here is still remarkable. Instead of reading the world as a natural whole, efforts to distinguish the realm of different meanings and to determine the path of our spiritual sublimation are sought. This kind of poetry is prominent in Western Symbolist poetry. Valéry is a poet who is closely related to Liang Zongdai. The "earth" in his eyes is also full of the will and the soul's kinetic energy:

> Closed, hallowed, full of unsubstantial fire,
> Morsel of earth to heaven's light given o'er --
> This plot, ruled by its flambeaux, pleases me --
> A place all gold, stone, and dark wood, where shudders
> So much marble above so many shadows . . .
> —"The Graveyard by the Sea"[161]

We may argue the religious and spiritual resources obtained by Liang Zongdai in his youth were an important reason for his closeness to the Western subjectivity of poetic thoughts. The selection of subjectivity in poetry was the main manifestation of his departure from the traditional Chinese poetry models.

Misreading of "Objectification"

However, did Liang Zongdai continue to follow this path of subjectivity? I'd like to remind readers to pay attention to his poetic masterpieces *Poetry and*

Truth and *Poetry and Truth II*. In past research, we have fully explored the important value of his poetic theories in these works, such as the important poetic concepts of "symbol," "pure poetry" and "match" as Liang Zongdai elaborated, the unique insights and in-depth understanding of Chinese and foreign poetics. In addition to these, however, we should continue to follow Liang Zongdai's unique poetry choice formed in his early years, to determine if he was strengthening or changing his position along the path of subjectivity. What is the relationship between his poetic attitude at that time and his poetry writing?

I think Liang Zongdai's poetics at that time had an important relationship with his identity as a poet, indicated by the fact he was not a scholar engaged in the construction of poetic buildings, but a poet obsessed with artistic writing and theory development. Liang Zongdai defined himself as the experimenter and explorer of new poetry. He was particularly concerned about the present and future of Chinese poetry. Comparing himself with Zhu Guangqian, a respectful friend who was also a colleague at Peking University and a poetry theorist, Liang Zongdai said: "Guangqian's goal is theory. It is a scholarship. He studied literature to confirm his theories, while my goal is to create literature and become involved with theories to confirm my writing and understanding of literature."[162]

However, unlike the simple boyhood poet identity in *Evening Prayers*, Liang Zongdai was immersed in the rich nutrition of Chinese and foreign poetics of the time. As a university professor and a scholar who studied Chinese and Western cultures, Liang Zongdai showed his familiarity and interest in Chinese and foreign poetic traditions. As an important member of the exploration of Chinese poetics in the 1930s, his primary task was not to allow his free spirit to fly but to answer important issues in the development of poetics. As a result, important concepts such as "symbol," "pure poetry," "match" and others affecting the development of Chinese poetics had become the main targets of Liang Zongdai's interpretations. The poetic achievements in these conceptual interpretations have been summarized in recent years and will not be repeated here. His discussion of "symbol" is more comprehensive and detailed than Zhou Zuoren's intuitive thoughts. It is more in line with the overall characteristics of poetry thinking than Zhu Guangqian's conclusions. His explanation of "pure poetry" is more specific and has a clearer practical meaning than that of Mu Mutian's "pure poetry" ideals. Liang Zongdai's discussion of "match" also goes deep into the poetic essence of Chinese-style Symbolist poetry, which has not been explicitly discussed by other Chinese poetry theorists. In all these explorations of poetics, Liang Zongdai fully demonstrated his rich, artistic experience as a new poetry practitioner.

What is most noteworthy is in these poetic elaborations, Liang Zongdai began to acquire more recognition and affirmation of the integration of Chinese and foreign poetry, which is different from his earlier literal understanding of the "subjectivity" of poetry. Although the three major poetic concepts elaborated by Liang Zongdai are the so-called "Chinese-Western integration," they are in line with the "objectification" pursuit of Chinese classical poetry. Like Zhou Zuoren and others, Liang Zongdai continued to use "*Xing*" to describe the foundation of "symbol," supplemented by the description of the Chinese characteristics of "emotions generated by immediate scenery and scenery generated because of emotions." This undermined the subjective will color of Western Symbolism. For Valéry, pure poetry is "absolute poetry" and "ideal poetry," insulated from reality and "has nothing to do with the reality order." Fundamentally speaking, this is "an unattainable goal."[163] Liang Zongdai also believes pure poetry is "something that has not existed or has not reached perfection ... It is a universe purer and immortal."[164] But he is more realistic and more optimistic than Valéry, with reasons from the Chinese classical tradition: "There are many pure poems in our classic poetry," such as Chen Zi'ang's "Ode to Mounting Youzhou' Terrace," Jiang Kui's "Dark Fragrance" and "Thin Shadow," etc.[165] Here, the difference between the objectification tradition of poetry and the subjectivity tradition is once again not mentioned. As for the "match," per the view of Liang Zongdai, it means that a poet (or readers) in writing (or appreciating) focused so much on the idea rather than form, forgets everything. The colors, fragrances, sounds of the world, and human senses became a symphony, and the poet "dissolved into the world."[166] In his "cosmic consciousness," which the poet advocated in these three important poetics theories, what we have seen is no longer the magnificent picture of life and self-transcendence in his earlier poetry:

> From this moment on, the curtain between the world and us has always been opened. Like the hometown, we restored a general picture of the universe. Or it can be said, returning to the arms of the universe, and not a lightning-like encounter only in drunk and dreams, but the reality experienced anytime and anywhere.
>
> When we abdicate the authority of reason and will, we completely entrust ourselves to the nature of disappointment. Let us imagine injecting objects, letting the atmosphere of the universe pass through our hearts; thus, forming a deep sympathy exchange. When we and the world get the same pulse and rhythm, what is standing in front of us is not fine sand, a wildflower, or a piece of broken tile, but an accidental

encounter between a free, lively soul and our soul: two identical destinies. At this moment, we nod to each other, with tacit understanding and smile.[167]

In such a cosmic consciousness, the world is no longer manipulated by God, no longer divided into the side of the light and the dark shore. The universe is "universal and complete." We are also equal and amiable with the universe. It does not work with every transcendental spirit and the individual "will" must be abandoned. The remainder is just harmony and tacit understanding between objects and people. This would be the experience as expressed in famous poetry, such as "Flocks of birds fly high and vanish; A single cloud, alone, calmly drifts on. Never tired of looking at each other— Only the Jingting Mountain and me."[168] "A silvery moon is shining through the pines, The limpid brooks are gurgling over the stones .... The scents of spring may go; that's Nature's will. This season here attracts the noble still."[169] This kind of cosmic consciousness is vividly shown in the objectification of Chinese classical poetry.

Liang Zongdai attached great importance to the Chinese and Western poetry spirit communication. On the one hand, it is directly related to his familiar expectations of the French literary world. Valéry admired Liang Zongdai and the Chinese poems he translated. "He thought Mr. Liang grasped the most delicate, ancient characteristics of the adjoining points of literature and arts almost as soon as he came into contact with French literature."[170] In addition, another French literature giant, Roman Roland, who was worshipped by Liang Zongdai, was also amazed by the "sanguine relationship" between Tao Yuanming and Latin poetry. He commented:

> This is not the first time I have found striking similarities between China's souls and one of the two spirits of France (the Latin French). I felt obliged to believe a mysterious sanguine relationship in anthropological elements—there is no other nation in Asia that shows such a relationship with our nation.[171]

As we all know, Chinese modern poetry, like Chinese modern literature, developed against the strong momentum of the constant influx of Western culture, which brought a wealth of information resources for the development of Chinese literature, but also caused a certain kind of great anxiety. Wen Yiduo, a famous poet, once expressed this anxiety vividly and the strategy for solving it at that time:

> From our contact with outsiders, it is found we lagged in almost every aspect of the material life, which gave an unbearable burden to the spiritual life of the nation

.... I think at least in these respects (referring to ancient Chinese philosophy and literature—the author's note) we are not weaker than others, so we feel some relief.[172]

Appreciation from the Western world undoubtedly brought incalculable encouragement and an "orientation" effect on Chinese poets. During the 1930s, Chinese poets, obsessed with the exploration of Chinese new poetry art, also "received" similar extraterritorial information promptly, and used this as an opportunity to "shift the focus on the absorption of Western poetry to concentrate on the inheritance of classic Chinese style poetry."[173] We can say this became an important reason for Liang Zongdai's eventual return to the position of Chinese classical poetry through the ideal of "Chinese-Western integration." Today, we can see both the appreciation from the French literary world and promotion from the domestic poetry community clearly show the essence of a "cultural misreading." Baudelaire's "match" leads to the discovery of "the glory behind the grave," and Mallarmé created "a palace built of untouchable stones." For Valéry, pure poetry is not a product of reality, it is an illusion. It is very similar to dreams.[174] Such a distinctive transcendental feature is difficult to blend with traditional Chinese poetry. If the misunderstanding of Valéry and Roman Roland is covered by the self-evident "subjectivity" of the Western tradition, Liang Zongtang and other Chinese modern poets used our deep-rooted "objectified" thinking to select and modify the Western Symbolism pursuit. At the same time, they even transferred the Western misunderstanding—turning the covering and wrapping of Western "subjectivity" thinking into a self-consolidation of Chinese "objectified" thinking. We should be vigilant about this misreading approach and its misreading process.

Interaction and Intertwining of Chinese and Western Poetics

There is more to explore about Liang Zongdai. In fact, as a poet with unique artistic feelings and unusual artistic practice in his early years, he can never ignore the new art nor fundamentally deny the different experiences of Western poetry, especially its new development operations.

Therefore, it is not difficult to find many contradictions in theoretical details in Liang Zongdai's seemingly complete and harmonious Chinese and Western poetic interpretations. This is inevitable for a poet who had different artistic experiences when he entered a collective mode of thinking, and the contradiction is precisely the product of his real artistic experience. For example, in the discussion of a series of Chinese classical poetry artistic ideals, the details of his artistic feelings mixed different elements at times. He explained the "match" with Zhuangzi's "forgetting everything," but a further description is like this: "The close connection of this color, fragrance, and sounds will bring us from the drunk and dreams of the gods and objects to reach a greater light—a light made of joy and wisdom."[175] The "drunk and dreams" here belong to Valéry, which means the poet had unconsciously mixed with the transcendental consciousness of Western Symbolism. And the "light of joy and wisdom" is the self-transcendence and self-sublimation of the Western subjectivity tradition. Here, Liang Zongdai seems to have returned to the spiritual experience of his early *Evening Prayers*.

Similarly, when Liang Zongdai quoted the works of Chinese classical poets with "cosmic consciousness," such as Wang Wei and Chen Zi'ang, he could not help but sigh: "But these are still traditional Chinese poems, too traditional! Let us talk about your typical Western poetry."[176] Thus, the example of "the fusion of Chinese and Western" poetry turned to the West. Here, it hinted at the poet's unique interest in exotic art. I believe it is from this unique perception that Liang Zongdai revealed many characteristics of Western poetry. For example, he pointed out Valéry's poetry is unique in that it proposes a series of "permanent philosophies, the permanent metaphysical question: Who am I? What is the world? What is my relationship with the world? What is its value? Is it the world, or me, or a soft, fragile onlooker that is important?"[177]

Liang Zongdai titled his poetics *Poetry and Truth*, which, according to him, was inspired by Johann Wolfgang von Goethe's autobiography *Dichtung und Wahrheit*. "Poetry" refers to fantasy, and "truth" refers to facts. Fantasy and facts are the "two sides of the object pursued throughout life."[178] Considering the sacred tribute of Liang Zongdai's *Evening Prayers* in his early years, and the longing for the "brightness" in the later poetics, I even suspected it always implied an understanding of another "transcendence" of "truth" in the eyes of Liang Zongdai, who was deeply influenced by Christianity in his youth, according to which God is truth itself, the supreme truth. "I am the way, the truth, the life," which is the cornerstone of all Christian faith. The *Gospel of John* said: "My mission is to testify to my truth. I was born for this purpose. I came to this world for this . . . . The person who works according to the truth goes to the light, so that people see his behaviors according to God's will." Of course, this does not mean Christian concepts dominated the thinking of Liang Zongdai, but having such a life experience seems to mean "truth" is at least not a simple "reality," but related to a certain transcendence experience of a soul.

I think Liang Zongdai's possible understanding of truth and fact is also fully expressed in his profound exposition of the relationship between poetry and life.

Liang Zongdai, after all, is a poet who had rich experiences in literary writing. Although his idea of "Chinese-Western integration" is more subject to the collective misunderstanding of Chinese poets from the Crescent to the Modernist School, Liang Zongdai's argument about the practical experience of poetry is directly related to his criticism of *Poetry Journal* with Xu Zhimo being the chief editor. "The authors' spiritual life of *Poetry Journal* needs to be enriched." Liang Zongdai was very outspoken:

> I think if today's Chinese poets would like to make a major contribution, on the one hand, you must pay attention to art cultivation and live a lively life. On the other hand, go out to the people, to nature, to your soul, or, if you think you have three heads and six arms, then you will go together, as you wish! Always live alive and enthusiastically.[179]

Some people think this reflects the "realism" in Liang Zongdai's poetic concepts. Using past realism to "correct" the issues of the "idealism" of so-called Symbolism was probably partial to a large extent. We must seek an explanation from the actual artistic experience of the poet and his perception of the development of poetry art. From early Symbolism to late Symbolism, to Liang Zongdai's concern about the practice of Rilke's "Poetry is experiencing," the development of Western modern poetry gradually revealed the dual meaning of inner and external experiences. Later, Yeats and Eliot's poetry pursuits proved the value of spiritual activity, while simultaneously deepening into the external world. In the fundamental sense, this choice conformed to the trend of Western poetry and was helpful to solve the modern Chinese new poetry problem during the 1930s: On the road of artistic consciousness, if people return to the emptiness of poetry created by classical artistic conception, they will finally fall into the trap of "poetic dryness." In this sense, only by investing in life, using the flesh and blood of real life to activate inner spirituality could Chinese new poetry acquire a bright future. The so-called "reality" here is certainly not the kind of "ism" that rejects the value of the soul but is part of the poet's self-experience. In the words of Liang Zongdai, the poet should be a "dual observer":

> He should look inside on the one hand, and look outside on the other.... The two are separate; they were born together. After seeing the heart, everything will find its

meaning displayed. The more accurate and clearer the understanding of the outside world, the more cheerful, more active, richer, and freer the mind.[180]

Liang Zongdai's interactive understanding of the real-life experience and the spiritual world connected the possibility of moving to the new Chinese poetry during the 1940s. There was some kind of very noteworthy relation between Liang Zongdai and Feng Zhi, and the pursuit of "new poetry modernization" during the 1940s. I think in a certain sense, Liang Zongdai's theory in the previous paragraph is no less important than his "three major poetic theories" in the history of Chinese modern poetry, and its pioneering value is even higher. Here, we see Liang Zongdai full of vitality and full of realistic quality. Though he is not famous for his study of Chinese and Western cultures, nor is he famous for revisiting the artistic world of Chinese classical poetry. He is an artist who confronted squarely the facts of the new Chinese poetry. Liang Zongdai is a poet who revealed the obstacles in current modern poetry writing.

Ai Qing: "An Abandoned Child" and Rebel of Chinese Tradition

I am "guilty,"
Here
A reed flute is banned.
I think of the reed flute,
It is my dearest memory of Europa.

—Ai Qing, "A Reed Flute"

There are many discussions about Ai Qing—how he is connected with Chinese realism new poetry, how he is connected with French Symbolism, how he is connected with the tendency of "prose beauty" of Chinese new poetry, how he influenced the Chinese new poetry during the 1940s ... However, as one of the many poets who embraced Western modern poetry during the 1930s, what distanced him from "pure poetry" which was so influential at the time? What made him so different from Chinese-style Modernist poets? These questions remain. Their answers are concentrated on such an issue, that is the relationship between Ai Qing and the Chinese poetry tradition. When Chinese-style Modernist poets reverse to the "pure poetry" of Chinese poetry tradition under the ideal banner of Chinese and Western culture integration, Ai Qing, who also identified with the modern poetry of the West, broke through this tradition in a larger scope and supported his pursuit of "prose beauty." This breakthrough finally established his position in the poetry community of the 1940s. Hu Feng, who discovered Ai Qing's talents as a poet, recalled his feelings when he read Ai Qing's poetry collection *Dayanhe—My Nanny*. He believed the "ideas and expression style of this work expanded the tradition of new poetry."[181] Hu Feng's short, precise comment inspired us to make a further interpretation of Ai Qing's poetry pursuit.

Ai Qing, "An Abandoned Child"

Just as Hu Feng knew Ai Qing through "Dayanhe—My Nanny," Ai Qing's poetry seems associated forever with Dayanhe, a poor, simple, peasant woman who served as Ai Qing's wet nurse. However, there lacks a deeper exploration of the meaning of Dayanhe, except for a recognition of Ai Qing's class awareness. Ai Qing could only receive a little precious maternal love from Dayanhe, because of the alleged curse that he would bring misfortune to his biological parents. This special experience cultivated sympathy for a landlord's son among the working people. It also guides his truest feelings about life and the emotional relationship between people—an innocent child lost the love of his parents because of the hard labor of his birth, becoming an abandoned child. His own family could not accommodate the weak child, and his father and mother had to be addressed as uncle and aunt. He was sent to live in another farmhouse without any relatives. What kind of trauma and humiliation is that?

The traditional Chinese regulation and molding of children begin with relationship training within the family. However, Ai Qing faced the reality that his biological parents rudely rejected this kind of usual warmth. At age five, Ai Qing, the "abandoned child," finally returned to his parents' home, but was greeted by his father's swearing and beating for no reason. In the young heart of Ai Qing, the dark clouds of depression grew even more intensely.

Ai Qing said: "When I grew older, I always wanted to leave home as soon as I could."[182] His father's indifference and discrimination interrupted his possibility of being fed into the relationship of traditional Chinese families. He attempted to break away from family bondage and resisted traditional human relations and moral values. Rebellion and independence grew in Ai Qing's spiritual world. Later, when Ai Qing studied in Paris, his father discontinued his financial support. Ai Qing worked tenaciously, which strengthened his rebellion to such a degree that even when his father was seriously ill and died, he refused to go home to pay his "filial piety." In his poems, he confessed, "I am afraid the responsibility of a family will destroy my young life .... I am on the opposite direction of my hometown [and] there is a better ideal in this world" ("My Father"). As the eldest son of his family, Ai Qing refused to assume "family responsibilities," rare in the ranks of the eldest son of modern Chinese writers! In the process of growing up alone, one's experience of the relationship between self and environment is first completed in his own family. A harmonious family may make him feel comfortable, learn to be obedient, tolerant, and adapt by sacrificing himself. In contrast, an indifferent family may make him feel lonely, but it may also stimulate rebellion and resistance, which leads to independence in his later life. Ai Qing, who had walked the path of rebellion, maintained more personality and self. It will be quite interesting if we compare Ai Qing, who rebelled against family, with another relatively gentle July School poet, Tian Jian, and look at their respective literary orientations!

Rebellion against the patriarchic authority seems too inherently cultural. Ai Qing's abandonment and challenges to his father are also reflected in his cultural rebellion.

> From the last semester of primary school, I learned to deny all of China's literary traditions. For me, Shakespeare, Goethe, and Pushkin are more familiar than Li Bai, Du Fu, and Bai Juyi. I hate old-fashioned poetry. I don't read traditional Chinese novels and plays .... The literary education I received was almost entirely Chinese new literature and foreign literature produced after the May Fourth Movement in 1919.[183]

An anecdote is often mentioned later. Ai Qing quoted Hu Shih's famous saying, "Each era has its literature" in his first essay in junior high school. He also strongly attacked classical Chinese writings. The teacher commented: "(the essay) shows little understanding. Hu Shih and Lu Xun's words could not be used as golden rules." Unexpectedly, Ai Qing dared to write a big "X" on the teacher's comment, a serious offense at the time!

Ai Qing did not recite all the classical poetry as usually required. However, he still became a poet, and such a "little understanding" may have guaranteed a kind of spiritual freedom after he rejected the pressure of traditional literature. Ai Qing became a poet not by reading Chinese ancient poems repeatedly, but by direct experience of the world through which he obtained the inspirations for his poetry. Furthermore, he was a genius painter first, and later wrote poems through the eyes and hands of the painter. Such a poet seems to be more natural.

Anti-tradition of the Avant-garde Art

Today, it is easier to notice the influence of painting on Ai Qing's poetry, but we may ignore the more important fact that Ai Qing originally did not intend to become a poet. What he showed in his childhood was a strong interest in art. A painter who did not intend to become a poet eventually became a poet. Doesn't this art path also challenge the traditional concept?

Ai Qing studied in the painting department of Hangzhou West Lake Art Academy at 18, and six months later he went to France to study at the advice of the Academy president, Lin Fengmian. His original intention then and the interest he showed had repeatedly proven that becoming a painter was Ai Qing's most persistent desire. Poetry seemed "amateur." It is well known Ai Qing was assigned to preside over the Central Academy of Fine Arts when Beijing was liberated in 1949. This "ignited his strong passion for artwork."[184] If it were not for a later change, it is difficult to say whether there would be an artist Ai Qing!

But, what makes more sense is the art path chosen by Ai Qing had an important influence on his poetry concepts. Such influence is rarely seen in other poets during the 1930s.

When Ai Qing lost his father's financial support in Paris, he studied painting while working part-time. As a result, he did not have the opportunity to enter formal art school. Instead, he bought tickets to learn painting in studios. At the time, several talented, rebellious, avant-garde artists were working in Paris, so he fell in love with "Monet, Mane, Reynold, Degas, Modigliani, R. Dufy, Picasso, Utrecht, etc. This experience led to his strong rejection of the "academy" combined with the anti-feudal and anti-conservative consciousness."[185] Working and studying at the same time also gave Ai Qing more free reading opportunities. He read the Chinese versions of Russian literature, the French translation of Russian poetry, and modern French and Belgian poetry. Gradually, "he began to note in the sketchbook some feelings that were fading and his ideas. He learned to capture the beauty of light, colors, shapes, and movements . . ."[186] A painter who did not intend to become a poet thus became a poet. In 1933 when the artist Ai Qing had no chance to continue to participate in the China Left-wing Artists League campaign and was unable to contribute to the Spring Land Painting Society in Shanghai, China, he started the first climax of poetry writing of his life. On an early morning on a snowy day, he created his masterpiece of 100 lines ("Dayanhe—My Nanny"):

Dayanhe, today I saw snow, reminding me of you:
Your grave is covered by snow-pressed grass,
The dead wild grass on the roof of your deserted former residence,
The one-square meter garden that had been pawned,
The stone bench with moss in front of your door,
...
I am a son of a landlord,
After I had drained the milk you could offer,
I was returned to my home by my parents.
Ah, Dayanhe, why are you crying?

Ai Qing was telling the vicissitudes of life through the distress he felt from Dayanhe. The unfortunate fate of Dayanhe also showed all the bitterness and humiliation of Ai Qing as a traditional "abandoned child." These complex emotions surged in an unstoppable manner, completely breaking the barrier of the harmonious ideal of traditional Chinese poetry. The thick melancholy and the free, prose-like passages are drastically different from the Modernist and left-wing poetry styles prevailing at that time. This is a precious contribution of an "abandoned child" who rebelled against tradition!

Ai Qing's poetry in the early 1930s had already shown the characteristics of this rebellion against Chinese poetry tradition. His unique way of art creation was closely related to his three-year life in France.

As mentioned previously, Ai Qing failed to enter a formal art school in France to receive a strict academy-style education for various reasons, but such failure just made his rebellious personality find colleagues in the Latin Quarter of Paris. The anti-academic rebellious pursuit of Western Modernist art encouraged Ai Qing's artistic choices to develop in a free, healthy, ad robust direction. This applied to his paintings, as well as poems, which used language to capture feelings. In almost every picture of Ai Qing's poetry, we can feel the turmoil and struggle of a modern artist: his will to move forward in Paris, his curse of love and hate in Marseille, the "transparent night" incited the wildness of those wanderers, and through the narrow window of the prison, he could also witness the "white shell/poetry-like universe" ("Scream"). Chinese Modernist poets identified with the choice of Western modern art to rebel against Western traditions, and then followed suit back to China's traditions. However, Ai Qing identified with their anti-traditional behaviors. This reinforced his rebellion against China's traditions—two completely different sets of ideas. Completely breaking the idea of Chinese poetry, which looks for balance and solemnness, the turmoil and struggle of Ai Qing's poetry highlighted a completely new, different life experience of a modern Chinese poet.

At the same time, Ai Qing abandoned some of the Western modern art concepts, such as its revelation of the human subconscious world, the questioning of human metaphysical issues, and the mystical colors associated with it. For a Chinese who ventured into a modern city from the "distant Eastern haystacks," these purely life-related topics seem a mystery. Ai Qing was concerned about the pain and spiritual fighting of modern people. Because of this, he also read Russian and Soviet literature, such as Vladimir Mayakovski, George Gordon Byron, Percy Bysshe Shelley, and Walt Whitman, whose passion also infected a Chinese youth who was pursuing life and resisting social oppression. Ai Qing's poetry is particularly tinted with the "depression" of Emile Verhaeren, a Belgian modern poet, who, like Ai Qing, had the turmoil and uneasiness of moving to the city from the countryside. The peasant-style melancholy and unyielding rebellion and unremitting pursuits constitute the rich poetry of Verhaeren. "Verhaeren's poems are my favorite or I'm deeply influenced by his poetry in my life." Ai Qing said.[187]

Ai Qing's "Reed Flute"

For Ai Qing, the recognition of the rebellious spirit of Western modern art, the acceptance of Western Soviet revolutionary poetry, and the abandonment of some modern Western poetry are all part of his pursuit of freedom and individual independence. Later, people followed the generalization of Hu Feng and labeled Ai Qing as "the poet who played the reed flute." The phrase "reed flute" comes from the famous quote of the French poet G. Apollinaire, which roughly means that "I had a reed flute in the past, and I don't exchange it for the scepter of the French Grand Marshal." Here, the reed flute represents the independence and freedom of the poet. In the poem "The Reed Flute," Ai Qing wrote Apollinaire's reed flute is his "dearest memory of Europa . . . . I have been hungry / but I still played the reed flute with grace. People laugh at my gesture, / because that is my gesture! / People are not used to my songs / because they are mine!" It is the poet's courage and the power to play his songs. In this sense, if we read "Dayanhe—My Nanny" again, we will find this poem was so moving at the time not only because it described the experience of a poor peasant woman, but more importantly, it was the inner passion that Ai Qing felt difficult to contain—a child abandoned by his parents found maternal love in a simple, honest, peasant woman, but her life path was such a huge difference from his. So here, the complex turbulence of love and pain, passion and pity, sorrow and remorse merged into an endless stream of poetry.

When many Chinese poems in the same era lost their own emotions and thoughts with the idea of "practice in society," Ai Qing's poem evoked the pleasure of reading with the most important trait of poetry—one's genuine feelings; thus, sprinkled countless dried hearts.

The influence of Western modern art also enhanced Ai Qing's attention to capturing "impressions" and refinement of "images" in his poems. For "post-impressionist" painters, such as Gauguin and Van Gogh, whom Ai Qing was familiar with, "impression" is a symbol and suggestion that permeates the artist's emotions. The French Symbolic poetry that aroused his great interest also advocated the "correspondences" of subjective and objective, and focused on creating a "symbolic forest." This had great inspiration for Ai Qing's writing. His debut "Meeting" brought the flavor of "impressionism" at the very beginning: "circular, circular, we are sitting in the smoke circles, treble, bass, noise, hugging the table, / mild, fierce, explosive ..." In poems, such as "Paris" and "Marseille," Ai Qing's ability to express complex emotions with complex images was fully demonstrated. What is valuable is such imagery art had not fallen into traditional harmony with the world. It still ran in Ai Qing's irregular language flow, allowing sentences to form in a variety of lengths and differences, vividly reflecting the complex feelings of modern Chinese people.

Ai Qing's poetry is sufficiently distinct from Chinese poetry, just in terms of the characteristics discussed above. His rebellion, his independence and freedom, his imagery art, and his free exile poems are very different from the Chinese poems of the time (including Modernist and left-wing poetries). The position of Ai Qing in Chinese poetry before the War of Resistance against Japanese Aggression reminds us of Tian Jian, whose early poems seemed similar to Ai Qing in his emotions, images, and free poem lines. However, to be fair, Ai Qing bequeathed more in terms of the feelings of poetry, and broad, far-reaching artistic exploration. It is no wonder when we read Hu Feng's "Preface to *Chinese Pastoral*" and "The Poet Who Played the Reed Flute," two critical readings of the works of Tian Jian and Ai Qing, we feel a subtle difference between the two. The former is rational, as if a far-sighted critic was facing a rookie and he was full of love and pity, but not forgetting to offer his guidance. But for the latter, the critic was so emotional, as if a solitary explorer suddenly found a rare confidant. He was so excited he seemed to have forgotten academic criticism. He was so involved with reading one poem after another. In the former, he rationally summarizes A, B, and C, while in the latter he was simply writing his emotions and feelings!

Maturity during the War of Resistance against Japanese Aggression

From the full outbreak of the War of Resistance against Japanese Aggression in 1937 to the arrival of Yan'an in 1941, Ai Qing traveled the country. This displaced life experience once again expanded the breadth and depth of his writing and promoted his maturity on the path of rebelling against the ideas of Chinese, traditional poetry and building modern concepts of new poetry.

Three new types of images appear in Ai Qing's poems: "North," "war," and "the country." The suffering in North China was as broad and thick as its land at the time. Ai Qing, who used to see the beautiful mountains and rivers in the south of the Yangtze River, felt a huge shock. Squeaking unicycle strollers and ancient Fengling ferry, gray desert storms, donkeys, camels, and beggars, all were related to the long history and painful memories of the nation. The North made Ai Qing become "solid." He drew portraits of the dead, tattered "human skin," flames of the cities, the "trumpet player," and soldiers who "died a second time." The fierce war presented Ai Qing with an unprecedented bloody landscape. Yet, the inner countryside and the wilderness, the buffalo, the pony, and the green pool, always inspired his imagination, reminding him of the hardships of survival, the meaning of civilization, and the "root" of the land that cannot be abandoned. Unlike those simple, self-expression, romantic poets, Ai Qing pursued a greater, higher coverage of the self in the world. In this way, it is in the process of "moving the scene" that the varied landscape of the world enriched Ai Qing's poetry and enhanced his poetry spirit.

The depth of Ai Qing's poetry also developed because of the War of Resistance against the Japanese. Life during wartime was complicated and chaotic, which enriched his soul. Here, joy and pain, hope and disappointment, excitement and frustrations often entangled with each other, tearing people and raising them. Ai Qing's poetry during this period continues to show his ability to grasp and deal with complex feelings. A pair of contradictory, interdependent "poetics" and "poetic power" flew with his pen: simplicity and sadness of the land, farmer's stupidity, and persistence, tragic and sublime soldiers, death and regeneration of the people. "Why do I always have tears in my eyes? /Because I love this land deeply ..." These classic poem verses conveyed the classic emotional intricacies and the modern charm of poetry is fully displayed.

Ai Qing's poetic practice is also in harmony with his conscious rational exploration. When summarizing his poetry writing practice, Ai Qing demonstrated a dynamic "poetic beauty" full of power. "The beauty in poetry is expressed through the emotions of poets, a kind of human upward spirit like sparks splashing in the darkness or spilled on the rock with a chisel and an axe." He summed up his struggle for freedom and independence, proposing: "freedom of speech is the most important thing in the old world—and these are often not achieved because any tyrant knows: a free speaker is even more terrible than a thousand people." Ai Qing pointed out the profound message: "Poetry is always the pastoral song of life," but "the so-called 'experiencing life' could only be successful with great efforts. It is by no means successful without much feelings in life." He fully affirmed the significance of imagery, symbolism, association, and imagination in modern poetry writing. At the same time, Ai Qing tried to promote the vernacular and prose beauty of new poetry. "The most natural language is spoken language."[188] "It is a progress that people now appreciated proses from enjoying verses . . . . The prose is a congenital rhyme."[189] All of this entailed his serious thoughts on the development of Chinese new poetry:

> The current mainstream of Chinese new poetry is based on free, simple language, with obvious rhythm and roughly similar rhyme as its forms; with a close, profound view of the rich reality as its ideas, it smashes all the personal sighs and gazes into the pale world.[190]

Life in Yan'an after 1941 seemed to bring some stability to Ai Qing, a child abandoned by the Chinese tradition established a stable life in a new type of interpersonal relationship, and he did not need to drift without a sense of belonging. Along with this change in his living environment, the rebellious edge of his artistic pursuit also showed obvious "passivation"—although among the poets who moved Yan'an, Ai Qing retained most of his self-consciousness and modern art spirit, still he hoped sincerely to deliver his original ideas to the future, and prepared to sacrifice for this future, which he was not completely familiar with. "Let the feet of the new era step on me like horseshoes . . . . For its arrival, I am willing to sacrifice my life / deliver it from my body to my soul" ("Times"). From this time forward, it would be not proper to use the "abandoned child" and "rebel" to label him.

Feng Zhi: Distant Metaphor and "The Most Outstanding Lyric Poet"

> We are prepared to embrace them wholeheartedly,
> Those unexpected miracles,

Suddenly in the long years
The comet appeared, and the wind swirled.

—Feng Zhi, "Sonnet One"

As is known to all, Feng Zhi's initial fame arose because Lu Xun evaluated him in the "Introduction, *Novel Collection II, Chinese New Literature Series*" in 1936 where the former was described as "the most outstanding lyric poet in China." Later, Chinese literature history reached a consensus that "Undoubtedly, this evaluation by Lu Xun established the status of Feng Zhi in the history of Chinese literature."[191] But what is the special meaning of "outstanding" for Lu Xun? Lu Xun did not elaborate on this, which led to a variety of speculations by future generations. Did Lu Xun discover Feng Zhi's quiet, subtle lyric style or the pursuit of the Chinese lyric tradition during the early days when the dominant new poetry tended to be straightforward and rational? For example, there is a view that Feng Zhi was "very skillful in incorporating the characteristics of classical poetry into new poetry, which was Lu Xun's ideal of poetry; thus, his high evaluation of Feng Zhi."[192] Of course, there are also doubts: Is this absolute judgment on Feng Zhi "over the border" since he was still in the early stages of his career at that time?

A study of this issue not only helps identify Lu Xun's poetry standards, and understand the characteristics of Feng Zhi, but it could also help us delve into the expectations of the representative of the Chinese new literary world at that time for the future of poetry, and the historical significance of Feng Zhi's choices.

In my opinion, to understand Lu Xun's evaluation accurately, it is necessary to understand the following three backgrounds simultaneously: (1) the true characteristics or potential of Feng Zhi's poetry in the history of Chinese poetry; (2) Lu Xun's basic understanding of Chinese poetry tradition, and (3) Lu Xun's expectations for the development of poetry.

Beyond Emotional Sensations

At the time of Lu Xun's comments, Feng Zhi had published two poetry collections, *Songs of Yesterday* and *Northern Tours and Others*. These works are different from the straightforward and rational early new poems, such as Hu Shih's, but did they win the favor of Lu Xun because they inherited the secluded, subtle lyric tradition of Chinese classical poetry? It is not so simple, because in 1936 when Lu Xun made his speech, Chinese new poetry had diverged far from the road of the early new poetry paradigm. A variety of lyric models had developed. The so-called secluded and subtle lyric style had been fully presented by the Crescent Moon School, such as Xu Zhimo's works. However, Lu Xun clearly stated he did not like Xu Zhimo's poems.[193] If indirectness and subtlety represented Chinese classical poetry in a certain sense, there is no evidence that Lu Xun expected this "emotional" style to become the "future" of modern Chinese new poetry. Lu Xun once criticized Xu Zhimo's ideas about poetry. When translating Baudelaire's "Death" in 1924, Xu Zhimo said: "The true beauty of poetry is not in its meaning but in its unpredictable rhythm. What it tried to prick is not your skin (which might be too rough and too thick!) but the unpredictable soul of yourself." He also said this mysterious musical rhythm is "the quietness of Heaven, earth, and humanity as Zhuang Zhou said."[194] In response to such "emotional" remarks, Lu Xun put forward his views in the article, "Music?" The article began with: "I can't sleep at night, and I plan to have some spicy chicken tomorrow, but I am afraid that I could not have the same one as I had before and I became wide awake with this haunting me."[195] This brief sketch showed the entangled material desire for human beings. Relatively speaking, these mysterious "feelings" are indeed a little illusory. In Lu Xun's view, it is unreliable to talk about the wonders of feelings without relating to the sharp-contrasted reality.

Today, people often quote Lu Xun's fragmented comments about poetry in the "Enemy of Poetry," such as "Poetry is the enthusiasm of the singer," and "poems must have forms easy to remember, easy to understand, easy to sing, and pleasant to the ears."[196] It seems Lu Xun advocated a kind of writing close to the paradigm of Chinese classical poetry. In fact, given Lu Xun's various comments on this, he started with the problems of tradition and attempted to promote renewal and change in Chinese literature. He appreciated the "devilish style" and "expressions without reservation," longing for "the vigor of blood," "the real evil voice of the macabre quirks."[197] He was against the "peacefulness of things" and questioned the beauty of "quietness."

Although Feng Zhi's early writings had not yet reached the maturity of the *Sonnets Collection*, they showed a different path from the Chinese classical poetry's sentimental lyric tradition. "Snake" did not show the sentimentality of the classical scholars. The sorrow in the "Silver Horse" is no longer the loneliness of "not knowing someone who could appreciate him." In addition to depression and loneliness, the "Silver Horse" has a thrilling power:

> For a moment, it is a phantom of youth.
> For a moment, it is the rush of the horse;
> At the moment when the earth is about to collapse,

The horse's hide wrapped around her whole body!

Similarly, we found loneliness and sorrow in "Snake." Yet, it is not the kind of sad confession, but a kind of long-lasting, persistent, firm thought:

> It is my loyal companion,
> Its heart is filled with warm homesickness:
> It missed that dense grassland—
> The rich silky hair on your head.

On the whole, "Snake" greatly surpassed the enthusiasm and compassion of traditional lyric poems. Loneliness and isolation may be a motif of traditional Chinese poetry, but Feng Zhi, who had just started writing poetry, empowered loneliness: with no friends and someone to love him, Nietzsche produced Zarathustra's roar when he is alone on the sick bed. Qu Yuan can only sing his eternal song after he was exiled and walked along the river banks bored.[198]

Therefore, although Feng Zhi claimed to write poetry under the influence of Tang and Song poetry and German romanticism sometimes,[199] some qualities that affect his deep view of life are undoubtedly Novalis, Hölderlin, Rilke, and other Western poets. And Feng Zhi rediscovered our traditions using these as a basis.

Not only that, when Lu Xun commented on Feng Zhi, he had already changed his direction in poetry writing, shifting from the emotional style in the 1920s to the empirical writing style, emphasizing the extraction and excavation of life experiences, which further distanced him from the lyric classical tradition. Feng Zhi also passionately quoted Rilke's *The Notebook of Malte Laurids Brigge*, in which the description of self-perception is beyond the traditional perceptual thinking of "initiate with objects" and "one's feelings flow with the change of the objects":

> We must observe many cities, people, and things, we must know animals, feel how birds fly, and know the posture of flowers in the morning when they blossom. We must be able to reflect on journeys to foreign lands, unexpected encounters, and imminent separations;—recall the years of blurred childhood; ... think of the diseases of children ... think of the daylight in a quiet, dull hut, and the mornings of a seashore. Think of the sea, think of many seas, think of the night of the journey, in these nights, the stars dance ... but this is insufficient, if all this could be imagined. We must remember the nights of lots of love, each night different from another, remembering the painful screams of childbirth, and the women in white who slept and relaxed. But, we have to accompany the dying, sitting next to the deceased ... there are some sudden sounds in the small units from the open window .... Wait

until they become the blood in our bodies, our eyes and gestures, and we can no longer distinguish ourselves from them. Only then our feelings will be achieved. At a very rare moment, the first words of a line of verse are formed in their center and spurt out.[200]

This is not the kind of expressing our feelings at the sight of a scene or our ideals through certain objects, which we are familiar with in the past. This is the deep dialogue between the world and our inner life experiences. The depth of space and the length of time ensure the dialogue does not slide on the surface of the feelings, but the passion, embrace, shock, and even torture of both sides. Although sometimes Feng Zhi borrowed Buddhist experiences to describe the relationship between people and objects he already used Rilke's philosophical thinking to inject a lot of new subjectivity into the objectified Chinese poetry tradition or to reshape the tradition in his mind. As Feng Zhi said later in his article, "Tradition and Decadent Palace," "It is not without reason that now there is often talk about inheriting traditional issues. I am only worried when we look back at the past. We see some only "destroyed palaces," and we cannot see the true colors of the tradition . . . . This is to dismantle those ruined palaces, not to let them contaminate a long tradition of purity."[201] Of course, this purity comes from the creation of Feng Zhi or the result of his creative activation.

Distant Metaphor and the Organization of Ideas

When critiquing Li Jinfa's poems, Zhu Ziqing put forward Near Metaphor and Distant Metaphor, which I think can also apply here. Distant and near refer to the distance between the vehicle and the tenor, which points to the strangeness and familiarity of our habits. This theory can also be used to analyze Feng Zhi's poetic thinking. He developed new possibilities in the direction of classical aesthetic forms. When Feng Zhi said his loneliness is a snake, we all think there is a long distance between loneliness and a snake. A lot of descriptions must be used to convince the readers. This is different from the lyric tradition of Chinese poetry. Feng Zhi had a strong desire to construct and express his rich thoughts. Xu Zhimo's poetry is a trace of his personal experience and did not intend to show the richness and singularity of his thoughts. He wanted to show his feelings. The display of ideas is to break away from the external world. When people feel relaxed and less serious, the spirituality of the human being is immersed in the world. The world always stimulates people's feelings. When a person is serious about the world, he or she may use more energy in developing one's thoughts. When we break away from the external world, our internal thinking begins to develop. In this sense, Feng Zhi's quality lies precisely in his emphasis on the internal construction of his thoughts. Along this path, German romanticism and modernism offered him new artistic resources.

Looking back, we can continue to ask: Why did Lu Xun praise Feng Zhi so profusely? Of course, there can be multiple explanations, including some shared moods, etc. However, both tended to deliberately develop the "idea organization" of the new poetry in a direction away from the classical aesthetic forms. Here, we should not only look at Lu Xun's fragmented comments on this but also study his early experiments in poetry. Although they may not be so successful in terms of artistic integrity, it is worth noting these not-so-coherent verses are very different from classical poetry. In almost every new poem by Lu Xun, we can feel the emotional connotations and spirit that cannot be tolerated by traditional poetry. "Dream" is a layered depiction of the unconscious world of chaos, very rare in new poems of the time; "God of Love" seems a declaration of modern love, and the extreme emotions of "I would rather die if there were no love" are completely different from the poetic tradition of "gentility and uprightness"; "Peach Blossom" implies the Chinese family relationship. The flamboyant peach blossom is used as a metaphor for narrow-minded humans, which is also a Distant Metaphor. "People and Time" expresses the straightforward, life-oriented attitude of life. Such writings show Lu Xun's preference for the complexity of self-thoughts, different from ancient Chinese poetry and lyricism. Therefore, Zhu Ziqing, editor of the *Chinese New Literature Poetry Collection*, argued: "Only the Lu Xun brothers completely got free from the chains of tradition."[202] Hu Shih, who first initiated the vernacular poetry during the same era, also admitted the early vernacular newcomers "were mostly born out of old-style poetry, *Ci*s, and songs, except the Zhou brothers from Kuaiji, Zhejiang Province."[203]

Why should we re-examine Lu Xun's evaluation of Feng Zhi? Because the modern construction of Chinese new poetry, including language art, is always a difficult issue with constant debates. Whenever our poetry encounters development difficulties, there would be a voice of "returning to tradition." Of course, in reality, the ambiguity and even the contradictory voices, cannot be easily explained. Distant Metaphor evokes the intimacy of our revisit of tradition, and may also lead to new ideas, eventually arriving at what Feng Zhi' called the "pure tradition." Through Feng Zhi, we may find that "tradition" is not necessarily obtained from "near." "Far" may also be a powerful or effective way.

Cycling of the Subjectivity Process

By observing Feng Zhi along such a direction as the Distant Metaphor—language construction far from the traditional lyrics, we can better understand his true contribution to the history of poetry.

It is generally believed the transition of Chinese new poetry from 1930 to 1940 was related to Feng Zhi and Bian Zhilin. It is the philosophical reasoning in their poetry that promoted the development of poetry and inspired poets, such as the Chinese New Poetry School. This is generally correct, but it is worth further exploration, specific to some historical details and the choice of individual poets.

Bian Zhilin's philosophy is quite different from that of Feng Zhi. Which form is more powerful to promote the turning point of history?

As we have already discussed earlier, there are more philosophical factors in Bian Zhilin's poetry, but it seems that such poetry cannot be called "philosophical poetry." It is difficult for some poems, such as "Fragment," to be defined as philosophical poems or lyric poems because there is a gray area here. If we focus on the relative relationship expressed in the poem, we could agree the poem is philosophical. If we focus on a kind of one-dimensional secret love expressed by the poem, then it can be regarded as a lyric. What is important is that Bian Zhilin did not intend to continue "long" philosophical thinking. He was only willing to present some of his own flashing thoughts.

If Bian Zhilin was willing to "present," then Feng Zhi moved on to the "starting and turning process of thinking," which are two different actions. The pursuit of the former is momentary, which can be called epiphany, while Feng Zhi conducted gradual thinking, a gradual realization, a process, the flow of thought in which the contradictions, including the thinking process, are presented. Feng Zhi was writing the reflection of a life actor. He acted, thought, and showed his struggles. This is a dynamic feeling, a feeling of acting, while Bian Zhilin was relatively more static with a unique spectator attitude. Bian Zhilin always denied a deep philosophy in his poetry. He was more inclined to think of it as a kind of "artistic conception," which has profound meaning, not just a casual expression of the artistic taste of poetry, as part of the category of Chinese classical aesthetics. Generally speaking, aesthetic conception is static, and it is always repeated around a center with the core meaning. It does not pursue the process of thinking, and there are no twists and turns in life. For example, Guo Moruo's "Tiangou," never could be described by the pursuit of "aesthetic conception," because the emotional flow of "Tiangou" is a whole process, a process with no beginning nor ending. Guo Moruo took a piece and accomplished a kind of emotional expression, a process of life action. We cannot see where it is going, nor can we accurately grasp it. Here, we can see the differences between modern poetry and classical poetry in their pursuit of aesthetics.

Guo Moruo portrays the process of emotions, while Feng Zhi shows the process of thoughts. In the span of thought, Feng Zhi's poems and Bian Zhilin's poems are significantly different. Bian Zhilin is just giving a touch, while Feng Zhi pushes ideas to all aspects. For example, Feng Zhi's "Departure":

> We waved our hands, and with departure
> Our world is divided into two,
> We feel cold around, and our vision is suddenly wide.
> Like two babies who have just been born.

Usually, the general lyric poems are written along the path of sorrow, that is, the "coldness" in poetry when writing about a departure. Feng Zhi made a twist, that while he felt cold, he was rewarded another world because of the departure. Then, he repeatedly deduced and explained:

> Ah, one departure, one birth,
> We are responsible for the hard work,
> Turn cold into warmth, grow raw into mature,
> Each plowed the world by himself.
> To see each other again, it seems to meet for the first time,
> Thinking about the past with gratitude,
> Like the first meeting, I suddenly felt the previous life.
>
> There are a few springs and a few winters in our lives.
> We only feel the rotation of time and seasons.
> We could not feel the age set by the human world.

Going beyond various characteristics of parting, Feng Zhi used it as a starting point to constantly ask questions about the meaning of life formed by separation, to imagine and further promote and expand the new world that had been unfolded because of separation. Another poem, "We Walk a Path Every Day" showed similar ideas. Since it is a road of daily routine, it should be quite familiar. Yet, Feng Zhi found unfamiliarity from familiarity:

> We walk a familiar path every day.
> Go back to where we live;
> But still hidden in this forest
> Many paths, deep and rarely walked.

When I walked an unfamiliar one, I was a little scared,
Afraid to go farther and farther, and get lost,
But unconsciously from the scattered trees
Suddenly our houses are in sight,

Just like a new island on the horizon
How many things around us
Ask for new discoveries?

Don't feel that everything is familiar,
Touch your skin when you die
And a question: Whose body is this?

From the path in life to the path of abstract life, and the questioning of the path goes deep into the doubts of life, such thinking ability is amazing! Usually, we write about the intimacy of familiar things. Of course, we may also feel bored or even exhausted, but Feng Zhi did not just stay on the surface of these feelings, he tried to discover multiple possibilities of familiar things until a strange "epiphany" from his body. This large space of thinking is the result of his constant questioning and cultivation of his thoughts. In the tradition of Chinese classical poetry, the poet's emotions often need to be stirred by constant contact with the world. The so-called "*Xing*" is needed. However, poets like Feng Zhi began to try another way in search of new, meaningful poems: through the excavation of self and asking questions. This is closer to the poetry thinking of what I call "subjectivity."

Mu Dan: Anti-tradition and New Traditions of Chinese New Poetry

A circle, how many years of labor,
Our despair will make it complete.
Destroy it, friends! Let ourselves
Be its incompleteness, worse than mediocrity;
Lightning and rain, new temperatures, and dirt
Will come to harass, maybe colder,
Because we are already a group being sieged
We disappear, then comes a "no man's land."

—Mu Dan, "The Besieged"

Like Ai Qing, Mu Dan also had a tense rebellious relationship with the Chinese classical poetry tradition. He established himself as a trailblazer of the "new tradition" of Chinese new poetry by distinguishing himself with the "modern characteristics" of Chinese classical poetry. Such a "new tradition" does not mean a disconnection from Chinese history and culture (like the poetry-style rebellious spirit existing in Chinese poetry of the Song Dynasties).

However, in the new entanglement of tradition/anti-tradition after the 1990s, our interpretation of Mu Dan is faced with many difficulties.

After the 1990s, with the introduction of a series of "anti-modernization" ideas in the West, there was a growing questioning and re-evaluation of modernization and modernity in Chinese academic communities. The "modern characteristics" of Chinese modern writers (i.e., modernity), along with our interpretation of them, seem somewhat embarrassing. It was at this time that some scholars' doubts and other scholars' responses reawakened people's thoughts about "modern," "modernity," and "modernization." Moreover, it appeared this kind of thinking could make a frequent review of the history of Chinese new poetry necessary, particularly the May Fourth vernacular new poetry that pursued the modernity of Chinese literature, as well as the full maturity of Chinese poetry during the 1940s. It seems very interesting Mu Dan's poetry was also involved in the questioning of this modernity. On the one hand, he is well-known as the most active practitioner of the "new poetry modernization" in the 1940s. Mu Dan's pursuit of modernity and the abandonment of traditional poetry was very striking. Furthermore, the same Mu Dan had become a successful model of modern poetry,[204] even for some modernity skeptics.

It is not difficult to find some skeptics of modernity, who nevertheless supporters of Mu Dan, share such a universal idea. That is, Chinese modern poetry with Mu Dan as a model of success is strikingly different from the May Fourth vernacular new poems which closely follow Western "modernity." Poets, such as Hu Shih and Liu Bannong, seem paranoid to pursue the comprehensibility of poetry. They abandoned the art of poetry for easy comprehension, while Mu Dan showed the artistic charm of modern poetry in "singular complexity." Mu Dan, who worked as a representative of Chinese Modernist poetry, rebelled against the May Fourth new poetry. This kind of thinking distinguishes the artistic differences between Mu Dan's poems and the May Fourth new poems, but completely ignores the consistency between Mu Dan's poetry and the May Fourth new poetry in the pursuit of modernity. It was the Symbolists of the 1920s and Modernists of the 1930s who turned criticism to Hu Shih. Yet, their rebellion is different from Mu Dan's. Here, it reflects a contradictory reality in poetic understanding. I believe it is time to discuss Mu Dan's poetry and the modern features of Chinese new poetry seriously. We should determine the characteristics of Mu Dan's modern poetry and its relationships with the literature's pursuit of modernization and modernity.

While the May Fourth new poetry abandoned the art of poetry because it was too clear and easy to comprehend, the new Chinese poetry from Symbolists and Modernists to the Nine Leaves School explored the core of art with its ambiguity, subtleness, and obscurity. Even if we say it is not simplification, but obscurity, that constitutes the distinctive features of Chinese Modernist poetry from Li Jinfa to Mu Dan, this does not mean a complete maturity path from Symbolism, Modernism to the Nine Leaves School. It does not mean all the modern poem obscurity, from the works of Li Jinfa to the works of Mu Dan, is the same. Mu Dan shows his unique ideas precisely in the process of transcending shallowness to rich obscurity. Hence, we first focus on Modernist poetry that transcends Hu Shih and consciously constructs modern features, more specifically, obscurity, the currently most discussed sign of modern poetry maturity.

Obscurity and Modern Poetics

First, we must remove some popular stereotypes and provide the term "obscurity" with a richer meaning, and admit it is, indeed, a conscious artistic pursuit in the development of modern poetry. Compared with romantic poetry that appeals to the senses, Western Modernist poetry since Symbolism falls on hints and lingo that fit in the depths of the soul. Hints take our spirit out of mediocrity and lead to a more distant, eternal existence. For example, "the transcendental Symbolist poetry is often ambiguous. This is a deliberate ambiguity so the reader's eyes are kept from reality and focused on the ontology (essential idea, which is a Plato's term favored by the Symbolists)."[205] The "hidden language" fully mobilizes the potential functions of the language, and conveys all kinds of potential meanings through different kinds of wonderful combination. Additionally, some poets even claimed the truth the poet wants to express can only be achieved through ambiguous language.[206] Since the development of Western modern poetry, some concepts, such as ambiguity, obscurity, and vagueness, have similar meanings. They all point to the same poetic choices—the exploration of rich potential meanings and the emergence of the power of language. According to William Empson,

> "Ambiguity" itself can mean an indecision as to what you mean, an intention to mean several things, a probability that one or other or both of two things has been meant, and the fact that a statement has several meanings. It is useful to be able to

separate these if you wish, but it is not obvious that in separating them at any particular point you will not be raising more problems than you solve. Thus I shall often use the ambiguity of "ambiguity" . . .[207]

Chinese Modernist poetry benefited from the modern Western "obscure" poetry when it attempted to correct an "easy comprehension" of the vernacular new poetry. People have long noticed the preference of Mu Mutian, Wang Duqing, Dai Wangshu, and He Qifang for French Symbolist poets, such as Verlaine, Rambo, Gourmont, Valéry, etc., and noted the preference of Bian Zhilin for Yeats and Elliot, as well as William Empson, who taught his "obscurity" theory at the National Southwest Associated University. Mu Dan became the most ardent follower of this poetic concept. Mu Mutian and Du Heng's discussions of "potential awareness" in their comments seem to indicate a profound modern psychological background of this poetic concept. Despite this, when we read the works by Mu Dan, Li Jinfa, Mu Mutian, Dai Wangshu, and Bian Zhilin, we still believe they are quite different in their respective "obscurity." This difference cannot only be attributed to the richness of the poet's artistic personality because many of the "obscurity" choices are very similar as if they are subject to some common poetic concepts. Among these, Mu Dan's poetry is the most special. Here, we can make a comparative interpretation.

Li Jinfa was the first poet who provided Chinese readers with a sense of eccentricity and obscurity in his poetry. In this regard, Mr. Zhu Ziqing commented, "His poetry has no regular rules. While their parts are understandable, the whole makes no sense . . . . This is the style of French Symbolist poets and Li was the first to introduce it to Chinese poetry."[208] This comment is undoubtedly classic in the case of the connection between Li Jinfa and French Symbolism. However, if we read Li Jinfa's work carefully, we know its eccentricity and obscurity seem to fall into another category. It is not difficult to grasp the combined meaning. Such verses summarize more than half of Li Jinfa's poems: "I feel I am the only lonely one, / Joy is as common as the air!" ("Fantasy"). What is difficult to understand is either a combination of certain images inside his poetry lines, or the meaning of some words. An example of the former: "One monk cloak cannot defend the cold air of South Russia / with the tremble of deep horns" ("To Fengming"). Readers might understand a lonely, desolate state of mind, but what exactly are "deep horns"? They might get lost. This image is only a meaningless obstruction for readers. An example of the latter is "the echo of the deep valley, the blood of the samurai, / the light that should be on the avenue of time / the light of the pale white" ("To Fengming"), "this is a rare evening scene, / even more so that they stop, stagnate" (Scene). The words "should" and "stagnate" in the above verses are vague rhetoric. In addition, his poems also include some arbitrarily succinct words compression, "To be feathered? What a bother!" ("To My Self-Portrait") and awkward classical Chinese words: "Glory diffused, / Thou commanded by the time" ("Under the Pine Tree"). Some attributed this quirkiness and obscurity to the limited Chinese and French proficiency of Li Jinfa. This forces us to ask such a question: will the aesthetic pursuit of ambiguity become a defense for all poetry to become obscure for it to be outstanding? It should be noted a Modernist poet's "intentional ambiguity" is one thing, while another poet's lack of ability to write properly is another. However, both cases may produce similar vagueness and obscurity.

There is indeed "deliberate ambiguity" in Li Jinfa's poems, especially when he described love in a foreign country. However, during these times, this "fuzziness," rather than the rich meanings as delivered by French Symbolism, made his poetry expressive, more definitive rather than ambiguous: "Your eyes are betraying your emotions// Like the butcher's imminent slaughter; / Your lips? What do you say! / I would rather trust your arms" ("Tenderness"). This is not so much obscurity behind Modernism as in line with the implicit and obstructing method of "implicitness in emotion expressions" in the Chinese poetry tradition. "The obstructing method means to show, but not straightforward. The so-called 'both the horse and the bow are ready in position without launching.'"[209] Although the obscurity of Western Modernism benefited quite a bit from the Chinese classical poetry tradition there are still subtle differences between the two. The ambiguity of Western Modernism used hints and hidden language to expand the meaning of poetry where "polysemy" and "richness" are used rather than "twisting" and "obstructing." In comparison, the subtlety of Chinese classical poetry is mainly about some kind of concealment and decoration of meanings, and strives to not reveal the meaning in a shallow way, but the bottom line is still relatively clear meaning. In other words, good poems are those with multiple meaning potential, while at the same time, ideas should be conveyed and the main theme is clear without ambiguity.[210]

The analysis of "ambiguity" and "subtleness" naturally reminds us of Dai Wangshu and several other poets of Chinese Symbolism, as well as Modernist poets, such as He Qifang and Bian Zhilin. All of these different "obscure" poems shared the same preference for "subtleness."

Many of the lyric poems written by Dai Wangshu before the full outbreak of the War of Resistance against Japanese Aggression, such as "Sleepless,"

"Worries," "Awkward Life," "Walks in the Mountains," "Changing Your Mind," etc., are also ambiguous and subtle. This is not a "singular complexity" but a deliberate natural cover-up. However, "Lane in the Rain" does not contain much obscure meaning. It is more like a kind of sentiment, which is quite clear for readers to feel the emotions. Du Heng's famous saying in "Preface to *Wangshu's Poem Collection*" is quite intriguing: "One reveals his subconscious mind in his dreams, and reveals his hidden soul in his poetry, which is also like a dream." This is certainly an application of modern psychoanalytic theory, but the phrase "reveal his hidden" is reminiscent of the "obstructing" of Chinese classical poetry. So, in the following, Du Heng continued: "From this, we learn poetry is ambiguous. Technically, its motivation is between expressing oneself and hiding oneself." Mu Mutian and Wang Duqing's poems are not as eccentric and awkward as Li Jinfa's. The "pure poetry" of musical and color sense comes from Verlaine, who is good at rhythm, and the "voyant," Rambo. But it seems also because of this, their poetry is much closer to the Chinese classical tradition. Verlaine and Rambo's obscurity lies in the fact they can reveal a deep vibration in the soul through seemingly plain descriptions. Mu Mutian and Wang Duqing chose the discourses of Symbolism but abandoned the bridge to the other side. "The water is singing in the mountains / The water is singing between the stone gaps / The water is singing in the ink willow trees shades / The water is singing on the tip of the flowering weeds."[211] This kind of ambiguous emotion is closer to the subtlety of China's artistic conception. Similar colors and sentiments can also be found in He Qifang's *Prophecy*.

Bian Zhilin's poetry is the most perplexing, which shows noticeable traces of 20th-century Western Modernist poetry. His famous poems, such as "Fragment," "Organization of Distance," "The Round Treasure Box," "Fish Fossil," "White Snail Shell" and so on, seem full of mystery, waiting for people to crack. In particular, works such as "Organization of Distance" are filled with old and new allusions, which would be associated with T. S. Eliot. But in fact, Bian Zhilin did not intend to make the poetry intricate and complicated and did not intend to induce us to think deeply. Different from the metaphysical speculation of Eliot's poetry, Bian Zhilin valued the idea of "just a touch" philosophy. He did not intend to develop complex ideas but to play in countless interesting worlds. When several great poets were perplexed by his mystery, Bian Zhilin smiled slightly, "There is a relationship between existence and consciousness. But the whole poem is not about philosophy, nor is it expressing mysterious thoughts, but follows the traditions of Chinese poetry to express a mood or image."[212] However, this mood is not intended to be explicit. Bian Zhilin said "[I am] quiet in the crowd and afraid of revealing my private feelings."[213] This seems to remind us of Du Heng's comments on Dai Wangshu's poetry, the ambiguity from Li Jinfa to Dai Wangshu, and also the moods and images by Mu Mutian, Wang Duqing, and He Qifang. So, we know under the Western shell of Chinese Modernist poetry, there is an implicit core of Chinese style.

However, Mu Dan has rather a deep understanding of the Western Modernist poetry. In his poetry, the obscure moods of Mu Mutian, Wang Duqing, and He Qifang could barely be found. The fierce screams of a "beast" broke the silence of the night; the emptiness and enrichment of life entangle and struggle with each other; hope and despair fluctuate, and countless contradictory forces are intertwined in Mu Dan's poetry. There is no such thing as obscurity, no disguise for personal affairs, because Mu Dan is going to surpass the suffering in "self-satisfaction," and the literary philosophical thoughts of Bian Zhilin seem unable to meet his needs. The flow of thought, his blood and flesh, and the feelings of his life melted into this rolling thought, flipping with it, swaying with it, and tearing or exploding with it. Readers might feel deeply confused when they read "The Eight Poems," "From Emptiness to Enrichment," and "Accusation," but this is precisely the result of a combination of rich, complex thoughts. When reading Mu Dan's poems, readers will realize the general language used to describe the meanings and situations of various poems does not work here. His poems have at least several complicated meaning structures. The first is the questioning and thinking about a certain living experience, but there is no clear orientation, only constantly interspersed with "fragments" of self-survival, constantly presenting the ups and downs of one's spiritual world. The gloom of historical ghosts is intertwined with the rhythm of real life, numerous thoughts and rich experiences correspond to the vastness of modern existence. Examples include "From Emptiness to Enrichment," "Childhood," "Song of Roses," and "The Eight Poems." The second is a retelling of a certain kind of life experience, but instead of objective realism, it contains much imagination and sentiments of Mu Dan, which are beyond ordinary people. Such examples include "Reduction," "Rat Den," "Accusation," "Departure," "Fantasy Passengers," "Survive," "Above the Line," and "The Besieged." The third is consciously showing a variety of meanings, which contrast each other, triggering people's multi-directional conjectures of life and the world, for example, "May." The fourth is to highlight a certain tendency while implying his more secretive, deeper doubts and confusions, such as "Flag." Such a complex combination of meanings, as analyzed by Madame Zheng Min, constitutes a huge magnetic field. "They fully express the division of the magnetic force he feels in life." This obscurity created by the division may have grasped the core of Western Modernism: "In general, since the 20th century, poets have become more sensitive and conscious to complicated thinking and emotional lineage. The structure of poetry is also enriched. Modernism seeks complex, multi-layered structures more consciously than classicism and romanticism."[214]

The expansion, richness, and even miscellaneous development of meanings do not seem unique to "obscure" Modernist poetics in terms of the development of Chinese poetry. It is an important trend of Chinese new poetry to break through the inherently implicit character of traditional poetry. (Only Modernism highlights the element of "obscurity.") Here, Mu Dan's choice did not conflict with the vernacular poets, such as Hu Shih. Rather, it had deep communication with them. At that time, Hu Shih considered the "top ideals and complex feelings" as a pursuit of the new vernacular poetry. His "Should" tried to construct the multi-layered meanings that Chinese traditional poems could hardly express.[215] Perhaps we are not satisfied with "Should" today, but we cannot deny Hu Shih's "Should," "One Thought"; Shen Yinmo's "Moon Night," "Naked"; Fu Xue's "Rain"; Huang Shengbai's "Farewell to Wei Shizhen" and other works indeed cannot be generalized by the "subtle" tradition of Chinese classical poetics. As far as the pursuit of Modernism is concerned, Mu Dan is, of course, in line with Li Jin, Mu Mutian, and Dai Wangshu, but he has a modern concept different from other Modernist poets. That is, Mu Dan's poetry is a successful practice of vernacular poetry ideal from its beginning. In the exploration and building of modern poetry, Mu Dan is closer to Hu Shih than Li Jinfa and Mu Mutian undoubtedly. The modern characteristics of his poetry are also more likely to make people think of the concept of modernity, a flaw of Hu Shih and his followers, who were the first trailblazers. But, the issue is Mu Dan achieved great success in the pursuit of modernity. People often argue the modernization of new poetry represented by Mu Dan is a further development of Dai Wangshu, Bian Zhilin, and Feng Zhi. Some poems by Dai Wangshu, Bian Zhilin, and Feng Zhi are more "Chinese," while Mu Dan is all for "Westernization."

Vernacular, Spoken, and Prose Poetry

The issues of vernacular, spoken, and prose trends in poetry also led to some discussions. In criticism of early vernacular new poetry, the use of vernacular is considered an imitation of the modernity of the West. Spoken language is accused of separating the necessary connection between poetry and the written language of classical Chinese. It is said the written language retains more spiritual and implicit information. According to this idea, Mu Dan's value is that he is "completely freed from the requirements of oral language." As for the prose trend, of course, it is far from the ideal of "pure poetry" in which poetry is poetry. These arguments make sense but still lack explanations on some key links. For example, Mu Dan greatly appreciated the prose beauty of poetry and the simplicity of language advocated by Ai Qing.[216] He criticized the rough language of the early vernacular new poetry. Chinese Symbolists and Modernist poets who advocated "pure poetry" were also drawn by Western Symbolism poetics. Do not they also show another kind of fate for the "other"?

So, we must face the complexity of the facts of poetry history: Mu Dan had similar language orientations with early vernacular poets, who identified with Western modernity, while the Chinese Symbolists and Modernists who intended to put things in order did not break away from the trends of Western-style modernity! So, how should we distinguish these different schools and poets? The miscellaneous facts enlighten us. The key to the problem is probably not in the Western way of modernity nor the construction of the "pure poetry" ideal. The real issue is how Chinese modern poets look at their literary traditions and strive to exert their creative abilities.

Spoken and written language in literary writing have different meanings. Written language is the result of the long-term development of language, which contains relatively rich, humanistic meaning, but it may also fall into a mechanical, rigid state. Spoken language is flexible and full of vitality, but it is not convenient to condense implicit messages. Literary writers use written language, but written literature must maintain long-term vitality through the continuous nutrition from the spoken language. In medieval Western literature, there was a time when Latin "unified" Europe, with written and spoken language used for different purposes. But since the Renaissance, these nations embarked on the road of reviving their national languages. After this, written literary languages also often learn from spoken languages, and the romantic poetry movement is a case in point. The prose tendency was to use the natural order of spoken language to disintegrate the rigidity and affectation of the written language. For Wordsworth, spoken language and prose came together. And Symbolism, especially the pursuit of "pure poetry" during early Symbolism, once again borrowed the power of non-spoken language. However, some late Modernist poets of the 20th century emphasized the importance of spoken and prose tendencies again. The choice of the 20th century is a better one. Throughout the history of language choice in Western poetry, we saw Western poets' abilities to mobilize the intrinsic potential of spoken or written language in their efforts to complete their writing as appropriate.

In contrast, Chinese poetry formed a tradition of rhythmical division of spoken and written language during the thousands of years of history. This makes the language of poetry lose the most basic vitality in the paranoid writing development. In comparison, the "vulgar" vernacular often used in plays made people feel more approachable. Chinese vernacular as a variant contains more oral elements. In the early days, the poets of the vernacular used the vernacular to counter the rigidities of classical poetry. They chose the prose tendency of poetry to deconstruct the tradition of classical poetry. Essentially, this does not identify with the Western way of modernity, but with the development of Chinese literature and the true understanding of the direction of Chinese poetry. We have no evidence that Hu Shih and other early vernacular poets failed to know well about the language of their poetry, although this ability may not be as high as we expected. If Western culture influenced Hu Shih as the "other," then the influence of this "other" is timely and correct. In the process of communication and development of human culture and literature, it is difficult to avoid this kind of inspiration from the "other," or it can be said to be inevitable! The modern language choice made by Hu Shih and others for the language of Chinese new poetry is the modern direction of modern Chinese literature. Or, for Hu Shih and his followers, it is Westernization that promotes the modernization of Chinese new poetry.

From the Symbolism of the 1920s to the Modernists of the 1930s, we see another language choice. On the surface, this is also a form of Westernization that follows the Western poetry, but it has a completely different poetic meaning.

The language of Chinese new poetry since Hu Shih's time matured step by step, but people soon discovered the cultural information contained in this written language is not as good as in classical Chinese. Compared with classical Chinese, the dryness and shallowness in vernacular increased the difficulties in poetry writing. As Yu Pingbo said, "I always feel the pain of writing poetry in today's vernacular." "The difficulty of vernacular poetry lies in the freedom. It is all free. There is no fixed form. There are no set models, but you cannot just make it up! If you do, what will it look like?"[217] Yu Pingbo's thoughts were popular among Chinese poets at the time: The vernacular text, which contains a lot of spoken languages, lacks "cultural information," but if it is measured by the "fixed form," does this still reflect people's attachment to the exquisite "refined language" of classical poetry? It is worth noting that the Symbolism and Modernism that decided to create "pure poetry" developed in such a context. Although "pure poetry" is the poetic ideal of Western Symbolism, it reflected people's beautiful memories of the "artistic" tradition of Chinese classical poetry. If we observe "pure poetry" writing from Symbolism to Modernism, we know many of their specific measures come from the language model of Chinese classical poetry. They attempted to "reshape" the Chinese "refined language" tradition with the vernacular: Some written vocabulary containing information about Chinese traditional culture was consciously "expropriated," such as willow, red leaves, white lotus flowers, swallow feathers, Autumn sickness, nostalgia, fallen flowers, morning bells, evening drums, ancient moon, residual candle, zither, and silky robes, etc. The typical super-syntactic and textual structures in Chinese classical poetry were also consciously simulated and imitated. This was to avoid the "chains" of language as much as classical poetry. "We crossed the river, but no bridge was offered."[218] Or just like the metaphor of Fei Ming, poetry is a plate of loose sand, and every grain of sand is a jewel, but it is difficult to thread them together.[219]

Western symbolic poetry guides the "pure poetry" ideals of Chinese Symbolists and Modernist poets, but it is a contradictory guide. The image choice of Western Symbolism poetry and the setting of verses is inconsistent with Chinese ancient poetry, but their understanding of the musicality of the sentences is similar to mysticism, which is difficult for Chinese poets to truly comprehend. Therefore, Chinese poets reinterpreted the musical pursuit of Western Symbolism, while quietly transforming it into a Chinese-style "artistic" ideal in practice,[220] to create a self-dividing reality of theory and practice. The division itself seems to prove these Chinese poets lack knowledge of the difficulties of the Chinese poetry language like Hu Shih. The memories of a deep-buried tradition were awakened by the new directions of Western poetry and the traditional language ideal was resurrected. But, this kind of resurrection is not out of deep thinking about the Chinese poetry language because the brilliant tradition of Chinese classical poetry language also constitutes a huge inert force, which interrupted the impact of spoken language and turned to the traditional camp of written language (refined language), which are not conducive to truly enriching the linguistic vitality of poetry. Sure enough, during the late 1930s, Chinese Modernist poetry fell into a poetic zombie state, so they had to shout "anti-tradition": "The poetry is so rigid, so civilized, there must be savage, vigorous efforts to resist the pressure of these thousands of years of tradition."[221]

In this context, we find Mu Dan's language choice cannot be explained at all by "completely getting rid of the requirements of oral language," because it is the Symbolism and Modernism of China that tries to rid the oral requirements. Mu Dan's linguistic contribution is precisely the transcendence of the "pure poetry" tradition practiced by Symbolism and Modernism. Beyond the "pure poetry" tradition, he reaffirmed the vernacular and the prose orientation of the vernacular Hu Shih created. Of course, this is a higher level of affirmation, which condenses his 20 years of a comprehensive summary of language achievements of Chinese new poetry from the May Fourth in 1919 to the 1940s. The new oral language is included as a new part of the written language.

In summarizing the achievements of the Nine Leaves School represented by Mu Dan, Mr. Yuan Kejia noted,

> Modern poets attach great importance to the application of everyday language and rhythm of speech because of the richness of both. Only changeable and flexible, fresh, vivid words and rhythms can properly and effectively express the singularity of modern poets' feelings, the dramatic changes of thoughts, and thus being used as a tool for creating the most conscious activities.[222]

Mr. Yuan Kejia's understanding and Mu Dan's view on Ai Qing's attitudes toward language indicated a conscious, rational exploration.

Mu Dan's poetry completely removes the quaint poetry vocabulary and replaces it with modern language full of modern life, such as Browning, Mauser guns, King Henry, coffee shops, inflation, industrial pollution, telephone, and medals .... There are no allusions nor historical and cultural contents of "implicit meaning in these words or phrases." They are ordinary, everyday, word-of-mouth words woven into new scenes of modern life. They quickly and effectively captured the true feelings of life and change. Readers already familiar with the many old vocabulary words of Chinese Symbolism and Modernist poetry would feel a "shocking amazement and appreciation" when they read Mu Dan's poems.[223] At the same time, the prose-style sentences also replaced "pure poetry." The expression of grammar replaces the super-logic and super-grammar "refined language." Instead of letting us linger and walk back and forth in the same place, Mu Dan's poetry pushes our feelings forward with the flow of words: "What do we do? What do we do? /Life will always seduce us. / In suffering, I am hungry for the trap of happiness, /

hey, for it comes only once, not again" ("Accusation"). The prose tendency of poetry created the flow of poetry, like the living water of life running to the sea. This created a brand new aesthetic effect undoubtedly in the camp of Chinese Modernist poetry.

Mu Dan had a much deeper understanding of spoken language and prose tendencies than the early vernacular poets. He made full use of the freshness of spoken language and the clarity of prose but avoided the issues of the revolutionary poets of the 1930s and 1940s, who considered spoken language so supreme that poetry became popular folk songs or slogans, and the prose tendency became indulgence in prose, losing the necessary spiritual cohesion. Mu Dan was soberly aware that literary language was ultimately a written language. All were merely efforts to inject new life into this written language. Therefore, in his writing, Mu Dan delved into the linguistic charm of modern Chinese, so it can be matched with a fresh spoken language and clear prose sentences to complete the best expressions. We see a large number of abstract written vocabulary words in Mu Dan's poems. The frequent use of conjunctions, prepositions, adverbs, modifiers and modifications, quantifiers and definitions, etc. brought the readers into the joy of philosophical thinking. Thus, the poetic power of written language is truly shown as belonging to modern Chinese. (All these "abstract thinking" belong to modern Chinese and have nothing to do with the "refined language" of the ancient Chinese written language.) At the same time, written language and spoken language are a pair of complementary forces. The proper functioning of modern Chinese written language suppressed the disorder of some spoken words and trimmed the sloppiness that prose may bring. Yuan Kejia repeatedly emphasized one should also break the "superstition" of spoken language and prose tendency to achieve a new understanding, which could be regarded as a kind of summary of Mu Dan's poetry achievements. Yuan Kejia argued:

> Even if we take the national language as the standard, there is still much to maneuver between spoken Chinese and the national language of literature. There is still room for meditation. And the "prose tendency" of poetry is a kind of special structure of poetry. It has nothing to do with the "prose tendency" of the proses.[224]

Mu Dan's efforts can be said to be full of discoveries about the relationship between the modern spoken and written Chinese language. It is not a simple "separation" from the spoken language but reaffirms the spoken language and prose tendency, endowed a new form of written language at a new height. Perhaps, we will still associate Mu Dan's efforts with the language movements of Western poets in the 20th century (such as Yeats and Eliot), but I think that Mu Dan's understanding of the new trends in Western poetry is much more superficial and secondary compared to his true understanding of the Chinese poetry tradition and the deep thoughts on the Chinese new poetry. If Mu Dan had a preference for the modernity of Western 20th-century poetry, it is entirely because the development of Chinese new poetry needed the creation of such modernity. Creation is what matters. Borrowing from others is nothing but a kind of communication methods. Compared with early vernacular poems, Mu Dan demonstrated the creative value of this modernity.

Traditions: Past, Present, and Future

Through the previous discussion, we see modern features of Chinese modern poetry, including Mu Dan's poetry, actually contain some recognition of the modern pursuit of Western poetry. What is interesting is the recognition of the modern pursuit of Western poetry did not lead to the same modernity. It is no wonder that some of the most typical modernization roads of Chinese Modernist poetry have been very bumpy starting with Hu Shih. He was pushed to one end of the spectrum, while Mu Dan was pushed to another end randomly by some critics. It is no wonder some people ignored intentionally or unconsciously the modernity of Hu Shih's critics when examining his modernity.

Now, we are interested in why the same pursuit of the development of Western Modernist poetry had such a different effect. Of course, we know in the previous analysis there is a more substantive issue; that is, how do modern poets face the inspiration of the West and complete their creative contributions? Is it a breakthrough in the existing creative pattern or is it a conscious return? Is it "turning to the other" or turning to "the other's other"?

Therefore, the question has led to a key point: how do Chinese poets understand their traditions? How do they deal with the relationships between their creative direction and traditions? These are important questions because the difference between understanding and processing finally formed the different modern features of China's new poetry.

What is tradition? What is the tradition related to us? I think tradition should be a historical, cultural form that can accommodate understanding and the spiritual world of future generations. This description of tradition contains two main points. First, it is a historical, cultural form. Only a cultural form with relative stability can be interpreted and sorted by future generations. As T. S. Eliot said, today's people can't think of the past as a mess. Second, it must be able to accommodate the understanding and spiritual world of future generations effectively, communicate with people whose living conditions have changed, and continue to activate and expand themselves with the cognitive changes of later generations. Otherwise, it could not be called tradition, if it is completely dusted in history and cannot make sense to future generations. These two points represent the power of the two directions of tradition. The former maintains a fixed, less varied cultural component and belongs to history. The latter is filled with infinite vitality and belongs to the most interesting, creative component of culture. It is inspired by the now and points to the future. The former seems to form an easy-to-understand dominant structure visible in history and culture, while the latter is an invisible hidden structure, which requires constant impact to sparkle. The former always shows the glory of history and is also admirable, but gives people psychological pressure, while the latter is transformed into reality and constitutes the "new tradition" of the future. "Consciousness of history also contains a kind of comprehension, not only to understand the past but also to understand the reality of the past . . . . It is this consciousness that makes a writer a traditional one . . . . The existing art classics themselves constitute an ideal order, which changes as new (real new) works are introduced."[225]

However, in the long-established concepts of the orthodox scriptures, the Chinese seem to pay more attention to the maintenance of tradition and neglect the stimulation and re-engineering of it. Often people cannot grasp the organic connection between "anti-tradition" and "tradition" accurately. They are not aware that the conscious anti-tradition is the examination and development of the traditional structure. It is a composition of new traditions. Of course, it is difficult to continue to promote a "new tradition" of "anti-tradition." Our criticism of the early vernacular poets, such as Hu Shih, is like this. Hu Shih's "revolution" of the increasingly declining Chinese classical poetry is a kind of meaningful dialogue with tradition. It is precisely in this unique "anti-tradition" questioning, the tradition was twisted and continued. The history of Chinese poetry continued to develop through Hu Shih's actions. Similarly, the value of Mu Dan has not been acknowledged accurately, because if the differences between Mu Dan and Hu Shih are exaggerated, one could not conclude that the value of Mu Dan's entire work is also the reactivation of traditional life. Neither could one be able to explain a new tradition of Chinese new poetry contributed by Mu Dan's new creation.

On the other hand, it seems easier for us to accept the Symbolism and Modernism of Chinese new poetry, because they directly inherited the glorious tradition itself. But, there is one serious fact we have neglected. That is, this simple identity is insufficient to provide a powerful impetus for the growth of Chinese new poetry because when we are admired for the glory of history, we also bear the same amount of psychological pressure that the glory of Chinese classical poetry tradition limits the free development of our thoughts and conceals our future dreams. T. S. Eliot said it well:

> If the only form of tradition, of handing down, consisted in following the ways of the immediate generation before us in a blind or timid adherence to its successes, "tradition" should positively be discouraged. We have seen many such simple currents soon lost in the sand; and novelty is better than repetition. Tradition is a matter of much wider significance. It cannot be inherited. If you want it, you must obtain it by great labor.[226]

Mu Dan worked with "great labor." Mu Dan's modernity has value because he expended great efforts in the construction of poetic meaning and the choice of poetry language; thus, breaking through the inherent pattern of classical poetry. When he rebelled against the classical "refined language" poetry tradition, he explored the poetry potential of modern Chinese. It is in Mu Dan that we are excited to see that modern Chinese undertakes rich, multiple-layered "obscurity" than the classical "subtlety." Modern Chinese poetry can still touch readers with free-running verses. It can still lead people to deeper thoughts in unmistakable communications. A profound understanding of the conveyance and deep thoughts can be compatible in this way. Poetry can also be full of philosophical and logical tensions, even when written in the abstract. Abandoning the sentimentality of the scholar-officials led to the awareness of the suffering in modern China. With quiet emptiness and bleak mentality behind them, Chinese modern poets live a more real, inartificial life. Without the emotional sensation of the natural scenery, Chinese poetry is still Chinese poetry and seems to have a more valuable vitality. In short, Mu Dan's attempt to establish a modern poetry model with the modern Chinese language has broadened the room for the free growth of new poetry and created good conditions for the development of Chinese new poetry in the future. In this sense, Mu Dan's "anti-tradition" is the new meaning of Chinese poetry tradition!

Yuan Kejia: Modernization in Chinese Context

> We have been waiting for a long time
> Roaring thunders of a dark, humid, summer's night;
> Blue lightning swept through the sky with stars falling and trees destroyed.
> Clatter! Dusty-sealed windows are open all at once!
> —Yuan Kejia, "Two Chapters Extra"

Yuan Kejia's "new poetry modernization" thought appeared during the late 1940s, but it was recognized by academic communities and widely commented on by literary historians during the 1980s,[227] more than 40 years later. At that time, when the modernization wave sufficient to inundate all social and cultural fields came to the fore, the discussion of such literary significance did not reveal its rich meaning and unique value. After the 1990s, the "end of modernity" declaration made the take-for-granted ideal of modernization a bit awkward because modernization as well as modernity are regarded as the inherent concepts of Western culture. Identification with them implied submission to Western cultural colonization. Yuan Kejia's "New Poetry Modernization" also stated at the beginning: "To understand the meanings and significance of this modernization tendency, we must first have a rough understanding of the meanings and significance of modern Western poetry."[228] At this time, there is little possibility of a calm discussion and an in-depth analysis of the theoretical significance of the new modern poetry and the modernization of literature.

However, Yuan Kejia's important poetics could not be measured in these "trends of the times." It has its path and its historical foundation. Re-examining his "new poetry modernization" argument will not only allow us to re-examine the historical contributions Chinese new poetry once had, but also help us observe our "modern twists and turns" in the 1980s and 1990s. This will clarify the origins of the modernization of Chinese new poetry and Chinese new literature, especially its relationship with the frequently discussed ideas of nationality and Chinese nature.

Modernization of Chinese New Poetry

"New poetry modernization" is a big issue of Chinese new poetry. Today, these thoughts on modernization may just hit the center of our disputes about modernization and modernity in more than a decade.

Why is the issue of "modernization of new poetry" posed? Is it to follow the trend of Western poetry and literature? The first sentence of Yuan Kejia's "New Poetry Modernization" is: "A new poetry of "modernization" has emerged since the 1940s, which has aroused readers' attention."[229] Then it is the sentence we quoted in the previous section: "To understand the meanings and significance of this modernization tendency, we must first have a rough understanding of the meanings and significance of modern Western poetry." The simple quote of this latter sentence may naturally provide people with the impression of "Western literature preference" first. However, when we read more, we know for Yuan Kejia, the priority is not to pay attention to and pursue the new trend of Western poetry. What triggered his modernization discussion is precisely the fact of China's new poetry development. This reminds us of Hu Shih's *On New Poetry*, which focuses on and explains "a big event in eight years," because "the achievements of the past two years showed the Chinese prose has passed the debate period and its time for most people to practice. Only the verses of the Chinese language, the so-called "new poetry," cannot take off many people's doubts."[230] That is to say, like the grass root writers of Chinese new poetry, Yuan Kejia's first concern is not "the introduction of culture and imitation," but how to understand and analyze the current phenomenon of writing. It is a new phenomenon of literature that stimulates the interest and interpretation of the theorists' thinking, and the theoretical impulse here does not come from "translatology." It is only "hermeneutics."

It is precisely because Yuan Kejia's poetics is an analysis of the phenomenon of Chinese poetry writing, rather than the translation of foreign poetics, he quotes the poetic conclusions of Western new criticism (such as Richards' Theory of Maximum Awareness State), not because of the integrity of the theories themselves, but Yuan Kejia intended to target the most important reality of Chinese new poetry development:

> ... The meanings and functions of artworks lie all in its deepening and the promotion of life experience, and the maximization of the conscious activity, not in any illusory (such as art for art's sake theory) or concrete purposes (such as art as a political struggle tool) ...

In the discussion of I. A. Richards' maximum awareness state, the poems that can achieve the maximally inclusive are characterized by being built out of sets of impulses which run parallel, which have the same direction, ... contrast experiences which win stability and order through a narrowing of the response with those which widen it.[231] This is an interaction of factors within the poetry, focusing on the semantic relationship in texts, the so-called "organization" and "form."[232] Yuan Kejia expanded them to the "promoting and deepening of life experience," and further forward the "realistic" problem of "the same strong social consciousness in the strong self-consciousness, the combination of realistic description and religious sentiment," etc., clearly different from the "texts" and the semantic world of new criticism. Although the word "experience" is one of the key words of Richards' poetry criticism,[233] connecting "life" to "experience" is entirely Yuan Kejia's idea, just like his poetic ideal—a combination of reality, symbol, and metaphysics. Using "reality" as the first word indicated the profound Chinese origin of Yuan Kejia's poetic thoughts.

As for his critique of the "illusory purpose" and "specific purpose" of poetry pursuit, they are derived from the important facts of Chinese new poetry development, different from the expressions of new criticism, and even different from Western Modernist poetry. Both the new criticism of art autonomy, self-sufficiency, and Symbolism's "pure poetry" ideals are defending rather than skeptical of poetry's "art for art's sake." Only in modern China, from the Crescent Moon School, Symbolist School, and the Modernist School in the 1930s, their pursuit of "art for art's sake" only borrowed the "pure poetry" banner of Western Symbolism, when they were trapped in the complex reality.

> Poetry is a form of life expressed in language. It is derived from the vast field of life, and modern life is closely related to modern politics. If a poet is still attempting to be free from any political life, he not only is immersed in the illusory prayers of the fish out of the water but also faces the threat of suffocation that will follow it. This would narrow his emotional radius, reducing the meaning and value of life. This self-restricted desire not only affects the value of his work but also seriously damages the valuable meaning of an individual life.[234]

Only in modern China, the "pure poetry" of "art for art's sake" turned out to be an obstacle to artistic development. The poetic stagnation and premature decline of Modernist poetry in the 1930s caused such a considerable crisis that some called for "barbaric, simple, bold, and rough" poems.[235]

At the same time, Yuan Kejia also warned people to be cautious of the idea that "poetry is a weapon of politics or a tool for propaganda." We could easily associate criticism of the "specific purpose" of poetry with our new criticism of the "purity" of literature. But for these Western poets, separating "moral" and "social" with other contents from the "ontology" of poetry is first and foremost a question of trying to return to the "text" of the art world. In their view, if one always understood literature from the perspective of "social history," it has seriously damaged the "meaning" of literature itself. In contrast, Yuan Kejia, although he maintains the independence of poetry, it is interesting that his poetic construction is to promote the development and transformation of Chinese new poetry rather than guiding us in the world of art self-sufficiency. For this purpose, Yuan Kejia has a sense of social mission. In other words, he is looking for the historical power of modern new poetry by promoting poetry to complete "independence." Yuan Kejia's "poetry independence" declaration does not lead us to enter closed "texts." On the contrary, he finally let poetry enter a broader historical process, and let us who care for the fate of new poetry also care for the operation of the world and literature. As some scholars noted, "Because of the inevitable concern about the social function of poetry, a whole set of text criticism theory of new criticism has evolved into a poetry writing guide according to Yuan Kejia. He used this theory to call for modern poems, which would take Eliot and Oden as art models, but also intervene in China's reality. Yuan Kejia attacked directly the slogans and conceptualized "political sentimental" writings simply subject to the political movement at the time. He explored the path of remedy as a problem solver. The review of the existing texts then gradually changed into Yuan Kejia's "forward-looking" of future texts."[236]

Modernization Is Not Westernization

Yuan Kejia's ideal is the "modernization of new poetry." So, what is "modern"? This is a concept of disputes. The Chinese academic communities since the 1990s have explored this issue seriously. The conclusion is this is a concept from Western culture. It was fully developed in the Western Renaissance-Enlightenment period and imported into the East, including China, with the global expansion of Western civilization. That is to say, the modern ideal of Chinese culture is a replica of the Western form, at least with the suspicion of self-defeating imitation. Yuan Kejia, who explored modernization based on the development of Chinese new poetry, paid considerable attention to the differences. He showed it is necessary to find the source of expressions and the actual artistic achievements in such an interpretation activity. On the one hand, "readers of modern poetry have too little experience in dealing with such poems. Like the enemies of unknown origin, they often regard it as a translated product in a panic. Many forms of Europeanization have long been part of the general knowledge of Chinese. Although originally from the West, it is not the original sample of the West." On the other hand, "the critics of modern poetry can only analyze the sources of this reform because of insufficient training. They fail to clarify its relationship with tradition and, therefore, create a general impression that modernization is Westernization."[237]

Yuan Kejia acknowledged the significance of Western poetry's origin to the modernization of Chinese new poetry but pointed out the fundamental differences between China's modernization and Westernization—China's modernity is a correspondence to China's tradition. Modernity is the modernity in the evolution of Chinese traditional forms, rather than the external modernity of input and transplantation. In the article "Dramatization of New Poetry," Yuan Kejia offers a brilliant discussion:

> There is an important concept that should have been clarified a year ago, but it has been forgotten because of the author's negligence. That is the new poetry modernization that I mentioned is not synonymous with the new poetry Westernization. New poetry has been influenced by Western poetry from the very beginning, and, thus, the demand for its modernization is closely related to our study of modern Western poetry and modern Western literary criticism. Yet, we have no reason to mix modernization with Westernization. From the most superficial point of view, modernization refers to growth in terms of time, while Westernization refers to change in terms of space. The new poetry does not have or cannot be Westernized just like this space is not and cannot become that space. The new poetry can or must be modernized, just as an organically grown thing would as part of the natural process of transformation. It is moving forward rather than being uprooted.[238]

Therefore, although Yuan Kejia's poetic thought has obvious connections with the new criticism of the West, his motivation to explore modernity is the phenomenon that modern Chinese poetry is different from traditions. The opening of "New Poetry Modernization" announced, "A modernized new poetry has appeared since the 1940s. . . . 'Appearance' is the key word of Yuan Kejia, and it is China's 'Forties,' rather than the end of the 19th and early 20th century in the West."

It is in this sense of time flow and the evolution of the times that Yuan Kejia used a series of vocabulary: experiment, reform, revolution, rise, new, and old . . . as descriptions of the modernity that came out of traditions. The modernity he understood and called for is the adjustment and reaction to poetry forms we have already had. Not only do the forms of ancient Chinese poetry need adjustment, but also some of the reviving ancient traditions disguised in the modern emerging concept of Chinese-Western communication. "We should try to abandon some old-fashioned, or seemingly fresh, but old-fashioned thoughts and habits."[239] For example:

After all the meanings of their experiments are exhausted, they are powerful as representatives to change the old and emotional revolutionary call; the germination of this emotional revolution is not from today. People who read poetry works, such as Dai Wangshu, Feng Zhi, Bian Zhilin, Ai Qing, etc. would be reminded of their precedents with no difficulty.[240]

It does not only represent the rise of a new sensibility, that is, it could be said that it will change the way of the overall mental activity dramatically.[241]

If readers can compare this with popular works, they will easily grasp the incomparable superiority of this indirect method; but it is slightly different from the "subtleness" of traditional poetry.[242]

On the contrary, the literati with traditional talents are most likely to fall into this self-made trap. There are many bad Cis and Qus that give us witnesses. Seeing the fallen leaves and responding with the self-pity of one's fate is a typical example. These sentimental qualities are hypocritical, almost shameless hypocrisy.[243]

When reviewing and comparing the various choices of modern poets, Yuan Kejia especially distinguished Mu Dan from Xu Zhimo, who "reconstructed the classic ideas in a modern way":

The features of Xu's poems include light in weight, strong in emotions, gorgeous in imagery, well-proportioned, and mostly used the repetition of emotions to create a heavy lyric atmosphere. In other words, Xu's poetry is good poetry of romance. Mu Dan's poems are heavy, entangled in feelings and reason, and struggled to overcome each other, the imageries are prominent, the rhythms are often abrupt and changeable, and the atmosphere is not heavy, but seeks a strong concentration. This is modernized poetry.[244]

Bian Zhilin is a poet applauded by Yuan Kejia as a representative of the modernization direction of the new poetry. However, because of the many transitional characteristics in his poetry, some critics argued Bian Zhilin as writing with a Chinese classical poetry style. These critics covered and confused his valuable, modern trend. Therefore, Yuan Kejia was very careful when he discussed Bian Zhilin's poetry. He picked out the classical tastes in Bian Zhilin's poems and placed them on one side. Then, he focused on those modern features easily overlooked.

People who have read *Ten Years of Poetry* have every reason to believe, as pointed out by several critics (such as. Wen Jiasi), that Bian Zhilin's feelings are extremely delicate and sensitive. However, our criticism of him should not stop here. To reveal the true value of his poems and to raise the alertness of imitators, we must further specify Mr. Bian's poems start with feelings, but they do not stop there. The main tone of his feelings, although very delicate and weak, often have width and depth. The most successful of his art in poetry does not lie in the piecemeal minor imagery nor the beautiful performance of articles and rhythm, but in the thorough emotional expressions through feelings.[245]

In particular, Yuan Kejia summarized the trend of escaping from modernity as a "primitive" pursuit. In his view, those who pursue simplicity, nature, and rural areas, and try to closer to Chinese classical poetry can be said to fall into the category of "primitive" art.

> Because of the uneasiness and irritability of modern urban life, people turn to simplicity and nature; because of resistance to the disharmony and instability of the industrial world, people recall and miss the past .... Because the various disadvantages of the capitalist civilization made us sensuously rigid, and life was becoming more boring, people turn to folk songs and dances to find fresh sentiments and powerful performances .... However, here we must note, although this primitive tendency has the meaning of correction in a negative way, it is insufficient to actively solve the problem of modern culture. I believe modern innocence has already disappeared with the passing of the century. Eden is no longer ours. Even if many talented people want to return to the primitive state and save humanity, it is impossible.[246]
>
> We can obtain some vitality and necessary crudity from folk songs, and folk dances, but obviously, we cannot stop there, the pressure of cultural progress will force us to abandon our simple desires and make great strides toward modernity .... Modern poetry accepts the complexity and richness of modern culture and expresses the same complexity and richness.[247]

From these descriptions, we can see Yuan Kejia's modern pursuit is to face the actual form of the current social life, instead of whitewashing or evading. He would face problems and solve problems, face complexities, and present complexity. This is the "modern" path for art.

Modernity, as Yuan Kejia understands and calls for here, is very profound both in terms of the classical form in which Chinese poetry needs to change and returning to classical poetry in the context of the integration of Western and modern Chinese poetry.

Yuan Kejia used the impressive term "new tradition" for the first time in Chinese new poetry criticism and new literary criticism as an overview of the "modern" form in Chinese. The subtitle of the first paper of "New Poetry Modernization" is "A Search for New Tradition." With his repeated discussion, we know such a non-traditional poetry form, a non-folk form of poetry art pursuit different from people's "primitive" tastes is on the stage of history. It is neither Western transplantation nor a simple continuation of ancient culture, but an "organic synthesis" that includes foreign inspirations and its cultural tradition. As an independent creation of modern poets, its appearance marks

Chinese poetry has taken shape in its independent form of pioneering significance during the 20th century. Yuan Kejia is the earliest theorist to discover and summarize this phenomenon.

Democratic Poetry and People's Poetry

If Yuan Kejia's above-mentioned conception of modern poetry is completed in the context of Chinese and foreign cultural exchanges and dialogues, and if the significance of China is also presented in the comparison of ancient and modern Chinese, and foreign art elements, then his discussion on democracy and the value of people of modern poetry directly show his concern and response to China's modernity issue.

An important feature of modern Chinese social culture is all major artistic choices cannot cover and replace a series of more important political issues in our real life. In addition, these social and political encounters will often affect and change our artistic tastes and choices. Such a volatile social and political environment does not apply to Western Modernist poets and new critics. It is a social problem in modern China. Also because of the reality of the mutual impact of social politics and art, it became a problem with art and poetry in modern China.

"In recent years, we read articles discussing the relationships between poetry and democracy at times. Regardless of how the authors differ in their opinions, everyone seems to have recognized a certain relationship between poetry and democracy."[248] This is the beginning of *Poetry and Democracy*, which depicts for us the context of Yuan Kejia's poetic conception: an era of passionate political issues. Such issues are not just external. They directly cut into our survival and life. In this regard, Yuan Kejia has a deep understanding. He is more willing to understand democracy as a kind of human culture and consciousness, rather than an external political system. The significance of democracy as a part of culture could be described as Yuan Kejia's unique social discovery. It is his wisdom that he can find a "direct, significant connection"[249] between modernized poetry from this culture. Similarly, as two different trends of the "new literary movement during the past 30 years," "human literature" and "people's literature" also promoted and clashed with each other in the "comprehensive" thinking of modern poetry. "I pointed out the truth of the trend of promotion and conflicts, the actual causes of conflicts, and the possible ways of compatibility. I believe only through a comprehensive understanding, and through the relative amendment of sincere cooperation can it be sufficient to guarantee the bright future for the Chinese literature."[250] The expressions of the subjective experience of individual poets should be considered as "the people's literature" and in line with the democracy principle we pursue. Therefore, such arguments undoubtedly greatly expanded our understanding of people and democracy:

> We can be realistic and get closer to the problem; we assume there are some "outdated" people, who, due to the limitations of personality and reality, actually cannot produce as some specific models did, although they desire the descriptions of the popular life to disclose and to eulogize. And, they are unwilling to show some empty gestures. More importantly, they (the number of people here should not have a fatal effect, even if only one person does not affect the inference) do have special abilities in feelings and presentation. Although they cannot write people's life in order forms, they can create poems not as expected, but originated from real life, or produce poems about human life larger than people's lives. Who has reason not to let them write, not allow them to write? If someone must limit them, is this to promote democracy or to betray democracy? Is this a murder of life or an embrace of life?[251]

In the history of Chinese modern poetry, this breaks through the so-called liberalization of the so-called liberals. Naturally, it is also different from the literary admonishment of politicians. It is also not a derogatory statement of eclecticism, because the mutual "comprehensive" way has gained effective support from modern poetry experience.

In an abstract view, connecting poetry with political democracy and exploring the different meanings of humans and people in poetry is quite special in the history of human poetic thought. Even for some Western scholars, it is somewhat confusing in fact. Some of these arguments are far-fetched.[252] However, if such thinking is placed in the unique context of the development of Chinese culture and the development of literature and art in the 20th century, we should admit this is precisely the result of the unique, keen, realistic experience of Yuan Kejia. It is the feeling that arises from the reality of China that makes it possible for him to rediscover the unique composition of Chinese art value outside the boundaries of poetry art—a basic fact about the cultural symbiosis of literature and social culture:

> When I made a bird's eye view of the past and present of the new literary movement, I think it has a trait different from other literature. That is, its cultural elements exceed its literary elements. That is to say, the emergence, existence, and development of the new literary movement are far more important as the main arena of the cultural movement than its value as pure literature.[253]

It was not until almost half a century later that the Chinese academic communities once again realized and discussed such facts in the sense of literature. Yuan Kejia's discovery of this issue is another important contribution to modern poetic criticism, a poetic questioning and idea conception that best shows modern Chinese characteristics.

Dramatization and Experience

Yuan Kejia stood out not only because of his modern poetry modernization thought of "significance for China" in the world of modern poetics but also because of his milestone contributions in the course of Chinese modern poetics exploration.

Constructing the "experience" theory of poetry on the level of art itself and perfecting the dramatization of new poetry is the outstanding contribution of Yuan Kejia to Chinese modern poetry.

Chinese new poetry started with many difficulties against the high maturity of Chinese classical poetry. Breaking through the old mode and looking for a new thinking space can be described as the basic choice of Chinese new poetry. Given the formalized path, how to rediscover new poetry inspiration, or how to re-engage the new life experience, is the core issue of Chinese modern poetic thought for a long time. The "experience" theory of new poetry writing is put forward in this context. The so-called "experience" is to allow the new poetry to accept and convey the ideas of new life experiences. The "experience" theory of Chinese new poetry was born from the early days of vernacular poetry, but it was Yuan Kejia who forwarded it into the logic of art.

"Experience" became an important term in Chinese modern poetics, first in Hu Shih's "empiricism." Emphasizing the meaning of "experience" in poetry writing is related to Hu Shih's opposition to "abstract writing" and advocacy of "concrete practices." In 1920, in the self-preface of *Dream and Poetry*, Hu Shih stated clearly:

> This is my "poetic empiricism". Simply put: dreaming would need experience as a foundation, let alone poetry. Nowadays, the big issue is poems are written without experience. A new poet in Beijing wrote, "The corn flour is sent one-by-one into the mouth," and one poet in Shanghai wrote: "The silkworm slept yesterday. Today silkworms sleep, tomorrow, silkworms sleep, silkworms sleep, but people cannot!" Isn't this a kind of common sense of corn flour and silkworm raising? But, people who do not have such experiences should stop rambling about flour or raising silkworms, not to mention writing poems about them.

The experience here is more like the real feelings of life. Ten years later, Hu Shih still had the same opinion as in "To Lu Xiaoman's Landscape Painting": "One needs to know a mountain well when drawing a mountain; one needs to be familiar with a horse before painting one. If one just shuts doors and creates artwork, it could not be called artwork." It can be seen the experience here has not yet entered the level of more conscious art logic.

Although the development of Chinese new poetry still considered new artistic experiences as important since Hu Shih's time, poets who have long been accustomed to Western/traditional dual choices seem to prefer some big words of art, such as emotions, feelings, metrics, rhythms and even times, society, the public, etc. The experience reflection is rather sparse and the extremely limited experience vocabulary still did not go beyond Hu Shih's "life feelings," such as the life experiences of Zang Keijia:

> All my poems are the crystallization of my experiences. They are all written under an urge. They were pressed by bitterness and pain, by sleeplessness in the cold. I stood in the cold courtyard with teeth clinching under the cold howling wind. Words and sentences were produced one by one. Those who do not have a deep experience in life will not fully understand my verses, and those who refuse to pursue them to the depths will not know the sweet bitterness of my poetry writing.[254]

A few poets, such as Liang Zongdai and Feng Zhi, discussed the unique meaning of personal experience in poetics and occasionally cited the "experience" of Western poets, such as Rilke, but they did not discuss in-depth the "experience" in their poetics.

After Hu Shih's pioneering attempt, it was Yuan Kejia who re-enabled the "experience" discourse and pushed it to the height of artistic thinking. "Experience" is a poetic term frequently used by Yuan Kejia. For example, "the qualities of a poem are purely based on the height, depth, and breadth of the value of their experience."[255] "The first problem modern poets encountered in their writings is how they properly and effectively communicate the greatest amount of experience activities with the restrictions from various artistic agents."[256] "Crystalizing one's own experiences."[257] What is more noteworthy is that Yuan Kejia's experience is entirely the concept of art itself. In his view, the abstract preaching and sentiment draining that prevailed at the time "is naturally a life experience. But they may not be a poetic experience. In the vast majority of cases, the will is just a series of abstract conclusions of understanding. A few phrases would make their meanings clearer. Emotions are just impulses and a few shouts are enough."²⁵⁸ Distinguishing the general life experience from poetry experience is vital to understand Yuan Kejia's contribution to Chinese modern poetics. He further stated:

> The experience of poetry comes from real-life experiences, but poetry does not equal experience or end with life experiences. There must be a process of transformation or digestion between these two kinds of experiences. Life experience expressed in the works is not only an improvement, promotion, or deepening of the original experience but often the synthesis or crystallization of many different experiences. An author's synthesis ability, on the one hand, depends on the breadth and depth of experience, especially in his ability to absorb and digest the experience, partially determined by the natural development of innate temperament and partially by spontaneous education and training. Individuals' tastes diverged here, the quality of the soul, and strengths and weaknesses would show themselves. All these are very natural and cannot be faked.²⁵⁹

Yuan Kejia's dramatization pursuit of new poetry is to present the poetry experience as well as possible. During the 1940s, he said:

> The problem of current new poetry is neither purely an idea issue, nor purely a technical issue, but the transformation of how to transcend the two. So how can we transform these wills and emotions into poetic experiences? The author's answer is the title of this article: Dramatization of New Poetry, that is, trying to make the will and emotions present like drama and avoid the bad tendencies of preaching or sentimentality.²⁶⁰

As a method to enrich Chinese poetry, modern vernacular poets had borrowed from the "drama element" for a long time. During the 1920s, the Crescent Moon School poets, such as Xu Zhimo and Wen Yiduo, used drama monologues and dialogues in their poems. Wen Yiduo even proposed in 1943, "In the era of a novel and drama, poetry should learn from novels and drama, and secure an audience by using the skills of the novels and drama."²⁶¹ Here, Wen Yiduo's idea is that such an approach can completely break through the inherent mode of classical poetry.

> The life of traditional poetry is already over, but is there no life for new poetry—which is almost a complete re-start? Right, unless it can really give up the tradition, completely forget the past and start again. But, this is almost equal to saying that it is not poetry. To be more precise, poems would not be like poems, but like novels or dramas, at least make them more like novels, less like poems. Too many poem-like poems and so-called "pure poetry" would only exist for a very small number of people in the future similar to ridicule and apology.²⁶²

Here, the internal problems of "the dramatization of new poetry" was not mentioned. Just like the writing of the 1920s, Wen Yiduo, and Xu Zhimo mainly used "drama" as a fresh, new technique.

In the 1930s, Bian Zhilin continued to use drama elements and explained this from the perspective of artistic origins of Chinese and foreign poetry: "I always mention the 'aesthetic conception' in China or the 'dramatic situation' in the West which tends to be novel-like, typical, non-personalized, and even occasionally parody."[263] This shows the profound connection between this artistic orientation and modern Western poetics. However, like these "Chinese and foreign integration" poetry ideas at the time, traditional Chinese "aesthetic conception" and modern Western "dramatic situation," through their communication with each other in the poetics concept, leaves more ambiguity, although there is no lack of depth. Until then, the concept of "drama" was not based on the "modern problem" of Chinese new poetry of the time. It did not yet interpret the rich potential meaning of "drama" from the higher level of the art concept.

Yuan Kejia was the first to complete a comprehensive, profound study and elaboration of the pursuit of the new poetry drama as a modern "poetry experience." It is through Yuan Kejia's elaboration that dramatization fundamentally crossed the level of general skills and became a "thinking mode"—connecting ideas and forms without being confined by them. Thus, "dramatization" as the basic mode of poetry thinking has the basic characteristics of objectivity, indirectness, inclusiveness, the richness of tension, and emphasis on structure, and formed styles like Rilke, Oden, and other forms. Yuan Kejia's discourse includes a wealth of Western cultural resources—including the poetic ideas of T. S. Eliot, I. A. Richards, Kenneth Burke, and the creation of modern European and American poetry during the 20th century. However, the use of these external resources could in no way conceal the clear realistic pertinence of his poetics.

> Regardless of which direction you want to dramatize the poetry, the superstition that poetry is only of passion must be broken. No theory harms poetry more than uncontrolled emotions, regardless of the purpose of the description of the will or the expression of enthusiasm. Whether you are complaining as an individual or collective, you must integrate your thoughts and crystalize your own experiences. Otherwise, even if you show a long face or make a scene of yourself, it is difficult to produce poetry.[264]
>
> According to the author's thoughts, reading poems and singing dances should be a good beginning of the poetic drama. Both are close to drama and dance, and they focused on dramatic effects. The recital stresses rhythm, tone, and expression, and so is Yangge dance (a kind of Chinese rural folk dance). The only concern is some

people are too superstitious, enthusiastic, and unwilling to add a little restraint and transform poetry into a deep dive into thoughts and sensitive feelings. They blindly satisfy the monotonous repetition of the original standard. This is not only a literary problem. I must think about it more carefully and hope to have the opportunity for further discussion later.[265]

Yuan Kejia's thoughts have a clearer and more specific "problem orientation" among all the "dramatization" discourses on the development of modern Chinese poetics. That is to say, regardless of how many foreign resources he borrows, we must admit his discourse confronts and responds to China's problems; thus, a creative contribution to the development of modern Chinese poetics.

Yuan Kejia not only put forward the idea of "the dramatization of new poetry" in response to the development of Chinese new poetry but also attempted to establish his own poetic theory and criticism approaches. As we all know, in the overwhelming introduction of Western literary thoughts, Chinese modern literary theorists and poets took great pains when dealing with and digesting foreign resources, which led to a serious inadequacy of China's theoretical development. Several complete "poetics" of modern systems in China—including the poetics of Zhu Guangqian and Ai Qing, despite their contribution—did not make more efforts to launch new poetic concepts. Although Yuan Kejia acknowledged the external traces in his poetic concepts, he can always freely employ all these foreign poetic concepts, make new combinations and transformations, and form his new thoughts. In addition to the independent creation of many aspects mentioned previously, Yuan Kejia also tried to re-integrate the imported concept of "drama" into a generalization of his pursuit of poetics. In the article "On Drama-ism," Yuan Kejia raised drama to "ism" and used it as "an independent system of criticism,"[266] as his unique contribution, which not only forms a dialogue with modern Western poetic thought but also lays a foundation for China's poetic criticism concept. If there are more Chinese modern poets who can have Yuan Kejia-style thoughts, then more would be expected of our thoughts. Half a century later, Lan Dizhi, a critic who put forward the new concept of "symptomatic analysis," said with emotion:

> "On Drama-ism" is the most important article in the poetics of Yuan Kejia (June 8th, 1948, *Ta Kung Pao*). The "dramatization" we just analyzed is Yuan Kejia's summary of his ideal and modern poetry, and "Drama-ism" is his naming of critical theory. I named my literary criticism theory "symptomatic analysis theory" in 1998 (*Symptomatic Analysis of Modern Literary Classics*, Tsinghua University Press, 1998

edition), and named my theory of poetry criticism "the theory of important sentiment analysis in poetry" (*Emotions and Forms of Modern Poetry*, Huaxia Publishing House, 1995). Therefore, I assumed that "Drama-ism" is Yuan Kejia's naming for his criticism theory. Yet, when he prepared these papers for publication in 1948, "New Criticism" was used, and then "On the Modernization of New Poetry" when he recollected the publication in 1988. Neither time did he use the term of "Drama-ism Criticism Theory" because he wanted to integrate into the literary trend of the times, not to stress individual innovation, nor to hide the unconventionality in the tides of the times.[267]

Ren Hongyuan: Choice of a Contemporary Academic Poet

Dark explosion
Glorious hieroglyphs, suddenly hit me.
—Ren Hongyuan, "I Just Want to Walk into a Chinese Character, Read and Write Perpetually for Life and Death"

Facing the tradition of Chinese classical poetry, we saw the modern inheritance of Xu Zhimo, Dai Wangshu, He Qifang, and Bian Zhilin, and also saw the Ai Qing and Mu Dan-style modern rebellion. Besides these attitudes, another poet, Ren Hongyuan's experiences and choices in contemporary poetry is also worth noting.

"Contemporary Poetry: A Double Transcendence of Western Modernism and Eastern Classical Poetics" is an article about Chinese new poetry by the contemporary poet, Ren Hongyuan, in the last decade of the 20th century (the article was originally published in the *Literary Review*, Issue 5, 1988). In my opinion, rather than being a factual description of the overall trend of Chinese new poetry, it was Ren Hongyuan's call, as a poet, for the future of ideal Chinese poetry. Or more accurately, it is a summary of his ideals as a poet, who worked in a higher education institute and was immersed in the elite culture. Here, he examined the artistic choices of Chinese new poetry within the context of the Chinese/Western cultural patterns, with a unique way of thinking of an intellectual in higher education. Ren Hongyuan was a poet, but at the same time, he was also a university professor who taught Chinese literature history. Like other senior intellectuals of the 20th century, he paid attention to Chinese culture from a rational perspective and wrote about the development and future possibilities of Chinese literature from a cultural perspective. I believe as a member of the 20th-century Chinese academic intellectual, Ren

Hongyuan's "double transcendence" could help us understand and interpret the cultural choices of similar Chinese poets, including the reasons for such choices and the problems with them. Of course, ultimately, it would also help us to understand the contributions of Ren Hongyuan to poetry history and the poet himself.

A Chinese Academic Poet

Our so-called academic poet generally has such characteristics: the poet undergoes strict academic education or teaches in higher education for a long time. Teaching and cultural studies are important parts of his career with knowledge and learning as his main life pursuits. Ren Hongyuan's choice of poetry is generally subordinated to such interests and pursuits. Wen Yiduo in the *Red Candle* period and the Modernist poet, Bian Zhilin, in the 1930s are important representatives of Chinese modern academic poets. During the *Red Candle* period, Wen Yiduo was calm, simple, self-cultivated, and self-disciplined, a model of traditional Confucian scholars. He refused to enjoy what ordinary people take for granted through his hard study and cultural studies. His serious thoughts on the art of Chinese and Western poetry, and academic criticism of poetry accompanied him to the poetry world, for example, his famous commentary on Yu Pingbo's *Winter Night* and Guo Moruo's *The Goddesses*. Bian Zhilin "always tended to restrain himself, as if deliberately to remain a 'cold-blooded animal.'"[268] So it was a good choice for Bian to teach at Sichuan University and Southwestern Associated University, or bury himself in translation work. He also attempted to leave the ivory tower and join the trend of social movements, but in the end, he returned quietly. Yan'an in 1938 was not sufficiently attractive for him. Bian Zhilin was in the "remote part of England, lost himself in the fog of the medieval mountain village of Cotswold, dozens of kilometers west of Oxford" at an important time in China's historical upheaval.[269] Compared with these academic poets, other writers we are familiar with seem to have other choices. Guo Moruo was stimulated by fiery social enthusiasm. Mu Dan's concern was precisely the truth and suffering of the broader survival for those outside the academy. ("The passengers who were unloaded from the fantasy route.") Influenced by Lu Xun, Mu Dan was also more like a writer who embraced society. Hu Feng, who was also deeply influenced by Lu Xun, supported the July School poets who did not receive a traditional academic education, although they did not have the same artistic interests as Mu Dan.

Truly, we find the more important difference between academic poets alienated from society by the academy and non-academic poets, who experience life in society, is their understanding of art. Poets who embrace society often prefer to capture the facts of their lives or the true rhythms of the soul. Their rational understanding of poetry is often an understanding of life and existence. Naturally, they are not without the taste and pursuit of culture, but relatively speaking, these cultures are not in the form of knowledge or rational guidance in their writing practice. Culture has melted as a part of their spiritual experience. They did not or were not accustomed to using such clear concepts as China Culture, Western culture, new culture, or traditional culture to explain the impulse of their artistic creations. For example, in the call of Guo Moruo, the poetry heritage of ancient and modern Chinese and foreign is presented as a whole:

> I called the *Yage* master of the Zhou Dynasty, / I called the *Lisao* master of Chu, / I called the poem master of the Tang Dynasty, / I called the *Ci* master of the Yuan Dynasty/ The ancient Indian poet who wrote *Vedas*! / Dante who wrote the *Divine Comedy*! / Milton who wrote *The Paradise Lost*! / Tragic Goethe who wrote *Faust*! ("The Creator")

Walt Whitman's magnificence, Rabindranath Tagore's serenity, Qu Yuan's deep sorrowfulness, Wang Wei's light spirit, so many different poetry styles swept through, but Guo Moruo did not suffer from the clashes, it is his inner passion that dissolved the boundaries of "cultures." In Guo Moruo's writings, different varieties of even distant poetry heritage were juxtaposed "for my use"; thus, forming the poet's variable and juxtaposed characteristics. Interestingly, Guo Moruo did not believe there was anything wrong with such mixing! Ai Qing, a pioneer of the July School, had his rational structure—*On Poetry*, but this theory is not so much a study of Chinese and foreign poetic systems as a summary of his artistic practices. Therefore, *On Poetry* is the poet's unique juxtaposition argument. It is well known not as a concept of rigor but because of its highly realistic sense. Ai Qing's writing is not to summarize the essence of Chinese and foreign poetry but to turn toward life and express the feeling of contemporary existence. "Just like the command of justice can organize the people's pace, the poet's pen must work hard for the strength and unity of the people's spirit."[270] Another poet of the July School, A Long, was also extraordinarily "biased" and full of emotions because of his stress on the significance of the practice of survival. In his view, "poetry is a red signal bullet that rises straight into the sky." There are two tasks for the poetry and poets: "First, work as a bomb for the War of Resistance against Japanese Aggression. Second, work as a member of the War of Resistance against Japanese Aggression."[271] Similarly, the Nine Leaves School poet, Mu Dan, who was well known as "anti-traditional," also consciously inherited the spiritual heritage of socialist Lu Xun. Some of his abandonment of the Chinese classical poetry tradition did not come from his academic research but was a result of his close observation of reality. Wang Zuoliang said Mu Dan "is best at expressing the torture and tormenting feelings of Chinese intellectuals. On the other hand, his best quality is completely non-Chinese."[272] It should be added, "on the other hand," quality is not the poet's far-thinking choice of thought, because "Mu Dan's victory is in his complete ignorance of ancient classics."[273] The pains of the countless dead bodies and the "besieged" on the battlefield of the War of Resistance against Japanese Aggression provided Mu Dan with new images and moods. The sincere expression of such artistic feelings produced an "anti-traditional" effect, and Mu Dan, as an art practitioner, obviously did not need to find more reasons for this strange effect. In 1940, Mu Dan published two commentaries on Ai Qing and Bian Zhilin in *Ta Kung Pao*, a newspaper in Hong Kong. His passionate writing and perceptual language allowed us to think of the style of Ai Qing, A Long, Hu Feng, and other July School poets, which showed Mu Dan essentially shared similarities with poets outside the academy.

Unlike the poets described previously, our so-called academic poets are more accustomed to linking the practice of art with their knowledge exploration and cultural development. Their vision of cultural development seems implemented as a specific literary (poetry) choice. The specific direction of poetry writing needs to be elucidated in the context of more profound cultural knowledge. For academic poets deeply influenced by academia, the choice of poetry art is often associated with the choice of cultural traditions and the choice of Chinese and Western poetry. "On Little Poetry" by Zhou Zuoren in 1922 is an example showing his way of thinking as an academic by discussing not only China but also Europe as well as India. A year later, when Wen Yiduo commented on the "local colors" of *The Goddesses*, he made the most comprehensive interpretation of Chinese/Western culture. Wen Yiduo's idea about the future of Chinese new poetry did not involve personal feelings. The uniqueness of his concern was the "cultural" issue between China and the West:

> I always think the new poetry is directly "new", not only newer than China's traditional poetry but also newer than the West's traditional poetry. In other words,

it is not about writing a pure, local poem, but about preserving the local colors. It should not be pure foreign poems, but should try to absorb the strengths of foreign poetry; the new poetry should be the baby after the marriage of Chinese and Western art.

In the 1930s, another academic poet, Bian Zhilin, was also inspired by the intersection of Chinese and Western poetry. The broad poetic vision of Bian Zhilin enabled him to use a series of characteristics of Chinese classical and Western modern poetry—such as implicit and non-personalized, artistic and dramatic techniques, making them an important foundation for his ideal of poetry with "Chinese-Western integration."

Under such a background, it is not difficult for us to understand Ren Hongyuan's "double transcendence." This kind of cross-cultural macro-level investigation is typical of an academic poet's thinking.

Ren Hongyuan as an Academic Poet

Then, in contemporary poetry, what is noteworthy about Ren Hongyuan's poems as an academic poet?

First, as a 60-year-old poet during the time of writing, Ren Hongyuan always paid attention to what happened in contemporary poetry with an open mind and attempted to keep pace with the times. His "new" poetry discourse and the "avant-garde" poetic criticism are sufficient to enable him to have dialogues with the "contemporary pioneers." Behind this phenomenon are Ren Hongyuan's strict academic education and the deep thinking of the intellectual elite on the history of the nation. His decades of life with poetry have made him witness too many changes and disasters. As an intellectual, who grew up during the early 1960s, Ren Hongyuan deeply understood that the self-blockade of nationalism means stagnation, which means China in the 20th century would experience the pain of Lermontov in Russia during the 19th century.[274] When the "classics + poetry" movement was in its peak time, Ren Hongyuan was fascinated by 19th-century Western romantic literature. In 1957, he said,

> I understood the hopes and disillusionment of Pushkin in the early spring ... I know more about Lermontov's language of "the cliffs and the thunder and the storm" in the dark ages of Nicholas I; George Gordon Byron's elegy to face the future, written on the ruins of ancient Greece and Rome, and Percy Bysshe Shelley's cloud, the skylark, the spirit of freedom in the west winds ... The poem I read most was Lermontov's *Contemplation*.[275]

In the early 1980s, he hunted for a copy of *The Humans* by Atoaldas Megeraitis, fascinated by *Leaves of Grass* by Walt Whitman. Of course, he also read Ezra Pound and T. S. Eliot. Although he did not follow the tide blindly, Ren Hongyuan agreed with the "horizontal transportation" of poetry basically, just as he later began to "re-recognize the tradition."

Second, Ren Hongyuan's position as an academic poet is also the key to his rejection of the superficiality in the poetry community at the end of the 20th century. The inherent tranquility, stability, and self-contained lifestyle of the academia distinguished him drastically from those poets who are non-academics.

At the end of the 20th century, the noisy debates among Chinese poets revealed the anxiety that came along with "embracing the world" during the last moments of the 20th century, which caused the impetuousness of poetry writing. Among the bustling crowds, Ren Hongyuan is quite lonely, "Those who are ten years older than me experienced the vague remnants of the postmodernism ebb in the 1940s, and those who are ten years younger than me happened to catch up amid the raging 80s. I lost both ends in isolation in the middle."[276] The 20th century was splendid, but he believed: "As long as the head of a generation of intellectuals is not at the mountains of Olympia, our 19th century has not yet finished."[277] Ren Hongyuan produced only a thin collection of poems after more than 30 years of hard work, including "The Horizon" in 1956, "The Second Universe" in 1957, "The Ancient Astronomy Site of Beijing" in 1966, "The Comet" of 1970, "Sail" in 1981, "The Earth, Rotating on My Shoulder" in 1982, "The Yangtze River" in 1985, a group of poems "Sima Qian's Second Genesis" in 1987, a group of poems "Chinese Characters, 2000" in 1988 and a group of poems ("Nü Wa 11 Images") in 1989. Besides, what is even more striking is that in the 30 years of his writing career, Ren Hongyuan's poetry style changed very little. From "The horizon line can't limit our vision" in 1956 to "the body of Xingtian without his head was erecting upright" in 1989, we recognize one of his consistent pursuits at a glance: the praise of individual life. Under the superficial atmosphere at the end of the century, his pursuit was more determined: "Why should we imitate others, saying "a lost generation," "a contemplative generation," "an angry generation," we are just a humiliated generation."[278] For poetry, loneliness is a kind of fortune. Perseverance is a rare, valuable quality. Ren Hongyuan's loneliness within the ivory tower and his long-standing persistence guaranteed he would not always chase after the change, nor would he turn a blind eye to the poetic difficulties of intercultural communication just because of the pressure of poetry writing.

Third, Ren Hongyuan is different from the poets who "embrace society," although he shared the sincerity of poetry and the persistence of poetry exploration. For example, Mu Dan's questioning and exploration of real life has never entered Ren Hongyuan's art world. The poet's refined intellectual temperament made him more willing to use poetry to push the suffering of survival to a distant state, although he had a hungry childhood. "Sichuan, in the deserted mountain village, except the grandmother's face, even the sunset that burned the green hills every day was cold." Ren Hongyuan was an orphan as a teen. "I did not have a father until 13 and not a mother until 40."[279] We see that Mu Dan is good at expressing the suffering of this kind of existence. For example, the inflation in 1945 became Mu Dan's subject: "Under your glory, justice only looks pitiful. /You are one spider web, only the locusts in the center, / If we want to live, they must die, / the weather is fine, your rule must be cleared!" ("Inflation"). The urban life in 1976 made him feel, "This is not a beautiful city, / in the corner of its dust, / like a spider weaving a net in the cave, / some people's lives intersect like spider threads. / I will be tied to that web, / I'm entangled: there is trouble here, / there is the empty hope there" ("Differences"). But, we can only see most glimpses of suffering in Ren Hongyuan's poems, such as the lonely figure that visited the ancient astronomy site ("The Ancient Astronomy Site of Beijing") or one distant comet split the sky ("Comet"). It is not that Ren Hongyuan turned a blind eye to the reality of suffering, but because he was more accustomed to pushing the judgment of reality to the distance, or to dislodging from the entanglement of reality to show his understanding of life and calling for his life's ideal. Using his own words, it is because "I don't want to kneel on the ground again." He always wrote poems of heaven. At the same time, it was also difficult to decline completely the traditional poetics as a poet who completed the literary enlightenment in the aesthetic conception of "Spring River Moonlight Night." Especially, after decades of isolation from classical poetics since 1949, poets like Ren Hongyuan were emotionally hoping to regain nutrition from traditional poetics. Compared to Mu Dan who was more radical toward Westernization, these poets would certainly strive to make a modern revival of Chinese traditional spirits.

In addition, Ren Hongyuan, who matured in the 1990s, also had more cultural thoughts than the poets during the 1920s and 1930s. It seems the "Chinese-Western poetry and art integration" that Wen Yiduo and Bian Zhilin relished was unable to completely represent the poet's choice of poetics because the "Chinese-Western integration" in the history of modern poetry is a relaxed "long-term tradition of intentional connection with Chinese poetry." The final destination is Chinese classical poetics which is bridged by the integration of Chinese and Western cultures.[280] On the one hand, Ren Hongyuan was touched by such a reality:

> While Chinese poets broke from the classical traditions and returned to the Western romantics and Modernists, Imagery school poets, such as Pound, were fascinated by Chinese classical poetics, and even regarded Chinese classical poetry as a tradition of their modernism … In the unprecedented, vast vision of contemporary Chinese poets, the horizontal look and the inevitable vertical review interacted. Then, the modern discovery of the aesthetics of Chinese classical poetry began like finding a lost world and discovering surprises.[281]

However, on the other hand, Ren Hongyuan, while pleasantly surprised, was worried because he felt the same pressure from the traditional culture at the same time: "We are only lingering in the literature of predecessors. The more we lost ourselves there, the farther we are from the reality of nature and the reality of life."[282] In his view, Xiang Yu's killing of himself is the last glory of traditional Chinese life. "Our life is beginning to age." The poetic achievements of the predecessors are precisely the trap for people today.

> After Qu Yuan wrote about the sunset of Mount Kunlun, it was difficult for you to have your sunrise. After Zhuangzi flew with his Kun Peng bird, you had difficulty in having your sky and flying. Under the Taishan Mountain of Confucius, you have already had difficulty becoming a mountain. With Li Bai's Yellow River and Su Shi's Yangtze River, it is difficult to be water. The chrysanthemum of Tao Yuanming of the Jin Dynasty blosomed and the flowers of your life will fade.[283]

These kinds of heavy cultural experiences come from the historical conservation of Ren Hongyuan as a scholar. It is the reserve of a scholar's historical wealth that makes him apart from the simple innocence of poets; thus, becoming more loaded, calmer, and even more difficult. Unlike his poetry friend Jiang He's obsession with his ancient dreams, Ren Hongyuan constantly questioned,

> Returning to the ancient East for transcendence is always an adventure for the modern soul. Perhaps, Jiang He was not clear whether he reached a kind of tranquility beyond the conflict and the solemnity of looking down at suffering or the stillness and silence, which drowned the impulse of modern life.[284]

In this way, in the so-called Chinese-Western integration, "returning to the East" still cannot represent Ren Hongyuan's voice. This can be seen as a conceptual disagreement between the movement of the times and the development of knowledge in an academic poet, even though they both use the China and the West dichotomy of thinking.

"Double Transcendence"

Ren Hongyuan would not ignore the contradictions between Chinese and Western poetry just for writing purposes, nor was he a stubborn xenophobe. He had doubts about the simple "return to the East," but it was impossible for him to deny the tradition and go with "Westernization." Then, how did he approach the poetics issue of academic poets? I believe Ren Hongyuan's new strategy was to accept both sides and then transcend both. Specifically, he held an open attitude to the West but was not limited by it. He was brave to criticize Chinese historical traditions and tried to explore them. Using poetic language, he portrayed the interaction of the Yangtze River and the Pacific Ocean. He should be the new shore of the mainland. Behind his back was the source and flow of the Yangtze River for thousands of years; in front were the vast tides of the Pacific Ocean. Facing the two sides of the river and the sea, contemporary Chinese poetry will hopefully achieve a double transcendence between Western modernism and Eastern classical poetics.[285]

Ren Hongyuan not only read Turgenev, Pushkin, and Lermontov, but also Whitman, Pound, Elytis, and Eliot. It is worth noting he "recovered the long-destroyed Tang poetry 'imagery' from Pound, recognized tradition and returned to the East in Elytis," and confirmed Zhuangzi's "instant eternity" in Eliot's "a simultaneous coexistence."[286] These Western poets (especially modern Western poets) pushed Ren Hongyuan to his poetry maturity. This contradictory maturity showed he had never been willing to be at the mercy of any Westerners. "A glimpse of Pound helped me regain my "imagery" and I hurriedly returned for fear of being lost again .... Walking into the wasteland of others can't help you escape your wasteland." He even boldly questioned: "Is there no more poet since Elliot? Otherwise, how can modern poets simply give up the spirituality of poetry so easily and strenuously lift the heavy thinking that philosophers have long desired to lay down?"[287] Reading through poetry written by Ren Hongyuan, we see that most of the images are not from the West but from the Chinese culture—Wang Wei's sunset, Zhuangzi's butterfly, Tao Qian's chrysanthemum, Li Bai's moon, various kinds of Chinese calligraphy writing styles such as Zhuan, Li, Kai and Cao and other ancient Chinese characters; Sima Qian and characters under his pen; Nü Wa

(According to one legend she was the creator of mankind) who mended the sky, the decapitated Xingtian, and others. An enthusiasm for life originated from Western romantic poetics and is realized through pure Chinese culture. In such moments, even the flashing Western images (Sphinx, Prometheus) submerged in the vast ocean of Chinese imageries, became a description of the Chinese cultural landscape:

> Sphinx
> Kneeling next to the pyramid on the bank of the Nile
> Asking the world
> > Mystery of the ages
> > An eternal question
> > I answer
> I answer with the mended sky
> I answer with the myriad forms of life created by the yellow dirt.
> > > —"Nü Wa 11 Images"

Nü Wa interpreted intuitive "human beings" with her magnificent life creation. The philosophical thinking of the Sphinx added to the cultural significance of Eastern practice. This is the transcendence of Western poetics.

Ren Hongyuan's rebellion against Chinese traditional culture is also obvious. In a certain sense, "anti-culture" is the inevitable trend of his breaking away from historical chains. "The problems of our survival in this land are not whether we can go into history, but whether we can get out of it."[288] However, Ren Hongyuan clearly distinguished himself from the "anti-culture" of the third-generation poets: "After all, people are "cultural animals." Life without culture and lifeless culture are not the essence of human beings. Isn't real poetry a life that rises to culture and culture transforms into life?"[289] That is to say, Ren Hongyuan did not rebel against the culture itself, but by presenting the decadence of tradition to activate (or create) a new life and a new culture.

How did Ren Hongyuan activate and how did he create? Ren Hongyuan first "restored" the "era of Nü Wa." At the time, this long history had not yet unfolded and the great pressure of culture had not yet come to a living life. The world was a wasteland. History and culture were a virgin land waiting for our exploration.

> The time surges from ahead / It rushed over today, rushed over/ I fell into the history of my 20-year-old, 30-year-old, and 40-year-old .... Drifting past the earliest history record / on the edge of the myth, the first moon rise / The first autumn / the first Nanshan / the first glass of wine" (*Time, Surging from ahead*). I became the first person in all history and culture! I became the creator of the Creator Nü Wa!

So far, his latest and most proud group of poems is "Nü Wa 11 Images" in which Ren Hongyuan presented us with a magnificent and grand creation picture, or more accurately, the picture of the poet's own life for the first time without any restraint. My head is coming out of the body of the beast as if it was a new round of sun for the world. The beast died and the first horizon appeared in front of the standing man. "I began with the world." The world "waited for me to name." I created life and history like God created the world. I solved secrets about people with the practice of life and even used my skull to hold ideas for 500,000 years later in the 21st century. Nü Wa is the one who has free thoughts. "It was the 'I' who owned the second universe: 'There is a fire in my mind / Kunlun snow is no longer just a white past. It is restored as hot rain from the sky. / It is restored into wavy flames'" ("Yangtze River"). "I am young. Every day I am nearing completion/one round of the sun, throwing it in the West/I am re-creating/turning to the East every day, I'm always facing a round in the East /new sun rising for me" ("Earth, Turning on My Shoulders"). "Restoration" is a recurring discourse in Ren Hongyuan's poetry, a spiritual trace tracked by the poet through history. Nü Wa is the avatar of the poet's own life dating from prehistoric times. In retrospection of thought, the material world also presented its original features (the stones in the Kunlun Mountain are restored to water and fire). For today's human beings, restoration also means a new creation and a new departure. So, the Pioneer No. 2 spacecraft flying away from the solar system is also a restoration. "Restoration is his and her first hieroglyph / human earth cannot explain this word / a search with no return / a nameless call" ("The Earth Cannot Explain This Word").

Ren Hongyuan not only longed for the freest creation in "restoration," but also tried to re-infuse history with modern life and activate our ancient tradition: "Life is only today" and "History is the experience of exhausting today . . . History is today rewritten . . . It is no longer Sima Qian who let me walk into his *Historical Records*, but I let Sima Qian and his children in *Historical Records* walk into my day."[290] Such "recognition of tradition" is still a kind of creation in the "restoration." The stone girl on the Daning River has nothing to do with any legend. "You are my discovery. I created you . . . . You are a statue I have carved / a dream / a beautiful concept /As my monument, representing today" ("Wuxi Girl"). Sima Qian "came into history for the second time" and "became a male creationist." *Historical Records* became "a record of history forever" ("Sima Qian's Castration Made Him a Male Creationist"). The men and women in *Historical Records* with the modern spirit interpretation seem full of vitality, away from the deadly historical tombs, each with its irreplaceable meaning of life. Xiang Yu's suicide near the Wu River preserves freedom of mind, and Wu Zixu (died 484 BCE, a model of loyalty in Chinese culture) "spent the darkest night in exchange for hundreds of years of glory," Nie Zheng (a Chinese Assassin who lived during the Warring States period) disfigured his face because he had the courage to "face himself," Gao Jianli (a musician who was made blind by Qin Shi Huang, emperor of the Qin State) "saw everything" because of blindness. Sun Bin (author of *The Art of Warfare* who lived during the Warring States period) "completely released himself" and became the man who "pursued the world" after feet disability ... The past is finally connected with the survival of modern people. And history created the future for us.

Ren Hongyuan's desire for creative "restoration" and "re-recognition of tradition" is presented in his language consciousness. He named his first collection of poems *The Language of Nü Wa*. The group of poems, "Chinese Characters, 2000," is at the beginning of the collection, which is particularly eye-catching. He deeply believed for a cultural person (poet), the "burden of all historical culture" is the burden of language. The titles of poems have clearly shown Ren Hongyuan's sensitivity to language pressure: "The Words, One After Another Brilliant into Wisdom of the Black Hole"; "The Sky is Old, the Atomic Cloud is Also the Original Cloud"; "Crossed the Ice and Snow of the Antarctic, Yet Can't Get to the End of the Autumn Border." It is under this premise that "restoration" and "recognition" are all meaningful. Ren Hongyuan's "restoration" is not simply a return to the ancient language state.

> Chinese, even ancient Chinese, can't save contemporary China ... Although the Chinese language has not completely died in terms of grammar, it has aged thousands of years: nouns don't mean anything. The verbs do not show movement. The adjectives lose their ability to modify. The quantifier words cannot quantify. The connectives are bound to themselves. The prepositions are dead in their positions.[291]

His restoration is to promote language for the first time, "Let language restore with life. Restore naming for the first time, restore the first adjective and the first movement."[292] In a word, he tried to break free from the language norms of his predecessors and rediscover the potential of the Chinese language, like his young daughter who named the new moon for the first time: "Words shoot down words / Naming for the first time / you as a new subject / a lonely birth / resist death through words / distant light years / recover all hieroglyphs" ("Words Shoot Down Words the New Moon First Named").

Still, the so-called "restoration" does not mean a return to an era where there was no language or culture. Restoration still needs and depends only on the characteristics of the Chinese. At this time, the freedom of super-grammar and super-logic of the Chinese language was also valued by Ren Hongyuan, "The Chinese language that has not completely died in terms of grammar is the talent of Chinese freedom."[293] In this sense, "restoration" and "recognition" have the same meaning. Restoration is the recognition of our mother tongue. We see a lot of new language forms with new meanings when reading Ren Hongyuan's poems.

For example, abstract words are used directly in the poems, interspersed with figurative words. Such language is a feature in Ren Hongyuan's poems: "the edge of Chinese characters," "the border of the character autumn," "the words' moon," "I just want to walk into a Chinese character," "I never throw a Chinese character / into the ellipse orbit of a star," "You are a new subject." Abstraction expands the semantic category of poetry and figurative language gives abstraction a basis for feeling.

In another set of examples, the parts of the speech of words are used creatively in the original Chinese contexts. Nouns are used in the position of adjectives or adjectives and function as verbs. For instance: "the *youth-ed* words," "the atomic cloud also *primitives* that cloud." "Cao Xueqin movement of words," "*lonely* into deep autumn," "beautiful every woman," "*intoxicated* in her song," "forty-eight kinds of curves, *curved* me."

For another set of examples, the poet rearranged the language from time to time, which constituted an unprecedented sequence of language: in "Red Mansions Dream Wakes Up," the word "dream" is embedded between "Mansions" and "Wakes Up," which has dual functions. The former refers to the text of a famous work and the second part refers to the poet's understanding of it, which can be said to be a combination of words. In addition, there is also the dismantling of words, such as "his every round of the moon / is still the same circle (*zhao-jiu*, the literal meaning is shine on the same old circle)" ("The Moon, A Circle Can't be Deconstructed"). Here in Chinese, "*zhao-jiu*" can function as one word meaning "remain the same," but when the "*jiu*" is connected with "circle" it implies the circle of the moon is still the same, causing the meaning of the word "*zhao-jiu*" to greatly expand. There is also the horizontal arrangement of words vertically arranged:

So many words
The moon has depressed my starry sky
None

> Fall from the sky
> Eclipse
> 　—"Words Shoot Down Words, the New Moon Named for the First Time"

The vertical arrangement lengthens the psychological time at which the words stay with the reader. The arrangement presents a subtle correspondence. The longer stay time of the fall and eclipse implies the poet bears the pressure of writing and the anxiety of eagerness for language freedom. The fall and eclipse, respectively, highlight their respective semantics, which cannot be achieved by simple horizontal arrangement.

The restoration and re-recognition of language constitute the "Ren Hongyuan Movement" of words, which is Ren Hongyuan's solution to the linguistic problems in 20th-century poetry.

Of Life and Culture

Ren Hongyuan's poetic ideal is built on the "double transcendence of Western modernism and Eastern classical poetics." Then, what is the basis of his double transcendence? I believe this is the word he repeatedly emphasizes—life. Although he repeatedly sighed with pain, "I am only being read and written, and being read and written by other people's words," he still pinned his hopes on "changing the order of the language subject. 'I' was born for the second time," because "when all the words are moved, chased, and hit by the subject, it is a moment of glimpse of light in the darkness of life in the language." Here, the meaning of the birth of the subject "I" is to peek into the darkness of life. Cao Xueqin's literary talent has been turned into poetry in the "Cao Xueqin movement of the words shift" by Ren Hongyuan. In his view, "Cao Xueqin is the first Chinese who looked back to reflect on life."[294] Reading Ren Hongyuan's poetry, we can clearly understand that in the "Cao Xueqin movement of words shift" the "Ren Hongyuan Movement of Words" actually displayed for us to break free again and again from the stagnant literary history, break the chain of words, re-summon the effort of word freedom with the new subject "I." All these efforts "I" create the world with Nü Wa, "named" the world together; "I" was born together with Sima Qian, suicide together with Xiang Yu at Wu River. They all highlighted a living life in the poetic world. It is the resurrection, and the vigorous, posture of life that temporarily announced the end of Western Modernism and the East classical poetics. Life has its own world. The "metaphysical" theory of glory is lost in the development of life regardless it is the West or classic!

It is "the unrest and vigor of life" that encourages Ren Hongyuan's desire to create. Similarly, the search for the independent meaning of life allows him to discover the new "Eastern wisdom." "Eastern" is no longer just an atmosphere, a sense of harmony and peace, but a reaffirmation of people. He believed: "With the wisdom of the East and the transcendental inheritance preserved in Chinese, Chinese poets can easily complete 'the return of people'." "The wisdom of the East is the talent of Chinese poets. Its center is time wisdom—the non-religious, even super-authentic, and clear life experience of time. Time consciousness is the first consciousness of life. The meaning of life is also in the meaning of time ... The meaning of life offered by the 'lifetime' of China's classical poetics, is far clearer than the 'Dasein' of Heidegger's modern existential philosophy."[295]

However, Ren Hongyuan, a poet immersed in the light of his own life, had to face the pressure of culture all the time and experienced a tremendous restraining power of culture for the free extension of life. In Ren Hongyuan's writing, the pressure of this culture was often described as the language of countless cultural imprints and inheritors. Human life cannot be separated from the forms of established culture, and all the poet's feelings must be subject to the culture constructed by language—the second nature:

> We were born into the language. Our whole lives are exile of a word and we can no longer escape from the border of a word. We reconstruct our second nature in language. From then on, we have eyes that look at the world through language and listen to the world through language. Our senses grow in the language. Losing language, we will be blind, and deaf, and all our senses will die.[296]

Or in the language of poetry, it is "After Zhuang Zi's Kunpeng the big bird/ I have difficulty in having my sky and flying. After Qu Yuan embraces the sunset of Mount Kunlun, I have difficulty having my second sunrise. Under the Mount Tai of Confucius, I have difficulty becoming a mountain. In Li Bai's Yellow River, and Su Shi's Yangtze River, it is difficult to be water. The chrysanthemum of the Jin Dynasty bloomed, and the flowers of my life will fade" ("I Just Want to Walk into a Chinese Character, Read and Write Repeatedly for Life and Death").

The contradiction between life and culture (language) was so dazzlingly presented to Ren Hongyuan and was more eye-catching because of his identity as an academic intellectual. On the one hand, in his pursuit of life freedom, he had experienced the pressure and erosion of culture (including the academic culture). He almost denied himself when this kind of pressure became unbearable for him. He shouted:

> I hate "writing in the study" and "writing in the library" very much. Don't you think there are too many books produced by books? I want to write from ... the body to the book. I just like to write the feeling that has become Chinese characters. I want to try, to turn "concepts" into "experiences", turn "thinking" into "experience", and turn "discourse" into "narrative". Is there a possibility theoretically to do such?[297]

But on the other hand, survival as an academic intellectual required him to be connected with the "study" and "library" all the time. Even more importantly, his mind had to suffer repeatedly from a large amount of cultural information from the "study" and "library," such as the historical stories about Nü Wa and Sima Qian. The words about Roland Barthes and Jacques Derrida were also "traces" indelible by the academic culture. We even find the topics that Ren Hongyuan, a poet who was so obsessed with life, often talked about—the topics of poetics and the topics of poetry were still culture. His interpretation of culture seemed to be more thorough and incisive compared with his many vivid, rich feelings about life.

The contradiction between the realization of life and cultural norms is a universal conflict for Chinese academic poets during the 20th century. Wen Yiduo felt the sharp contradiction between his cultural ideals and his real feelings deeply during the period when he wrote *Dead Water*. He finally revealed the difficult artistic dream to the world by giving up poetry writing. Since then, Wen Yiduo evolved from "academic-oriented" to "society-oriented." Bian Zhilin's poetry as a "cultural" reference value is more important than the impact of his art. The cultural value of Bian Zhilin's poetry art is at the expense of his intentional or unintentional "omission" of the reality of existence. When reading Ren Hongyuan's poems, while we can appreciate some of his singular "word movements" and beautiful cultural images, we might also have the impression that the "double transcendence" pursued by him is more a search for an attempt at other possibilities than an accomplished reality.

Let us continue to pay attention to the academic poet Ren Hongyuan as well as other contemporary Chinese poets to see how they enter the 21st century with their sincere artistic exploration, because as Ren Hongyuan said:

> Now, we are at the end of a century. There has never been such a bright end of a century. God who has died in this century does not have to die again in the next century. The culture that has collapsed in this century does not have to collapse again in the next century.[298]

Lu Xun: "Cheering for New Poetry" against Tradition

> If you believe in the past, go back yourself.
> If you believe in the future, come with me.
>
> —Lu Xun, "People and Time"

Strictly speaking, Lu Xun is not a member of the Chinese new poetry history. However, at the beginning of the new Chinese poetry's break away from the "classical tradition," we witnessed his "cheering and support," or in his own words, "drumming the side drum" (being supportive). Facts proved this "drumming" was not a work of the scene, nor a boring pastime from onlookers. Instead, it contained many intriguing thoughts, especially for those deeply involved in poetry and style creation. Lu Xun's soberness and wisdom as a peripheral observer deserve our considerable attention. In the face of "traditions," Lu Xun's choice of refusal is inspiring. At least, this is another important way to transform traditional pressures and start new artistic traditions.

Lu Xun did not deny his position in the modern novel world, nor did he deny his research results in classical literature. He also showed his sympathy for some essays some people despised, and even defended his own "rigid translation." But he never admitted he was a modern poet, and never positioned himself as a theoretical authority in the modern poetry research community. He wrote several new poems, but emphasized he "does not enjoy writing new poems," just "playing the drum and having some fun."[299]

He commented on modern poetry sometimes, but he also repeatedly stressed that he was a layman[300] who did no research.[301] I believe such statements should not be regarded as simple modesty. In a certain sense, this is precisely Lu Xun's sincere self-report of his artistic ideal. In other words, Lu Xun realized the distance between his artistic preference and poetry, and thus, avoided it promptly. Naturally, these occasional writings, these few comments, and such conscious alienation from poetry may not be thought of high cultural value. But, it can inspire us at least. There is an indirect relationship between Lu Xun and the Chinese poetry tradition. It is more like mutual exploration and mutual dialogue under certain rational control. If the artist and the language form are essentially a dialogue relationship, then the dialogue between Lu Xun and the Chinese poetry tradition is completely rational. Lu Xun limited his involvement in the artistic world of Chinese new poetry, but he took this involvement as part of the grand goal of exploring modern Chinese culture and regarded it as a sample of rational research of

Chinese culture. He used its success or failure as an artistic display of the difficult transformation of Chinese culture from tradition to modernity. Lu Xun built the relationship between him and modern new poetry not from the perspective of pure poetry, but from the perspective of culture. He pondered and made choices of Chinese poetry tradition. In this rational dialogue, Lu Xun's new poetry writings and reviews are unique, and could not be measured with a single poetic standard.

I believe that only by fully affirming the logical premise of the dialogue will it be possible to make a new, useful interpretation of the true relationship between Lu Xun and the Chinese poetry tradition.

Rationality and Dialogue

The view that Lu Xun wrote new poetry mainly in 1918 and 1919 excludes the four "simulated folk songs" including the "*Introduction to Eryi Collection*" in 1928 and the "*Songs of Good Things*" in the 1930s. Strictly speaking, Lu Xun only wrote six or seven pieces. This period is the first peak after Lu Xun embarked on the literary road. In two years, he also wrote five novels, two long essays, more than 30 short essays and notes, and seven prose poems, translations, and several ancient text studies. Along with the publication of the first three new poems in the *New Youth* are the later, well-known masterpiece works, "A Madman's Diary," "Kong Yiji," "Medicine," "Tomorrow," "A Small Incident," etc. which are mature works. Among his essays, there are famous pieces, such as "My Opinion on Chastity" and "How to Be a Father Now." In terms of the quantity and quality of the works, these six new poems in Lu Xun's overall writing are insignificant. More importantly, I think this shows Lu Xun himself did not intend to consider them as important as his novels and even sociological commentaries. In his own words, this is "only because the poetry was lonely at that time, so I played the drum to cheer people and once those poets appeared, I would stop playing."[302] I think this self-report vividly depicted the rational spirit of the author's involvement in the new world of poetry and the overall cultural concept that transcends poetry. On the one hand, as an important part of new culture growth, the new poetry practice can best show the modern trend when resisting the traditional literature, which had a relative advantage of poetry culture. Therefore, Lu Xun, like other new literary writers at the time, attempted to use the achievements and the power of poetry "to consolidate the status of new literature." On the other hand, when new poetry became accepted by the world as part of modern culture (some people are called "poets"), when some "aspiring people" admire the virgin land of new poetry and claimed themselves poets, Lu Xun once again withdrew wisely from it. This entry and withdrawal is not a poet's emotional activity, but a prudent, mature intellectual's rational thinking and careful choice of history, future, and self. Lu Xun always deliberately put himself at such a distance that was convenient for dialogue.[303]

In Lu Xun's practice of new poetry, the effects of this rationalism and dialogue are twofold. First, the "non-rhyming" characteristics of Lu Xun's new poetry, which is very eye-catching, are different from the essence of the so-called "poetry." What is "poetry"? This is probably one of the many concepts difficult to pinpoint in human culture. Of course, this book does not focus on its interpretation. But in the sense of rhetoric, it is universally understood there is a distinction between verses and proses. This distinction is particularly rooted in Chinese literature and has a decisive significance. In Chinese literature, the essence of poetry as rhythmed means a series of formal features, such as rhyme, metrics, coupling, and rhythm. Therefore,

> ... According to this, it is known that the metrics are a necessary condition for poetry. At least it can be recognized that the formal feature is a major condition for the verses. Especially the Chinese verses, where the differences with prose depend on the rhythm and format in any case.[304]

We see that Lu Xun's new poetry showed many characteristics of "non-rhyming" different from these inherent poetic standards in many aspects:

1. Prose tendency of sentence patterns. In the selection of sentence style, Lu Xun's new poetry has more narrative prose-like verses, such as "The spring rain is over, the sun is very good, and I just had a walk in the garden ... . The peach blossom is so angry that her face reddened like the 'Famous Concubine Yang'" ("Peach Blossom"). "When they were taking home, they added some extra color to the holder with the reflections on their face." "These verses were very different from traditional Chinese verses, such as 'Over old trees wreathed with rotten vines fly evening crows.'"
2. Very distinct logic in semantics. For example, "When the previous dream is squeezing out the dream before the previous dream, the dream after drove away the previous dream" ("Dream"). The logic is quite clear. In "Peach Blossom," there is "I said, Excellent! 'Peach blossom red, Plum blossom white.' (Instead of saying peach blossoms are not as white as plum blossom)." Lu Xin even used brackets to make his

meaning explicit and several levels of thinking are displayed to readers, thus leaving little room for the imagination.
3. The "hard" processing of rhyme. Lu Xun's new poetry paid much attention to rhyme, with one rhyme for the entire poem, or a change of rhymes in the middle. But, it seemed difficult to understand his rhymes, which often showed the inflexibility of rational control. For example, "God of Love":

> A little boy, unfolding his wings in the air,
> With an arrow in one hand and bow in another,
> Somehow, an arrow hit the chest.

The three consecutive sentences all rhymed "ong" in Chinese, it appears to be crisp and neat but lacks the necessary twists and turns found in poetry in a way. "Inflexibility" is more negative than positive here.

4. The arbitrariness of poetry and tone structures. The melody of Chinese poetry stems from its organic treatment of the word beats. There are many monosyllabic words in classical literature, so its beat always falls on a single word, which leads to the "*Ping-Ze (flat-or-fall)*" flow change of the words. According to this law, the modern vernacular has a large number of two-syllable and three-syllable words, so its beat should naturally fall on simple words, or fall on compound words. Because of this, "*flat-fall* patterns would be realized through 'pauses.'"[305] Correspondingly, the "pauses" of the vernacular new poetry generally remain roughly the same in the corresponding two sentences. For example, He Qifang's *Prophecy*: "You must / come from / the /warm / south! /Tell me / the moonlight / there, the daylight / there!" There are five pauses in each of the two sentences; in addition, the number of words constituting each pause of the same sentence is preferably different. The number of words for the corresponding pauses in different sentences must be different, especially the ending pause. In Bian Zhilin's words, the "humming type" of three-character and the two-character "reciting type" should be used in balance.[306] For example, we can divide these two sentences in Xu Zhimo's "Season and Climate" as follows: the first sentence "but / spring flowers / had long become / mud," the second sentence "spring breeze / also / had been / long gone." For the first sentence, its rhythm is the singer-song type "one-two-three-one" (one character and three-character), and for the second sentence its rhythm is the speech type "two-one-two-two." Within

each sentence, there are also variations; thus, creating a corresponding flow.

Quite different from the inherent tone and melody structure of Chinese poetry, Lu Xun's new poetry did not pay much attention to the equal number of pauses, such as "A little boy, with curling hair, / on his silvery yellow face there is slightly red,—looks like he is the hope" ("Their Garden"). There is a big pause difference between the two sentences with fewer variations and corresponding flows. For example, in "People and Time": "If you believe in the past, you return yourself. If you believe in the future, come with me." Both sentences use the same two-character pauses in the original.

All in all, I think because Lu Xun maintained a highly stable, distance-oriented rational attitude from the moment he was involved in the new poetry writing, it was not as easy for him to be stirred and excited as some poets around that period. His uniqueness and unbelievable rationality distinguished him from those who were ruled by their emotional impulses. If in the overall framework of literary writing, the uniqueness of poetry is just the uniqueness of style, the uniqueness of language structure, and the uniqueness of domain writing, the emotional impulses that made our poets excited are the meaningful forms of the poetry language and poetry style. If this is the case, then, Lu Xun is someone who is hard to excite by the inherent stylistic features of Chinese poetry. Under the unmistakable condition of the Chinese language, in the cultural atmosphere of the "expected structure" of Chinese poetry, Lu Xun's new poetry is indeed far from our mental requirements. His excessively strong cultural rationalism restrained and twisted his sensibility and manipulation of the language of the new poetry. Therefore, Lu Xun indeed cannot be regarded as a "true" modern poet.

Divergence from Early Vernacular New Poetry

Strong cultural rationalism distanced itself from Chinese poetry culture in the sense of cultural introspection and cultural comparison. Therefore, it almost decisively led to the rebellion against the poetry ideal. Therefore, we can also see that early poets, such as Hu Shih, Liu Bannong, Zhou Zuoren, etc. are mostly a group of rationalists who were keen on culture. They shared many similarities with Lu Xun in the new poems. Hu Shih said: "Where does the poetry revolution begin? It is necessary to write poetry as prose" ("Preface to *Experimental Collection*").

However, it should be noted this similarity is only one aspect of the issue. As a product of cultural rationalism, Lu Xun's new poems are profoundly different from other early vernacular new poems. If early, new poetry shares the features of being shallow and straightforward, Lu Xun's poems dug deeper. If we say Lu Xun drew on the inherent folk color of medieval poetry to oppose the rigid literati, he seemed reluctant to give up the literati's cultivation and mind. If reference to the ancient poetry works is a customary practice, then Lu Xun did not do it. Although Lu Xun's new poems provide some unfamiliar experiences for readers, including many of the above-mentioned "non-rhyming" and "non-poetic" features, we can never say these works are superficial and childish, or not worth mentioning (similar judgment can be applied to some early new poems). In fact, in Lu Xun's new poems, we can feel the emotional messages and spiritual heights that cannot be entailed by traditional poetry. "Dream" made a delicate, layered expression of the unconscious world of dreams and chaos, unique in the new poetry at this time.[307] (Some commentators who try to find the realism of "dreams" from all sides, I am afraid, would find it difficult to understand the uniqueness of this poem.) "God of Love" is like a declaration of modern love: "If you love someone, you could love him hard. /If you don't love anyone, you can die yourself hard." It is hard to accept the extreme sentiment of "rather dies than have no love" in a "gentle, honest" poetry tradition. "Peach Blossom" is an allusion to the Chinese people's relationship that values hypocrisy rather than sincerity in Chinese society. It is unprecedented to use gorgeous peach blossoms to hint at narrow-minded people. "Their Garden" describes the hard time a little boy experienced when he received a lily from the neighbors, hinting at the difficult journey for a generation of young people transplanting into exotic cultures. "People and Time" demonstrates the passerby style outlook of facing reality directly, embracing life.

Among these new poems, the most confusing and difficult to understand is "He." The "rusty iron chain" in the first paragraph seems to indicate that "he" is in the house, but the "window curtain is open" in the second paragraph showed he is not there. Why? There is no answer in the third paragraph. "If come back this is still my home." What does this mean? Some people think that "he" is a "fantasy"; "I" is "some young people who are addicted to fantasy." And "If come back this is still my home" is "the rule that one should return to sober reality." I think it is somewhat reasonable to reveal the existence of "he" as "untouchable," but whether the pursuit of "I" is "unimaginable" should be further discussed. The imagery of the chains and the white wall in the poem contains some of incomprehensible conceptions that cannot be explained by pure fantasy. Some think "he" is a new thought introduced into China and the three stanzas of the poem described the unfortunate fate of this new thought in feudal China—imprisoned, exiled, and buried.[308] I think this interpretation is more in line with the general state of mind, but it seems the poetry is too real. The biggest feature of Lu Xun's poem is to create a fascinating atmosphere hard to pin down. "He" is a kind of beautiful, valuable thing in "I" ("like flowers"), rather than a fantasy hard to pinpoint (thus, we could understand it as the advanced Western culture or thoughts), but "he" does not exist in the reality around us, but mainly exists in the thinking and feeling of "I"—"He fell asleep in the room" is just what "I" feel, "I" think he should fall asleep in the room (in fact, a self-comfort in the subconsciousness). So after all, no one is there when the window is open in autumn (or we also think that "he" is indeed in the house in the summer, but time has passed, and "he" has left.) In this way, the "I" who is still obsessed with "him" searched for him in the snow, but then quickly gave up. "He is like a flower. How would it be worthwhile here for him!" This seems to contain the fear of "I" in the face of the cold of the wilderness. In the end, "it's better to go back and find him." It also shows "I" have no idea about his whereabouts; thus, "I" could invent a reason to return home. In Chinese culture, "home" has a special symbolic meaning. This "I" pursued what he wanted with hardship by leaving home but ended with feeling comfort with "return to my home." This is a tragedy from self-transcendence to conformity. *He* is the whole process of how "I" got excited and summoned for the ideal, but finally gave up the ideal. In the more idealistic sense, we can also interpret it as a typical relationship between modern China and Western culture.

Lu Xun accommodated such a profound, rational spirit and cultural awareness, which indicated his ingenuity. From this, we see Lu Xun's break from the taboo and deviance in the inherent stylistic features of poetry are intentional after rational thinking. He seems to break the boundaries of poetry and narrative style deliberately to seek new development in poetry. For example, narrative and logical prose-style sentences are used instead of the "intentional" blank space of traditional poetry. The poems explore from space beauty to time beauty. New rhythm forms are used to break the traditional rhymes to set up new forms. These stylistic transformations, although it cannot be said they are successful, provide a way of thinking. At least they show Lu Xun has deep thoughts on the development of modern Chinese new poetry. This development of new poetry with cultural reflection was rarely tried then and later. This is also the second most important effect of Lu Xun's unique rationalism and exploration. Cultural rationalism is not only a way of thinking, but also the conscious goal of the development of thought. That is, all choices must make new estimates and new rational decisions under the overall goal of progress within the general goal in cultural reflection, cultural comparison, and cultural progress. This is the profound difference between Lu Xun and other general rationalists. For example, for Hu Shih and other cultural rationalists engaged in early, new poem writing, ration functions mainly in a form of thought in their new poem writings rather than far-reaching cultural orientation. Therefore, in practice, they rarely used the results of cultural reflection. There is little Lu Xun-style cultural meaning in their works and they quickly gave up all efforts of "prose as poetry" after the failure of the rational operation. Then, the ideas that they thought of as new poetry still fell into the categories of classical poetics.

Lu Xun was different. His goal was always the same. His pursuit remained unchanged. In the difficulties caused by the rational twist, he went deeper into thinking. Therefore, even if it is a mistake, it is also a profound mistake. Zhu Ziqing, editor of the *Chinese New Literature Collection*, insisted "only the Lu Xun brothers are completely free from the traditional chains."[309] Even Hu Shih admitted the early vernacular newcomers "are mostly born out of oldstyle poetry, Cis, and Qus" except for "the Zhou Brothers from Kuaiji."[310] It is very rare for an intellectual who did not intend to become a poet, to receive such positive comments from these two experts.

Lu Xun's New Poetry Criticism: An Evaluation

In an article "Can't Tell" in 1924, Lu Xun said,

> I think the most proper for critics is not to write poems at the same time. You might be happy if you bring your pen like a sword and sweep all the weeds in the literary world. However, if you think there is no poem in the world and you start to write, you might produce something like: "How vast is the universe? I can't tell; /How deep is parents' grace? I can't tell; / Love of the one who loves, I can't tell. /Ah, oh, oh, oh, I can't tell!"[311]

This passage was written under a particular context when Zhou Lingjun, a critic who wrote "Deleting Poems," dismissed almost all the popular poem collections of the time as "poor," "not poems," or "immature work," but his poems are mostly "cannot tell" type. However, I still believe the meaning of such "critique" is limited. If considering the context, Lu Xun did not overthrow Zhou Lingjun's basic arguments (such as his evaluation of the new poetry), but merely refined a rule in a relaxed manner: "I thought the critics ...." Compared with the sharpness he wrote in his essays, this critique is much milder. Such a concise summary is also the result of Lu Xun's reflection on his cultural path. Therefore, the stable relationship between critics and writers, especially poetry critics and poets, applies not only to Zhou Lingjun but also to Lu Xun.

Lu Xun's new poetry writing peaked between 1918 and 1919. At this time, he had no special criticism of the new poetry. Later, when he wrote as a critic, "The Enemy of Poetry," he had long since "washed his hands and stopped writing poems." Naturally, this is not an easy way to take refuge, but a choice made according to the situation. Or it can be said when Lu Xun discovered his consistent cultural rationalism made it difficult to work on new poetry writing, he turned to the field of new poetry criticism and new poetry theory exploration immediately. Of course, even at this time, poetry and new poetry had not become his main concern. The problem of new poetry is still part of Lu Xun's grand goal of transforming the old culture and building a new culture. The rationalism and dialogue posture at a distance is still an important way for him to enter the new poetry criticism and study new poetry theory. Because of this, Lu Xun's arguments on the new poems are piecemeal and indirect. There is no such strict system as some Lu Xun researchers have claimed. I even think some arguments are insufficiently accurate and inconsistent with modern poetics. However, compared with other grand criticisms of some "poetry philosophers" who wrote profusely, borrowed only from the West, or claimed to be learned from both the East and West, Lu Xun's piecemeal critics are self-contained and his unique cultural criticism often hits the nail on the head. He captures the key to the development of new poetry in the cultural sense. In this sense, it is not necessary to discuss a particular poetic conclusion. The value of Lu Xun's new poetry criticism and new poetry ideas are the values of his perspective, his thinking mode, and overall cultural progress.

To understand Lu Xun's new poetry criticism and new poetry theory, it is necessary to first identify Lu Xun's basic valuation of the achievements of Chinese modern poetry. Xu Zhimo has far-reaching influence on the history of Chinese modern poetry. "*The Goddesses* started a new chapter in the history of Chinese poetry, consolidated by *The Zhimo's Poetry* published shortly after."[312] The influence of Xu Zhimo on modern Chinese new poetry has surpassed that of Guo Moruo, author of *The Goddesses*. "Many scholars in the past who used to read Chinese traditional poems (*Ci, Qu*) and even Western poems without writing poems (such as Lin Yutang, etc.) believed the new poetry of the vernacular is poetry after they read Xu Zhimo's new poems."[313] It is striking that Lu Xun did not agree with the poetic style represented by Xu Zhimo from the beginning, including his poetics.[314] In 1934, he made it clear, "I don't like the poems, such as those written by Xu Zhimo."[315] Given Xu Zhimo's actual position and influence in the history of Chinese modern poetry, I think Lu Xun's attitude also determined his basic valuation of the overall achievements of Chinese modern poetry to a great extent. However, what deserves our deep thought is we do not attach great importance to this position for a long time and a variety of reasons. Or subconsciously, it may be difficult to understand and believe Lu Xun would make such a biased judgment! In 1987, a very important document of studies on Lu Xun, "Lu Xun's Talk with Snow in 1936" was disclosed. One of the questions caught our attention. In response to Edgar Snow's question, Lu Xun believed even the works of some of the finest Chinese modern poets "have nothing to praise, and they are just part of the experimentation .... So far, China's modern new poetry has not been successful."[316] From our inherent interpretation of the development of new poetry, it is natural for us to be puzzled by these arguments. Wang Yao recalled later, because of Lu Xun's poor evaluation of the new poetry, this document caused quite a stir in the Chinese literary and art fields.[317]

I think if people today still have difficulty understanding and accepting Lu Xun's conclusions on Chinese modern poetry, it shows how different our thinking and observational perspectives are from Lu Xun's. From the unique dimension of the modernity transformation of traditional culture, Lu Xun estimated the value of modern new poetry is modernity, which differentiates it from traditional poetics. Lu Xun believed the achievements of Chinese modern poetry can only be built on the transcendence of Chinese classical poetry. That is to say, its value should be manifested in its divorce from the ideal of classical poetics and into the visionary world of an unfamiliar nature. Its mediocrity means it does not come out of the trap of traditional culture.

From this point of view, the most important characteristic of Lu Xun's new poetry criticism is the historical perspective. All poetry phenomena in modern society should be re-examined in the long river of historical and cultural development. Xu Zhimo's poetry is a sign of the maturity of the new poetry. However, the "Parnassianism" represented by Xu's new poems is nothing more than the traditional Chinese *pianfu* style, a style in between prose and poem. Its historical limitations are quite obvious in terms of transcending traditional culture.

There are two basic trends in the production and acceptance of human art. The first is recognition. According to Jung's theory, artworks can resonate and excite millions of people because it shows the historical accumulation of our deeper hearts across generations. Without it, art cannot enter the hearts of traditional people; thus, losing the foundation of existence. However, on the other hand, if art is driven by acceptance, it will eventually become increasingly rigid and lose its vitality. Therefore, the second transcendence trend is also inevitable. In transcendence, art constantly seeks defamiliarization and the recipients continue to meet the new stimuli. Excellent works of art are the dialectical combination of such an acceptance, non-personalized tradition, and the rebellious tradition of personalization. According to Frye, it is the interaction of pure tradition and pure variability.[318] According to Eliot:

> Poetry is not a turning loose of emotion, but an escape from emotion; it is not the expression of personality, but an escape from personality. But, of course, only those who have personality and emotions know what it means to want to escape from these things.[319]

On another occasion, he also pointed out the most important task of poetry is to express feelings and emotions. Unlike thoughts, feelings, and emotions are personal, and thought is the same for all people.[320] Binary dialectical thinking has always been the basic thinking of Westerners, as well as in the so-called "non-personalized" and go-back-to-tradition modern trends. The Chinese classical poetics produced by the original yin and yang complement philosophy different. It pays more attention to mutual complementation, mutual explanation, and mutual utilization of things. In the development of poetry art, it tends to identify with traditions and consider the ideal of reviving traditional poetry as one's responsibility. According to the interpretation of Ye Xie (a literary critic in the early Qing Dynasty), it is the cycle of "if there is a root then there will be sprouts" and "trace the sprouts you will find the roots." From the *Book of Songs* to the poetry of the Song Dynasty, poetry "is just like the trees planted in the former era and finished its journey in the latter. Since the Song Dynasty, poetry is like flowers, which blossomed and then faded, blossomed again and faded again. Although there are layers of changes, it must be born from the roots."[321] Modern poets and poetry critics go back to traditional poetics on the road of nationalization, which is "born from the roots." In Lu Xun's view, such "returning to the roots" is tragic. He believed "all good poems have been written during the Tang Dynasty."[322] As a result, we distanced ourselves from Lu Xun's view of poetry and culture, and a barrier is set up with Lu Xun's thoughts.

A Critique of History and a Reflection of Reality

Then, what are the defects of the Chinese poetry tradition according to Lu Xun? Please read Lu Xun's comments on the *Book of Songs* and *Chu Ci*, the source of Chinese classical poetry.

> The three hundred poems in the *Book of Songs* are from the north of China, with the Yellow River as the center. . . . The people there were down-to-earth, so even though they were outspoken, they would respect ritual and righteousness; they were dissatisfied without being violent, they were complaining without being angry, they were sad without being hurting, and they were happy without being frivolous. Their poems also contain lessons.[323]

Lu Xun also said: "The Chinese poetry is used to talk about their wishes, but later scholars imposed emotions and called the three hundred poems in *Book of Songs* innocent. How could it be about wishes and innocence?"[324] Here, Lu Xun analyzed deeply the beauty of the harmony of the *Book of Songs*. He believed its original form was a result of "the down-to-earth people there," but the reason it continued in the history of classical poetry was purely the result of distorted interpretation. As to the tradition of Qu Yuan's of *Chu Ci*, although "it spoke what others dare not say, there were also many worries and complaints, and no resistance to the challenges could be found in the book. It was not sufficiently strong to move later generations."[325] In short, these traditions drew Chinese classical poetry into the limited space of emotional restraint and depression.

Lu Xun proposed the constraints of these aesthetic rules must be broken to develop Chinese modern poetry and even modern Chinese culture. Lu Xun's first poetry commentary, "On the Influence of Unorthodox Poets" published in 1905, has two main characteristics: one is to introduce the development of poetry into the overall cultural framework, and to expand the poetics problem discussion to "raise the true meaning of origin." The second is to assert "when the ancient source dried, a new source would be sought." That is to say, to get rid of the old and develop the new from the perspective of the overall cultural spirit, the new spirit, rather than "seeking new voices in foreign countries," the inherent "peace and harmony" of China should not be replaced by the

Western devil spirit. Lu Xun said, "Peace and harmony are not seen in the world . . . . Since humans were born, they can't live without threats. Evolution might halt, but the creatures could not go back to their original." Because of this, first, "spiritual warriors" who "intend to rebel and take actions" should be called to contribute to the development of Chinese modern poetry and Chinese modern culture. Such poets and cultural scholars will all have "beautiful strength," "and the filthy stagnation will be swept away."

Since "peace and harmony" are "not in the world," why is this poetic aesthetic pursuit so deeply rooted in China? Lu Xun believes this is because in the era of civilization, "the law has changed to a new one. Knowing the dangers of being pioneers on the battlefield, yet, withdrawing, would be considered an act of cowardice. When one knows there is no retreat, they created an ideal world as part of their self-deception . . . ." That is to say, the self-deception of the Chinese when faced with challenges is indifference and betrayal of real life.

This deception is shown in two aspects: The first is to pretend to be detached, that is, to embrace nature and forget the self as a living entity. If the Confucian ethical political view of "writing for a purpose" has a greater influence on China's essays, then the Taoist detachment from Laozi and Zhuangzi has a greater impact on Chinese poetry. Especially in modern China, there are few poets and poems that defend the Confucian utilitarian literary and artistic view, while there are many who sincerely devoted themselves to the Taoist aesthetic tastes. In 1920, Zong Baihua defined the new poetry as: *"Use a beautiful literature—the painting of the temperament—to express the aesthetic conception in the emotions of humankind."* The so-called "meaning of poetry" is "an intuition caused by the mutual contact of the soul of the poet with the mystery of nature."[326] This is probably the first step for Chinese modern poetry to return to the Taoist culture. Later, Kang Baiqing, Mu Mutian, Zhu Xiang, Zhou Zuoren, Liang Zongdai, Dai Wangshu, Zhu Guangqian, and others all affirmed and developed the poetic theory of embracing nature and seeking subtle resonance between things from different angles and to varying degrees. If there is some difference from traditional poetics, it is some modern poetic theories introduce the concept of Western mysticism in expressions. Yet, most of them do not accept the religious spirit behind the Western concept of poetics, in fact, the "mystery" is Chinese, another description of Heaven and Man. When Xu Zhimo translated Charles Baudelaire's "Death" in 1924, he said: "The true beauty of poetry is not in its word meaning but in his unpredictable rhythms. What it pricks is not your skin (It is too rough and too thick anyway!) It is the unpredictable soul of yourself." He further added this mysterious music is "the music of heaven, of earth and humans by Zhuang Zhou."[327] To this comment, Lu Xun published "Music?" to critique and at the very beginning, he said: "Sleepless at night, I plan to eat spicy chicken tomorrow, but I am afraid that I can't have the one with the same taste I had before. I can't sleep anymore."[328] This revealed the reality of people's failure of super-detachment just in a few words! People are not detached, and poetry is also the same. Modern Chinese poetry should express the "blood vapor" of real life. What we need is not mystic but "the really bad voice of the shocking quirks." The influence of unorthodox poets! If we do not understand the unique historical consciousness of Lu Xun's poetry theory, it is difficult to accept his criticism of Xu Zhimo.

For the same reason, Lu Xun published a long article in 1936 in the *Haiyan*, a monthly magazine in Shanghai, criticizing the "serenity" of Zhu Guangqian's poetics. Zhu Guangqian who studied both Chinese and foreign literature proposed serenity is the highest ideal of poetry. Lu Xun argued, "The ancient Greeks may regard peace and serenity as the best poetry. I do not know of this. But in the existing Greek poetry, Homer's epic is magnificent and lively. Sappho's love song is clear and enthusiastic, rather than serene. I think proposing serenity as the best of poetry, but not seen in poetry is just like proposing egg forms as the highest human forms which can't be realized." "Whenever literature and art are tied with an "extreme atmosphere," it would fall into a dead situation."[329] When looking back at ancient Chinese poetics, a remarkable feature is the tendency of leading the poetry into some kind of "extreme atmosphere." Here lies the unconscious inheritance of Zhu Guangqian's poetics, and Lu Xun's alert, sharp eyes see this.

Another evidence of Chinese modern poetry's indifference to real life is the aristocratization of poetry. From the lively and active to the highly narcissistic, from the broad coverage to the ivory tower, this seems to be a nightmare of Chinese poetry that has a long history and cycled itself. Lu Xun said, "I thought songs, poetry, *Ci*s, and *Qu*s are all part of folk culture. The literati took it for themselves and made them more difficult to understand until they became dead, and they grab another and strangle it again."[330] Sure enough, Liang Shiqiu commented as soon as the folk song development of the New Poetry faded. "Poetry must not be built on the real, universal life . . . . Poetry is aristocratic."[331] In response to such a new poetry culture mentality, Lu Xun agreed with the popularization trend of literary writing: "The illiterate writers may not be as delicate as the literati, but they are robust and fresh."[332]

However, Lu Xun never abandoned the thinking and values a cultural person and a new cultural enlightener should have, while agreeing to civilization and popularization. There is no lack of folklore pursuit in the history of Chinese classical poetry. "According to the new development of the traditional road, new poetry should arise from folk songs."[333] But no folk movement has transformed the essence of Chinese poetry spirit, rather it proves the necessity of aristocratization. Thus, popularization–aristocratization constitutes an endless vicious cycle. According to Lu Xun,

> This occurs because such popularization disregards the appetite of the masses and intellectuals become the "parasite literaries" (traditionally referred to as those who depend on the rich and the powerful) of the masses and lose the cognition they should have ... The masses are still not as enlightened as some of the educated in terms of insights ... As history has proven, it has always been the task of enlightened intellectuals to initiate reform.

Lu Xun also pointed out insightfully,

> Some intellectuals often look down on the masses, thinking they can understand the newer, more difficult words, while the public cannot. So, for the benefit of the public, they think new or difficult phrases must be thoroughly deleted. When one writes, the more popular, the better.[334]

It can be seen that the "parasite literaries" who cater to the public's appetite look down on the public in subconsciousness and consider themselves aristocrats. There is such a consistency between the "parasite literaries" (who traditionally depend on the rich and the powerful) and aristocratic tendencies!

Here, Lu Xun not only exposed the aristocratization in the so-called "bourgeois and petty bourgeoisie" poetry but also paid special attention to disclosing the aristocratic thoughts in some so-called proletarian revolutionary poems:

> In my opinion, it is not correct if a poet or writer, who participated in the revolution for the masses, expects the working class to pay him back in special preferential treatment, inviting him to sit in special cars, eat special meals, and offer butter and bread to him at the success of the revolution in the future, saying: "our poet, please enjoy it". This is not right.[335]

The traditional poet's conscious and unconscious hypocrisy is the psychological factor that forms Chinese poetry's indifference to real life, and the hypocrisy of the writers then leads to the hypocrisy of the recipients. Lu Xun once analyzed how "cover-up" and "deceit" are widespread in the whole society: "Chinese people always dared not to face up to life. They must swindle and deceive. From this generated the literary art that swindles and deceives, which further trapped the Chinese more deeply in shackles and deceit, so prevalent that even they fail to notice."[336] In 1925, Lu Xun spoke to Xu Guangping about his impressions of modern poetry: "Previously the hypocritical poems talking about "flowers" "love" dominate, now the hypocritical poems talking about "dead" or "blood" dominate. Alas! What a headache!"[337]

Therefore, "truth" became Lu Xun's first requirement for Chinese modern poetry. "Those who call for blood and fire, sing for wine and women, and enjoy the scent of the forest and the autumn moon, should be really in the mood for that. Otherwise, it is empty."[338] "Only the real voice can touch the Chinese people and the people of the world."[339] Yin Fu's poem collection *Baby Tower* is not skillful in terms of techniques, but Lu Xun wrote its preface, the only one he wrote to a modern poetry collection. It is not so much a political struggle, but rather a leap forward in cultural character. Although Yin Fu's poems are still slightly naive, they have heartfelt sincerity, sincere anger, and sincere struggles, if compared to the other schools of Chinese poets in the 1920s. The real ugly voices of owls are much better than the traditional weak poems, which only paid attention to the flowers, snow, moon, and breezes! Once this poetic path could continue healthily, it may be the future of Chinese new poetry, so Lu Xun emphasized: "This birth of *Baby Tower* is not to compete with current poets. Rather, it has its unique significance."[340]

The call for the sincerity of poetry also formed different attitudes of Lu Xun to modern love poems at different periods. Immediately before the May Fourth era in 1919, he praised a young boy's prose poem "Love" against arranged marriages as "steam of blood" and "the true voice of those who wake up."[341] In 1922, Lu Xun defended Wang Jingzhi's "Hui's Wind" and criticized the so-called "critics in tears."[342] Later, when modern love poetry fell into an empty, even mundane trap, Lu Xun felt much regret by showing a strong dislike. He published a "new poem parody of ancient poems" in 1924, which intended to play a joke on the popular poetry of lost love at the time.[343]

Regarding the stylistic features of the new poems, Lu Xun also offered his opinion. Generally speaking, Lu Xun advocated a less strict style. On the one hand, he opposed the "block" poems of the Crescent Moon School.[344] On the other hand, he insisted the new poems

> Should have a rhythm and rough metrics.... There must be forms that make them easy to remember, easy to understand, easy to sing, and pleasant to the ears....

While poetry has two kinds—one to read and one to sing, it is better to use the latter."[345]

Today, when we analyze this poetry calmly, it should be said being obsessed with "singing" is not necessarily in line with the actual trend of modern poetry. The formal innovation of Chinese new poetry seems mainly not a question of "singing." The outstanding modern new poetry represented by Mu Dan is not "easy to understand, easy to sing, and pleasant to the ears." We also see this claim of Lu Xun in poetry theory is not consistent with his early new poetry writing. (This also showed Lu Xun had no intention of concealing every artistic thought of his own, even if some thoughts may contradict each other, hindering the integrity and thoroughness of his poetic system.) However, I think we do not need to correct Lu Xun's theory because Lu Xun never claimed himself a modern poetry critic, nor did he intend to develop a profound, harmonious "Lu Xun New Poetics" through his fragmented comments!

More importantly, we saw Lu Xun's theory is based on his sincere vision of transforming Chinese modern poetry. He believed: "Without the rhythm and rhyme, one can't sing it; if one can't sing it, one can't remember it. If you can't remember it, one can't squeeze out the traditional poem from people's minds, and take up its position."[346] It can be seen that cultural transformation and cultural progress are still the consistent pursuits of Lu Xun, although there may be some mistakes in this pursuit in specific procedures. The reform of culture is a career full of hardships, and twists and turns. The combination of goals and procedures is complicated. For example, while some Chinese poetic theories conform to the trends of modern poetry, there is little profound significance of cultural progress if their goals did not challenge traditional poetics.

All in all, Lu Xun established a distant, unique relationship with China's modern new poetry. Not a skilled poet, he gave us the inspiration of another world with his short practice. Although unlike typical poetry theorists, who worked long and deep to make his theories perfect, Lu Xun was unique in modern poetry theory, pointed out what others did not, and left with us a more powerful theoretical impact. All of this is rooted in Lu Xun's unique cultural rationalism. In modern times, emotional understanding is the main way of thinking of modern poets and poetry theorists. It is probably in this kind of perceptual sensation and experience without consciousness of the mind the traditional Chinese poetic culture spirit is faintly and flexibly regenerated. In particular, when modern Western poets and philosophers also showed admiration for Chinese poetry culture, it was difficult for more people to awaken from emotional reliance and enter rational cultural reflection. It is harder for them to start a distant meditation on the intrinsic differences between Chinese and Western cultures, modern Western poetics, and traditional Chinese poetics.

Culture is a barrier that all modern Chinese artists are faced with. Culture is the primary issue in modern Chinese history, and its power is greater than in other countries after modernization. The difficult rational dialogues between Chinese traditional culture and Western culture hone and mold the hearts of every modern Chinese artist. "They should shoulder against the dark gates and let the children go to the wide, bright places."[347] This is Lu Xun's courage and vision.

Notes

1. In addition to the traditional-style poems in *Staying Abroad Collection* and *An Experimental Collection*, there are more than 90 traditional-style poems in Hu Shih's early writing period (see *Hu Shih's Anthology*).
2. The interpretation of Hu Shih's poetic theory from the perspective of "Intermediary" begins with Mr. Dong Bingyue. I think this is an extremely important perspective (see Dong Bingyue's *Intermediary: Historical Characteristics of Hu Shih's Theory of New Poetry*, *Chinese Modern Literature Research Series*, no. 2 1990).
3. See Zhu Wenhua, *A Biography of Hu Shih* (Chongqing Press, 1988), 68.
4. Wen Yiduo, "The Local Colors of *The Goddesses*," *Creation Weekly*, no. 5 (June 1923).
5. Hu Shih, "On New Poetry," in *Collection of Theory Development, China's New Literature Series*, 295–299.
6. Hu Shih to Ren Shuyong, July 1916. *Selected Letters of Hu Shih* (Zhonghua Publishing House, 1979).
7. "Reply to Mei Guangdi," included in the *Notes of Canghui Study* (Yadong Library, 1st edition, 1939).
8. Hu Shih, "On New Poetry," in *Collection of Theory Development, China's New Literature Series*, 294.
9. Hu Shih, "Literature Revolution Theories," in *Collection of Theory Development, China's New Literature Series*, 129.
10. Hu Shih, "Forced Rebellion," in *Collection of Theory Development, China's New Literature Series*, 8.
11. Hu Shih, "On New Poetry," in *Collection of Theory Development, China's New Literature Series*, 294.
12. Hu Shih, Preface to *An Experimental Collection*, 135.
13. It is generally acknowledged that Hu Shih's "eight issues" were influenced by Pound's *A Few Don'ts*. Study also showed Hu Shih copied Lowell's *Manifesto of Imagism* in his diary of studying abroad on December 26, 1916.
14. Hu Shih, "Preface to *Lao Luobo*," in *An Experimental Collection*, 33.
15. Hu Shih had different Chinese names for Wordsworth, Keats, and Browning.
16. Hu Shih, "Preface to *An Experimental Collection*," stress by the author in the original, 144.

17 Hu Shih, "Preface to *An Experimental Collection*," 193.
18 Kang Lin, "The Art History Value of *An Experimental Collection*," *Literary Review*, no. 4 (1990).
19 Hu Shih once said, "I initially love to use the rhythms of *Ci* and *Qu*, such as the style of *Dove* is a *Ci*" ("Preface to the Second Edition of *An Experimental Collection*"), *An Experimental Collection*, 187.
20 Guo Moruo, "Literary Theories, A Declaration," in *Moruo's Collected Works*, vol. 10, 101.
21 Guo Moruo, "Theories in Poetry," in *Moruo's Collected Works*, vol. 17, 266.
22 Guo Moruo, Preface to *Qu Yuan* (Kaiming Bookstore, 1935).
23 Guo Moruo, "Painting Inscriptions, Pu Jian, Past and Present," in *Complete Works of Guo Moruo*, vol. 19 (People's Literature Publishing House, 1984), 229.
24 See Guo Moruo, "My Childhood," in *Collected Works of Moruo*, vol. 6, 35; "My Poem Writing Experience," in *Collected Works of Moruo*, vol. 11, 147; "*Feigeng* Collection Preface: My Poems," in *Collected Works of Moruo*, vol. 13, 117.
25 Guo Moruo, "Guo Moruo on Poem Writing: About the Goddesses and Starry Heaven," *Present World*, no. 1 (Aug. 1936).
26 Guo Moruo, "Painting Inscriptions, Past and Present," in *Collected Works of Moruo*, vol. 12, 235.
27 Guo Moruo, "My Poem Writing Experience," in *Collected Works of Moruo*, vol. 11, 147.
28 Guo Moruo, "Ten Years' Writing Experience," in *Collected Works of Moruo*, vol. 7, 67.
29 See Guo Moruo's well-known articles: *Our New Literature Movement, Eulogy to Wang Yangming, On Chinese and German Cultures*.
30 Guo Moruo, "On Poetry Writing," *Literature*, 2 (1944).
31 Guo Moruo, "Preface to Literary Theories," in *Collected Works of Moruo*, vol. 10, 3.
32 For information on this, please refer to *Diary of Yilao* (1919) by Wen Yiduo during his teaching in Tsinghua University, *Wen Yiduo's Forty Years of Research* (Tsinghua University Press, 1988).
33 Wen Yiduo, "The Local Colors of *The Goddesses*," *Creation Weekly*, no. 5 (June 1923).
34 Wen, "The Local Colors of *The Goddesses*."
35 Zhu Ziqing, "Patriotic Poetry," in *Miscellaneous Remarks on New Poetry*, 51.
36 Wen Yiduo, "A Study on Metrical Poetry," in *Complete Works of Wen Yiduo*, vol. 10, 158, 159, 161.
37 Wen Yiduo, "The Rhyme of Poetry," *The Morning Post Supplement Poetry (Shi-Juan)* (May 13, 1926).
38 See Lan Dizhi, "Crescent School Poetry Exploration," in *The Orthodox and the Heretical*, 333.
39 Mu Mutian, "On Poetry—A Letter to Moruo," *Creation Monthly* 1, no. 1 (Mar. 1926).
40 Bian Zhilin, "Preface to *Dai Wangshu's Poetry Anthology*," in *People and Poetry: Retrospect and Prospect*, 64.
41 Liu Xuan, *Biography of Wen Yiduo* (Beijing University Press, 1983), 6.
42 Zhu Ziqing, "Preface to the Complete Works of Wen Yiduo," in *The Complete Works of Wen Yiduo*, vol. 12, 443.
43 Shen Congwen, "On the Dead Water of Wen Yiduo," *New Moon* 3, no. 2 (April 10, 1930).
44 Zang Kejia, "The Artistic Features of Wen Yiduo's Poetry," *Journal of Poetry* (April 1929). It's about "shock."
45 Wen Yiduo, "To Zang Kejia," in *Complete Works of Wen Yiduo*, vol. 12, 381.

46 When discussing *Laundry Songs*, Wen Yiduo said something similar to Wen Jiasi. See Sun Yushi, *Chinese Modern Poetry Art*, 93.
47 Quoted from Chen Congzhou, "Preface to *The Chronicle of Xu Zhimo*" (edited and printed by Chen Congzhou in 1949, reprinted by Shanghai Bookstore in 1981).
48 Fan Ni and Xiaochun, *Xu Zhimo, Human and Poetry* (Lijiang Publishing House, 1992), 7.
49 Xu Zhimo, "Youth Movement," *Morning Post Supplement* (Mar. 13, 1925).
50 According to my statistics, about 67.9% poems of *The Goddesses* are directly about natural scenery.
51 Wen Yiduo, "The Structure of Art," *Journal of Tsinghua University* 5, no. 1 (Nov. 1919).
52 For example, his naivety in dealing with interpersonal relations, and his carelessness and superficiality in social and political comments.
53 Wen Yiduo, "The Metrics of Poetry," *The Morning Post Supplement Shi-Juan*, no. 9 (May 1926).
54 Wen Yiduo, "The Local Colors of *The Goddesses*," *Creation Weekly*, no. 5 (June 1923).
55 See, respectively, *Wen Yiduo's Poems*, *Lonely Goose* and *Two-Month Sojourn Hut*.
56 Xu Zhimo, "Self Reflection," *Morning Post Supplement* (April 1926).
57 Xu Zhimo, "On Revolution on Lenin's Memorial Day," *Morning Post Supplement* (Jan. 21, 1926).
58 *Fiction Monthly* 14, no. 9 (Sept. 1923).
59 Xu Zhimo, "Thoughts during Florence Sojourn," *Literature Section, Morning Post Supplement* (Aug. 25, 1925).
60 Xu, "Thoughts during Florence Sojourn."
61 Xu Zhimo, "Cambridge as I Know It," *Morning Post Supplement* (Jan. 16 and 25, 1926).
62 Xu Zhimo, "Mansfield," *Fiction Monthly* 14, no. 5 (May 1923).
63 Chen Mengjia, "Commemorating Zhimo," *New Moon* 4, no 5.
64 Pu Feng, "A Bird's-eye View of Chinese Poetry from the May Fourth Movement to the Present," *Poetry Quarterly* 1, no. 1–2 (Dec. 1934–Mar. 1935).
65 See Bian Zhilin, "Xu Zhimo's Anthology Preface," in *People and Poetry: Retrospect and Prospect*, 21.
66 Xu Zhimo, "Political Life and Sister-in-Law of Neighbor Wang," *Capital Newspaper Supplement* (Jan. 4–6, 1925).
67 Xu Zhimo, "Russell Is Talking," *East Journal* 20, no. 23 (Dec. 1923).
68 Xu Zhimo, "Talk," in *Fallen Leaves* (Beixin Publishing House, 1926).
69 Xu, "Thoughts during Florence Sojourn."
70 Most of *Zhimo's Poetry* were written between 1922 and 1924; Most poems in *A Night at Florence* were written in 1925, 1926, and the first edition in 1927; poems in *Fierce Tigers*, *Travelogue* were mostly written around 1927, with the former first published in 1931 and the latter in 1932.
71 See respectively *In Front of Exeter Church*, *A Night at Florence*, *Autumn Moon* (*Fierce Tigers*) *Travelogue* (*Travelogue*).
72 Mr. Lan Dizhi had a great point: "If Zhimo had not died, Crescent School would have evolved into a Modernist School." See *The Orthodox and the Heretical*, 24.
73 Lü Jiaxiang, *Poetry Tides, Poets, Poetic Art* (Jiangsu Literature and Art Publishing House, 1991), 112.

17 Hu Shih, "Preface to *An Experimental Collection*," 193.
18 Kang Lin, "The Art History Value of *An Experimental Collection*," *Literary Review*, no. 4 (1990).
19 Hu Shih once said, "I initially love to use the rhythms of *Ci* and *Qu*, such as the style of *Dove* is a *Ci*" ("Preface to the Second Edition of *An Experimental Collection*"), *An Experimental Collection*, 187.
20 Guo Moruo, "Literary Theories, A Declaration," in *Moruo's Collected Works*, vol. 10, 101.
21 Guo Moruo, "Theories in Poetry," in *Moruo's Collected Works*, vol. 17, 266.
22 Guo Moruo, Preface to *Qu Yuan* (Kaiming Bookstore, 1935).
23 Guo Moruo, "Painting Inscriptions, Pu Jian, Past and Present," in *Complete Works of Guo Moruo*, vol. 19 (People's Literature Publishing House, 1984), 229.
24 See Guo Moruo, "My Childhood," in *Collected Works of Moruo*, vol. 6, 35; "My Poem Writing Experience," in *Collected Works of Moruo*, vol. 11, 147; "Feigeng Collection Preface: My Poems," in *Collected Works of Moruo*, vol. 13, 117.
25 Guo Moruo, "Guo Moruo on Poem Writing: About the Goddesses and Starry Heaven," *Present World*, no. 1 (Aug. 1936).
26 Guo Moruo, "Painting Inscriptions, Past and Present," in *Collected Works of Moruo*, vol. 12, 235.
27 Guo Moruo, "My Poem Writing Experience," in *Collected Works of Moruo*, vol. 11, 147.
28 Guo Moruo, "Ten Years' Writing Experience," in *Collected Works of Moruo*, vol. 7, 67.
29 See Guo Moruo's well-known articles: *Our New Literature Movement, Eulogy to Wang Yangming, On Chinese and German Cultures*.
30 Guo Moruo, "On Poetry Writing," *Literature*, 2 (1944).
31 Guo Moruo, "Preface to Literary Theories," in *Collected Works of Moruo*, vol. 10, 3.
32 For information on this, please refer to *Diary of Yilao* (1919) by Wen Yiduo during his teaching in Tsinghua University, *Wen Yiduo's Forty Years of Research* (Tsinghua University Press, 1988).
33 Wen Yiduo, "The Local Colors of *The Goddesses*," *Creation Weekly*, no. 5 (June 1923).
34 Wen, "The Local Colors of *The Goddesses*."
35 Zhu Ziqing, "Patriotic Poetry," in *Miscellaneous Remarks on New Poetry*, 51.
36 Wen Yiduo, "A Study on Metrical Poetry," in *Complete Works of Wen Yiduo*, vol. 10, 158, 159, 161.
37 Wen Yiduo, "The Rhyme of Poetry," *The Morning Post Supplement Poetry (Shi-Juan)* (May 13, 1926).
38 See Lan Dizhi, "Crescent School Poetry Exploration," in *The Orthodox and the Heretical*, 333.
39 Mu Mutian, "On Poetry—A Letter to Moruo," *Creation Monthly* 1, no. 1 (Mar. 1926).
40 Bian Zhilin, "Preface to *Dai Wangshu's Poetry Anthology*," in *People and Poetry: Retrospect and Prospect*, 64.
41 Liu Xuan, *Biography of Wen Yiduo* (Beijing University Press, 1983), 6.
42 Zhu Ziqing, "Preface to the Complete Works of Wen Yiduo," in *The Complete Works of Wen Yiduo*, vol. 12, 443.
43 Shen Congwen, "On the Dead Water of Wen Yiduo," *New Moon* 3, no. 2 (April 10, 1930).
44 Zang Kejia, "The Artistic Features of Wen Yiduo's Poetry," *Journal of Poetry* (April 1929). It's about "shock."
45 Wen Yiduo, "To Zang Kejia," in *Complete Works of Wen Yiduo*, vol. 12, 381.

46 When discussing *Laundry Songs*, Wen Yiduo said something similar to Wen Jiasi. See Sun Yushi, *Chinese Modern Poetry Art*, 93.
47 Quoted from Chen Congzhou, "Preface to *The Chronicle of Xu Zhimo*" (edited and printed by Chen Congzhou in 1949, reprinted by Shanghai Bookstore in 1981).
48 Fan Ni and Xiaochun, *Xu Zhimo, Human and Poetry* (Lijiang Publishing House, 1992), 7.
49 Xu Zhimo, "Youth Movement," *Morning Post Supplement* (Mar. 13, 1925).
50 According to my statistics, about 67.9% poems of *The Goddesses* are directly about natural scenery.
51 Wen Yiduo, "The Structure of Art," *Journal of Tsinghua University* 5, no. 1 (Nov. 1919).
52 For example, his naivety in dealing with interpersonal relations, and his carelessness and superficiality in social and political comments.
53 Wen Yiduo, "The Metrics of Poetry," *The Morning Post Supplement Shi-Juan*, no. 9 (May 1926).
54 Wen Yiduo, "The Local Colors of *The Goddesses*," *Creation Weekly*, no. 5 (June 1923).
55 See, respectively, *Wen Yiduo's Poems, Lonely Goose* and *Two-Month Sojourn Hut*.
56 Xu Zhimo, "Self Reflection," *Morning Post Supplement* (April 1926).
57 Xu Zhimo, "On Revolution on Lenin's Memorial Day," *Morning Post Supplement* (Jan. 21, 1926).
58 *Fiction Monthly* 14, no. 9 (Sept. 1923).
59 Xu Zhimo, "Thoughts during Florence Sojourn," *Literature Section, Morning Post Supplement* (Aug. 25, 1925).
60 Xu, "Thoughts during Florence Sojourn."
61 Xu Zhimo, "Cambridge as I Know It," *Morning Post Supplement* (Jan. 16 and 25, 1926).
62 Xu Zhimo, "Mansfield," *Fiction Monthly* 14, no. 5 (May 1923).
63 Chen Mengjia, "Commemorating Zhimo," *New Moon* 4, no 5.
64 Pu Feng, "A Bird's-eye View of Chinese Poetry from the May Fourth Movement to the Present," *Poetry Quarterly* 1, no. 1–2 (Dec. 1934–Mar. 1935).
65 See Bian Zhilin, "Xu Zhimo's Anthology Preface," in *People and Poetry: Retrospect and Prospect*, 21.
66 Xu Zhimo, "Political Life and Sister-in-Law of Neighbor Wang," *Capital Newspaper Supplement* (Jan. 4–6, 1925).
67 Xu Zhimo, "Russell Is Talking," *East Journal* 20, no. 23 (Dec. 1923).
68 Xu Zhimo, "Talk," in *Fallen Leaves* (Beixin Publishing House, 1926).
69 Xu, "Thoughts during Florence Sojourn."
70 Most of *Zhimo's Poetry* were written between 1922 and 1924; Most poems in *A Night at Florence* were written in 1925, 1926, and the first edition in 1927; poems in *Fierce Tigers, Travelogue* were mostly written around 1927, with the former first published in 1931 and the latter in 1932.
71 See respectively *In Front of Exeter Church, A Night at Florence, Autumn Moon* (*Fierce Tigers*) *Travelogue* (*Travelogue*).
72 Mr. Lan Dizhi had a great point: "If Zhimo had not died, Crescent School would have evolved into a Modernist School." See *The Orthodox and the Heretical*, 24.
73 Lü Jiaxiang, *Poetry Tides, Poets, Poetic Art* (Jiangsu Literature and Art Publishing House, 1991), 112.

74 Xu Zhimo, "Poets and Poems," *New People's Newspaper, Morning Glow* 6 (June 1926).
75 Xu Zhimo, "Poetry and Break," *The Morning Post Supplement Shi-Juan*, no. 11 (June 10, 1926).
76 Li Jinfa, *The Diner and the Fierce Year* (Beixin Publishing House, May 1927).
77 Du Geling and Li Jinfa, "Responses to Poetry," *Art Pictorial* 1, no. 3 (1935).
78 Sun Zuoyun, "On Modernist Poetry," *Tsinghua Weekly* 43, no. 4.
79 Du and Li, "Responses to Poetry," *Art Pictorial* 1, no. 3 (1935).
80 Alfred de Musset, "The Night of December," in *Alfred De Musset's Nights*, trans. Norman Cameron (Fifth Season Pr, 1999).
81 Richard Taylor, *Understanding the Elements of Literature: Its Forms, Techniques, and Cultural Convention* (Palgrave Macmillan, 1981).
82 From https://lyricstranslate.com.
83 Translated by Ellen Marriage.
84 Stéphane Mallarmé, *Oeuvres Completes*. Ed. Henri Mondor and G. Jean-Aubry (Paris: Bibliothèque de la léiade, Gallimard, 1945).
85 Quotes by Sun Xizhen, See Bian Zhilin, *People and Poetry: Retrospect and Prospect* (Joint Publishing Company, 1984), 190.
86 Quotes by Sun Xizhen, See Bian Zhilin, *People and Poetry: Retrospect and Prospect*.
87 Bian Zhilin, *People and Poetry: Retrospect and Prospect* (Joint Publishing Company, 1984), 189.
88 Paul Valéry, *Collected Works of Paul Valery*, Vol. 7: *The Art of Poetry* (Princeton University Press, 1989).
89 See Dai Wangshu, "On Lin Geng's Views on Poetry and Quatrains," *New Poetry* 1, no. 2 (1936).
90 Lü Jiaxiang, Dai Wangshu, "A Special Political Lyric Poet," in *Poetry Tide, Poet, Poetic Art*, 170.
91 Du Heng said, "One may reveal his subconsciousness in his dream and his secret soul in his poetry which would be dreamlike."
92 See Du Heng, "Preface to *Wangshu's Poem Collection*," in *Complete Works of Dai Wangshu* (Zhejiang Literature and Art Publishing House, 1989), 50.
93 Charles Chadwick, *Symbolism* (Routledge Kegan & Paul, January 1, 1971).
94 Charles Pierre Baudelaire, "Further Notes of Edgar Poe," in *Selected Writings on Art and Literature* (Penguin Classics, Mass Market, 1993).
95 The Chinese versions of these two poems were translated by Dai Wangshu.
96 See Baudelaire's "The Albatross" and "Evening Harmony," *Flowers of Evil* (a recent publication see CreateSpace Independent Publishing Platform, 2011). (Chinese version translated by Dai Wangshu).
97 Charles Chadwick, *Symbolism* (Routledge Kegan & Paul, January 1, 1971).
98 Paul Valéry, "The Place of Baudelaire," in *Collected Works of Paul Valéry*, vol. 8 (Princeton University Press, 1972), 193.
99 Yu Guangzhong, "On Dai Wangshu's Poems," *Appreciation of Masterpieces*, no. 3 (1992).
100 See Dai Wangshu, "On Lin Geng's Views on Poetry and Quatrains," *New Poetry* 1, no. 2 (1936).

101 Literally means "beauties and precious plants," which may refer to the qualities of not yielding and keeping high moral standards in life, particularly *"Fangcao."*
102 He Qifang later believed his *Nocturne* was still lustful, sad, utopian, and fragile.
103 He Qifang, "Street," in *Collected Works of He Qifang*, vol. 2, 78.
104 He Qifang, "An Ordinary Story," in *Collected Works of He Qifang*, vol. 2, 215–216.
105 See Zhou Yang, "Preface to *Anthology of He Qifang*," in *Anthology of He Qifang*, vol. 1.
106 Ai Qing, "Dream, Fantasy and Reality," *Literary Front* 3, no. 4 (June 1939).
107 Sha Ting, "Preamble to Selected Works of He Qifang," in *Selected Works of He Qifang*, vol. 1 (Sichuan People's Publishing House, 1979), 4.
108 See, respectively, *Prophecy, Seasonal Sickness, Footsteps, Lamentation*.
109 Fang Jing, He Pinjia, *A Short Introduction to He Qifang* (Sichuan Education Publishing House, 1990), 27.
110 Fang Jing, He Pinjia, *A Short Introduction to He Qifang*, 22, 32.
111 Fang Jing, He Pinjia, *A Short Introduction to He Qifang*, 22, 32.
112 Matthew Arnold, "To Marguerite: Continued." https://www.poetryfoundation.org/poems/43609/to-marguerite-continued.
113 Théophile Gautier, "Preface of *Enamels and Cameos*," trans. Agnes Lee. See https://themista.com/freeebooks/enamels.htm.
114 A Dwight Culler, *Poetry and Criticism of Matthew Arnold* (Houghton Mifflin College Division, January 1, 1961).
115 Fang Jing, He Pinjia, *A Short Introduction to He Qifang*, 36.
116 Fang Jing, He Pinjia, *A Short Introduction to He Qifang*, 36.
117 Lan Dizhi, "Preface to *Anthology of Modern Poetry*," in *Anthology of Modern Poetry* (People's Literature Publishing House, 1986).
118 He Qifang, "Poem Writing and Reading," in *Collected Works of He Qifang*, Vol. 4.
119 Luo Hanchao, "Lyric Personality of He Qifang's Early Poems," in *Thirty Lost Poems by He Qifang* (Chongqing Press, 1985).
120 Liu Xiwei, "Reading the Dream of Painting," *Literature Monthly* 1, no. 4.
121 He Qifang, "The Road in a Dream," in *Collected Works of He Qifang*, vol. 2, 66.
122 He Qifang, *Poetry Writing Process, An Ordinary Story* (Baihua Literature and Art Publishing House, 1982), 101.
123 Bian Zhilin, "Preface to *Diao Chong Ji Li*," in *Diao Chong Ji Li* (Anthology of Bian Zhilin's Poems), 1, 3.
124 Bian, "Preface to *Diao Chong Ji Li*," 1, 3.
125 Bian, "Preface to *Diao Chong Ji Li*," 5, 8, 9, 3.
126 Bian, "Preface to *Diao Chong Ji Li*," 5, 8, 9, 3.
127 Bian, "Preface to *Diao Chong Ji Li*," 5, 8, 9, 3.
128 Bian, "Preface to *Diao Chong Ji Li*," 3, 16.
129 Bian, "Preface to *Diao Chong Ji Li*," 3, 16.
130 Bian Zhilin, *Ten Years of Poetry* (Hong Kong Tomorrow Society, 1942).
131 See Dai Wangshu's *Anthology of Translated Poems* (Hunan People's Publishing House, 1983).
132 Bian Zhilin, *Vicissitude Collection, On Music* (Jiangsu People's Publishing House, 1982).
133 Ye Jiaying, *Jialing's Essays on Ci* (Shanghai Classics Books Publishing House, 1980), 18–19.

134 Wen Yiduo once praised Bian Zhilin for not writing love poems. In fact, *Untitled* is a love poem.
135 These poems have always been debated by critics.
136 Bian Zhilin, "Preface to *Diao Chong Ji Li*," in *Diao Chong Ji Li* (Anthology of Bian Zhilin's Poems), 3, 15.
137 Bian, "Preface to *Diao Chong Ji Li*," 3, 15.
138 Thomas Stearns Eliot, "Tradition and the Individual Talent," *Perspecta* 19 (1982): 36–42.
139 Eliot, "Tradition and the Individual Talent," *Perspecta* 19 (1982): 36–42.
140 Rainer Maria Rilke, *Letters to a Young Poet* (W. W. Norton; rev. edition, 1993).
141 Bian Zhilin, "Preface to *Dai Wangshu's Poetry Anthology*," in *People and Poetry: Retrospect and Prospect*, 63.
142 William Butler Yeats, "The Symbolism of Poetry," in *Essays and Introductions* (Palgrave Macmillan, 1961).
143 Feng Wenbing (Fei Ming), *On New Poetry Ten Years of Poetry*.
144 Bian Zhilin, "Completion and Beginning: In Memory of the 80th Birthday of Wen Yiduo," in *People and Poetry: Retrospect and Prospect*, 10.
145 Bian Zhilin, "Preface to *Diao Chong Ji Li*," in *Diao Chong Ji Li* (Anthology of Bian Zhilin's Poems), 15.
146 Bian, "Preface to *Diao Chong Ji Li*."
147 Wai-Lim Yip, "Syntax and Horizon of Representation in Classical Chinese and Modern American Poetry," in *Diffusion of Distances: Dialogues between Chinese and Western Poetics* (University of California Press, 1993), 47.
148 Bai Yuntao and Liu Xiao, "The Cultural Spirit of Chinese Classical Poetry," *Literature and Art Research*, no. 1 (1987).
149 Bian Zhilin, *Vicissitude Collection, On Music*.
150 Bian, "Preface to *Diao Chong Ji Li*," 16–17.
151 Bian, "Preface to *Diao Chong Ji Li*," 17.
152 Bian, "Preface to *Diao Chong Ji Li*," 17.
153 Feng Wenbing (Fei Ming), "On New Poetry," in *Ten Years of Poetry*.
154 Wang Wei, *Sitting Alone on an Autumn Night Thinking of my Brother-in-law Cui Xingzong*.
155 Wang Wei, *To Pei Shidi*.
156 Chen Zi'ang, *A Night Stay at Qipanling*.
157 Heinrich Ott, "Prayers as Monologues and Dialogues," in *Reden vom unsagbaren: die frage nach Gott in unserer zeit* (Kreuz Verlag, 1978).
158 Sun Jin, *Christianity and Aesthetics* (Chongqing Press, 1990), 196.
159 Refer to my work: *Modern Chinese New Poetry and Classical Poetry Traditions* (Southwest Normal University Press, 1994).
160 See *Liang Zongdai's Translated Poetry Anthology* (Hunan People's Publishing House, 1983), 53.
161 Paul Valéry, *Collected Works of Paul Valéry* (Princeton University Press, 1968).
162 Liang Zongdai, "On Sublime," in *Poetry and Truth, Poetry and Truth II* (Foreign Literature Press, 1984), 116.
163 Paul Valéry, *Collected Works of Paul Valéry* (Princeton University Press, 1968).
164 Liang Zongdai, "Poetry, Poet, and Critic," in *Poetry and Truth, Poetry and Truth II* (Foreign Literature Press, 1984), 204.

165 Liang Zongdai, "On Poetry," in *Poetry and Truth, Poetry and Truth II*, 95.
166 Liang Zongdai, "Symbolism," in *Poetry and Truth, Poetry and Truth II*, 76.
167 Liang, "Symbolism," in *Poetry and Truth, Poetry and Truth II*, 78, 81.
168 Li Bai, *Sitting Alone on Jingting Mountain*.
169 Wang Wei, *Autumn in My Mountain Abode*.
170 Paul Valéry, "Preface to *Les Poèmes de T'ao Ts'ien*," in *Les Poèmes de T'ao Ts'ien*, French version Trans. Liang Zongdai (Lemarget, 1930).
171 Liang Zongdai, "In Memory of Romain Rolland," in *Poetry and Truth, Poetry and Truth II*, 214.
172 Wen Yiduo, "Going back to Past" *Complete Works of Wen Yiduo*, Vol. 2 (Hubei People's Publishing House, 1993), 351.
173 Bian Zhilin, "Preface to *Dai Wangshu's Poetry Anthology*," in *People and Poetry: People and Poetry: Retrospect and Prospect* (Joint Publishing Company, 1984), 63.
174 Paul Valéry, *Collected Works of Paul Valery*, Vol. 7: *The Art of Poetry* (Princeton University Press, 1989).
175 Liang Zongdai, "Symbolism," in *Poetry and Truth, Poetry and Truth II*, 77.
176 Liang Zongdai, "On Poetry," in *Poetry and Truth, Poetry and Truth II*, 33.
177 Liang Zongdai, "Mr. Paul van Leech," in *Poetry and Truth, Poetry and Truth II*, p. 22.
178 Liang Zongdai, "Preface to *Poetry and Truth*," in *Poetry and Truth, Poetry and Truth II*, 5.
179 Liang Zongdai, "On Poetry," in *Poetry and Truth, Poetry and Truth II*, 29.
180 Liang Zongdai, "About Poetry," in *Poetry and Truth, Poetry and Truth II*, 91.
181 Hu Feng, *Memoir of Hu Feng* (People's Literature Publishing House, 1993), 70.
182 Ye Jin, Ai Qing's Talks on His Two Previous Works, *Ai Qing's Special Collection* (Jiangsu People's Publishing House, 1982), 63.
183 Ai Qing, "Popularization and Old Forms," in *Ai Qing's Special Collection*, 192.
184 Ai Qing, "Why do Hens Lay Duck Eggs," in *Ai Qing's Special Collection*, 59.
185 Ai, "Why do Hens Lay Duck Eggs," 56, 57.
186 Ai, "Why do Hens Lay Duck Eggs," 57.
187 Dong Xiao, "Poetry Discussion by Ai Qing and New Plans of Novels," in *Ai Qing's Special Collection*, 59.
188 Ai Qing, "On Poetry, On Poets," See *Ai Qing's Special Collection*, 112, 143, 120, and 133 respectively.
189 Ai Qing, "Prose Beauty of Poetry," in *Ai Qing's Special Collection*, 153.
190 Ai Qing, "Poetry and the Times," in *Ai Qing's Special Collection*, 159–160.
191 Yang Tangchen, "On Lu Xun's Evaluation of Feng Zhi's Poetry," *Journal of Xuzhou Normal University*, no. 3 (2007).
192 Wang Dui, "An Analysis of the Reasons Why Lu Xun High Evaluation of Feng Zhi's Poems," *Journal of Mudanjiang Institute of Education*, no. 2 (2010).
193 Lu Xun, "Preface to *Collection beyond Collection*," in *Complete Works of Lu Xun*, vol. 7 (People's Literature Publishing House, 1981), 4.
194 *Yu Si Weekly*, December 1, 1924.
195 Lu Xun, "Preface to *Collection beyond Collection, Music?*" *Complete Works of Lu Xun*, vol. 7, 53.
196 Lu Xun, "To Cai Feijun (350920)," see *Complete Works of Lu Xun*, vol. 13 (People's Literature Press, 1981), 220.

197 Lu Xun, "Preface to Bai Mang's Children's Tower, Qijieting Essays," in *Complete Works of Lu Xun*, vol. 6 (People's Literature Publishing House, 1981), 494.
198 Feng Zhi, "Best Flowers Bloom in the Loneliest Garden," in *Complete Works of Feng Zhi*, vol. 3 (Hebei Education Press, 1999), 170–171.
199 Feng Zhi, Speech at the Ceremony of the Literature and Art Award, International Exchange Center of the Federal Republic of Germany, On Poetry Creation, *Complete Works of Feng Zhi*, vol. 5, 196, 247.
200 See Feng Zhi, "Rilke," in *Complete Works of Feng Zhi*, vol. 4, 86.
201 See Feng Zhi, "Rilke," 26.
202 Zhu Ziqing, "An Introduction to Poems," *China's New Literature Series*.
203 Hu Shih, "On New Poetry," in *Collection of Theory Development, China's New Literature Series*.
204 See Zheng Min, "A Review at the End of the Century: Chinese Language Change of and the Creation of Chinese New Poetry," *Literary Review*, no. 3 (1993).
205 Charles Chadwick, *Symbolism* (Routledge Kegan & Paul, 1979).
206 Cleanth Brooks, "The Language of Paradox," in *The Well-Wrought Urn: Studies in the Structure of Poetry* (Harcourt, 1947).
207 William Epson, *Seven Types of Ambiguity* (Chatto and Windus, 1949), 5–6.
208 Zhu Ziqing, *An Introduction to Poems*, *China's New Literature Series* (Shanghai Friend Book Publishing, 1935).
209 Fang Dongshu (Qing Dynasty), *Zhao Mei Zhan Yan (Poetry Issues)*.
210 Fang Xun (Qing Dynasty), *Poetry Talks at Shanjingju*.
211 Mu Mutian, *Sounds of Water*.
212 Bian Zhilin, *The Organization of Distance*, notes, See *Diao Chong Ji Li (Anthology of Bian Zhilin's Poems)* (People's Literature Publishing House, 1984).
213 Bian Zhilin, *Diao Chong Ji Li (Anthology of Bian Zhilin's Poems)*, Preface.
214 Zheng Min, *Poets and Contradictions, A Nation Has Risen* (Jiangsu People's Publishing House, 1987), 31, 39.
215 Hu Shih, "On New Poetry," in *Collection of Theory Development, China's New Literature Series*.
216 See Du Yunxie, *Behind Mu Dan's Translation, A Nation Has Risen*, 115.
217 Yu Pingbo, "Psychological Views on New Poetry," *New Trend* 3, no. 1.
218 He Qifang, "Road in the Dream," in *He Qifang's Collected Works*, vol. 2 (People's Literature Publishing House, 1983).
219 Feng Wenbing (Fei Ming), *On New Poetry* (People's Literature Publishing House, 1984).
220 See Wu Xiaodong, From "Prose Poetry" to "Pure poetry," *Chinese Modern Literature Research Series*, no. 3 (1993).
221 Ke Ke (Jin Kemu), "On New Poetry," *New Poetry*, no. 4 (Jan. 1937).
222 Yuan Kejia, "New Poetry Modernization," in *On Modernization of New Poetry* (Joint Publishing Company, 1988).
223 Tang Shi, "Remembering the Poet Mu Dan," see *A Nation Has Risen*.
224 Yuan Kejia, "Superstition on Poetry," in *On Modernization of New Poetry*, 67.
225 Thomas Stearns Eliot, "Tradition and the Individual Talent," *Perspecta* 19 (1982): 36–42.
226 Eliot, "Tradition and the Individual Talent," *Perspecta* 19 (1982): 36–42.

227 The discussions were collected in *On Modernization of New Poetry* (Joint Publishing Company, 1988).
228 Yuan Kejia, "New Poetry Modernization," in *On Modernization of New Poetry* (Joint Publishing Company, 1988), 3.
229 Yuan, "Modernization of New Poetry," 3.
230 Hu Shih, *On New Poetry—A Major Event in the Past Eight Years*. Ed. Yang Kuanghan and Liu Fuchun, Vol. I (Huacheng Press, 1985), 2.
231 Ivor Armstrong Richards, *Principles of Literary Criticism* (Routledge, 2004), 234, 233.
232 Richards, *Principles of Literary Criticism*, 229.
233 When Richards talks about experience, he focuses on people's intelligence and emotions. Eliot's tradition and personal ability also focus on artistic experiences. It is Yuan Kejia's thoughts to regard real life as the determiner of experience.
234 Yuan Kejia, "New Poetry Modernization," in *On Modernization of New Poetry* (Joint Publishing Company, 1988), 4. 5.
235 Ke Ke (Jin Kemu), "On New Poetry," *New Poetry* 2, no. 3–4 (Jan. 1937).
236 Jiang Fei, "Domestication of New Criticism and Modernization of Chinese Poetics," *Journal of Qinzhou Teachers College*, no. 3 (2003).
237 Yuan Kejia, "Dramatization of New Poetry," in *On Modernization of New Poetry* (Joint Publishing Company, 1988), 22.
238 Yuan, "Dramatization of New Poetry," 21.
239 Yuan, "Dramatization of New Poetry," 22.
240 Yuan, "Dramatization of New Poetry," 4.
241 Yuan Kejia, "Another Analysis of Modernization of New Poetry," in *On Modernization of New Poetry* (Joint Publishing Company, 1988), 10.
242 Yuan, "Another Analysis of Modernization of New Poetry," 16.
243 Yuan Kejia, "Political Sentimentality in Modern Poetry," in *On Modernization of New Poetry* (Joint Publishing Company, 1988), 16.
244 Yuan Kejia, "Poetry and Democracy," in *On Modernization of New Poetry* (Joint Publishing Company, 1988), 48.
245 Yuan, "Poetry and Democracy," 71.
246 Yuan, "Poetry and Democracy," 49.
247 Yuan, "Poetry and Democracy," 50.
248 Yuan, "Poetry and Democracy," 40.
249 Yuan, "Poetry and Democracy," 41.
250 Yuan Kejia, "Literature of Human Beings" and "People's Literature," in *On Modernization of New Poetry* (Joint Publishing Company, 1988), 123.
251 Yuan Kejia, "Random Thoughts on Criticism," in *On Modernization of New Poetry* (Joint Publishing Company, 1988), 164.
252 For example, he thinks: "writing a good modern poem, as I call it, not only requires a poet to have democratic habits and democratic consciousness (otherwise, his poem must be not be modern, such as many political sentimental poems at present), but also creates democratic value." "Poetry and Democracy," in *On Modernization of New Poetry* (Joint Publishing Company, 1988), 43.

253 Yuan Kejia, "Our Challenges," in *On Modernization of New Poetry* (Joint Publishing Company, 1988), 179.
254 Zang Kejia, "My Poetic Life," in *Collected Works of Zang Kejia*, vol. 4 (Shandong Literature and Art Publishing House, 1994), 554.
255 Yuan Kejia, "New Poetry Modernization," in *On Modernization of New Poetry* (Joint Publishing Company, 1988), 6.
256 Yuan, "Another Analysis of Modernization of New Poetry," 11.
257 Yuan, "Dramatization of New Poetry," 29.
258 Yuan, "Dramatization of New Poetry," 24.
259 Yuan, "Random Thoughts on Criticism," 160.
260 Yuan, "Dramatization of New Poetry," 24. 25.
261 Wen Yiduo, "Historical Trend of Literature," in *Wen Yiduo's Complete Works*, vol 10 (Hubei People's Publishing House, 1993), 20.
262 Wen, "Historical Trend of Literature," 20.
263 Bian Zhilin, "Preface to *Diao Chong Ji Li*" (*Anthology of Bian Zhilin's Poems*, edited version), *Collected Works of Bian Zhilin* (Anhui Education Publishing House, 2002).
264 Yuan, "Dramatization of New Poetry," 28, 29.
265 Yuan Kejia, *Dramatization of New Poetry*, originally published in no. 12, *Poetry Writing* (June 1948). This part of description was deleted in the 1988 version by the Joint Publishing Company.
266 Yuan Kejia, *On Drama-ism, Dramatization of New Poetry* (Joint Publishing Company, 1988).
267 Lan Dizhi, *Exploring the Origin of Poetry Criticism Theory of Nine Leaf School, Modern Poetry Theory: Origin and Trend* (Tsinghua University Press, 2002), 52.
268 Bian Zhilin, "Preface to *Diao Chong Ji Li*" (*Anthology of Bian Zhilin's Poems*) (People's Literature Publishing House, 1984).
269 Bian, "Preface."
270 Ai Qing, "Poetics," in *Modern Chinese Poetics*, vol. I (Huacheng Press, 1988), 337.
271 A Long, *Where Arrow is Pointing, Human, Poetry, Reality* (Joint Publishing Company, 1986), 3.
272 Wang Zuoliang, "A Chinese Poet," London, *Life and Letters* (1946).
273 Wang, "A Chinese Poet."
274 Ren Hongyuan, "Three Literary Centuries in My Life," *Foreign Literature Review*, no. 4 (1988).
275 Ren Hongyuan, "My Second 20 Years Old," *Hunan Literature*, no. 2 (1992).
276 Ren Hongyuan, "Finding the Language of Nü Wa," *Poetry Trends*, no. 3–4 (1990).
277 Ren Hongyuan, "Three Literary Centuries in My Life," *Foreign Literature Review*, no. 4 (1988).
278 Ren, "Three Literary Centuries in My Life."
279 Ren, "My Second 20 Years Old."
280 Bian Zhilin, "Preface to *Diao Chong Ji Li*" (*Anthology of Bian Zhilin's Poems*) (People's Literature Publishing House, 1984).
281 Ren Hongyuan, "Contemporary Poetry: Double Transcendence of Western Modernism and Eastern Classical Poetics," *Literary Review*, no. 5 (1988).

282 Ren Hongyuan, "Finding the Language of Nü Wa," *Poetry Trends*, no. 3–4 (1990).
283 Ren, "Finding the Language of Nü Wa."
284 Ren Hongyuan, "Contemporary Poetry: Double Transcendence of Western Modernism and Eastern Classical Poetics," *Literary Review*, no. 5 (1988).
285 Ren, "Contemporary Poetry."
286 Ren, "My Second 20 Years Old."
287 Ren Hongyuan, "Three Literary Centuries in My Life," *Foreign Literature Review*, no. 4 (1988).
288 Ren, "Finding the Language of Nü Wa."
289 Ren Hongyuan, "Contemporary Poetry: Double Transcendence of Western Modernism and Eastern Classical Poetics," *Literary Review*, no. 5 (1988).
290 Ren Hongyuan, "Finding the Language of Nü Wa," *Poetry Trends*, no. 3–4 (1990).
291 Ren, "Finding the Language of Nü Wa."
292 Ren, "Finding the Language of Nü Wa."
293 Ren Hongyuan, "Luo Fu's Poems and the Tragedy of Modern Creation," in *Songs of a Poetry Dovotee* (Huacheng Press, 1994).
294 Ren Hongyuan, *The Black Yellow River* (Beijing Normal University Press, 1998).
295 Ren, "Luo Fu's Poems and the Tragedy of Modern Creation."
296 Ren Hongyuan, *The Black Yellow River* (Beijing Normal University Press, 1998).
297 Ren, *The Black Yellow River*.
298 Ren, Hongyuan, "Luo Fu's Poems and the Tragedy of Modern Creation."
299 Lu Xun, "Preface to *Collection beyond Collection*," in *Complete Works of Lu Xun*, vol. 7 (People's Literature Publishing House, 1981), 4.
300 Lu Xun, "Preface to *Collection beyond Collection, Enemy of Poetry*," in *Complete Works of Lu Xun*, vol. 7 (People's Literature Publishing House, 1981), 235.
301 Lu Xun, "To Dou Yinfu (341101)," in *Complete Works of Lu Xun*, vol. 13 (People's Literature Publishing House, 1981), 556.
302 Lu Xun, "Preface to *Collection beyond Collection*." 4.
303 Wang Yao, *Manuscript of Chinese New Literature History* (1) (Shanghai Literature and Art Publishing House, 1982), 68.
304 Sawada Sokiyoshi, *History of Chinese Rhyme* (1) (The Commercial Press, 1937), 2.
305 There is no unified name for the beat unit of modern poetry. He Qifang and Bian Zhilin call it "dun" (pause), Wen Yiduo "yin chi" (sound ruler), Sun Dayu "yinzu" (sound group), etc.
306 Bian Zhilin, "Humming Rhythm (singing) and Speaking Rhythm (reciting)," in *People and Poetry, Retrospect and Prospect* (Joint Publishing Company, 1984).
307 Lu Xun paid attention to Freud's theory early on. He was interested in subconsciousness and tried to apply it to writing for a long time.
308 Refer to Zhou Zhenfu's notes: *Collection of Lu Xun's Poems* (Zhejiang People's Publishing House, 1980, rev. edition).
309 Zhu Ziqing, *An Introduction to Poems*, *China's New Literature Series*.
310 Hu Shih, "On New Poetry," in *Collection of Theory Development, China's New Literature Series* (Friend Book Publishing, 1935).
311 Lu Xun, "*Collection beyond Collection*: Speechless," in *Complete Works of Lu Xun*, vol. 7 (People's Literature Publishing House, 1981), 39.

312 Bian Zhilin, "Rereading Xu Zhimo," in *People and Poetry, Retrospect and Prospect* (Joint Publishing Company, 1984), 34.
313 Bian Zhilin, "Preface to *Selected Works of Xu Zhimo*," in *People and Poetry, Retrospect and Prospect* (Joint Publishing Company, 1984), 25.
314 Lu Xun, "Music?" written in 1924, *Collection beyond Collection, Complete Works of Lu Xun*, vol. 7 (People's Literature Publishing House, 1981), 53.
315 Lu Xun, "Preface to *Collection beyond Collection*," in *Complete Works of Lu Xun*, vol. 7 (People's Literature Publishing House, 1981), 4.
316 Originally published in *New Literature Materials*, no. 3, 1987, annotated by An Wei.
317 Wang Yao, "Thoughts on Lu Xun's Talk with Snow," *Lu Xun Studies Annals* (1990).
318 See *Selected Works of Ye Shuxian: Myth-Archetypal Criticism* (Shaanxi Normal University Press, 1987), 56.
319 Thomas Stearns Eliot, "Tradition and the Individual Talent," *Perspecta* 19 (1982): 42.
320 T. S. Eliot, "The Social Function of Poetry (1945)," in *On Poetry and Poets* (Farrar, Straus and Giroux, 2009), 3–16.
321 Ye Xie, *The Internal Side of Poetry* (2).
322 Lu Xun, "To Yang Jiyun (341220)," in *Complete Works of Lu Xun*, vol. 12 (People's Literature Publishing House, 1981), 612.
323 Lu Xun, "Chinese Literature History Outline," in *Complete Works of Lu Xun*, vol. 9 (People's Literature Publishing House, 1981), 356.
324 Lu Xun, "On the Influence of Unorthodox Poets," in *Complete Works of Lu Xun*, vol. 1 (People's Literature Publishing House, 1981), 68.
325 Lu Xun, "On the Influence of Unorthodox Poets," 69.
326 Zong Baihua, "A Brief Talk on New Poetry," *Youth China* 1, no. 8.
327 See *Yu Si, Weekly*, no. 3 (Dec. 1, 1924).
328 Lu Xun, "Music?" 53.
329 Lu Xun, "Qiejieting Essays II, Drafts without Titles (Six to Nine)," in *Complete Works of Lu Xun*, vol. 6 (People's Literature Publishing House, 1981), 427–428.
330 Lu Xun, "Letters to Yao Ke (340220)," in *Complete Works of Lu Xun*, vol. 12 (People's Literature Publishing House, 1981), 339.
331 Liang Shiqiu, "On the Restoration of the Evolution of Poetry," *Supplement of Morning Post* 5 (1922): 27–29.
332 Lu Xun, "Qiejieting Essays: A Layman's Thoughts," in *Complete Works of Lu Xun*, vol. 6 (People's Literature Publishing House, 1981), 95.
333 Zhu Ziqing, "Miscellaneous Remarks on New Poetry, True Poetry," in *Writer's House*, 1947 edition (People's Literature Publishing House, 1981).
334 Lu Xun, "Qiejieting Essays: A Layman's Thoughts," in *Complete Works of Lu Xun*, vol. 6 (People's Literature Publishing House, 1981), 101–102.
335 Lu Xun, "Erxin Ji: Opinions on Left Wing Writers' Union," in *Complete Works of Lu Xun*, vol. 4 (People's Literature Publishing House, 1981), 234.
336 Lu Xun, Grave: "On Opening Your Eyes," in *Complete Works of Lu Xun*, vol. 1 (People's Literature Publishing House, 1981), 240.
337 Lu Xun, "Letters to Her, Thirty-four," in *Complete Works of Lu Xun*, vol. 11 (People's Literature Publishing House, 1981), 100.

338 Lu Xun, "Preface to *Collection beyond Collection, Postscript of The Twelve*," in *Complete Works of Lu Xun*, vol. 7 (People's Literature Publishing House, 1981), 300.
339 Lu Xun, "Idling Collection, Silent China," in *Complete Works of Lu Xun*, vol. 4 (People's Literature Publishing House, 1981), 15.
340 Lu Xun, "Preface to *Bai Mang's Children's Tower, Qiejieting Essays, 1936*," in *Complete Works of Lu Xun*, vol. 4 (People's Literature Publishing House, 1981), 15.
341 Lu Xun, "Hot Wind, Forty," in *Complete Works of Lu Xun*, vol. 4 (People's Literature Publishing House, 1981), 15.
342 Lu Xun, "Hot Wind, Against the Tearful Critic," in *Complete Works of Lu Xun*, vol. 1 (People's Literature Publishing House, 1981), 403.
343 Lu Xun, "Idling Collection, I and the Beginning of *Yu Si*," in *Complete Works of Lu Xun*, vol. 4 (People's Literature Publishing House, 1981), 166.
344 Lu Xun, "To Yao Ke (340220)," "Miscellaneous Talks," See respectively *Complete Works of Lu Xun*, vols. 12 and 5 (People's Literature Publishing House, 1981), 325, 339.
345 Lu Xun, "To Dou Yinfu (341101)," "To Cai Feijun (350920)," See, respectively, *Complete Works of Lu Xun*, vols. 12 and 13 (People's Literature Publishing House, 1981), 220, 556.
346 Lu Xun, "To Dou Yinfu (341101)," in *Complete Works of Lu Xun*, vol. 12 (People's Literature Publishing House, 1981), 556.
347 Lu Xun, "Grave, How to Be a Father Now," in *Complete Works of Lu Xun*, vol. 1 (People's Literature Publishing House, 1981), 130.

APPENDIX: MODERN CHARACTERISTICS OF CHINESE MODERN POETICS

I

Just as the approach to many problems in the study of Chinese modern literature and culture, the study of the emergence and development of Chinese modern poetics is often set within the great historical background of Chinese and foreign cultural exchanges. Due to the imbalance of this exchange, a series of Chinese literature issues, including Chinese modern poetry, is "naturally" described time and again as the Eastward shift of Western culture and literature. If we follow the modernity questioning in recent years, then Chinese modern literature and culture, along with Chinese modern poetics, are only the result of the Eastward shift of Western cultural hegemony. Therefore, all modern characteristics of Chinese literature, to a large extent, have become a reflection of the problems of modernity in the West. Therefore, it is necessary to further study modernity in West culture to explore the modern characteristics of Chinese literature.

It is undoubtedly important to fully affirm the legitimacy of this idea because it does reflect a crucial fact that determines the image of modern Chinese culture. Our mainstream academic achievements so far have also benefited from this magnificent vision. However, further thinking revealed some doubts about this idea: Where does the fundamental driving force for cultural and literary writing come from? Is it the abstraction of the "tradition" or the writer's subjectivity? As Wang Furen noted:

> Man is creative and every culture is a kind of human creation. The nature and role of China's modern and contemporary culture cannot be determined only from its sources. Therefore, the dualistic model based on China's inherent cultural traditions and Western culture cannot make fruitful research on its independence .... It is the Chinese intellectuals who have absorbed ancient Chinese culture or Western culture for their survival and development in the modern and contemporary eras, rather than the opposite. They are completely free in the face of all human cultural achievements, a fact we cannot ignore.[1]

The same is true of the understanding of the characteristics of Chinese modern poetry. Strictly speaking, when Chinese modern poetics developed, it was not the question these poetry theorists must inherit or reject ancient Chinese or Western poetics. It should be how these people who care about poetry interpret the changing status of poetry writing. Like Hu Shih's *On New Poetry*, the concern and explanation of the earliest Chinese modern poetics is "a big event in eight years" because "in the past two years, the achievements in essays in Mandarin ended any debate. It is time for most people to practice it. Only Mandarin verses—the so-called 'new poetry'—still are questioned by many people."[2] The poetics of the May Fourth era raised the banner of "evolution," but it is obvious that under their respective "evolution" concepts, there are various reasons for these new changes in the current poetry. In their eyes,

> The natural trend is gradually realized without intentional advocacy. This is a natural evolution. Natural trends are sometimes hindered by human habitual conventions and failed when implementation should have been achieved. It must be promoted with deliberate advocacy to promote this realization. That is revolution.[3]

The poetry theorists in the May Fourth Movement used the "voice" of Western evolutionism to "intentionally advocate" the revolution of Chinese new poetry. It is the rich facts in the literature that inspired the theorists' impulse for explanation and the desire for new theoretical development. Chinese modern poetry explains and explores new topics about poetry first rather than offering simple input to some classical or Western poetics theories. In such a context of structuring of the new rational framework, our theorists were also completely free. We also cannot ignore their freedom. The reason Hu Shih regarded the form of the text as the focus of new poetry discussion is not because he mastered the Western imagery of poetry. Rather, Hu Shih believed he must break through the shackles of the "refined words" of Chinese poetry to realize "the great liberation of poetry," which had come to a dead end. We find some deviations between Hu Shih's poetics and Western imagery poetry that influenced him, but it is precisely this deviation that shows the complete freedom Hu Shih had as a Chinese poetry theorist. Hu Shih's poetry proposition was fiercely criticized by Mu Mutian and others. After Hu Shih was rebuked as "the biggest sinner in the new poetry movement in China," Mu Mutian and Wang Duqing introduced the French concept of "pure poetry." The root cause for this was "the Chinese are now writing vulgar poetry and this is what I hate."[4] "The Chinese who wrote poems recently are just like those who do social work. They do not take it seriously nor work hard for it. As a result, they only produced inferior products even in terms of techniques."[5] It is this clear, Chinese consciousness that made "pure poetry" of Mu Mutian, Wang Duqing, and others full of the "national elements,"[6] deviated from the original meaning of "pure poetry" in Western poetics. In a certain sense, Hu Shih's "freedom," "oral style," and "poetry liberation" represented an important side of Chinese modern poetics. Questions and criticism on Hu Shih's claims from Mu Mutian and Wang Duqing, and their "pure poetry" ideal of "art for art's sake" represented another aspect of Chinese modern poetics. Yet, they all took the basic development of Chinese modern poetry as their starting point. These theorists constructed their poetry claims according to their feelings, absorbing, eliminating, and even "misreading" a series of poetic concepts in the West.

The new poetry modernization theory represented by Yuan Kejia embodies the most conscious "modern characteristics" pursuit of Chinese modern poetics. The goal of such pursuit is also expressed by our theorists in solving "problems of the current new poetry." "The problems of the current new poetry are neither purely ideas nor purely techniques. They are more than the transformation of the two, including the two. Then, how to transform these wills and emotions into a poetry experience? The author's answer is the "Dramatization of new poetry"; that is, trying to make both will and emotions presented in the drama style, while dodging the negative tendencies of preaching or sentiments."[7] Yuan Kejia also clearly noted the so-called "modernization" should not be confused with "Westernization." "It is not necessary nor impossible for new poetry to Westernize as it is impossible for this space to become that space. The new poetry may or must be modernized just as an organically grown plant is close to a natural process of transformation. It is moving forward rather than uprooting . . . . A Chinese gentleman, regardless of how fluent he is in a foreign language, how well-dressed he is in his Western suit, even his knowledge of the Western exceeding his knowledge of his own country, it is difficult for him to be confident that he is already a foreigner or determined a foreigner. People's general impression of him is not his excessive Western intellectual knowledge, but his lack of intellectual knowledge of his home country. On the other hand, he can learn to be a modern Chinese without hesitation, trying to abandon some old-fashioned or seemingly fresh, but essentially old-fashioned, thoughts and habits." The next few words seem fresh after half a century. It's like special reminder to some "modernity" skeptics. "The critics of modern poetry can only explain the sources of this reform because of insufficient training. Yet, they failed to note its relationship with traditional poetry, creating a general impression that modernization is Westernization."[8]

In this sense, I think, the fundamental significance to understand and evaluate the modern characteristics of Chinese modern poetics is not to clarify the modernity of the West, which affects Chinese modern culture and literature (although this is still an important question), but what the modern poetry environment offers to poetry theorists. How did modern Chinese poet-critics feel and interpret such an environment? What kind of theoretical design did they produce? Or, in addition to the existing poetic system in China, what kind of poetic tastes and poetic topics did they discover in modern times? What kind of new theoretical discourse model was gradually formed in the process of expressing their respective views? In the words of Yuan Kejia, attention should be paid to the "transmutation of natural procedures" in the organic growth of poetry theory within our "space." I believe this is the "issue" that truly constitutes the modern characteristics of modern Chinese poetry.

II

To understand and elaborate in what sense the "problems" of Chinese poetics solve after the 20th century are "new" and "modern," we must first return to ancient Chinese poetics for a review. What is the "new" about the "old" of ancient Chinese poetics? How did the ancient Chinese poetics discover and understand the "problems" of poetry? What is the new style formed? Why is there a change in these inherent "problems" after the 20th century? How did the changes in the "problems" of poetry lead to changes in the forms of poetry?

An overview of this series of questions is an illustration of the rise of Chinese modern poetry.

In the ecological environment of Chinese classical poetry and the special cultural mentality of ancient Chinese intellectuals, ancient Chinese poetics gradually emerged. In brief, the important "problem" ancient Chinese poetry theorists first faced is Chinese poetry (especially lyric poetry) experienced considerable artistic maturity and social influence in its first stage of development. Wen Yiduo said: "The era of *Three Hundred Poems* (*Book of Songs*) is indeed a great one, in which our culture has generally been shaped from this very beginning."[9] It is worth noting this "great era" has a precocious humanistic character, that is to say, our poetry art was not developed toward the metaphysical divine world, but was loaded with more real life. In this realistic society, our poetry theorists also have a rather realistic poetic attitude.

In the face of the amazing texts of the *Book of Songs*, the separation of the critics, appreciators, and the actual writing process of poetry is formed almost instinctively. Such a mentality may have encouraged and supported the Confucian utilitarian poetics as the representative, which focused on the social roles of poetry in the "distant" observation and examination of these popular pieces. For instance, "One's personality should start with the *Book of Songs*, mature in rituals, sublimed in music" (*The Analects of Confucius*, *Taibo*). "One could not talk properly if one does not learn the *Book of Songs*" (*The Analects of Confucius*, *Mr. Ji*). "Poetry can develop one's emotions, be used to observe the world, make one a good member of a group, and be used to express injustices. It can be used also to get along with one's father as well as one's sovereign, which started from the names of birds and beasts" (*The Analects of Confucius*, *Yanghuo*) and so on. These are the starts of ancient poetics and the use of poetry concepts in ancient Chinese poetry. These utilitarian poetic theories became the first stage of the development of ancient Chinese poetics. In the *Poetry* by Zhong Rong of the Liang Dynasty, ancient Chinese poetry theorists began to appreciate and evaluate poetry works from the perspective of ideas and art, but the objects of appreciation and evaluation are undoubtedly the "finished products." Thus, this evaluation is a sensory activity outside the artistic creation process. Therefore, the "distance" posture from the poet's actual creative process was also preserved and became an extremely important feature of classical Chinese poetry in later development. The history of classical Chinese poetry theory shows: "there are two kinds of poetics: one is derived from Zhong Rong's *Poetry*, the other is based on Ouyang Xiu's *Liu Yi Poetry*. All later poetics can be traced to either of these two."[10]

If Zhong Rong's *Poetry* reflected a more serious style of theoretical criticism, then *Liu Yi Poetry* by Ouyang Xiu of the Northern Song Dynasty is more casual and discusses "poetry and other things" just "for fun." It conveys the poetry theorist's "distant" attitude toward poetry writing. This "distance" gesture once again vividly reflects the basic artistic environment in which classical Chinese poetry scholars engaged in poetry criticism: Chinese poetry criticism followed a high maturity of poetry writing, and ancient Chinese poet-critics did not grow with the growth of poetry, but with the introduction, dissemination, and appreciation of poetry. The great prosperity of ancient Chinese poetics occurred during the Song Dynasty when Chinese intellectuals were pressured by the unpredictable artistic peak of Tang Dynasty poetry. "When one reads the classical poems extensively, he would recite the lines of his favorites. They became part of the memory. It often occurred that people might confuse these quotations as one's verses" (*Shilin*, *Poetry* by Ye Mengde). For the artists who advocated originality, how dreadful it would be when they found they could not go beyond their predecessors? "The Tang people are good at poetry and there are few poetics. There are fewer poems produced in the Song Dynasty than those of the Tang Dynasty, and there are more poetics."[11] This is also an accurate description of the helplessness of the Song Dynasty literati and the helpless writing transformation. Indeed, when the current peak of artistic creation is insurmountable, what could a poet do? What can poetry theorists do? Probably accumulating knowledge, all kinds of knowledge about poetry. Exploring some experience in reading poetry became a natural phenomenon.

So our ancient Chinese poetics do not directly think about the subjective writing rules, reveal the mystery of artistic creation, nor explore the complex spiritual activities of the writers. Rather, focusing on the reading of finished products, bringing together the knowledge of finished products, and conveying personal appreciation became their main features. In this sense, ancient Chinese poetics can be called a reader's "appreciation theory" of poetry, or a specific reader's "interpretation theory" for poetry from social needs. We may find the vast majority of influential poetics were not written by poets with outstanding achievements even though almost all of the literati were poets in such a huge country of poetry producers as China. This shows the division between poetry writing and poetics in the sense of "generation."

This practicality and appreciative pursuit of ancient Chinese poetics is quite different from the Western poetry criticism tradition since ancient Greece. The ancient Greeks believed poetry came from gods, which effectively blocked the possibility of Chinese-style utilization in reality. First, the divine adoration and rational brilliance of ancient Greece, as well as the later wisdom, will, and inner life, continue to attract Western poetry theorists to follow a path of longing for mystery, longing for wisdom, and exploring spiritual creation. We can find quite clearly the feelings of poets are always the center of Western poetics, from the divine nature of ancient Greek poetry to Aristotle's view of poetry as techniques using specifics to reflect the general until the Renaissance, Romanticism, and the poetic theories since the 20th century. In the West, a set of "poetics" about the experience of poetry writing developed. Aristotle's *Poetics* discussed how poets can succeed in imitation, and Wordsworth's *New Edition of The Lyrics* "made everyday things present to the soul in an unusual state." Samuel Taylor Coleridge talked about the use of imagination, genius, and use of words. T. S. Eliot studied the relationship between tradition and the poet's talent. Heidegger asks "What are poets for?" As some scholars already noted:

> Both classicism poetics in terms of techniques and romantic poetics in terms of aesthetics in the West are based on the writing process and are established in the assumption of the author's mental functions. In other words, the essence of poetry (art) is discussed by focusing on the author's psychological mechanism.[12]

This can also explain the fact that more famous poetic criticisms are written by famous poets in Western history in comparison with China.

The attention to and tracking of the human spiritual world, and the creation of mysteries also enabled Western "poetry" theories to have an opportunity to go beyond the specific stylistic criticisms and expand into the more universal spiritual fields. Aristotle's "poetics" in ancient Greece is the "theory" of the entire literary and artistic activities. His "poetry" is essentially a rich concept different from history and scientific discourses, including epics, tragedies, comedies, harp songs, Aulos songs, and so on. In the 20th century, Heidegger also discussed the meaning of *Sein* (existence) in "poetry thoughts." In his view, the initial occurrence, persistence, variation, and disappearance of meaning are closely related to the activities of "poetic language." In contrast, ancient Chinese poets always used poetry and read poetry, which quite specifically made poetry discourse concrete and definite. As a result, all we have are specific poem comments rather than more abstract "poetics."

New changes in Chinese modern poetics and the establishment of the meaning of modern characteristics of Chinese poetry stem from a fundamental change in the ecological environment of poetry and the special cultural mentality of intellectuals. That is to say, Chinese poets in the 20th century can no longer express their feelings in "distant" reading of the intrinsic classic texts because all the background knowledge about Chinese classical poetry has been exhausted by the predecessors. All classic reading experiences are constantly elucidated by the ancients and they may not be able to speak more in detail, more uniquely than the predecessors. More importantly, the reality of Chinese poetry has undergone drastic changes. A new style of poetry—modern vernacular new poetry came on stage and this new literary style, sufficient to arouse people's great interest, is still growing. The relationship between poetry theorists and poetry is no longer "distant." The new texts that seem far from mature are insufficiently strong to place a lot of pressure on them with a "classic" posture and force them to express their reading experiences carefully. Modern poetry is a kind of collective literary activity of participation and development of modern Chinese literati. The new poetry writing and the destiny of poetry development are often linked to the choice of many literati's own survival and artistic careers. That is, before the critics put forward comments on other people's works, they are likely to be the first active advocates of the new poetry movement and the pioneers of modern new poetry writing. Poetry was a part of their life and career. The commentary on poetry is naturally no longer a detached "appreciation" or "taste" issue, but the process and way of their value and life. Such a profound historical change ultimately determines the modern transformation of Chinese poetics.

III

I think the characteristics of this modern transformation can be shown in the following aspects.

From the "readers" poetics to the "authors" poetics, although the authors of ancient Chinese poetics can also be called poets, they clearly showed readers' attitudes of appreciating poetry from the standpoint of their poetics writing. That is to say, these poem commentators, although writing poems themselves, engaged in poetics not from the perspective of a writer, but as a reader. Then, we have the situation we mentioned above: the vast majority of influential poetics does not come from outstanding poets. In modern times, the problem of the actual writing of new poetry has become a common concern of many literati. First, poetry writers need to discuss this issue, so their position and attitude in writing modern poetics naturally occur. The more productive and the more experienced poets are, the more likely they are to become involved in poetics. In the history of modern Chinese poetry famous poets who have produced famous pieces on poetics are also outstanding poets, such as Hu Shih, Guo Moruo, Kang Baiqing, Wen Yiduo, Mu Mutian, Wang Duqing, Dai Wangshu, Liang Zongxi, Fei Ming, Ai Qing, Hu Feng, Tian Jian, Yuan Kejia, etc. The reports from these authors of the new poetry constitute the most important component of Chinese modern poetics, which is fundamentally different from that of ancient China.

The focus on the "problems" of poem writing became the starting point for poetics writing. "Poetics is to write about the insiders as an outsider" (Wu Xiu's *The Preface to Long Shoutang Poetics*). The position of this outsider of ancient Chinese poetry determines the incomplete standing positions for current poem-writing activities. In other words, because what they are "appreciating" are often the famous masterpieces of previous generations, they do not directly discuss current problems. For Chinese modern poetry theorists, paying attention to poetry is to look at themselves. They discussed poetry because they encountered a series of problems. Hu Shih "discussed the new poetry" given the eight-year new poems "still being questioned by many people." Zong Baihua also discussed the new poetry because "there has been a big problem in the Chinese literary and art communities recently, which is about the new style poetry practices. That is, how could we write good new poetry?"[13] Cheng Fangwu called for the "defense of poetry" because he witnessed "We pulled down the decaying palace (of traditional poetry) and rebuilt the palace of the new poetry ... during the past few years. However, now, there is wild grass everywhere in the palace. How sad and painful!"[14] Mu Mutian advocated pure poetry because he believed Hu Shih's writing "created a kind of prose in verse in China. It is like dressing proses in rhymes."[15] Wen Yiduo commented on Guo Moruo's *The Goddesses* and raised the "local colors" issue because he was not satisfied with reality. "The current new poets—new here means what is in fashion—seem to develop European envy. Their purpose for writing new Chinese poetry was to imitate entirely the Western style."[16] To solve this problem, Wen Yiduo systematically conceived creating modern metrical poetry through his *"Three Beauties."* Xiao San and Wang Yaping discussed the popularization and nationalization of poetry because they discovered the "problem" of aristocratization and Europeanization of Chinese new poetry. Yuan Kejia argued for the dramatization of the new poetry, because he believed "the problem of the current new poetry" is that the poet's will and emotions are not "revealed in the dramatic performance."[17] As an important representative of the Chinese modern academic poetry theory, Zhu Guangqian's poetic theory should be different from the general poetry theory, but if compared with the "outsiders" of the "reader poetry theory" in ancient China, Zhu Guangqian still cared more about the writer's mentality, although as an "outsider." His discussion still belongs to the typical modern "author's poetry theory." Mao Dun is unknown for his poetry, but as an "outsider" he found the problem of the current writing as an "insider." For example, he discovered in 1937, "In the past two years, there has been a new tendency of Chinese new poems—from lyrics to narrative, from short to long." As to specific authors' works, Mao Dun commented:

> I think Tian Jian is too broad in perspective, while Zang Kejia pays too much attention to details. It is meaningful to examine the long pieces of these two poets. We could say the future of long narrative poetry is in the harmony of the two. I have never written poetry, but I want to boldly suggest, first, building the general structure all at once. Then, we can come to scrutinize the words. The general structure would remain intact, but the lines or stanzas could be meticulously examined. How about such experimenting?[18]

As someone who claimed to have never written poems, Mao Dun dared to follow the internal laws of poem writing by finding "problems" and solving "problems." This reflected the unique thinking of modern poetics had been formed. Attention to current "problems" became a basic starting point for all poetics writing.

Attention to current "problems" of poem writing makes the discussion and revelation of the psychological state and writing method in the specific creative process the main concern of modern poetics. To solve the current "problems," Chinese modern poetics devoted the most important space to "how." Hu Shih elaborated on how the new poetry can achieve metrical harmony. As to how to "be specific rather than abstract," Yu Pingbo put forward a series of suggestions, such as "increasing the weight of poetry" and "not into the old souls." Zong Baihua discussed "ways to train poetry art" and "methods of poet personality development." Mu Mutian put forward "poetry thinking" and "the method of poetry thinking." Liang Zongdai discussed how "symbolism" could be created. Hu Feng's famous suggestion is: "The person who is interested in being a poet must have the willingness to be a real person . . . . The poet must never have a "frivolous" approach to poetry."[19] All of these "how" reveals the mystery of the artistic creation process in its different aspects. Different from the ancient Chinese "poetic method" introductory textbooks, quite contemptuous of techniques, Chinese modern poetics mainly explored the author's subjective consciousness and creative mentality, which introduced Chinese poetics to an unprecedented psychological perspective. Guo Moruo proposed in 1921 "people who want to study poetry may start from psychological aspects."[20] Words such as "emotion," "mood," "thinking," "potential consciousness," and "inspiration" appear in the poetics of Guo Moruo, Yu Pingbo, Zong Baihua, Mu Mutian, Wang Duqing, Liang Zongdai, Dai Wangshu, Du Heng, Zhu Guangqian, etc. Poetry theorists, such as Yu Pingbo and Zhu Guangqian, also discussed people's attitudes toward the new poetry and the psychological differences and appreciation of poetry. From these aspects, Chinese modern poetics is probably closer to the tradition of Western poetics and quite different from the pure techniques of poetic law in Chinese traditional poetics.

The creative value of poetry and the spirit of the times received special attention. In ancient China, the literary thoughts of knowing the Way, learning the classics, and writing and following the saints' thoughts influenced almost all literary criticisms, as did poetics. On the one hand, ancient Chinese poets and poetry theorists deeply felt the pressure from the predecessors' classics. On the other hand, they were unable to justify their artistic pursuits beyond the writings of their predecessors. Most of their poetic ideals can only be expressed in various "retro" slogans—the entanglement and circulation between "Tang Poetry as the ideal" and "Song Poetry as the ideal," but the current appeal of poetry was not strongly affirmed and extended. China's modern poetics has a completely different value trend on the whole. For Chinese modern poetry theorists, how to prove the "newness" of new poetry, how to find the difference between Chinese new poetry and classical poetry, and how to stimulate and nurture the "spirit of the times" of Chinese new poetry are precisely the centers of their discourse and the basic ways to establish the academic value of their research objects. How do Zhou Zuoren's "Little River" and Hu Shih's "Should" express "fine observation" and "twisted ideal" not found in classical poetry? How does Chinese new poetry derive different spirits from Chinese classical poetry because of "the great liberation of poetry style"? These are important parts of Hu Shih's *On New Poetry*. The idea of Hu Shih's initiation of the modern value of poetry in "difference" and "variation" occurred through the development of Chinese modern poetry. Poetry theorists like Zhou Zuoren, who claimed to be one of the traditional, also "believed the power of tradition cannot be scorned." Still, they all acknowledged "Chinese poetry has always been bounded too tightly, and dramatic change is inevitable. Freedom and extravagance are indeed important new developmental factors. The trend of new poetry is very healthy."[21] Despite his criticism of *The Goddesses* for lack of "local colors," Wen Yiduo commented with passion and admiration in the early 1920s:

> When talking about new poetry, Guo Moruo's poetry is worthy of being called new poems. Not only is his work farthest from the old poetry, the most important is it is full of the spirit of the times—the twentieth century. It is said literary and artistic works are the offspring of the time. Indeed, *The Goddesses* is a good son of such a time.[22]

Chinese modern poetics gradually established a set of more philosophical and rigorous theoretical systems in transcending the appreciation tradition of ancient poetics and turned to psychology and philosophy to open a new path. It distinguished itself from the vague concepts of ancient Chinese poetics. The establishment of this theoretical system benefited from the modern literati's conscious pursuit of precision thinking—such as "fine observations" and "twisted ideals" that Hu Shih observed as characteristics of modern vernacular poetry. It is also an inevitable result of the introduction of a series of Western philosophy and social sciences terms. It should be noted ultimately these terms met the need of the very individualistic theoretical development of Chinese poetry theorists. That is, they often lose their inherent meanings. The specific context is different and they present new, colorful meanings, such as the "pan-theism" in Guo Moruo's poetics, the "symbols" in Liang Zongxi's poetics, the "image" and "aesthetic conception" in Zhu Guangqian's poetics, the "subconsciousness" in Li Jinfa and Du Heng's poetics, and so on. Such individual differences also reflect the efforts of Chinese modern poetry theorists when developing their poetic systems.

IV

Going beyond the tradition of readers' commentary style poetics and establishing a new author-style speculative theory system is one of the modern characteristics of Chinese modern poetry, although this pursuit is not unimpeded. First, this is manifested in the fact that a mature philosophical system belonging to a modern culture is still missing in modern China. China does not have a platform similar to the Western Renaissance either. That is, there is a deficiency in the universally agreed thoughts and concepts, which could truly support Chinese modern poetry. Therefore, Chinese modern poetry theorists are more likely to move from individual meaning differences to some kind of "incommensurable" reality. Repeatedly modern poetry theorists are entangled with a series of basic problems and it is difficult to detach themselves, such as the debates between "popularization" and "aristocratization," the disagreement on "nationalization" or "Westernization," and the tension between "personalization" and "popularization," the ambiguity of "regularization" versus "liberalization," the choice of romanticism, realism, or modernism, the writing by intellectuals' versus the "writing by the public," and so on. The inconsistencies of these basic cognitive systems of Chinese modern poetry make us lose the possibility of continuing to sublimate our thoughts to a metaphysical level. In modern China, we have our theoretical poetics, but there has not been a poetics about the existence of human beings similar to Heidegger's being. Chinese modern poetry theorists often speak to themselves in the scope of their respective concepts, and have not yet shown us the connection between each other nor built the glory of the philosophical "poetry and thinking" and "being and poetry."

Moreover, due to the ultra-left tendencies in China's social and political climate at that time, a non-artistic conceptual system replaced the individualized poetic discourse. On the surface, this substitution has temporarily reached the identification of the conceptual vocabulary that we have dreamed of, but such recognition is premised on the denying and deleting basic perception of art. In this way, our poetic theory not only further interrupts the possibility of going to poetics but also loses the ability to feel poetry texts as fine as ancient Chinese poetics. If we say that China's modern poetics has lost something after entering the contemporary era, then this loss is twofold: we have lost the depth and rigor of the psychological mechanism of the Western inquiry into authors (because we do not need to pay attention to the individual writer's creative talent and psychological state, except to implement the "order"); we also have lost the "joy" of classical Chinese poetry reading (the interpretation of all works must be included in the established political thought model). For a long time after the end of the Cultural Revolution, contemporary Chinese poetics needed to be rebuilt. The illusory discourse identity collapsed, but the new platform of identity recognition has yet to be established. At the same time, we have lost the ability and habit of artistic feelings. This is a very sad situation! During the new period, the restructuring of Chinese poetics is not just a question of the introduction of Western theory. There are still many we need to do. For instance, there is too much rootless noise in the boisterous Chinese poetics discussions in the new era. They are either from the author's self-talk because it lacks a series of basic ideological identities and is difficult to form the "author's poetry theory" thriving during the first half of the 20th century. Or, it becomes a game of concepts after a loss of the specific artistic sensibility. Here, there are similarities between playing fashionable foreign concepts and the stubborn persistence of the old political cliche, because both have lost the vivid artistic understanding at the same time. The dilemma of Chinese modern poetry has reached its peak in the "modern transformation"!

At the dawn of the 21st century, it is quite arduous to restructure modern Chinese poetics. It not only needs to restore the textual abilities of poetry theorists but also requires us to build a platform for broader consensus. It is necessary to continue to draw from Western poetics, it is also necessary to restore the artistic understanding of classical poetics. Of course, in this way, our poetics will not be the revival and repetition of the West or ancient China. The modern characteristics of Chinese modern poetics continue to come from the Chinese modern poetry's thinking of life, art, and their own complex choices.

Notes

1 Wang Furen, "Questions on a Research Mode," *Journal of Foshan University*, no. 1 (1996).
2 Hu Shih, "On New Poetry—A Major Event in the Past Eight Years," in *Modern Chinese Poetics*, ed. Yang Kuanghan and Liu Fuchun (Huacheng Press, 1985), vol. I, 2.
3 Hu, "On New Poetry—A Major Event in the Past Eight Years," 6.
4 Mu Mutian, "On Poetry—A Letter to Moruo," in *Modern Chinese Poetics*, vol. I, 6.
5 Wang Duqing, "On Poetry Again—To Mutian and Boqi," in *Modern Chinese Poetics*, vol. I, 109.
6 Mu, "*On Poetry—A Letter to Moruo*, 94.
7 Yuan Kejia, "Dramatization of New Poetry," in *Modern Chinese Poetics*, vol. I, 500.
8 Yuan, "Dramatization of New Poetry," 499, 500.
9 Wen Yiduo, "Historical Trend of Literature," in *Complete Works of Wen Yiduo*, vol. 10 (Hubei People's Publishing House, 1993), 17.
10 Guo Shaoyu, "Preface to *Poetics of Qing Dynasty*," see Ding Fubao's *Poetics of Qing Dynasty* (Shanghai Classics Publishing House, 1978).
11 Wu Qiao, "Reply to Wan Jiye's Questions on Poetry," in *Poetics of Qing Dynasty*, vol. I.
12 Yu Hong, *Chinese Literary Theories and Western Poetics* (Joint Publishing, 1999), 75–76.
13 Zong Baihua, "A Brief Talk on New Poetry," in *Modern Chinese Poetics*, vol. I, 29.
14 Cheng Fangwu, "Defense of Poetry," in *Modern Chinese Poetics*, vol. I, 70.
15 Mu Mutian, "On Poetry—A Letter to Moruo," in *Modern Chinese Poetics*, vol. I, 99.
16 Wen Yiduo, "Local Colors of the Goddesses," in *Complete Works of Wen Yiduo*, vol. 2, 118.
17 Yuan Kejia, "Dramatization of New Poetry," in *Modern Chinese Poetics*, vol. I, 500.
18 Mao Dun, "The Future of Narrative Poetry," in *Modern Chinese Poetics*, vol. I, 315, 319.
19 Hu Feng, "People and Poetry, Secondary Poets," in *On Modern Chinese Poetry*, vol. I, 403.

20 Guo Moruo, "Three Essays on Poetry," in *On Modern Chinese Poetry*, vol. I, 53.
21 Zhou Zuoren, "Preface to *Yangbian Ji* (*Spurring Collection*)," in *On Modern Chinese Poetry*, vol. I, 129.
22 Wen Yiduo, "The Times Spirit of the Goddesses," in *Complete Works of Wen Yiduo*, vol. 2, 110.

POSTSCRIPTS FOR THE PREVIOUS CHINESE EDITIONS

Postscript for the First Chinese Edition

The idea of studying new poetry by focusing on the poem noumenon is only a proposal and this book is only the beginning because it is still clearly insufficient to fully demonstrate the three-dimensional image of Chinese new poetry in the multicultural exchange from the perspective of the modern evolution of Chinese classical tradition. At least, we should approach both China and the West to make it possible to draw closer to the truth of the object. However, the influence of Chinese poetry tradition on modernity is too complicated, and non-exhaustive discussions cannot present its rich details, which led to the topic of this book. If some parts need further elaboration or clarification, they will be continued in the next project, *Modernization of Modern Chinese Poetry*.

Some senior experts paid quite some attention to the writing of this book. Among them, especially worth mentioning, are Professor Qian Liqun from Peking University, Professor Lü Jiaxiang from Shandong Normal University, and Professor Song Yiqiao from Liaocheng University. These kind professors encouraged me and reminded me of the possible difficulties in writing. Professor Lü Jiaxiang reminded me of using "prototype" with caution. In a letter of thousands of words, Professor Song Yiqiao elaborated on the "not yet finalized" issue of the new poems and made a sincere statement: "As far as this topic is concerned, I think it is necessary to avoid a strict distinction between the local roots and external influences, especially the degree of certainty of the former." At the beginning of the book's conception, Professor Qian Liqun provided great support and paid continuous attention to its writing process. In the meantime, he made many important, frank critiques, especially reminding me to pay attention to avoiding the trap of "historical determinism." Today, upon completing and publishing the book, I have complicated feelings when I reread the letters from these mentors. Perhaps the current manuscript still has not integrated the guidance of my professors, and even mistakes or regrets can still be found. Then, let these insights be the new foundation for my next thoughts.

In 1987, quite unassured, I submitted a paper "A Short Comment on Li Jinfa" to *Modern Chinese Literature Studies*. It was from that moment that my splendid "writer's dream" gradually faded, and another so-called "academic path" began to extend under my feet (I still can't say whether it's lucky or unlucky). In this extraordinarily lonely journey, I have received the care of many mentors. Those who were far away in Beijing gave me the first, most selfless help, including Hou Yuzhen, Wang Xin, Lu Ji'en, Wang Shijia, Gao Yuandong, Wu Fuhui, Qian Liqun, Liu Na, Huang Houxing, Tong Qingbing, Wang Yichuan, and Wang Chaobing. The editors of *Modern Chinese Literature Studies, Literary Review, Masterpieces Review, Lu Xun Research Monthly, Journal of Southwest China Normal University*, and *Academic Journal of Zhongzhou* also supported my research continuously. It is worth mentioning that many of these mentors and friends were known only by correspondence. Five years after I publicized "A Short Comment on Li Jinfa," I happened to know the editor of the article was Professor Qian Liqun, who had been caring about my career for five years. Perhaps this is the "Chinese modern literary spirit," which is a life attitude and academic attitude aggregated under the common idea and belief, a refusal of the principle of utilitarianism, which is there for thousands of years. At the end of the 20th century, in the powerful whirlpool of rapid development of material civilization, when our survival once again fell into the utilitarianism trap, and when the nihilism followers dominated the stage, the "Chinese modern literary spirit" was the light of academics and the hope of history!

The teachings of Professor Wang Furen and Professor Lan Dizhi of Beijing Normal University are especially memorable.

My interest in new poetry is directly influenced by Professor Lan Dizhi, who provided me with guidance in the writing of many of my papers. His new poetry monograph, *The Traditional and Unconventional*, is one of the most frequently read books of my life. I receive new inspiration every time I read it.

My academic research was guided by Professor Wang Furen, whose teachings and influence on me are self-evident. However, today, I deeply feel that what I have gained from him is far beyond academics, which seems more worth cherishing. It has been nearly 10 years since 1985. At every important moment in my life, I feel great willpower and emotional support from him. It is sincere friendship and love valuable to me in a country with a long history of civilization. It shows another personality beyond the familiar faces (complex cold faces and exaggerated flattering faces). Now, when my first book is about to publish, it is difficult for me to express my feelings in words. When the world "crawls in the weak, human-to-human relationship/innumerable maliciousness for self-nutrition" (Mu Dan), is there anything more precious than sincerity?

Li Yi
Longjiang Village,
Southwest Normal University
Lunar New Year, 1994

Postscript for the Third Revised Edition in Chinese

"Contemporary Chinese Humanities Series" by the China Renmin University Press focuses on the development of contemporary Chinese scholarship since the reform in the 1970s. I am very grateful that Dr. Liu Ting, the editor for this series, offered to include my work because nowadays, it is difficult to obtain a copy in the market even with multiple prints and editions. I feel regretful that I could not make it available to new and old friends who often ask for it.

With this opportunity, I revised the original book once more. Apart from a few textual corrections, I further add to this edition Feng Zhi, and Yuan Kejia, two important contributors to modern Chinese poetry. A wish is fulfilled. By now, the framework of Chinese modern new poetry and classical poetry tradition can be said generally complete. Since the first edition of this book 20 years ago, I have witnessed the changes in Chinese academics. My thoughts also developed, which are truly memorable along with the reading experience of Chinese new poetry.

I am grateful to China Renmin University Press, especially Dr. Liu Ting and Ms Luo Xiao for their efforts in the publication of this book!

Li Yi
Liyun Residence,
Beijing Normal University
August 2014

INDEX

Airs of the States 14, 67, 107, 112–124, 126, 184
Ai Qing 5, 58–59, 62, 99–100, 104–105, 107, 140, 146, 152, 163, 171, 217, 285–293, 301, 309, 312, 322, 330–331, 333–334, 385
An Experimental Collection 26, 100, 138, 179–181, 185, 187, 188
art for art's sake 79–80, 83, 92, 118, 254–255, 260, 318–319, 379

Baihua (daily speech, vernacular) 7
Ban Gu 120, 194
Baudelaire 35, 65, 105, 230–235, 243, 246, 262, 367
Bi 26, 47, 52, 56, 65, 113, 187
Bian Zhilin 5, 26, 30, 38–39, 42, 60, 68, 83, 87–88, 90–91, 126, 139, 147–149, 161–162, 165–168, 171, 225, 239, 245, 251–252, 257–274, 299, 300, 304–308, 322, 329, 331–332, 334–335, 337, 346, 350
Bing Xin 14, 33, 38, 143

Book of Rites 36, 49

Chen Mengjia 2, 21, 24, 44, 129, 148, 165, 170
Chinese People's War of Resistance against Japanese Aggression/ the War of Resistance against Japanese Aggression 4, 71, 100, 109–111, 116, 118, 121, 169, 198, 245, 261, 291–292, 305, 334
Chinese Poetry Association 2, 4, 14, 56, 100, 103, 107, 109–110, 115, 121
Chu Ci 47, 156, 170, 193, 196, 358
Ci 63, 67, 78–79, 82–86, 88–90, 94, 113, 121, 123, 126, 128, 134–137, 139, 143, 154, 156, 164–165, 170, 183, 203, 247, 263, 333, 356, 358
Complete Poems of Dai Wangshu 241
Conscious Forms of Modern Chinese New Poetry 79
Crescent Moon School 2, 5, 14, 16–17, 21, 27, 29, 38, 53–54, 59, 80–81, 83, 86, 89–90, 98, 115, 125, 139, 151, 158,

161–162, 164, 170, 172, 182, 205, 219, 227–228, 240, 247–249, 254, 274, 276, 295, 319, 328, 362

Dai Wangshu 30–31, 39, 54, 68, 79, 90–91, 108, 118, 125–126, 131, 139, 148–149, 151, 161–162, 167, 176, 225, 240–252, 257–263, 266, 272, 304–305, 307–308, 322, 331, 359, 367, 385, 387
Distant Metaphor 36–39, 43, 45–46, 293, 297–299
Du Fu 46, 72, 155, 287

Eliot, T. S. 42, 87, 92, 129, 269, 271, 306, 315–316, 329, 336, 375, 383

Feng Zhi 30, 68, 151–152, 167, 285, 293–294, 296–301, 308, 322, 327, 371
French Symbolism 32, 89, 234, 240, 242–248, 250, 255, 263, 285, 304–305

Goddesses, The 4, 8, 13, 21–22, 24, 26, 28, 37, 58–59, 62, 73, 87, 151, 193, 196, 198, 203, 206, 217, 219–220, 225, 228, 249, 332, 334, 355, 364–366, 385, 388
Guo Moruo 4, 8, 13, 20–22, 24, 26, 32, 43, 45, 59, 62, 64–65, 68, 73–74, 76, 78–79, 86, 117, 127–128, 151, 171, 173, 192–205, 207–209, 214, 217–221, 225–226, 228, 244, 300, 332–333, 355, 365, 385, 387, 391

He Qifang 30–31, 39, 54, 82, 88, 90, 121, 125–126, 139, 148, 151–152, 161–162, 167, 175–176, 225, 245, 251–263, 266, 304–305, 307, 331, 368, 371, 374
Huang Tingjian 94–96, 155, 175
Hu Shih 1–2, 8, 13, 20–21, 24–26, 86, 89, 92, 98–102, 108, 129, 130, 137, 143, 157, 160, 167, 170, 175–176, 178–192, 205, 226, 287, 298, 302–303, 308, 310–312, 314–315, 326, 351, 354, 364–365, 371–372, 374, 378–379, 385–386, 388, 390

Jiang Kui 263
July Poetry School 4

Kang Baiqing 24, 32–33, 64–65, 172, 181, 359, 385

Late Tang and Five Dynasties 253, 255, 262–263
Liang Zongdai 5, 33, 64–65, 68, 128, 274–275, 277–285, 327, 359, 369–370, 386, 387
Li Bai 51, 84, 136, 155, 170, 192, 205, 210–211, 287, 370
Li Guangtian 2, 21, 90, 133
Li Jinfa 30, 38, 44, 46, 59, 68, 80, 83, 127–129, 167, 171, 229, 230–240, 247, 303–305, 307–308, 367, 388
Li Sao 63, 68, 74, 113, 187, 193, 196
Li Shangyin 83, 87, 155, 210, 243, 247, 250, 253, 262
Liu Bannong 100–102, 108–109, 114–115, 119, 121–123, 131–132, 302, 351
Liu Dabai 58, 100, 102, 108–121
Lu Xun 2, 21, 119, 131, 181, 294–296, 298, 332, 334, 347–349, 351–356, 358–363, 370–371, 374–376

Mallarmé, Stéphane 81, 128, 255, 367
Mao Dun 99, 109, 117, 129–131, 386, 390
May Fourth Movement 2, 21, 24, 27, 58, 60, 73–74, 80, 82, 107, 109, 116, 151, 182, 185, 196, 254, 287, 366, 378
Modernist School 5, 14, 16, 29, 38, 53, 80–81, 83, 90, 115, 125, 139, 143, 274, 284, 319, 366
Mu Dan 5, 14, 18–19, 44–45, 59–60, 62, 65, 105, 107, 140, 167, 171–173, 217, 301–304, 307–309, 312–316, 322, 331–332, 334, 337, 363, 371
Mu Mutian 14, 16–17, 58–59, 92, 100, 104–105, 107, 140, 182

Near Metaphor 36, 38–39, 45–47, 54, 297
New Youth 19, 115, 131–132, 176, 348

Nine Leaves poets 25, 27, 29, 31, 33, 35, 37, 39, 41, 43, 45, 47, 49, 51–53, 55–57, 59, 61, 63, 65, 274, 278

Objectification 2, 5, 8, 21, 24, 32, 38, 53–54, 64, 80–81, 83, 90, 103, 115, 128–130, 148–149, 163, 167, 171, 250, 304, 306–308, 359, 365, 371, 379, 385–387, 390

Parnassianism 81, 83–84, 90, 356
Ping (flat or level) 153, 157–158, 189, 350
Pu Feng 3–4, 21, 55, 60, 103–104, 108–109, 115, 119, 123, 130–132, 222, 366

Qu 154, 164, 183, 356, 365
Qu Yuan 13, 67–71, 73, 76–79, 125, 127, 192–194, 196, 207, 253, 296, 338, 345, 365

Red Candle 62, 91, 151, 209–210, 213–214, 226, 332
Ren Hongyuan 331–332, 335–341, 343–346, 373–374
Richards, I. A. 41, 318, 329

Song Dynasty 10, 13–16, 23, 27, 63–64, 67, 78–79, 82–85, 88, 92–107, 112, 121, 123–124, 134–137, 139, 141–143, 145, 153–155, 184, 263, 357, 382
Subjectivity 31, 56, 58, 61, 274, 299
Su Shi 94–95, 137, 165
Symbolist School 5, 14, 16, 29, 38, 53, 80, 83, 89–90, 115, 125, 139, 164, 274, 319

Tagore, Rabindranath 192, 195–196, 205, 221
Tang Dynasty 12, 14–15, 26, 42, 75, 82, 84–85, 88, 94–96, 98, 101, 121, 134–137, 139, 143, 145, 153–155, 164, 184, 194, 203, 210, 219, 243, 247, 253, 266, 333, 358, 382
Tao Yuanming 13, 79, 192–194, 202, 205, 225, 281, 338

Tian Jian 55, 60, 71, 76, 100, 107–109, 119–121, 125, 128, 131, 217, 287, 291, 385–386

Valéry 239, 248, 250, 255, 262, 273, 278, 280–283, 304, 367, 369–370
Verlaine, Paul 41, 81, 89, 230, 233, 235, 242–243, 246, 248, 255, 262, 277–278, 304, 306
Vigny, Alfred de 81

Wang Duqing 2, 21, 80, 115, 125–126, 128–129, 131, 250, 304, 306–307, 379, 385, 387, 390
Wang Wei 14, 44, 51, 136, 192–194, 205, 283, 369, 370
Wen Tingyun 83, 86–87, 136, 243–244, 247, 250, 253, 262
Wen Yiduo 8, 14, 21–22, 24, 28–29, 42, 44, 59–60, 62, 80, 86, 89–91, 108, 118, 129, 151, 158, 162, 165–167, 176, 205–220, 225–226, 228, 244, 248, 254, 264, 269, 273, 281, 328–329, 332, 334, 337, 346, 364–366, 369–370, 373–374, 381, 385, 388, 390–391
Wenxin Diaolong (*The Literary Mind and the Carving of Dragons*) 26, 39, 48–49

Xing 23, 26–27, 29–36, 47, 52–53, 56, 63–64, 113, 187, 210, 280, 301
Xu Zhimo 16, 17, 25, 28–29, 54, 59, 64, 80, 86, 108, 118, 125–126, 128–129, 147–149, 151, 158–159, 162, 167, 170, 176, 207–208, 217–229, 244, 247, 249, 254, 274, 284, 295, 322, 328, 329, 331, 355–356, 359–360, 366–367, 375

Yeats, W. B. 92, 262, 267, 273, 284, 304, 314, 369
Ye Gongchao 12, 21
Yuan Kejia 43, 99–101, 104, 124, 129–130, 132, 175, 312–313, 317–327, 329–330, 371–373, 379–380, 385, 390

Yuefu 14, 67, 74, 107, 112–124, 126, 153, 187

Yu Pingbo 12, 16, 21–22, 24, 65, 68, 100, 114, 127, 157, 167, 176, 181, 310, 371, 386–387

Ze (fall or downward) 153, 157–158, 189, 350

Zheng Min 2, 8, 21, 44, 60, 140, 166–167, 175, 308, 371

Zhimo's Poetry 224–225, 355, 366

Zhou Zuoren 13, 21, 24, 29, 34, 64, 108, 114, 119, 131, 181, 280, 334, 351, 359, 387, 391

Zhu Guangqian 31, 108, 167, 279, 330, 359–360, 386–387

Zhu Ziqing 24, 37–38, 65, 108, 114, 129, 131, 150, 171, 176, 206, 218, 264, 269, 297, 298, 304, 354, 365, 371, 374–375

Zong Baihua 14, 33, 53, 64–65, 86, 129, 359, 375, 385–387, 390

Milton Keynes UK
Ingram Content Group UK Ltd.
UKHW021025170524
442783UK00006B/72